The Long Book of Sewing in pictures

The Long Book of Sewing in pictures

Money saving sewing jobs explained and illustrated

Violet K. Simons

Drawings by Alan Burton

Wolfe

First published 1975 by
Wolfe Publishing Limited
10 Earlham Street WC2H 9LP

SBN 7234 0587 5

Printed by
C. Nicholls & Company Ltd,
The Philips Park Press Manchester

contents

introduction

This book is different from most other sewing books because it not only tells you what to do, but why you have to do it. It assumes that you are short of gadgets, short of money, and totally lacking in experience.

The purpose is to give you confidence by explaining with text and illustrations the easiest ways of getting good results, and to prove that you can do it if you try.

No attempt is made to tell you how to make a dress or coat because pattern instructions tell you that, but you will find explained some of the technical terms found on patterns, and how to put them to use, even if you are not nimble fingered.

When home made dresses look home made, it's often because insufficient time has been given to the finishing touches, things like pressing, cutting and clearing up. A well made dress should look as tidy inside as it does outside. Although the instructions in this book are the most simple, they will help you to achieve a professional look.

Repairing and altering are even more necessary as a result of the increasing cost of replacing. Properly renovated clothes can be worn for work and play, thus saving pounds towards the morale-boosting more expensive items. A section is devoted to the alteration of children's clothes because a great deal of money can be saved by adapting clothes that are not worn out but simply grown out of.

Sewing is a relaxing pastime, and a most satisfying one, whether you have made a new garment or have given an old one a new lease of life. There is nothing more enjoyable than knowing you look expensive, especially when it only costs you a few pounds to do so. These pleasures can be yours if you follow the hints and advice contained in these pages.

tools of the trade

PINS AND NEEDLES
These must be sharp and clean. They can deteriorate, so make sure they are not rusty or blunt. Blunt needles, particularly on a sewing machine, and blunt pins, will tear threads in fine fabrics and, even worse, will pucker the threads, leaving marks which no amount of pressing will ever eradicate.

Sewing needles are numbered. The lower the number the finer the needle.

With a sewing machine you may get away with a fine needle on a thick fabric but you would not get away with a thick needle on a fine fabric like silk or even Tricel.

The finer the fabric the finer the needle.

If in doubt, before machining, consult your sewing machine manufacturer's booklet, or a good haberdasher.

SEWING THREADS
For really neat and professional sewing the correct threads must be used.

The fine fabrics which require a fine needle, also require a fine thread.

If you are machining with the wrong type of thread the machine stitches will not lock, and the thread will very likely tangle.

Always do a little test sewing on the fabric you propose to use before you start on the garment.

It is important to match your sewing thread to the main colour of the fabric. If you cannot get an exact match then take a shade darker.

For Crimplenes, Terylenes and other man-made fibres it is now recommended to use Terylene or nylon threads. These have the same durability as the fabric and are not so likely to wear away as would cotton or silk.

There is a special coarse, strong thread for sewing on buttons, known as button thread.

NEEDLE THREADER
Saves time and eyesight (see page 13).

SCISSORS
These must be sharp. You cannot cut well with blunt scissors, so keep one pair specially for cutting out. Blunt scissors can also drag the threads of some fabrics and spoil the garment before it is made.

PINKING SHEARS
These are not a necessity, but are certainly a great help. They save time, too, because if the edges are pinked they may not need any further finishing off.

SEWING MACHINE
Before you start sewing make sure there is no oil or sticky dust to soil the fabric.

Check the tension for the particular fabric you are using by first doing some test runs on scraps. Consult the manufacturer's leaflet if in doubt about altering the tension.

Always keep a sewing machine covered when not in use.

TAILOR'S CHALK
This is for marking up darts, sewing lines and other things on fabrics. It is better used in the hands of professionals because if you are slow, or handle the work too much, it is inclined to rub off. For beginners it is safer to make your marks with tailor's tacks (see page 148).

TAPE MEASURE
You are bound to need one of these at some time. Buy a good one and, like the scissors, keep it in a safe place just for dressmaking.

SEAM RIPPER
If you do have to unpick any stitching it is safer to use this small gadget. But be careful – it can slip!

OLD REELS OF THREAD
These are invaluable, not only for repairing the garments on which they were originally used, but for use as tacking thread. You need contrasting colours for tacking, so keep a good supply in hand.

THIMBLE
This is optional, but better to have one than a sore finger.

IRON
You will see on page 153 the importance of pressing as you go, so an iron is really a necessity in the sewing room.

SLEEVE BOARD
This is more important than a full-sized ironing board and has the added advantage of taking up less space. Very necessary for pressing armholes, necklines, cuffs and lots of other awkward spots.

IRONING BOARD
You will need this ultimately, but the smaller sleeve board is the one you will find most useful.

1 Cut the thread to ensure there are no fine wisps to prevent it going easily through the eye of the needle.

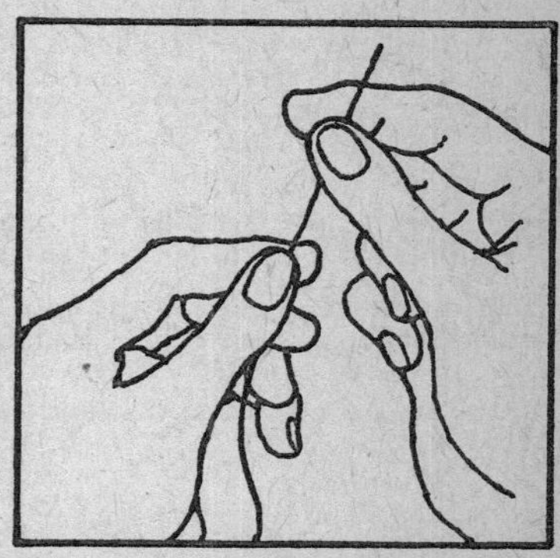

2 Moisten end of thread by passing it between the lips, or between dampened fingers.

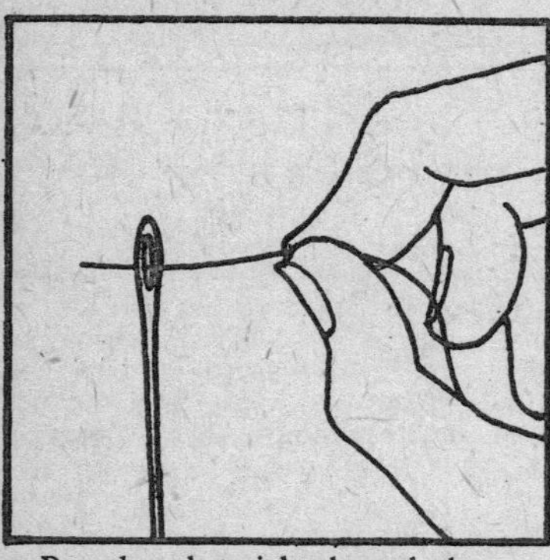

3 Pass thread straight through the eye. Do not knot or twist it.

4 Nylon and Terylene threads are inclined to fray, so it is advisable to use a threader.

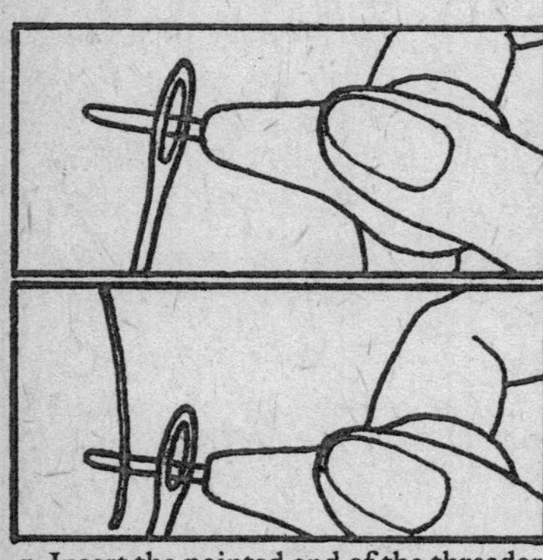

5 Insert the pointed end of the threader through the eye of the needle, and pass thread through the large wire loop of the threader.

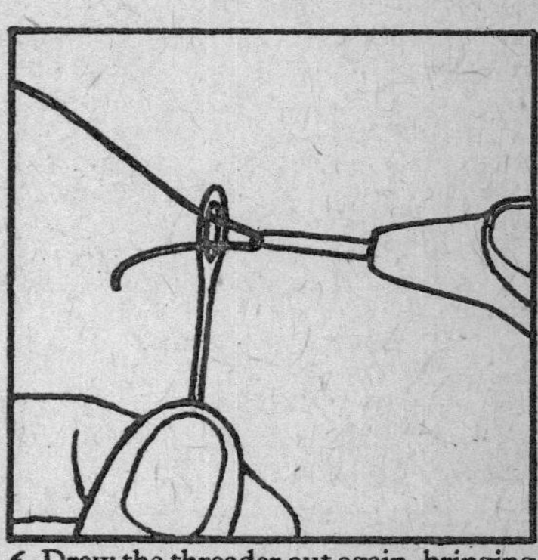

6 Draw the threader out again, bringing the thread with it.

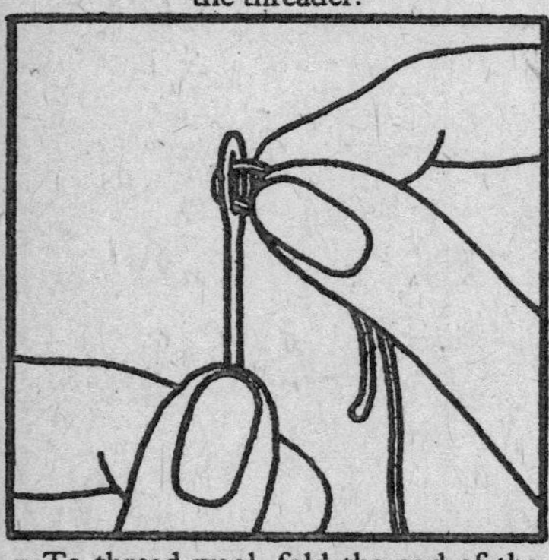

7 To thread wool, fold the end of the wool back and press the fold through the eye. Or use the threader.

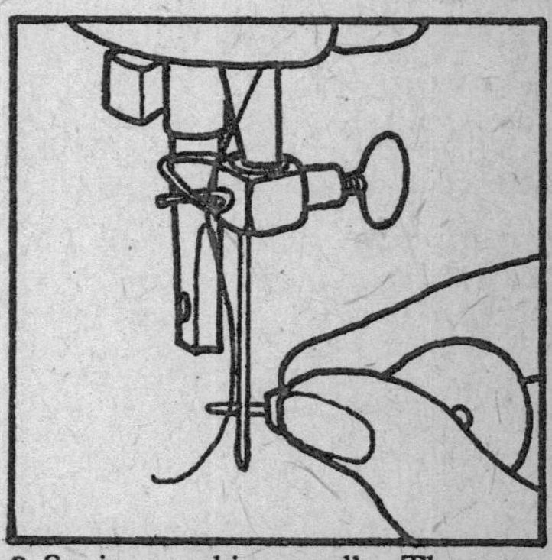

8 Sewing machine needle: The same principles apply as for any other needle and thread, but the threader saves a lot of time.

basic hand sewn stitches

Even though you have a sewing machine you must be able to do all the basic hand-sewn stitches because there are many occasions in the making-up of a garment when hand sewing is necessary and machining is impossible. This is especially so for beginners. For instance, saddle stitching, tacking and catch stitching are done by hand. Fastenings are mostly sewn on by hand. If you haven't got a special fitting for the machine, zip fasteners are neater when sewn in by hand.

running stitch

The most basic stitch of all. Used for sewing two pieces of fabric together or for sewing down a hem, if you wish. Also used in darning and embroidery. Unless using a variation, such as saddle stitch or tacking, it must be kept very small.

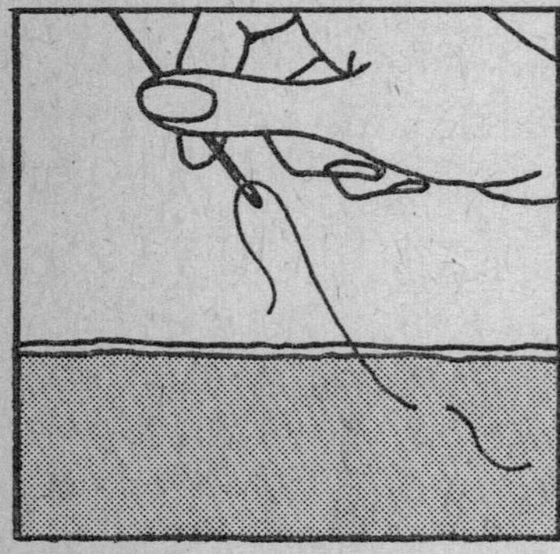

1 Insert the threaded needle through the thicknesses of fabric to be stitched, and bring it out again a fraction of an inch farther along.

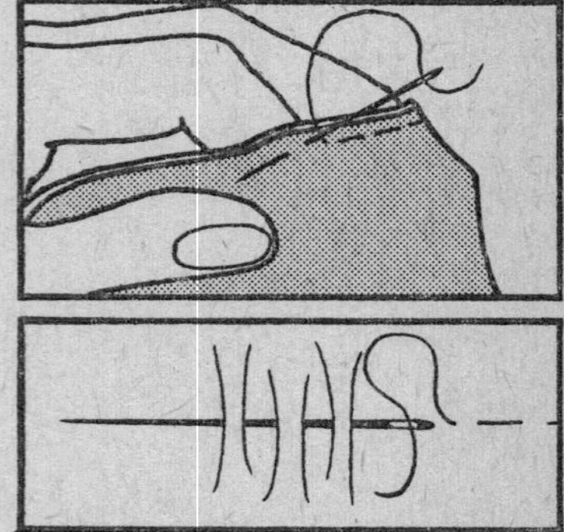

2 Make a few more stitches in this way and pull the thread right through. Do not pucker. For speed, make two or three stitches and store them on the needle before pulling the thread through.

back stitch

Has the same uses as running stitch but makes a stronger seam. It is a good substitute for machining. Where it is used for a main seam it is important to keep it small and neat.

1 Make one small running stitch.

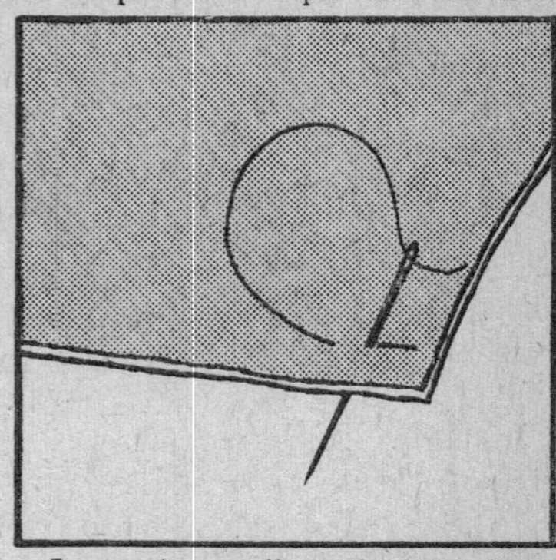

2 Insert the needle again behind the thread at the end of the previous stitch.

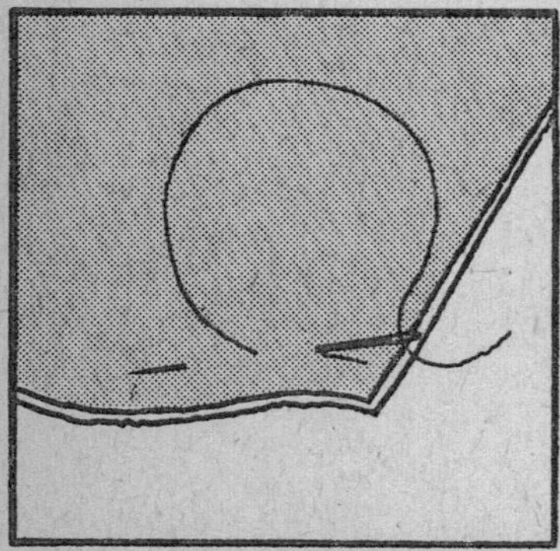

3 Bring it out again just in front of the thread.

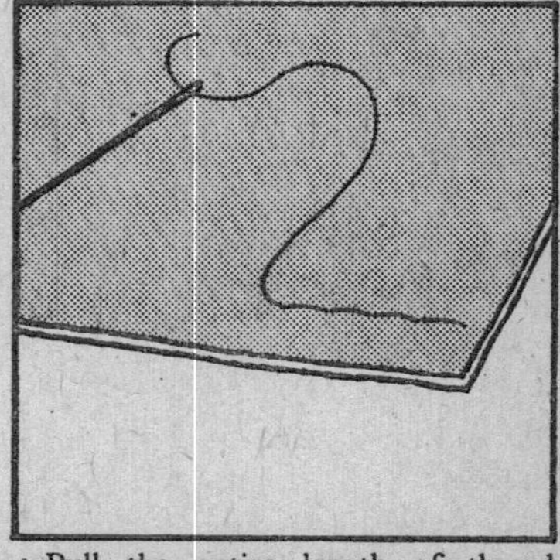

4 Pull the entire length of thread through each time you make a stitch. You can't save time by storing stitches with this one.

hem stitch (or felling)

Used for sewing down one edge of fabric on to another piece.

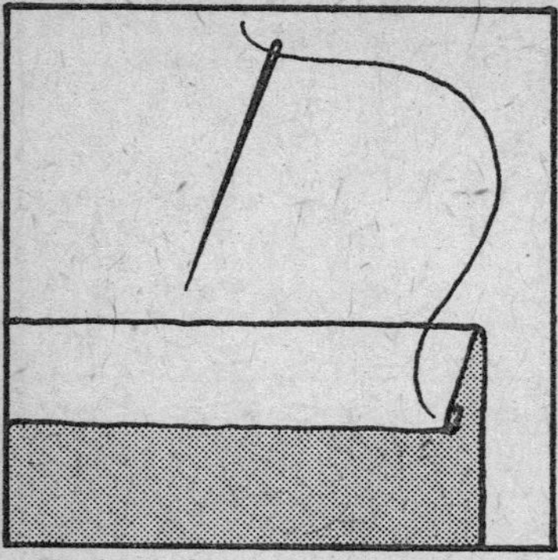

1 Working from right to left, start with the thread pulled through to the upper side of the work.

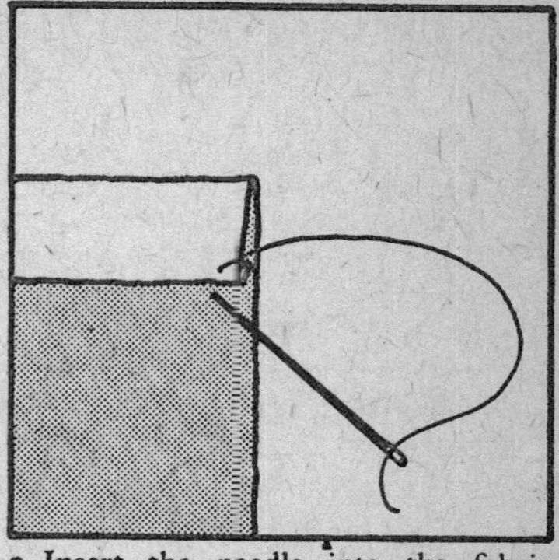

2 Insert the needle into the fabric immediately below the upper fold.

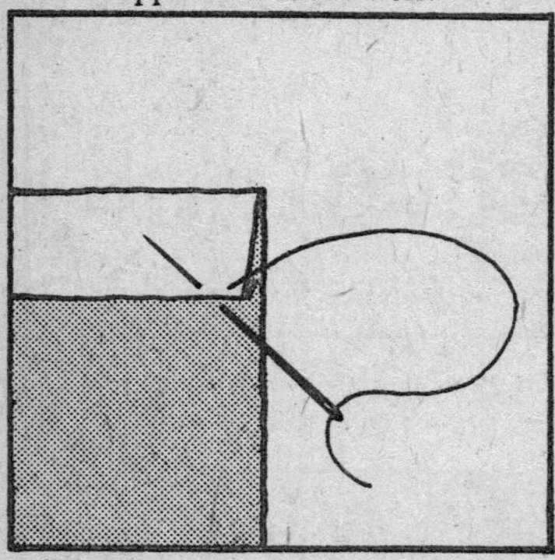

3 Bring it out just above the fold a little farther along. Pull the thread through. Do not pucker.

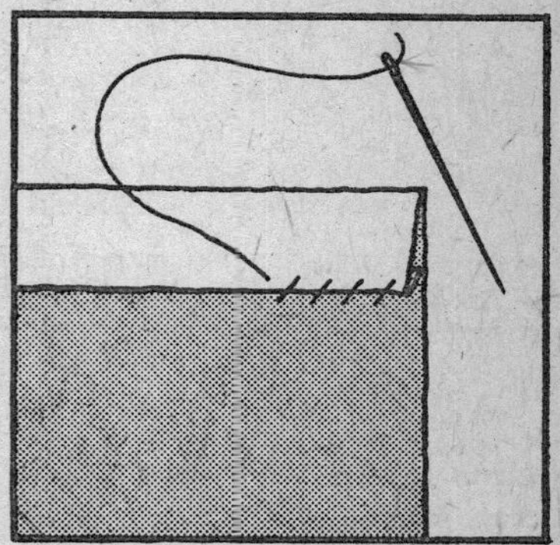

4 You can't store hem stitches on the needle, but store a few on the thread, pulling it through its entire length every four or five stitches.

slip stitch

Used in the same way as hem stitch, but where great delicacy is called for and where little or no sign of stitching should be seen on the outside. Start above the upper fold as for hemming.

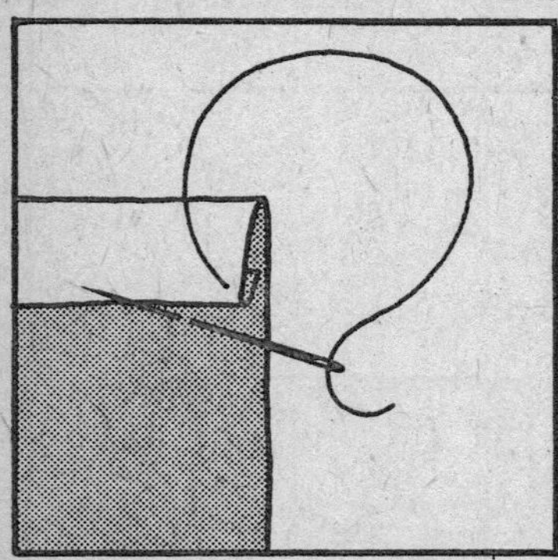

1 Slip stitch is well spaced out, so about $\frac{1}{4}$ in. farther along take up a thread or two of the fabric immediately below the fold.

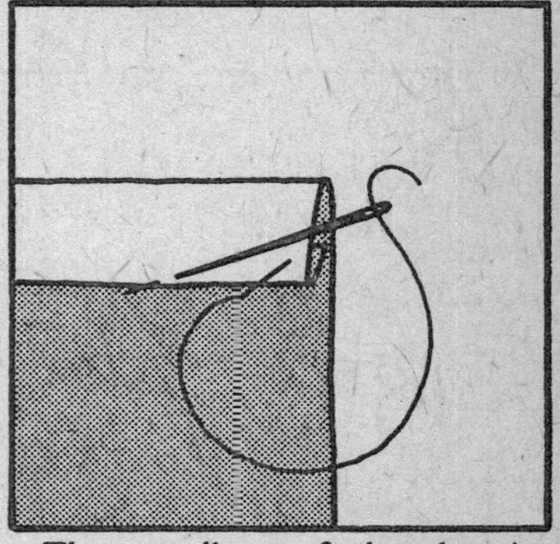

2 The same distance farther along insert the needle into the fold, on the fold, and bring it out again without letting it pierce the outer side of the fabric.

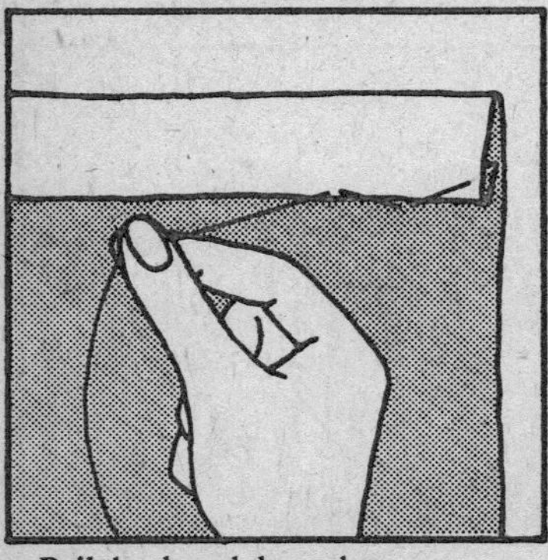

3 Pull the thread through.

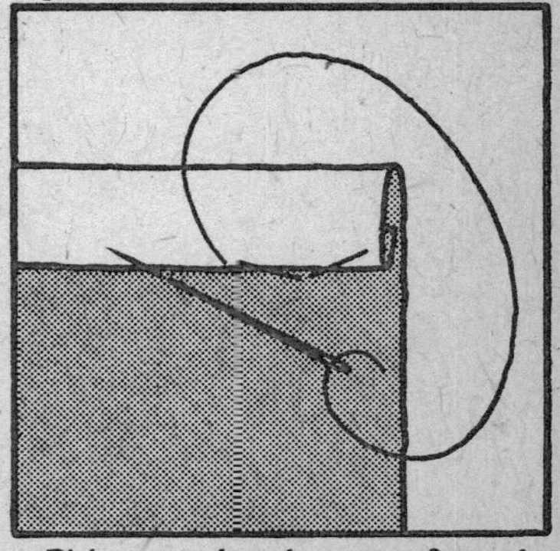

4 Pick up a thread or two from the fabric immediately below the fold, again an equal distance farther on.

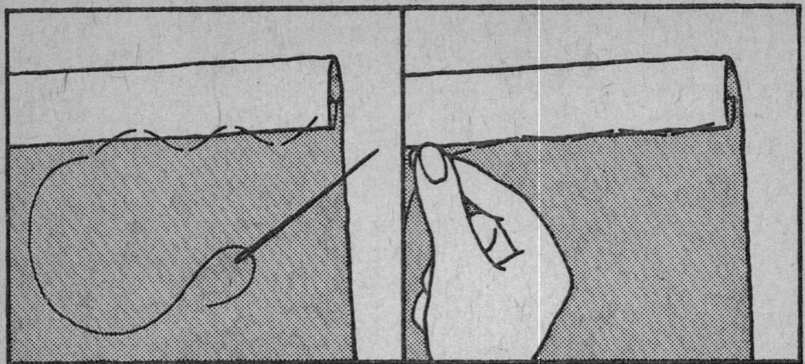

5 You can store a few stitches at a time on the thread. Do not store on the needle, and do not pucker.

oversewing (or overcast stitch)

Used for attaching any two pieces of fabric face to face, or for neatening a raw edge. Also used in a slightly varied form for sewing on fastenings like press studs.

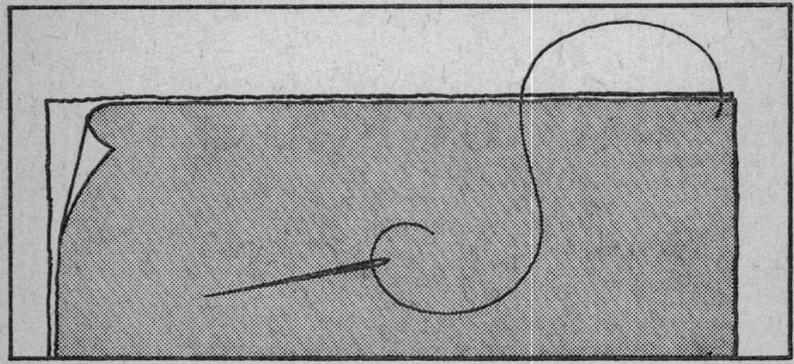

1 Working from right to left, start with the thread on the upper side of the fabric.

2 Insert the needle into the back of the fabric through to the front, about $\frac{1}{8}$ in. from the edge and about the same distance away from the previous stitch. Pull the thread through.

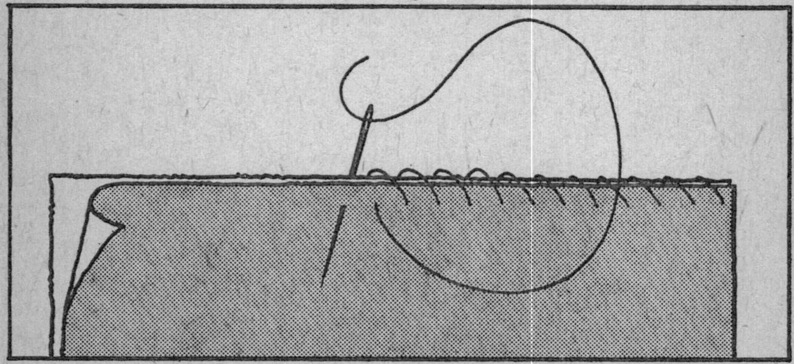

3 Continue. Store a few stitches on the thread if you like, but not on the needle. Do not pucker.

tacking or basting stitch

Used as a temporary measure to hold fabric pieces together until final stitching, or to mark a planned fold or line of sewing.

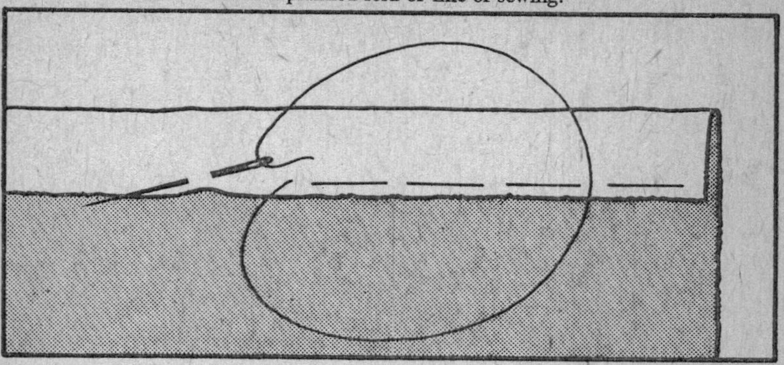

1 The same principle as running stitch but take long stitches with short spaces in between, for speed.

herringbone, cross or catch stitch

Used for hems or for 'inside' work on garments such as attaching interfacing.

1 Work from left to right and start with thread on the upper side of the fabric.

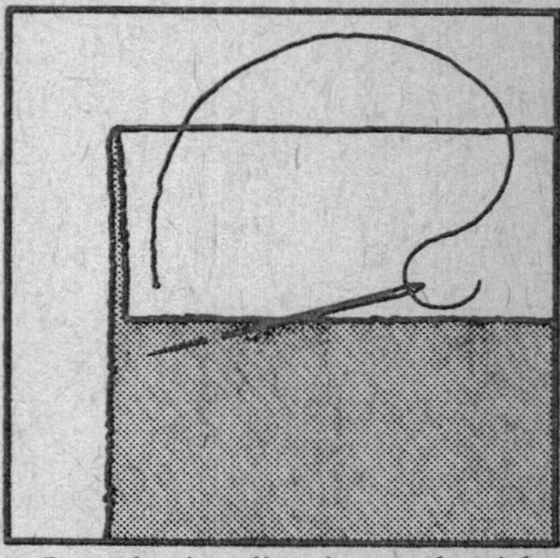

2 In a slanting direction to the right, with the needle pointing to the left, pick up a few threads below the hem.

3 Pull the needle and thread through.

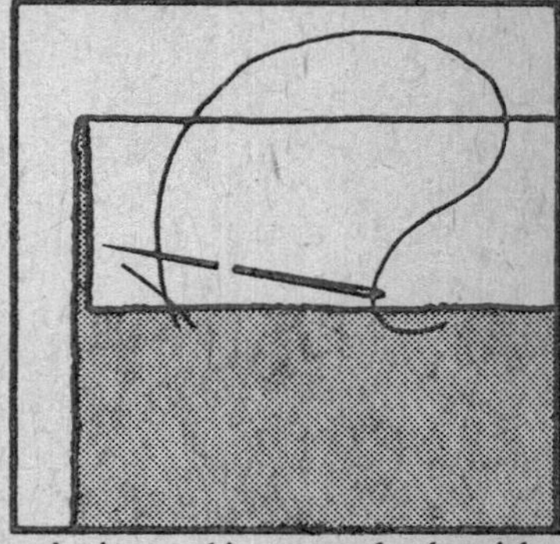

4 Again, working towards the right, with the needle pointing to the left, pick up a few threads from the fold.

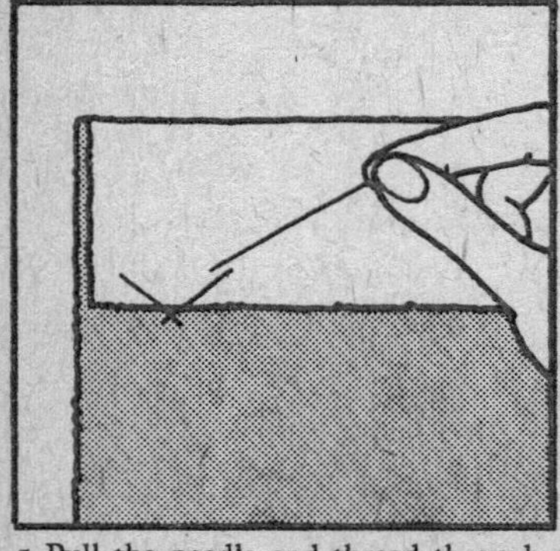

5 Pull the needle and thread through.

6 Continue working alternately above and below the hem, pulling the thread through to its entire length for each stitch. Do not attempt to store stitches.

blanket stitch

So called because of its use on thick woollen fabrics, but also useful for attaching fabrics face to face without a hem, and in a miniature form for buttonholes. Used extensively with minor variations in embroidery. Unless required for decoration, all the stitches must be the same size. If working without a fold, use an imaginary line to keep the bottom edge of the stitches straight.

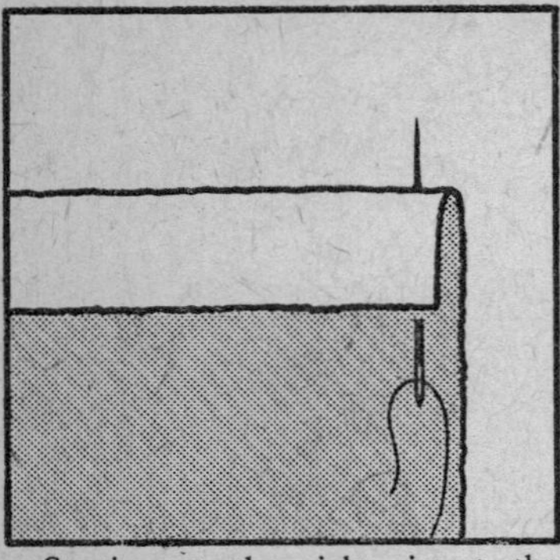

1 Starting at the right, insert the needle and thread under the fold (if no fold take the needle through the fabric) and bring it out at the outer edge.

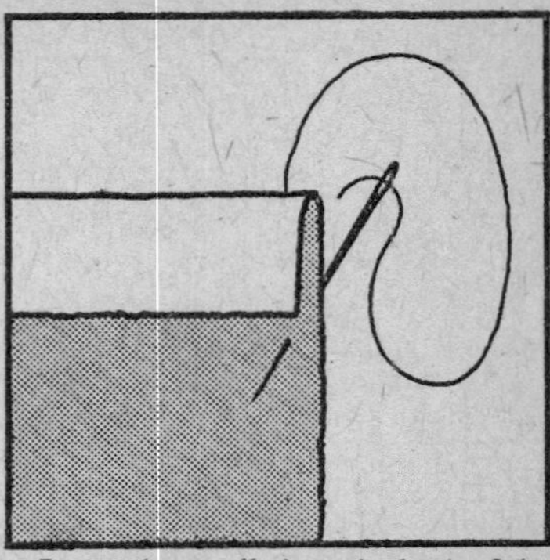

2 Insert the needle into the back of the fabric at the bottom edge of the fold and immediately underneath the point where the thread emerges.

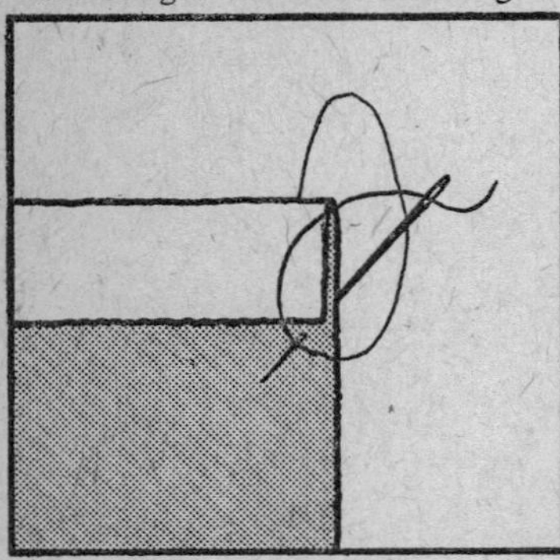

3 While the needle is half in and half out of the fabric take hold of the thread near the eye of the needle and wind it once under the pointed end of the needle, from left to right.

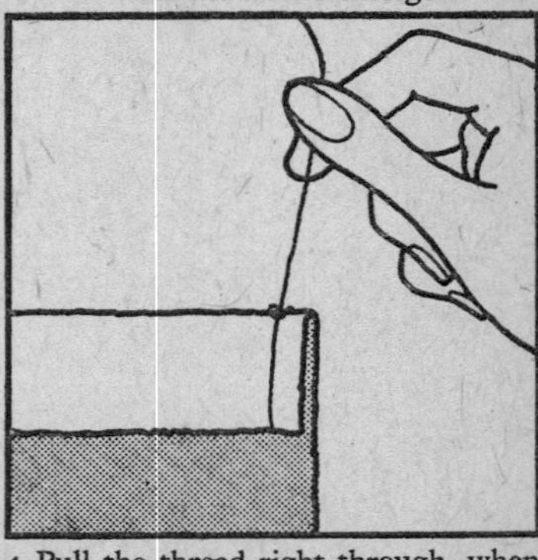

4 Pull the thread right through, when it will be caught by a loop on the outer edge, and at the same time will hold the hem down firmly.

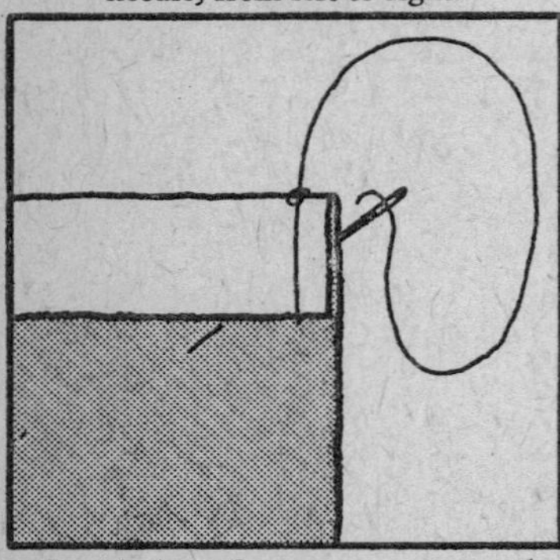

5 Decide how far apart you want the stitches and insert the needle again at the back of the fabric, bringing it out at the front, at the bottom of the fold.

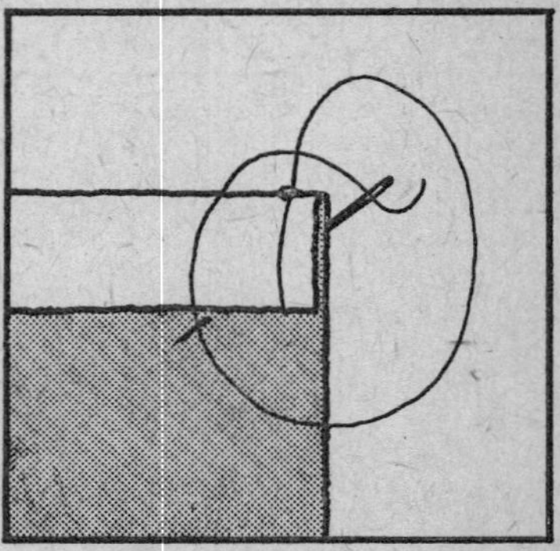

6 Again, wind the thread round the point of the needle before you push it right through.

7 Pull the thread through to its entire length.

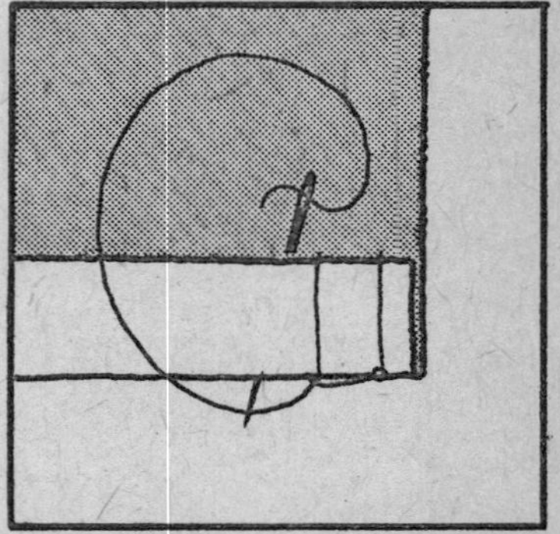

8 Some people work blanket stitch downwards like buttonhole stitch. The principle is the same – it's just a question of how you hold the fabric.

buttonhole stitch

This works on the same principle as blanket stitch, but whereas blanket stitch can be worked with the loops at the top, buttonhole stitch is always worked with the loops at the bottom. If you are working a buttonhole, for instance, turn the work so that the loops come at the bottom edge. It is always worked on the right side of the fabric.

1 The stitches must be small and very close together, so begin by inserting the needle a tiny distance from the edge and bring it out below the edge.

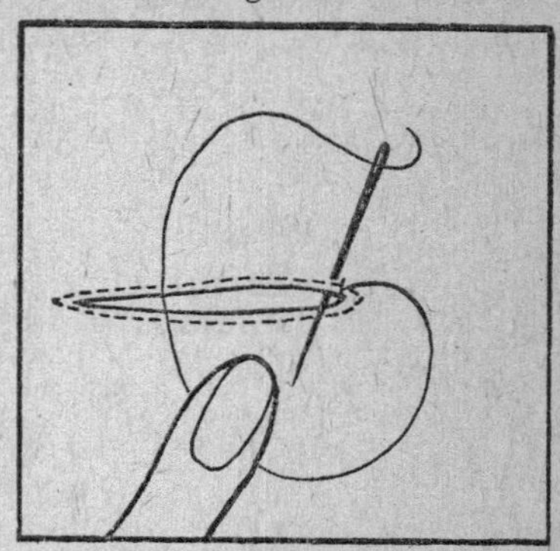

2 Hold the thread forwards with your left thumb.

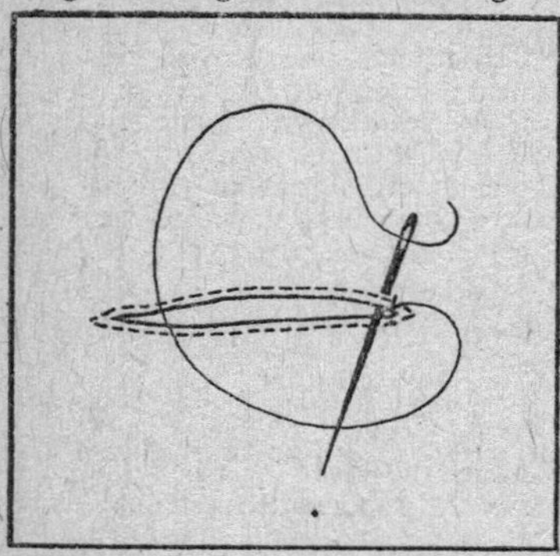

3 Bring the needle through over the thread, which will form a loop when pulled to its fullest extent.

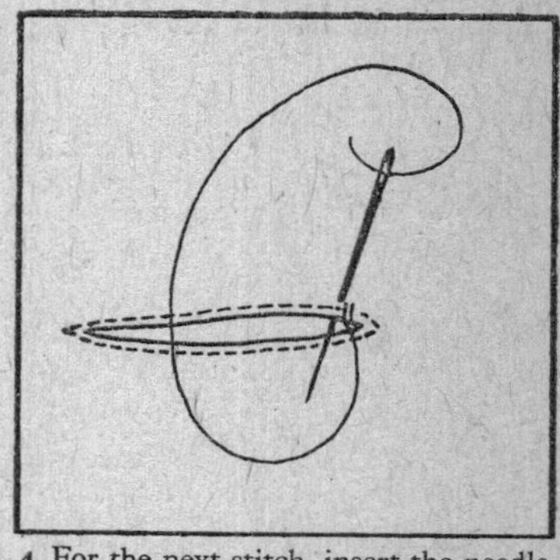

4 For the next stitch, insert the needle close up against the previous stitch.

gathering

Exactly as a running stitch but sewn either with double thread or two separate lines of running stitches. Secure the thread very firmly to start and do small, even running stitches for the required length. To gather, do not fasten off but gently pull the thread through the fabric, at the same time easing the fabric in the opposite direction. Spread the gathers evenly and fasten off securely.

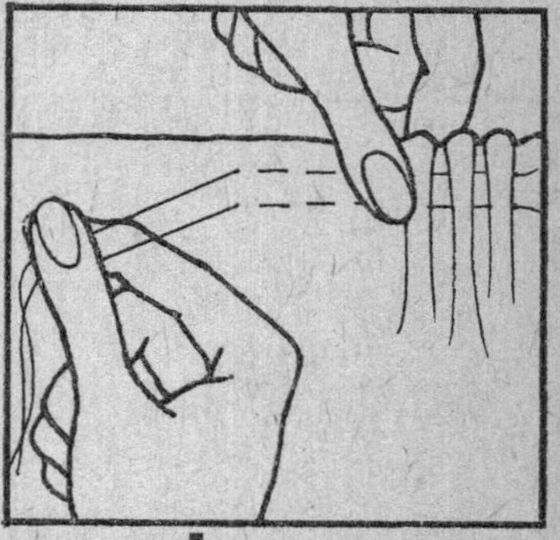

fastening off and on stitch

This is not given any identity or dignity in any sewing books, but it is in fact one of the most important stitches. It's a mixture of running stitch, back stitch and oversewing.

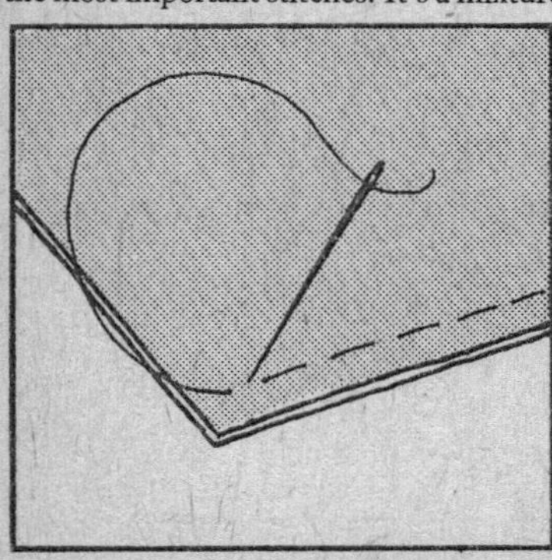

1 Insert the needle behind the point where the thread emerges from the fabric.

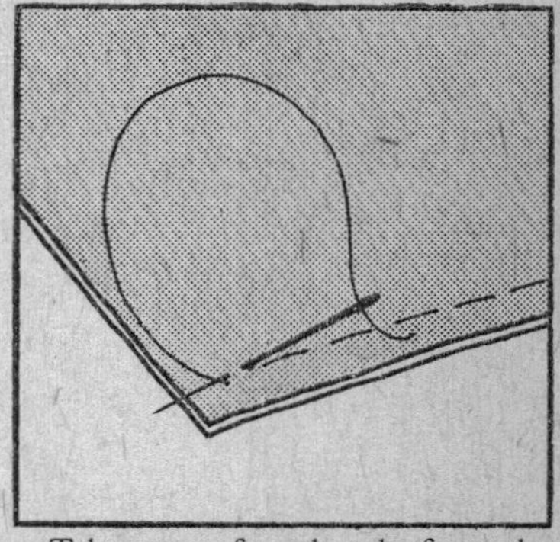

2 Take up a few threads from the fabric and bring the needle out on top again. Pull the thread right through.

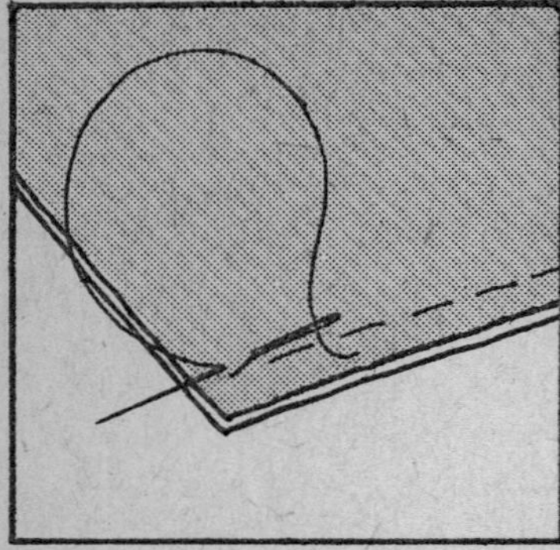

3 Insert the needle again where you did last time, and bring it out at the same point as last time. Pull the thread through.

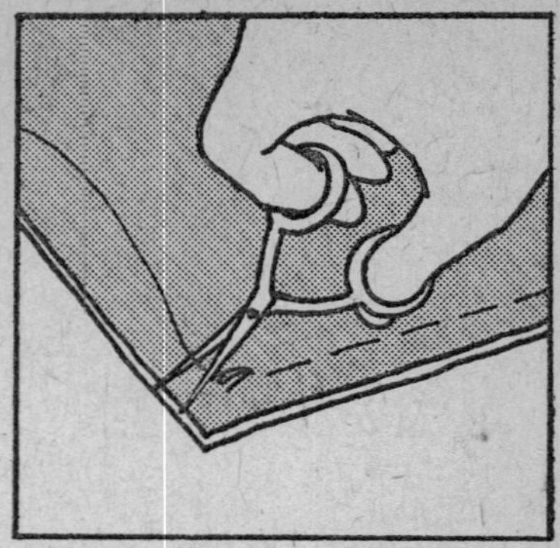

4 Do this at least three times, and try not to let the needle penetrate deeper than the seam allowance, so that nothing shows on the outside.

seams

To the uninitiated any line of sewing is a seam, but strictly speaking there is a difference between seams and hems. A seam is a join, but a hem is made when you sew down one piece of fabric on to another. For instance, you have a seam down the side of a dress to join the front and back together, but you have a hem at the bottom where you fold the fabric and sew it down. This chapter concerns seams only.

It is important when making garments to press all seams as you go along because it will never be as easy once the garment is completed (see page 153).

seam allowance

Never sew too near the edge. Leave about $\frac{1}{2}$ in. between the line of sewing and the edge of the fabric. This $\frac{1}{2}$ in. is known as a seam allowance. All paper patterns are made with at least $\frac{1}{2}$ in. seam allowance (see page 138).

plain seam

Can be hand sewn in running or back stitch, or machined.

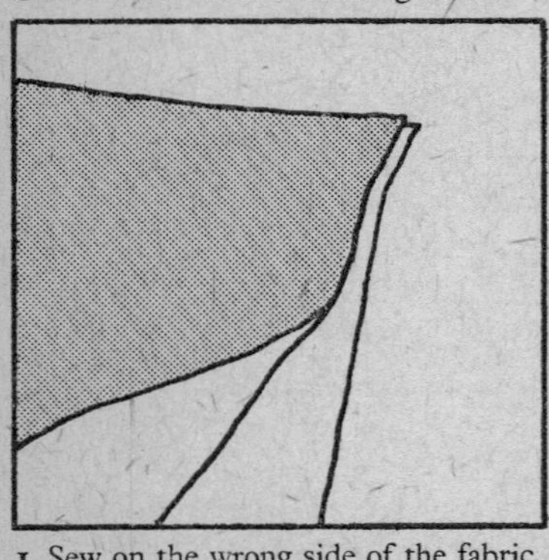

1 Sew on the wrong side of the fabric, with the right sides together facing inwards.

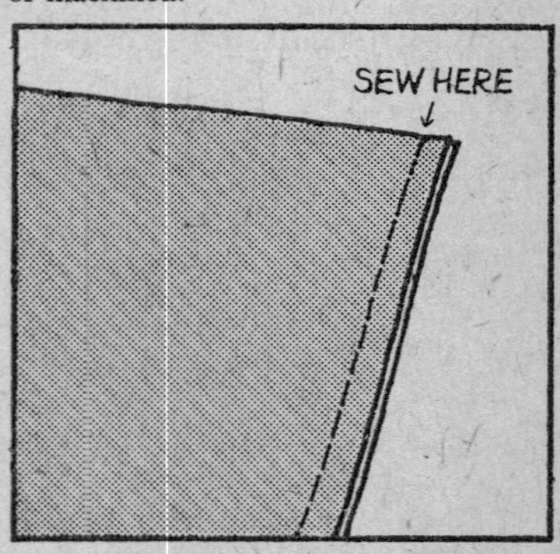

2 Sew $\frac{1}{2}$ in. in from the edge all the way along.

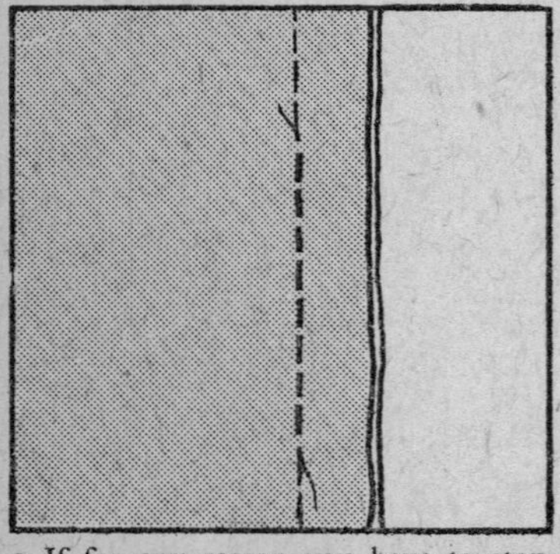

3 If for any reason you have to stop in the middle of a seam, start again $1\frac{1}{2}$ in. farther back and sew on the original line to prevent gaping.

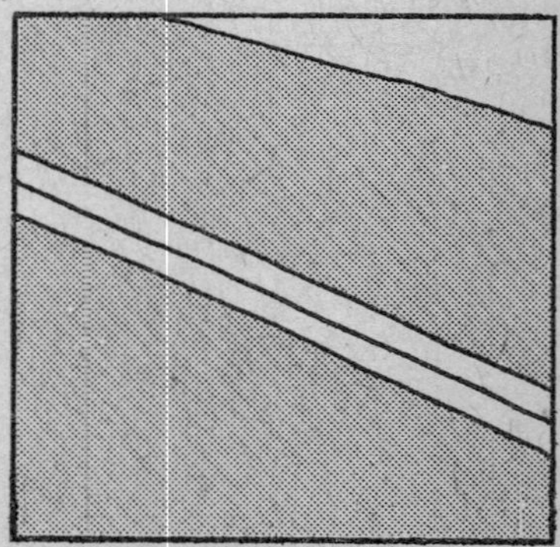

4 When completed, open out the seam and press flat.

run and fell

Fell is another word for hemming, so this seam consists of two operations, a running seam and a hemmed seam. It is used mainly on nightwear, underwear and blouses, where constant washing would make a ragged mess of seam allowances no matter how well finished off. You can, of course, do it all on a machine if you wish instead of hemming.

1 Work on the wrong side of the fabric by placing the two pieces face to face, right sides inwards, with one edge about ¼ in. below the other.

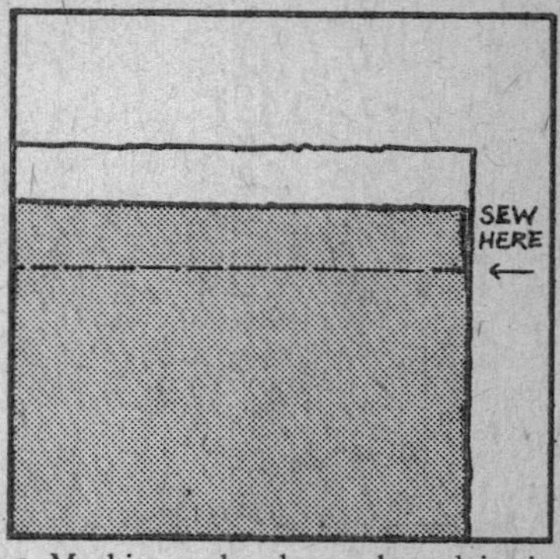

2 Machine or hand sew about ¼ in. in from the lower edge.

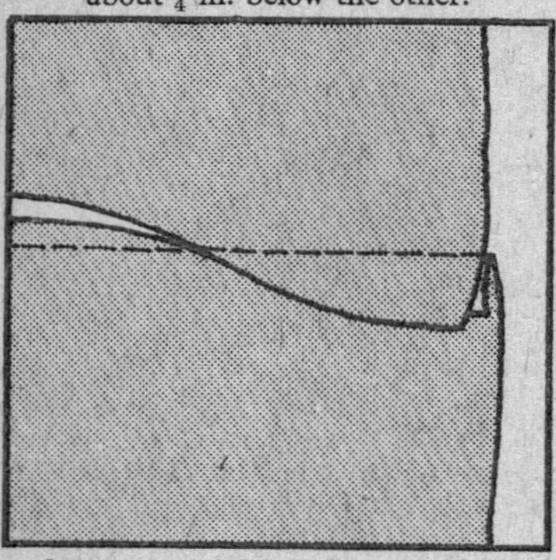

3 Open out the fabric flat and fold the two edges towards you, the fold being on the line of stitching. Press.

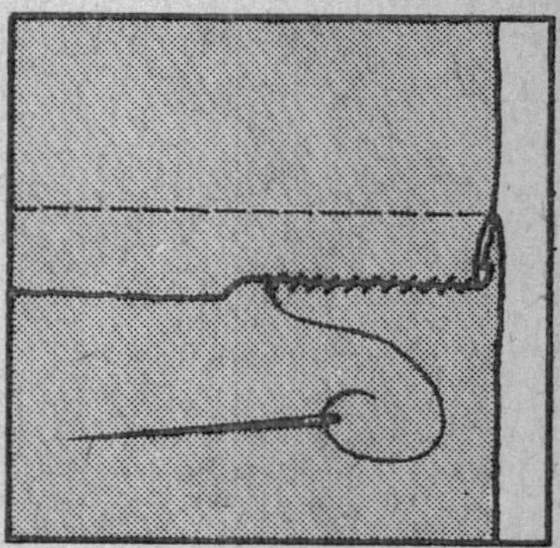

4 Tuck the raw edge under and either hem (fell) or machine stitch it to the main piece.

french seam

This consists of two separate running (plain) seams and is used on very fine or fraying fabrics, particularly chiffon, voile and lace where a folded-back seam allowance would show through and be unsightly.

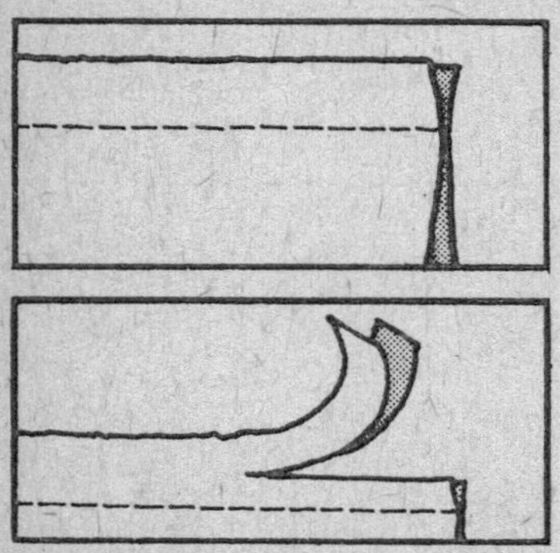

1 The first seam is sewn on the right sides of the fabric. Place the two edges together, right sides out, and sew a plain seam about ½ in. in from the edge. Trim off the seam allowance to about ¼ in. Make sure it is straight and even.

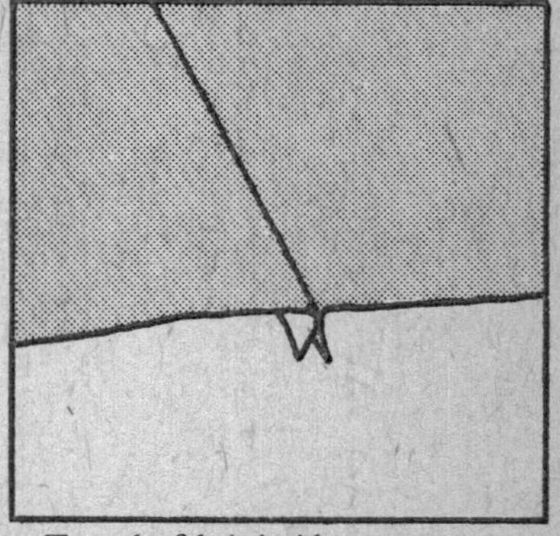

2 Turn the fabric inside out.

3 Fold on the seam you have just made. The wrong side of the fabric will be on the outside.

4 Sew a plain seam far enough in from the edge to completely cover the seam allowance inside.

top stitched seams

This is generally done for decorative purposes, and can be single or double, either sewn by hand or machined.

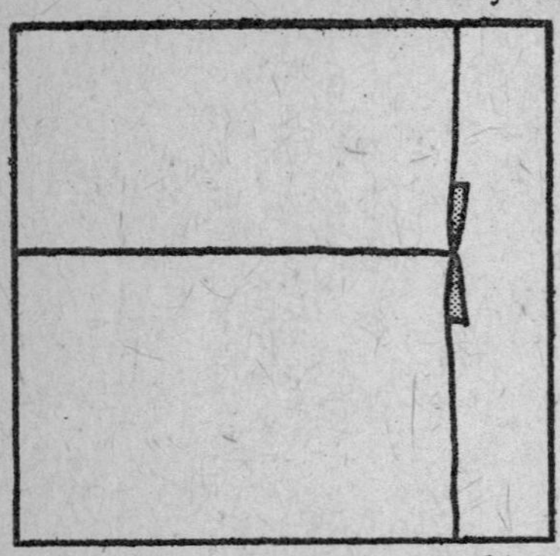

1 Sew a plain seam, open out the fabric and press.

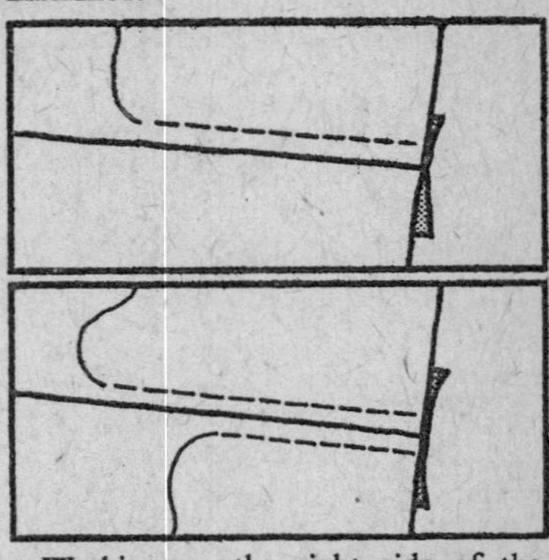

2 Working on the right side of the fabric, sew another plain seam, either by hand or machined, one side or both sides of the first seam.

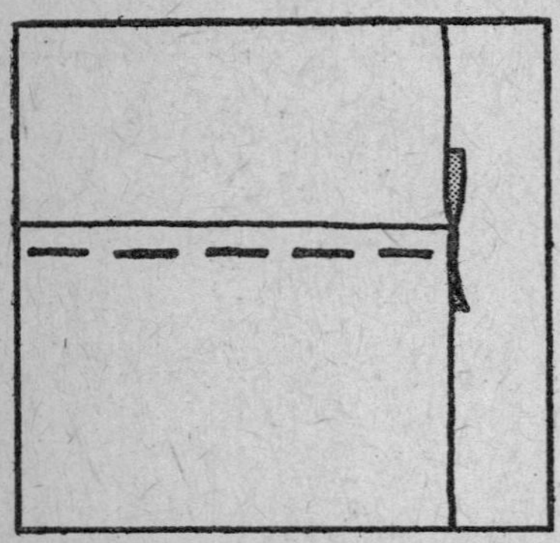

3 To give a saddle stitched effect, work by hand with a contrasting thick thread, in large even running stitches.

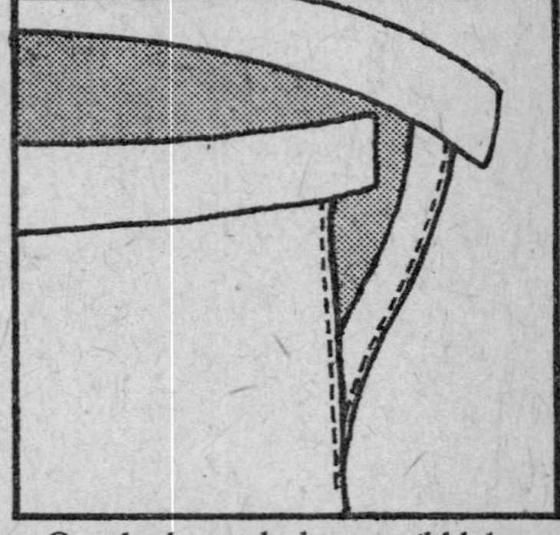

4 Can also be used when you fold down facing. On the fold, on the right side, run a plain seam. This helps to hold down the facing without further stitching.

welt seam

This has the outward appearance of a run and fell seam, but it is not, although it is used on coats and heavy fabrics. First of all make a single plain seam, then proceed as follows:

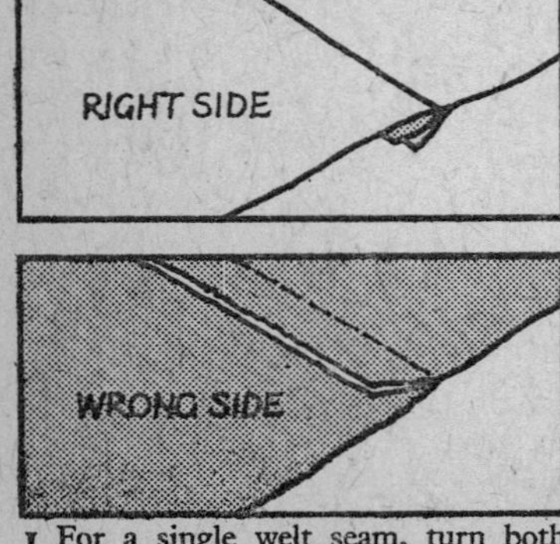

1 For a single welt seam, turn both seam allowances to one side.

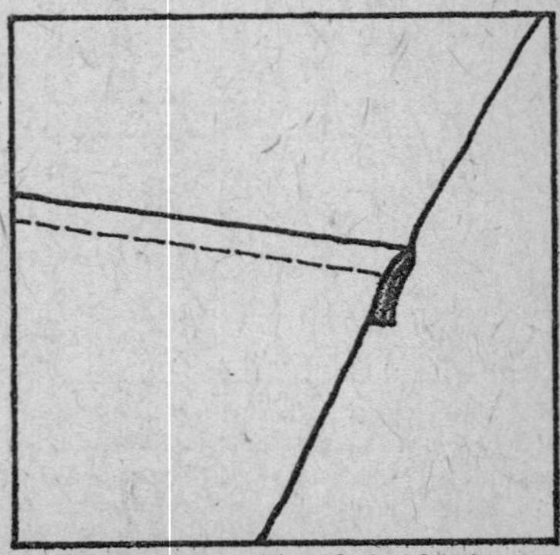

2 On the right side of the fabric sew another line of stitching over the folded back seam allowance, about ¼ in. away from the first seam.

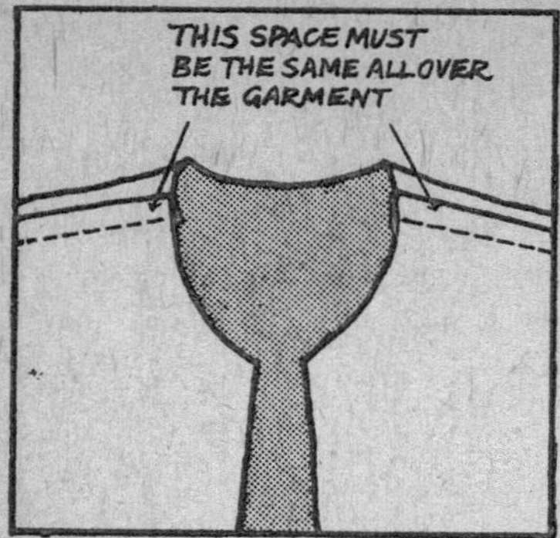

3 You must be consistent with this seam, all over the garment.

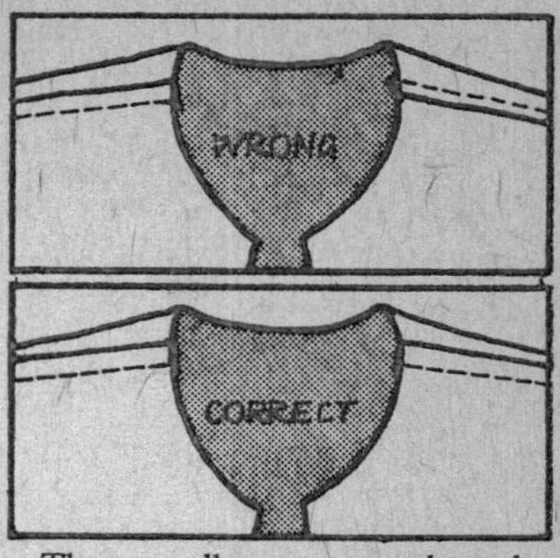

4 The seam allowance must always be turned in the same direction.

5 Your second line of sewing must be the same distance from the first seam.

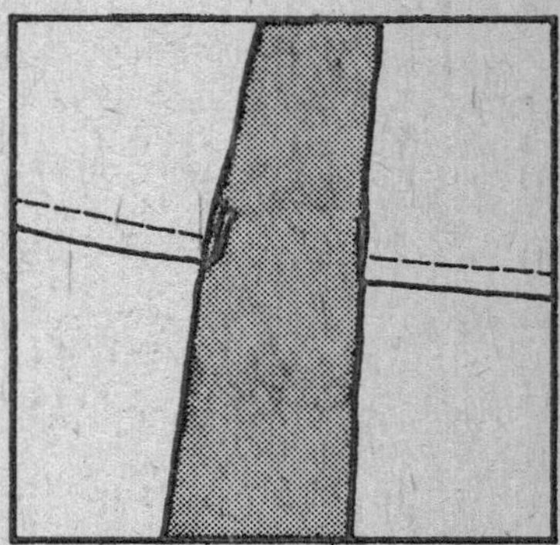

6 And the same side of the first seam.

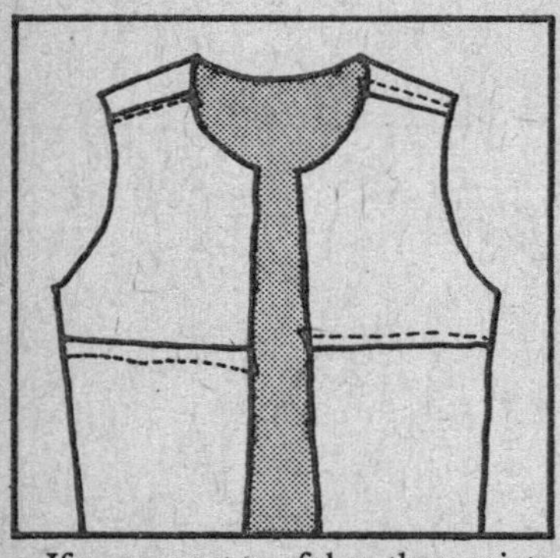

7 If you are not careful on these points you could have a coat looking like this.

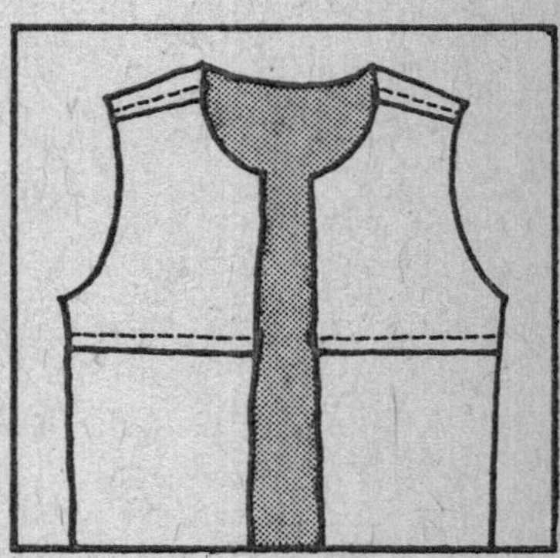

8 Instead of like this.

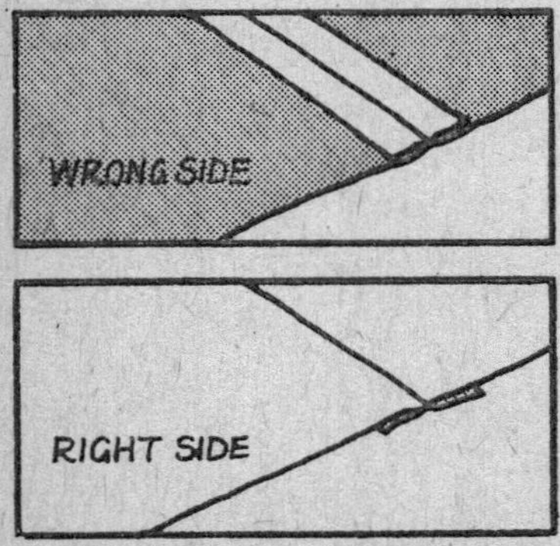

9 For a double welt seam, open out the seam allowances and press.

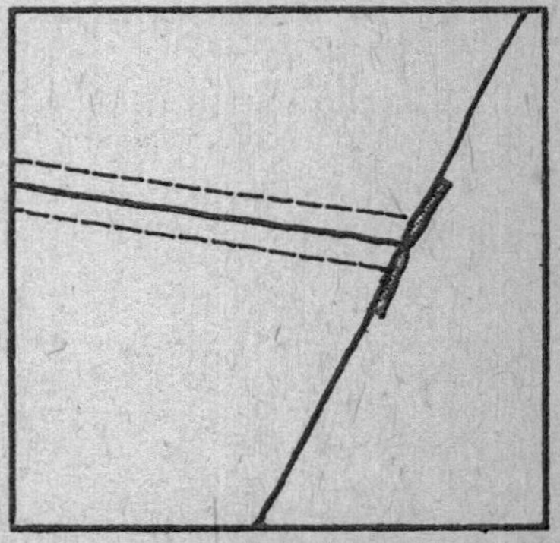

10 Sew a line of stitching either side of the original seam, both exactly the same distance away from it.

slot or open seam

This is a very smart touch and is used only for a pleasing effect.

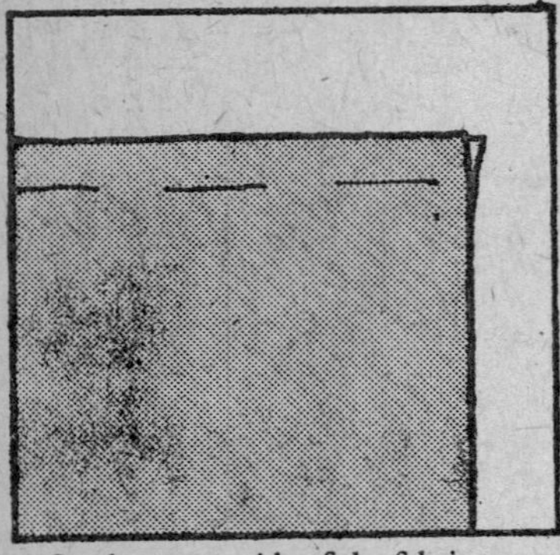

1 On the wrong side of the fabric sew a single seam in tacking stitches, which will later be removed.

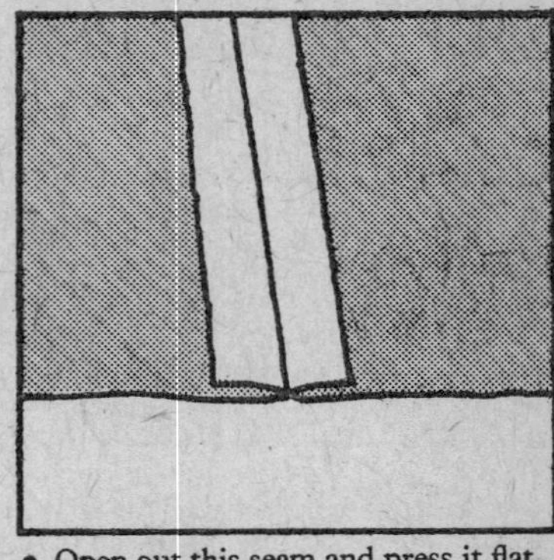

2 Open out this seam and press it flat.

3 Cut a strip of matching fabric the same width as the folded back seam allowances, and the same length as the seam.

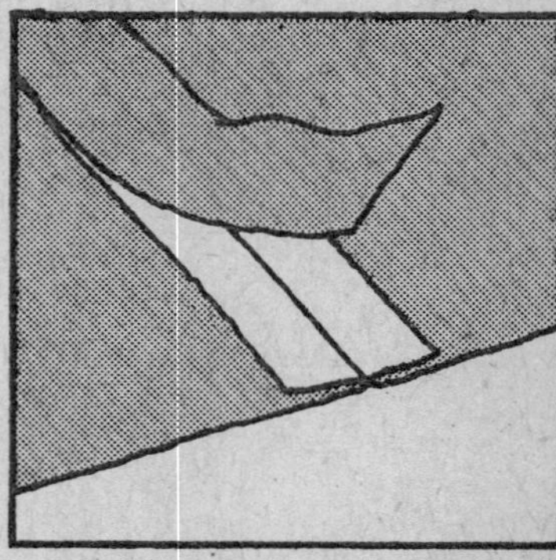

4 Lay this strip right side downwards over the wrong side of the seam allowances.

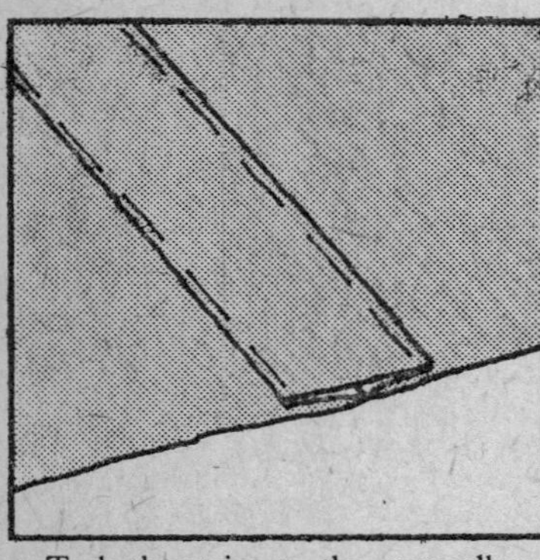

5 Tack the strips to the seam allowances along both edges.

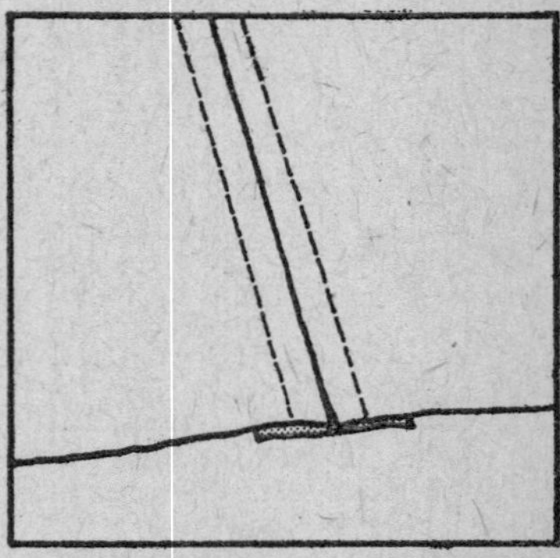

6 On the right side of the fabric do a single line of sewing on either side of the centre seam, both lines an equal distance away from it.

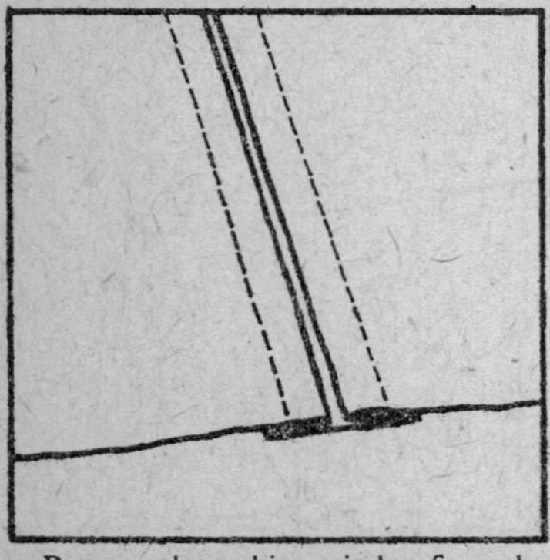

7 Remove the tacking stitches from the centre seam.

fabrics

It would be impossible to list all the different types of fabrics, but they can be grouped into four sections, thin, thick, fancy and household, or (perhaps more homely) summer, winter, evening and household.

THIN FABRICS consist of cotton, rayon, Tricel, Crimplene and in fact everything lightweight that is not made of wool. Most of these, with the exception of Crimplene, are made in 36 in. widths. Some man-made fibres such as Crimplene and Terylene come in 54 in. widths.

THICK FABRICS are all the woollens, coat and suit weights, bonded jerseys and all the things you would not make a summer dress of. These come in widths of 54 in. and 60 in.

FANCY FABRICS. These are lace, brocades, velvet, lurex and all the things you wouldn't put in the washing machine. They come in varying widths – the cheap ones 36 in., the good ones 54 in. and 60 in.

HOUSEHOLD FABRICS, better known as soft furnishings, consist of curtaining, loose cover fabrics and stout upholstery fabrics. You can get cheap curtaining in 36in. widths but most of it is 48 in., with some 54 in. and 60 in.

RIGHT AND WRONG SIDES. Sometimes it isn't easy to tell the difference. Look for lumpy threads, and wisps of thread particularly near the selvage. With patterned fabrics, the colouring is never so bright, or the pattern so decisive, on the wrong side.

grain of fabric

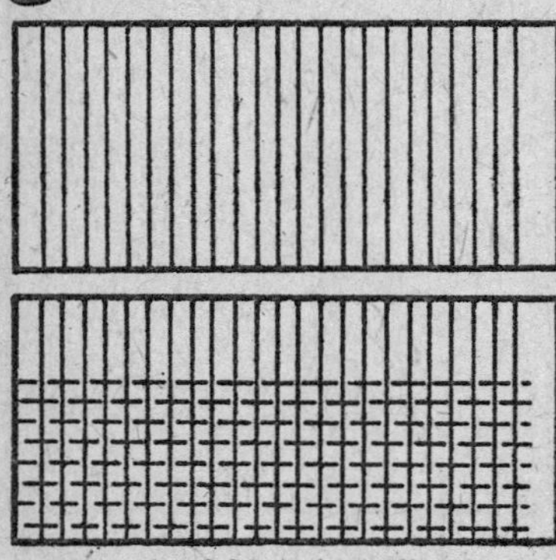

1 A length of fabric basically consists of hundreds of threads going down, and hundreds more going across, all woven like a darn (see page 131) on a much more minute and refined scale.

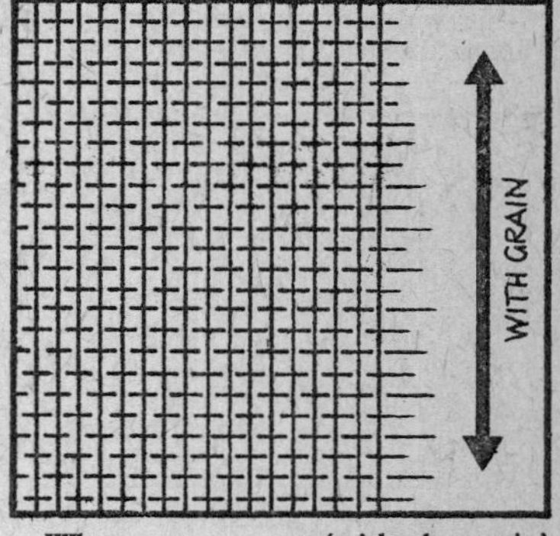

2 When patterns say 'with the grain' they mean the downward grain.

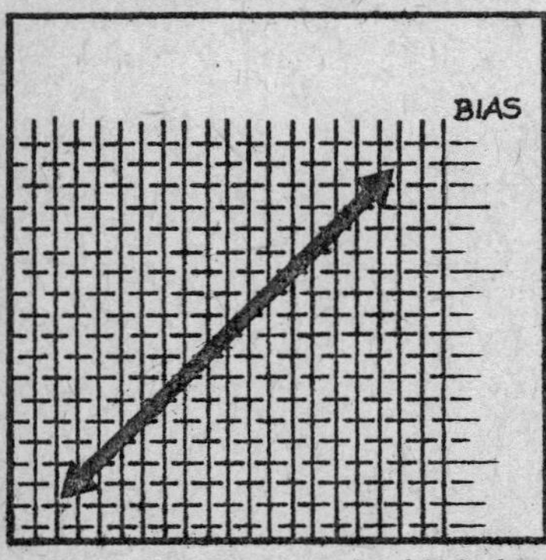

3 When they say 'on the bias' they mean diagonally across the grain.

Apart from large patterned fabrics and velvet, most modern materials can be handled easily by the home sewer.

velvet

This beautiful fabric is a tricky one to work on because (a) you can't iron it like other fabrics, and (b) it has a pile, which is shiny or dull according to which way up the pile is. You must lay your pattern pieces all facing in the same direction, so allow for a little wastage when buying, unless the pattern specifies velvet and shows you how to lay out the pieces on this fabric.

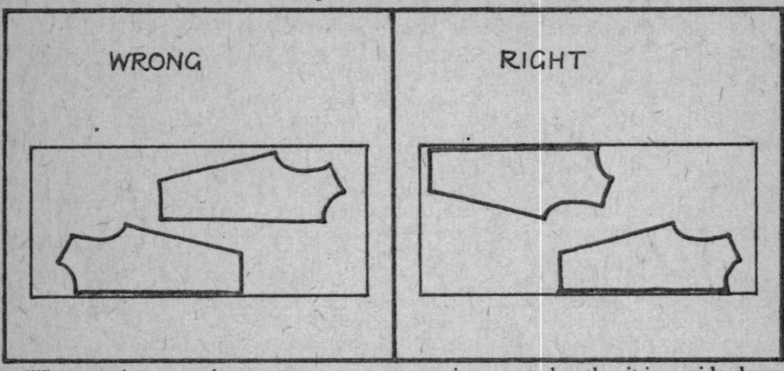

1 When cutting out velvet, never turn a pattern piece around so that it is upside down compared with the others.

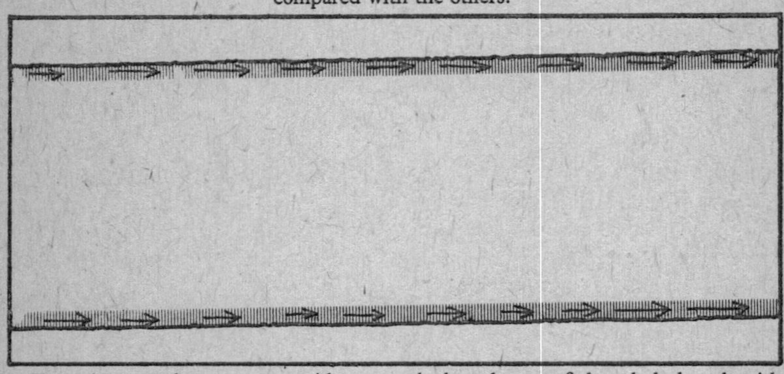

2 To make sure there are no accidents, mark the selvages of the whole length with arrows all pointing in the same direction. Use either tailor's chalk or a felt pen, or even pins all pointing the same way.

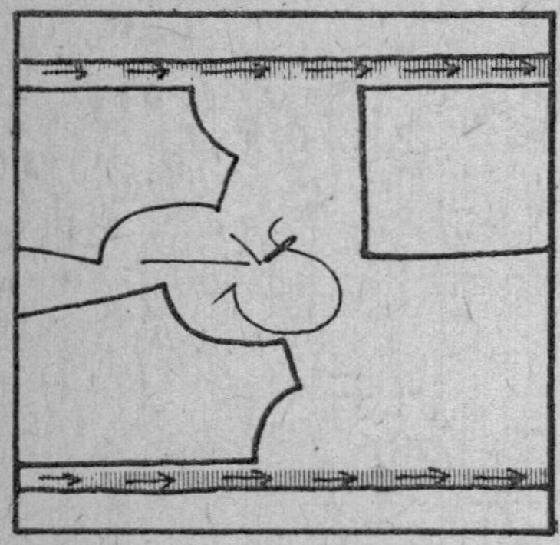

3 If you have sizeable scraps left between the pattern pieces, which might be needed on the garment somewhere, sew a rough arrow in contrasting thread on them before actually putting them on one side.

4 To press, never treat it like any other fabric.

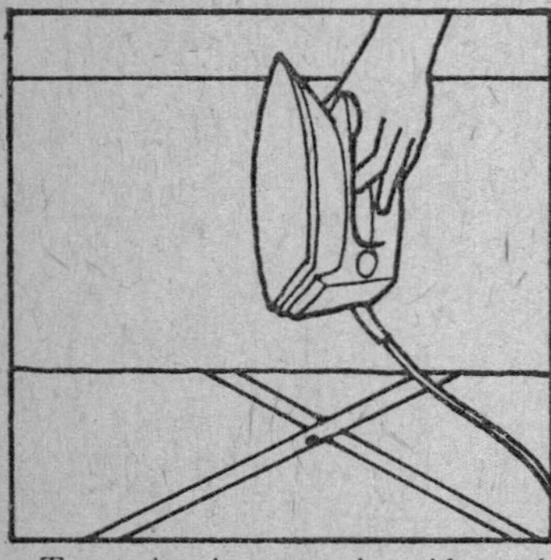

5 Turn the iron on its side and preferably get someone to steady it for you. Use a moderate heat.

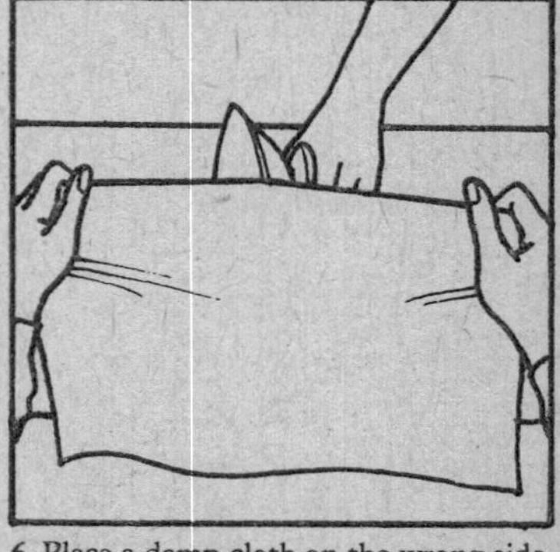

6 Place a damp cloth on the wrong side of the velvet, pick up the two together, and with the damp cloth against the iron, pass the velvet firmly backwards and forwards across the side of the iron.

If this does not give the smartness you would like, take the finished garment to a good valet cleaner or other professional for pressing, but don't take risks yourself.

corduroy

Treat in exactly the same way as velvet. Unless stated by the manufacturer to be washable treat it just as carefully.

large patterned fabrics

Patterned fabrics must match on made-up garments (see page 146) and on soft furnishings. Sometimes with the latter the designs are large, so when buying allow for wastage in matching the design. Consult the shop assistant if in doubt.

If the pattern is large and you are making a housecoat you will not be able to cut as economically as you would on plain fabric.

1 This is a typically large patterned fabric.

2 You must not make up a garment to look like this.

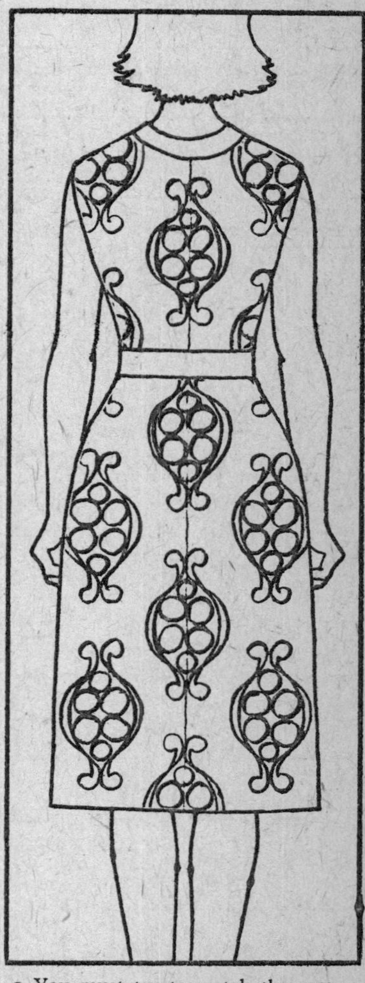

3 You must try to match the pattern like this.

In all cases where you have to cut to suit the pattern on the fabric instead of cutting economically to suit yourself, buy extra fabric to allow for the wastage involved.

sewing curves and angles

It is impossible to get a curved or angled seam to lie flat when it is opened out without some clipping, notching or cutting somewhere in the seam allowance. A good pattern is wasted unless you do this.

The two cardinal points to remember are (a) an inward curve only needs to be snipped with a straight cut, and (b) an outward curve has to have Vs cut into it because the seam allowance must be stretched to a greater length than the seam itself. In either case you can cut to within ⅛ in. of the sewing line.

Cutting or slashing is required to get a neat angle, but for beginners it takes a little courage. Once you have mastered the fact that seam allowances can be cut you will no longer produce garments that look home made.

Another rule to remember when slashing to form an angle is to reinforce the machine stitching at the angle with a few hand sewn stitches.

curves

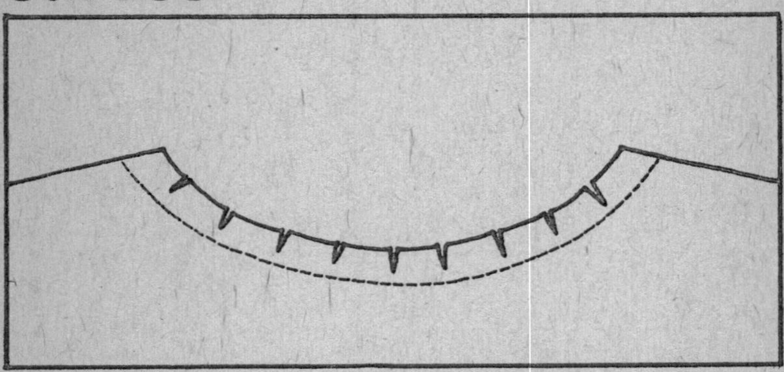

1 For an inward curve snip the seam allowance with sharp scissors. Be careful not to cut the stitching.

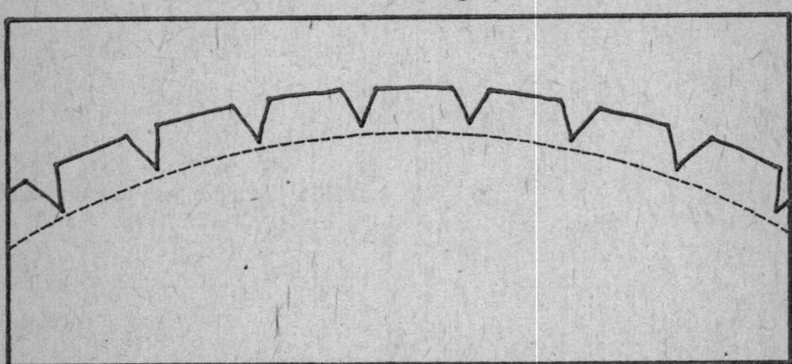

2 For outward curves cut tiny wedge shapes in the seam allowance.

angles

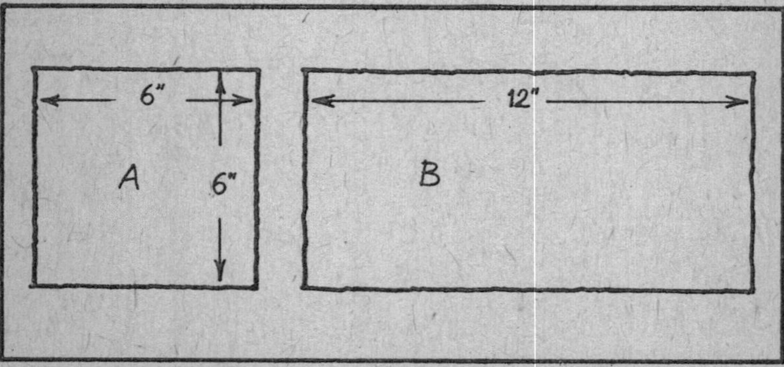

1 It is possible to sew the right-angled piece A to the straight piece B in one seam.

2 Pin one edge of the angled piece to the straight piece.

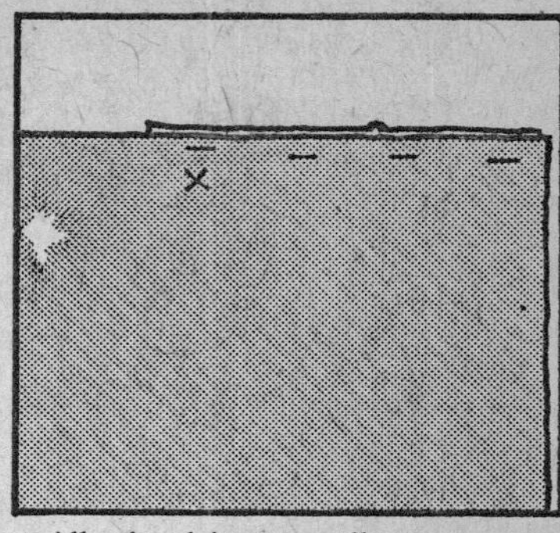

3 Allowing ½ in. seam allowance, make a mark on the straight piece where the angle will come.

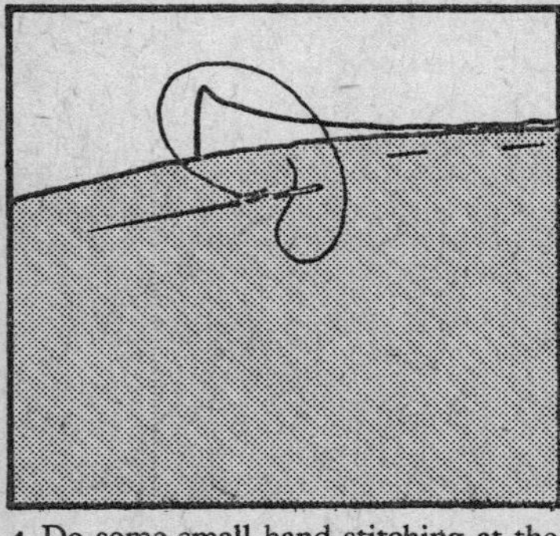

4 Do some small hand stitching at the spot you have marked on the straight piece as reinforcement.

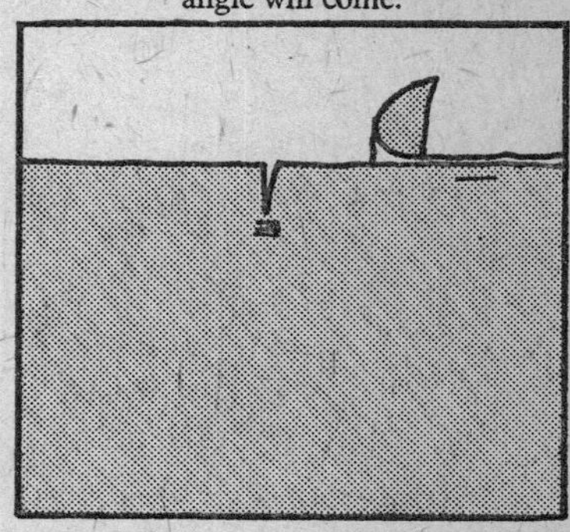

5 Cut (slash) the seam allowance of the straight piece from the edge to the hand stitching.

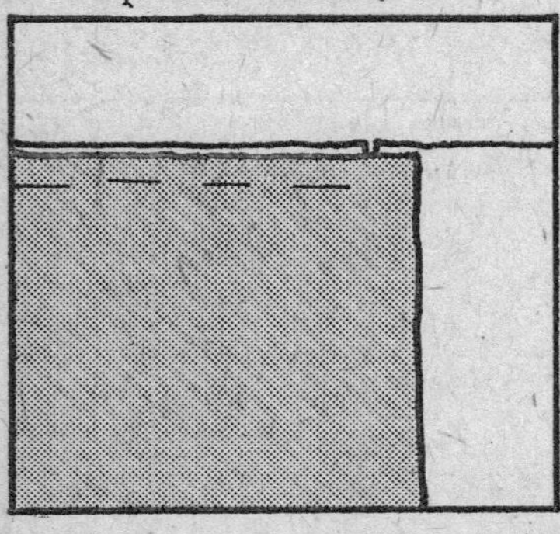

6 Tack the edge you had originally pinned, from the slash to the edge.

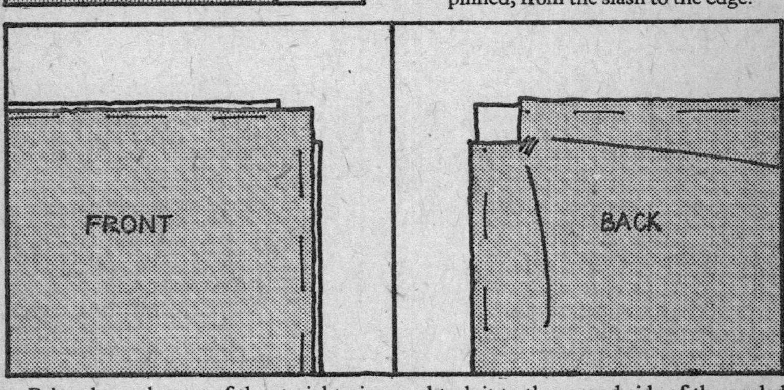

7 Bring down the rest of the straight piece and tack it to the second side of the angled piece.

8 With the straight piece uppermost sew one edge as far as your hand stitching.

9 At this point turn the work in the machine, smooth out any folds in the fabric, and continue sewing along the other edge.

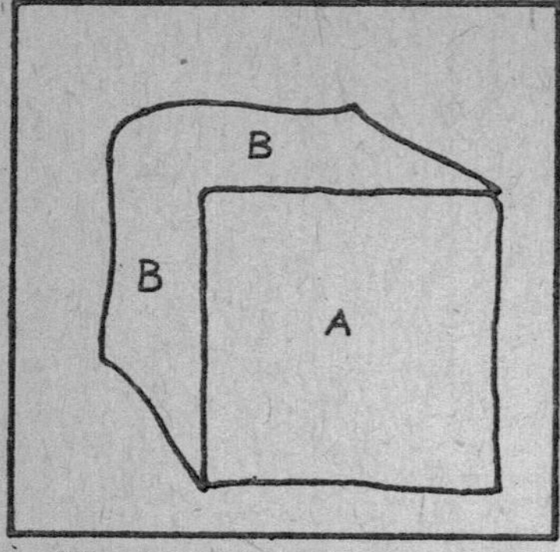

10 When turned inside out you will have a sharp, right-angled bend.

The same principle applies over and over again in dressmaking.

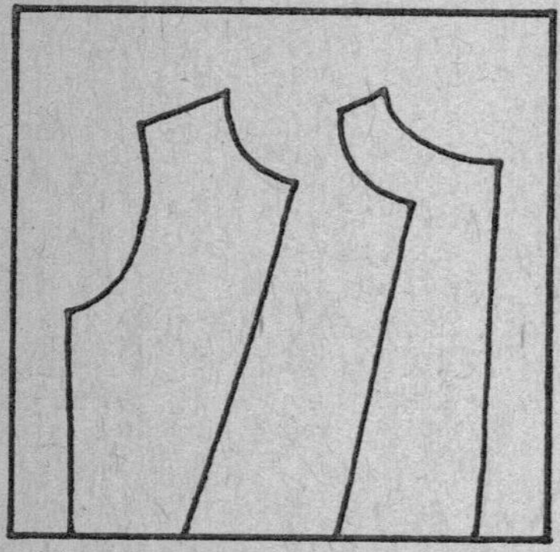

11 Here you have two angles to join together which would not lie flat without cutting (slashing) somewhere.

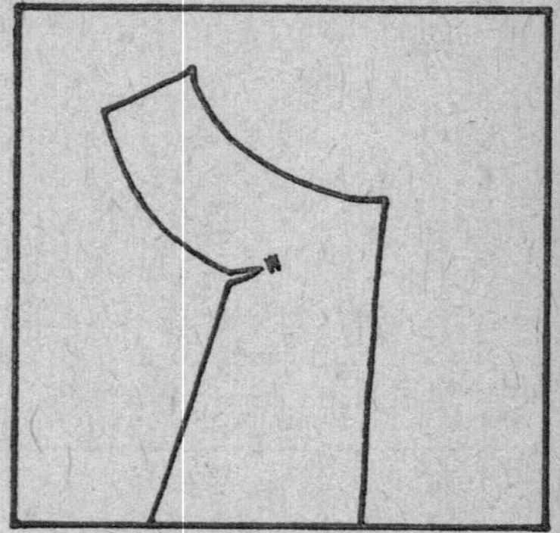

12 Cut (slash) into the seam allowance of the angle, inside which you are going to fit the other piece.

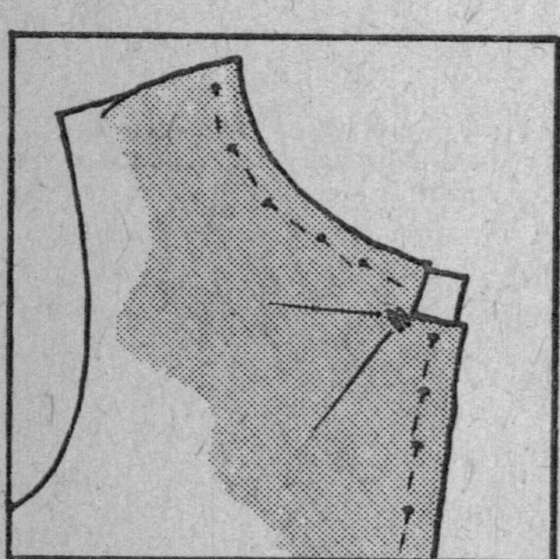

13 Now pin the other pattern piece to the one you have slashed, matching the actual spot where the point of the angle will come.

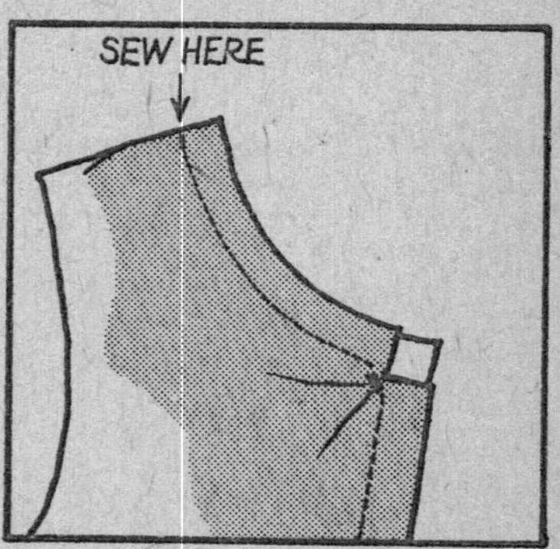

14 Sew with the slashed piece uppermost and turn slightly at the point of the slash.

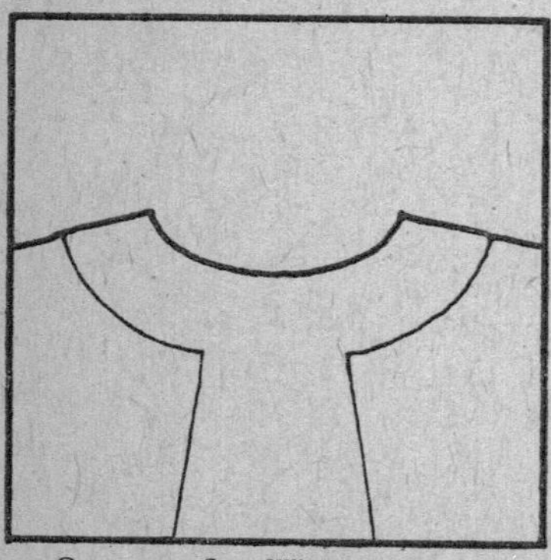

15 Open out flat. When you have repeated the process on the other half of the bodice you will have effected a very pretty but tricky neckline.

sewing darts

Darts are necessary in practically every garment. They are the difference between a sack and a dress. Even the 'sack' style of dress is darted at the bust. And they must always match in length.

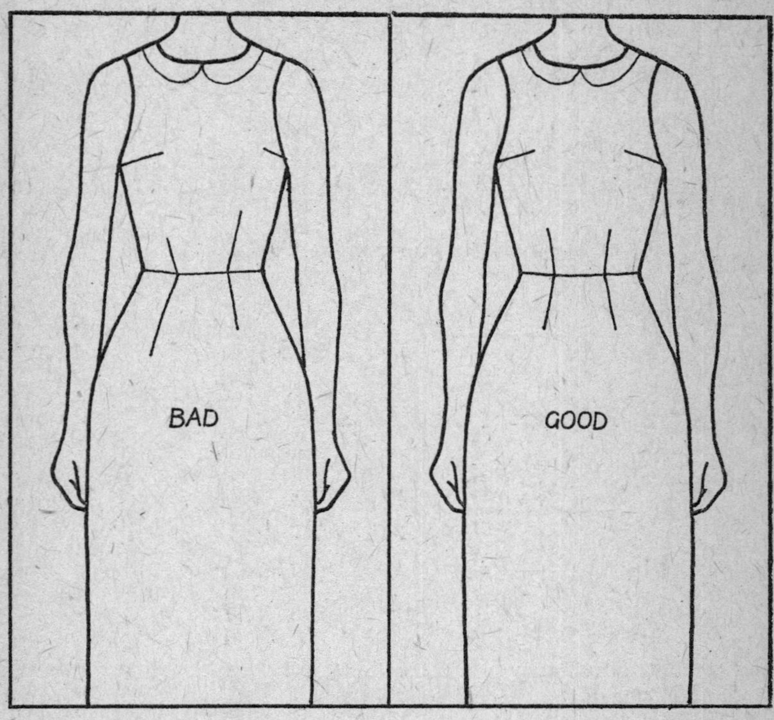

working from a pattern

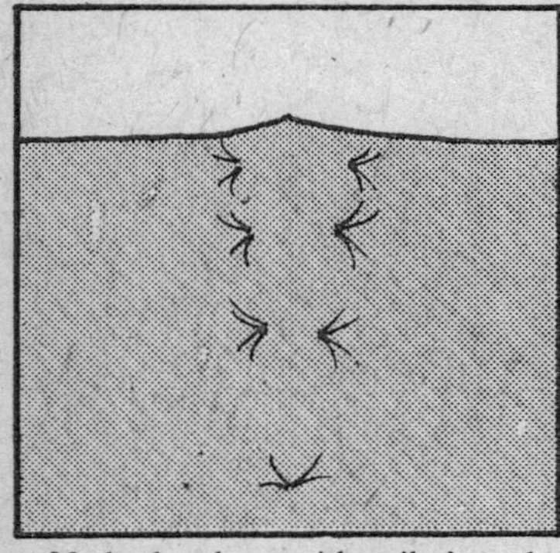

1 Mark the darts with tailor's tacks (see page 148-149).

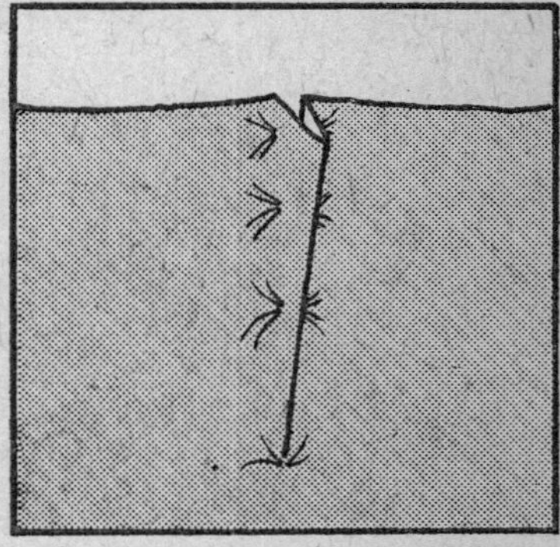

2 On the wrong side of the fabric, make a fold down the middle of the dart so that the two rows of marks meet.

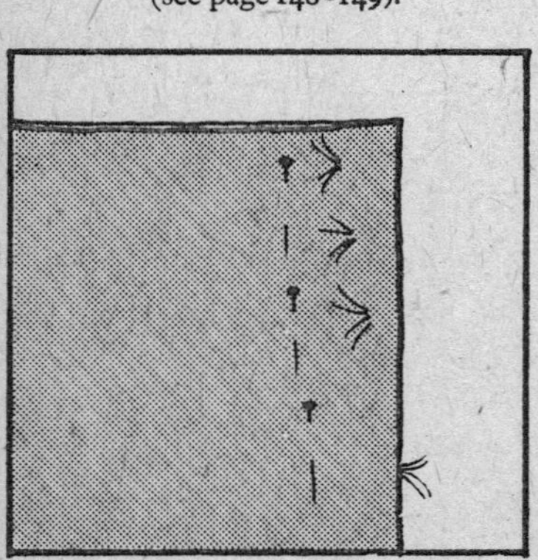

3 Pin or tack in place.

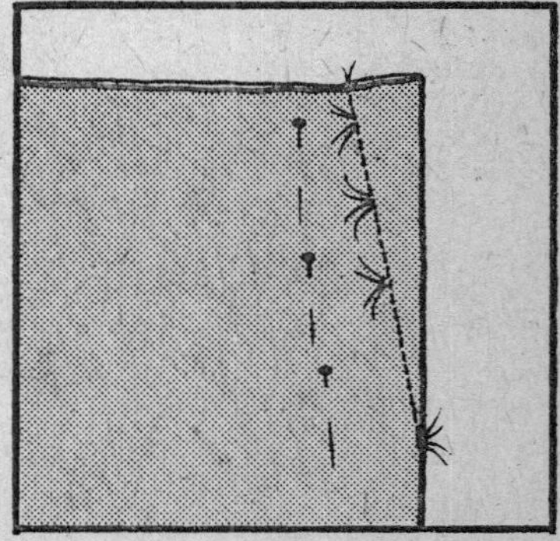

4 Starting at the top, sew a straight line through each of the marks, meeting the fold at the last mark.

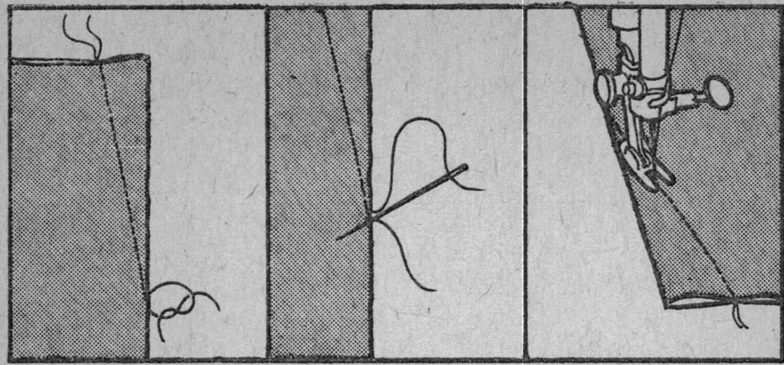

5 Fasten off the point of the dart securely by
(a) tying the two ends of thread in a knot, or
(b) sewing them down with tiny hand stitches, or
(c) swivelling the work round in the machine and sewing back again on the same line for about an inch.

6 At the top of the dart tie the ends in a knot and cut them off to keep the sewing neat.

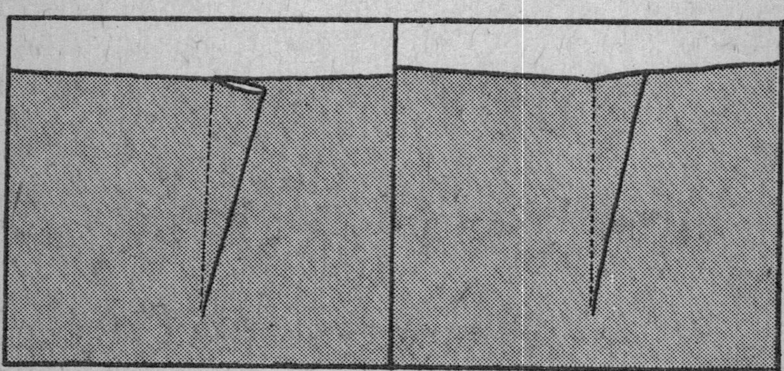

7 The top of the dart is shaped, the fold rising slightly. When you press, lay the dart sideways so that it lies level with the main piece along the top.

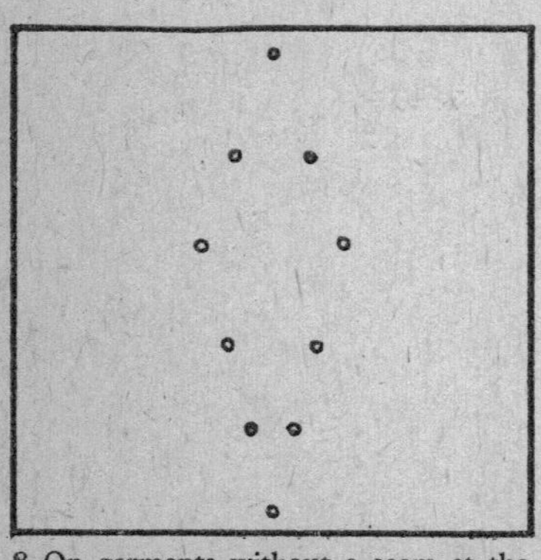

8 On garments without a seam at the waist you get a double dart, outlined on the pattern piece like this.

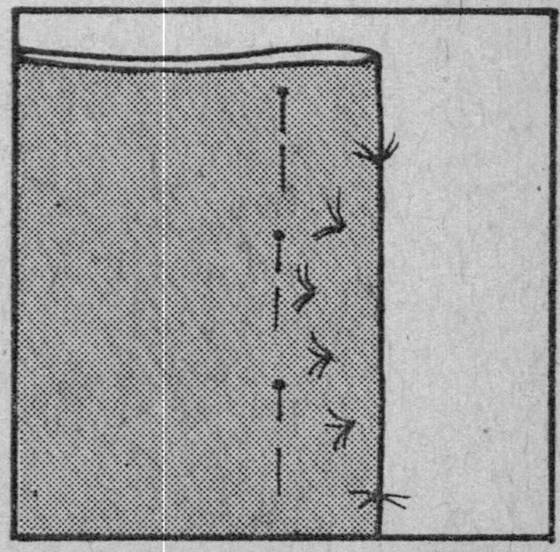

9 Fold the dart in half, on the wrong side, from the top 'o' to the bottom 'o', and pin.

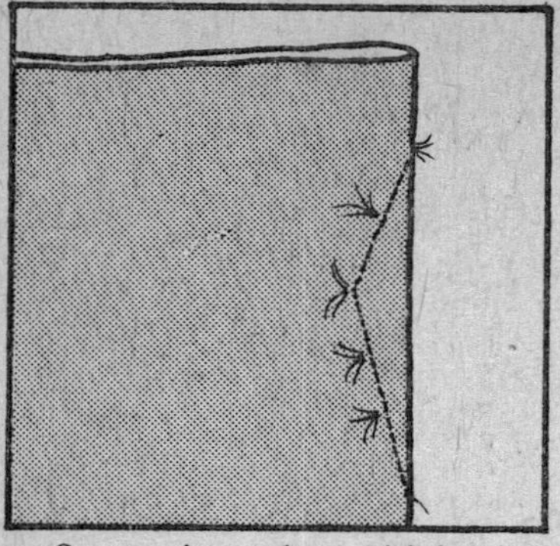

10 Start sewing at the top 'o', keeping a straight line to the outermost 'o', then straight down to the bottom 'o'.

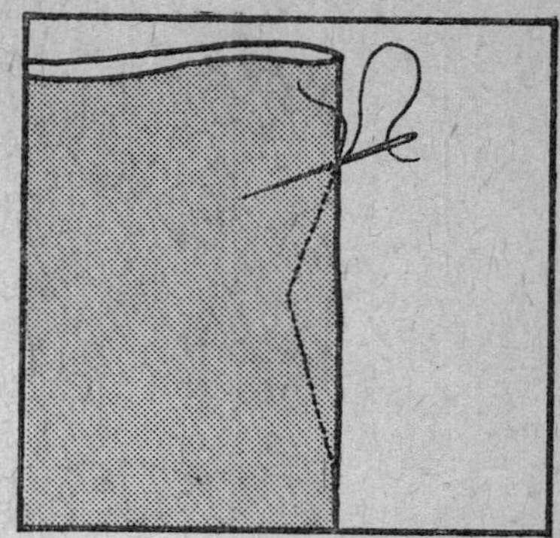

11 It is most important to finish off securely at both ends of the dart.

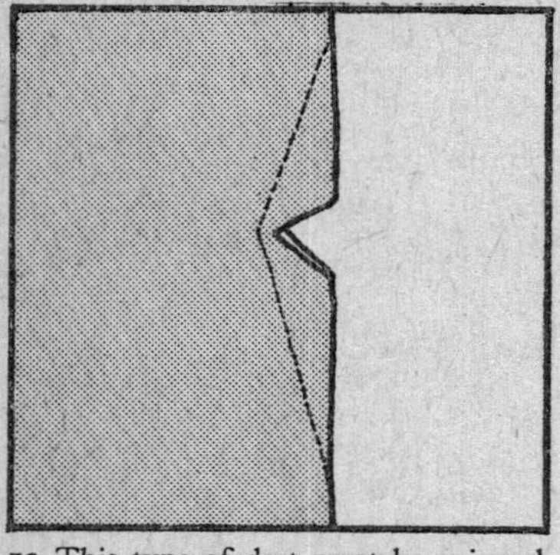

12 This type of dart must be snipped in the middle, otherwise it will never lie flat.

working without a pattern

1 The rule with darts is that the wider they are at the top, the longer they have to be, because they must taper into the garment, rather than stick out in a point.

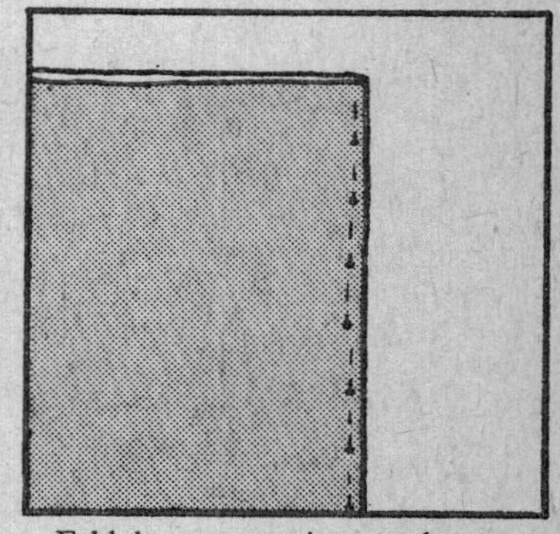

2 Fold the garment piece, on the wrong side, right down its entire length and pin it.

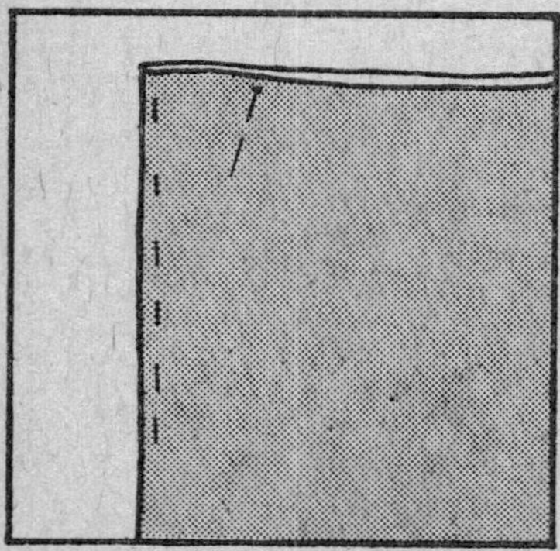

3 Place a pin in a downward direction where you will require the top of the dart to come.

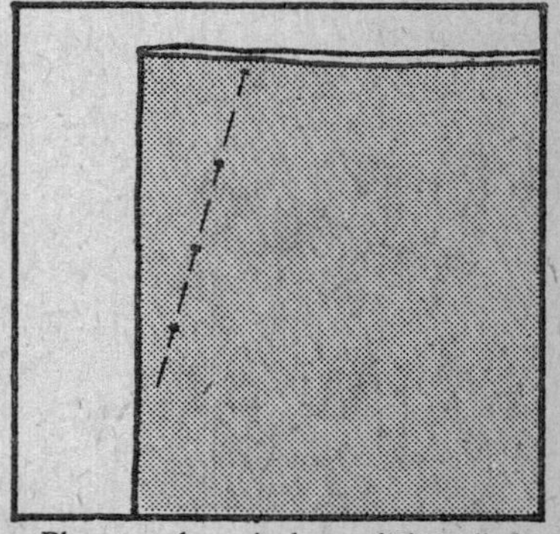

4 Place another pin beneath it, a little nearer to the fold, and another and another, until you have made a line which will taper into the fold.

5 Check this by turning to the right side of the fabric and laying it out. If it lies flat you are all right, if you have a lump you must extend the dart a little more.

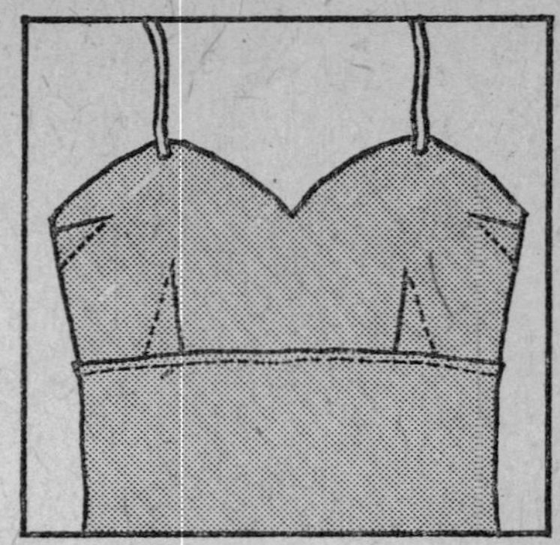

6 The only time this would not apply would be at the bust, where you may wish the dart to accentuate fullness, but fitting before you sew will guide you.

Always sew the dart from the top to the bottom because it is easier to taper into the fold.

sewing hems

You might as well embroider the words 'home made' on the back of your dress as be careless about the hemline. It must be straight, and smooth, with not a stitch showing on the outside

The first step is to get the length right.

on your own

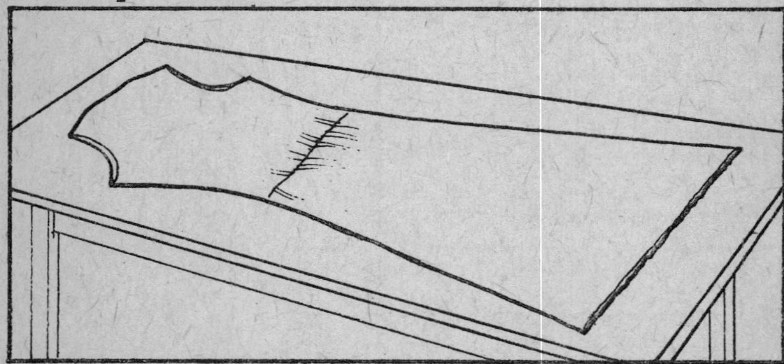

1 Lay the garment flat on the table.

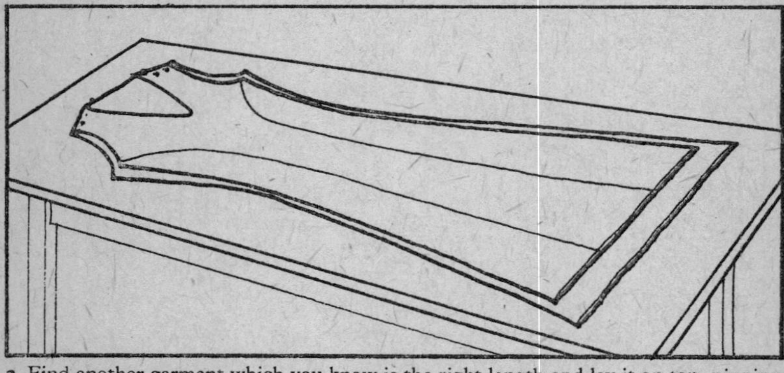

2 Find another garment which you know is the right length and lay it on top, pinning together both lots of shoulder seams.

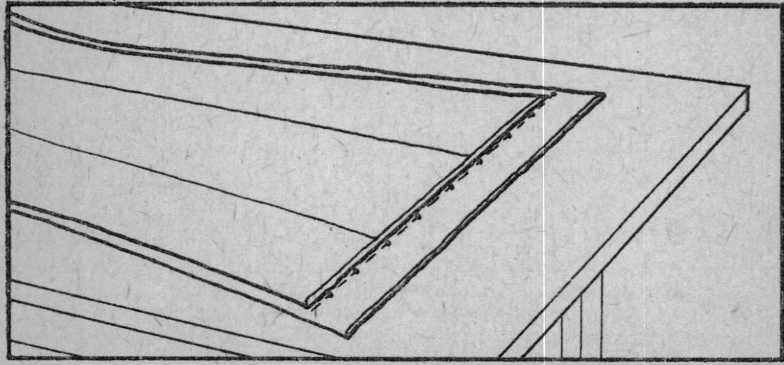

3 Smooth out and make sure they are both absolutely flat, then make a line with pins on the new garment where the lower hem of the other garment comes.

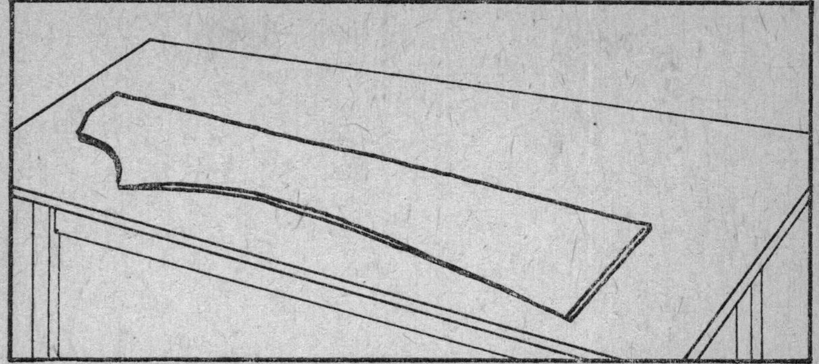

4 Turn up the hem on this line, pin and fit. Fold the garment in half lengthways to make sure both sides are the same length. Put it on and stand in front of a mirror to get the right effect.

with help

5 Take a piece of cardboard long enough to reach from the hem of your dress to the floor, and get your helper to mark on it the point to which the hem reaches. Cut off the cardboard at this mark.

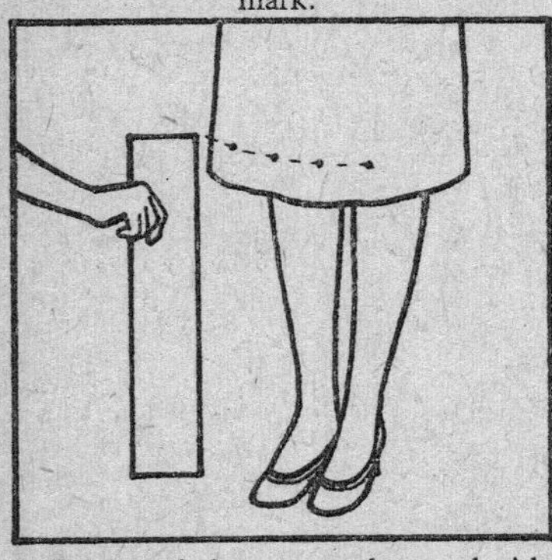

6 Get your helper to crawl around with this piece of cardboard, marking your skirt with pins on a level with the top of the cardboard, or

7 Buy an old walking stick and get your helper to mark it at the correct point. Provided you always use the same stick you will have a permanent hem definer, and you can use it for as many different lengths as you like.

turning up hems

1 Before turning the hem all vertical seams must be opened out and pressed flat.

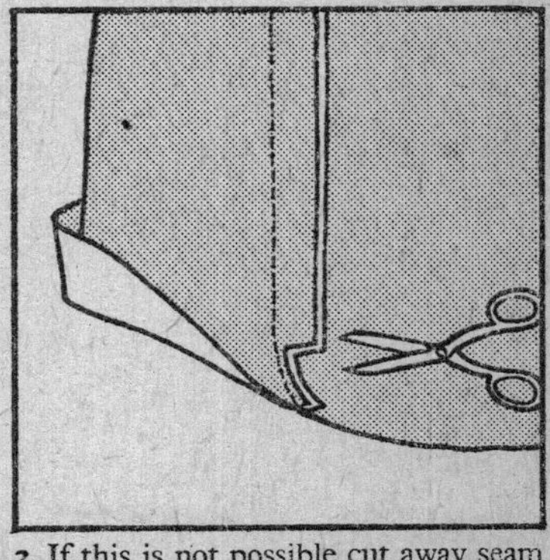

2 If this is not possible cut away seam allowances inside fold as page 154-156.

blind hemming

3 Don't turn under the edge because this will show a ridge on the outside. Oversew the raw edge.

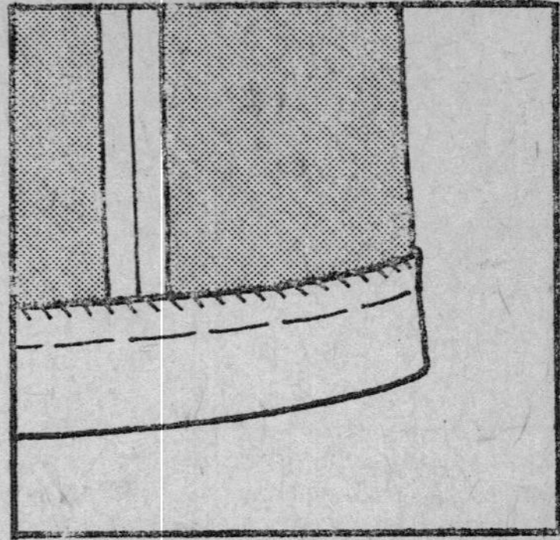
4 Turn the hem to the wrong side and tack all the way round about ½ in. below the oversewing.

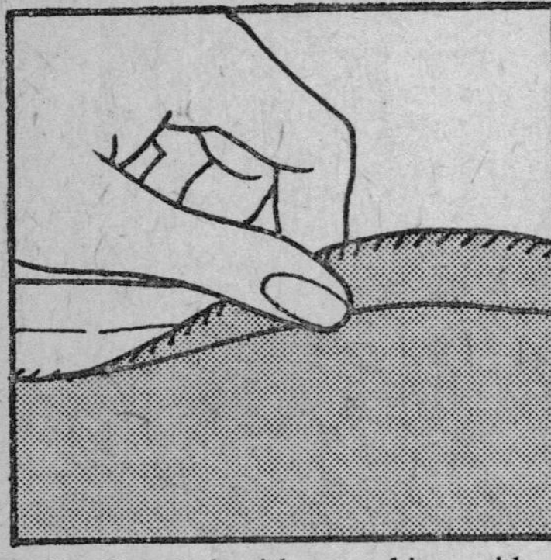
5 To slip-stitch without making a ridge on the outside, fold back the oversewn edge.

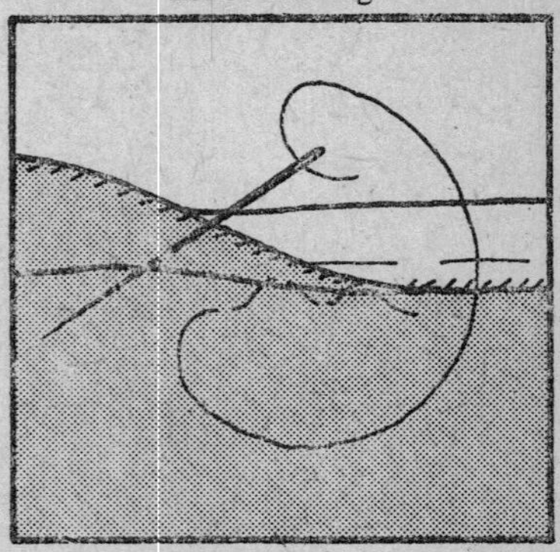
6 Take a few threads from the upper surface and then the merest scrap of thread from the lower surface. Do not pull the thread too tight.

straight skirt, lined dress

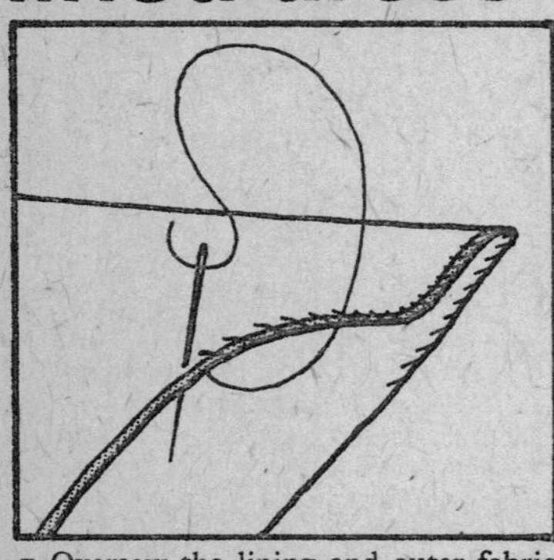
7 Oversew the lining and outer fabric together to neaten the raw edge. Turn and tack as 4 above.

Slip stitch under the hem as 5 and 6, but take up only threads from the lining on the lower surface.

skirt with a vent

8 The outer edges of the vent must be neat, so you fold down the facing at the vent after you have turned up the hem.

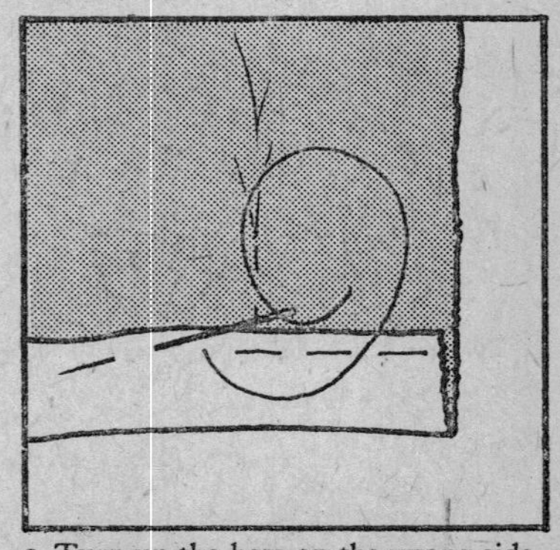
9 Turn up the hem on the wrong side, right to the outer edge of the vent. Tack.

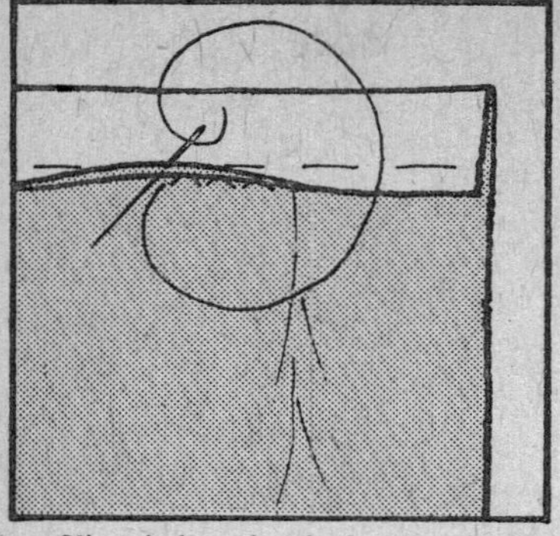

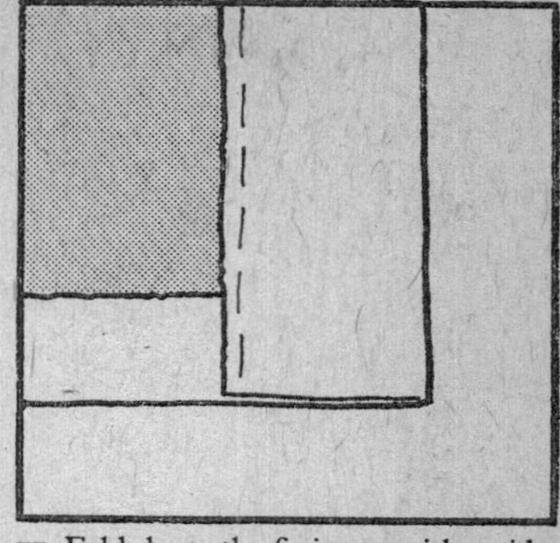

10 Slip stitch under the hem as page 40.

11 Fold down the facing on either side of the vent, and tack.

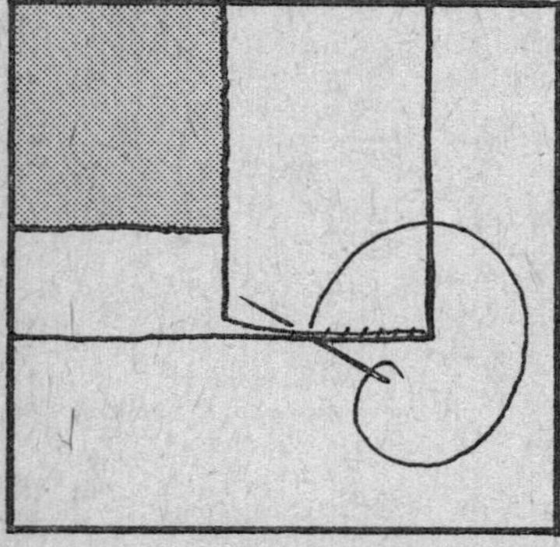

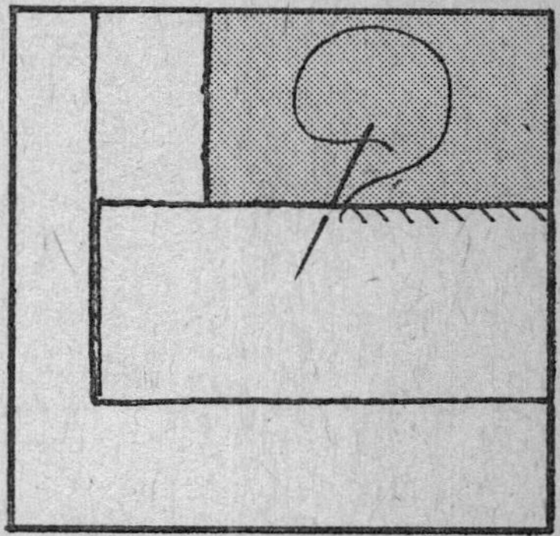

12 Neatly hem the facing to the bottom of the hem.

13 Oversew the side edge of the facing and slip stitch this to the skirt as on page 40.

skirts with pleats stitched to a panel

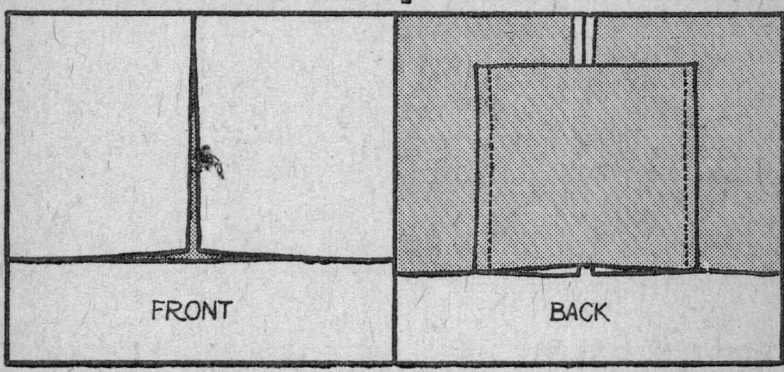

Don't stitch the pleat and turn the hem afterwards. You must turn the hem first and stitch the pleat afterwards.

1 Leave the lower half of the pleat seam unsewn.

2 Turn up the hem to the wrong side, including the pleat in the dress but not the backing piece.

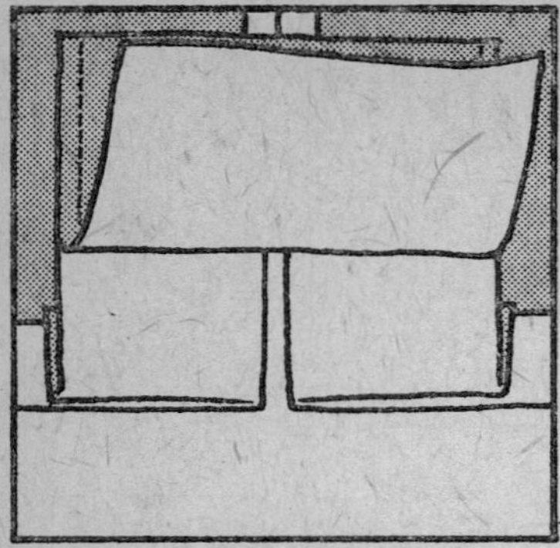

3 Match the pleat folds exactly.

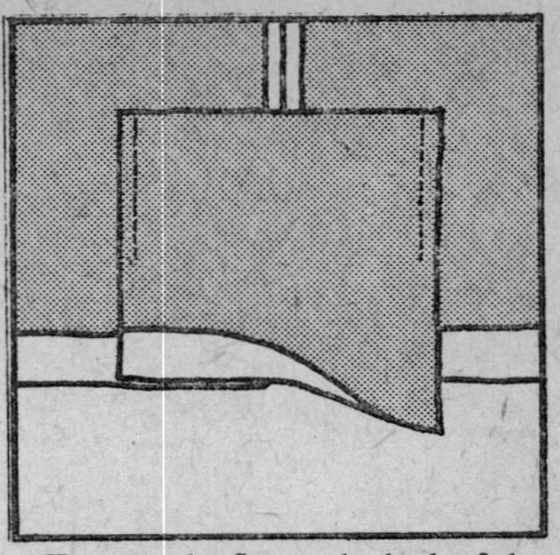

4 Turn up the flap at the back of the pleat. Match length. Blind hem the skirt and flap as on page 36 .

5 Now finish sewing the pleat seams, overlapping the existing line of sewing by 1½ in.

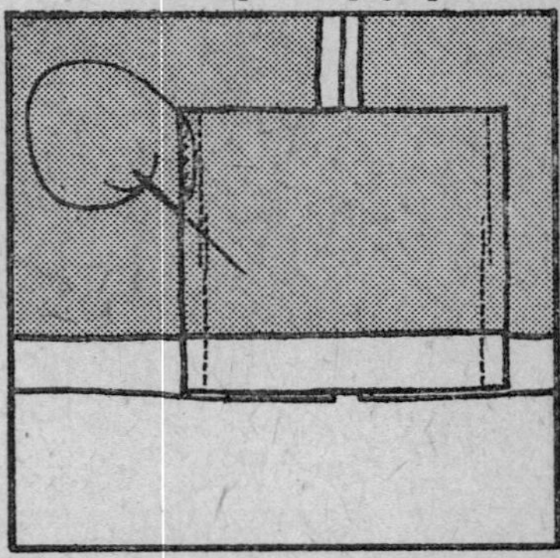

6 Fasten off all threads neatly and securely. Oversew all the raw edges together down the pleat seam allowance.

flared skirt or trouser bottom

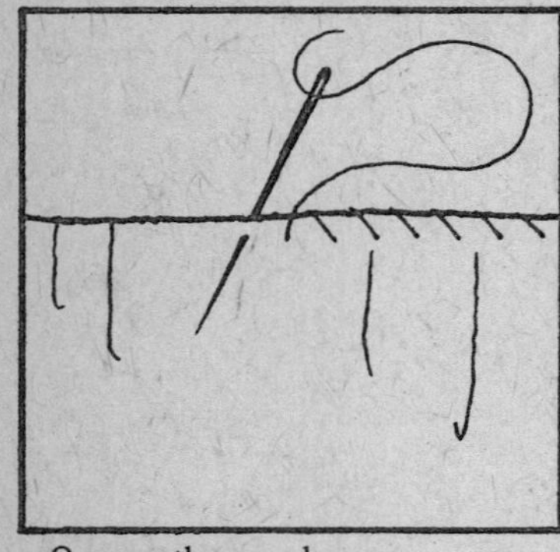

1 Oversew the raw edge.

2 Turn up on the wrong side at the required length, and pin near the fold.

3 You must pin near the fold in the first place otherwise you will have points in the hem line.

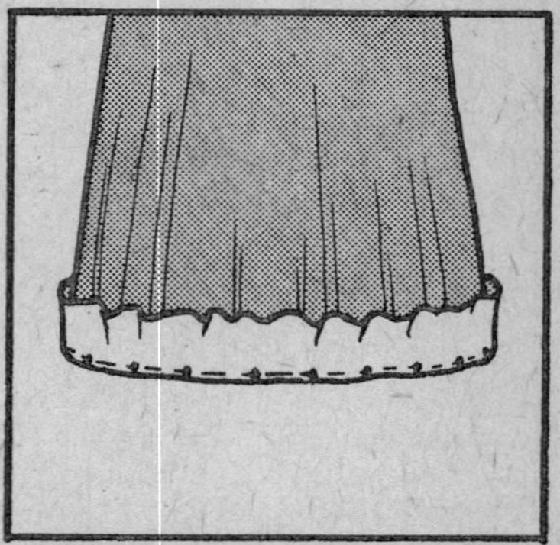

4 As the skirt gets narrower towards the waist you will have excess fabric in the turned-up hem, so get the actual hem line smooth.

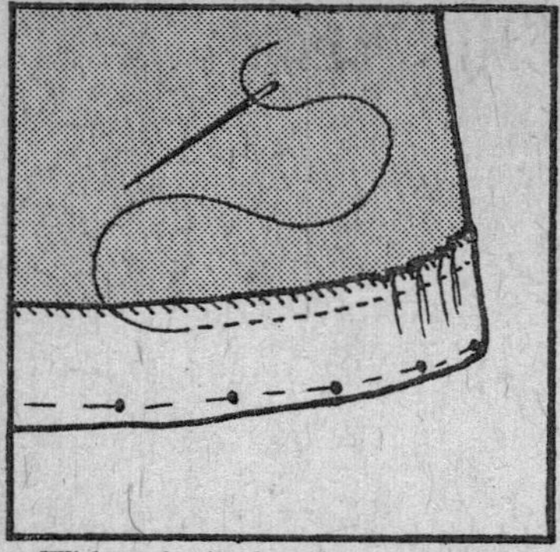

5 With a single thread, run along just below the oversewn edge and gently gather the surplus hem until it lies flat, with the hem smooth.

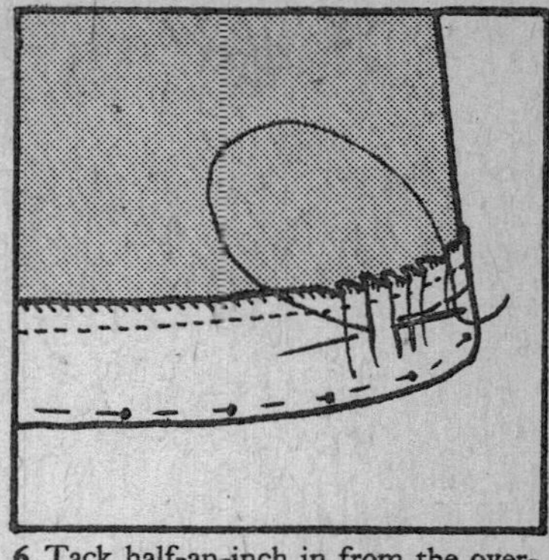

6 Tack half-an-inch in from the oversewn edge and, where the fabric is gathered, back-tack to make sure the gathering is firmly held down.

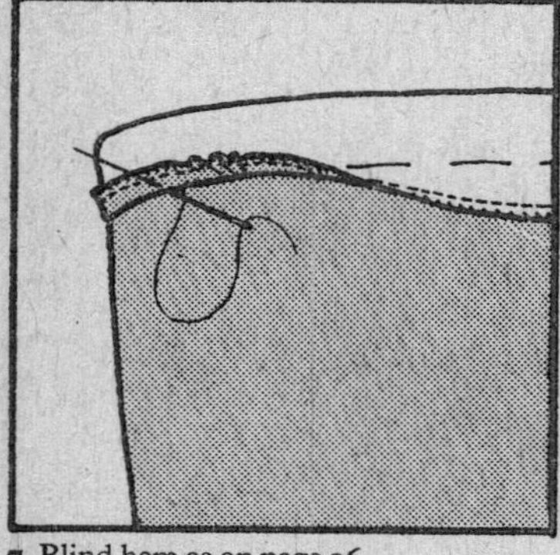

7 Blind hem as on page 36.

coat hems

The difference between a coat hem and a dress hem is that the coat opens and you have facing to contend with.

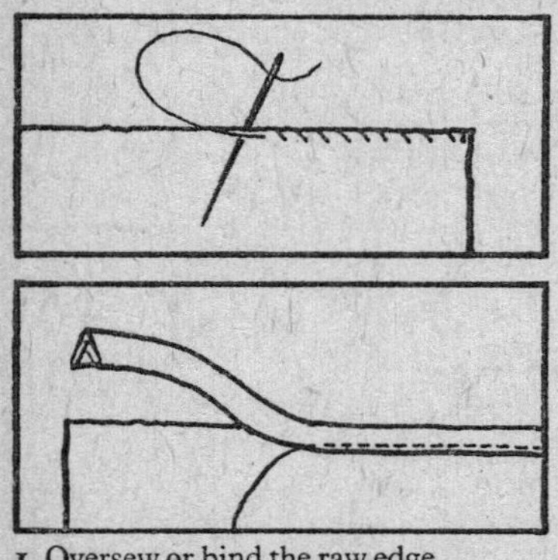

1 Oversew or bind the raw edge.

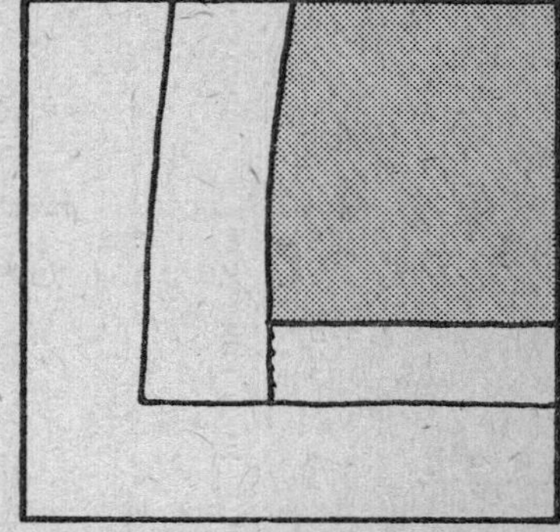

2 The facing must overlap the hem.

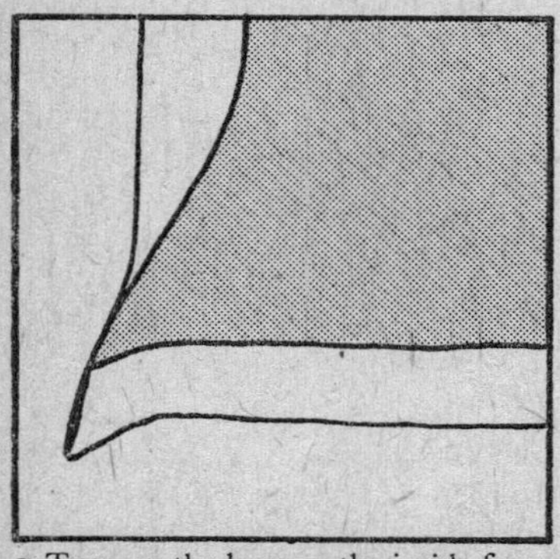

3 Turn up the hem on the inside from edge to edge, including the facing.

4 Fold down the facing. If the double thickness of facing creates too much bulk see page 156 for cutting away.

5 Slip stitch the facing down the side and along the bottom.

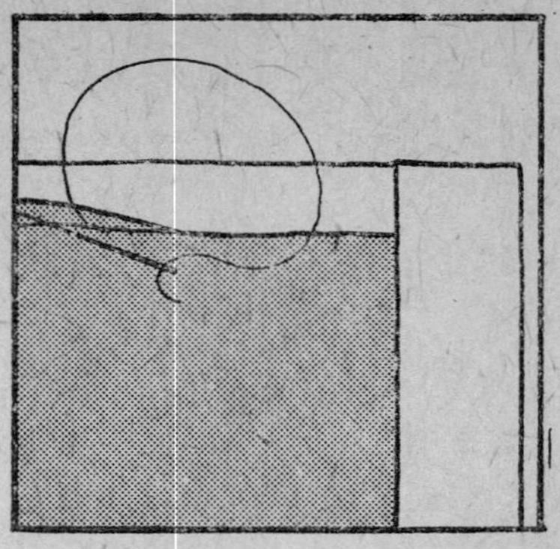

6 Blind hem the bottom of the coat as on page 36.

children's coats and dresses

1 Children grow so you may like to allow for letting down.
Oversew the raw edge and fold up, on the wrong side, only a modest hem of about 1½ in.

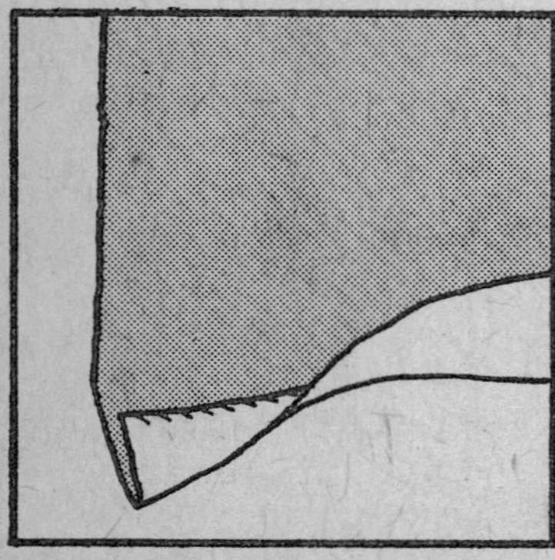

2 Fold again at the required length. Tack and bind hem as on page 36, and sew down facing as above.
Do not cut anything away. This is better than having an abnormally deep hem.

3 Only press the bottom fold, otherwise the inside fold will make a ridge on the outside.

hems stiffened with vilene

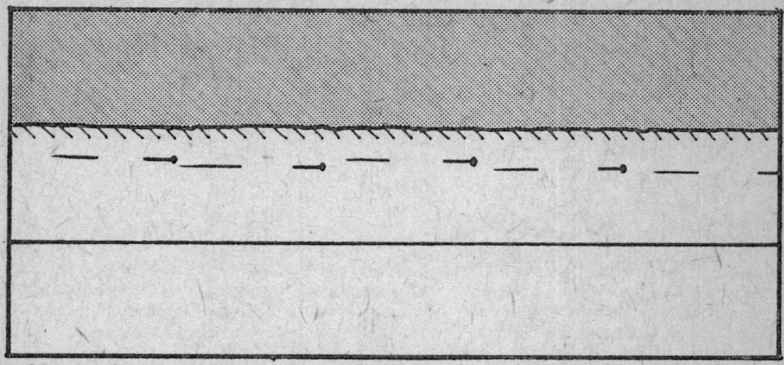

1 Measure for length, oversew the raw edge and pin up the hem as on page 34-35.

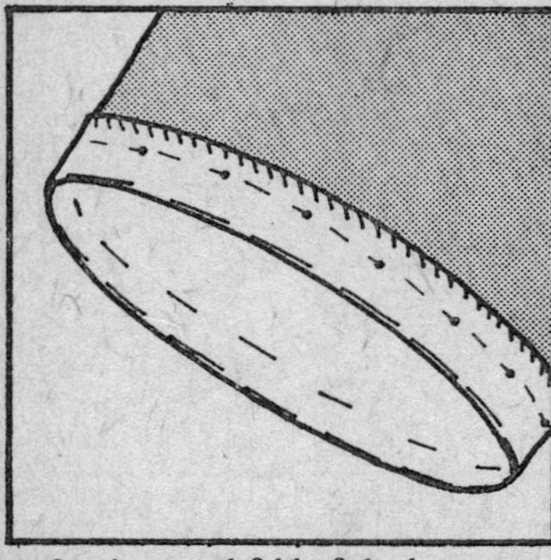

2 On the actual fold of the hem sew a line of tacking stitches in a contrasting thread.

3 Take out the pins and unfold the hem.

4 Cut your strip of stiffening ½ in. narrower than the hem, and lay it right against the line of tacking, on the wrong side, between the tacking and the oversewn edge.

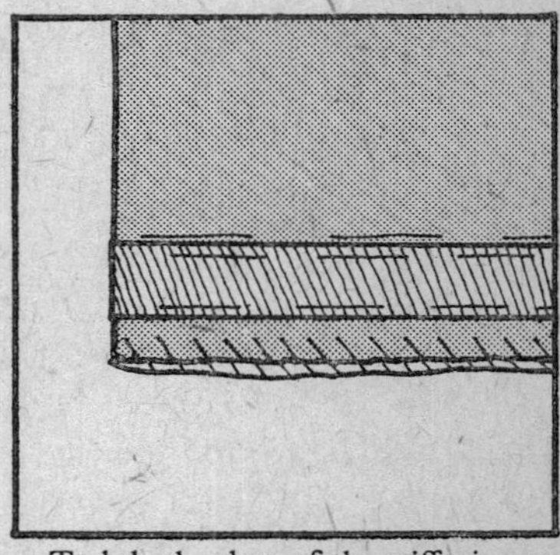

5 Tack both edges of the stiffening to the hem.

6 When you fold up the hem you will fold in the stiffening as well.

Tack and blind hem as on page **36** .

fastenings

Haberdashery stores and departments are full of sewing aids. Among the newest gadgets are buttons which don't need to be sewn on, and buttons you can cover yourself by clipping two pieces together. The list is endless, but this book is about sewing, so the proper use of the new patented fastenings which don't need to be sewn is left to the manufacturer's instructions

buttons

Buttons should never be sewn tight to the fabric unless they are purely for ornamentation. If you are going to put them through a buttonhole you must sew them sufficiently far away from the fabric to allow for the thickness of the buttonholed piece to go under the button. The thicker the fabric the more 'stalk' you must leave under the button.

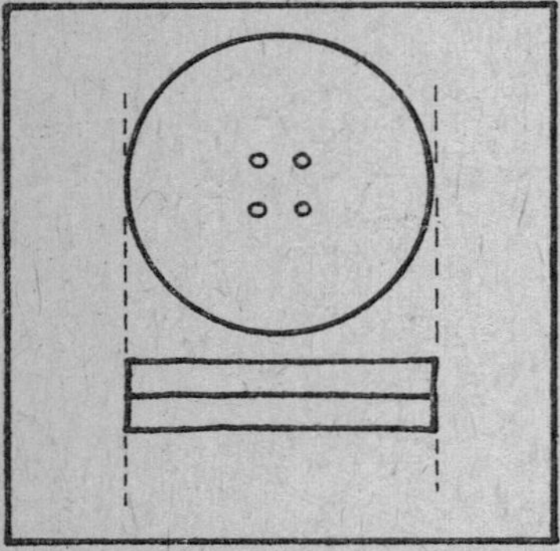

1 The button and buttonhole must be the same size otherwise the button will slip too easily out of the buttonhole. If it is too big it will break the ends of the buttonhole.

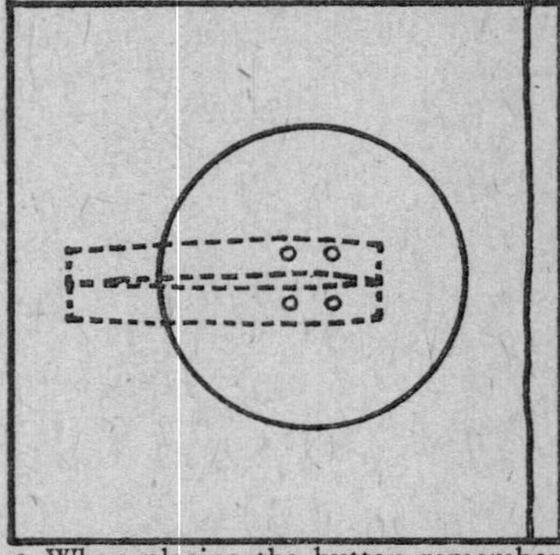

2 When placing the button remember that it will not remain in the centre of the buttonhole – movement will draw the buttonhole backwards until the button stops it – so you must sew on the button towards the front end of the buttonhole.

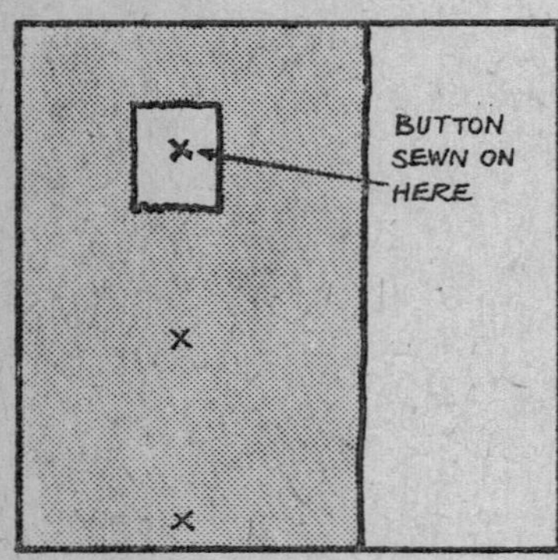

3 Never sew a button on a single thickness of fabric. If you are working on single fabric place a piece of tape under the fabric where the button will be sewn. If the buttons are fairly close together, one length of tape can be carried down the buttoned area if it won't show through from the outside. (see page 170).

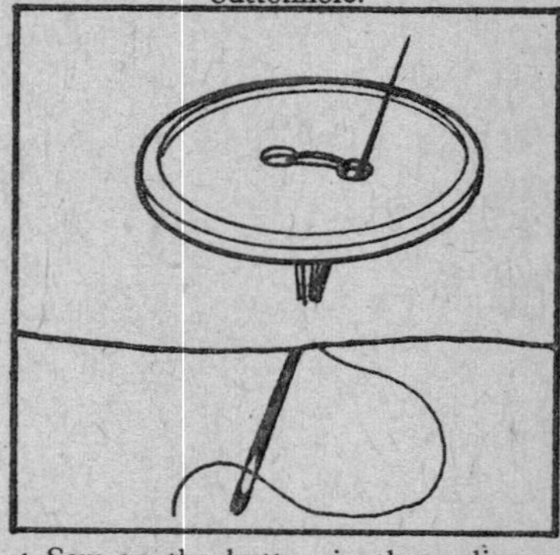

4 Sew on the button in the ordinary way by making loops through the fabric and over the button, but hold the button away from the fabric. Keep the first few loops very loose and after about three, pull the thread until the stalk is just the length you want it.

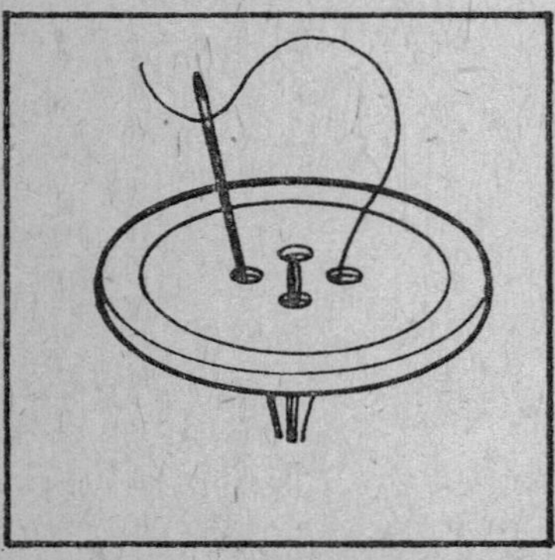

5 If there are four holes in the button, work two of them and then work on the other two.

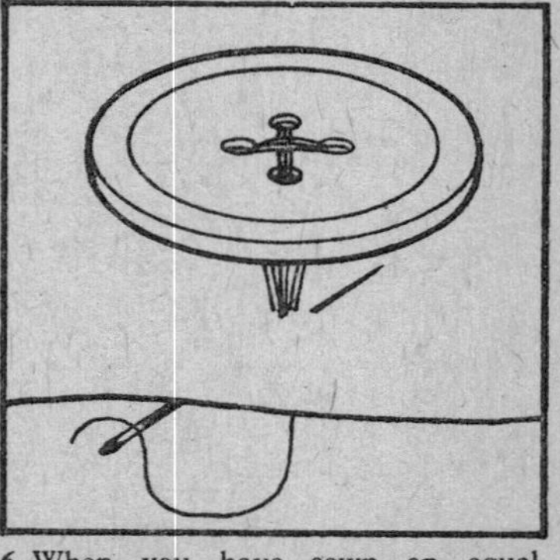

6 When you have sewn an equal number of loops through each pair of holes bring the needle through to the under side of the button.

7 Wind the thread round and round and up and down the loops between the button and the fabric until it makes a tight little stalk. Fasten off on the underside of the fabric.

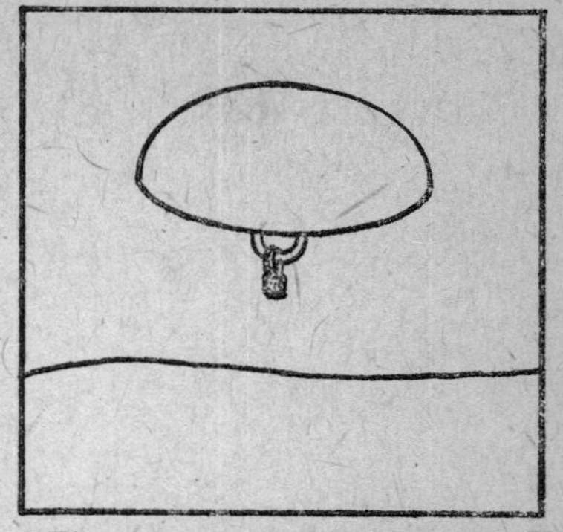

8 The same principle would apply to a button with a metal loop on the back instead of holes, but the stalk would be proportionally shorter.

9 On coats and jackets a small button is sewn at the back to take the strain off the fabric. Proceed as 1–4.

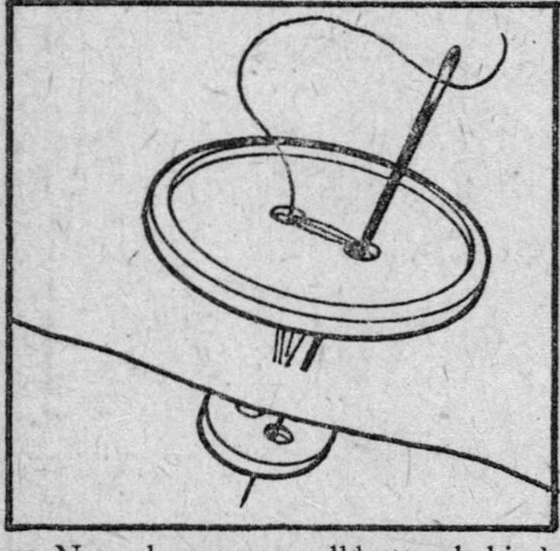

10 Now place your small button behind the outer one and insert the needle through the hole of the outer button and the small one.

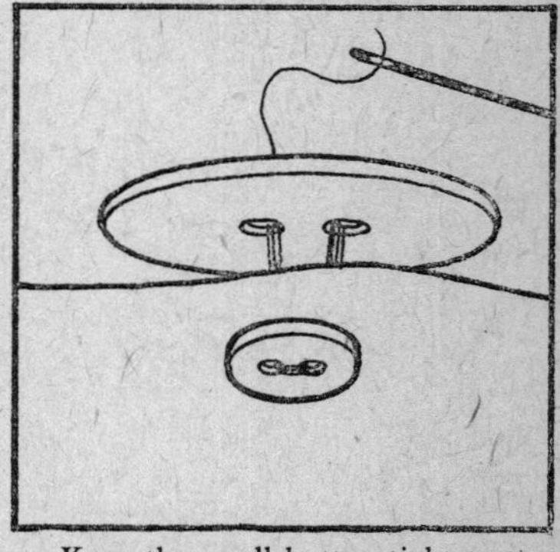

11 Keep the small button tight to the fabric while making a stalk for the outer one.

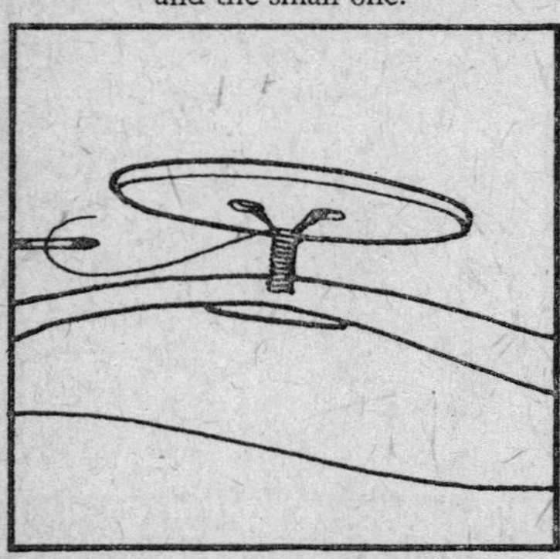

12 When you wind the stalk as in 7, this will bring the small button into place.

press studs

Like buttons, these should never be sewn on a single thickness of fabric (see 3 page 42). They are used for fastening one piece of fabric on top of another.

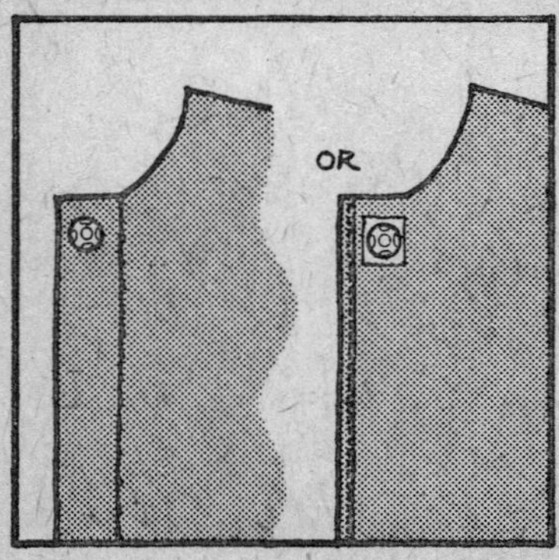

1 Unlike buttons, which are sewn on the outside of a garment, one half of a press stud has to be sewn on the inside or underside. In this case you cannot put reinforcing tape on the outside, so you either sew the press stud on a hem where there is a double thickness, or place the reinforcing tape between the press stud and the fabric.

2 Oversew down through the fabric and up through the hole in the stud, about six or seven times for each hole.

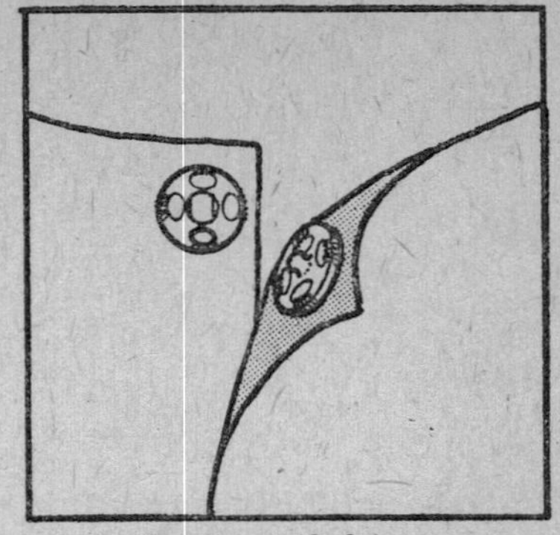

3 Place the other half of the press stud in the correct position and sew it in the same way.

zip fasteners

Zip fasteners should match the main colour of the fabric where possible. If you cannot get an exact match always choose a shade darker. It will tone in much better than a lighter or brighter shade.

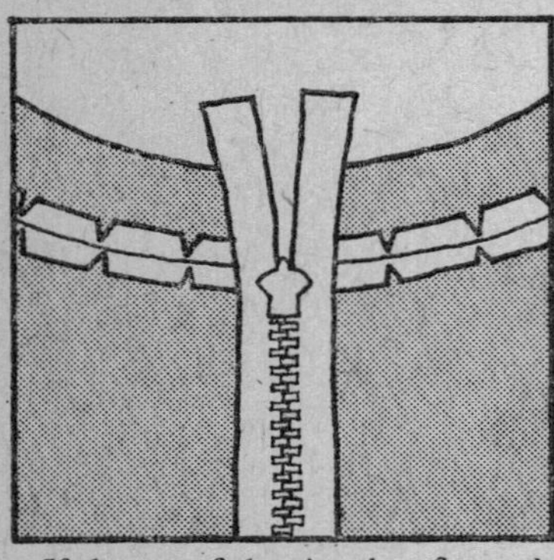

1 If the top of the zip when fastened is either at the neck of a dress, or the waist of a skirt, you must put in the zip before the facing or the waistband is finally sewn down, in order to get a neat, secure finish.

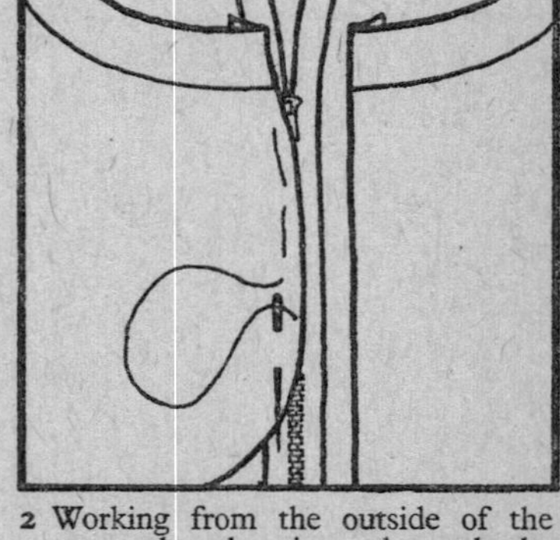

2 Working from the outside of the garment, lay the zip underneath the opening so that the metal or plastic part is just underneath the left hand side of the opening, and the top of the metal or plastic part is just below the fold of the facing. Tack this in position.

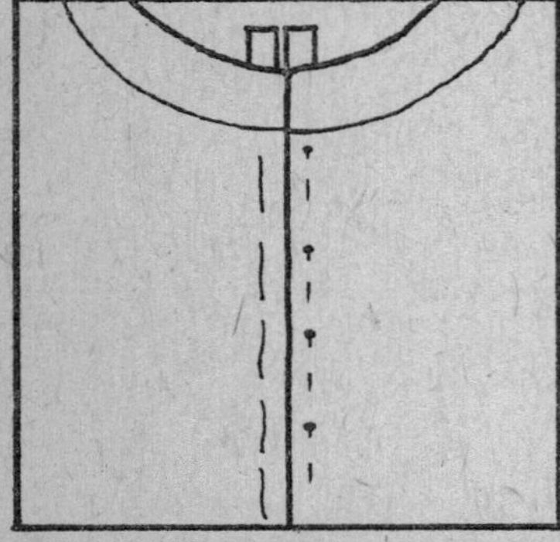

3 Pin the right hand side of the opening in position so that the two edges just meet, and the zip cannot be seen from outside.

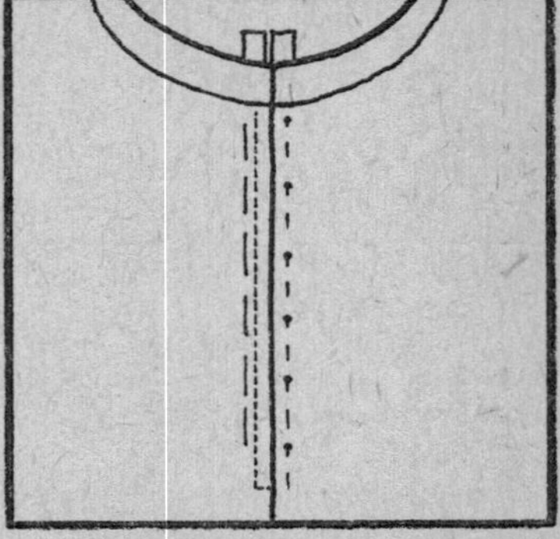

4 Machine sew if you have a special foot for the machine, otherwise it is neater to sew by hand. On the left hand side of the opening sew just clear of the metal part to allow room for the slider to go up and down until you are level with the end of the metal. Leave some good ends of thread for finishing off.

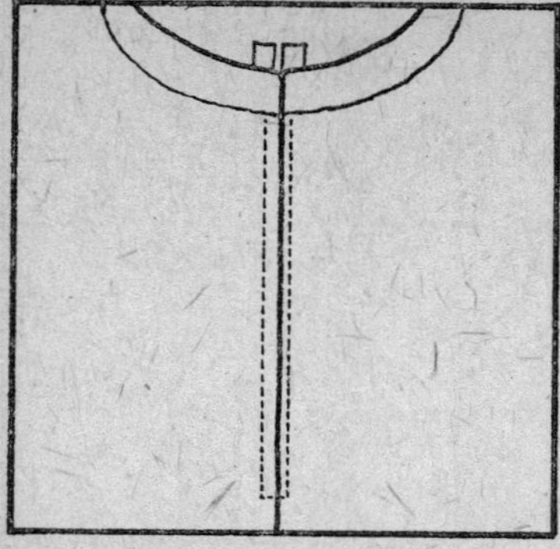

5 Sew the right hand piece just clear of the metal, which will be much nearer to the edge than the sewing line on the left hand piece. Finish on a level with the left hand piece. If you are satisfied that the zip will open and close easily take all loose threads to the back of the garment and finish off securely by hand.

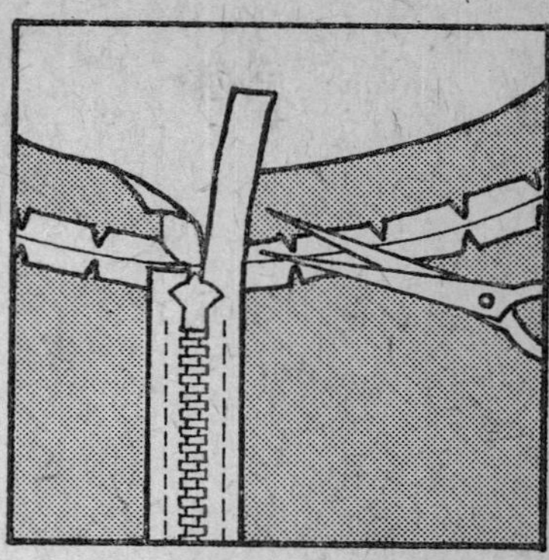

6 Now turn to the wrong side of the garment to finish off the neck edge (or waistband). Cut off surplus ends of webbing.

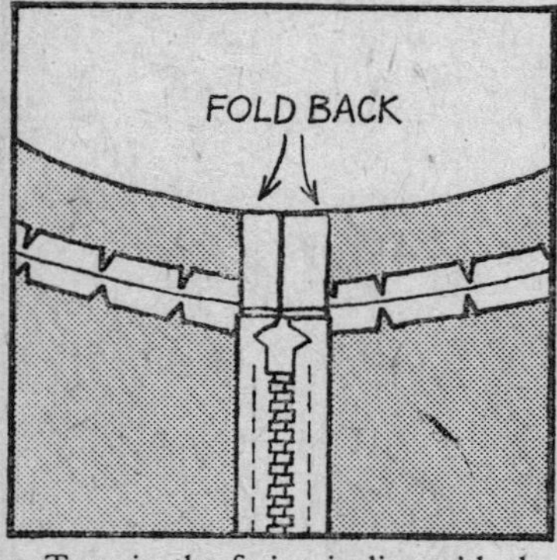

7 Turn in the facing in line with the opening.

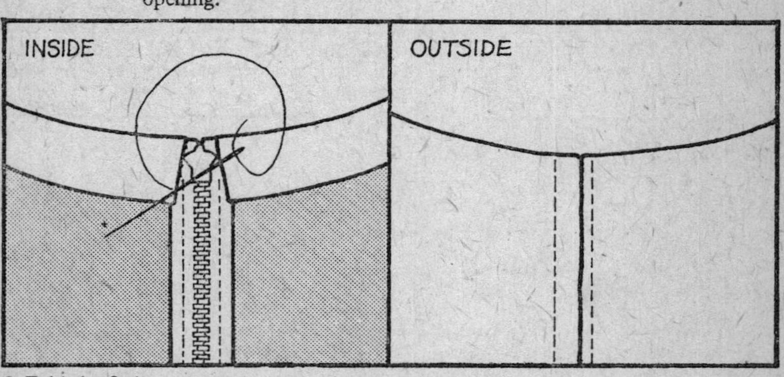

8 Fold the facing over and sew it down to the zip webbing.

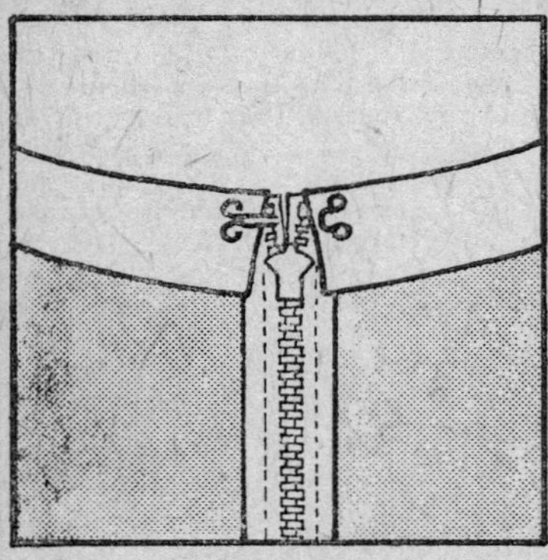

9 Sew a small hook and eye at the top of the back of the garment, or the waistband (see page 46).

hooks and eyes

These are bought on cards and come in varying sizes, but some people prefer to sew loops rather than use the 'eye'. Nowadays these are mainly used at the neck edges of dresses or on the waistbands of skirts and slacks.

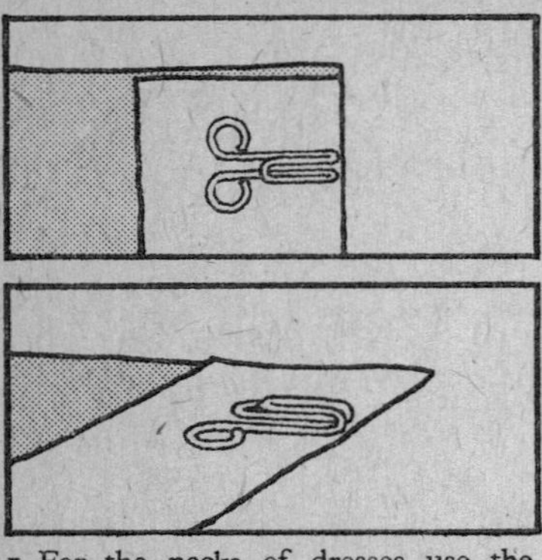

1 For the necks of dresses use the tiniest hook you can find and sew it in place with the arch of the hook on a level with the edge of the fabric. Don't let it protrude beyond the fold. The hook lies with its back to the fabric.

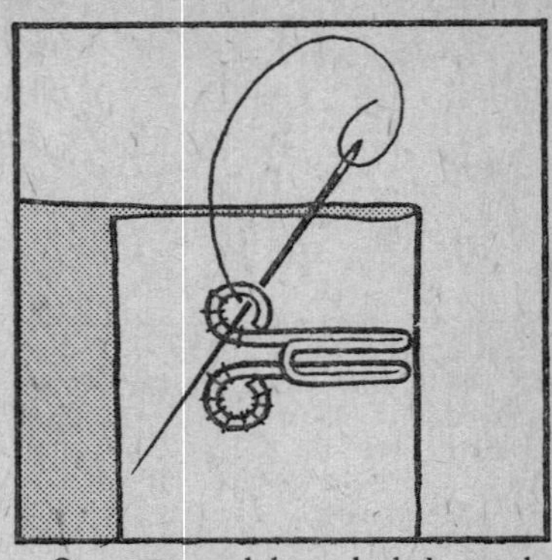

2 Oversew round the eyelet holes neatly being careful not to take big ugly stitches through to the outside.

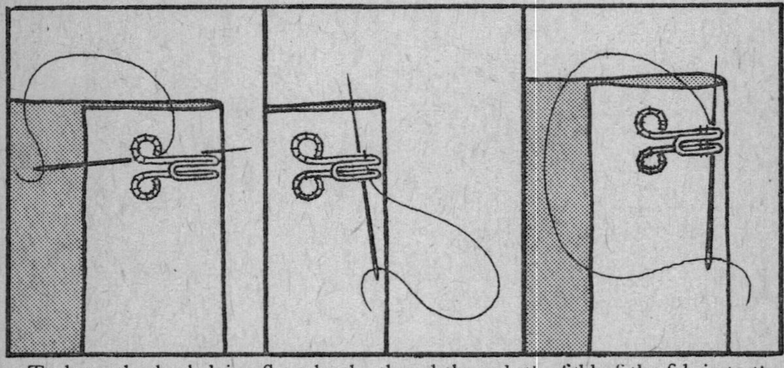

3 To keep the hook lying flat take the thread through the fold of the fabric to the edge and oversew the back of the hook to the fabric two or three times. Fasten off on the wrong side.

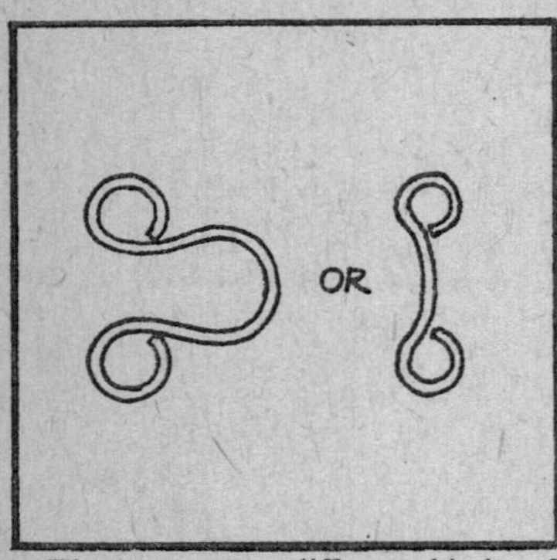

4 There are two different kinds of eyes – round ones and flat ones.

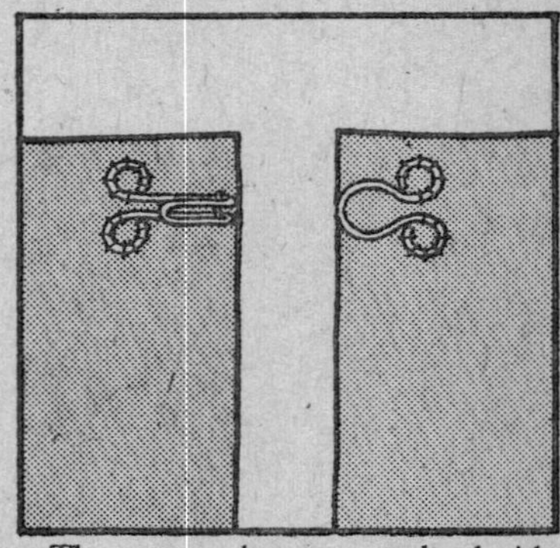

5 The eye must be sewn on a level with the hook and for a neck edge a round eye is recommended. The eye must be facing the hook with the rim against the edge of the fabric. Sew round the eyelet holes as in 2 above.

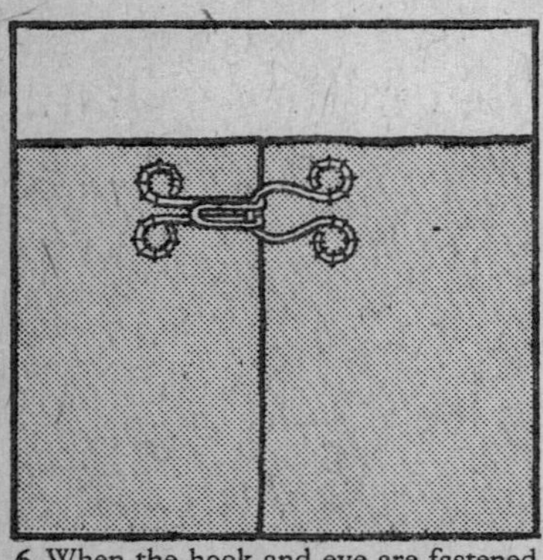

6 When the hook and eye are fastened the two edges of fabric should meet and lie smoothly.

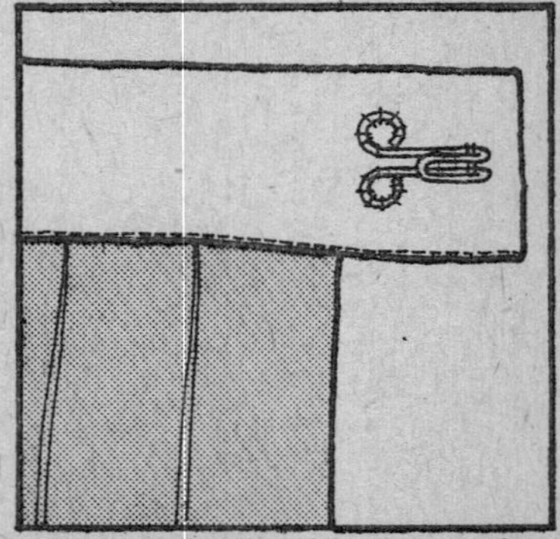

7 For waistbands where one surface is lying on top of another a straight eye is best. The hook is sewn underneath the top or overlapping piece.

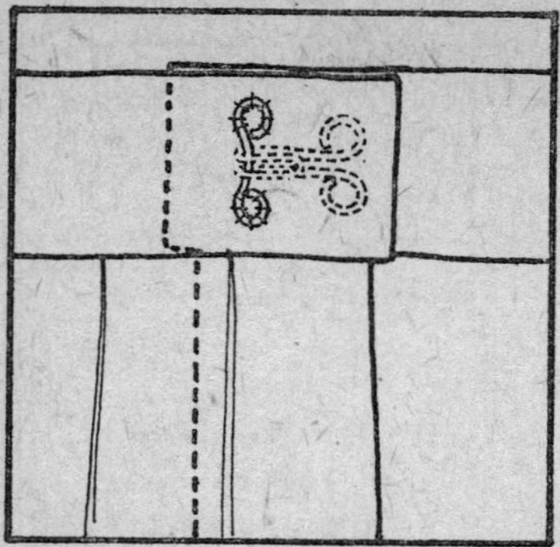

8 The eye is sewn on a level with the hook but you must allow for the hook to slide along to its tip. Sew as in 2 page 46.

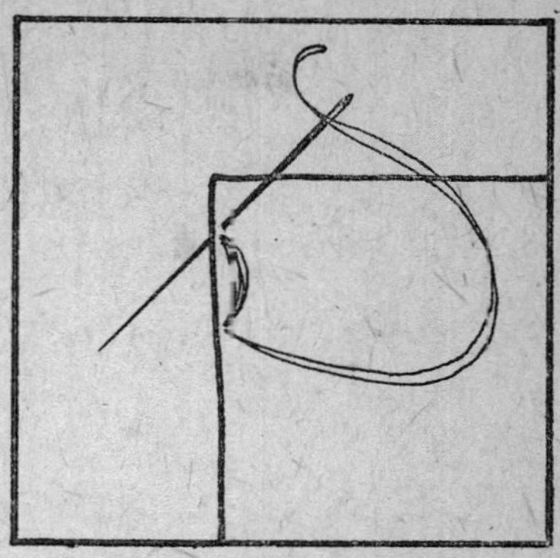

9 If you prefer to sew your own loops, they need only be the size of the hook and must line up exactly. Use double thread and make a few loops far enough apart to allow the hook to go through without puckering.

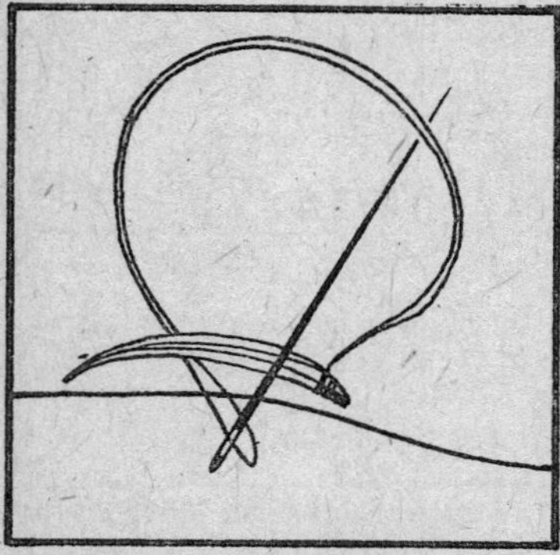

10 Make tiny buttonhole stitches along the loops by taking the thread over the loop and passing the needle underneath it. Pull the thread right through after each stitch.

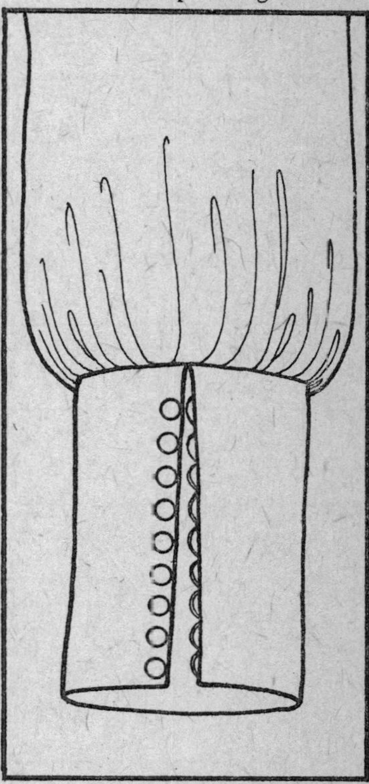

11 If you have a row of tiny buttons and wish to sew loops instead of buttonholes, these are done as in 9 and 10 above, but make sure each loop is big enough for the button to go through, but not so big that it keeps coming undone.

threading elastic

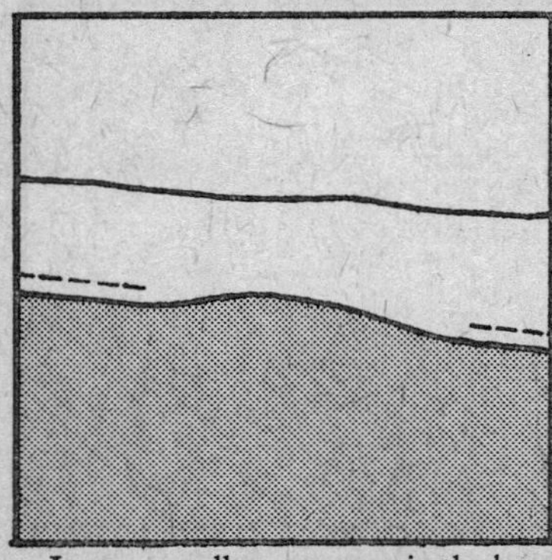

1 Leave a small gap unsewn in the hem of the turning through which you wish to thread elastic (or tape).

2 Make sure you have the correct length of elastic, and thread one end through a bodkin.

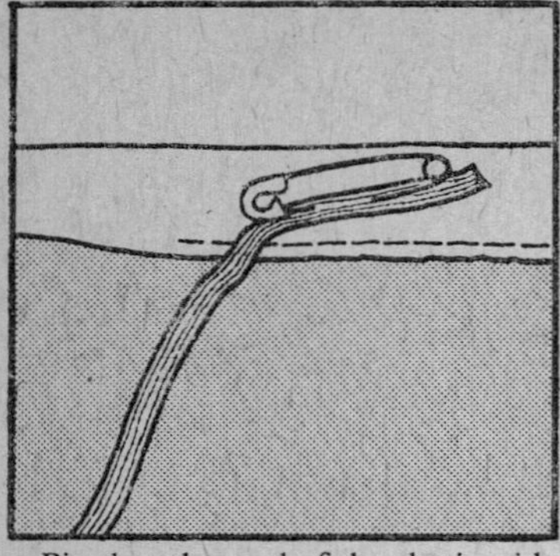

3 Pin the other end of the elastic with a safety pin to the hem near the gap.

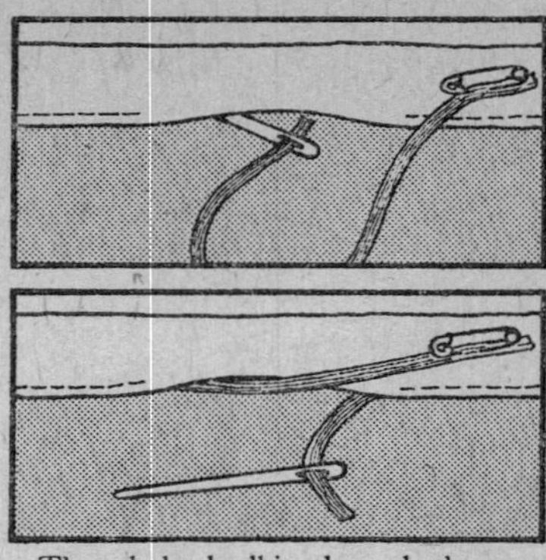

4 Thread the bodkin through the gap and feed it along inside the hem until it comes out again from the other direction.

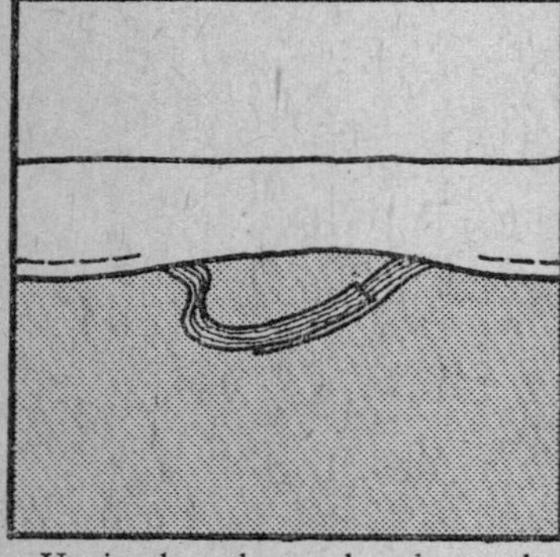

5 Unpin the other end and sew the two ends together by overlapping them about an inch.

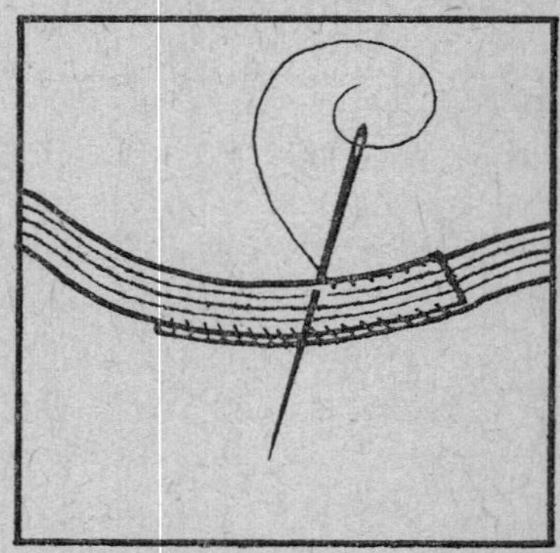

6 Oversew the two ends together along both sides.

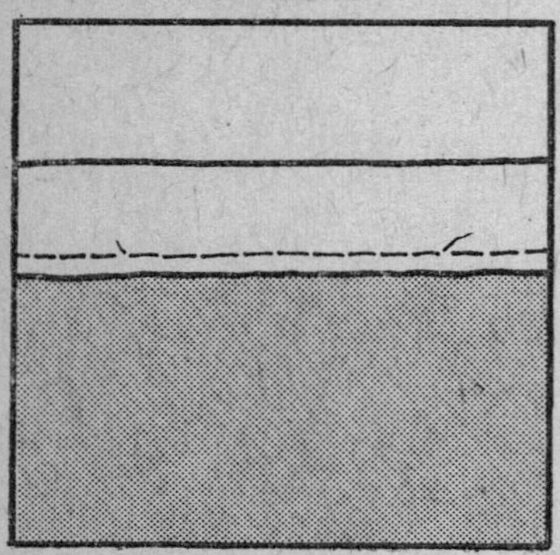

7 Sew down the gap.

making a belt

You will neea a firm base on which to make the belt. It is best to buy petersham, which is sold by the yard, in varying widths. Buy enough to allow for turning in and overlapping. Cut a strip of fabric at least 2 in. longer than the petersham and three times as wide.

1 Turn towards the wrong side one narrow fold at one end of the strip of fabric, and pin.

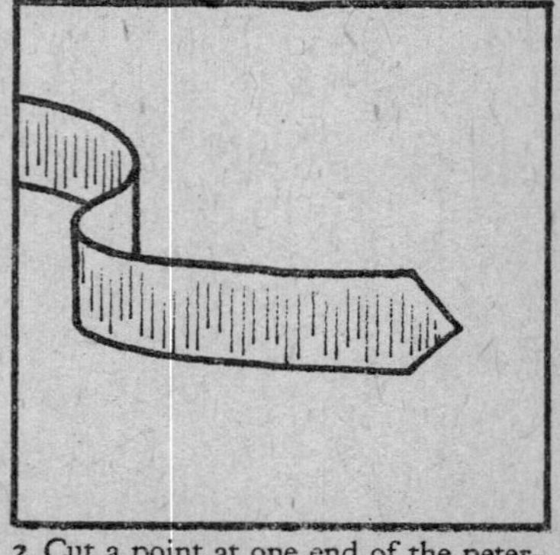

2 Cut a point at one end of the petersham.

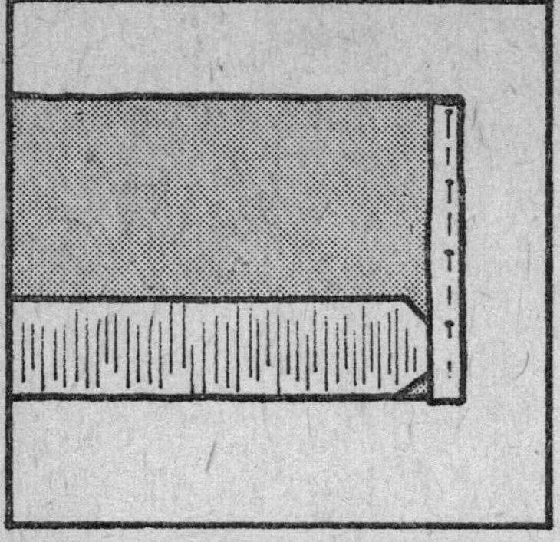

3 Lay the petersham on the wrong side of the fabric, with the lower edges matching, and tuck the point of the petersham under the fold you have pinned down.

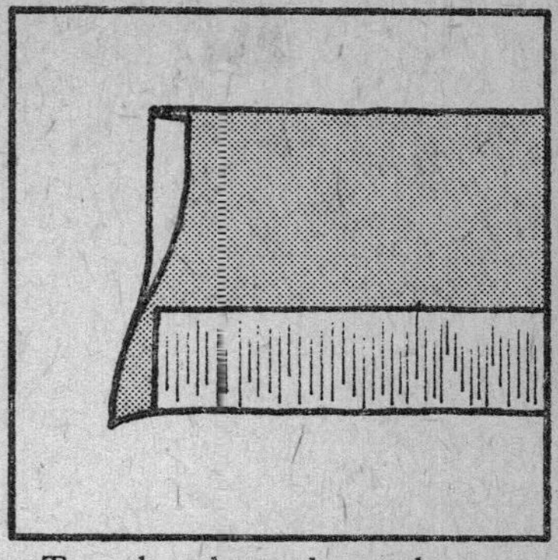

4 Turn the other end over the petersham, and tack it down.

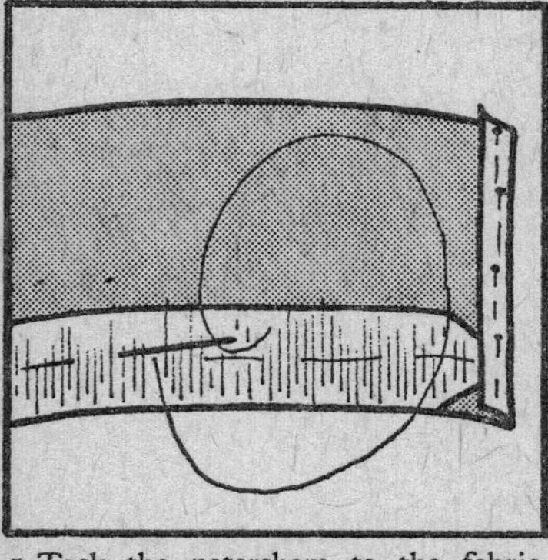

5 Tack the petersham to the fabric along the middle.

6 Cut away the bottom corner of the *fold* at the pointed end to reduce bulk.

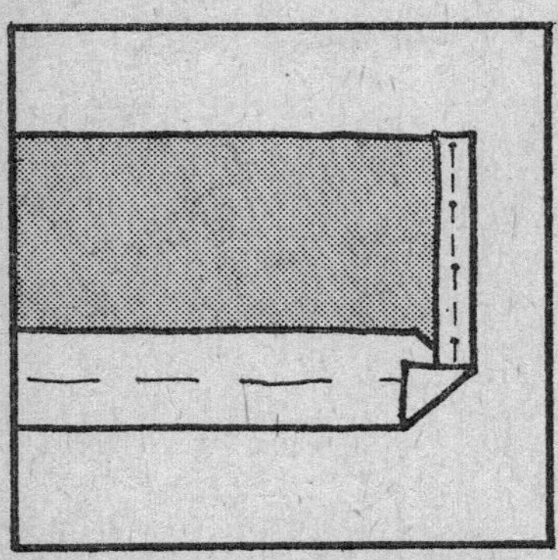

7 Fold the bottom corner of the fabric over the petersham, along one side of the point.

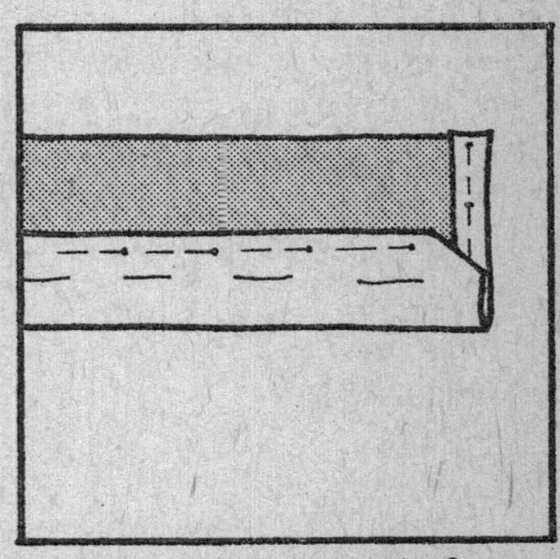

8 Fold over the whole length of petersham along its inner edge. Pin.

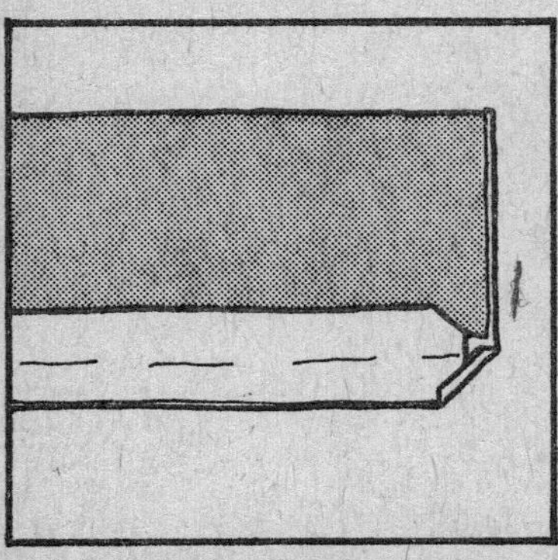

9 After removing the pins cut away the inside of the fold, and the bottom corner leaving $\frac{1}{8}$ in. for turning, so that only the point is covered.

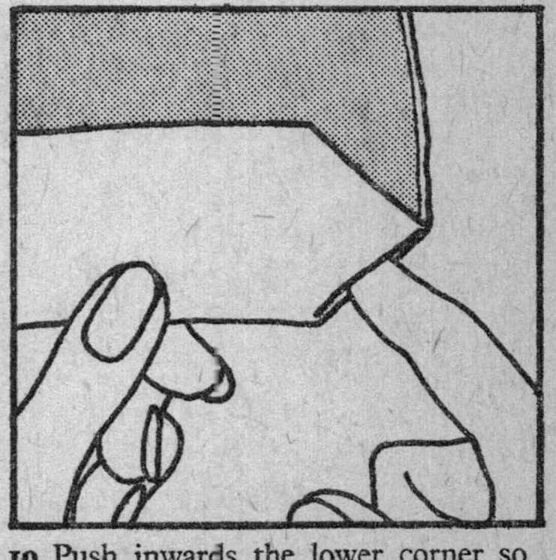

10 Push inwards the lower corner so that it lies smooth along the cut edge of the petersham.

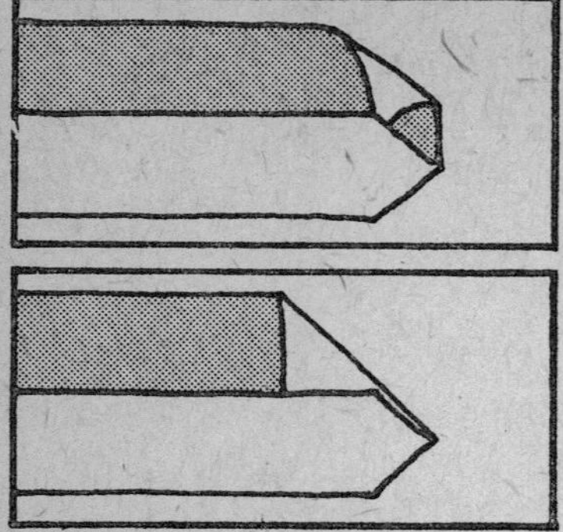

11 Fold down the top corner of the fabric *behind* the petersham.

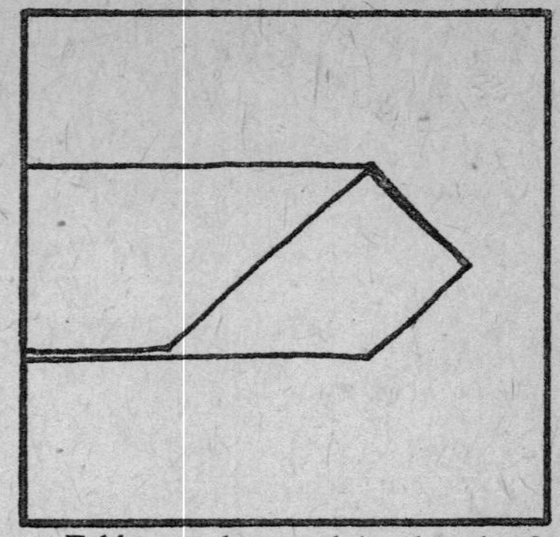

12 Fold over the remaining length of fabric, and press it.

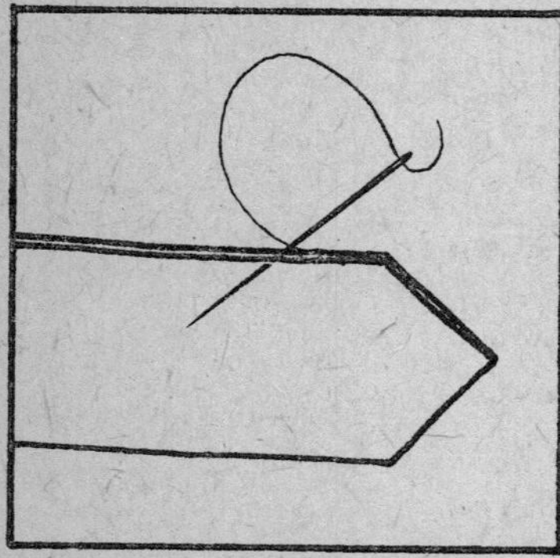

13 Open out the belt and fold in the last turning *behind* the covered petersham.

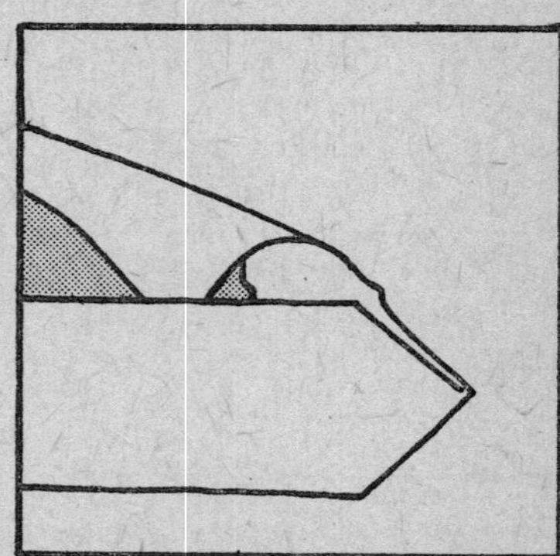

14 Slip stitch round the point and along the side where you have tucked in the fold.

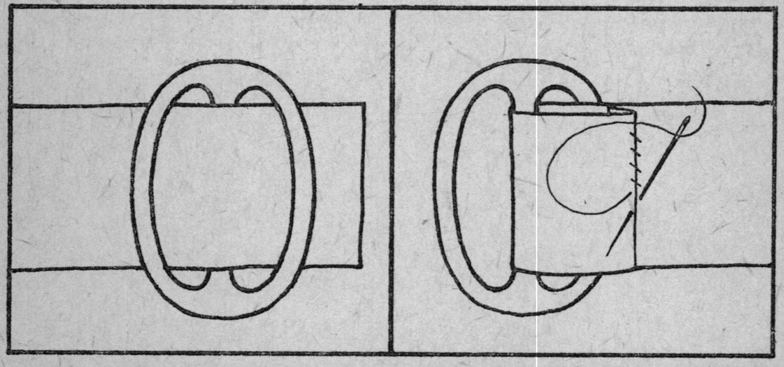

15 Fix the buckle to the flat end by passing that end of the belt through the buckle, right side uppermost, and sewing down the end on the wrong side.

buttonholes

There are several different ways of making buttonholes, and there are no strict rules about which sort goes where. Since they are nearly always in the front of a garment, neatness is of first importance. They must all be exactly the same size, all in a straight line, and they must lie flat without any puckering.

marking up

Great care must be taken, because buttonholes are worked on the right side of the fabric and are therefore marked up on the right side.

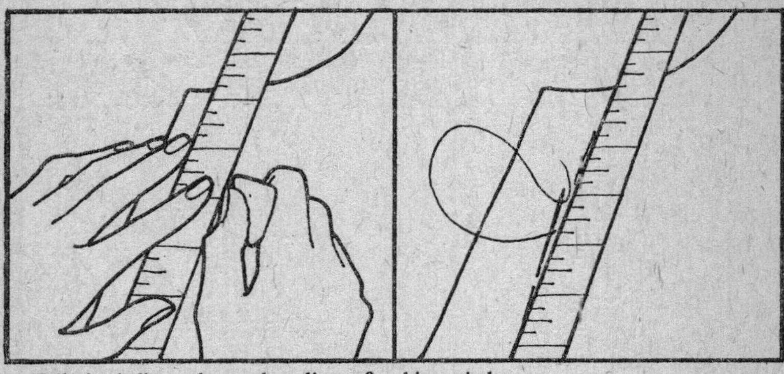

1 Tailor's chalk can be used, or lines of tacking stitches.

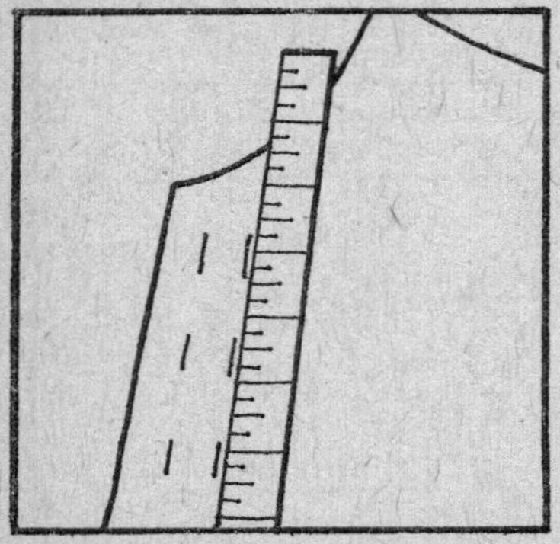

2 With the help of a ruler make a vertical mark at either end of the buttonhole.

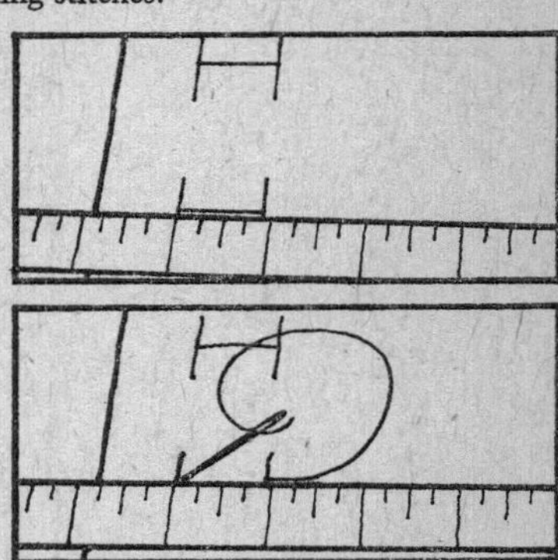

3 Using the ruler, mark a horizontal line between the two vertical ones, which will be the actual buttonhole.

hand stitched

Hand stitched buttonholes are better sewn with the facing and interfacing, if any, as one operation, so that you can leave them until after you have sewn down the facings.

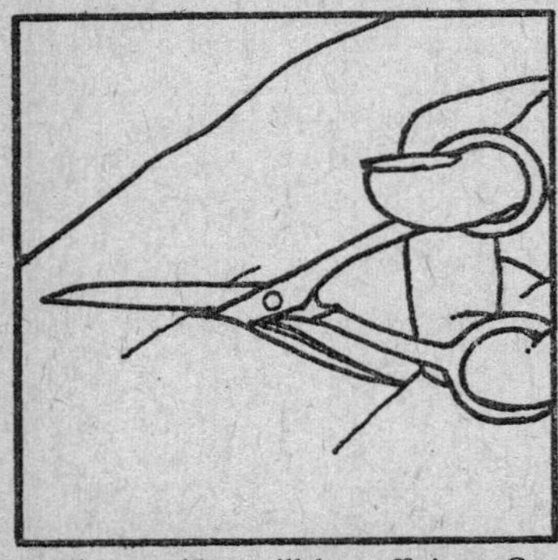

4 This marking will be sufficient. Cut the fabric on the horizontal line between the two vertical ones.

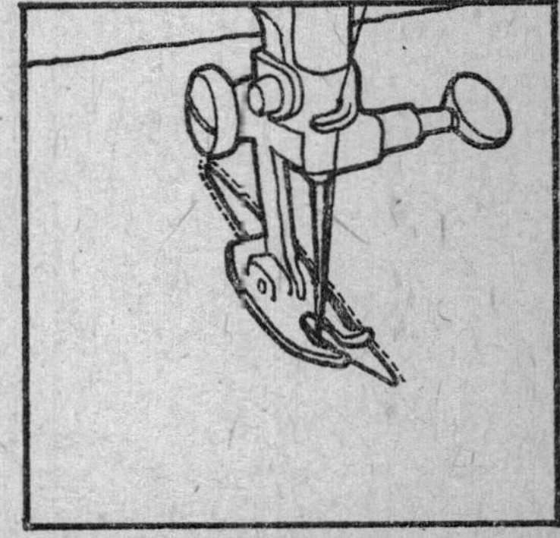

5 Machine stitch as close to the edge as you can, along both sides of the buttonhole.

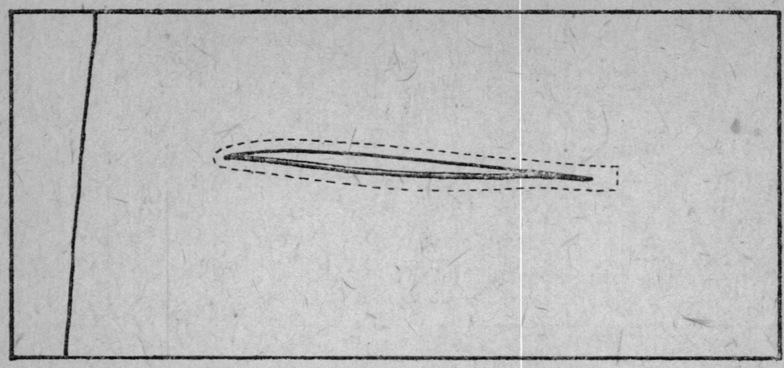

6 Go round the end nearest the outer edge of the garment, and straight across the other end.

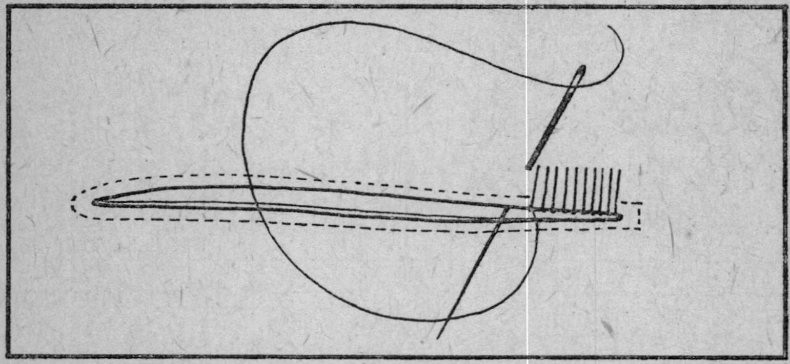

7 On the right side of the fabric, using buttonhole stitch (see page 19) start at the straight end of the buttonhole and work along one side.

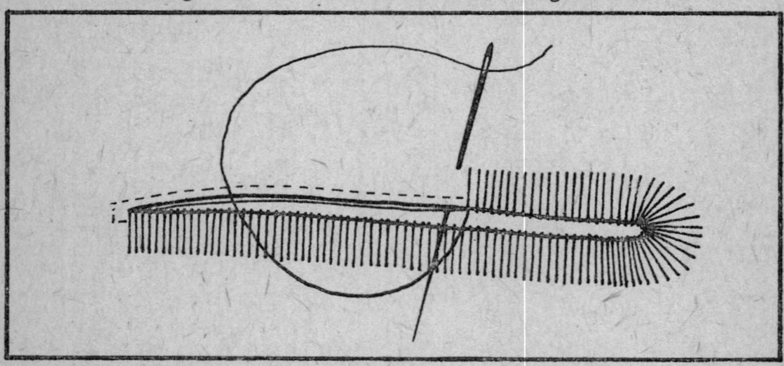

8 Work round the rounded end, and along the other side.

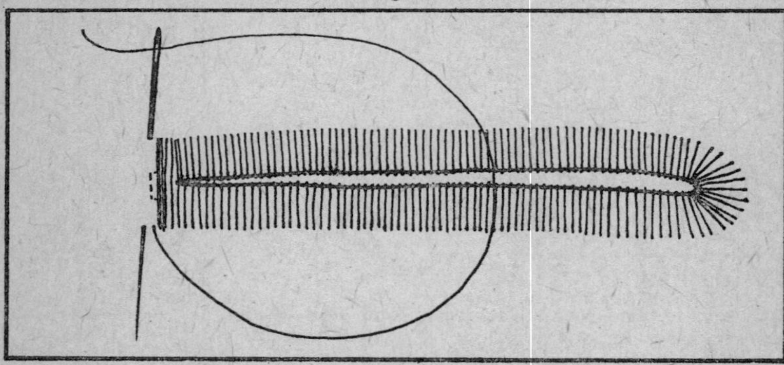

9 When you get back to the straight end work four stitches on top of each other across the end.

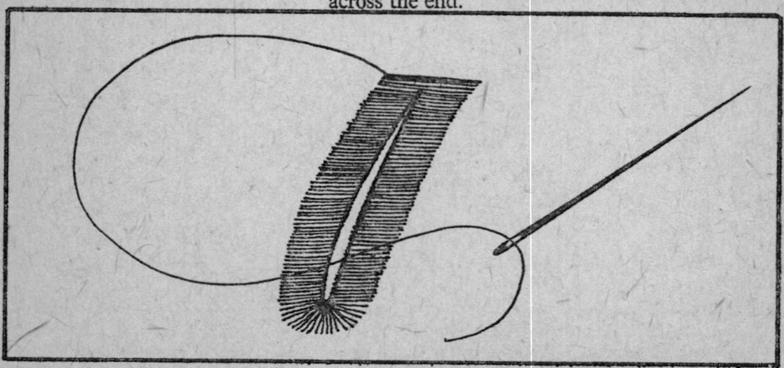

10 Turn the work round.

11 Work tiny buttonhole stitches across the four straight stitches with the looped ends worked in towards the buttonhole.

bound

Bound buttonholes should be done first, on single fabric, before you attach the facing. They are finished off as a second operation when the facing is in place.
The principle here is that you will have a strip of binding on either edge of the buttonhole instead of buttonhole stitching. It is therefore necessary to make sure both strips of binding are the same width, and this width will vary according to the size of the buttonhole. Generally, delicate fabrics have the smaller buttonholes.

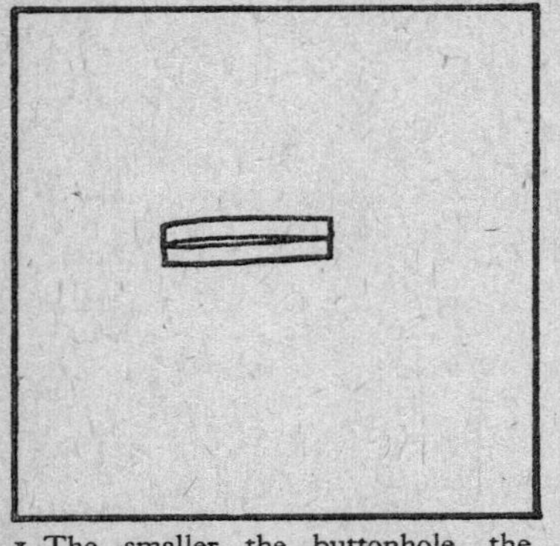

1 The smaller the buttonhole, the narrower the binding.

2 The larger the buttonhole, the wider you can have the binding.

3 You can if you wish have a narrow binding on a long buttonhole.

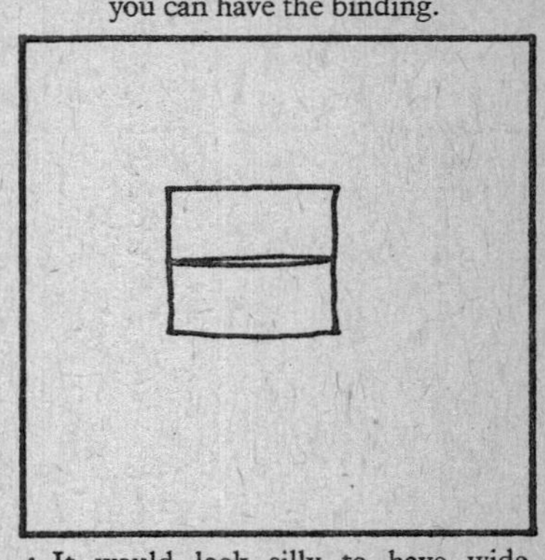

4 It would look silly to have wide binding on a small one.

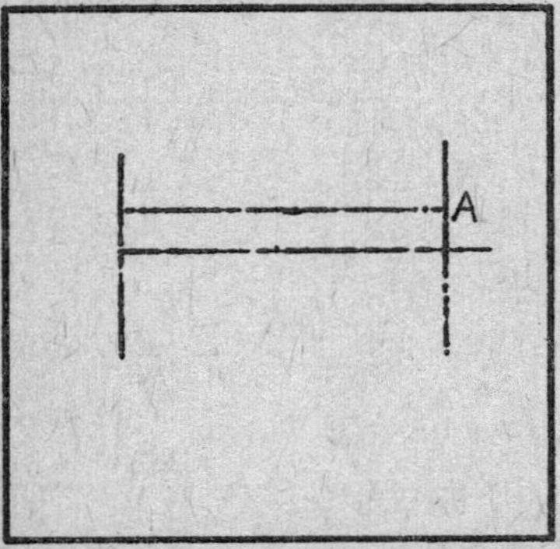

5 Decide the width you want and mark a line (A) on one side of the centre line of the buttonhole, the same distance away from it as the proposed width of the binding.

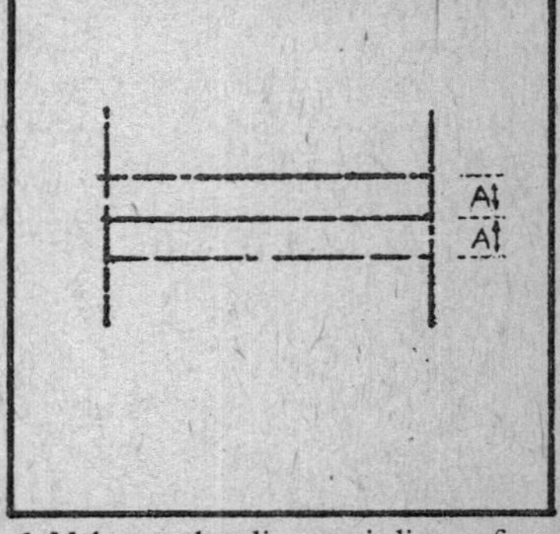

6 Make another line equi-distant from the centre on the other side.

There are two ways you can make a bound buttonhole, and you may find one easier than the other

METHOD ONE

First stage

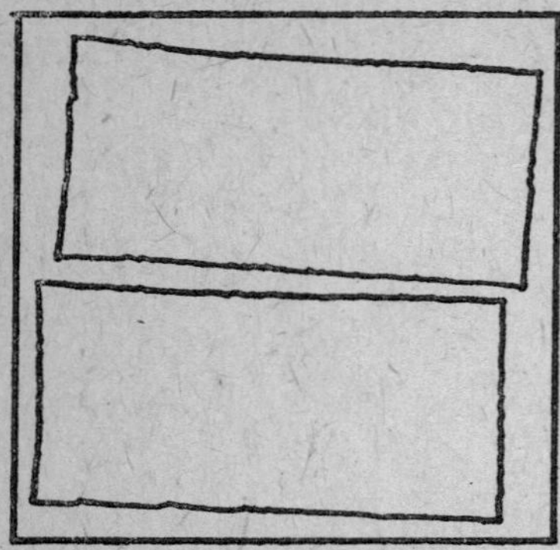

1 For each buttonhole cut two small strips of fabric, both a good inch longer than the buttonhole.

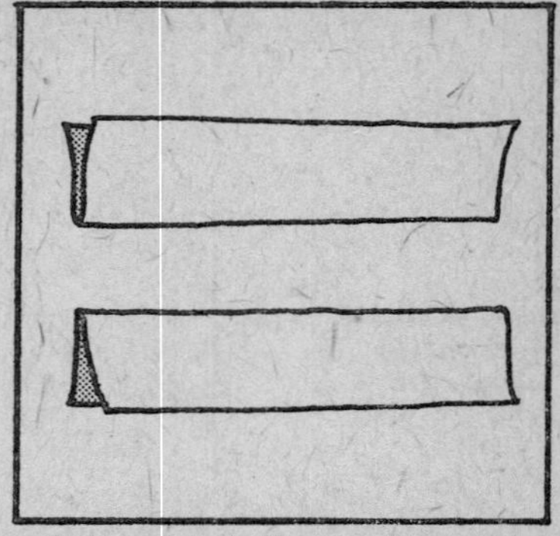

2 Fold each in half, right side outside, and press.

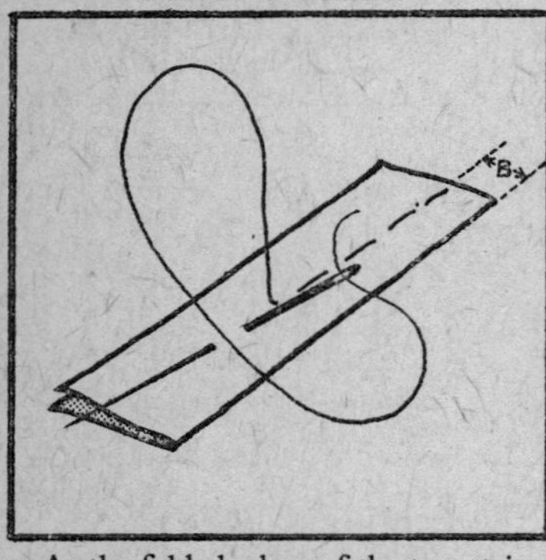

3 As the folded edges of the two strips will eventually form the inner edges of the buttonhole, sew a line of tacking stitches as far from the fold as the width of the binding (B).

4 These two pieces are sewn over the buttonhole back-to-back because they are eventually turned inside out.

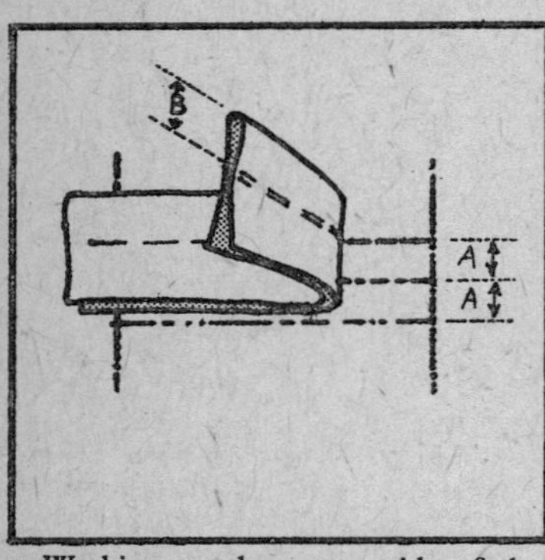

5 Working on the wrong side of the fabric place one of your pieces in position with lines A and B together, and the fold facing away from the centre.

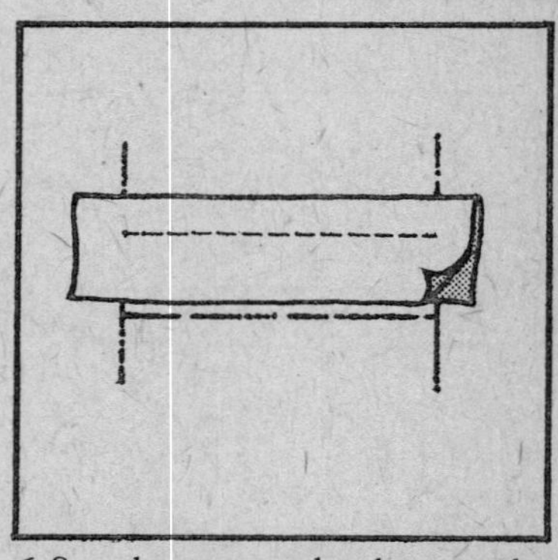

6 Sew the two together between the two vertical marks.

7 Sew a second piece to the other side of the buttonhole.

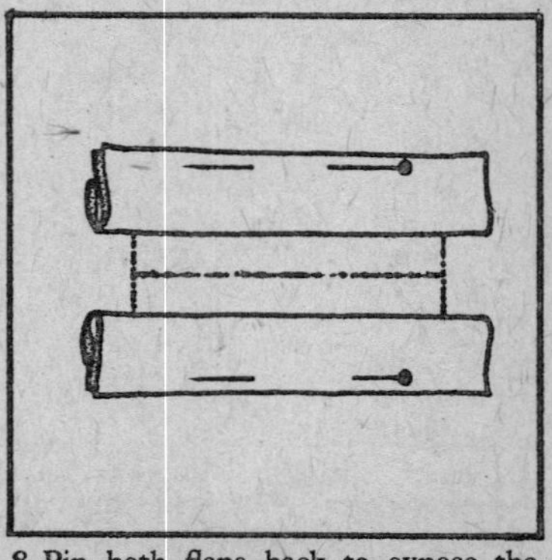

8 Pin both flaps back to expose the centre line.

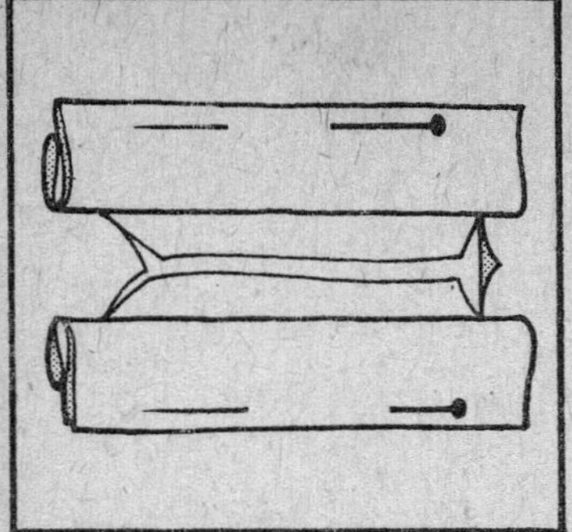

9 Snip along this centre line to within about ¼ in. of each end, and at each end cut diagonally out to the corners.

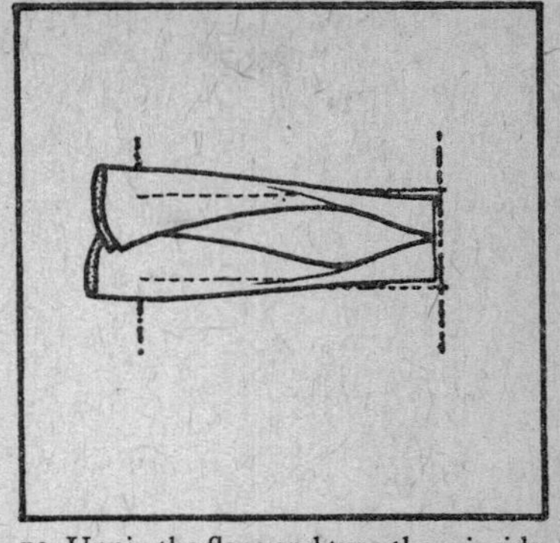

10 Unpin the flaps and turn them inside out through the buttonhole.

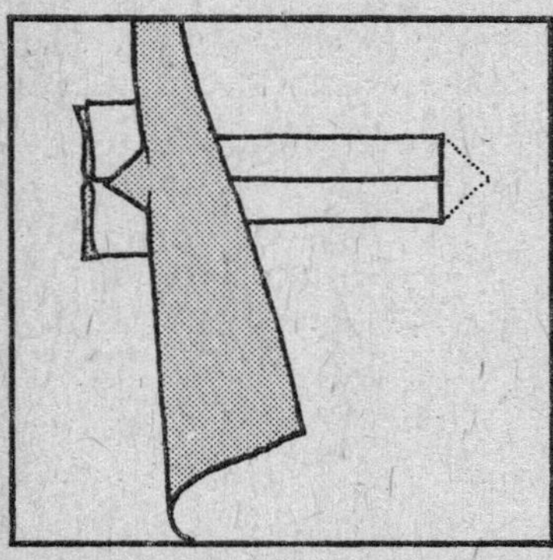

11 Tuck in the little triangular flaps at each end.

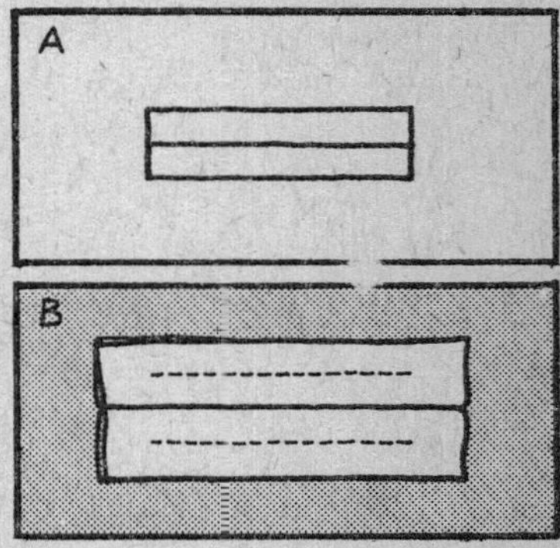

12 It will then look like A on the outside and B on the inside.

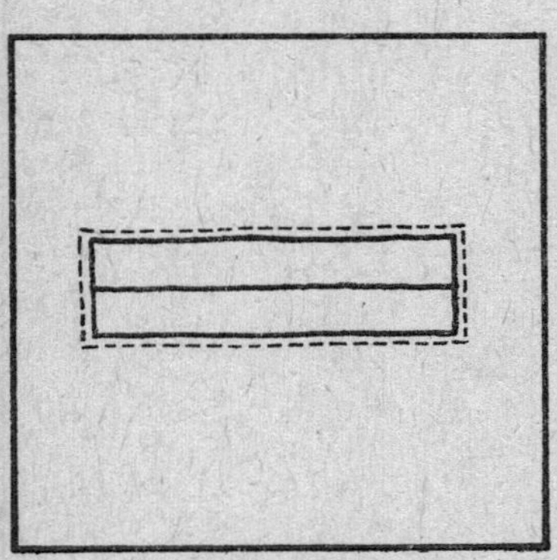

13 Stitch all the way round the buttonhole, on the right side, either by hand or by machine.

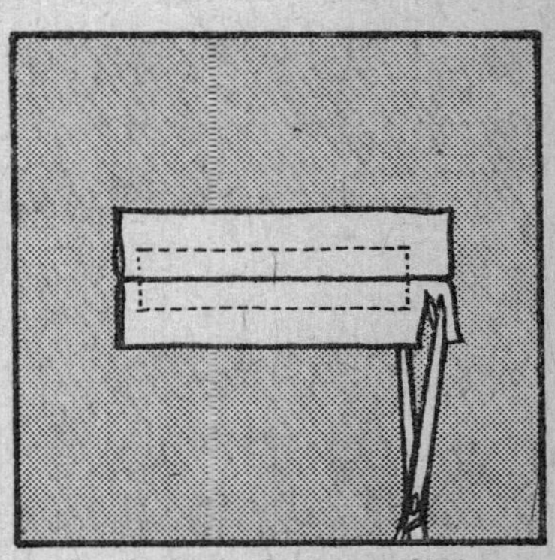

14 On the back of the buttonhole, cut away excess allowance on the flaps, but not too much.

Second stage

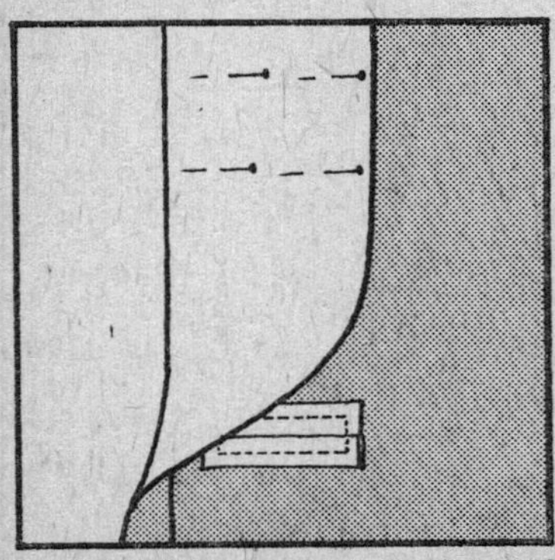

15 Fold the facing (and interfacing if used) into position and pin in place round the buttonhole.

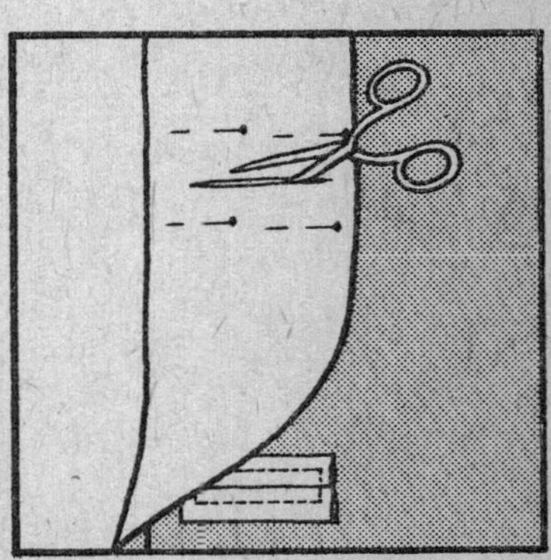

16 Make a corresponding cut in the facings for each buttonhole.

17 Turn in the edges of this cut all the way round the buttonhole.

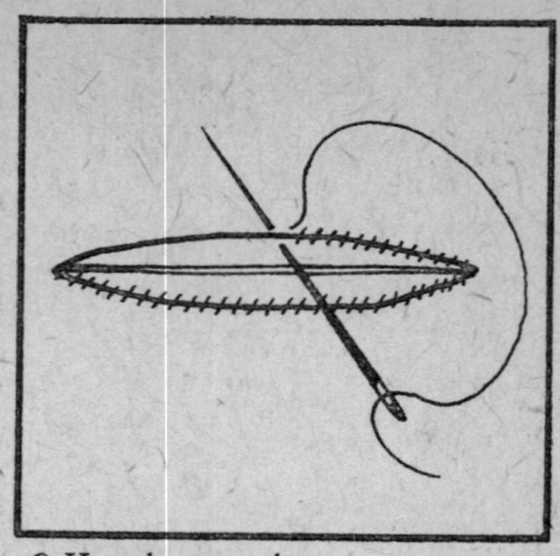

18 Hem down neatly.

METHOD TWO

This time mark up on the *wrong* side of the fabric. Work as far as BOUND BUTTONHOLES 6 page 53.

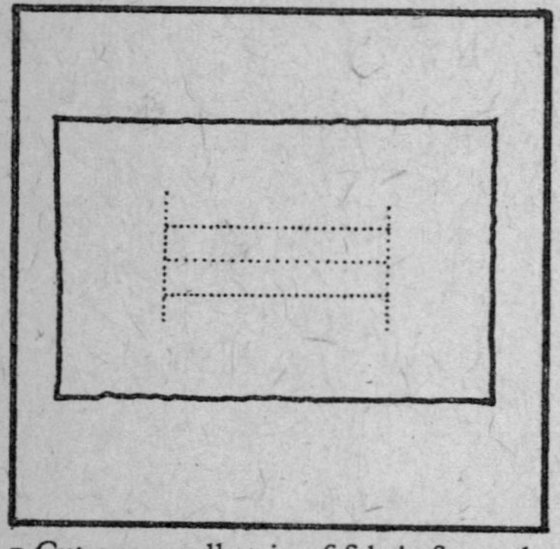

1 Cut one small strip of fabric for each buttonhole, 1 in. longer than the buttonhole, and $1\frac{1}{2}$ in. wide.

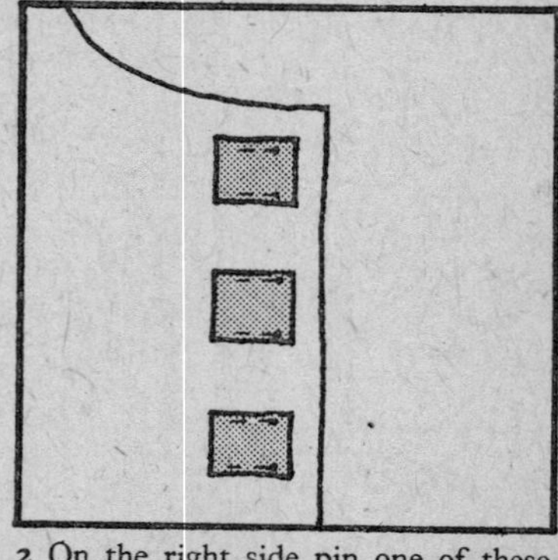

2 On the right side pin one of these pieces over each buttonhole area, with the right side downwards.

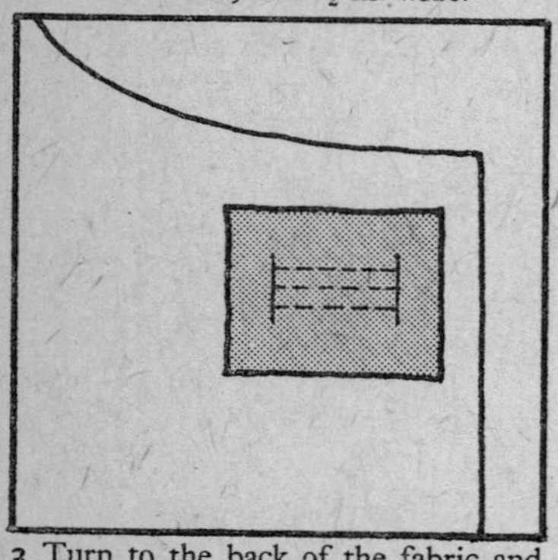

3 Turn to the back of the fabric and sew with a contrasting thread an outline of the buttonhole mark so that you can see it on the right side.

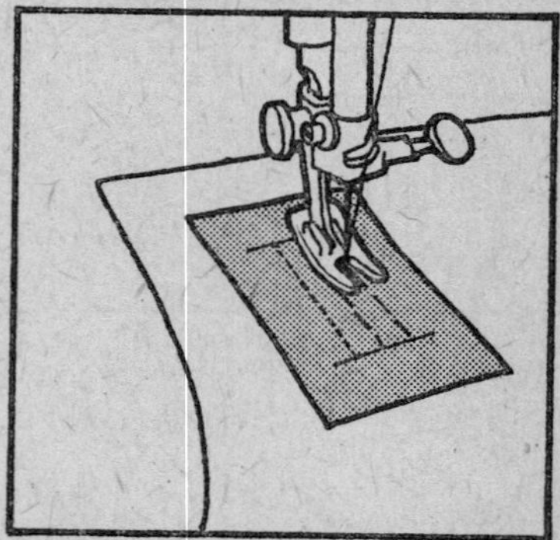

4 Sew along the two outer horizontal lines between the two vertical ones.

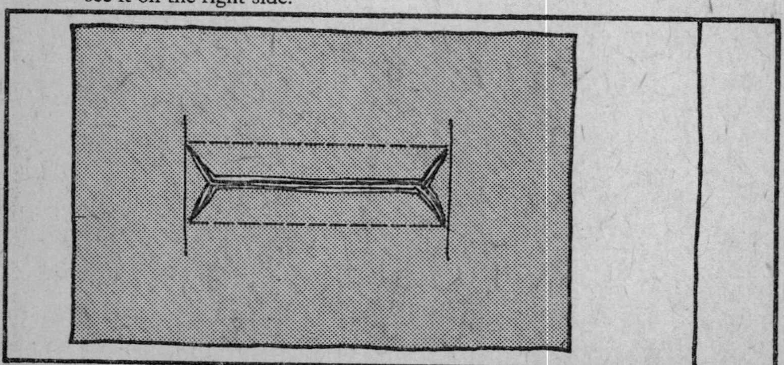

5 Snip centre line as in Method 1, Step 9.

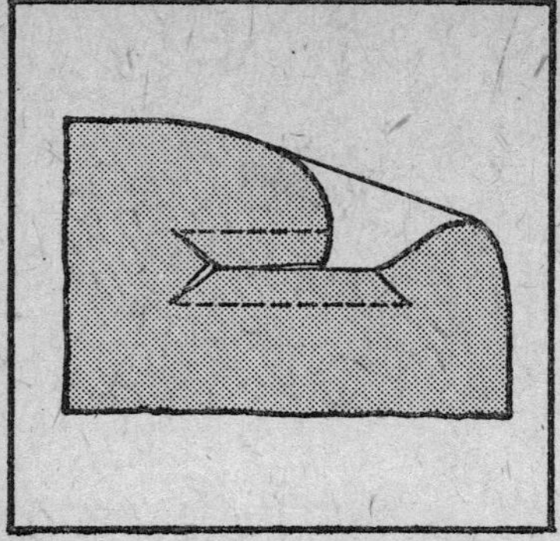

6 Remove all tacking threads and turn the flaps to the inside.

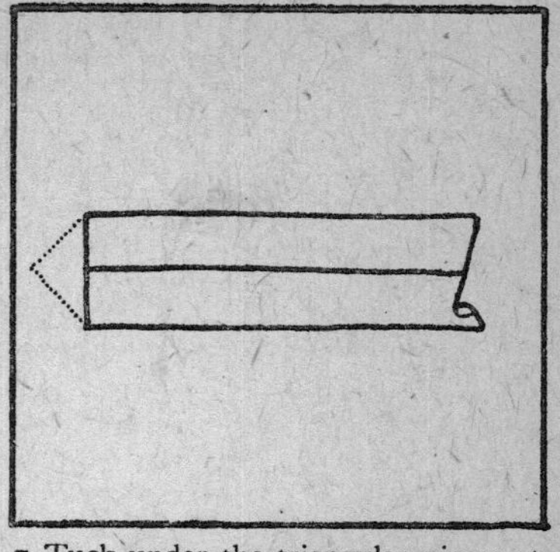

7 Tuck under the triangular pieces at each end.

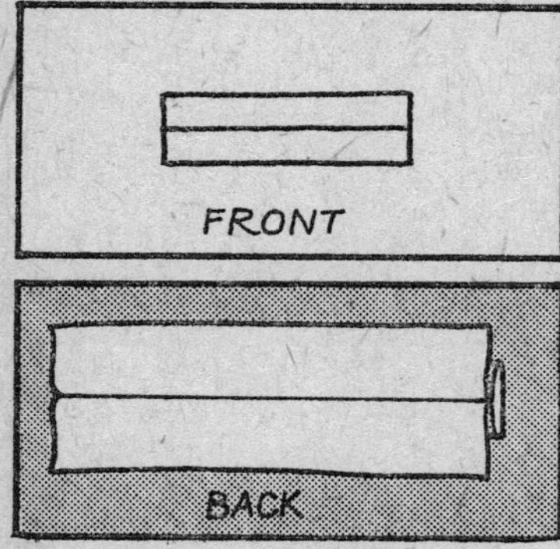

8 It will now look like this. Finish off front and back as for Bound Buttonholes, Method 1.

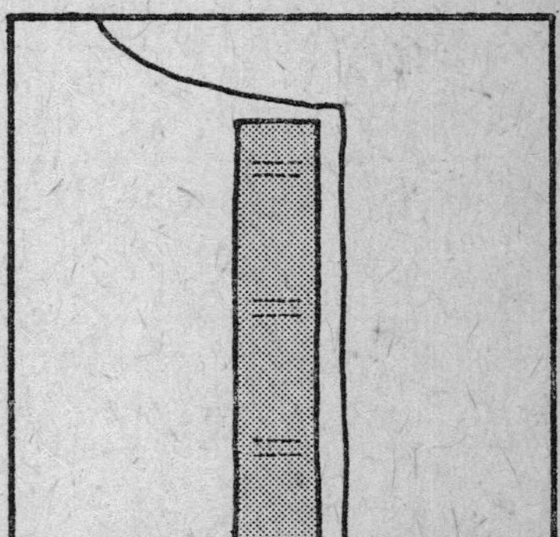

9 You can save a little time with this method by taking one long strip instead of a small one for each buttonhole, and tack this down the entire buttonhole area.

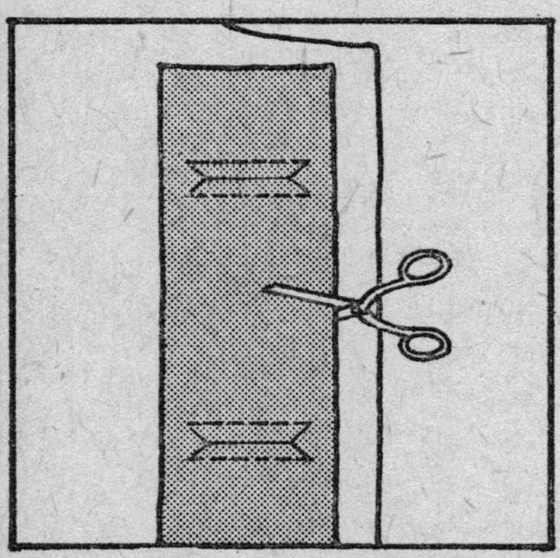

10 Cut this strip between the buttonholes after you have completed 5 above.

looped buttonholes

It would need a professional to make the tiny, rolled binding which you find on ready-made clothes. The home dressmaker would be better advised to buy narrow elastic, narrow braid or cord. The quantity you buy will depend on the size of the loop, which must be just the size of the button, and the number you propose to make.

1 Cut the braid into suitable lengths to go round the button, plus 1 in. (½ in. each end) seam allowance. Wherever the buttonholes are needed, these little loops must be hand sewn into place before the facing is attached.

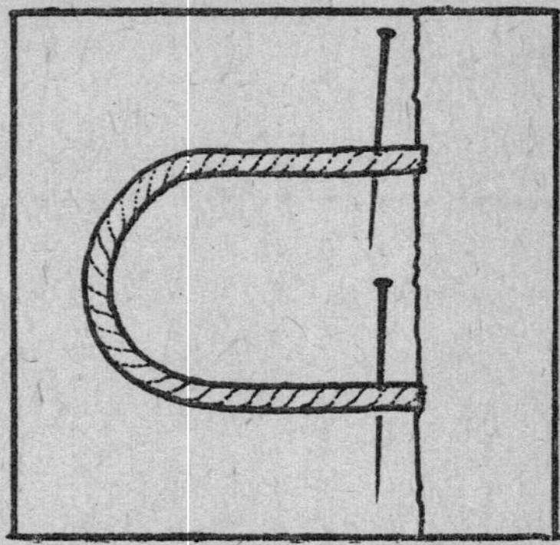

2 Working on the right side of the fabric, take the first loop and pin it with its ends meeting the raw edge of the fabric and the loop facing inwards, and with a space the width of the button between the two ends of braid.

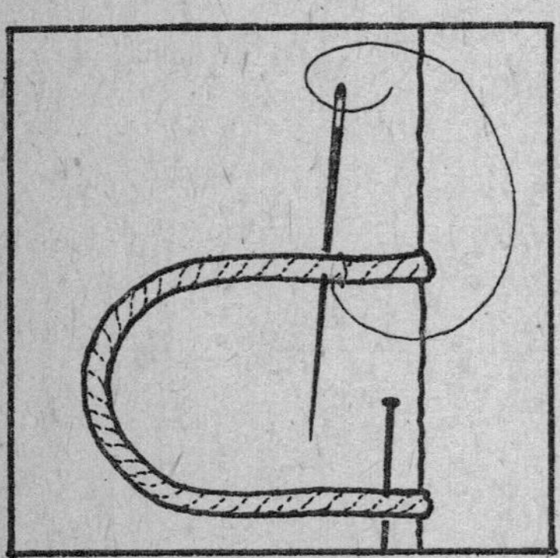

3 Make a couple of hand stitches on the sewing line to anchor it. Sew down as many loops as you need in this way.

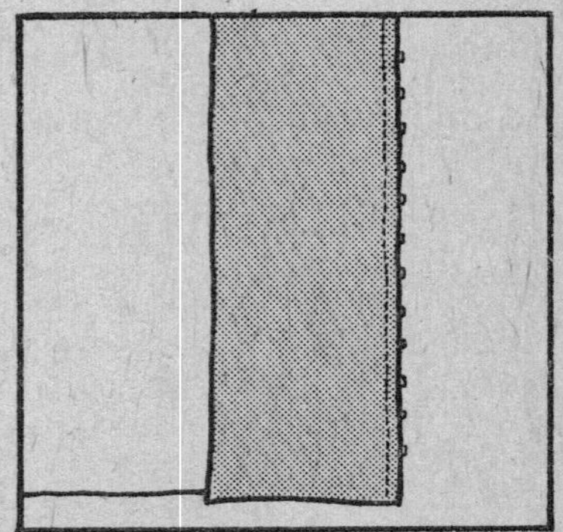

4 Lay the facing, right side down, on top, and sew along the sewing line.

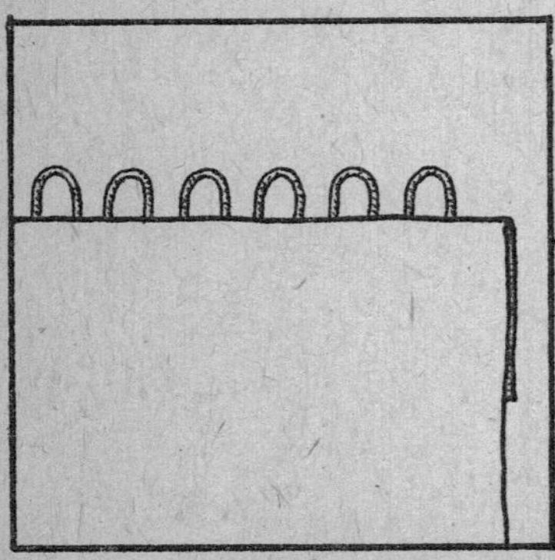

5 When the facing is turned inside out, the loops will be firmly in place.

binding

Binding is a very attractive way of dealing with edges, and every budding dressmaker should know how to both make it and apply it. You can buy it ready made, but that won't help if you want it to be the same as the dress.

making bias binding

Binding is always cut on the bias, that is to say, diagonally across the weave of the fabric. It is then equally suitable for curved and straight edges.

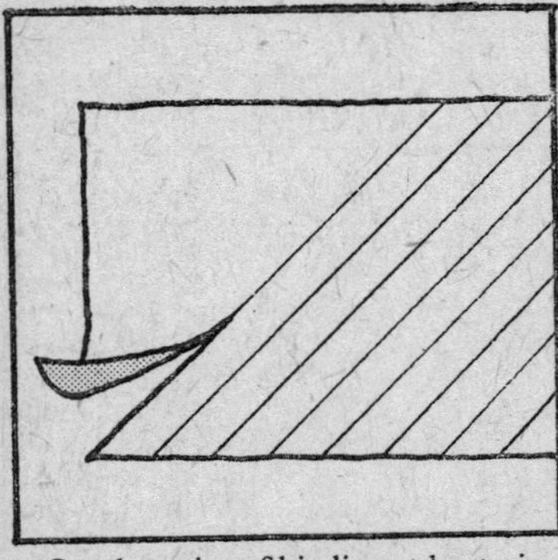

1 Cut the strips of binding at least 1 in. wide. You can always trim off a little.

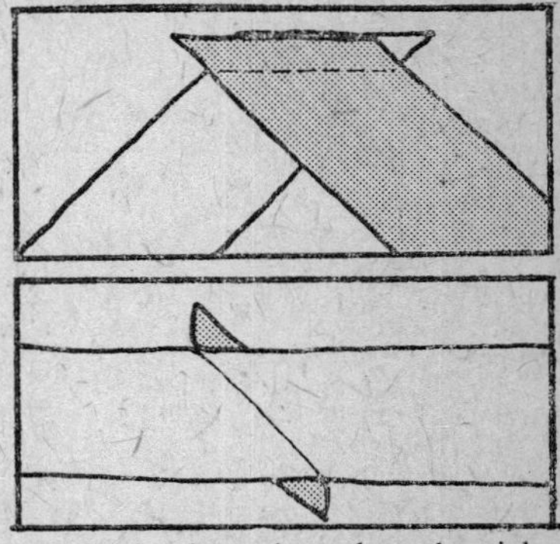

2 To join the strips, place the right sides of the fabric together, work on the wrong sides, and match the straight ends so that when they are opened out the sides will be even.

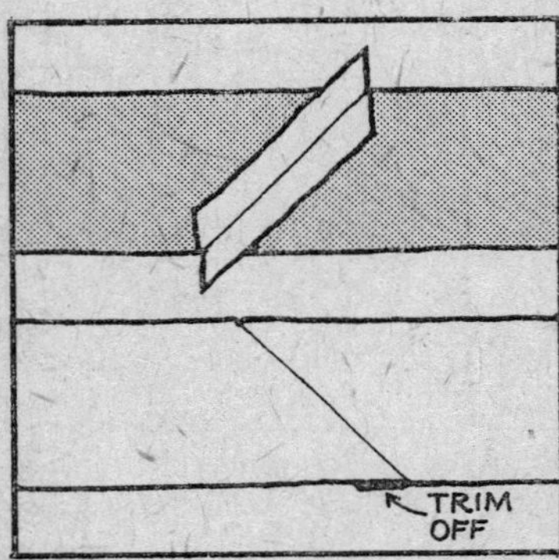

3 Sew with a plain seam, fasten off securely, open out and press flat. Join as many pieces as you will need.

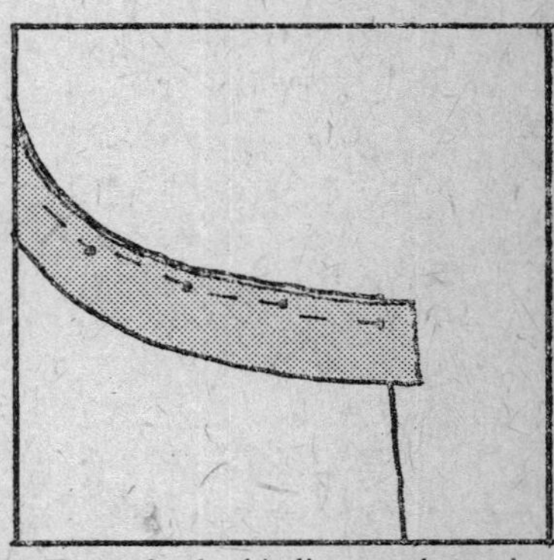

4 To apply the binding, work on the right side of the garment. Pin one edge of the strip to the edge of the garment, right sides together.

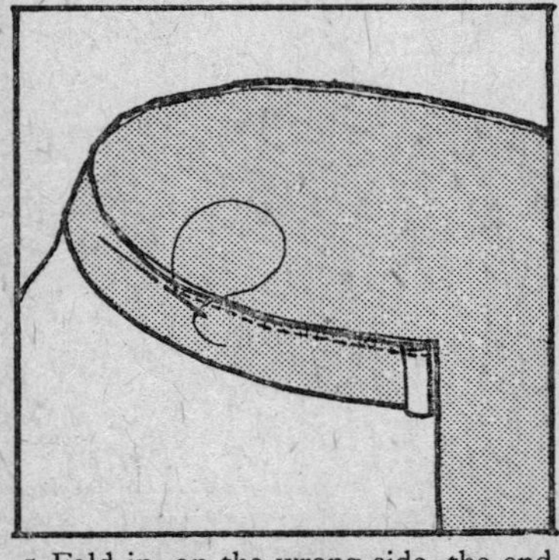

5 Fold in, on the wrong side, the end of the strip before you start sewing.

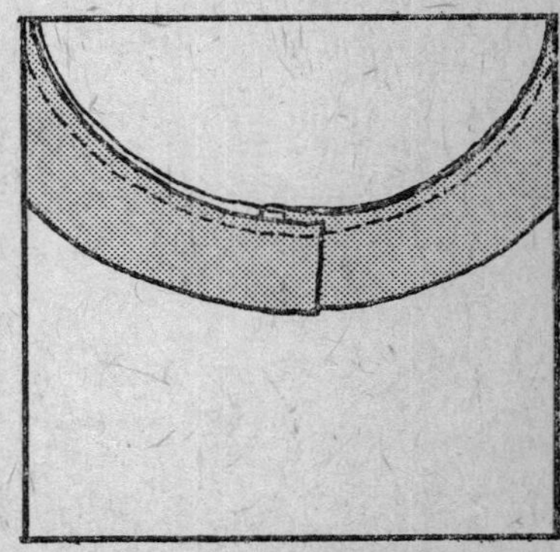

6 If you are binding a complete circle, overlap the point where you started by about $\frac{1}{2}$ in.

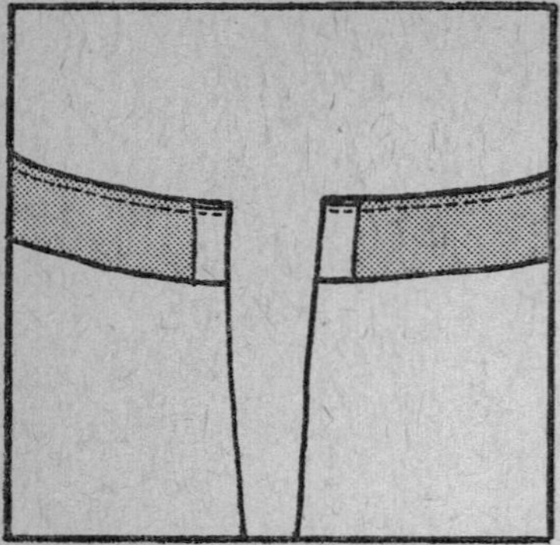

7 If you are not joining the two ends of the binding, fold the end as at the beginning.

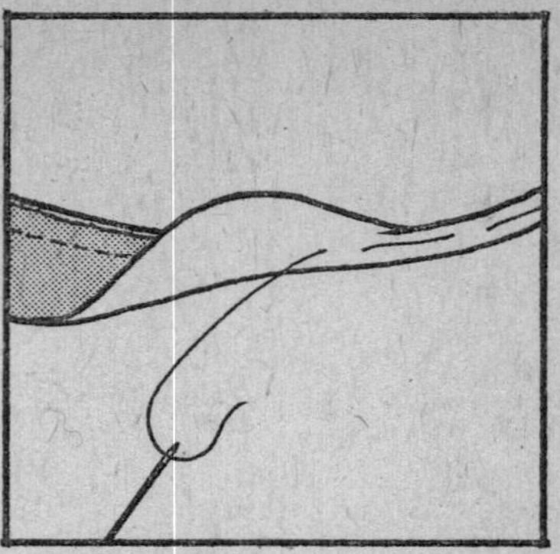

8 Turn the binding towards the wrong side and tack it to the seam allowance behind.

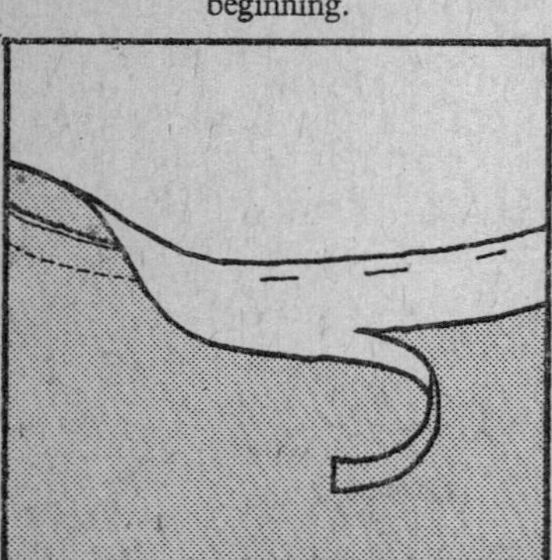

9 Turn to the wrong side and fold down the binding. If it is too wide trim off a little all the way round.

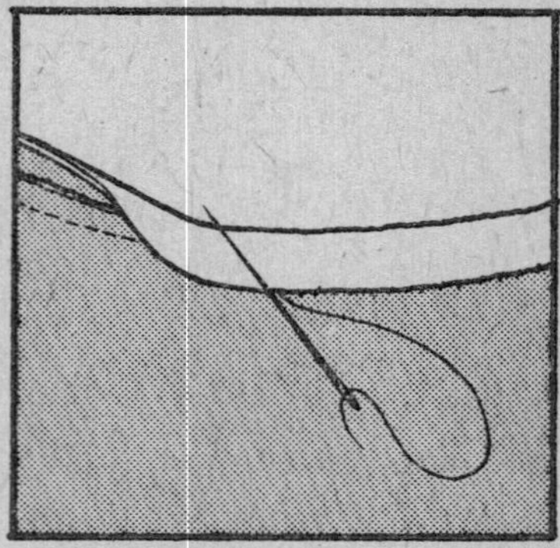

10 Turn under the edge and hem neatly without the stitches showing through on the outside.

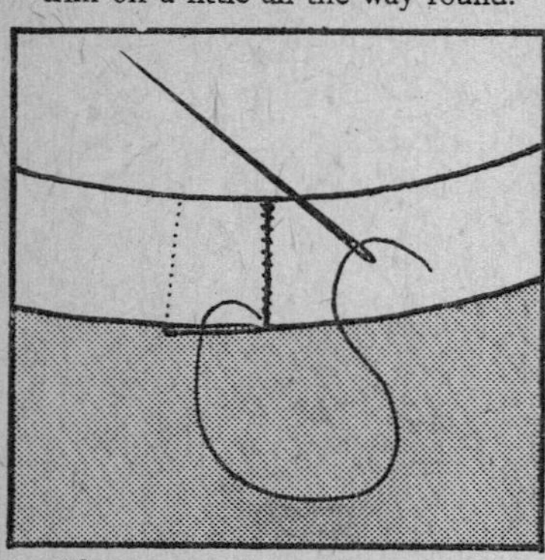

11 If you are joining the ends of the binding, when you get to the point at which you started, the folded in end will overlap the other end. Put a few stitches in this folded edge to keep it in place.

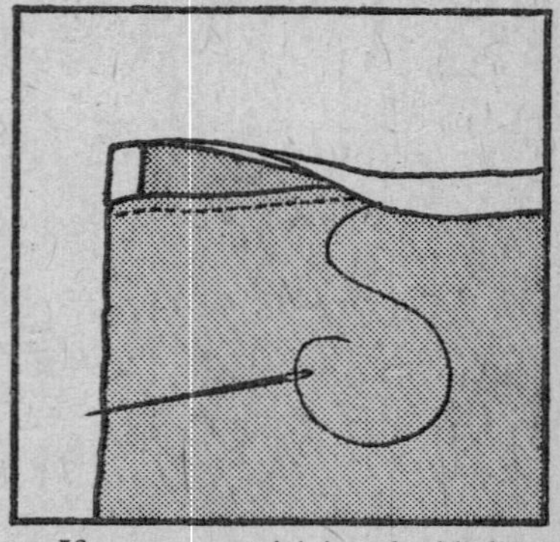

12 If you are not joining the binding it will be neat when you fold over the turned-in end.

ready-made bias binding

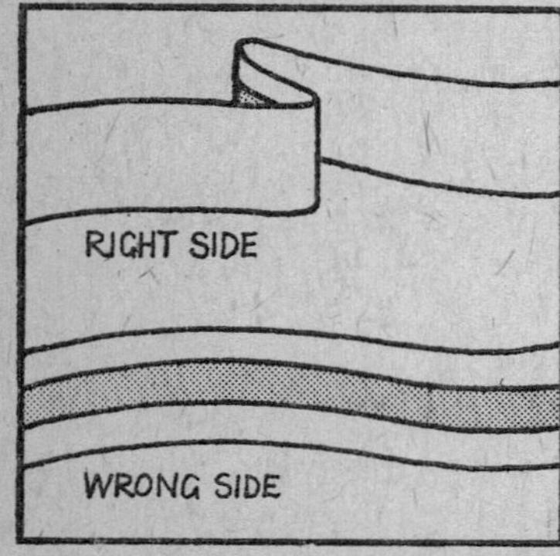

1 This is bought ready packed and is already turned in. The outside is smooth and the wrong side has two turnings.

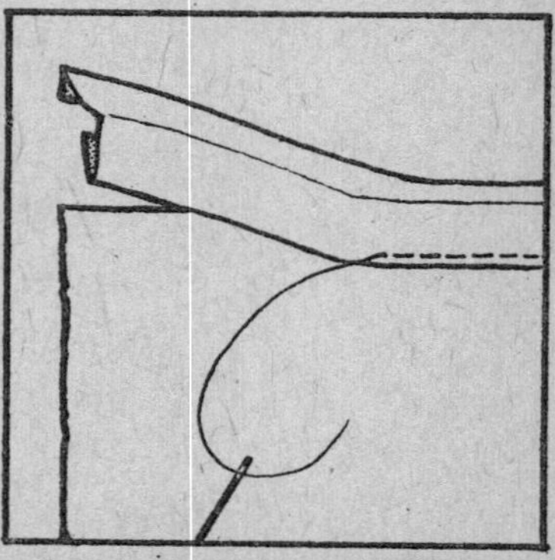

2 It can be applied to each edge separately by machining or hemming the outside first. This time overlap the binding and the edge to be bound, on the right side of the garment.

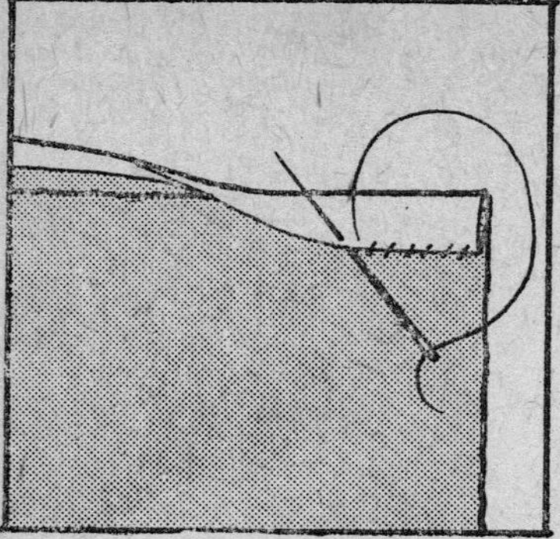
3 Turn to the wrong side and hem down the other edge, or

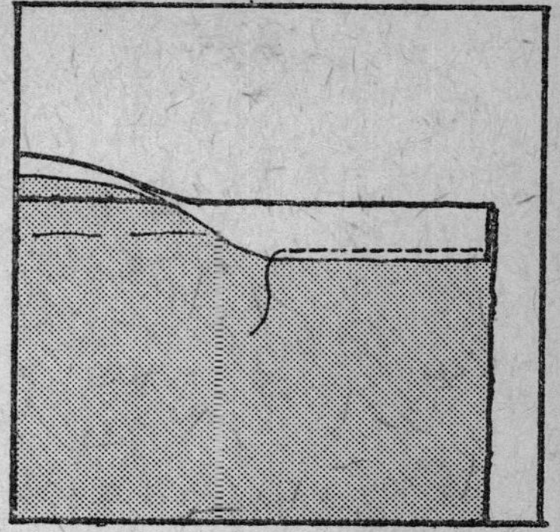
4 Tack the binding to the front of the garment, turn over to the back, fold down the binding, and machine both front and back with one seam.

frilling and piping

Frilling is neater sewn between two surfaces so that the gathered edge doesn't show. If the surface is only a single thickness it would be better to use a piece of facing.

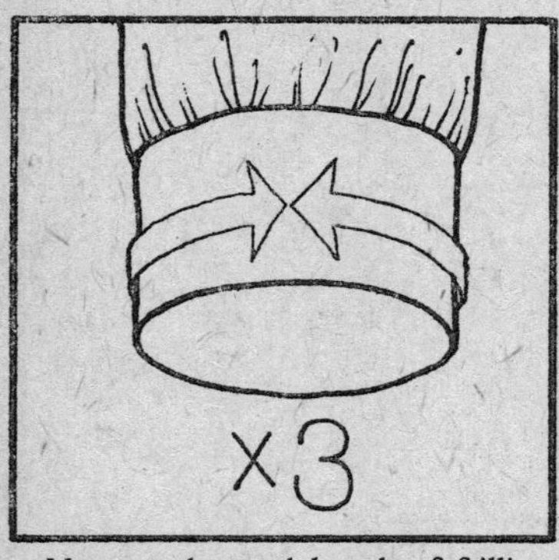

1 Measure the total length of frilling you will require, and allow three times as much.

single thickness frilling

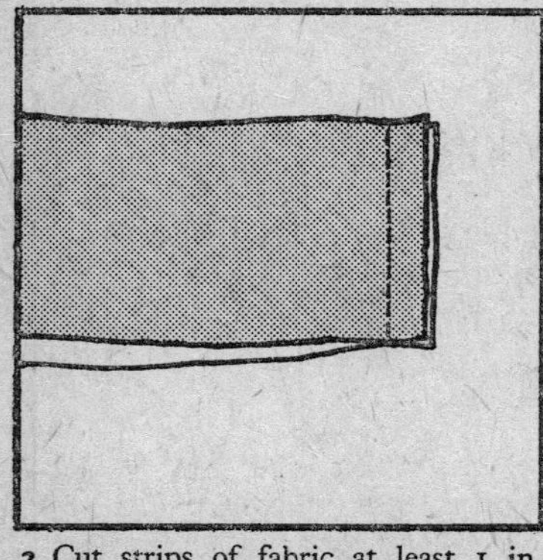
2 Cut strips of fabric at least 1 in. wider than you will want the frill to be, and join them together with a single seam, on the wrong side.

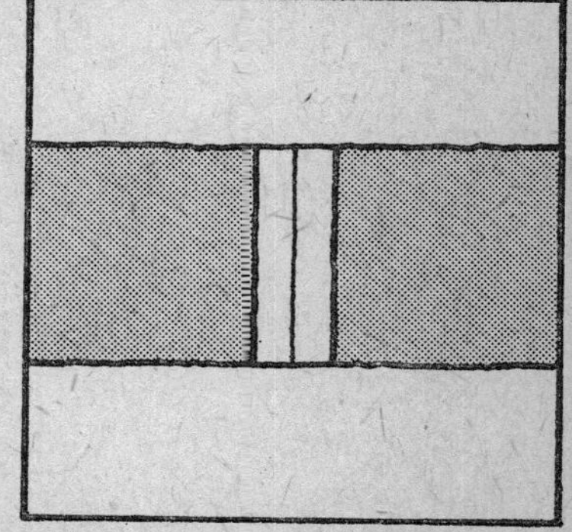
3 Open out these seams and press flat.

4 Turn a narrow hem on one edge of the frilling on the wrong side and sew it down, either by hemming, machining or by shell edging.

double thickness frilling

Cut your strips twice the width you want the frill to be, plus 1 in. Join the strips as above.

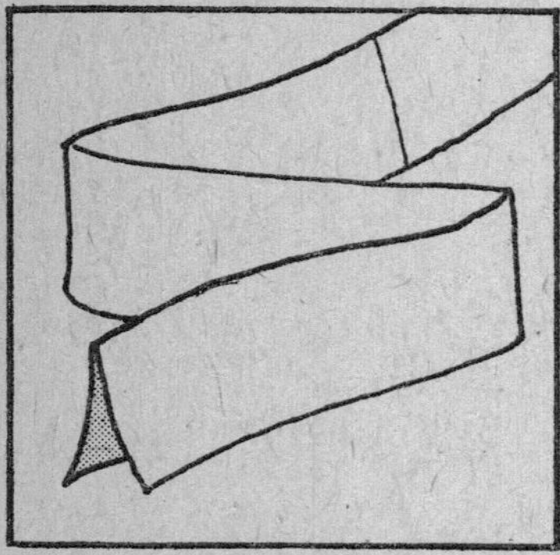

5 Fold the strip in half lengthways, right side out, and press.

gathering and attaching both types

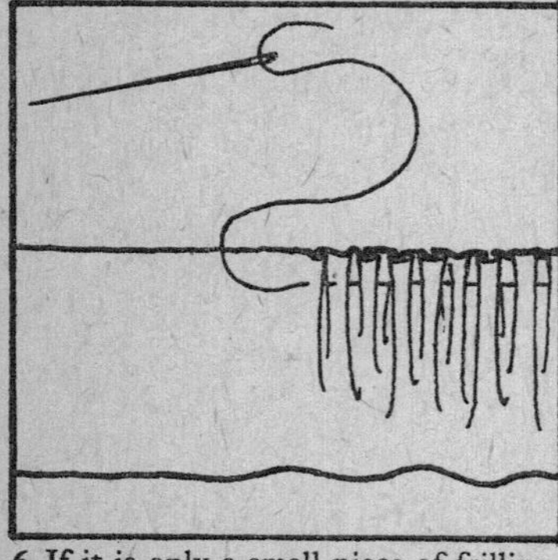

6 If it is only a small piece of frilling, say for a cuff, do a row of running stitches $\frac{3}{8}$ in. in from the raw edge, and gather (see page 19).

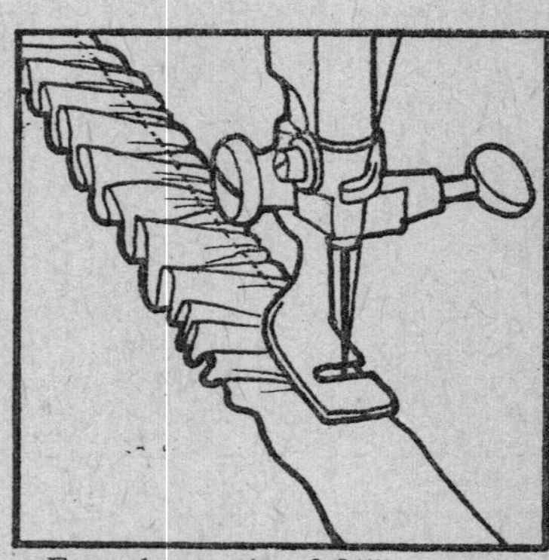

7 For a long strip of frilling use the gathering foot on the machine, if you have one, otherwise gather by hand as on page 19.

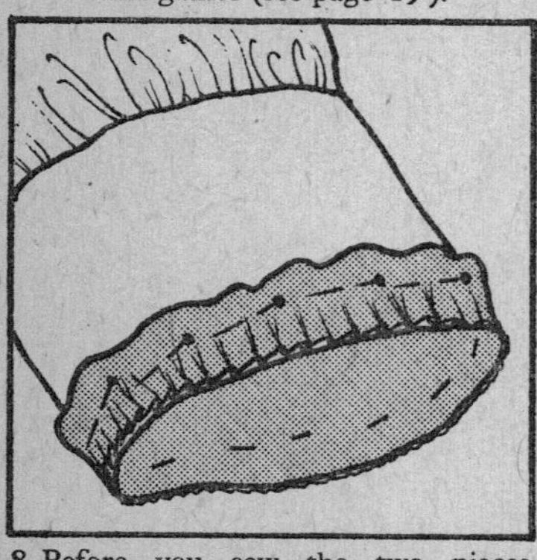

8 Before you sew the two pieces between which you are inserting the frilling together, pin it, wrong side uppermost, to the right side of one of the other pieces, with the bottom edges together.

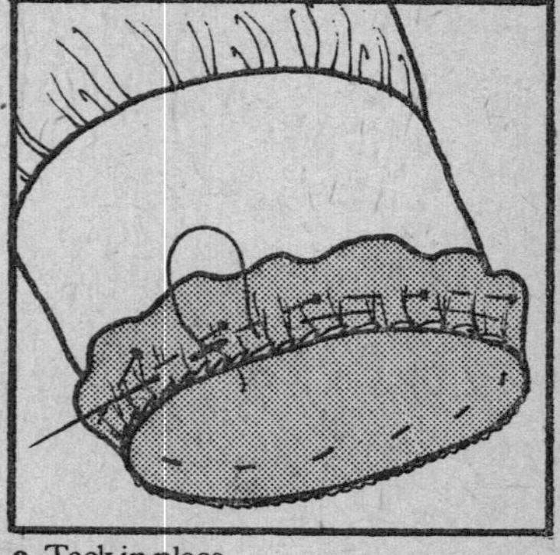

9 Tack in place.

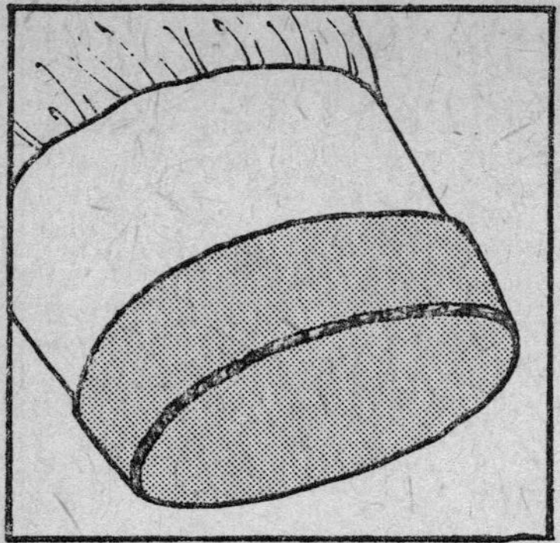

10 Place the other piece, wrong side uppermost, on top of this, with the bottom edges together.

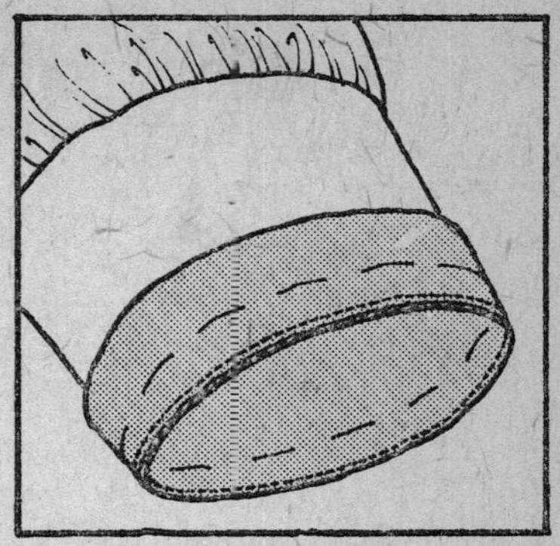

11 Tack in place and then sew.

12 Turn the two pieces inside out, and the frilling will be in place.

13 If you are attaching a piece of facing, turn in the outer edge of the facing and slip stitch it lightly to the main fabric.

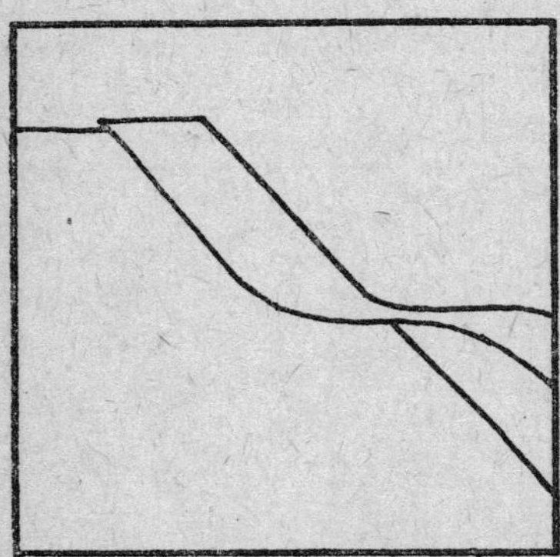

14 Alternatively, here is a quick method for a larger article, such as a cushion cover. Take one piece of the main fabric right side uppermost, and lay the frilling along the edge, with the unsewn edges together.

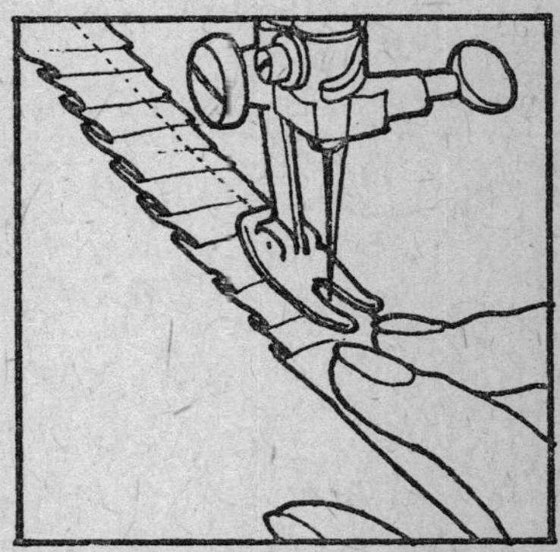

15 As you sew, push the strip of frilling forwards to make tiny tucks.

corded piping

In order to sew this by machine you will need a special fitting – the one you use for sewing in zips. It is not possible to get good results without. The other alternative is to sew it in by hand, because you must get the seam tight up to the cord.

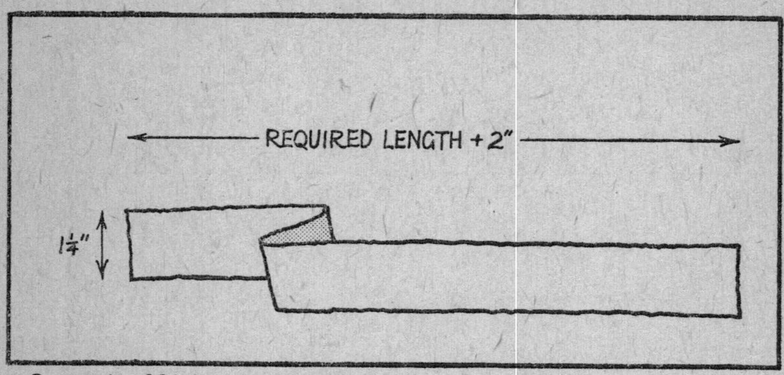

1 Cut a strip of fabric 1¼ in. wide, and as long as required, plus 2 in. for joining.

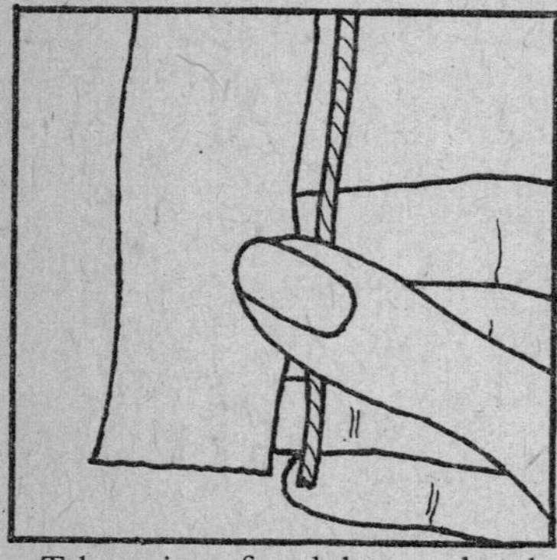

2 Take a piece of cord the same length.

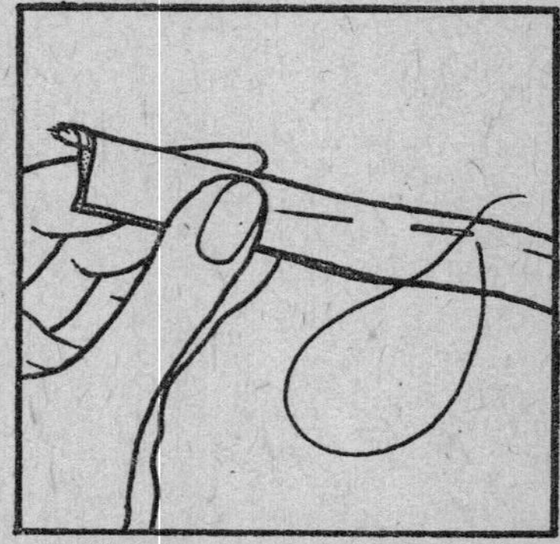

3 Fold the strip round the cord, right side out, and tack close up against the cord.

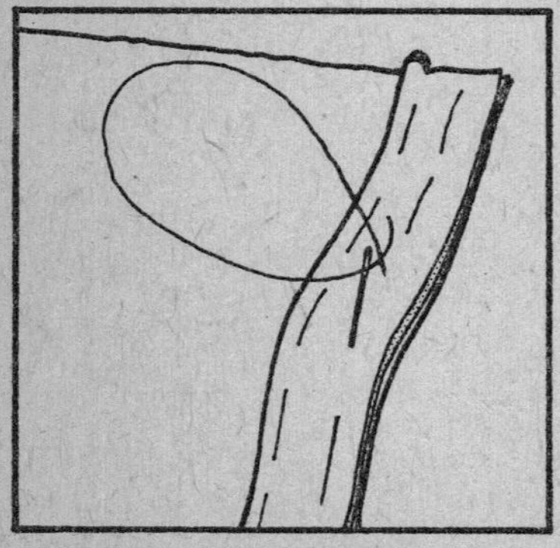

4 Lay the corded strip on the right side of your main fabric, with the corded edge inwards and the raw edges together. Tack in place.

5 Lay the facing or second piece of fabric on top of this, right side down, and sew a plain seam as close to the cord as you can.

a few things to make with frilling and piping, without a pattern

These items are included because you don't need a pattern, and can use up left-overs if you feel like a little relaxation.

frilled cushion cover

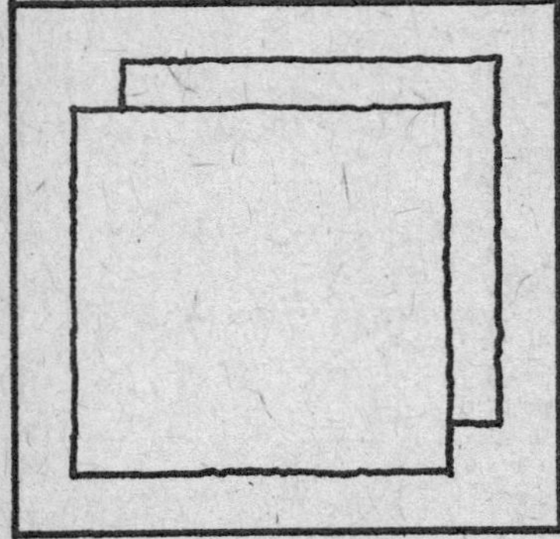

1 Cut two identical pieces of fabric.

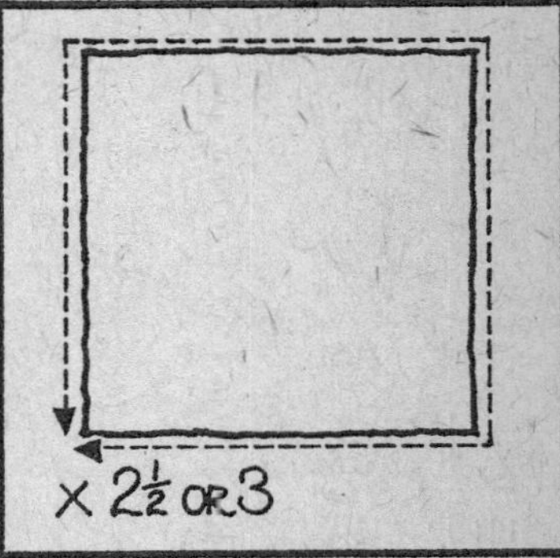

2 Measure the distance round the four edges and multiply by 2½ or 3 for your strip of frilling.

You must use double thickness frilling to make a good job of it, so make the strip twice as wide as you require the frill, plus a seam allowance. See page 62.

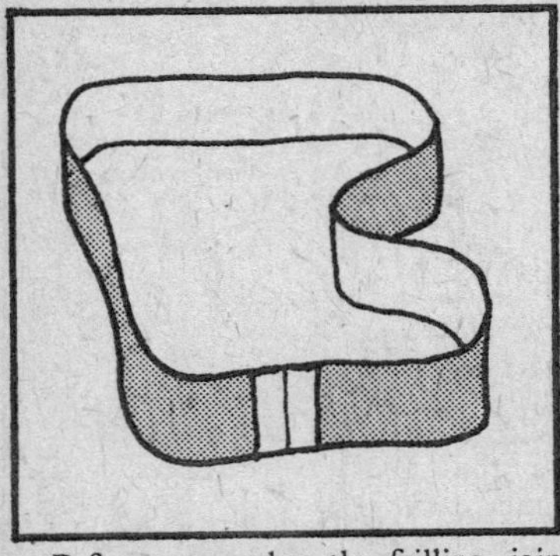

3 Before you gather the frilling, join the two ends of the strip with a single seam, open out and press.

METHOD A

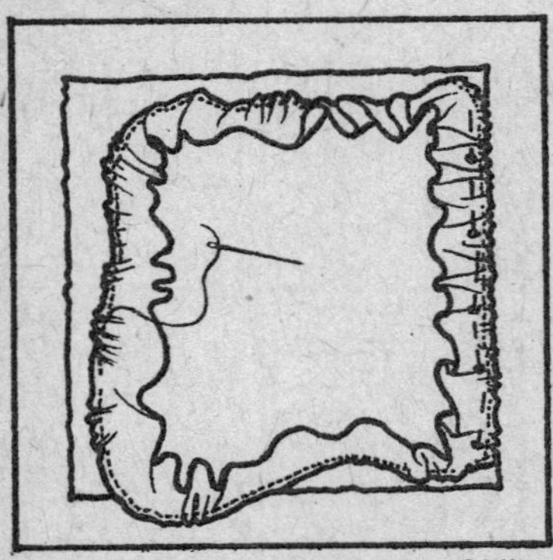

4 After you have gathered the frilling as on page 62, do not fasten off, but pin it in place by laying it on the right side of one cushion piece, with the frill facing inwards and the raw edges together.

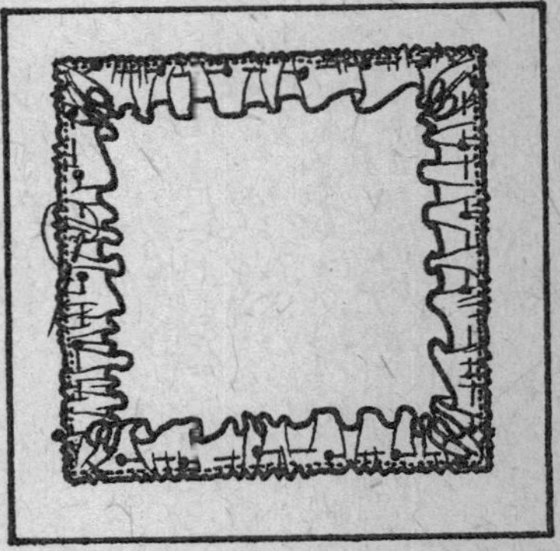

5 When you get round to the point at which you started, adjust the gathers to fit the cushion, and then fasten off.

6 Even out the gathers and tack the frill all round.

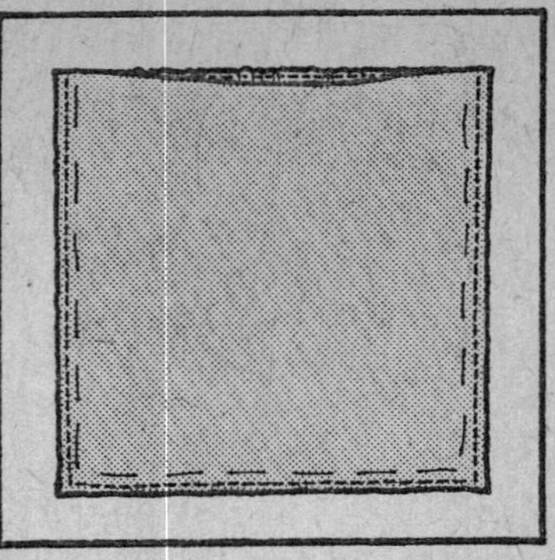

7 Lay the other cushion piece on top, right side downwards. Tack and sew three sides only.

8 On the fourth side, which must be left open, sew the frilling to the piece to which it is tacked.

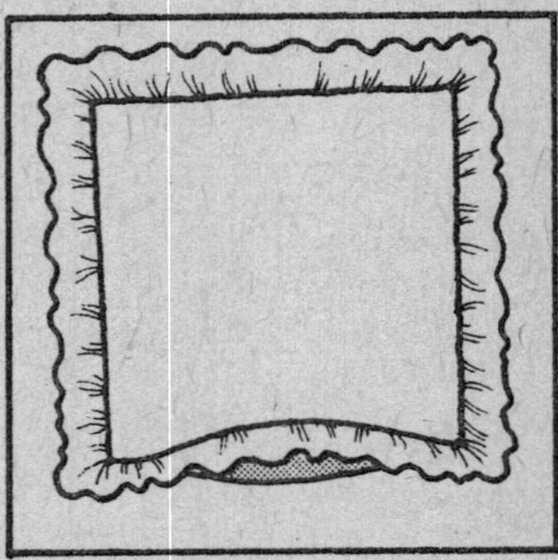

9 Finish off all ends of thread and turn inside out.

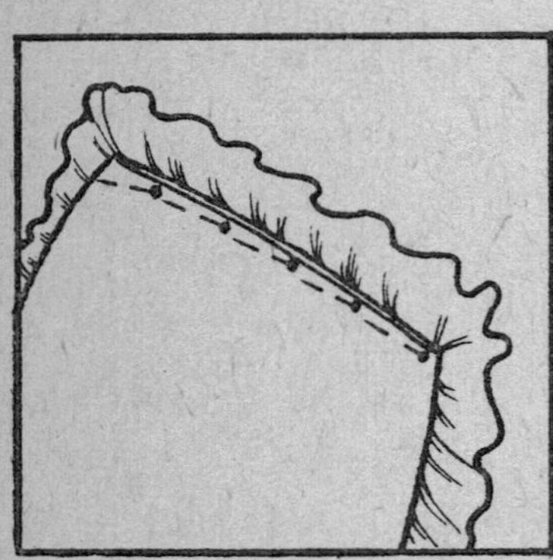

10 After the stuffing has been inserted, turn under the edge without the frill ½ in. and pin to the other half of the cushion.

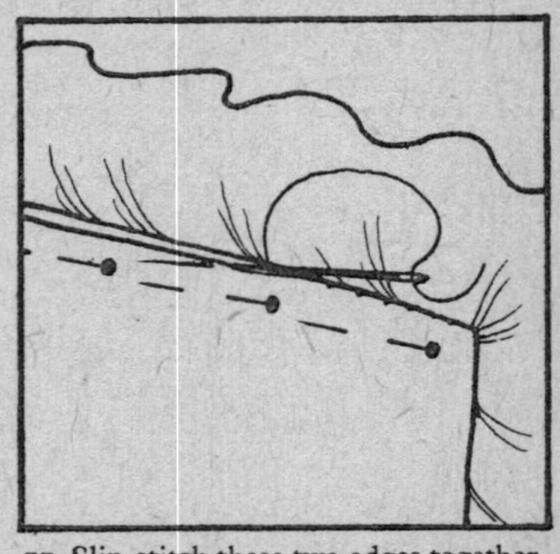

11 Slip-stitch these two edges together.

METHOD B

You could work as suggested on page 63.

12 Lay the folded strip on the right side of one cushion piece, raw edges together, and make tucks as you sew it.

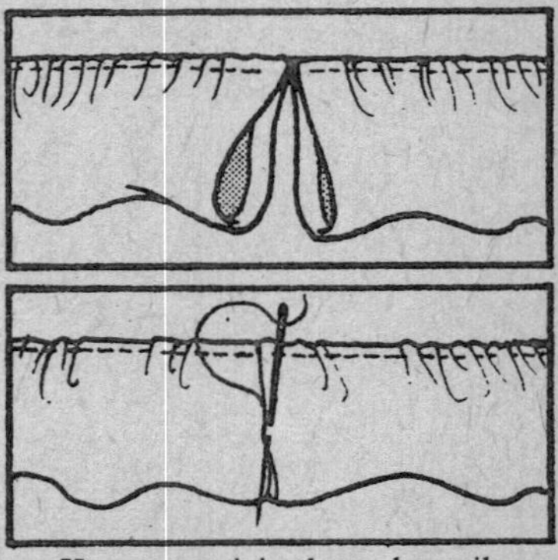

13 You cannot join the ends until you have sewn on practically all the frilling, so when you do, turn in the ends and catch them lightly together.

Continue as 9, 10 and 11 above.

cushion cover with piping

Take two identical pieces of fabric for the cushion, plus a strip 1¼ in. wide, long enough to go round the four sides, plus 2 in. Cut a piece of cord the same length as the strip. Cover the cord as on page 64, and proceed as follows:

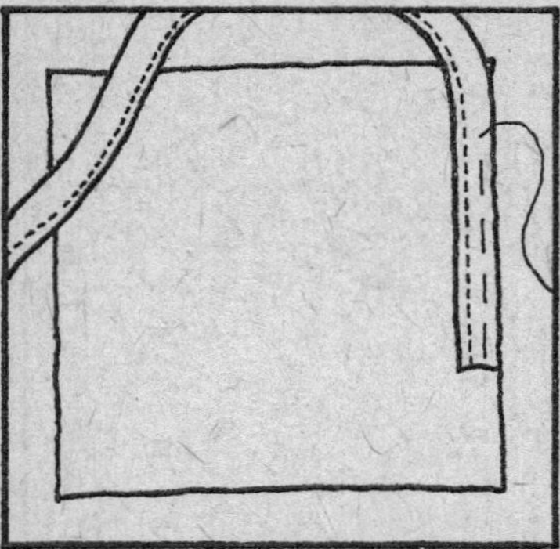

1 Tack the corded piping along one edge of one cushion piece, on the right side.

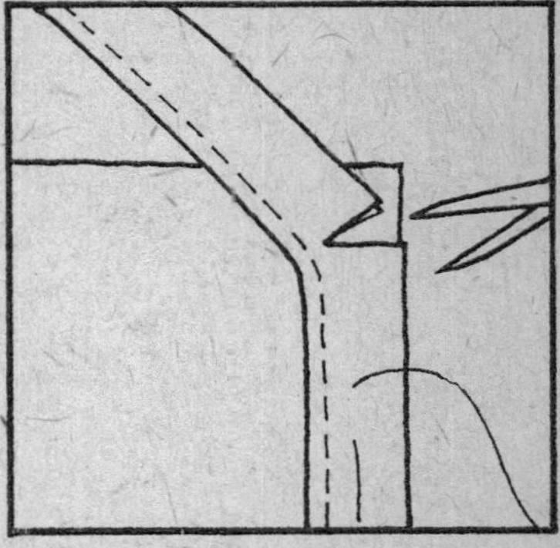

2 At the corner, cut the seam allowance of the piping to within ⅛ in. of the cord.

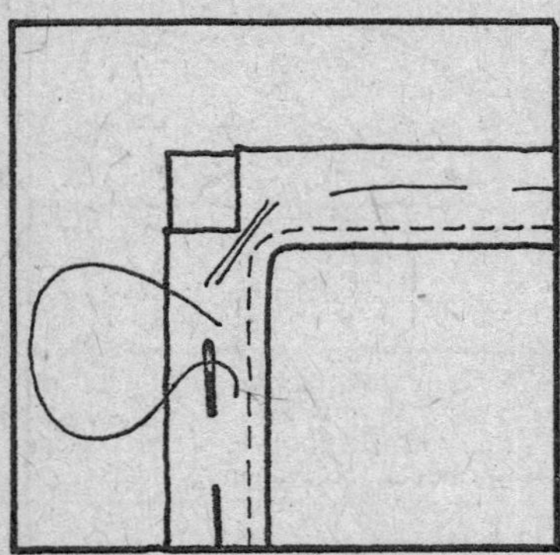

3 Tack the piping firmly at the corner, and continue to tack it along the next side.

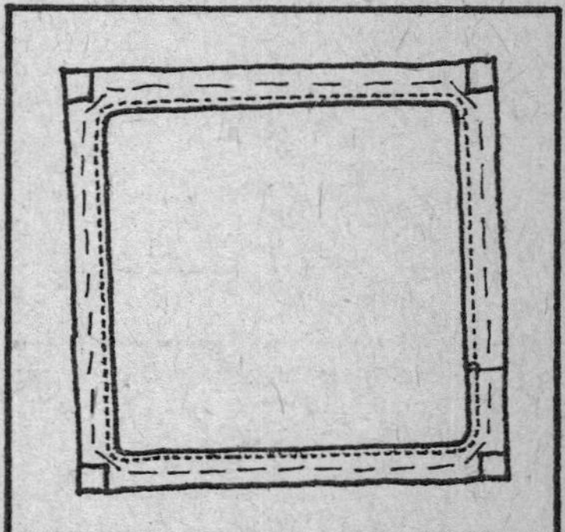

4 At the next corner snip again, and continue round the cushion piece in this way.

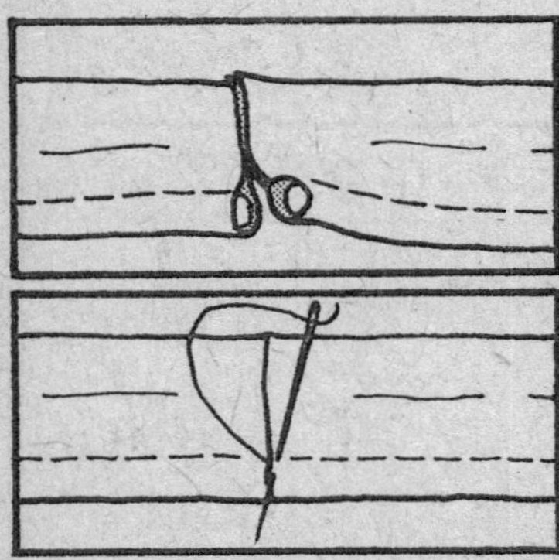

5 Where you join the two ends of piping together, cut the cord so that the two ends just meet but do not overlap. Turn in the ends of the piping and slip stitch them together.

Lay the other half of the cushion on top, right side down, and complete exactly as for Frilled Cushion, Method A, 7–11.

teacosy, with frilling or piping

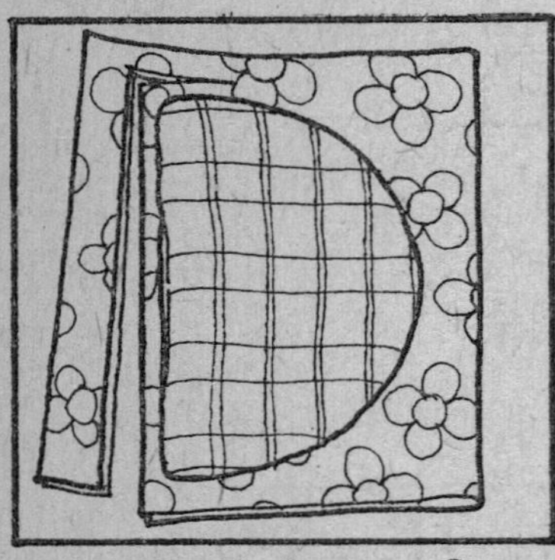

1 Use a teacosy for the pattern. Cut two identical pieces, allowing an extra $\frac{1}{2}$ in. all round for turnings.

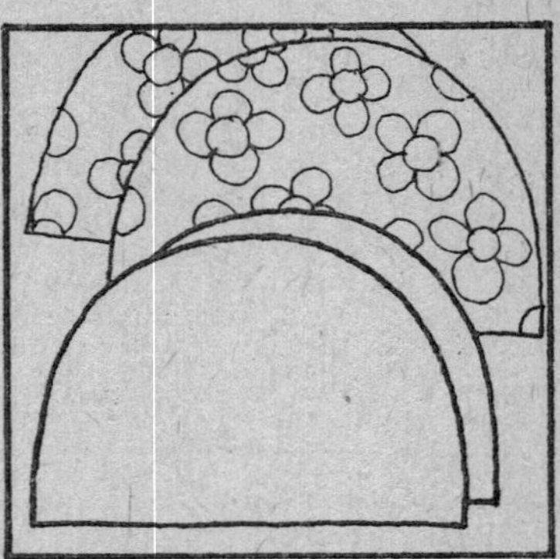

2 Cut two pieces the same size for lining.

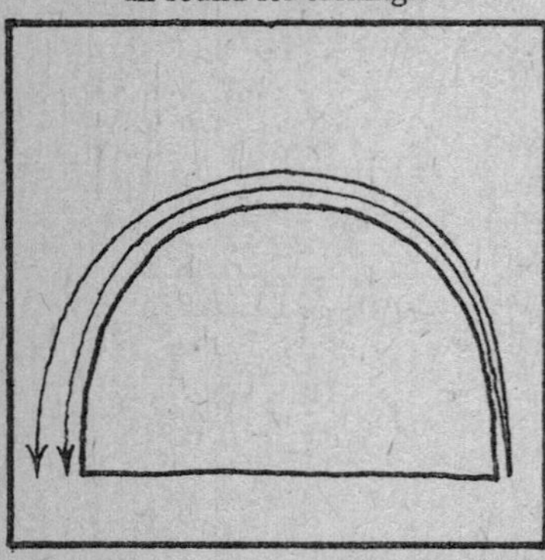

3 Measure round the top for the frilling or piping, and allow at least twice as much if you are going to use frilling.

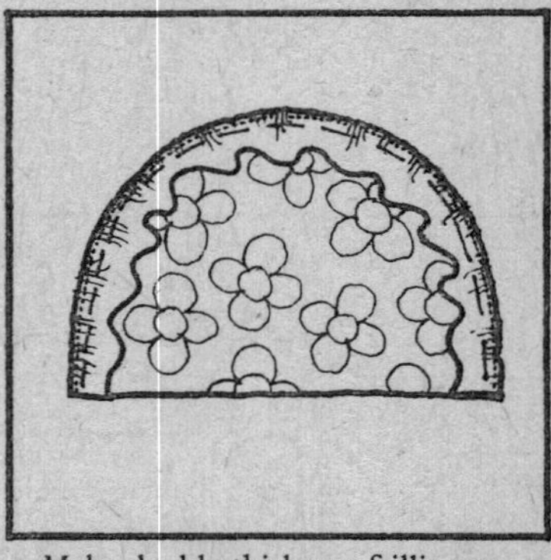

4 Make double thickness frilling as on page 62, or piping as page 64, and lay this on the right side of one teacosy piece, as for a cushion. Tack.

5 Lay the other piece right side down on top, and sew.

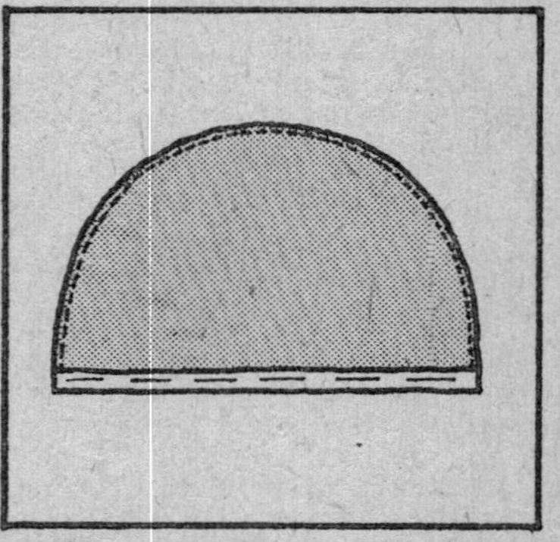

6 While the work is wrong side out, turn up the bottom hem $\frac{1}{2}$ in. and tack.

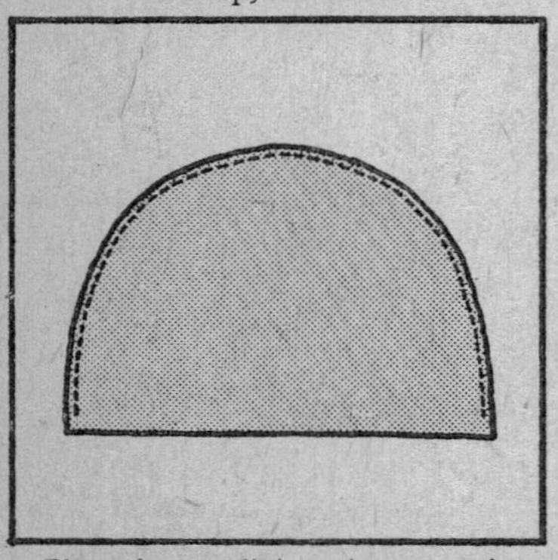

7 Place the two lining pieces together, right side inwards, and sew round the top.

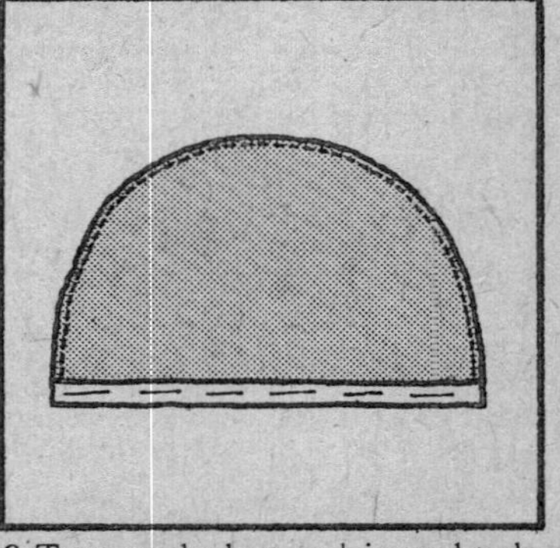

8 Turn up the bottom $\frac{1}{2}$ in. and tack. Turn inside out.

9 Use the lining as a pattern for cutting out the padding and cut exactly to size.

10 Turn the lining back to the wrong side and tack a thickness of padding to each side of it.

11 Turn the outer teacosy to the right side and fit the padding and lining inside it.

12 Oversew the lining to the outer teacosy round the bottom.

alterations

These alterations apply to ready made garments, hand-me-downs, or something you have made which is not quite as good a fit as you hoped for.

ironing out creases

In order to make alterations unnoticeable you must remove as much evidence as you possibly can of the original sewing, including the folds, which are inevitable wherever there is a seam. It is necessary to get rid of the old folds completely and start afresh on smooth fabric.

Even with finer fabrics like cotton, old creases can be stubborn. The following method generally works very well, with the exception of velvet, which does not take kindly to normal ironing procedures.

1 Take a damp cloth and lay it over the fold.

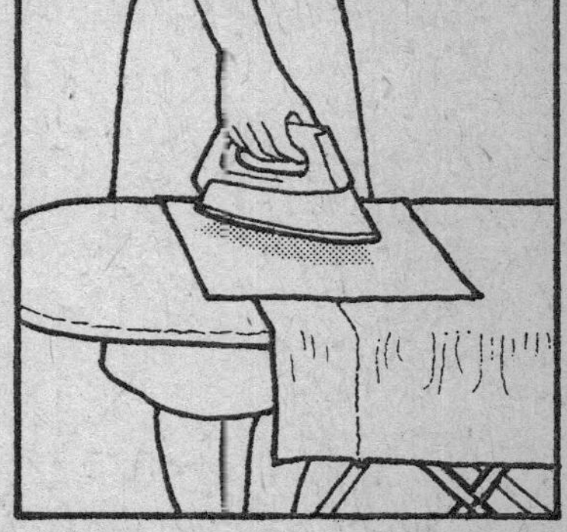

2 Use the iron only moderately hot and let it hover over the damp cloth above the crease, a matter of a hair's breadth away.

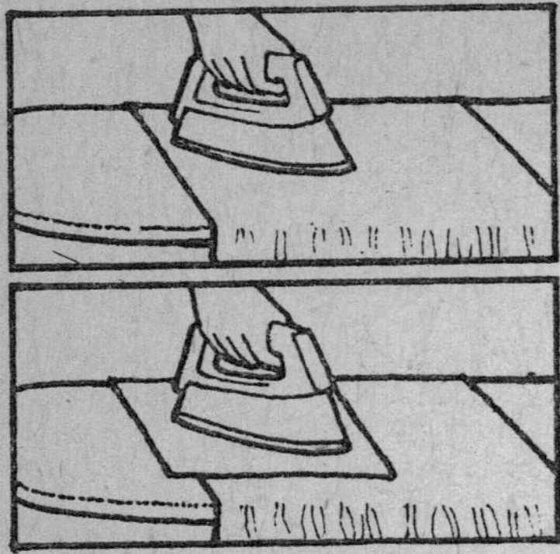

3 The steam thus created will go a long way towards removing the crease. After a little of this treatment, either iron the fabric direct, or, if a woollen fabric, iron over a damp cloth in the ordinary way.

sagging boat neckline

This can happen if you are slightly narrow on the shoulders and were afraid to alter the paper pattern, or if you bought a ready made garment which isn't a perfect fit. There are two ways of dealing with this.

METHOD ONE

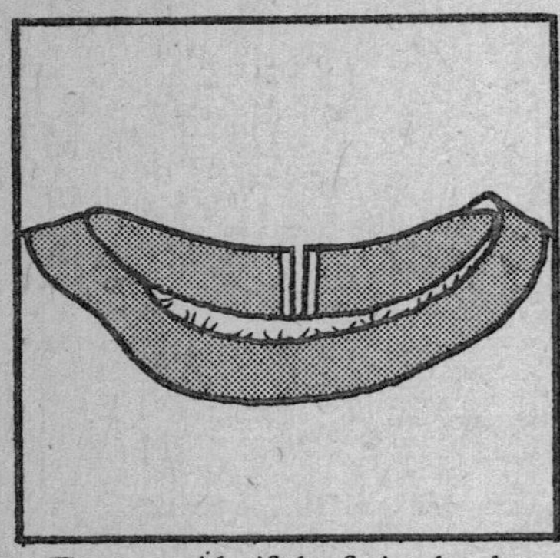

1 To start with, if the facing has been sewn in place, unpick it.

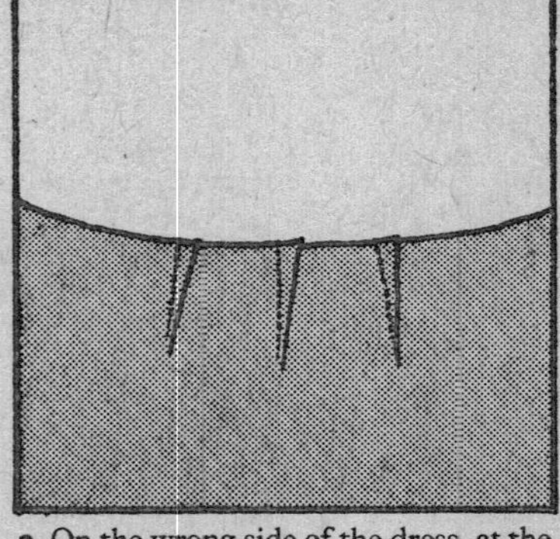

2 On the wrong side of the dress, at the front, make three small darts, evenly spaced with the middle one dead centre. (See page 33 for making darts).

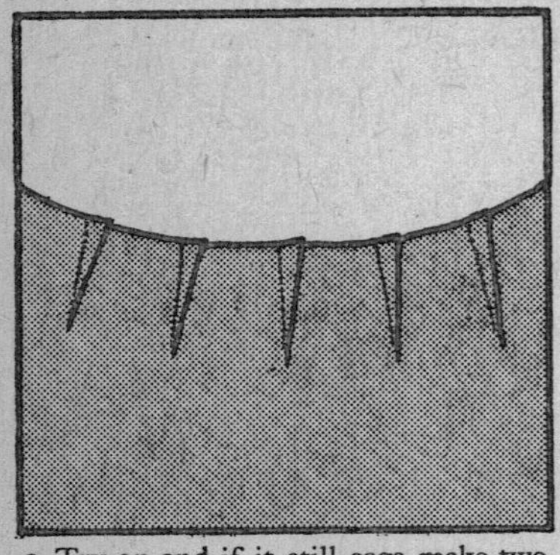

3 Try on and if it still sags make two more darts, one either side of the other three, an even space away. The idea is to make the dress look as if it were designed that way.

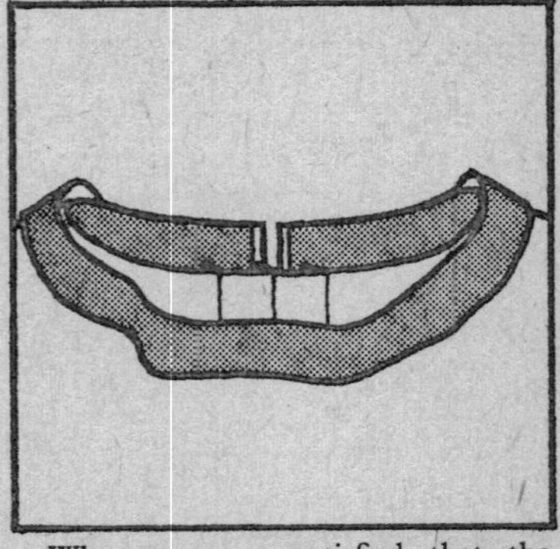

4 When you are satisfied that the neckline is correct you will have too much facing.

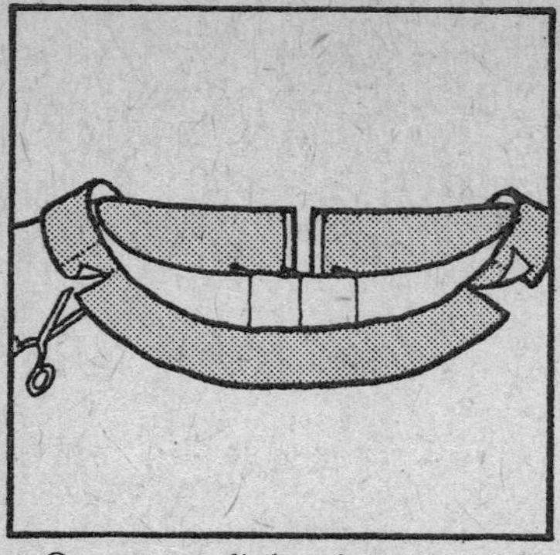

5 Cut out a little piece, near the shoulder on each side.

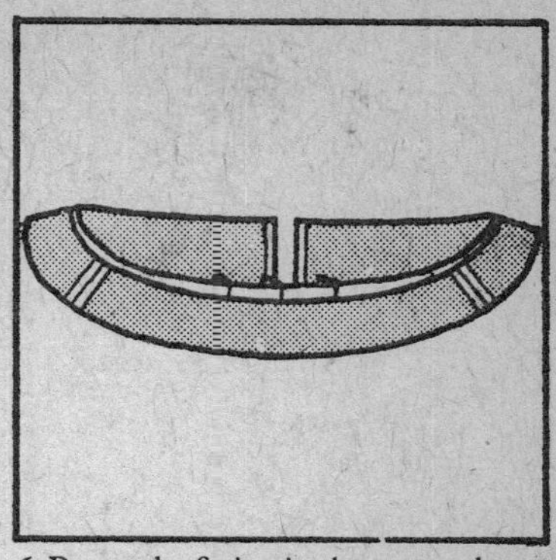

6 Resew the facing in these two places, open out the seams, and press flat.

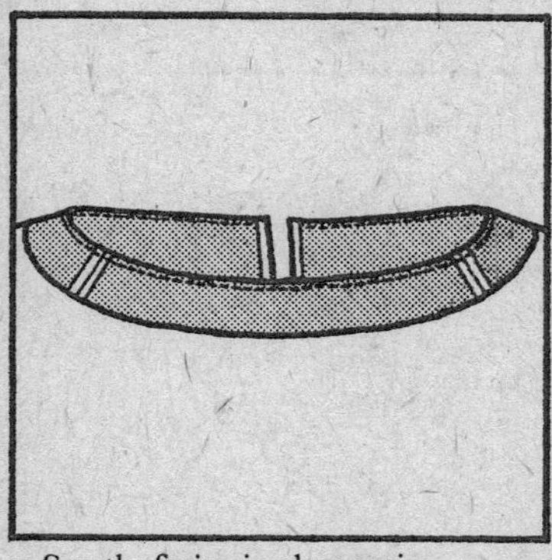

7 Sew the facing in place again.

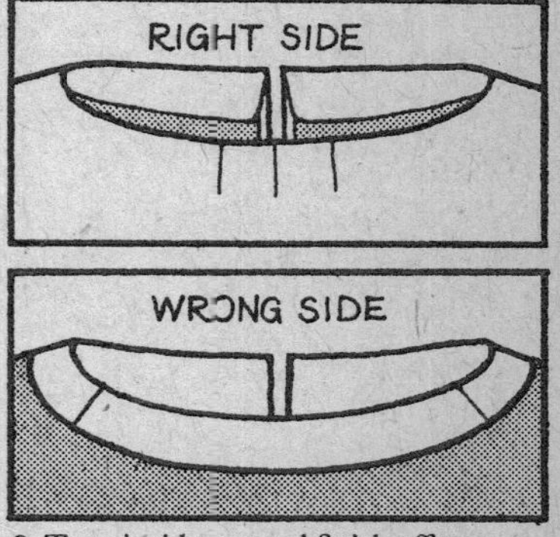

8 Turn inside out and finish off.

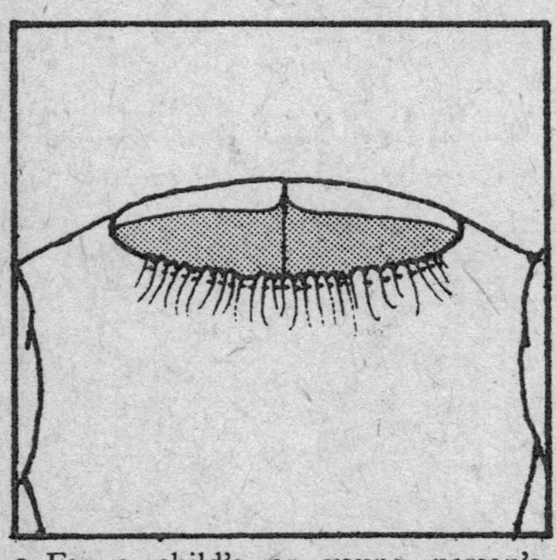

9 For a child's or young person's dress you can just gather the front neckline by going round with running stitches in double thread, and puckering.

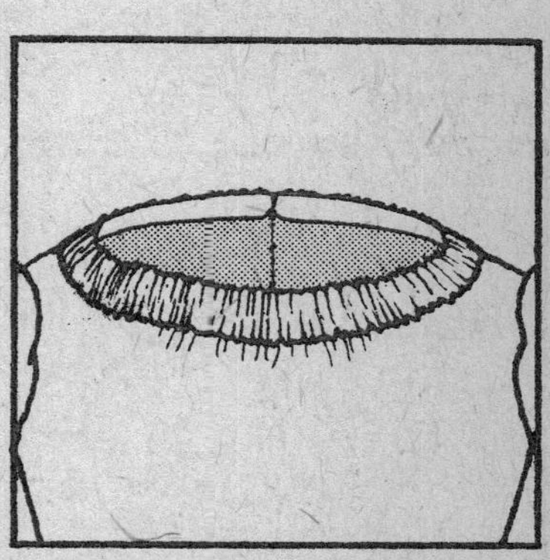

10 Then cover this with a band of braid or ruching.

METHOD TWO

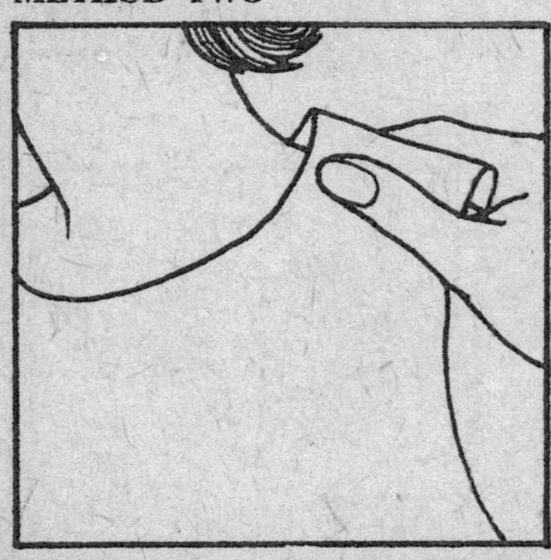

11 With the dress on try lifting the shoulder seams an even amount each side, pin them and take a good look in the mirror to see how it looks. Keep adjusting until you are satisfied with the result.

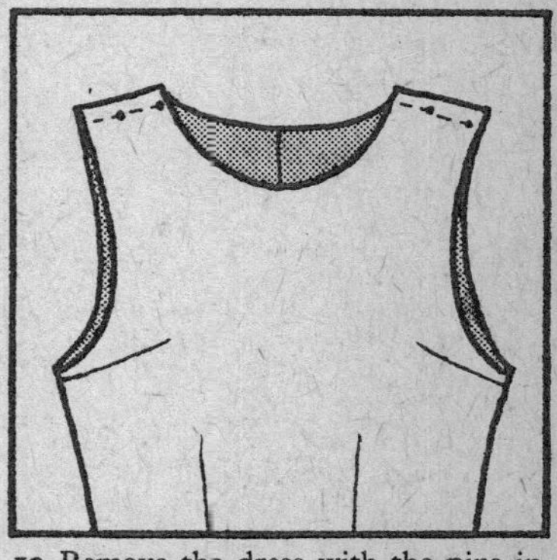

12 Remove the dress with the pins in place.

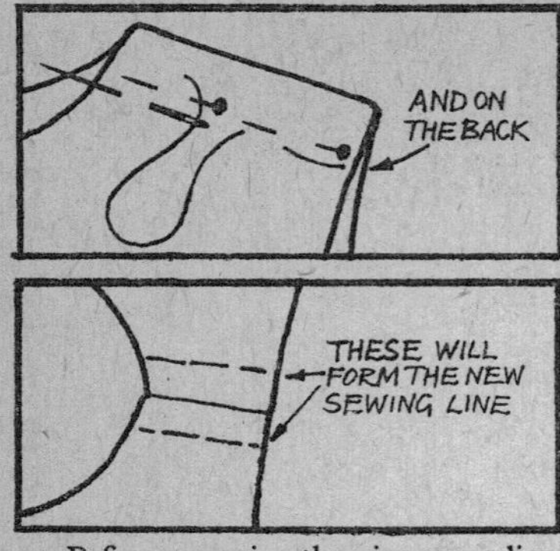

13 Before removing the pins sew a line of tacking stitches on both front and back, in the outer fabric only, as a guide for your sewing line.

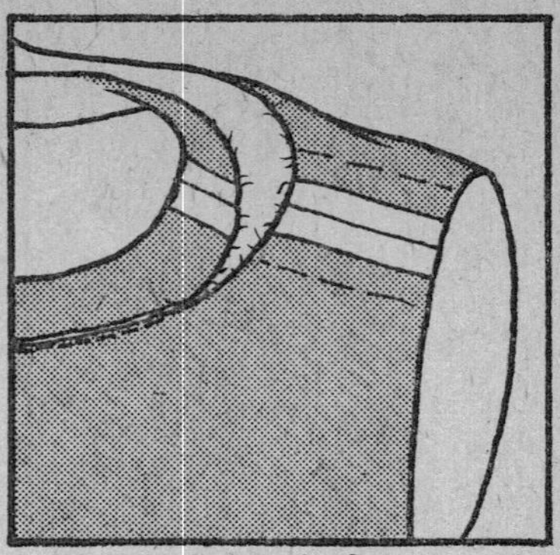

14 Unpick the neck facing at the shoulders.

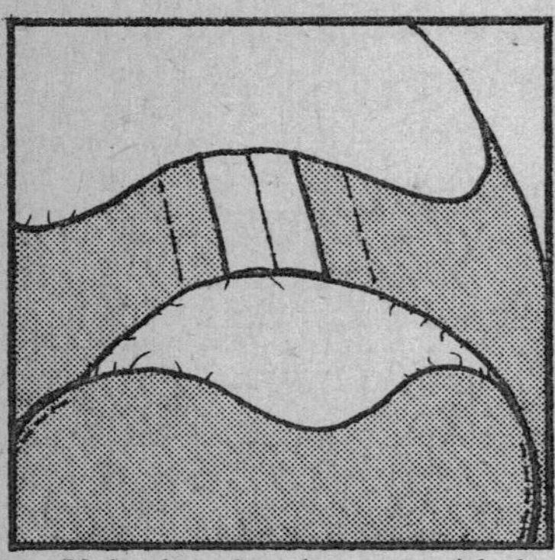

15 If the dress has sleeves, unpick the top of the sleeves.

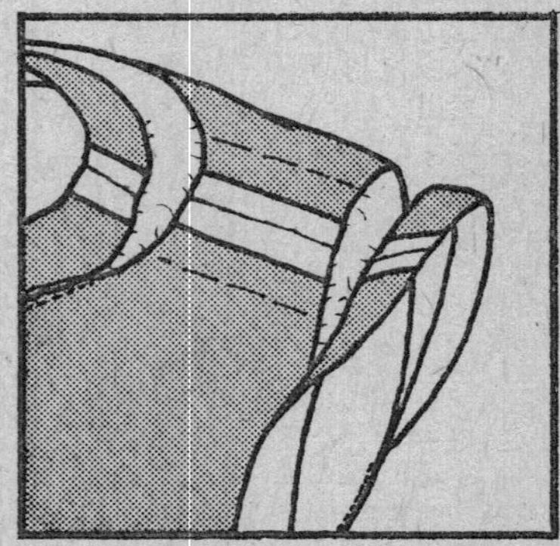

16 If the dress is sleeveless unpick the facing at the top of the armhole.

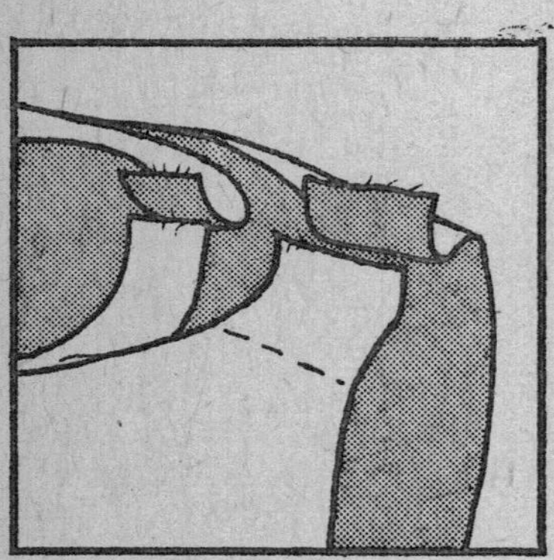

17 Unpick the shoulder seam of the dress and the facing.

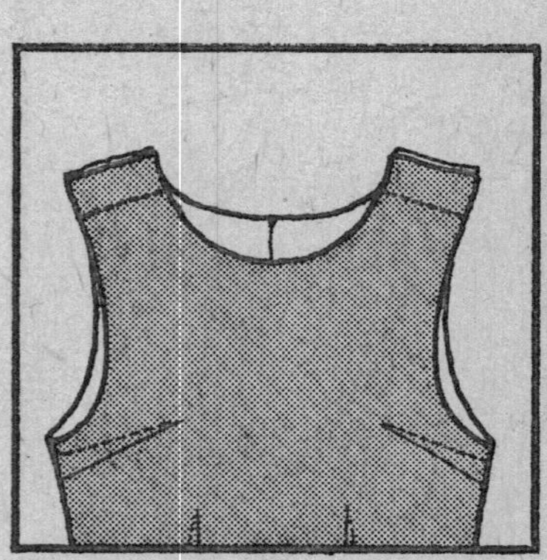

18 Turn the dress inside out and resew the shoulder seams on the lines you have marked.

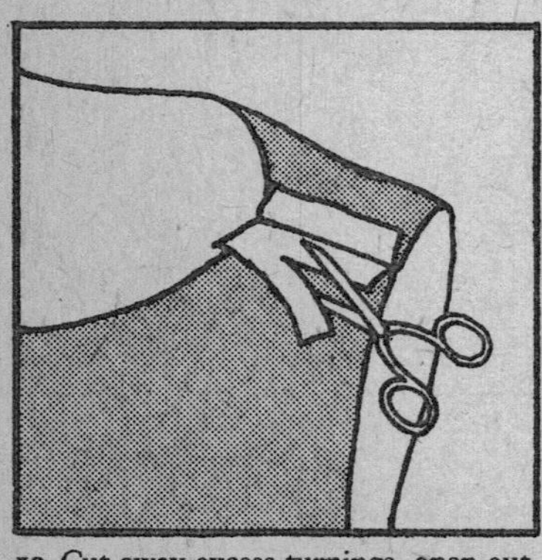

19 Cut away excess turnings, open out and press.

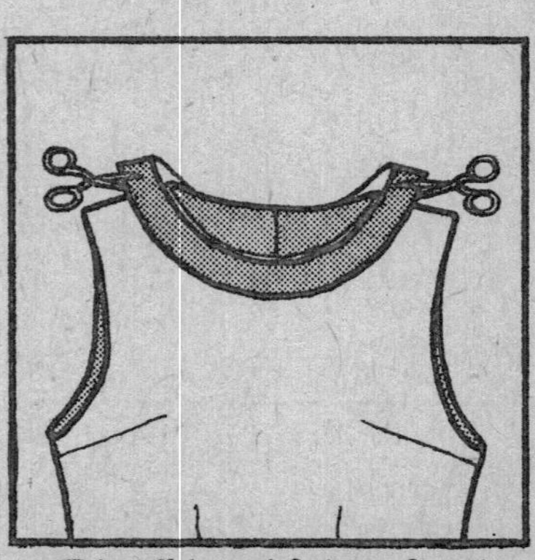

20 Trim off the neck facing to fit against the outer layer.

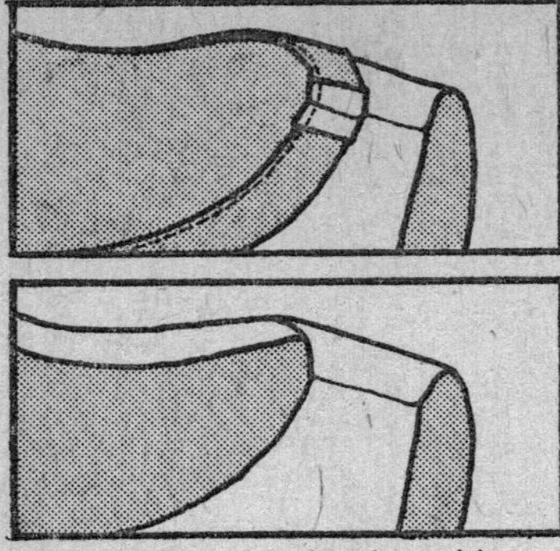

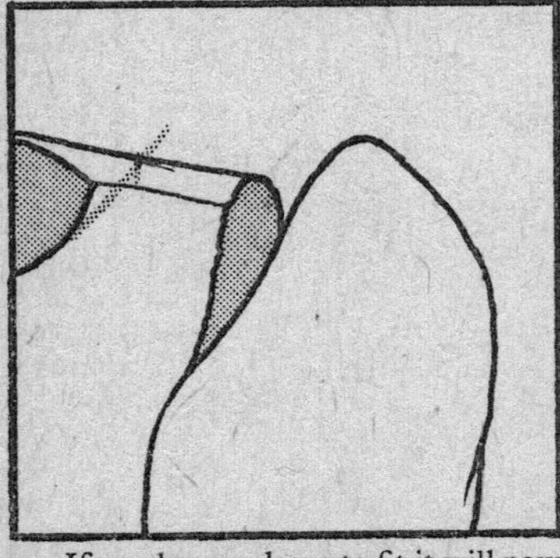

21 Press out and replace in position.

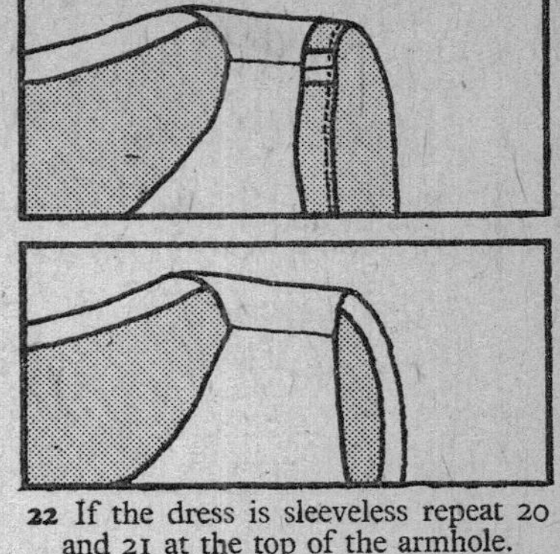

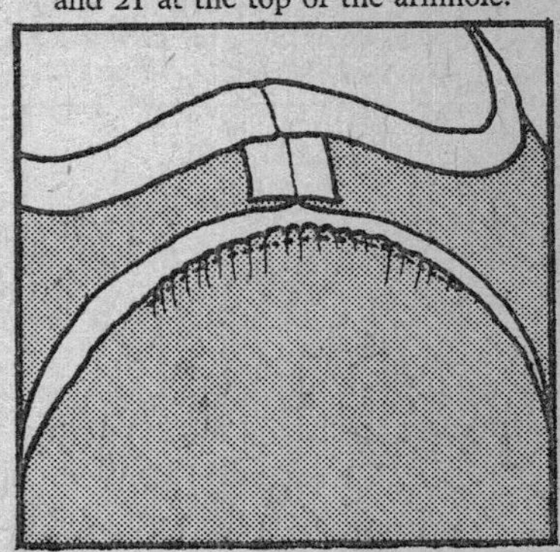

22 If the dress is sleeveless repeat 20 and 21 at the top of the armhole.

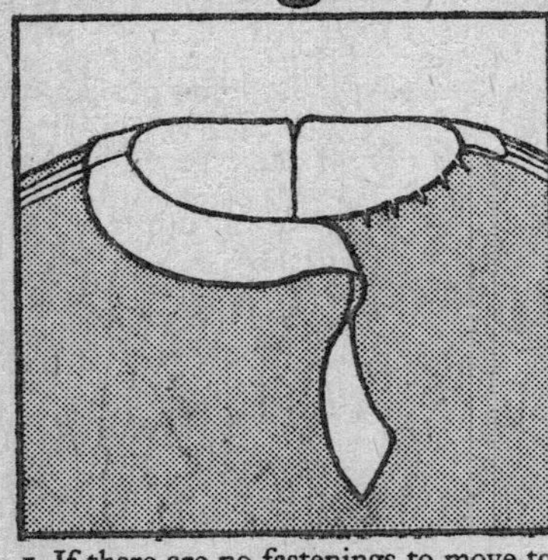

23 If you have a sleeve to fit it will now be bigger than the armhole and will have to be eased in.

24 Do a row of tiny running stitches, with double thread, round the top of the sleeve and gather it gently until it fits the armhole.

Method Two can be used for other necklines which are not quite snug, but it is important to test first by pinning before cutting.

round neckline too tight

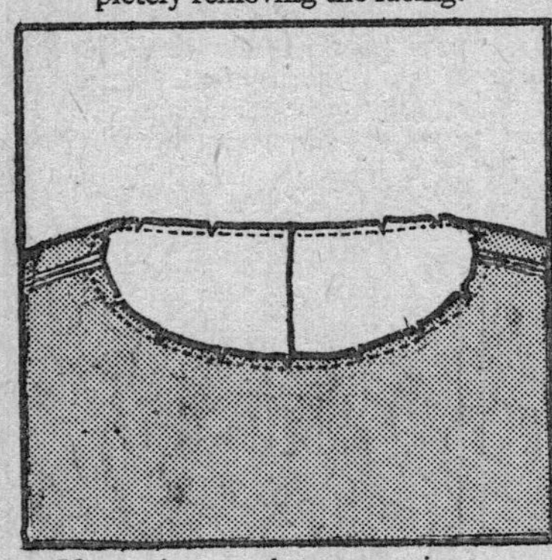

1 If there are no fastenings to move to ease the situation then you must trim a little off the neckline. Begin by completely removing the facing.

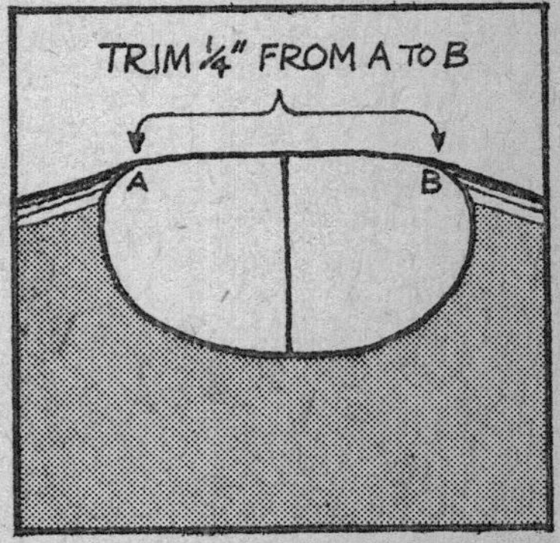

2 Did you snip the seam allowance round the neck before you sewed down the facing?

3 If not, do so and try on again.

4 If it is still too tight trim very carefully not more than ¼ in. off the neckline, starting just behind the shoulder seam and finishing an equal distance behind the second shoulder seam. Do not cut the centre back if there is a zip fastener.

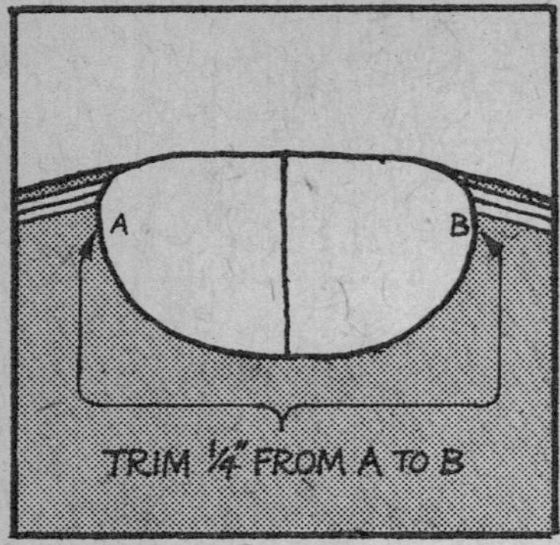

5 If the neck is still too tight trim off a further ¼ in., but this time start just in front of the shoulder seam and finish an equal distance from the other side.

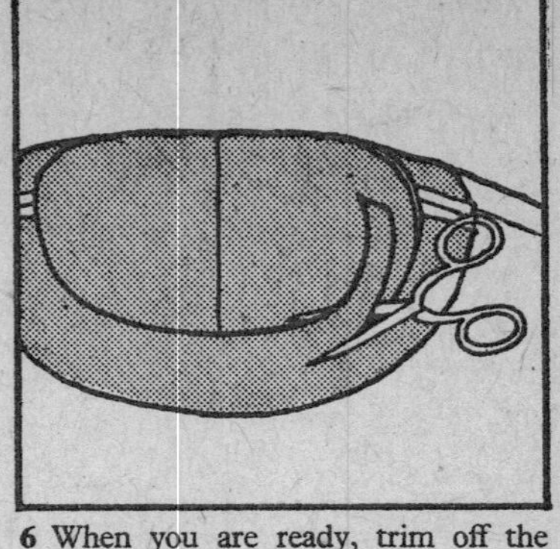

6 When you are ready, trim off the facing so that it fits the outer layers and replace.

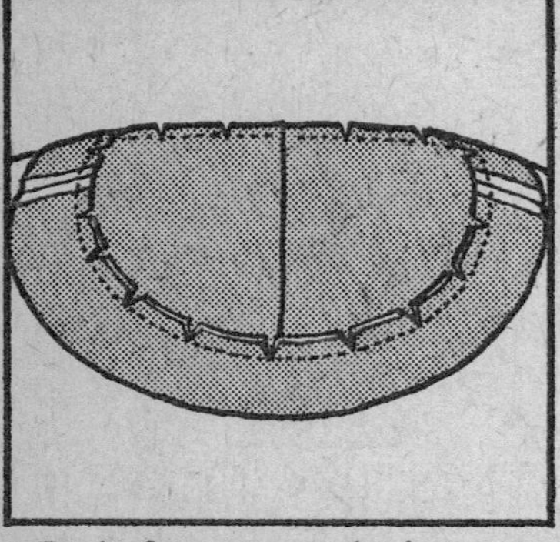

7 Don't forget to notch the curves before turning back and sewing down, otherwise it will still be too tight.

tight armholes

Insert a piece of fabric. If you haven't any matching fabric try and cut a small piece from the inside of the hem or pocket. It is not recommended to use anything other than a good match.

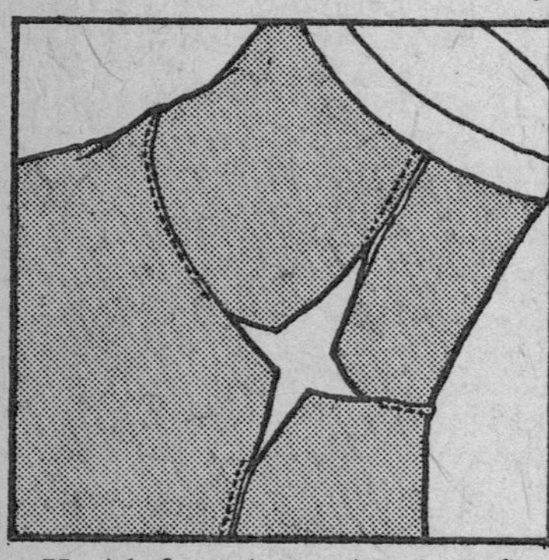

1 Unpick for at least 2 in., depending on how tight the armhole is, the sleeve seam and side seam under the arm.

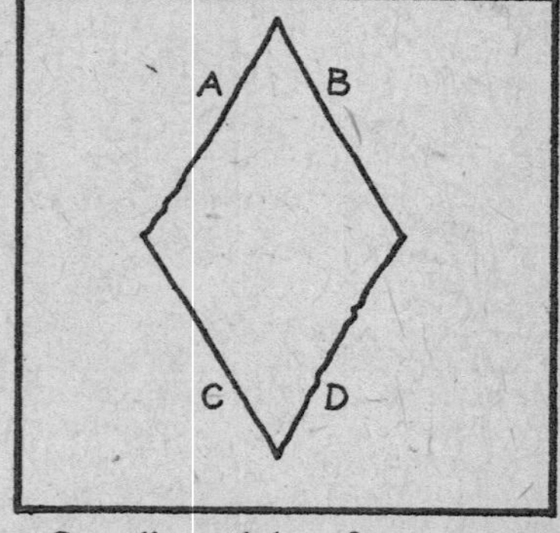

2 Cut a diamond shape from a separate piece of fabric of a suitable size to fit into the unpicked seams.

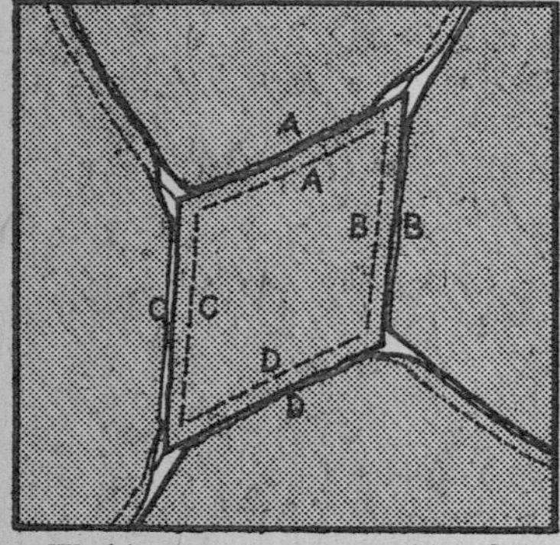

3 Working on the wrong side of the garment, sew in this diamond, an edge of the diamond to an edge of the garment.

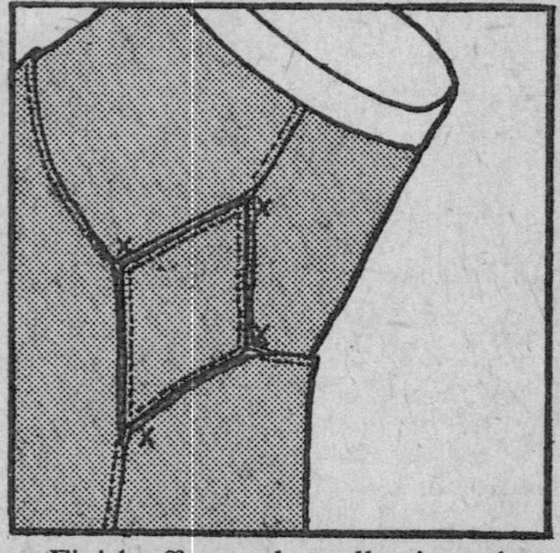

4 Finish off securely at all points where you unpicked.

shortening a bodice

1 Remove the zip if there is one. Unpick the waist seam completely.

2 Cut off from the bottom of the bodice the required amount, all the way round, leaving ½ in. seam allowance.

3 The bodice will now be slightly bigger at the waistline than the top of the skirt.

4 Unpick what is left of the darts and make fresh ones, wide enough to absorb the width and long enough to give the bodice shape. Sew the two pieces together again.

5 The zip fastener will also be too long, so unpick the back seam by a small amount where the bottom of the zip will come. Replace the zip as on page 44, 45.

lengthening a bodice

Unless you have a very wide seam allowance this can only be done by inserting a strip of fabric. If the result can be made to look as if it is part of the design all well and good, if not, a belt can be worn to hide the alteration. Remove the zip and unpick the waistband as in 1 page 75.

1 Unpick about $1\frac{1}{2}$ in. of the side seams.

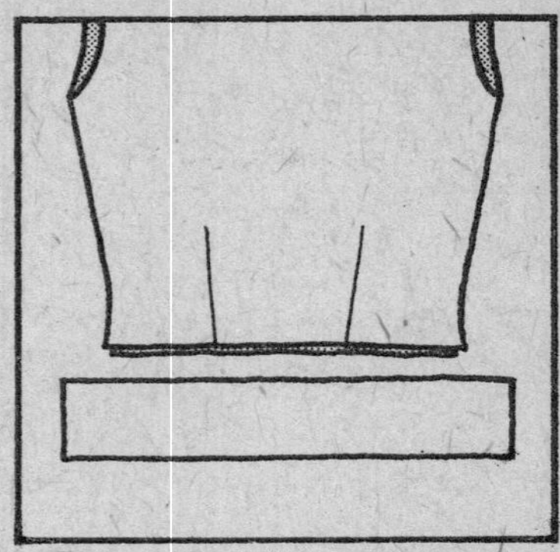

2 Cut a strip of fabric of the required depth plus seam allowance, long enough to go across the front bodice plus about 3 in.

3 Cut two more pieces the same depth, each wide enough to match the back bodice pieces, plus about 3 in. on each.

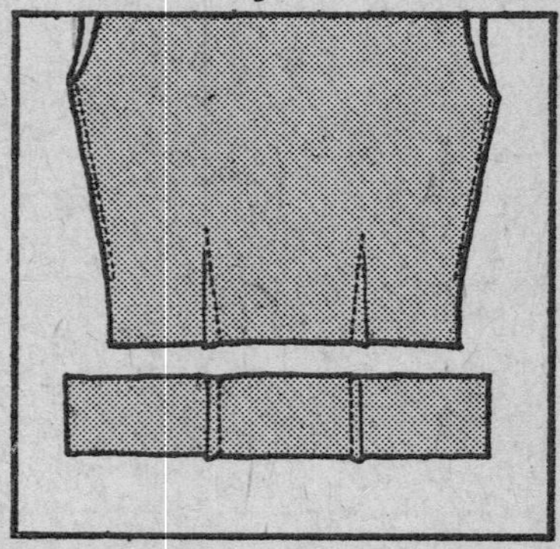

4 If there are any darts in the front bodice make small vertical tucks on the wrong side of the new piece to line up with them.

5 Do the same on the two back pieces, if there are any darts at the back.

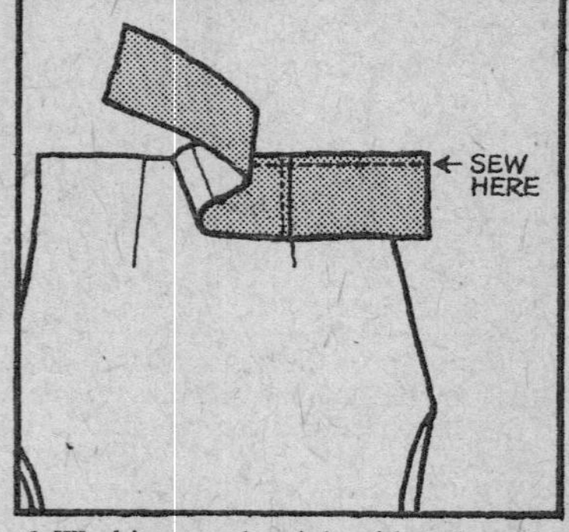

6 Working on the right side, place the extra front piece on the front bodice, right side downwards, matching the tucks with the darts. Sew in place.

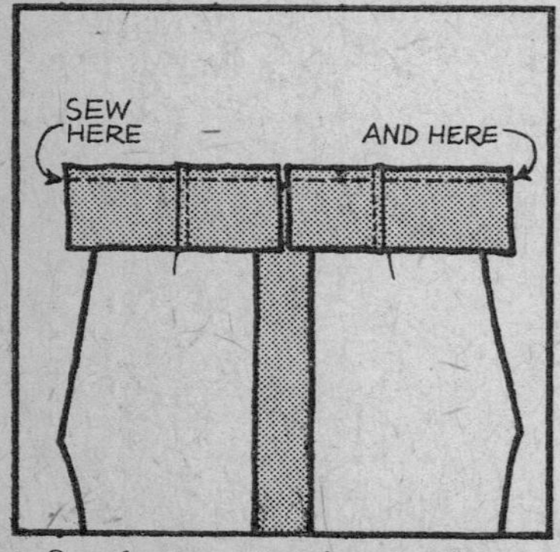

7 Sew the two extra pieces on the two back bodice pieces in the same way, matching tucks to darts if there are any.

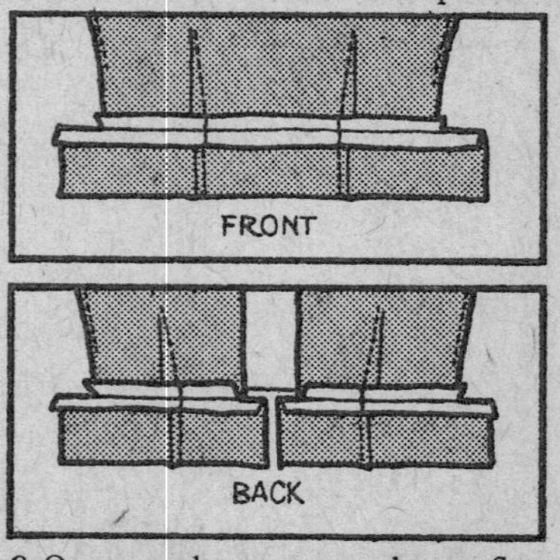

8 Open out these seams and press flat.

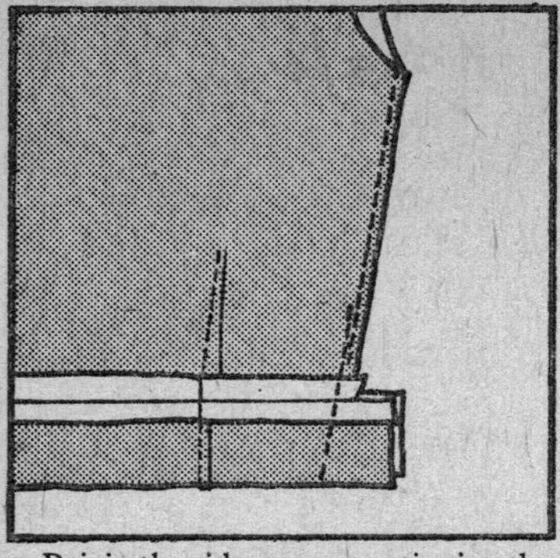

9 Rejoin the side seams, continuing the one already there. Overlap the sewing lines as on page 20 .

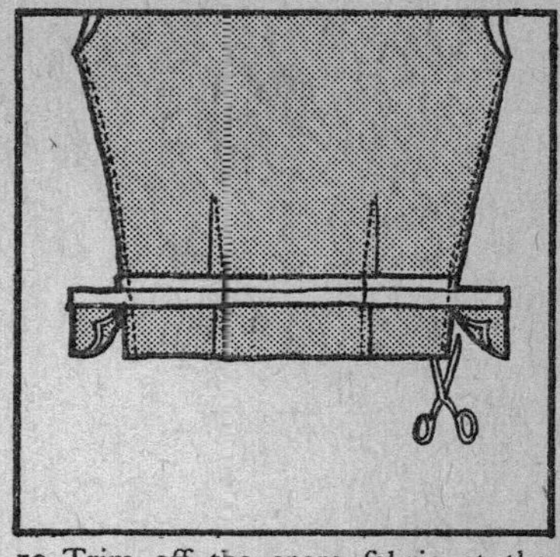

10 Trim off the spare fabric at the sides.

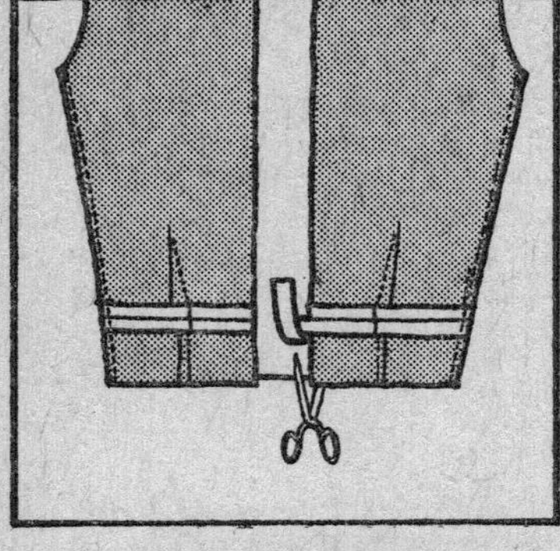

11 At the back opening, trim the extra pieces back to match the original edges.

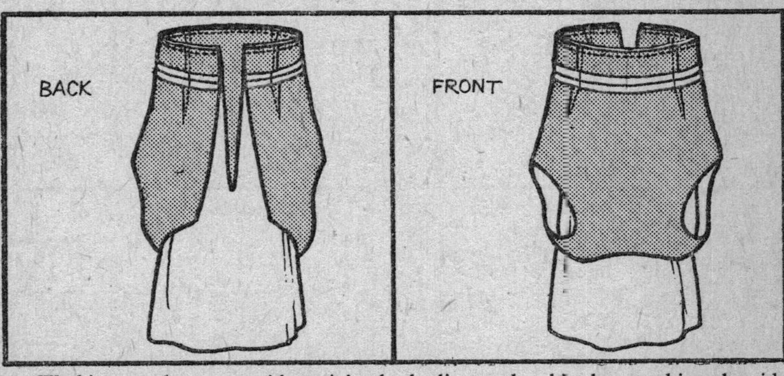

12 Working on the wrong side re-join the bodice to the skirt by matching the side seams, and the tucks to the darts.

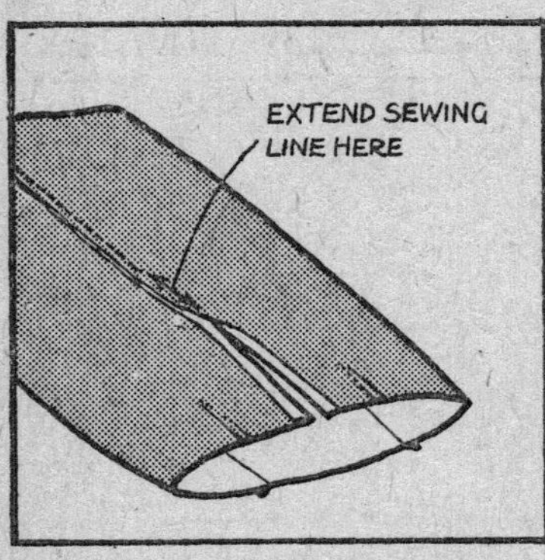

13 The original zip will now be too short so either buy another, or, if you can get the dress over your hips, shorten the vent at the back of the skirt by sewing the centre back seam a little higher.

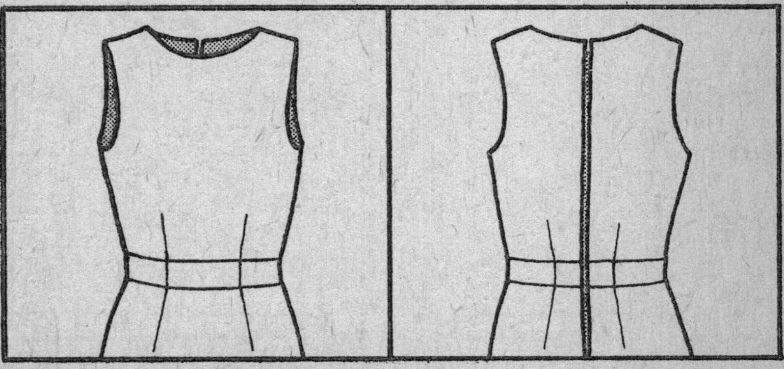

14 The finished effect will be quite neat.

shortening a skirt

It is not always advisable to shorten a skirt at the hem. This can spoil the line, especially if the skirt is pleated. It is better to shorten at the waist, but both methods are given here.

AT THE HEM

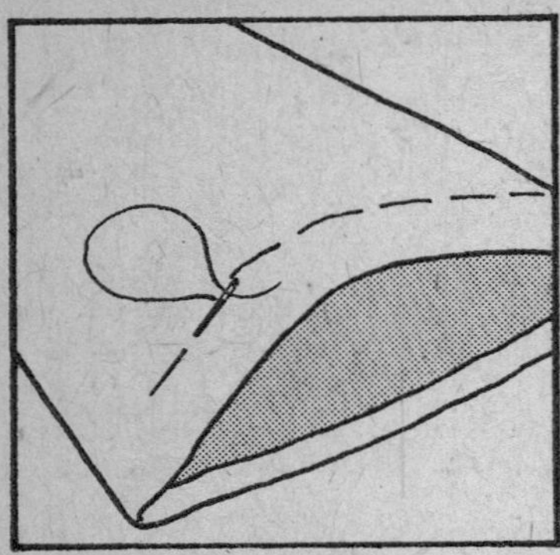

1 When you have decided the exact length you require make marks all round the skirt at this point with a contrasting thread, which can be removed afterwards.

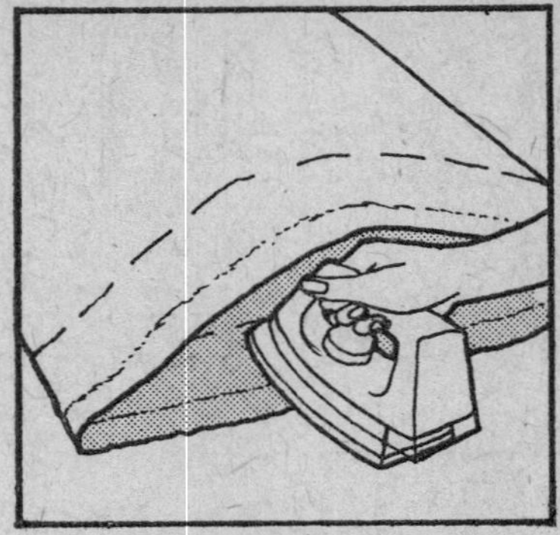

2 Unpick the original hem, open out and press flat.

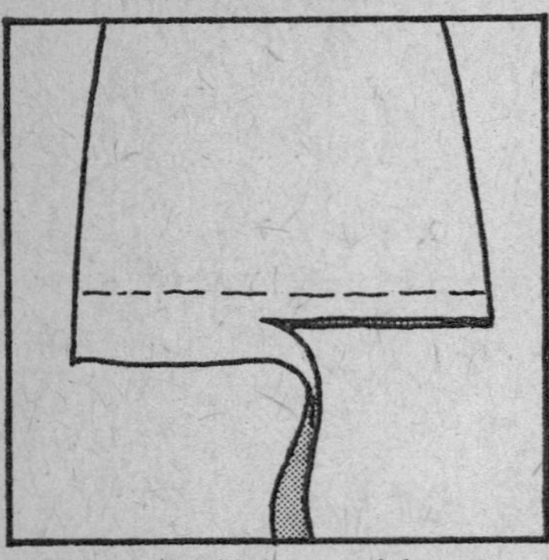

3 Unless you think you might want to lengthen the skirt again, cut a strip from the bottom edge equivalent to the amount by which you are shortening.

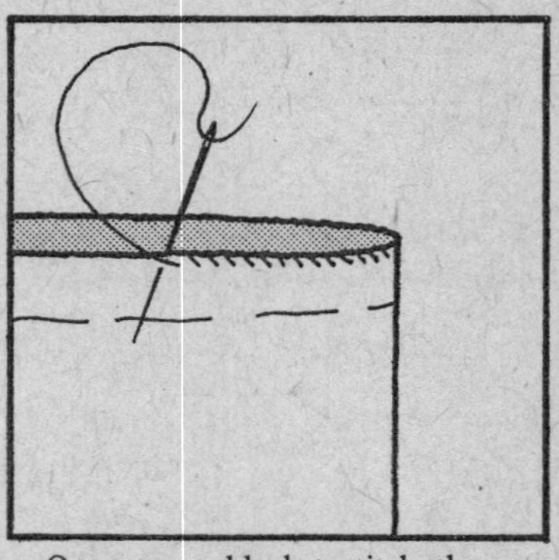

4 Oversew or blanket stitch the raw edge.

5 Turn a new hem on the line you have marked. Check that it is straight. Blind hem as shown on page 36 .

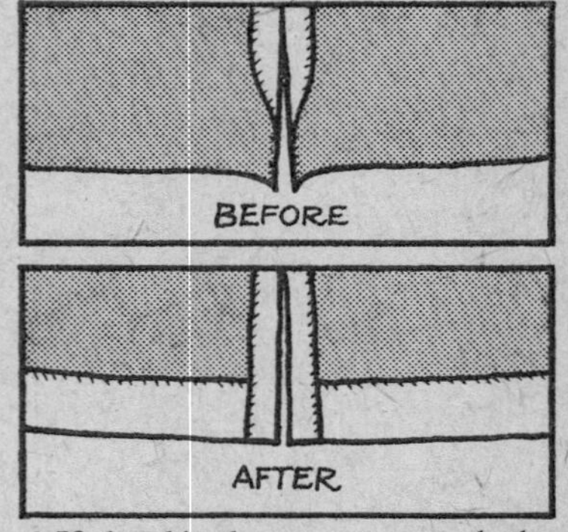

6 If the skirt has a vent, unpick the facings, work as in 2 to 5, sewing down the facings last of all. (See page 36).

AT THE WAIST

1 If a dress, unpick the waist seam.

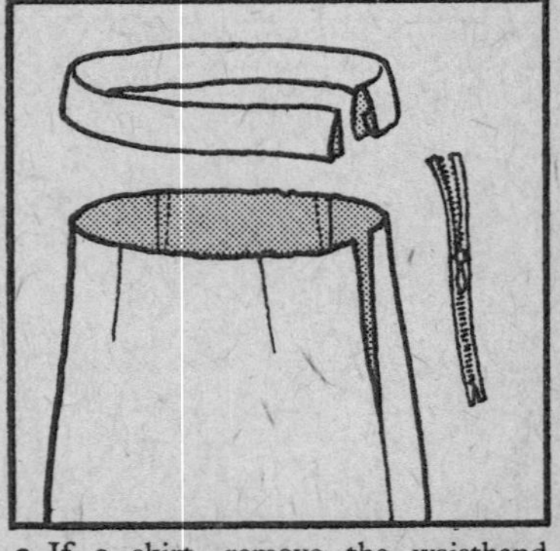

2 If a skirt, remove the waistband completely. In both cases remove the zip.

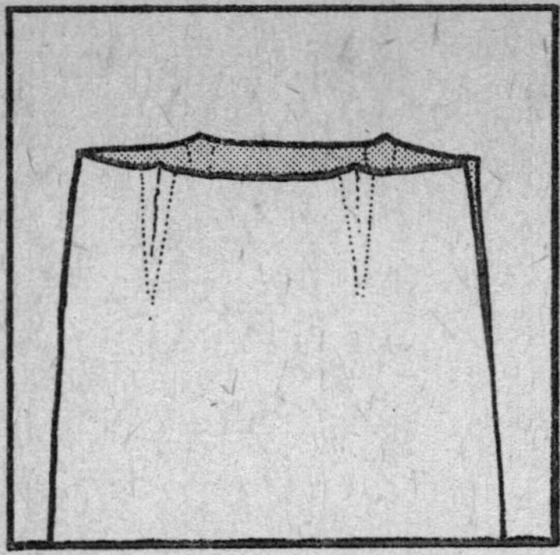

3 Unpick all the darts in the skirt, and press flat.

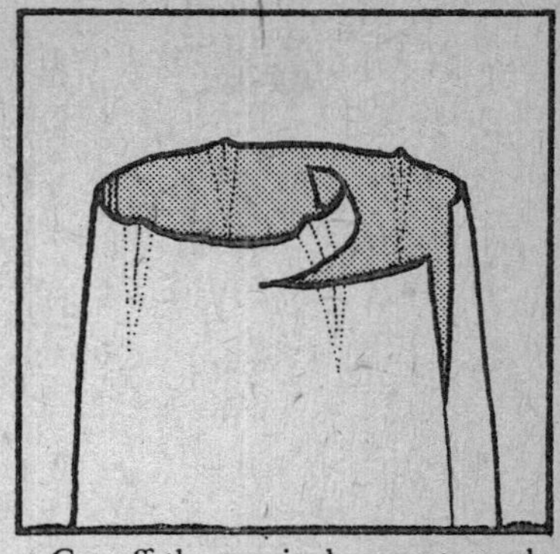

4 Cut off the required amount evenly from the top of the skirt allowing at least ½ in. seam allowance for when you re-sew it.

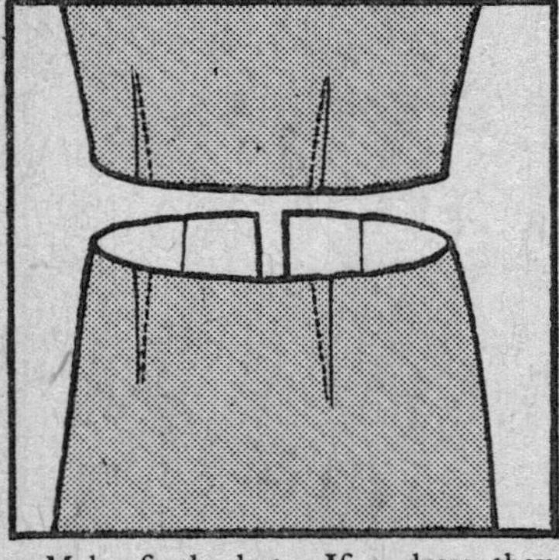

5 Make fresh darts. If a dress they must line up with darts on the bodice.

6 If a skirt only they must be in the same place as they were before but of a size to fit the skirt top into the waistband as before.

If a dress, re-join the bodice and the skirt as on page 77 and replace the zip as on pages 44-45 . If a skirt only, sew in the zip as on page 44 - 45 and replace waistband as follows:

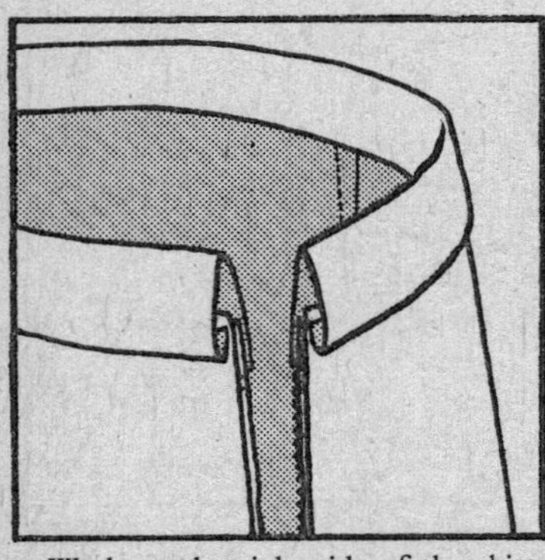

7 Work on the right side of the skirt. Lay the outer side of the waistband over the top of the skirt, overlapping by ½ in.

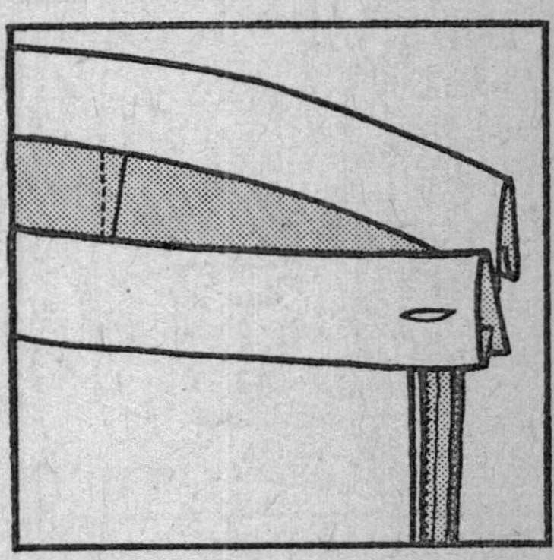

8 If there had previously been an overlap for fastenings then set the skirt into the waistband to allow for this.

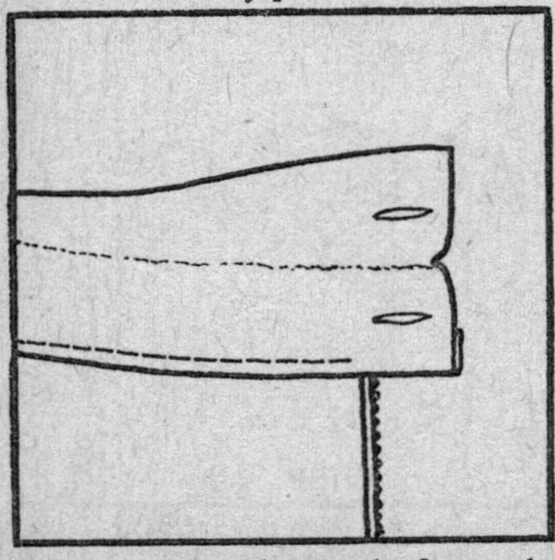

9 On the right side, sew the front only of the waistband in place, on the same sewing line as before.

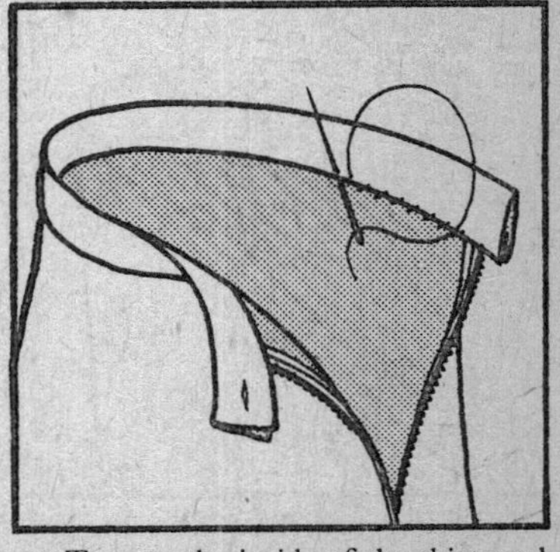

10 Turn to the inside of the skirt, and hem down the back of the waistband.

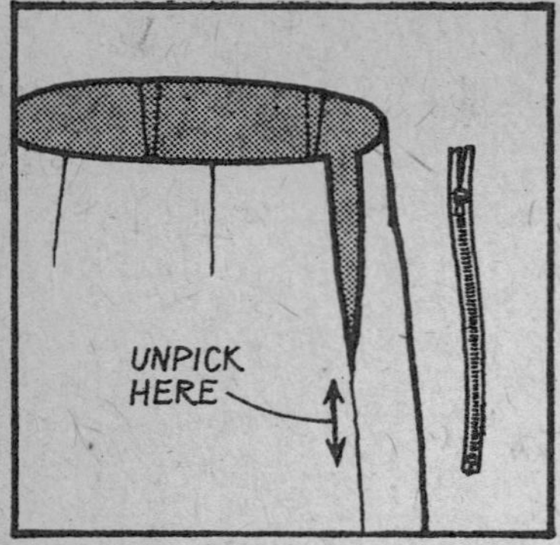

11 In either case the zip will be too long so extend the opening for whatever length you need by unpicking the seam. Fasten off securely and replace the zip as on page 44 or 45.

lengthening a skirt or dress at the hem

1 (a) If you have sufficient fabric to make a good hem fold at the required length, check length and straightness, and blind hem as on page 36.

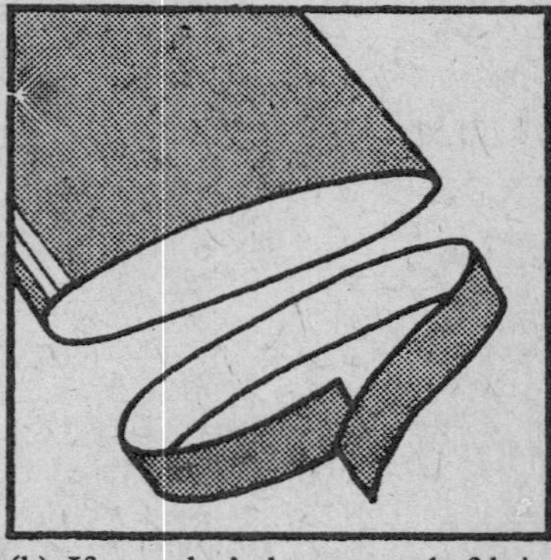

(b) If you don't have enough fabric to turn a hem you must make a false one. Cut a strip of fabric not less than 3 in. wide, long enough to go right round the hem.

2 Pin this strip round the bottom of the skirt in the first instance, because when joined it must fit perfectly.

3 Mark clearly where the join should come and sew the ends of the strip together on the wrong side, open out and press flat.

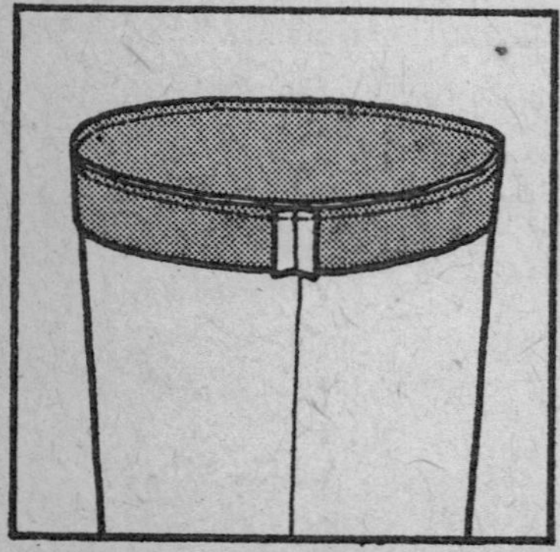

4 Lay the right side of the false piece to the right side of the skirt, edge to edge at the bottom, and sew it right round.

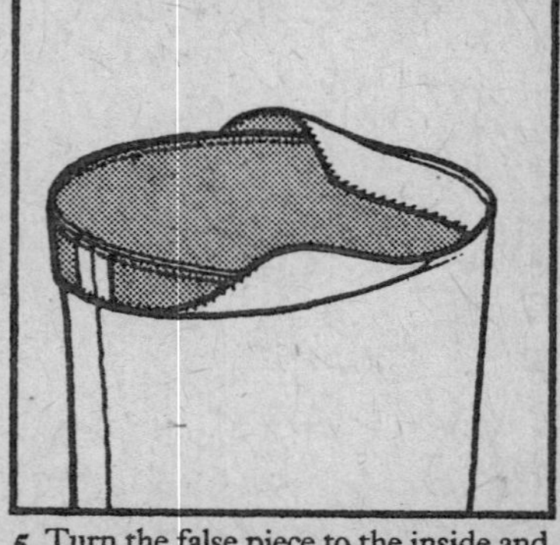

5 Turn the false piece to the inside and fold immediately above the sewing line. Oversew the raw edge of the false piece and blind hem as on page 36.

lengthening a skirt by letting in contrasting bands

This can be done very carefully by inserting strips of braid or contrasting fabrics.

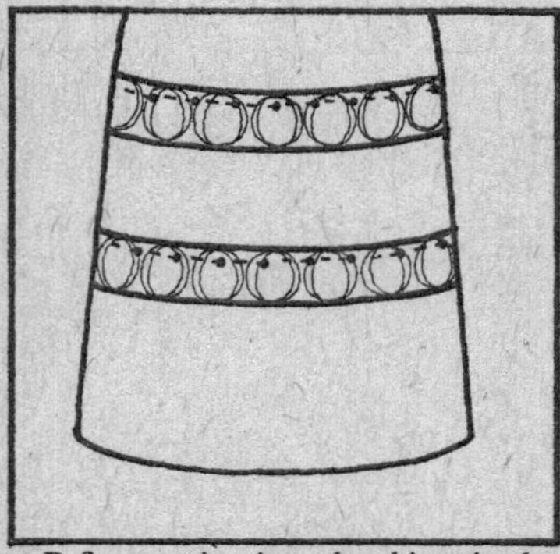

1 Before cutting into the skirt pin the contrasting pieces where you propose to insert them. Make sure they are absolutely straight all the way round. Keep them pinned securely as a guide for cutting, and proceed as follows (If you have more than one insertion cut and insert one completely before you start the next).

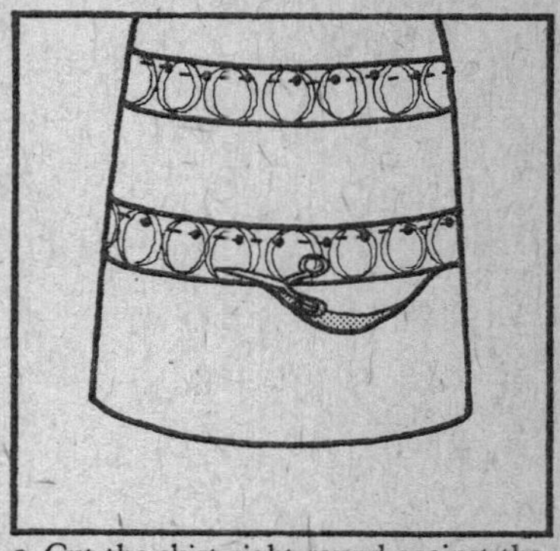

2 Cut the skirt right round against the lower edge of the contrasting band.

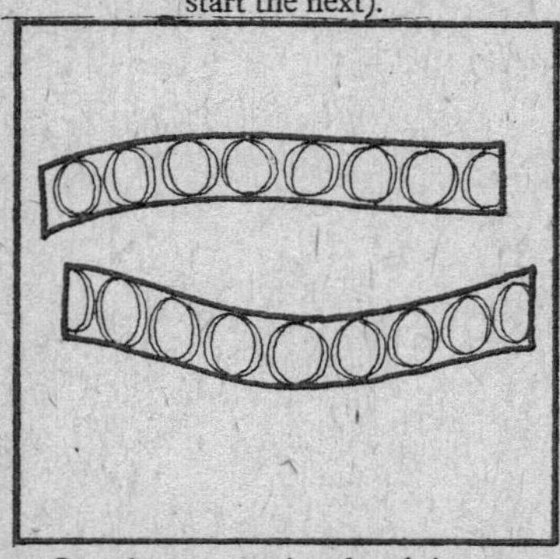

3 Cut the contrasting band into two pieces, allowing a small amount for seam allowance at each end of each piece.

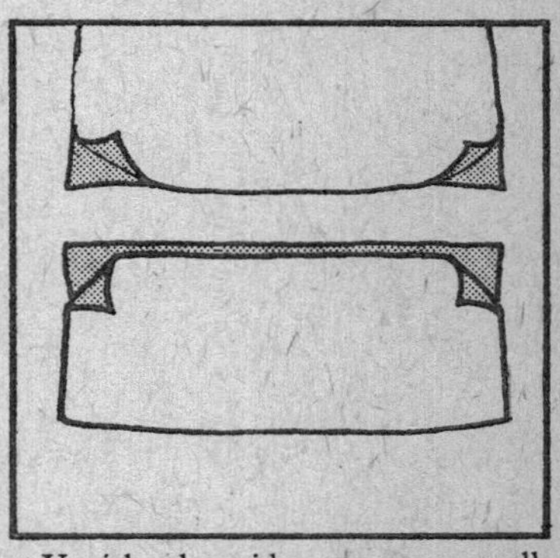

4 Unpick the side seams a small amount at each side of the cut edge, above and below it.

5 If you are inserting braid, on both the front and back of the skirt, overlap the lower edge of the braid over the upper edge of the lower skirt piece, and sew it in place.

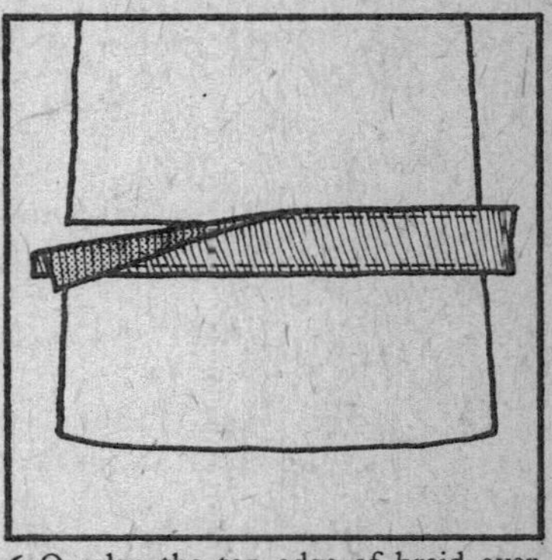

6 Overlap the top edge of braid over the lower edge of the upper skirt piece, and sew in place.

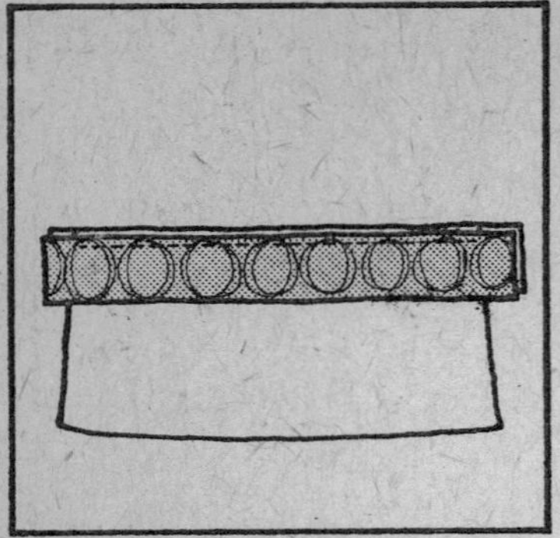

7 If you are inserting a piece of fabric, lay the insertion right side downwards on the right side of the skirt, both back and front. Sew it across, open out and press flat.

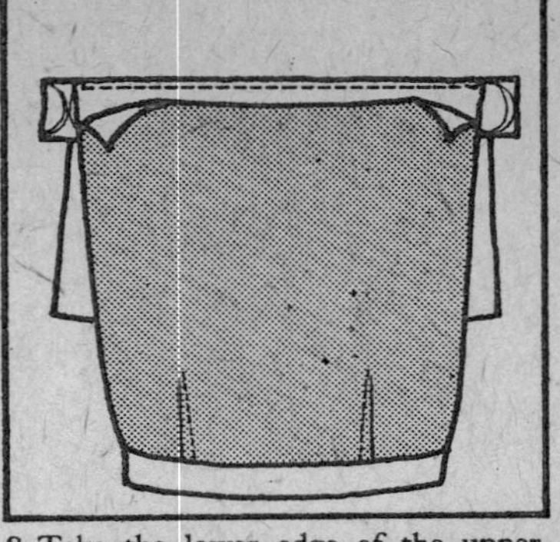

8 Take the lower edge of the upper piece of skirt and lay it wrong side down on the right side of the top edge of the insertion. Sew in place, open out and press.

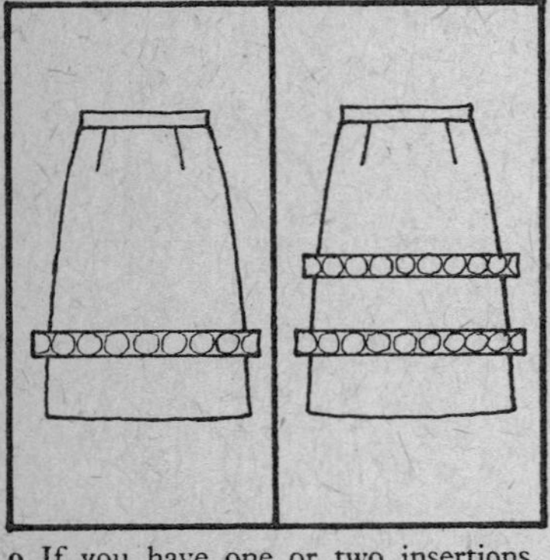

9 If you have one or two insertions, your skirt will look like this.

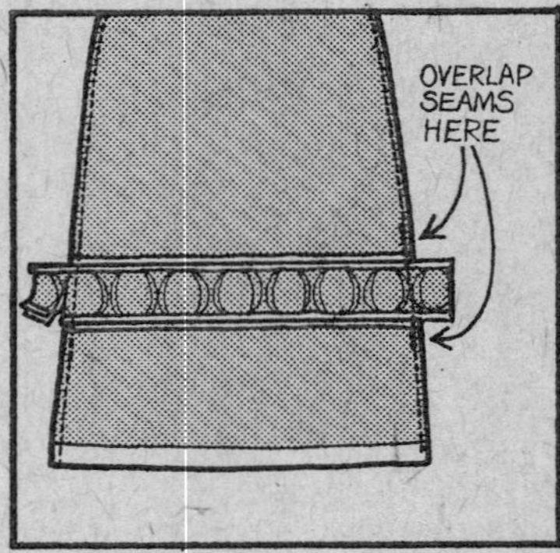

10 Whichever kind of insertion you used, turn the skirt inside out and re-sew the side seams, overlapping the original seams by at least an inch. Cut away excess seam allowance.

letting out skirts and dresses

After unpicking anywhere, press out old folds before re-sewing.

THE BODICE

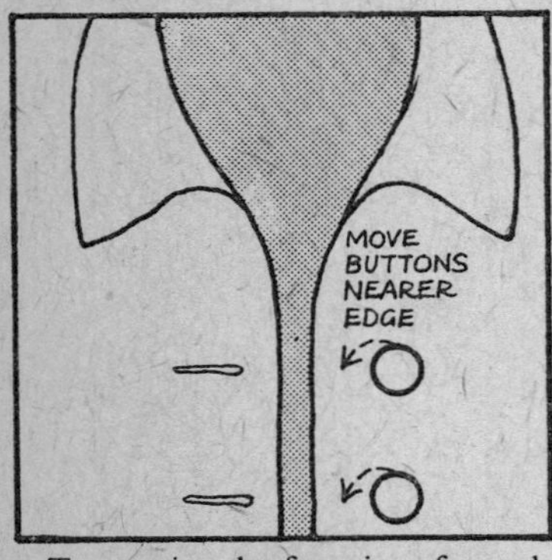

1 Try moving the fastenings forward.

2 If this is not the answer, unpick the waist seam, side seams and darts. Remove the zip but leave the sleeves in if possible. Fit as page 151 and make suitable darts, smaller than the previous ones, as page 33. Re-sew the side seams, if necessary with less seam allowance than before.

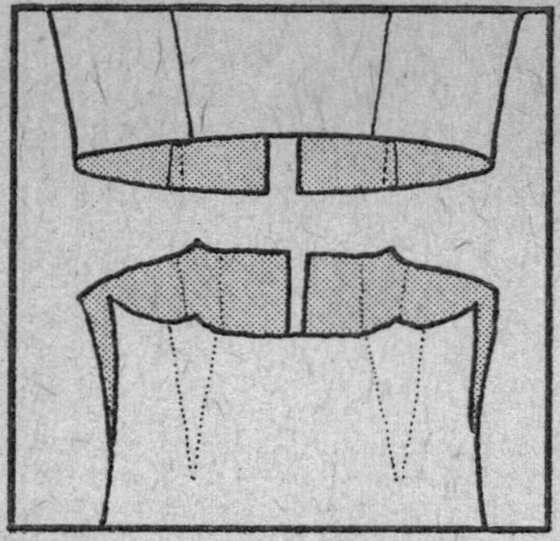

3 If the bodice is now larger than the skirt at the waist, unpick the darts in the skirt, and the side seams for a depth of about 6 in.

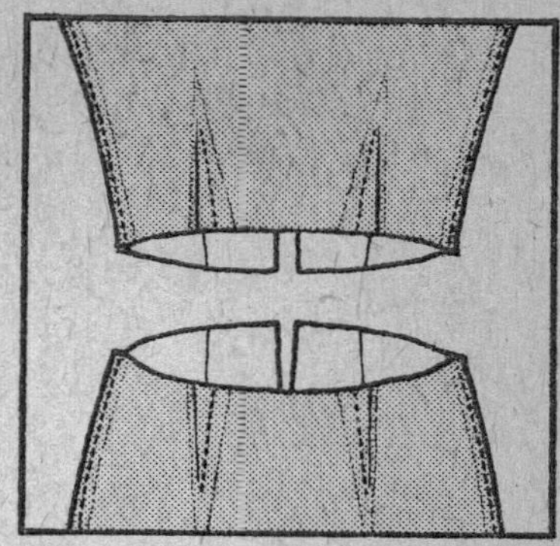

4 Re-fit the skirt as page 151 so that it matches the bodice at the waist. Re-make suitable darts as page 33 and re-sew the side seams.

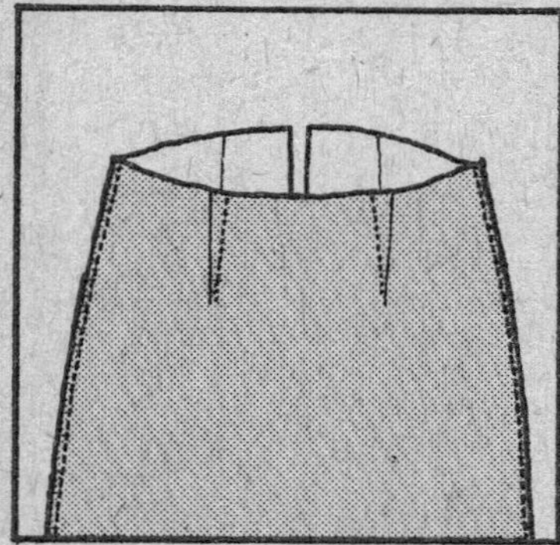

5 Re-join the bodice to the skirt by turning the skirt to the wrong side.

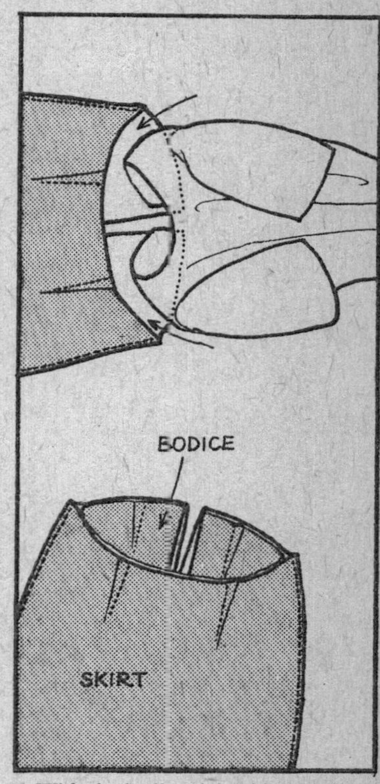

6 With the bodice right side out, place it inside the skirt so that the raw edges, darts and seams at the waist all match up.

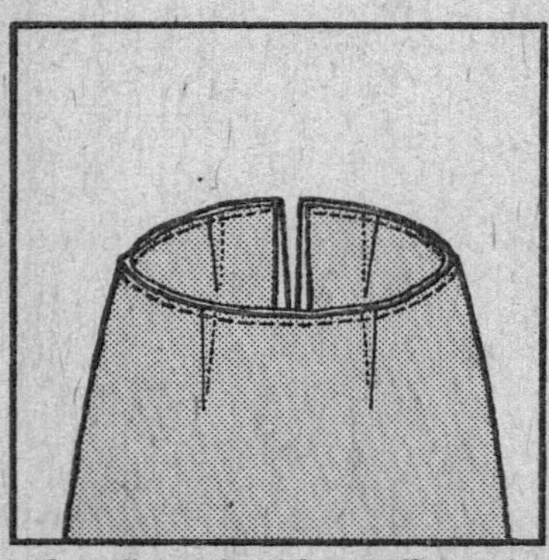

7 Sew all round and fasten off securely. Replace the zip as page 44-45.

8 Turn the dress back to the right side. It should look as good as new.

AT THE WAIST

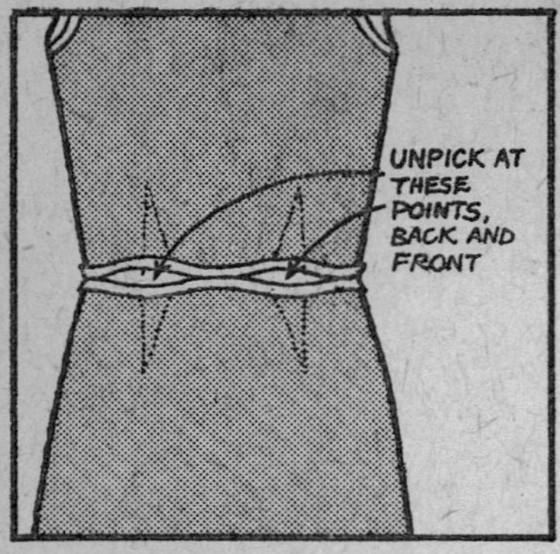

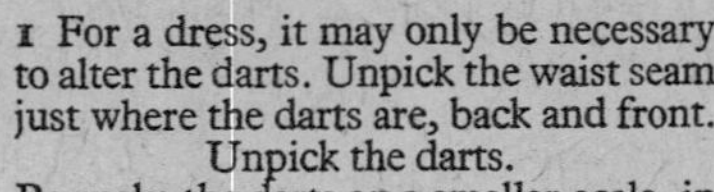

1 For a dress, it may only be necessary to alter the darts. Unpick the waist seam just where the darts are, back and front. Unpick the darts.

Re-make the darts on a smaller scale, in both the bodice and the skirt, as shown on page 33 and re-sew the waist seam as in 5–7 page 83

If altering the darts is not sufficient, also unpick the side seams.

When alteration involves the side seams:

Remove the zip if it is at the side, and unpick both side seams to at least the depth of the zip opening, and up to the armhole. Re-fit as page 151. Make new darts and new side seams.

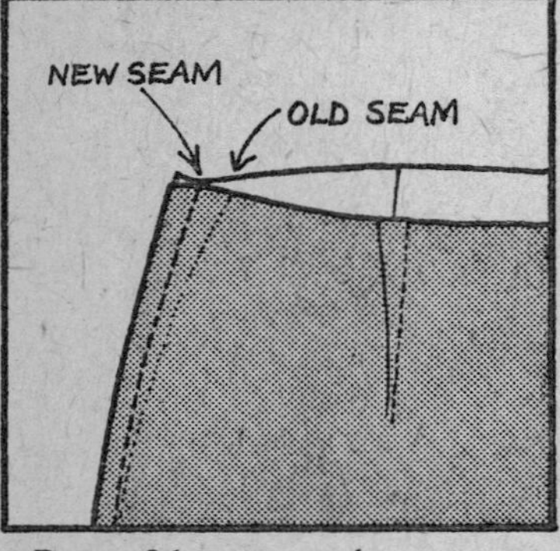

2 Be careful to merge the new seam into the old one to give a smooth line.

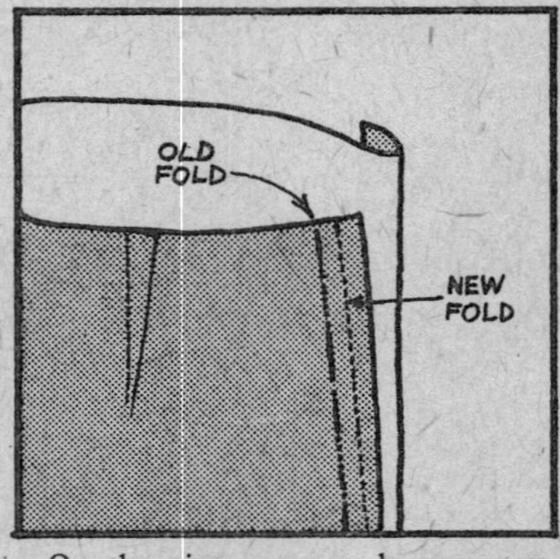

3 On the zip seam, mark your new sewing line with tailor's chalk or tacking stitches, and press the folds back on those marks. Replace the zip as page 44. 45 and re-sew the waist seam.

at the waist–skirt only

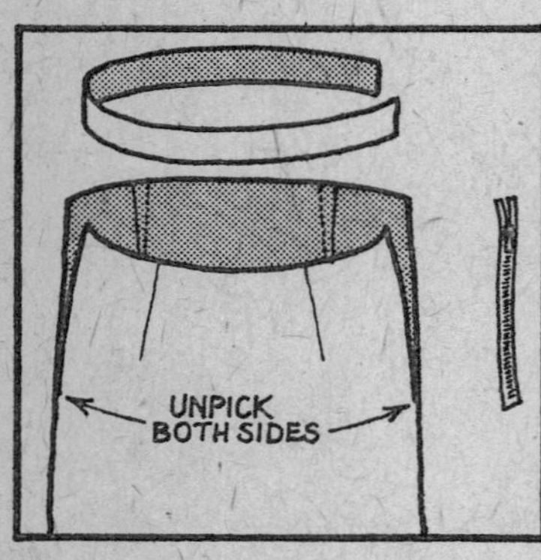

4 Remove the waistband completely by unpicking the stitching. Only remove the zip if the alteration is going to involve the side seams.

If altering darts only, unpick old darts, press out and re-fit the skirt. Make new darts as page 33.

If the alteration involves the side seams work as far as 3 above.

Replace the waistband as Steps 7–10, page 79.

If, as a result of the alteration the original waistband is not long enough, make a new one as instructed for Ladies' Slacks, 1–4 on page 92, 93.

pleated skirts

Remove the waistband and deal as for Children's Alterations, page 106.

at the hips

Hip alterations can't be done without also altering the waist seam or the waistband, whichever is appropriate. Unpick all seams to below hip level. Remove zip if there is one.

Re-fit as page 151 and re-sew all seams.

Re-make darts if necessary, as page 33.

Replace bodice and zip, or waistband and zip, as shown on pages 79 and 83.

taking in skirts and dresses

Prepare exactly as for letting out, but work in reverse.

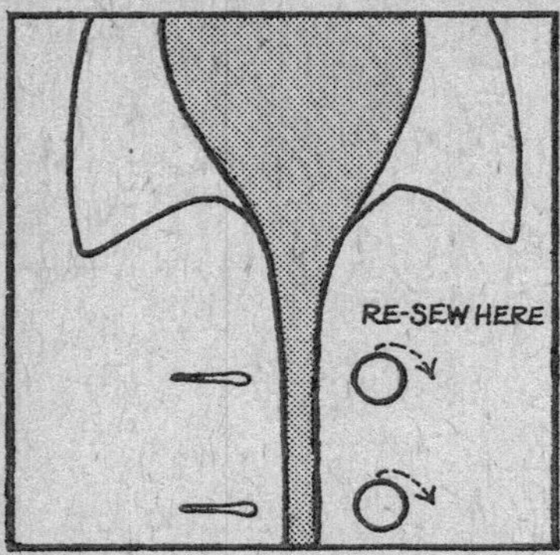

1 Move fastenings back instead of forwards.
Re-make darts, but make them larger instead of smaller, and if necessary sew farther in than the previous side seams.
Match up the skirt and bodice at the waist as on page 83.

when alterations involve sleeves

It could be easier to make adjustments by either taking tucks or widening by insertion, as for Children's Alterations, page 104-107.

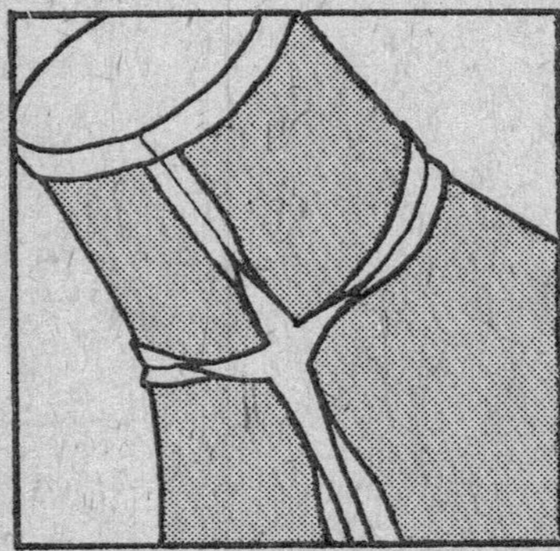

1 If you have to unpick the side seams, as a result of which the armhole is larger than the sleeve, also unpick 2 in. or so of all the other underarm seams, and insert a diamond as on page 122.

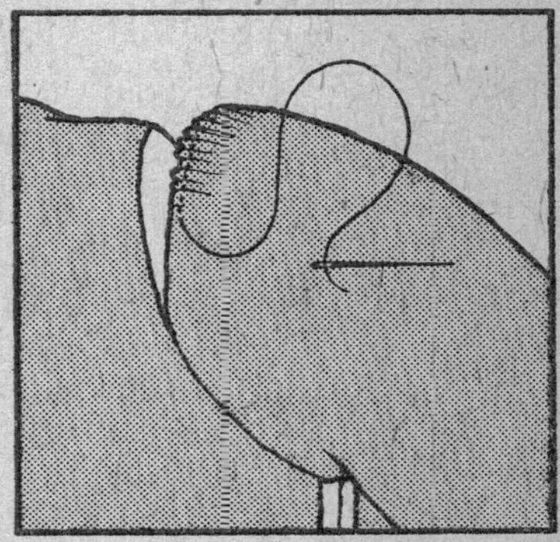

2 If the armhole is fractionally smaller than the sleeve, it is a simple matter to ease the sleeve in with a little gathering.

shortening and lengthening a coat

1 Unpick the lining either side to about 6 in. above the hem.

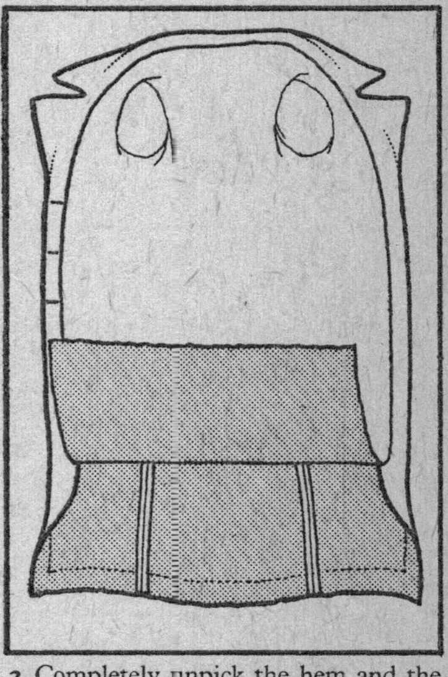

2 Completely unpick the hem and the facing at the sides, and press out the fold mark.

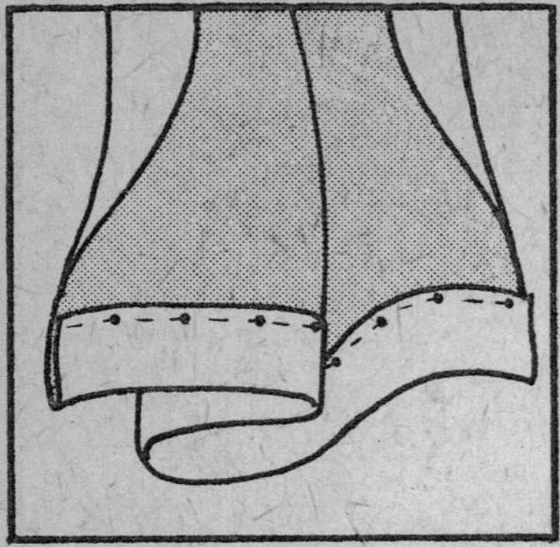

3 Whether you are shortening or lengthening, fold up the hem to the new length all the way across, and pin.

4 Check for evenness and make sure both fronts are the same length.

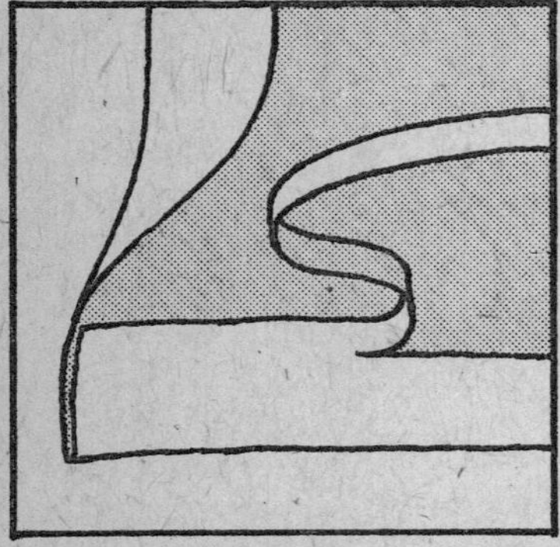

5 If you are shortening and the hem is too deep, trim off a small amount.

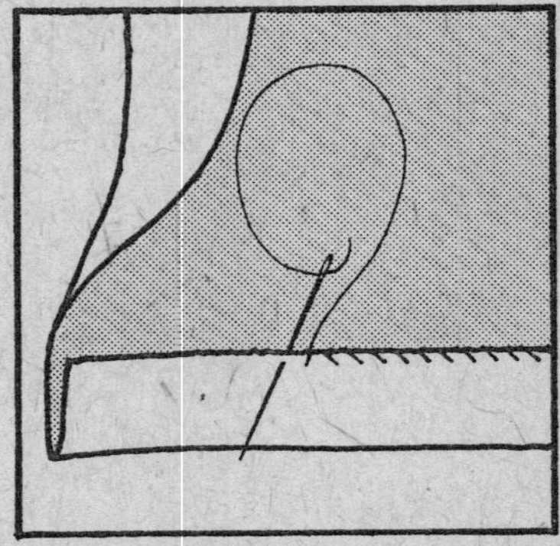

6 If you trim off, oversew the raw edge.

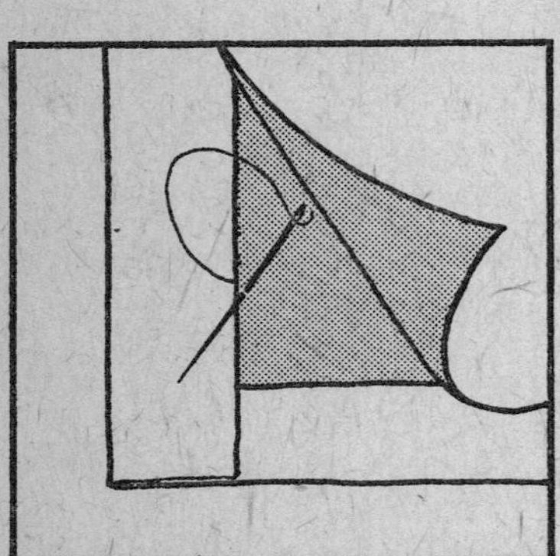

7 Fold the facing back into place and slip stitch in position. Blind hem the hem of the coat as on page 36.

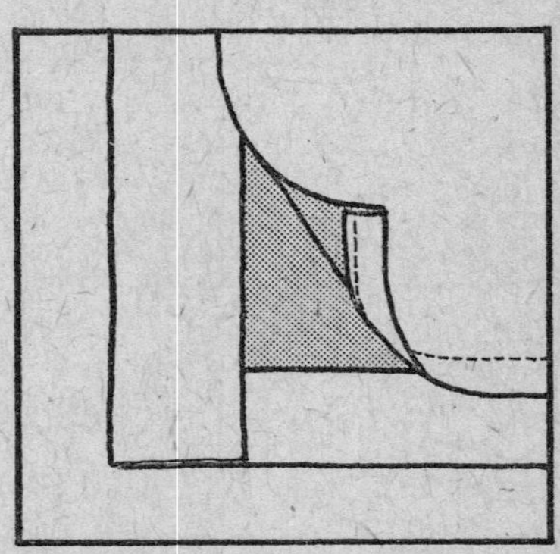

8 If you are shortening, turn up the lining by a sufficient amount to be 1 in. above the hemline of the coat.

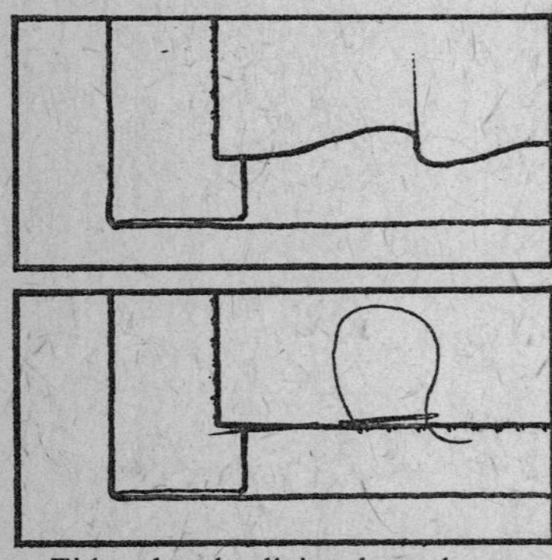

9 Either let the lining hang loose or slip stitch it to the top layer of the inside hem.

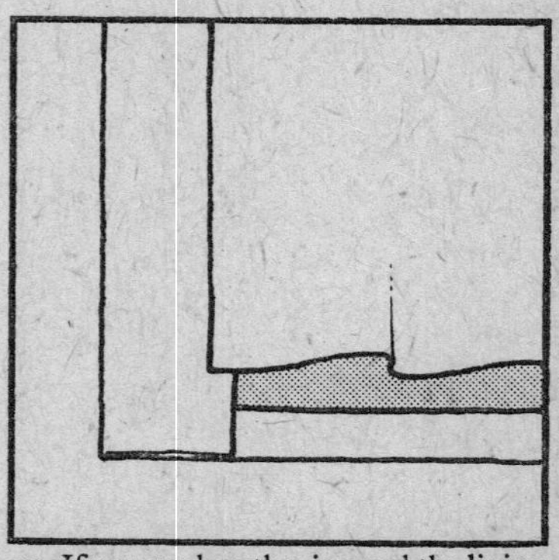

10 If you are lengthening and the lining hangs loose, don't alter it.

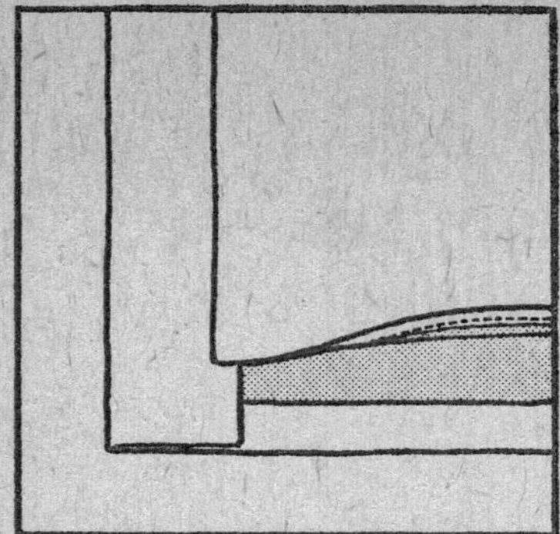

11 If the lining was attached at the bottom, but you now have insufficient length to sew it as it should be, to the inside hem, sew a hem to the lining and let it hang loose.

12 Slip stitch the lining into place at the sides.

lengthening a coat with a false hem

This happens when you don't have a very big hem to start with and, by lengthening it, there is not sufficient fabric to turn up. Start off as 1, 2 page 85 and proceed as follows:

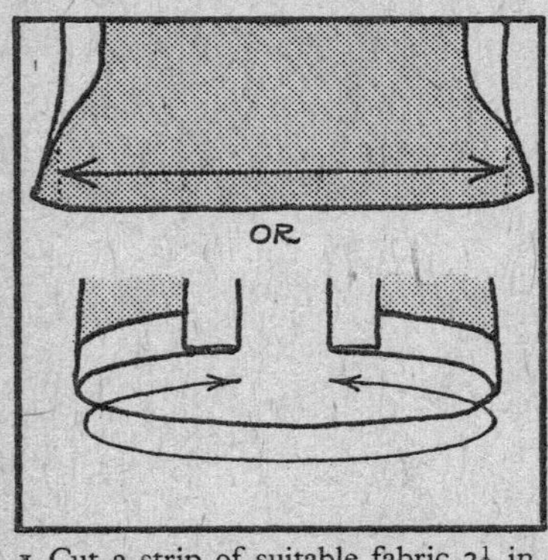

1 Cut a strip of suitable fabric 3½ in. deep and long enough to go round the bottom of the coat from front fold to front fold. It need not be sewn to the facing.

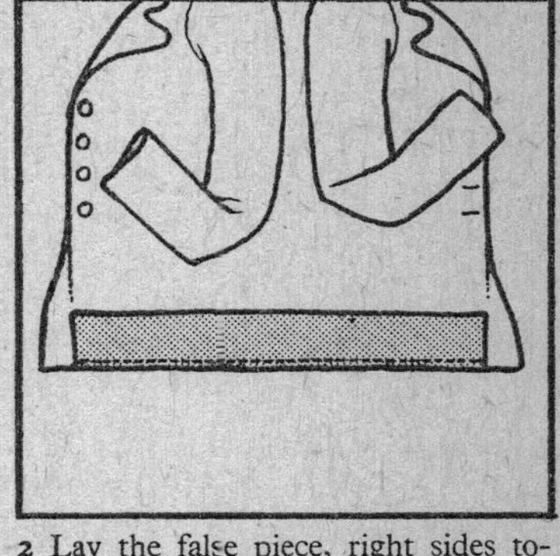

2 Lay the false piece, right sides together, on the outside of the coat, matching the bottom edges. Tack into position and sew.

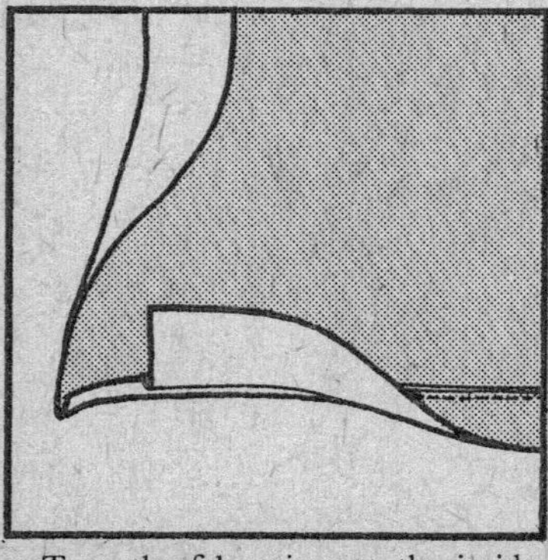

3 Turn the false piece to the inside, folding it just above the sewing line, oversew and blind hem as on page 36.

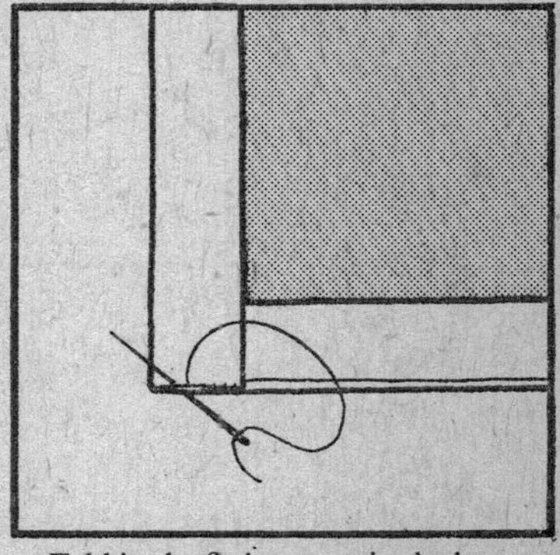

4 Fold in the facing, turn in the bottom edge and hem it neatly. Finish off as on page 86.

reducing width of shoulder seam

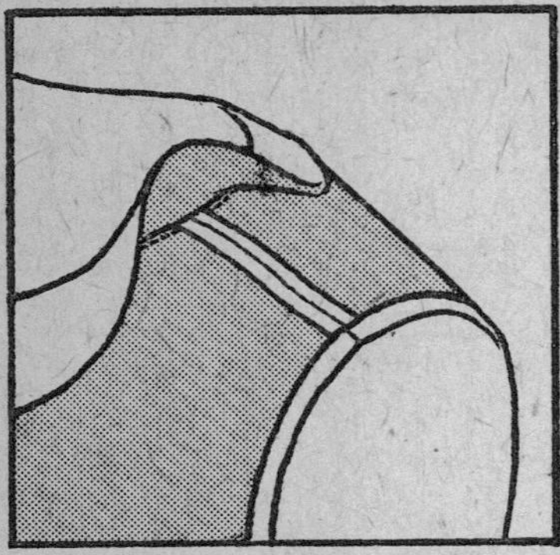

1 Unpick the facing, if any, where it is slip-stitched to the shoulder.

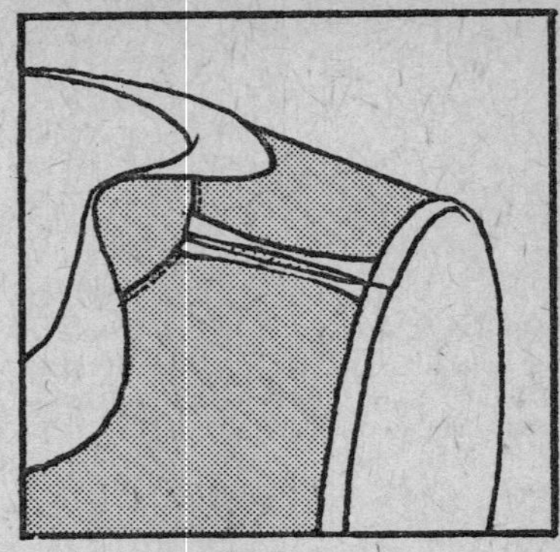

2 Unpick the shoulder seam.

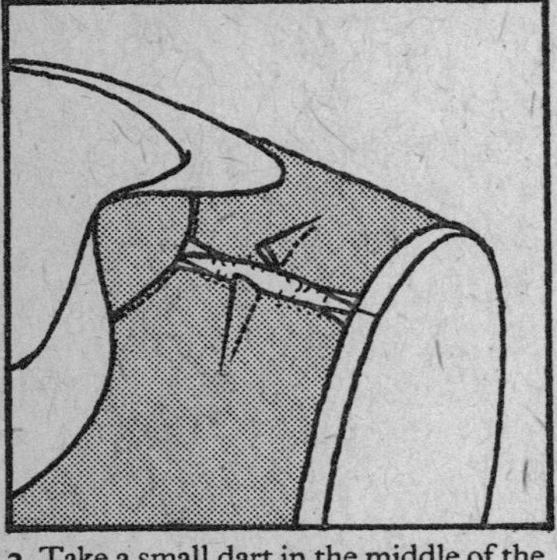

3 Take a small dart in the middle of the shoulder on the front and back bodice.

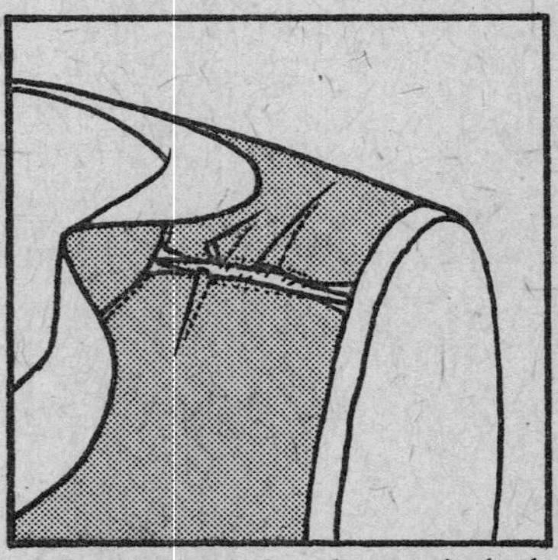

4 If there is already a dart on the back bodice, work beside it on the neck side. (See page 33 for making darts).

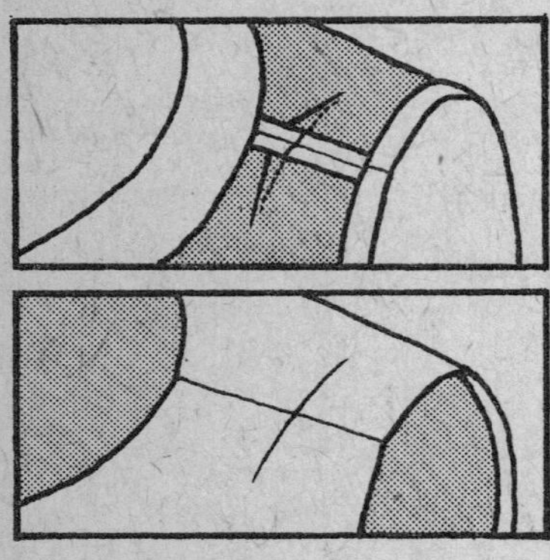

5 Press the darts flat, resew the shoulder seam, and replace the facing.

widening the shoulder seam

This is not possible unless generous seam allowances have been left untrimmed. If this is the case proceed as follows:

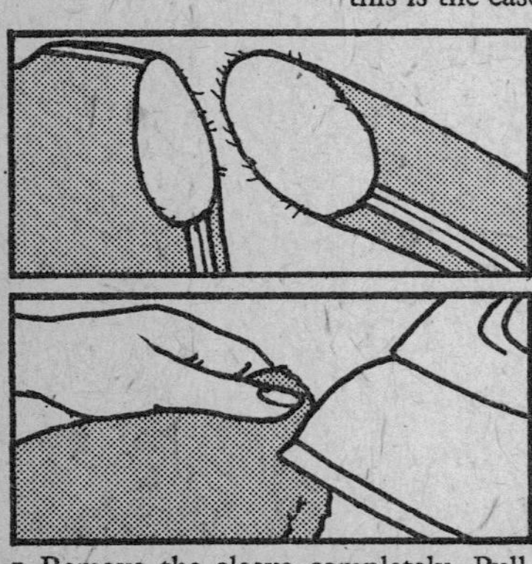

1 Remove the sleeve completely. Pull out any loose ends of thread and press the old sewing line out as page 69-70.

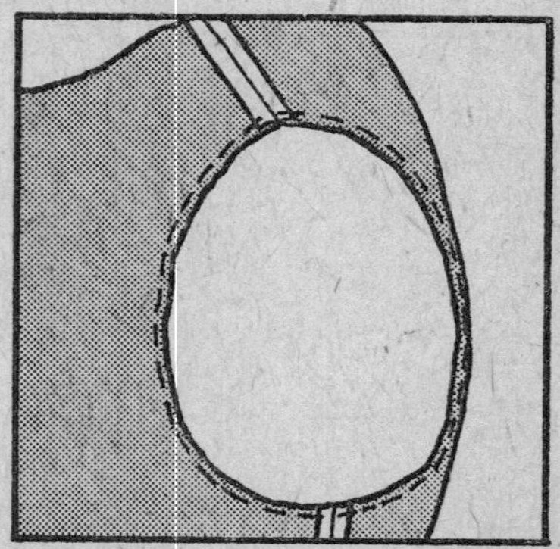

2 With a contrasting thread and small tacking stitches, mark out a new sewing line round the armhole much nearer to the edge than previously.

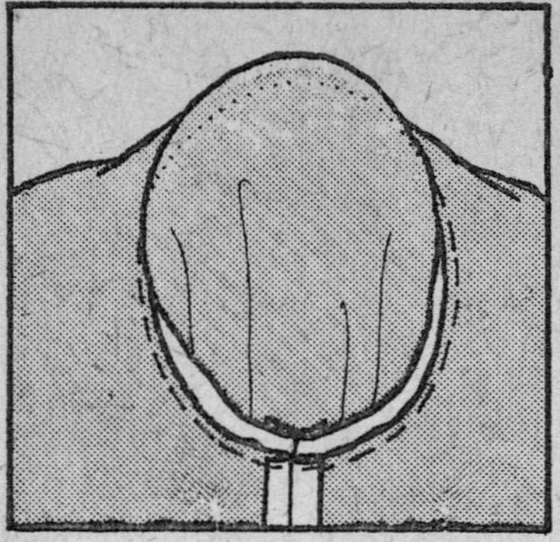
3 Re-set the sleeve into the armhole, matching the old sewing line on the sleeve to the new one you have marked on the bodice.

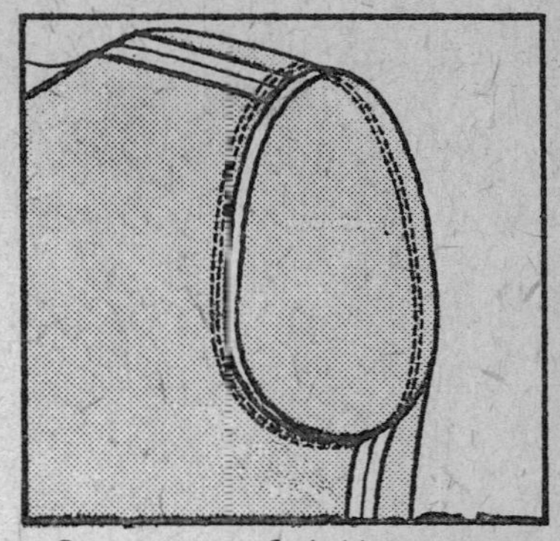
4 Sew two rows of stitching as you are working near the edge on one piece.

shortening sleeves

PLAIN HEM

1 Unpick the existing hem.

2 Fold again where required, which will pucker the sleeve, as a sleeve gets narrower towards the wrist.

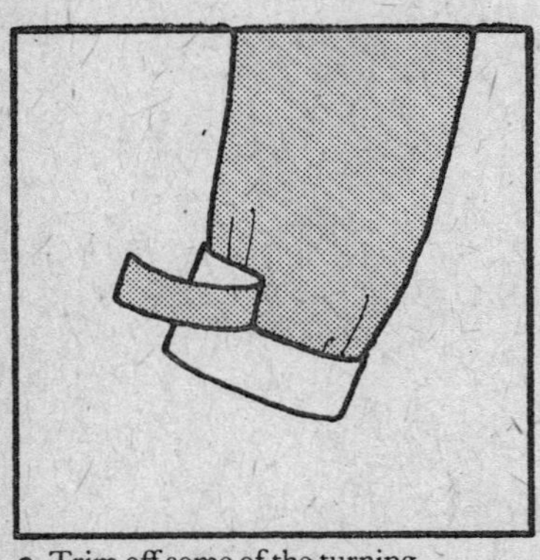
3 Trim off some of the turning.

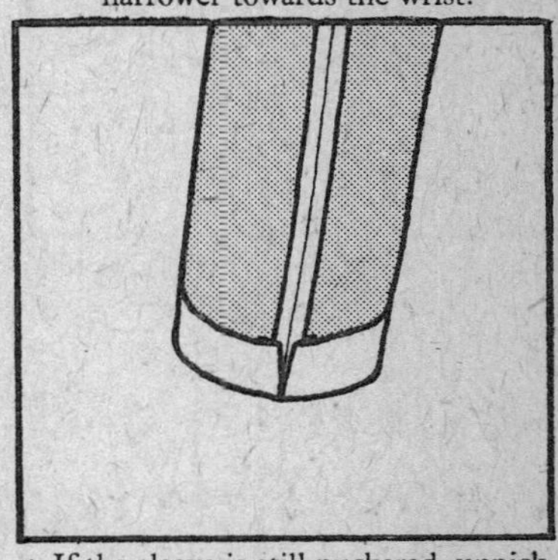
4 If the sleeve is still puckered, unpick the seam or seams in the folded back piece.

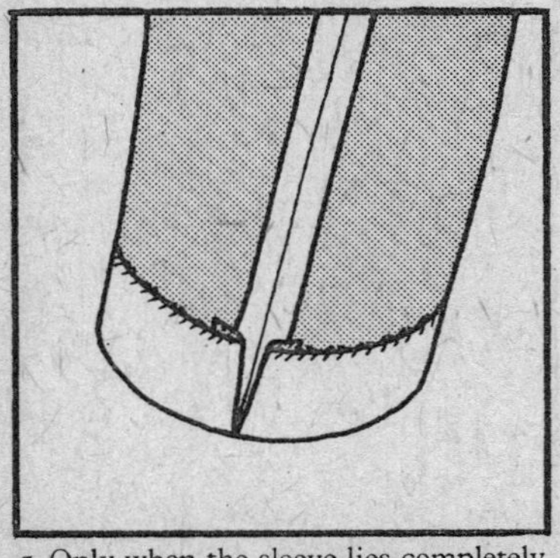
5 Only when the sleeve lies completely flat under the turn-back, oversew the raw edge and slip stitch in place.

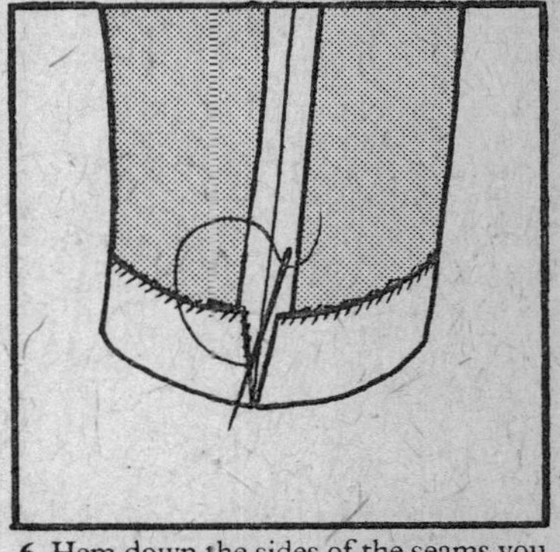
6 Hem down the sides of the seams you unpicked.

WITH CUFFS

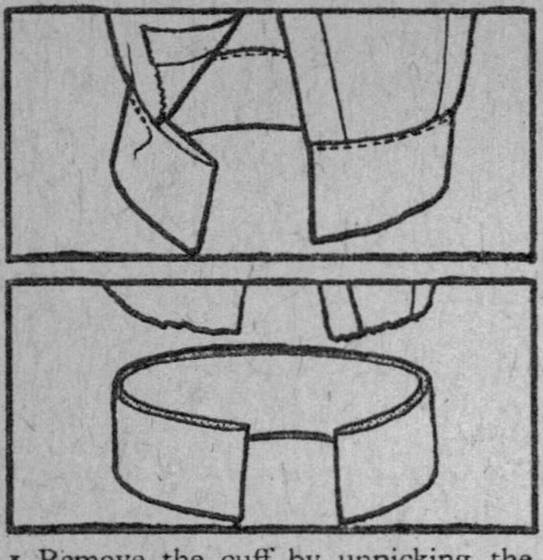

1 Remove the cuff by unpicking the seams joining it to the sleeve.

2 If the sleeve is gathered at the bottom, unpick the gathering, flatten out pleats, and press smooth.

3 Cut off from the bottom of the sleeve the required amount, less about ½in. seam allowance.

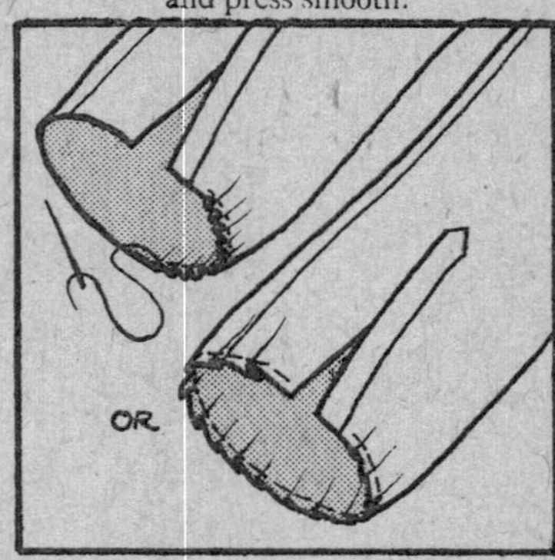

4 Re-gather the sleeve bottom as shown on page 19 or tack into small tucks so that it is the correct size to fit back into the cuff. Do not gather or pleat the facing of the sleeve opening.

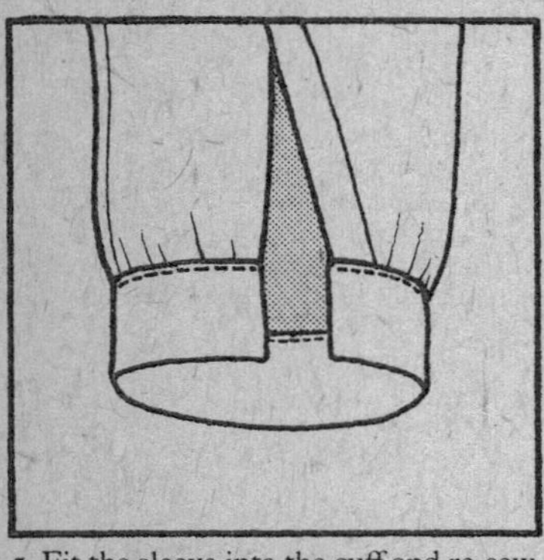

5 Fit the sleeve into the cuff and re-sew on the original sewing line.

See also
CHILDREN'S ALTERATIONS.

men's trousers

The most common alteration is to let them out! This is always done at the centre back seam by inserting a triangular shaped piece of near matching fabric.

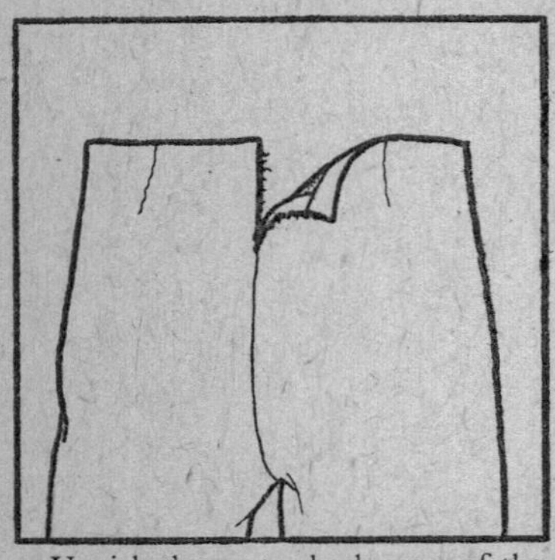

1 Unpick the centre back seam of the trousers and the lining for a few inches. Remove any buttons.

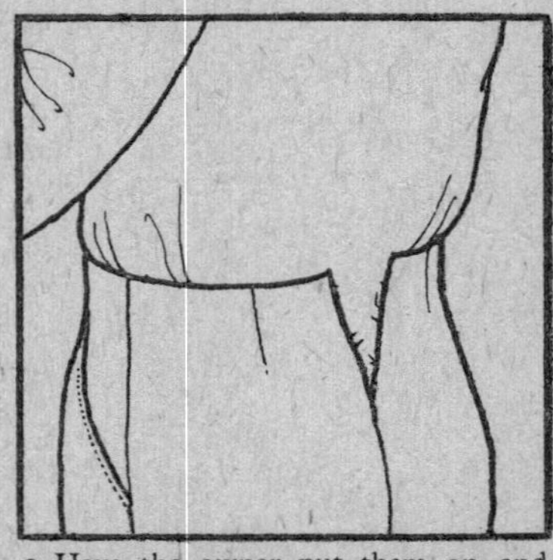

2 Have the owner put them on and fasten them up (if possible).

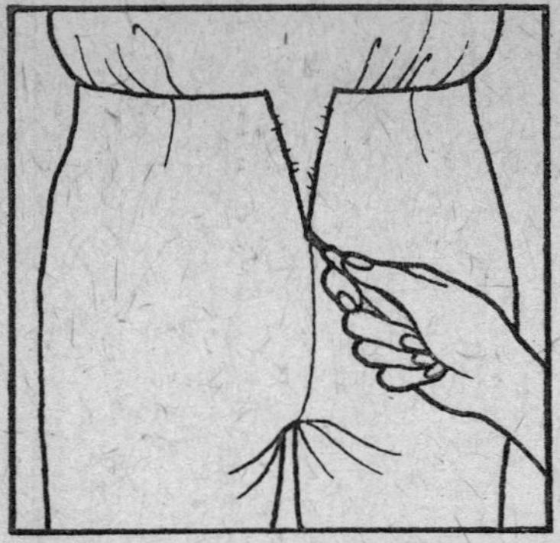
3 Keep unpicking the centre back seam until there is no tightness.

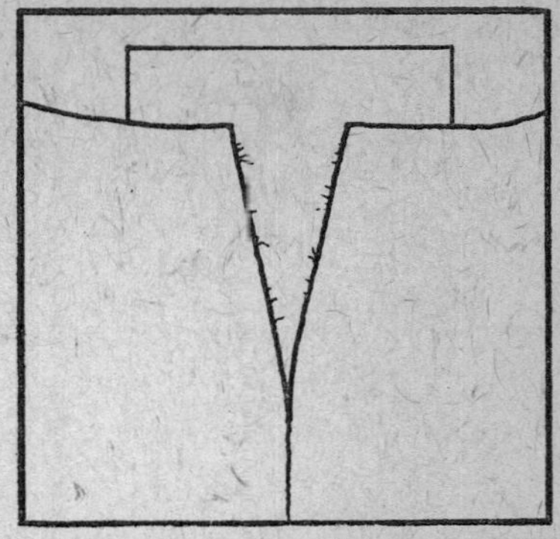
4 Slip a piece of stiff brown paper behind the gap in the back of the trousers.

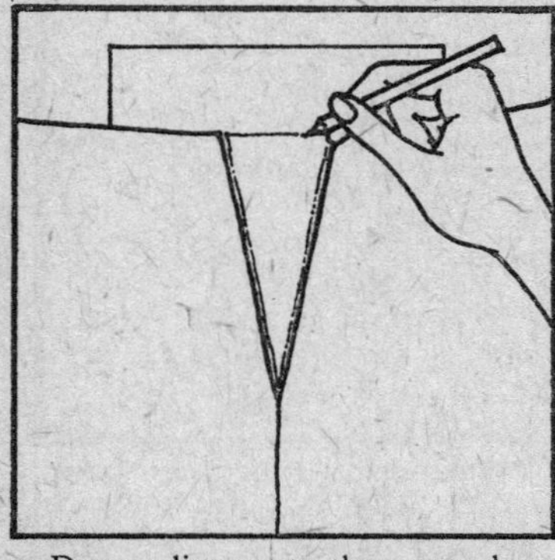
5 Draw a line on to the paper down each side of the gap and across the top.

6 Remove the paper and draw another line round the first one, ½ in. away from it. This ½ in. will be the seam allowance.

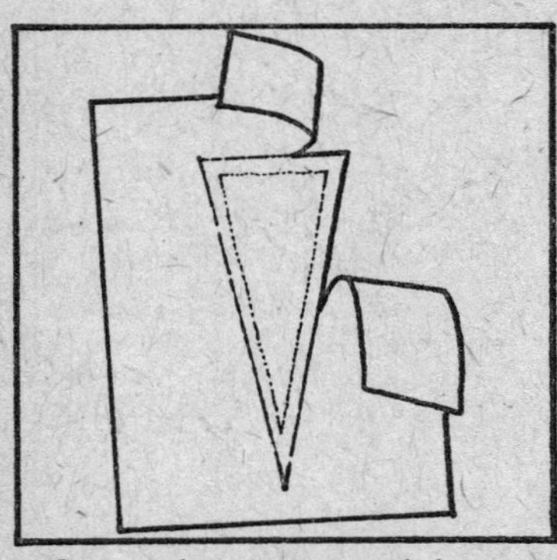
7 Cut out the pattern round the outer line which will give you the exact size of the piece to insert.

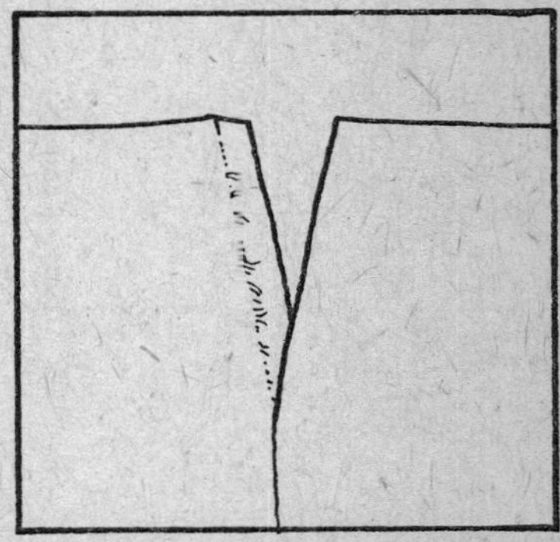
8 To insert the false piece, work on the right side and open out the seam allowance down one side of the gap.

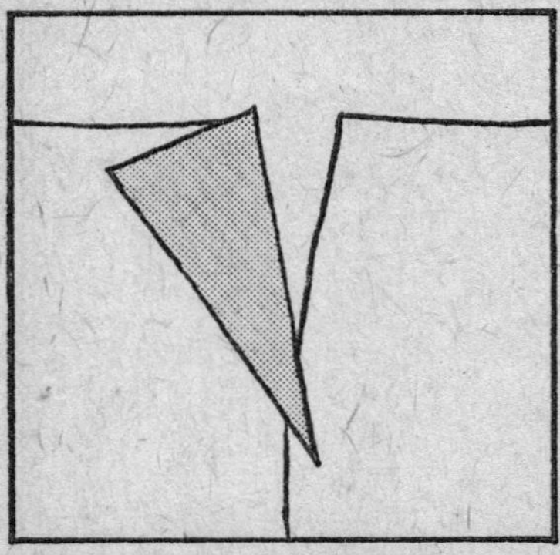
9 Lay one edge of the false piece, right side down, along the unfolded edge of the trousers.

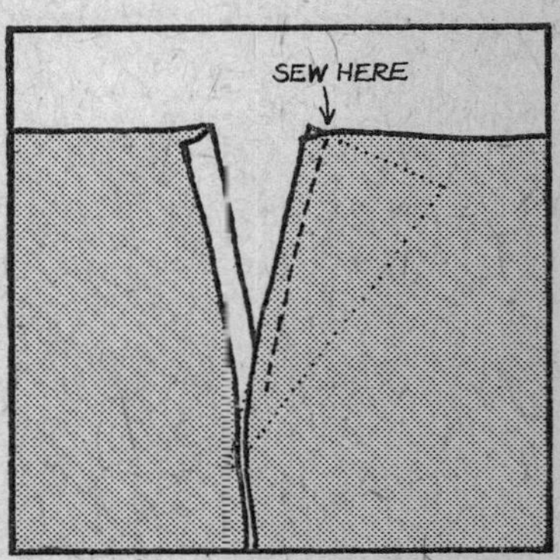

10 Sew the two together along the original sewing line.

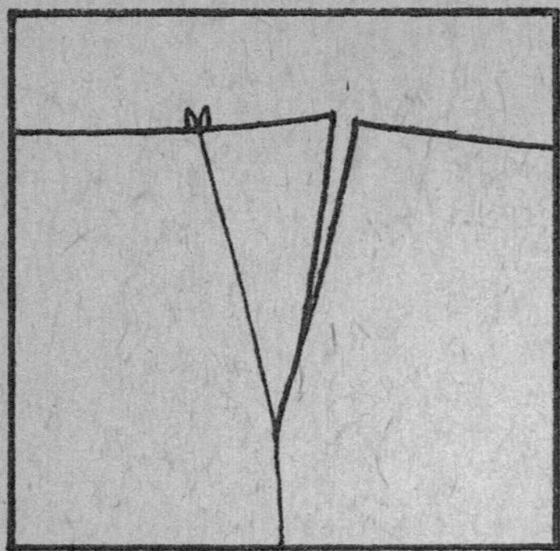

11 Turn the false piece forwards and tuck to the inside the pointed end of the triangle.

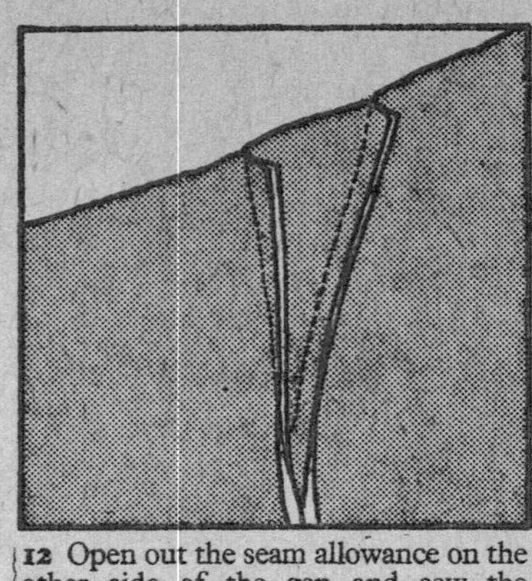

12 Open out the seam allowance on the other side of the gap and sew the second side of the false piece on the old sewing line as before.

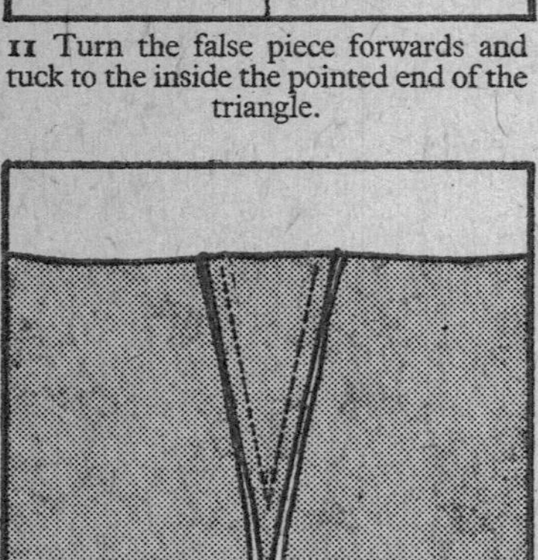

13 Trim off any excess seam allowance and press both seams away from the centre.

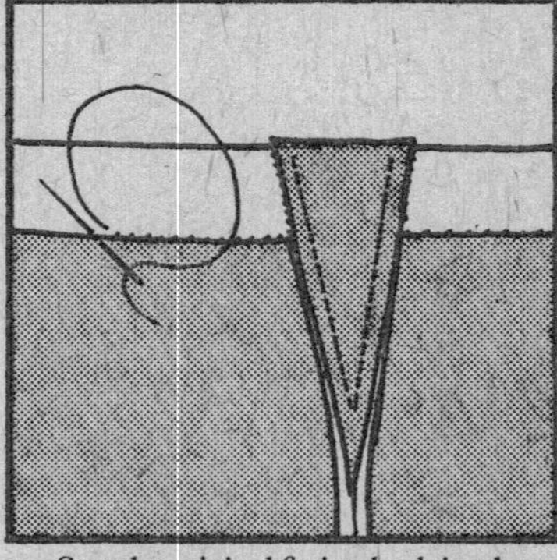

14 Sew the original facing back in place.

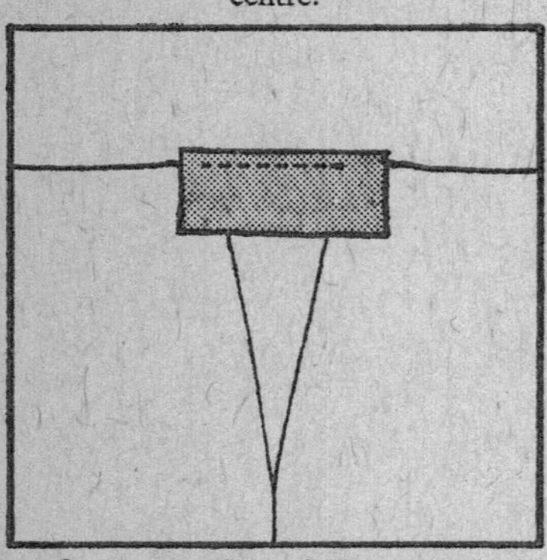

15 Cut a strip of thin fabric with which to face the false piece, at least 2 in. wider than the insertion, and sew it along the top on the right side.

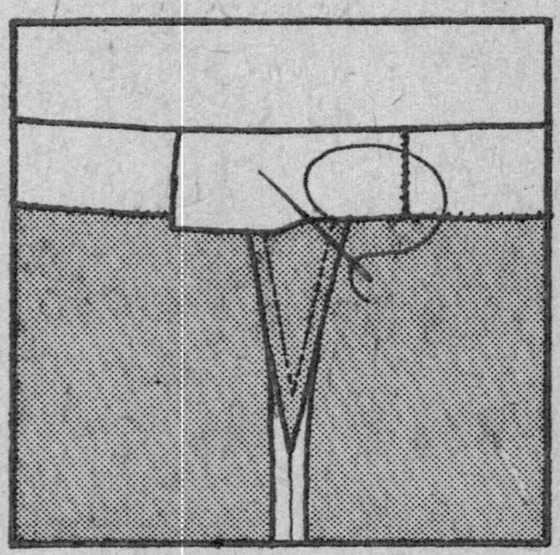

16 Turn the facing over to the wrong side. Turn under the side edges and the bottom edge, and hem it down. Replace buttons.

ladies' slacks–letting out

These are usually made with a waistband, so any alteration to the waistline can be done as for a skirt. See page 84. Any further extending could be dealt with by removing the waistband as on page 84 and inserting a false piece as for men's trousers.
If the waistband is too short after letting out, make another from the nearest match you can get, or a completely contrasting fabric.

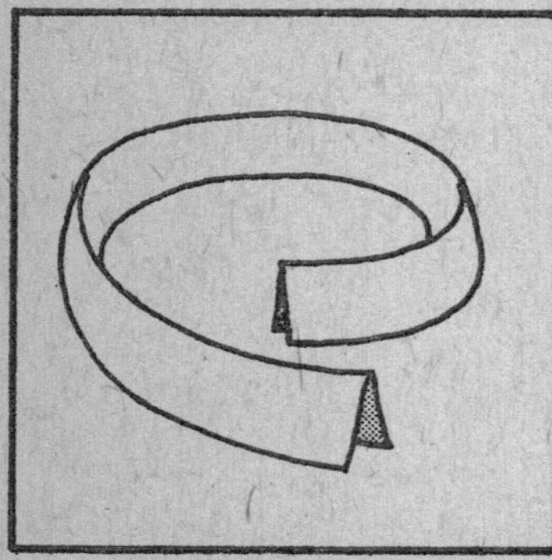

1 Cut a strip of fabric 4 in. wide and long enough to go round the waist plus an overlap. Fold this in half and press.

2 Allowing for the overlap, lay the right side of the waistband to the right side of the slacks, and sew on the original sewing line.

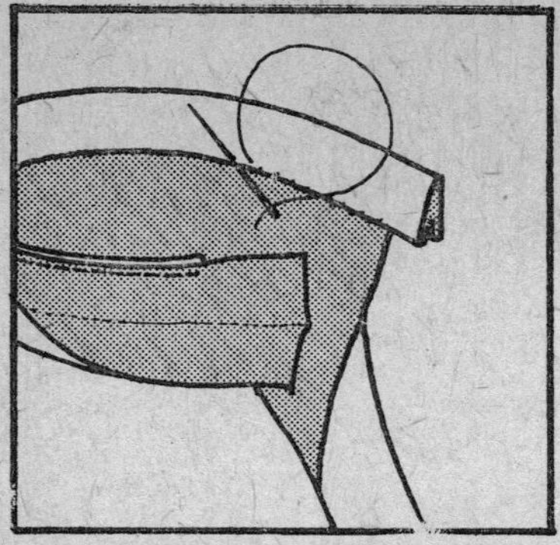

3 Turn the waistband over to the inside, tuck under the edge, and hem it down.

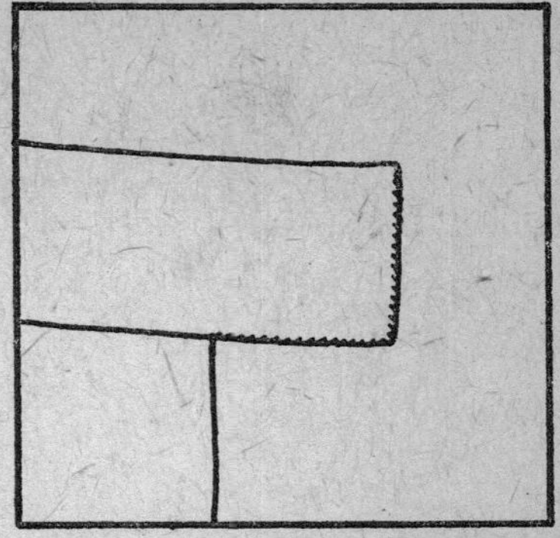

4 When you get to the overlap, tuck under both edges and oversew. Oversew both ends. Insert the zip, if any, as in page 44, 45.

ladies' slacks – taking in

Work as for a skirt, page 84. If making darts is not sufficient:

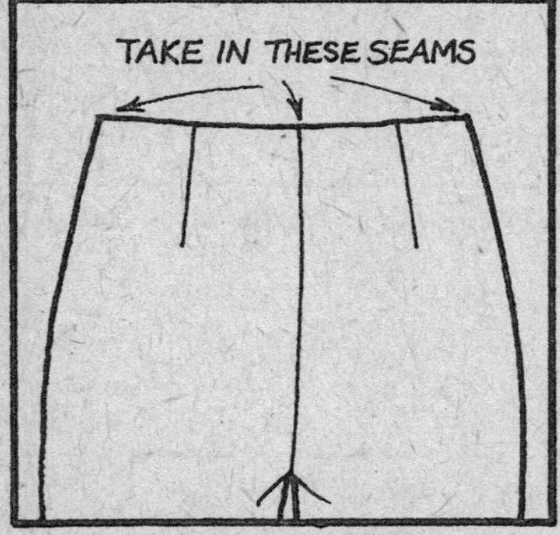

1 Take in the centre back seam and the side seams.

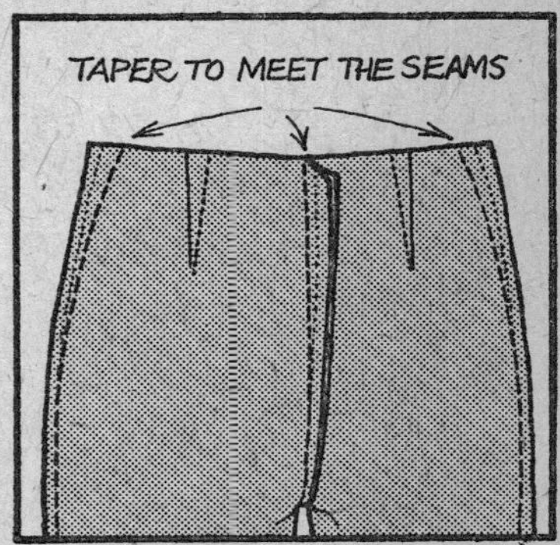

2 On the wrong side, start an appropriate distance from the seam, tapering to meet the seam.
Replace the waistband as on page 79.

trouser legs – shortening

If the trouser bottom has a plain folded hem deal with it as for a sleeve. Page 97.

WITH TURN-UPS

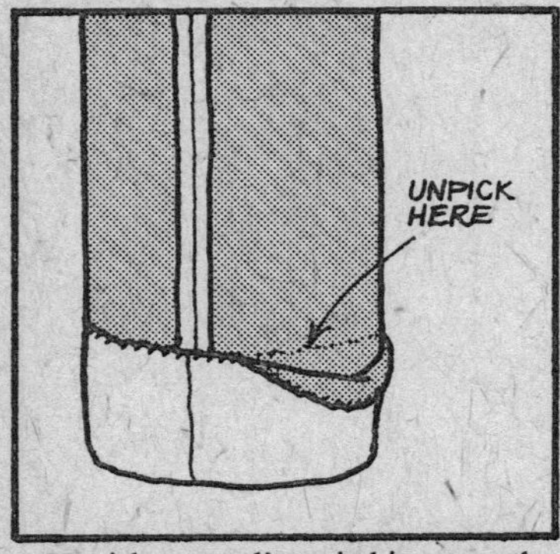

1 Unpick any slip stitching on the inside of the trouser bottom.

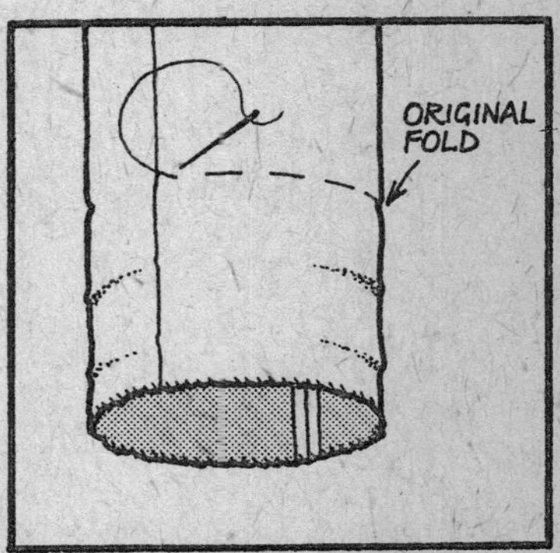

2 Pull out straight and sew in a contrasting thread a line of tacking stitches on the original bottom fold.

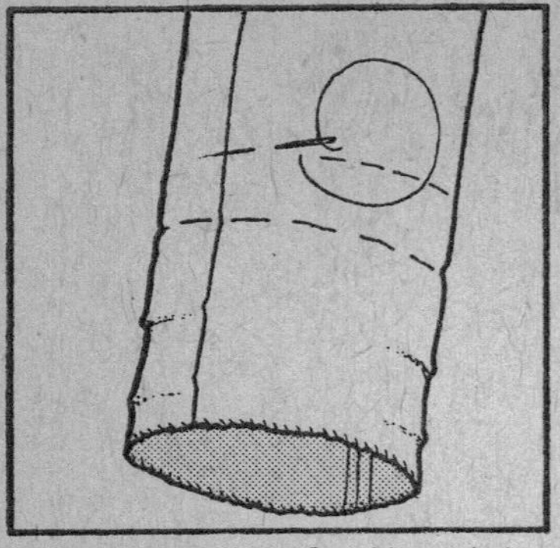

3 Now sew a line of tacking stitches above it where you wish the new fold to come.

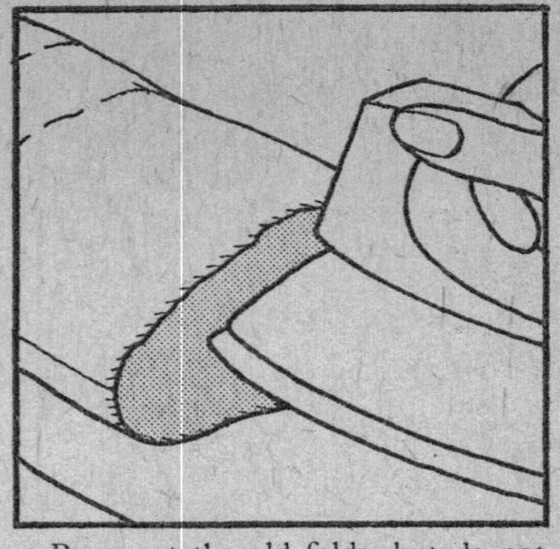

4 Press out the old folds, but do not make a centre crease.

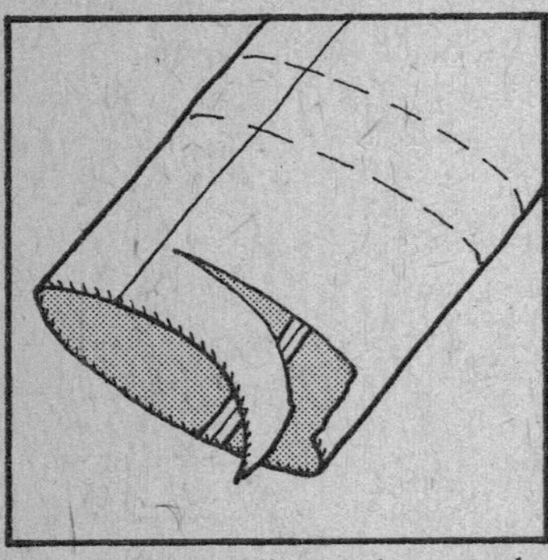

5 Whatever the distance between the two lines of tacking stitches, cut the same amount away from the bottom edge.

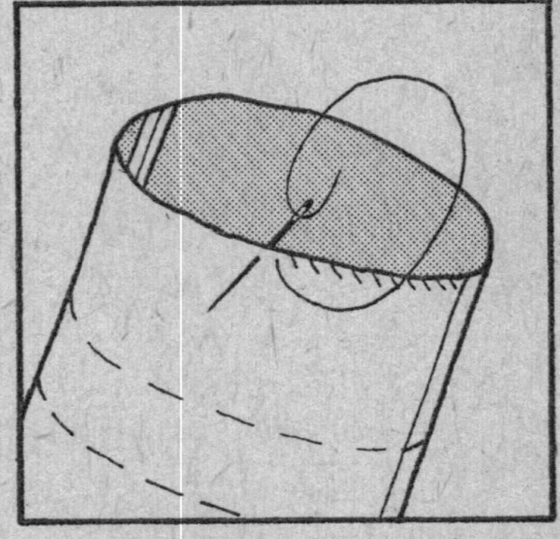

6 Oversew the raw edge at the bottom.

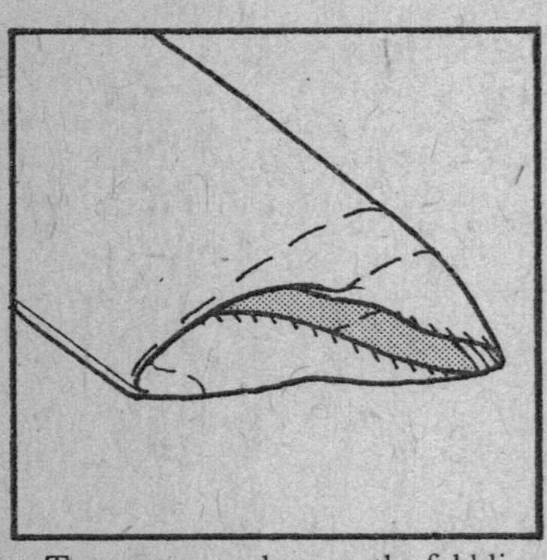

7 Turn up a new hem on the fold line you have marked.

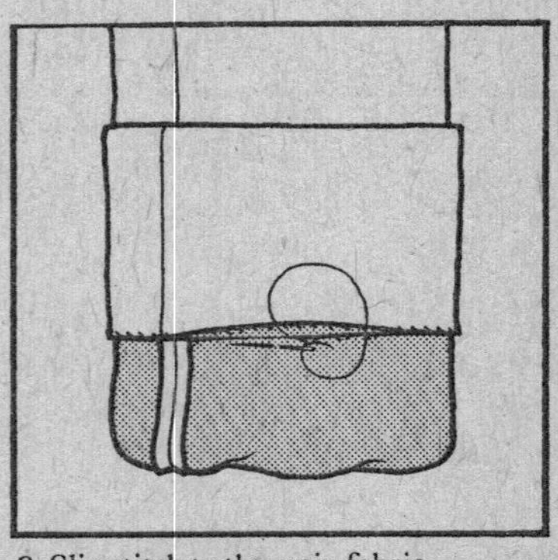

8 Slip stitch to the main fabric.

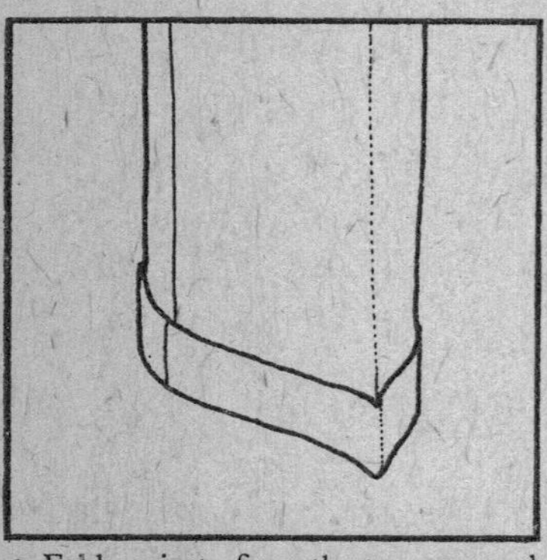

9 Fold again to form the turn-up, and press a centre crease, on the right side of the garment.

trouser legs lengthening

If there are no turn-ups proceed as for a sleeve, page 97.

WITH TURN-UPS

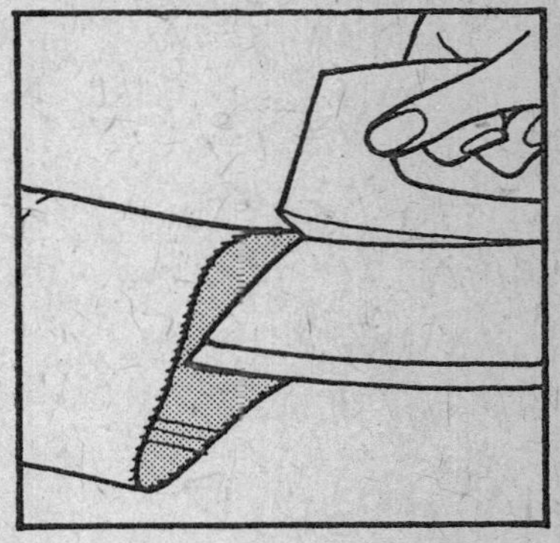

1 As there is always a large turning at trouser bottoms proceed as 1 and 2 page 93 except that you need only mark one new line with tacking stitches, below the old fold line.

Press out without making a crease and proceed as 6 to 9 page 94.

tapering flared bottoms

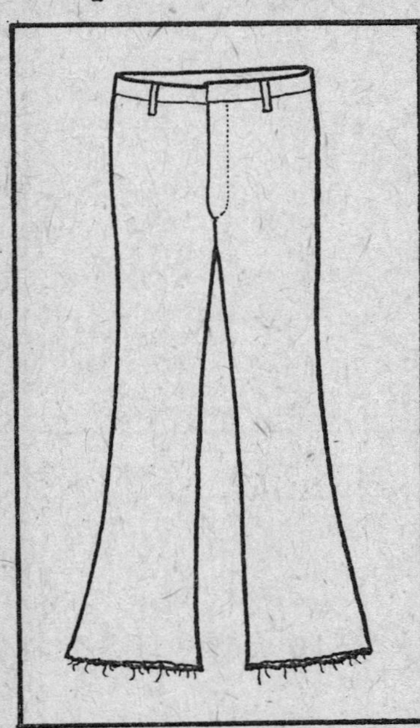

1 Unpick the bottom hems. Press the opened out seams flat again so that you can see the sewing lines.

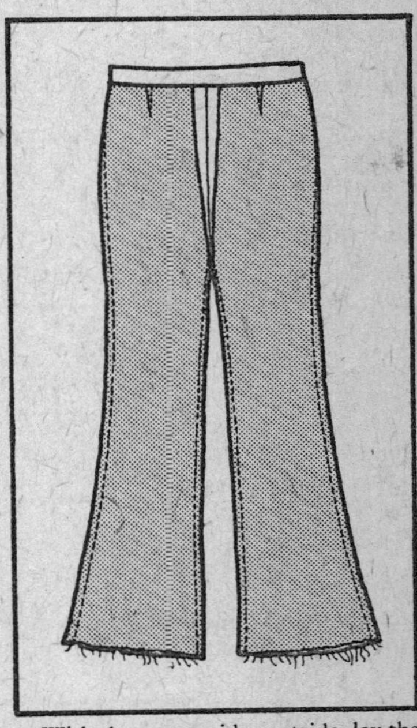

2 With the wrong sides outside, lay the trousers on a flat surface with all edges matching.

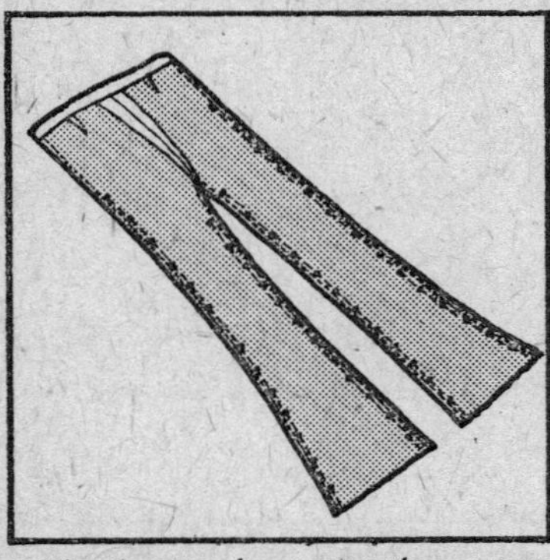

3 Pin the two layers together wrong sides outside.

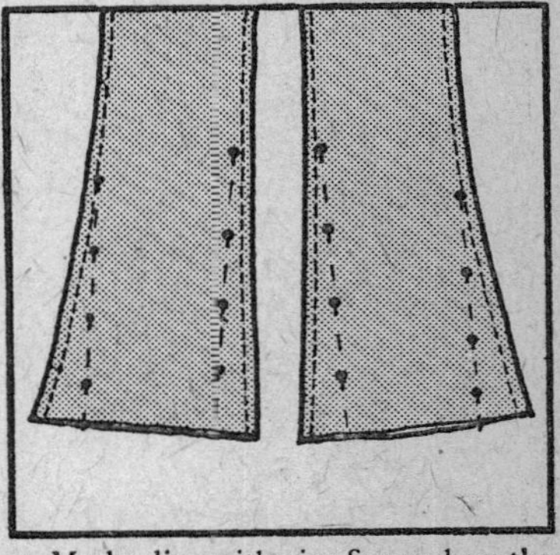

4 Mark a line with pins from where the flare begins down to the bottom edge, in a straight line.

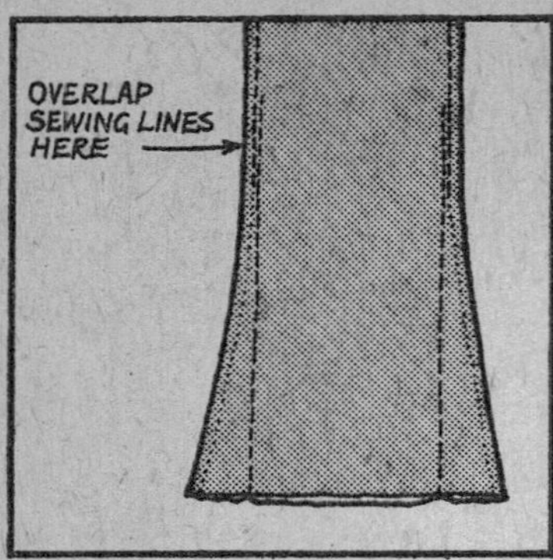

5 When you are sure it is straight, tack it, and then sew, overlapping the previous sewing line by an inch or so to secure.

6 Cut off waste fabric at the sides.

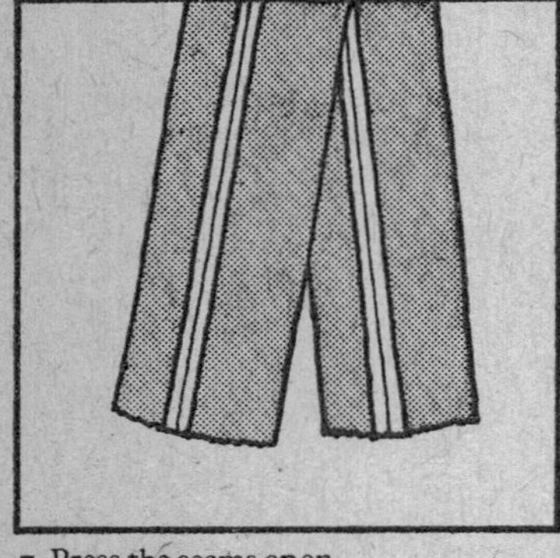

7 Press the seams open.

8 Turn up the bottom and slip stitch as page 15.

tapering straight trousers

The same principle will apply as for the previous section, so work as 1, 2, 3 page 95.

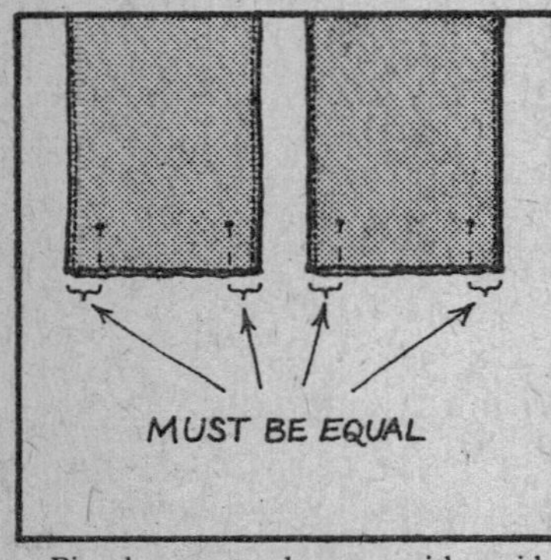

1 Pin the trouser bottoms either side to give you the size you require. Take an even amount off each side of the leg.

2 With the trousers laid on a flat surface mark a straight line with pins from a point on the outer edge level with the crotch to the pin at the bottom nearest the outer edge.

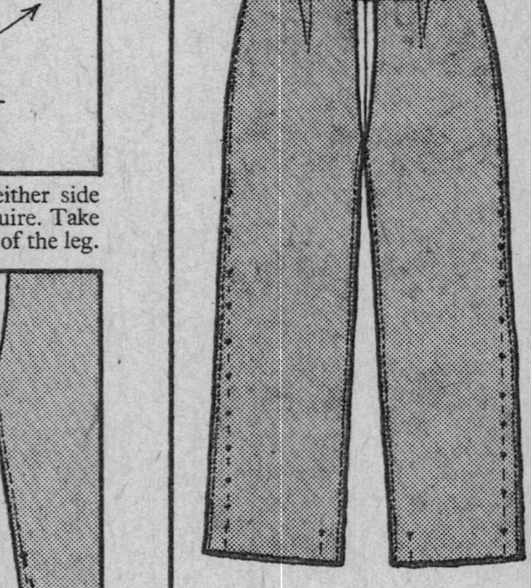

3 Mark another straight line with pins on the inside leg from 6 in. below the crotch to the pin at the bottom nearest the inside edge.

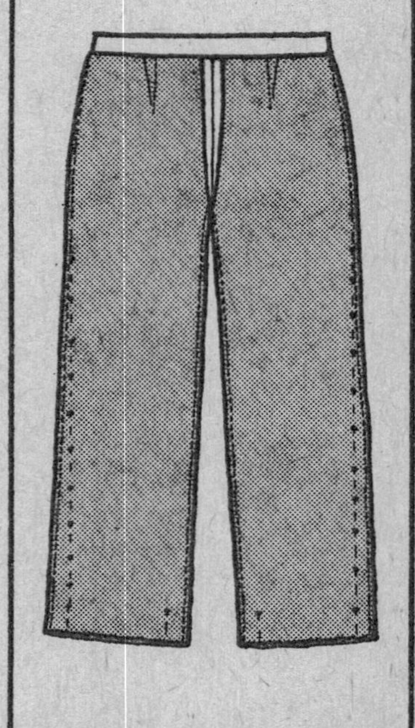

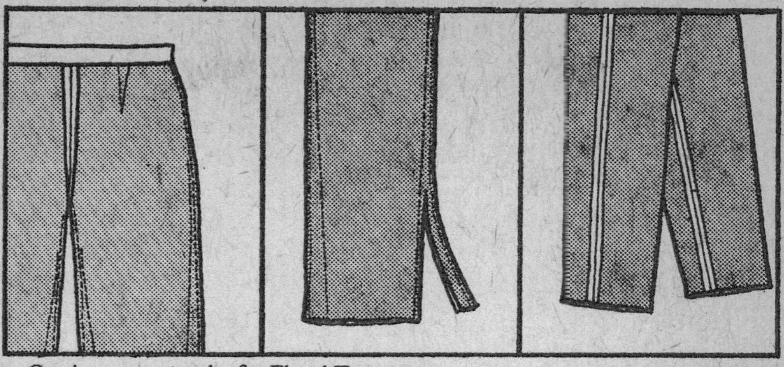

4 Continue as 5, 6 and 7 for Flared Trousers.

5 When you turn up the bottom hem, deal with the tapered turnback as for sleeves.

coat sleeves – shortening

Work one sleeve at a time and keep the second one to peep at if you are not sure how the professionals did the job in the first place.

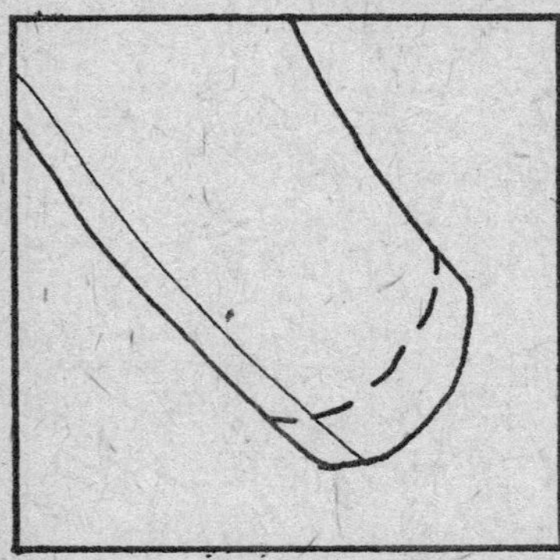

1 Sew a line of tacking stitches in contrasting thread around the sleeve at the correct length. Just catch the outer layer of fabric.

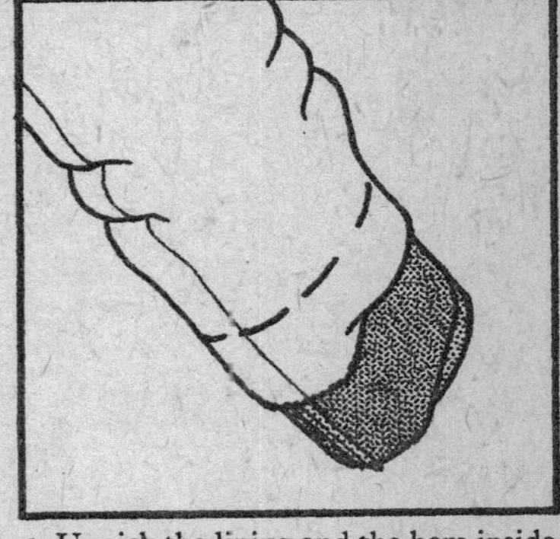

2 Unpick the lining and the hem inside the sleeve.

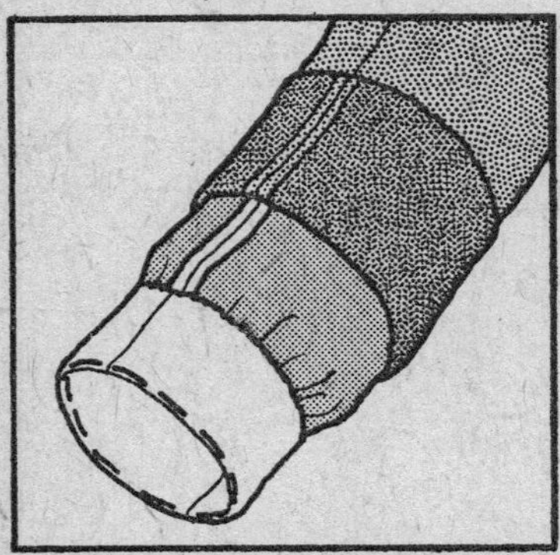

3 Fold back on the line you have marked.

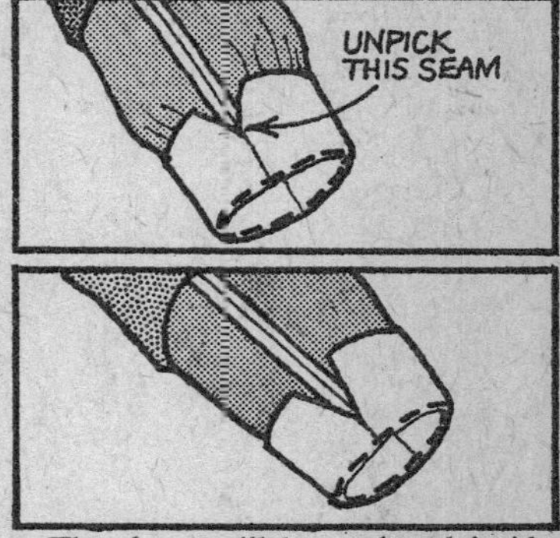

4 The sleeve will be puckered inside the fold. Unpick the sleeve seam or seams gently, a little at a time from each one if there is more than one, until the sleeve lies flat inside the fold.

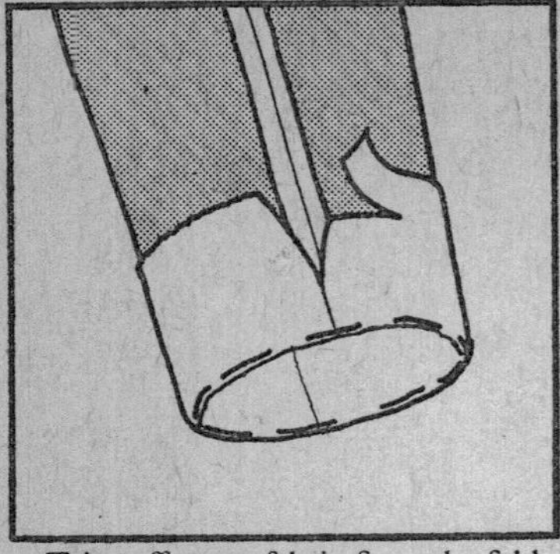

5 Trim off spare fabric from the fold-back, from the point where the edges slope away from the seam allowances.

6 Slip stitch the edges of the fold-back to the seam allowances, and slip stitch the fold-back to the sleeve.

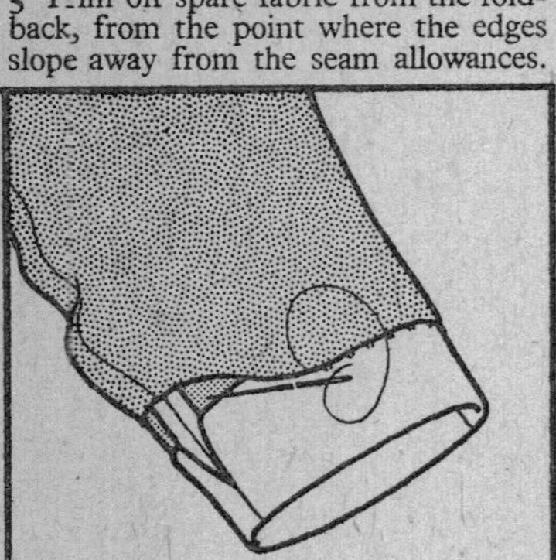

7 Turn up the lining by an equivalent amount and replace it by hemming it down to the sleeve the same distance from the edge as it was before. (Match up with the other sleeve for this).

coat sleeves lengthening

The amount by which you can lengthen a sleeve depends on the amount of turning available to let down, and also the seam allowance of the lining. You must show at least ½ in of the main fabric, and you must bring the lining over the sewn edge to give a neat finish. At the same time you must not drag the lining, which has to have plenty of fullness.

1 Unpick the lining and the hem inside the sleeve and press out the fold mark on a sleeve board, as on page 69 .

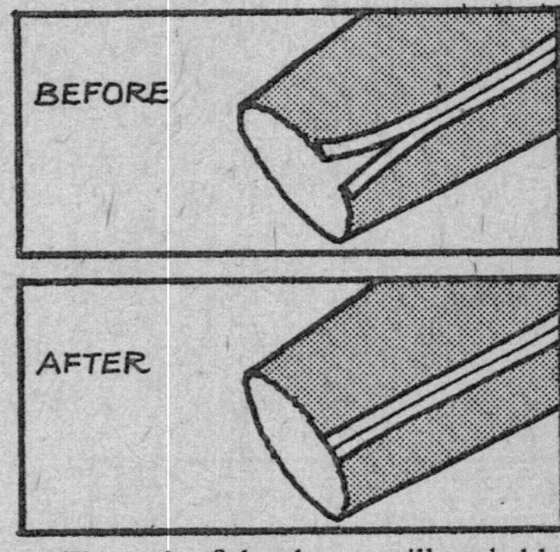

2 The ends of the sleeves will probably not be stitched in order to lie flat, so you must sew them together.

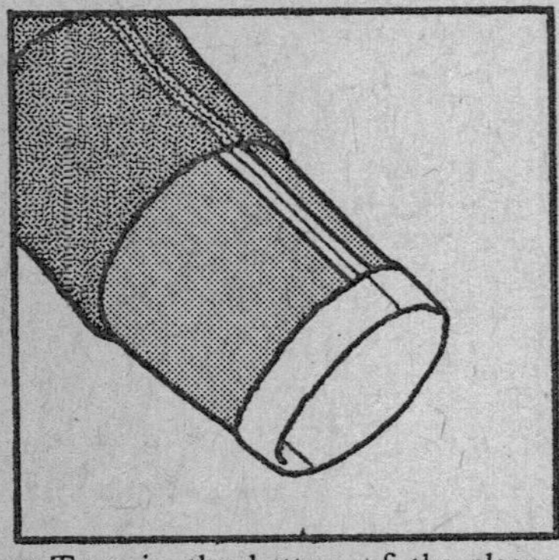

3 Turn in the bottom of the sleeve making sure the hem is not less than ½ in.

4 Slip stitch the turning to the outer fabric.

5 Pull down the lining and turn it under by the smallest possible amount.

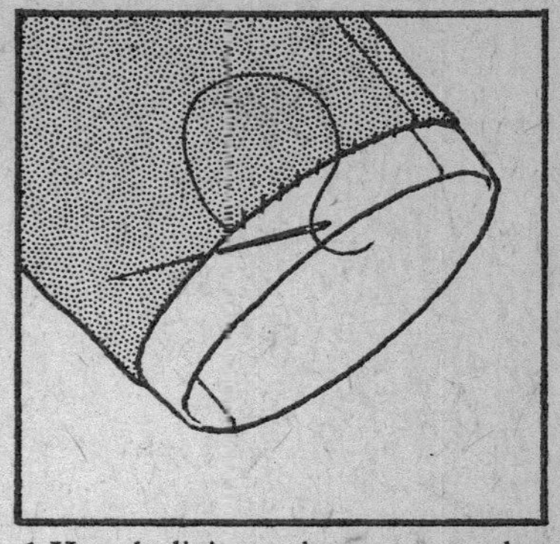

6 Hem the lining to the outermost edge of the fold-back.

cutting and facing a v neck

You can re-style an existing dress this way.

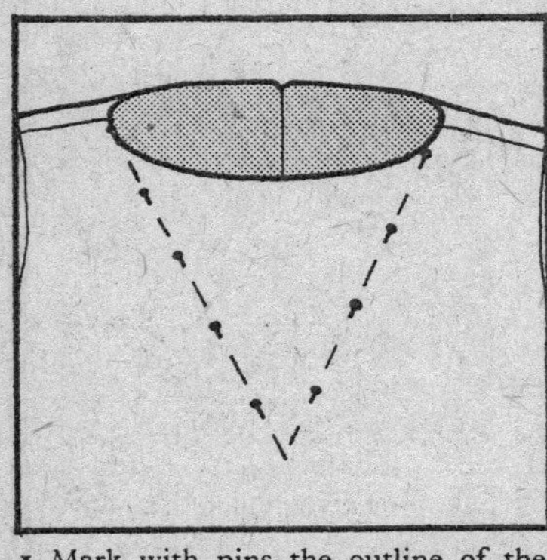

1 Mark with pins the outline of the neck and make sure it is right before you cut.

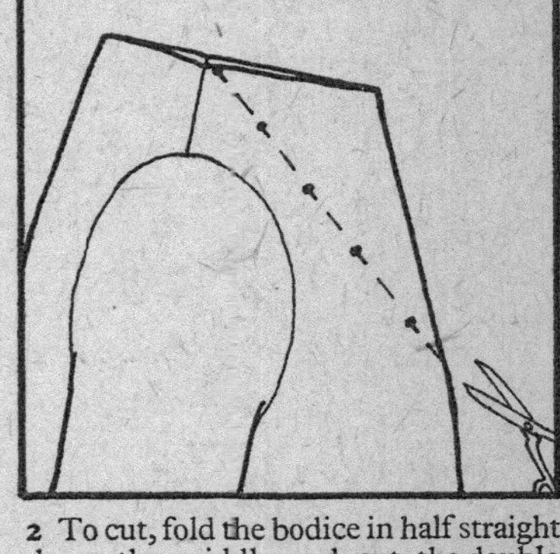

2 To cut, fold the bodice in half straight down the middle and cut the double fabric from the base of the V to the shoulder seam.

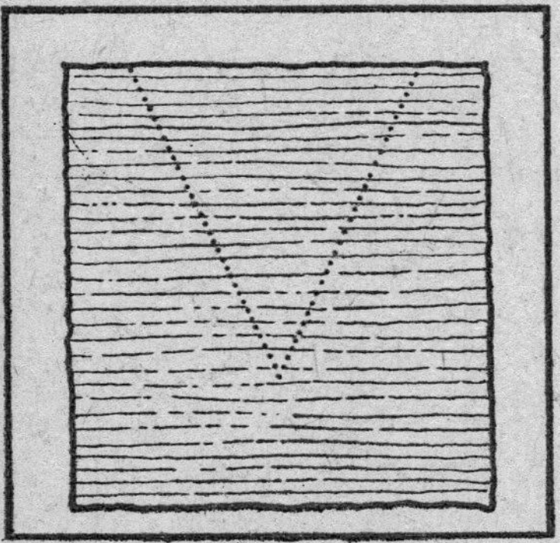

3 For the facing, cut an oblong of fabric 3 in. wider than the neck, and 3 in. longer than the V.

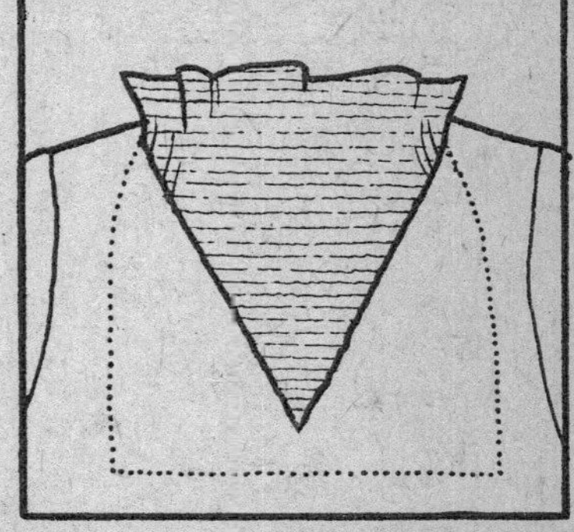

4 Lay the garment down flat, front uppermost, and place the oblong of facing underneath the front bodice with the bottom edge $1\frac{1}{2}$ in. below the point of the V.

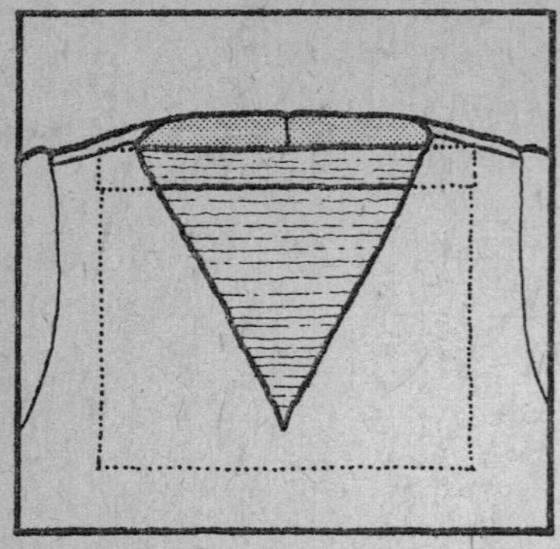

5 Fold over the top edge to tuck under the shoulder seam.

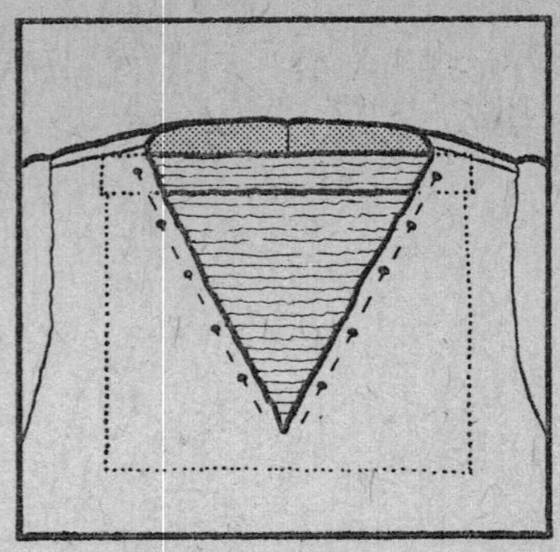

6 Pin in position either side of the V.

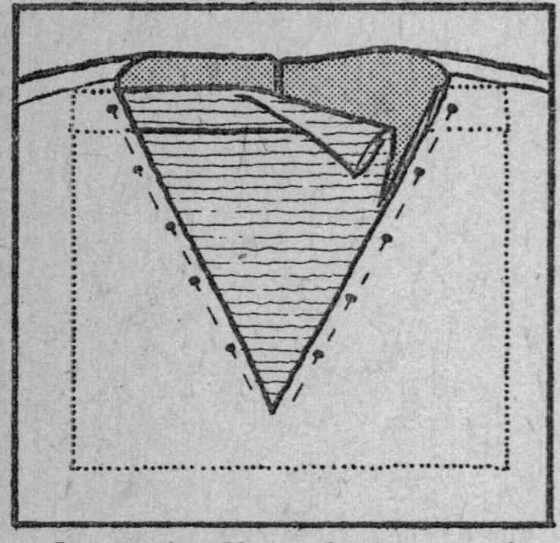

7 Cut another V exactly the same size out of the oblong of facing.

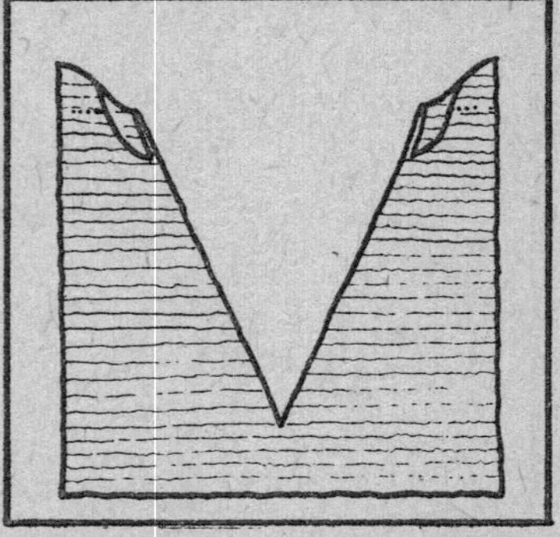

8 Discard the middle piece and open out the fold at the top of the other piece.

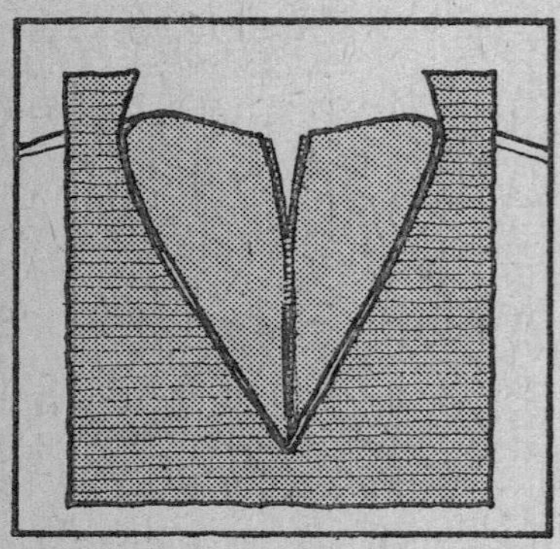

9 On the right side of the dress, place the facing right side down, matching the point of the V and the neck edges.

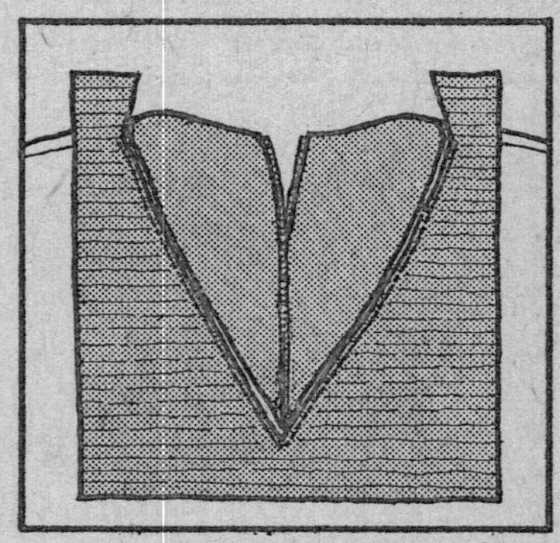

10 Sew the two together $\frac{1}{8}$ in. in from the edge to $\frac{1}{8}$ in. below the point of the V.

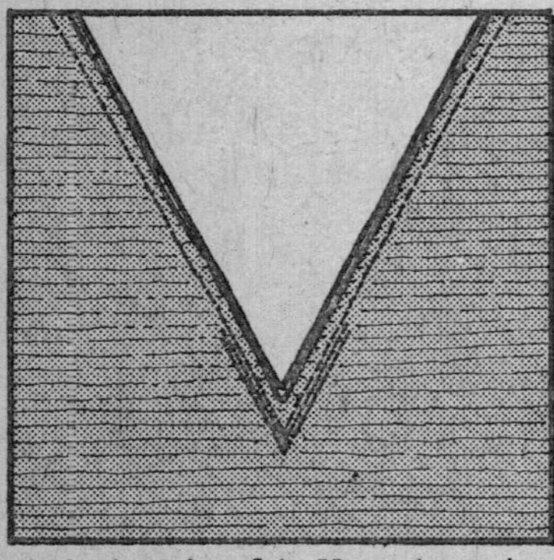

11 At the point of the V put the sewing back in the machine and sew round the V twice more for strengthening.

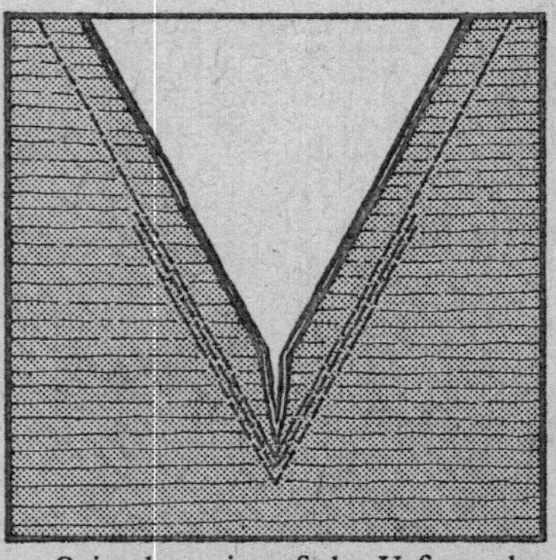

12 Snip the point of the V from the edge to the sewing line.

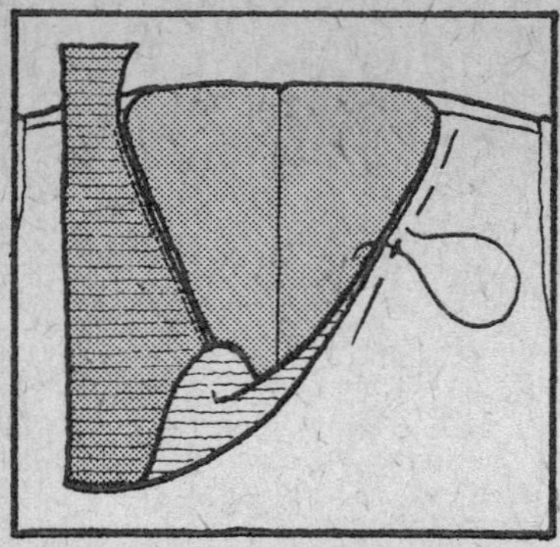

13 Turn the facing to the back of the bodice and tack it down.

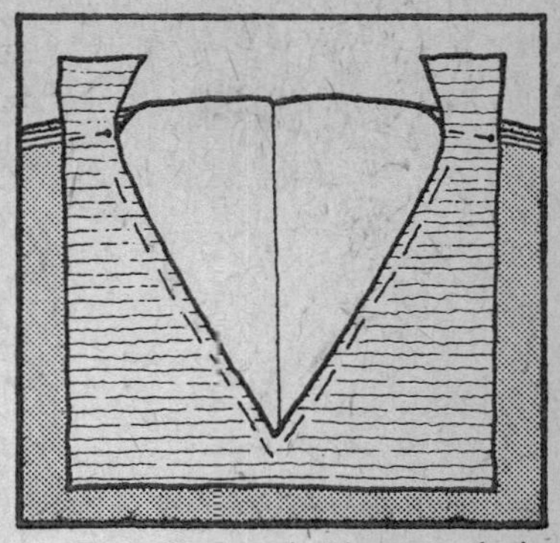

14 Turn the dress inside out and pin the facing to the shoulder seam.

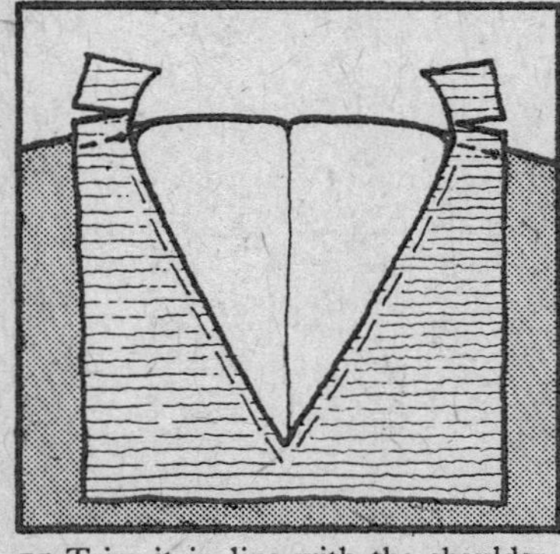

15 Trim it in line with the shoulder, leaving ½ in. seam allowance.

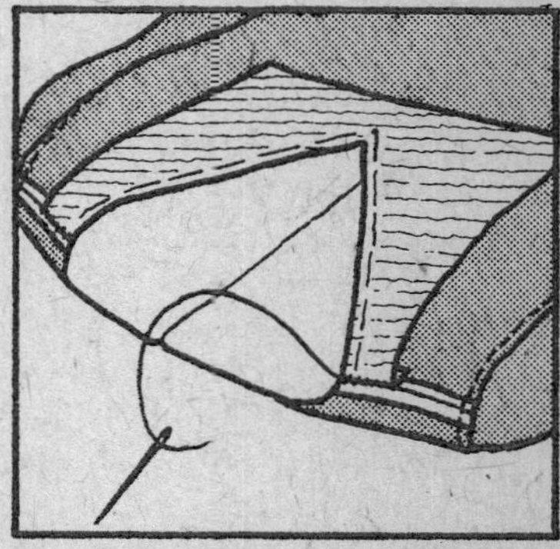

16 Turn under the seam allowance on both shoulders and hem down at the previous seam.

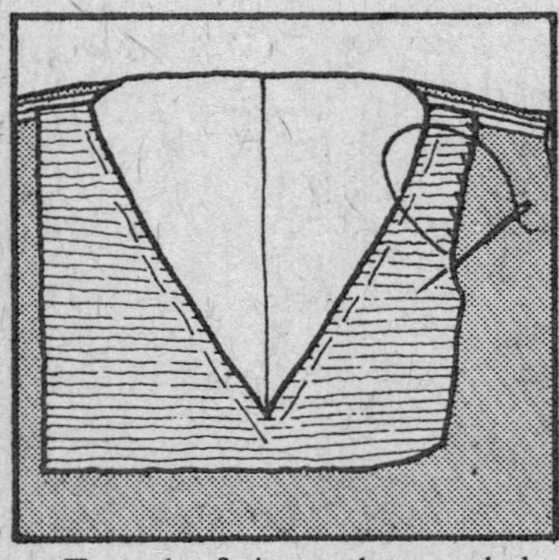

17 Turn the facing under round the other three edges and oversew for neatness.

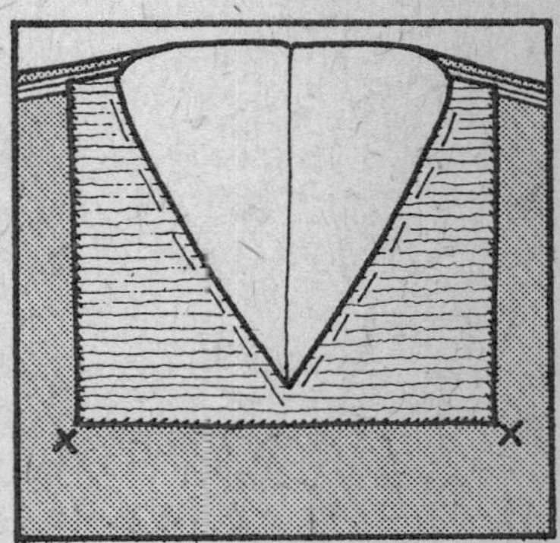

18 Catch the facing very lightly to the bodice at the corners only.

If you wish to make a firmer neckline by inserting interfacing, proceed as far as 8.

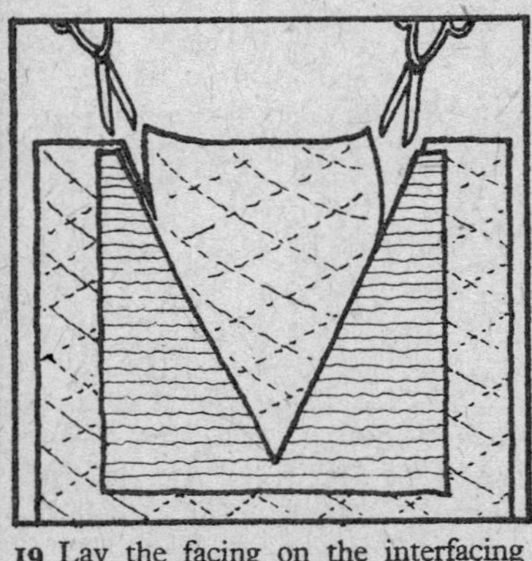

19 Lay the facing on the interfacing and cut out a V.

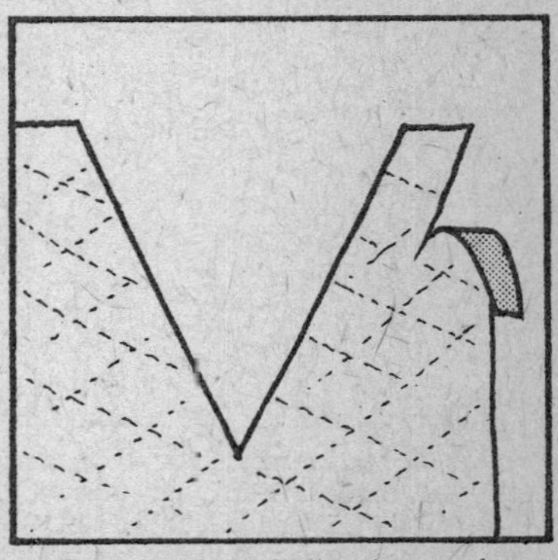

20 Remove the middle piece and cut the interfacing again 2½ in. from the first cutting line.

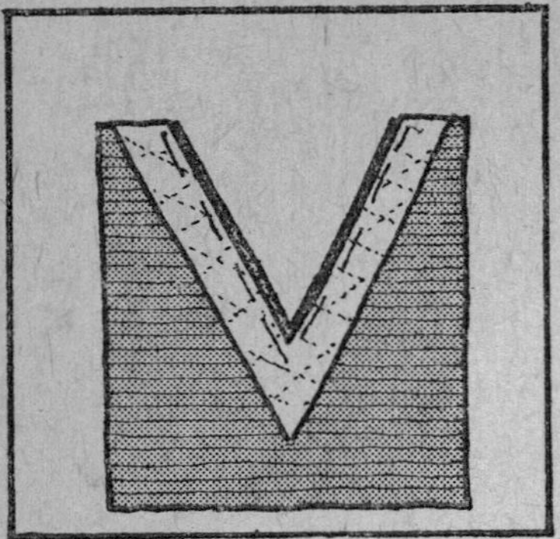

21 Tack the interfacing V to the wrong side of the facing V, matching at the point of the V and along the sides. Proceed as 9 onwards.

lengthening or shortening where top stitching or a welted seam is used

The top stitching must be done *after* the hem has been turned, and matching thread must be used.

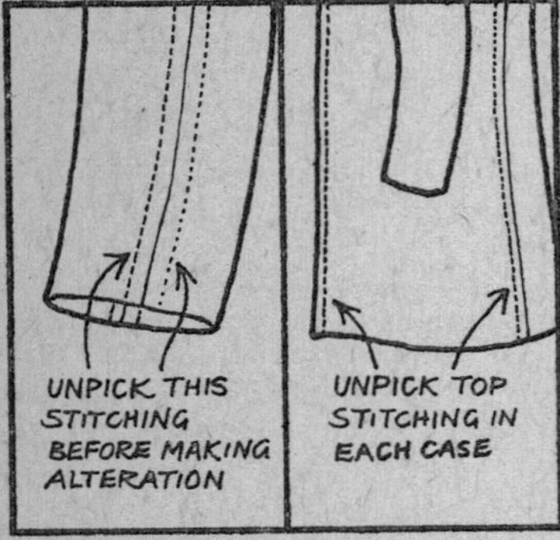

1 The same principle applies whether at the hem of a garment or the sleeve, and whether lengthening or shortening.

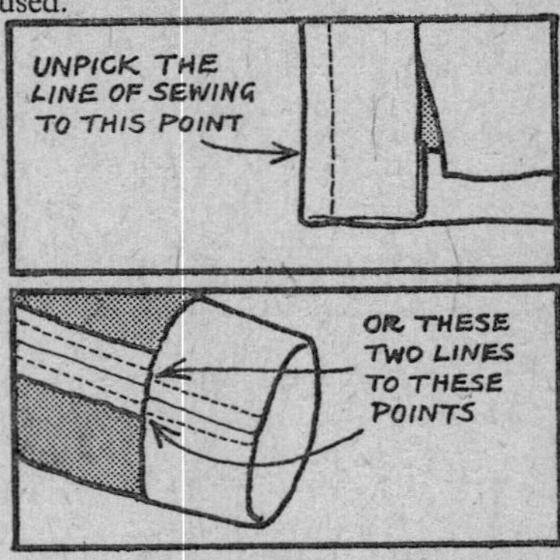

2 Unpick very carefully the top stitching or welt seam for the depth of the existing hem.

3 Unpick lining and facing as required. Shorten or lengthen the hem as appropriate.

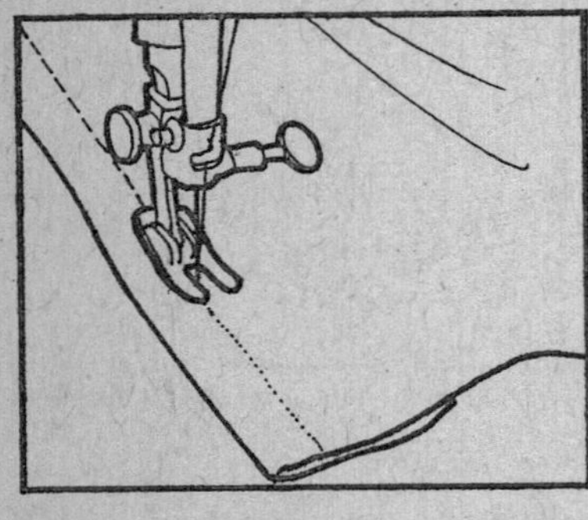

4 At hem of a coat work as page 85-86 until facing has been replaced, then re-sew on the machine, on the right side, the line of top stitching in the groove which will already be there.

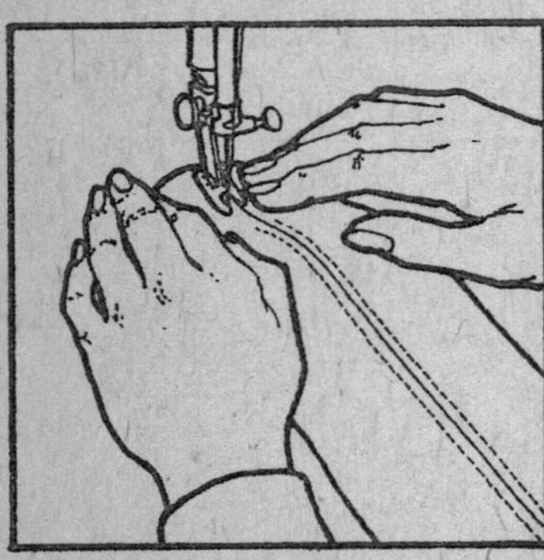

5 For a sleeve, when you have slip-stitched the new turning, place the work in the machine and re-sew the top stitched seams. If you are a novice it will be easier to work from the edge back to the original sewing.

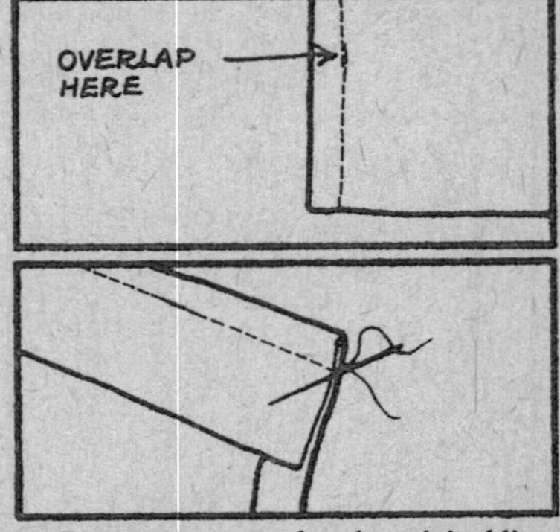

6 In every case overlap the original line of sewing as on page 20 and fasten off ends of thread securely.

alterations to children's clothes

Children's clothes are comparatively easy to alter because of the lack of shaping. The following are a few of the most common adjustments, but others will be found in the appropriate sections which can easily be used for children's clothes.

shortening sleeves

Do not cut anything away. Children grow and you may want to let them out again.

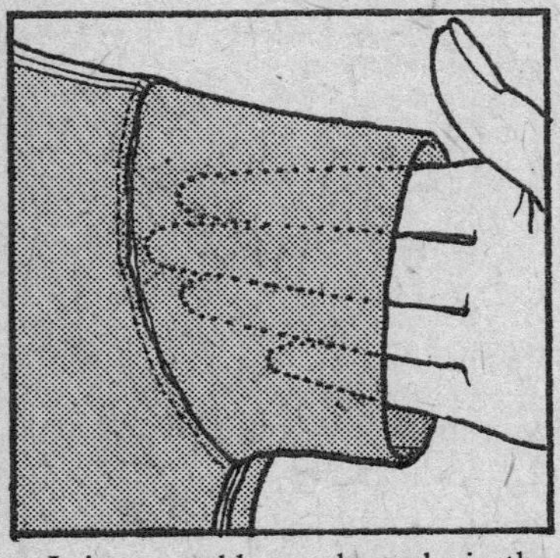

1 It is acceptable to take tucks in the upper sleeves of shirts. Turn the sleeve inside out and then turn all but a quarter of it back again.

2 Sew about $\frac{1}{2}$ in. in from the fold (which will shorten the sleeve by 1 in.) all the way round, preferably by hand as this will show less sign of previous stitching if you have to let it out again.

You can also shorten at the cuff:

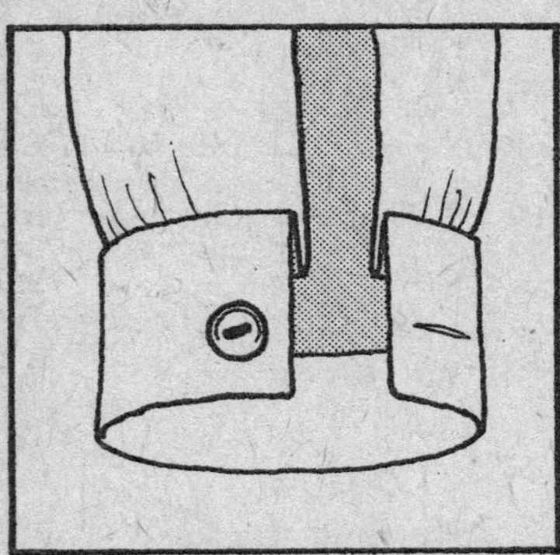

1 Take a tuck on the inside of the sleeve where it joins the cuff.

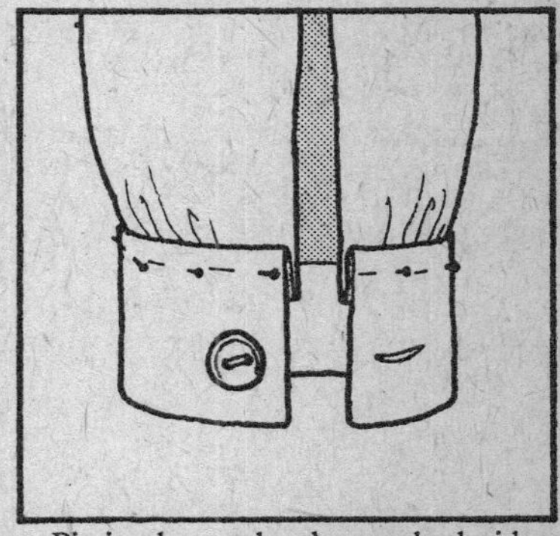

2 Pin in place and make sure both sides of the opening match.

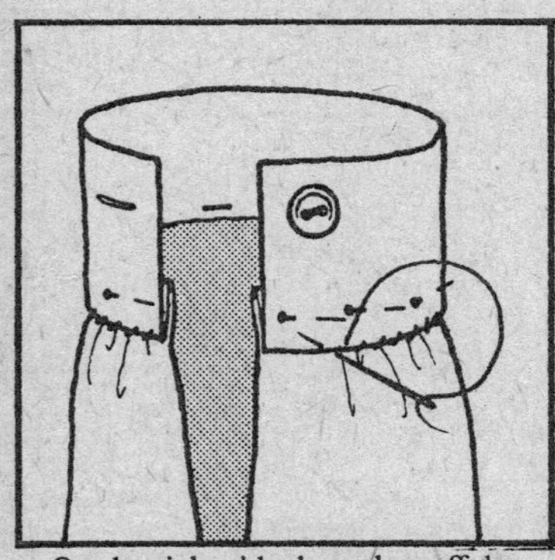

3 On the right side, hem the cuff down to the sleeve neatly

If necessary you can take tucks in both places, letting out one at a time as the child grows.

waisted dress too tight

There is more scope for the unskilled here because there is little or no bust shaping. The best way is to insert a pretty braid or lace.

Buy lace or braid narrow or wide according to how much bigger you want to make the bust, bearing in mind that you will be inserting four widths.

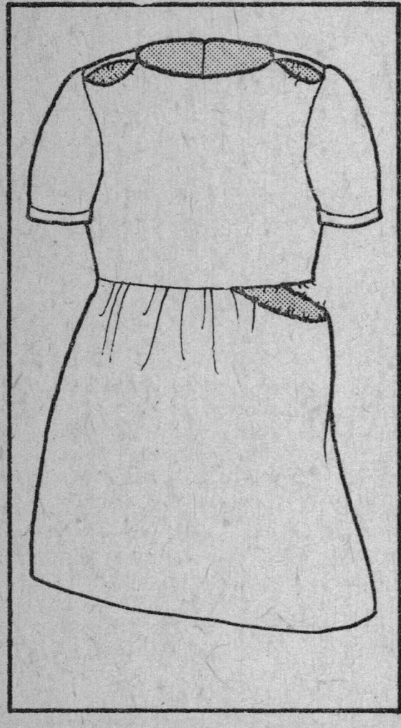

1 Unpick the shoulder and waist seams.

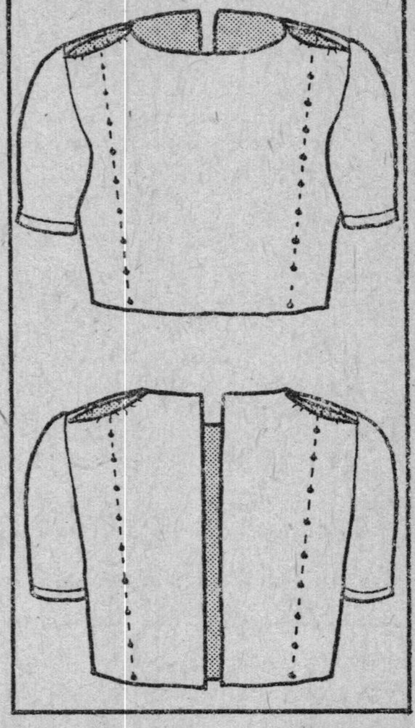

2 Mark, with pins, a straight line from the centre of the shoulders to the waist on either side of the front and also the back.

3 When you are satisfied that the lines are straight, cut the fabric from top to bottom, back and front separately.

4 Turn under, towards the wrong side, a very small hem, about $\frac{1}{8}$ in. down each of the cut edges.

5 Sew with plain stitches for strengthening.

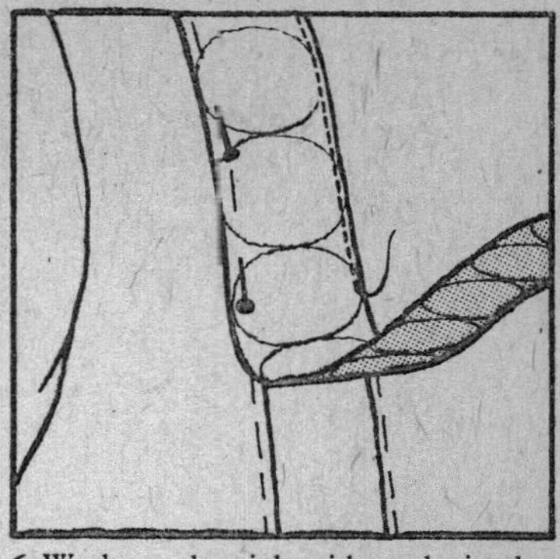

6 Work on the right side and pin the edges of the braid or lace over the small hems you have made. Sew in place.

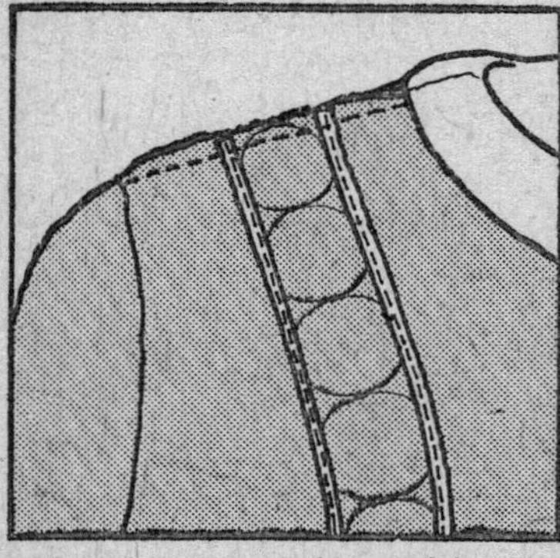

7 On the wrong side re-join the shoulder seams.

8 The bodice will now be bigger than the skirt at the waist.

Proceed with whichever of the following alternatives is appropriate:

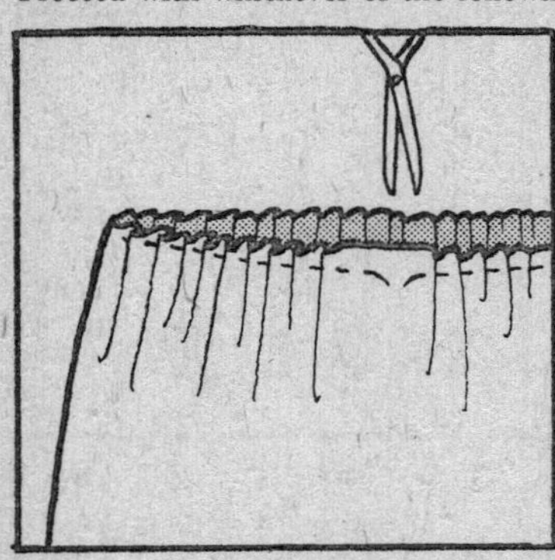

9 If the skirt is gathered, unpick the previous gathering by snipping the thread and pulling out.

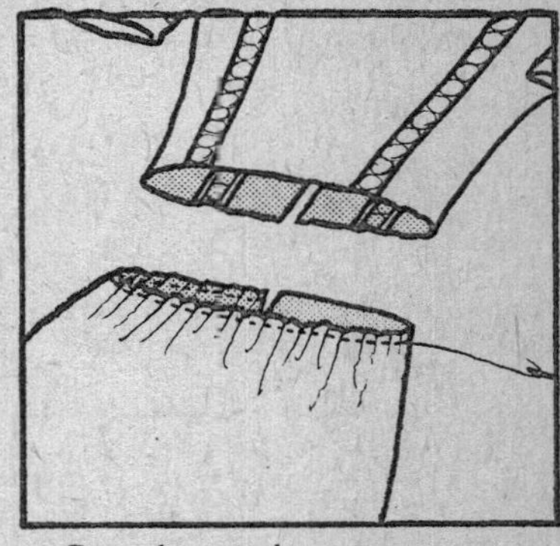

10 Re-gather as shown on page 19, and adjust to fit the bodice.

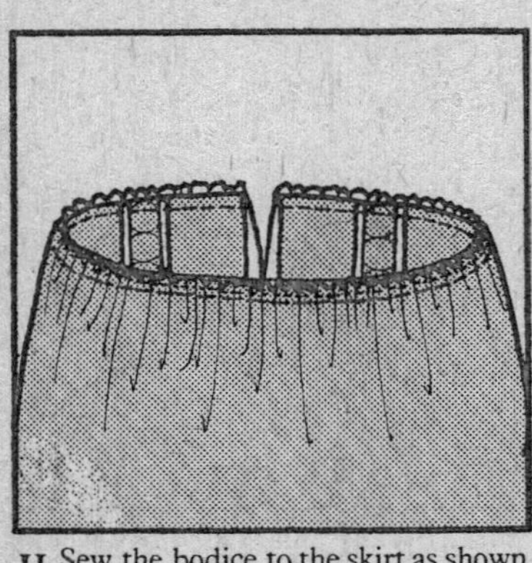

11 Sew the bodice to the skirt as shown on page 77.

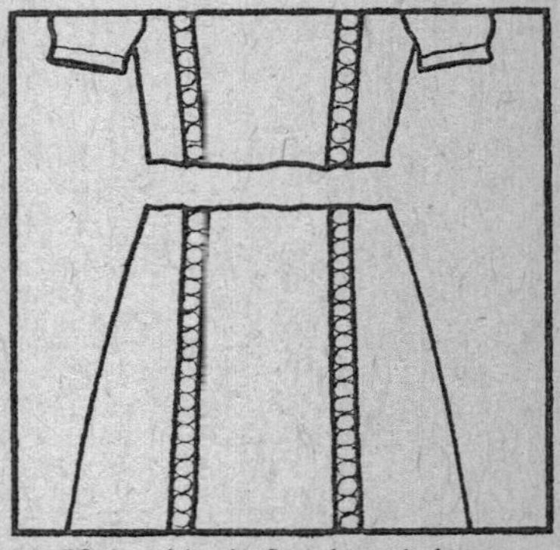

12 If the skirt is flared, and the seam allowances are not sufficient to let out, insert strips as for the bodice, so that they line up with those in the bodice.

13 Flared skirts are cut on the cross, or bias, so the sewing edge will be stretchy. Before you turn under the ⅛ in. hem as in 4, machine sew each cut edge. Re-join the bodice to the skirt as on page 77.

14 The insertion must come to the bottom edge of the fabric and be turned up with the hem, as part of it.

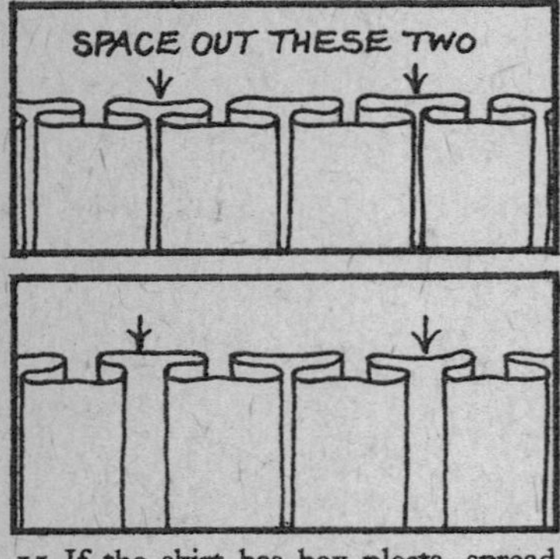

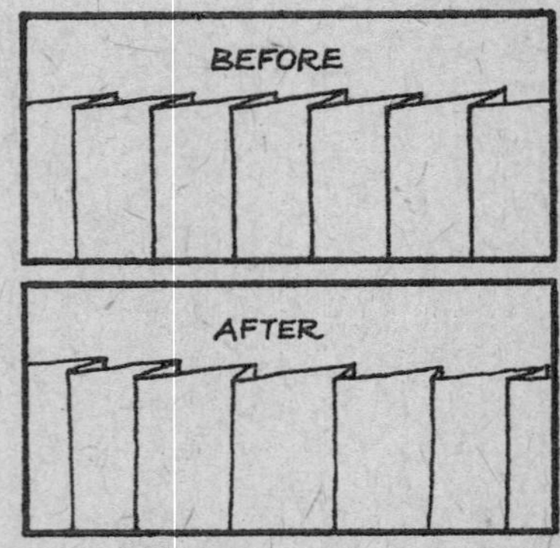

15 If the skirt has box pleats, spread out the space between the two pleats either side of centre, back and front.

16 For kilt-type pleats, spread the middle three back and front by bringing forward the folds at the back of the pleats.

Whichever type of skirt, re-join to the bodice as on page 77, and blind hem the skirt bottom as page 36, if necessary.

straight dress too tight

1 Unpick the shoulder seams and the hem.

2 Insert braid or lace from shoulder to bottom edge as instructed on 104-5.

Re-sew shoulders as for bodice, page 105. The insertion must come to the bottom edge of the fabric as 14 above. Blind hem the bottom as page 36.

taking in a waisted dress

Tucks, on the outside, are the answer here but make two or more in order to create design rather than have a make-do-and-mend look.

1 Start by unpicking the shoulder and waist seams as on page 104.

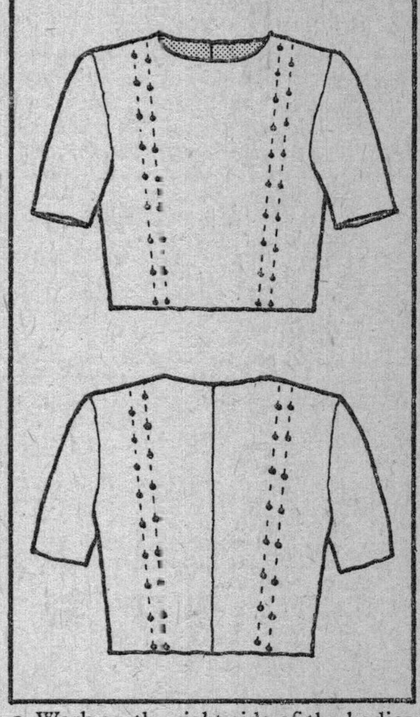

2 Work on the right side of the bodice and mark two straight lines with pins, 1 in. apart, from the shoulder to the waist, on the front and back.

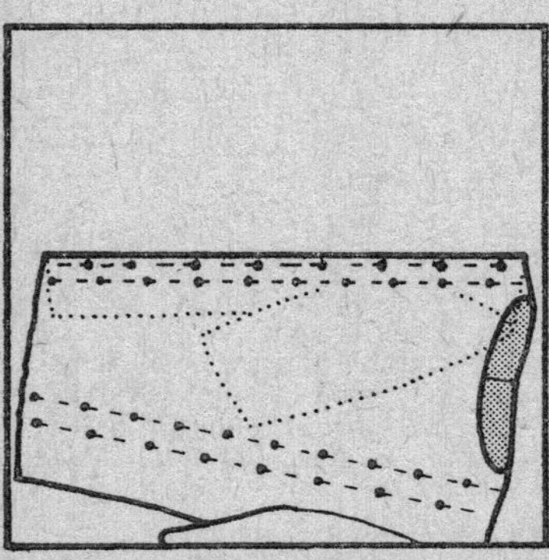

3 Turn the garment so that you are working sideways. Fold the bodice from shoulder to waist on the outer lines first. Pin.

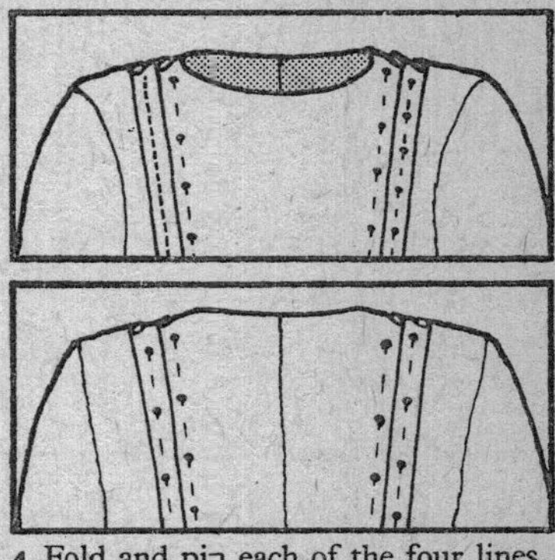

4 Fold and pin each of the four lines, fit, adjust and sew.

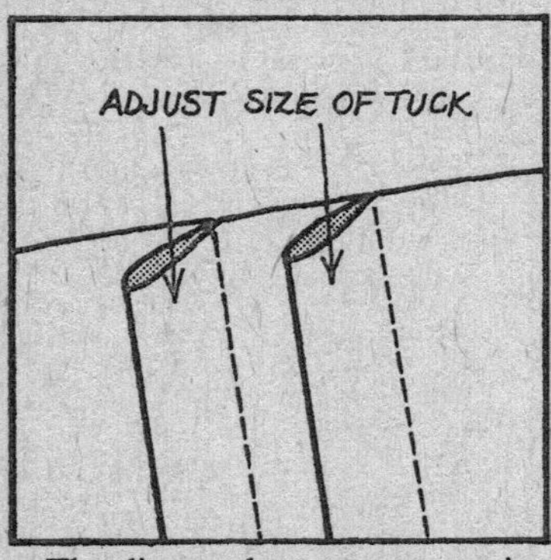

5 The distance between your sewing line and the fold depends on how much you are taking in, but they must all be the same.

The skirt will now be bigger than the bodice, so reduce the waist by one of the following alternatives:

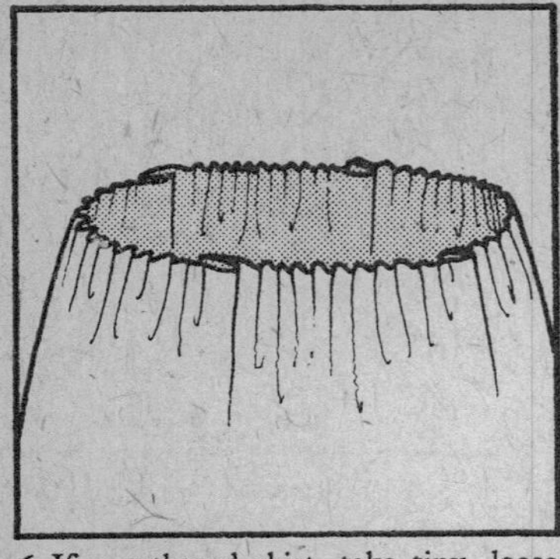

6 If a gathered skirt, take tiny, loose tucks in the gathering here and there If they are tiny, they will never show among the gathers.

7 Make small darts as shown on page 33.

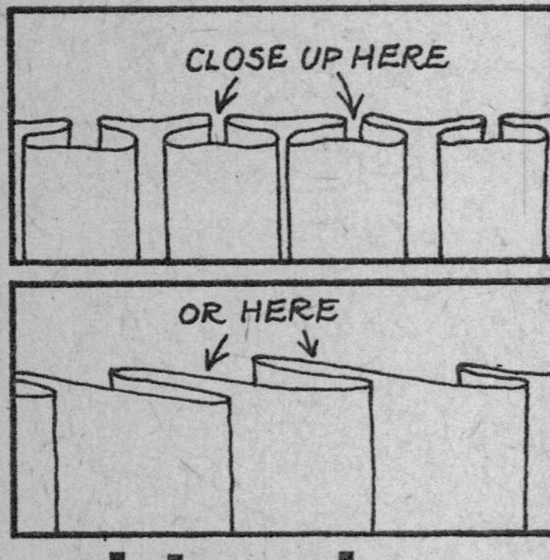

8 If a pleated skirt, increase the size of some of the pleats by a very small amount by adjusting the back folds.

taking in a straight dress

Unpick shoulders and hem as page 106. Make tucks as for bodice, page 107.

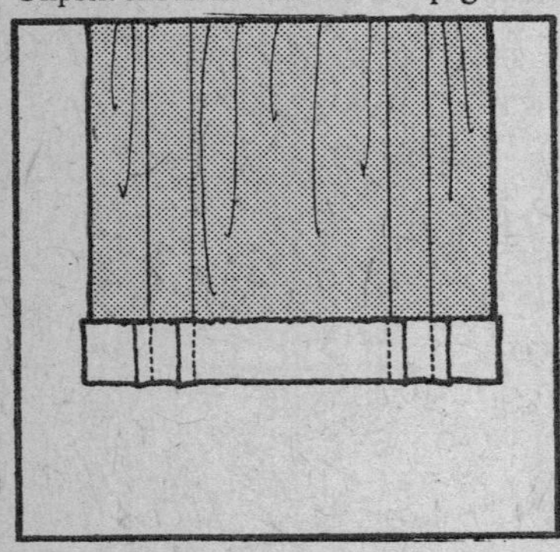

To get a neat effect it is necessary to take the tucks right down to the fabric edge, and fold them with the hem. Do not take tucks before you undo the hem, otherwise it will look too much like an alteration.

lengthening by adding a frill

This is a pretty effect suitable for children, but not necessarily for adults.
If you can't match the fabric use something which is a complete contrast.

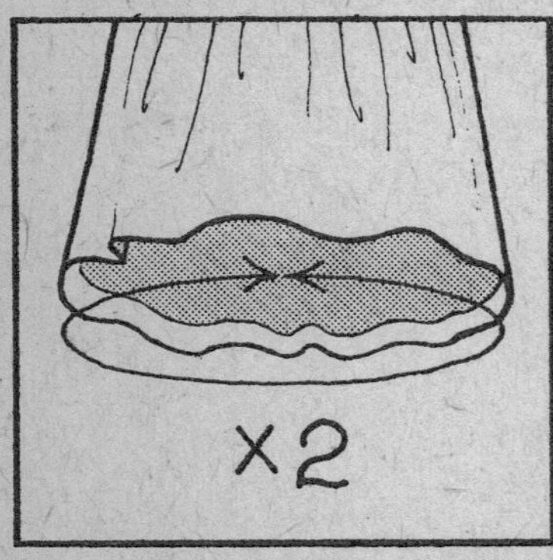

1 To make the frill, measure round the bottom of the skirt and allow at least twice this. Cut to whatever width you require. Join the ends and press open.

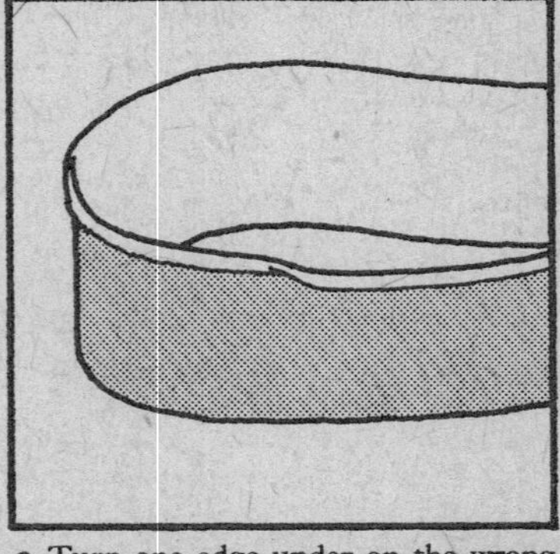

2 Turn one edge under on the wrong side by a very small amount, then turn again to make a tiny hem. Either sew on the machine or hand stitch a shell edging.

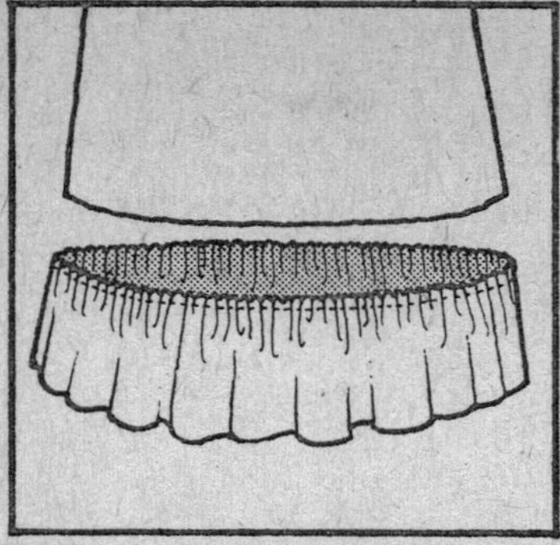

3 With double thread gather the other edge as page 19, until it fits the hem.

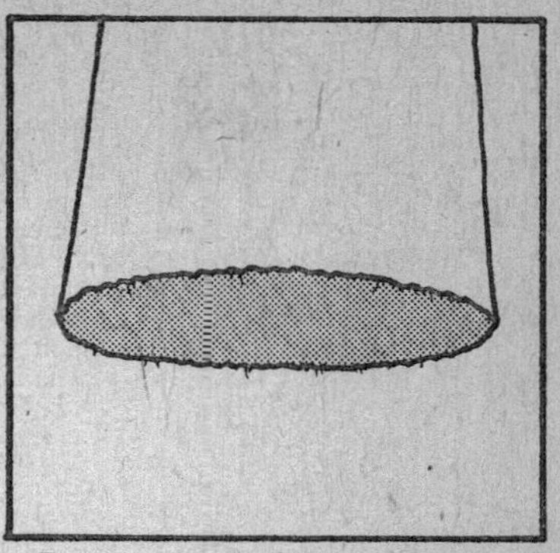

4 Do not sew the frill on to a turned up hem, it will look too amateurish. Unpick the hem and press out the old crease.

5 On the right side of the skirt pin the frilling, right side downwards, raw edges together. Tack in place.

6 Sew a plain seam $\frac{1}{2}$ in. in from the edge.

7 On the right side, fold the skirt back on the seam, so that the seam allowance is lying under the skirt and not under the frilling.

8 Top stitch $\frac{1}{4}$ in. in from this fold, all round, to anchor the seam allowance in its upward position.

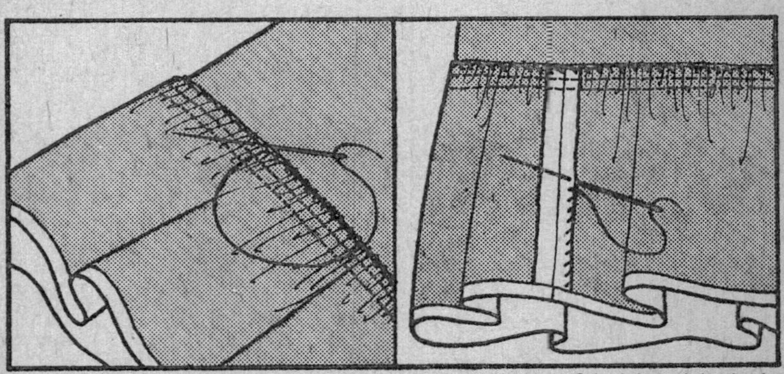

9 Oversew the raw edges together, and oversew the raw edges of the join or joins in the frill.

shortening a dress by taking tucks

This is a pretty and easy way of shortening flared and gathered skirts. There is also the advantage that as the child grows the tucks can be let out again.

Remember that each tuck will reduce the length by twice the size of the tuck. For instance, if the tuck is $\frac{1}{2}$ in. deep, the length will be reduced by 1 in.

1 It looks better if you have two small tucks rather than one big one.

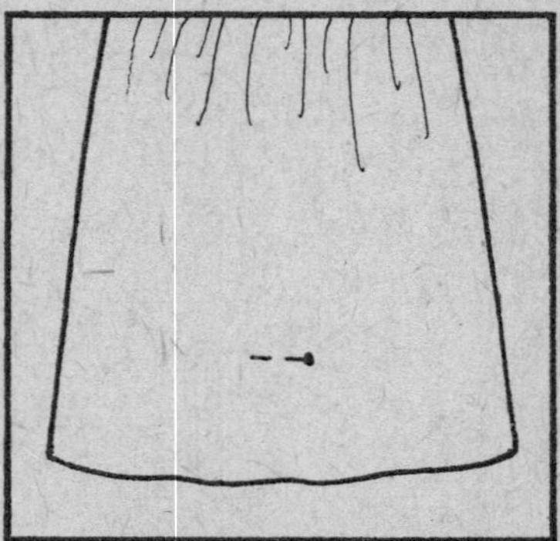

2 Put a pin in the centre front skirt at the point where you propose to fold the lower tuck.

3 Mark on a piece of cardboard the space between the lower hem and the pin.

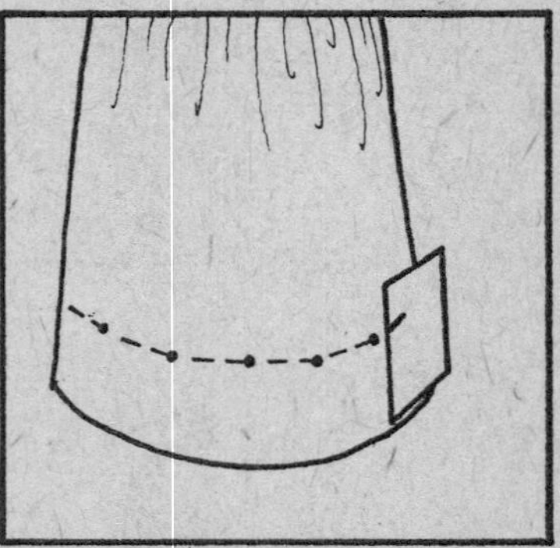

4 Using this marker continue round the skirt with pins to mark a straight line.

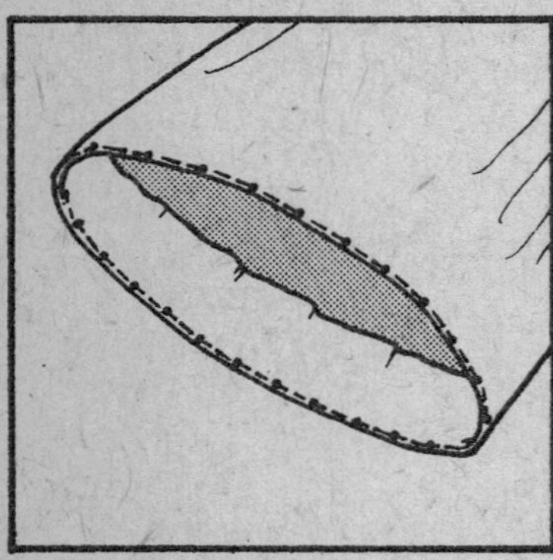

5 Working on the right side, fold in the skirt all the way round on the line you have marked.

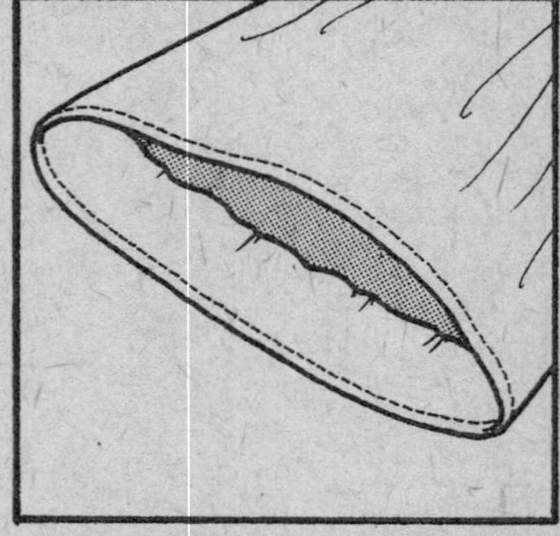

6 Sew a plain seam an appropriate distance from the fold. For instance, to reduce by 1 in. at this point, sew $\frac{1}{2}$ in. away from the fold, or as required.

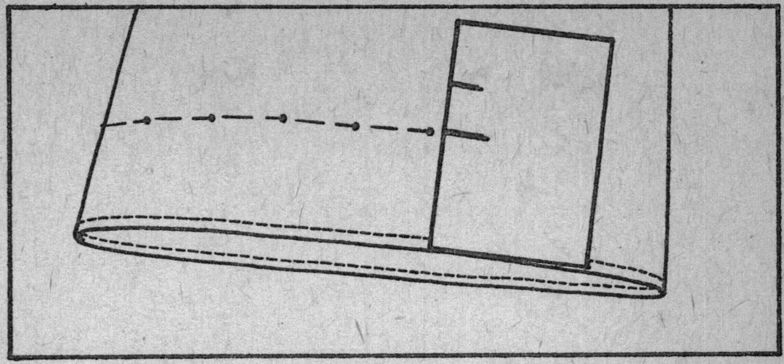

7 Make another mark on the cardboard an appropriate distance from the fold you have just made, and mark the second fold with pins. Sew as in 6.

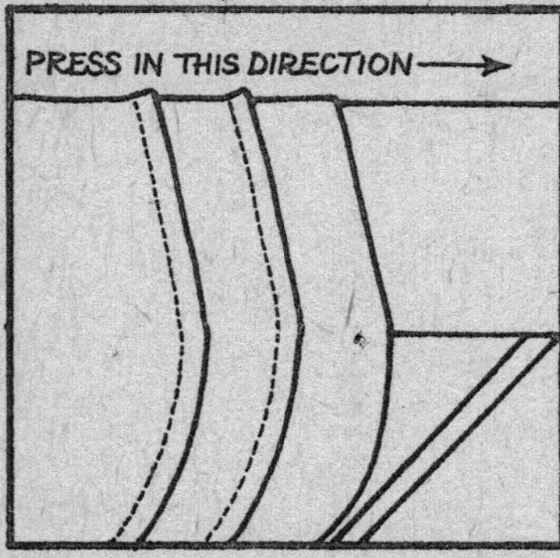

8 Press the tucks towards the hem.

mending

reinforcing worn areas to prevent tearing

This is necessary on sheets, pillowcases, serviettes and tablecloths, elbows, boys' trouser seats and lots of other things.

1 Use double cotton thread for strength and work on the right side of the fabric to keep it neat.

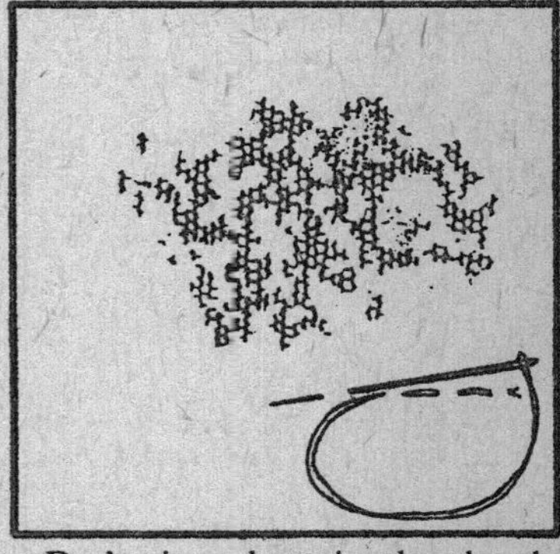

2 Don't tie a knot in the thread. Starting below and to the right of the worn area make a few small running stitches and pull the thread through until the ends are about to disappear.

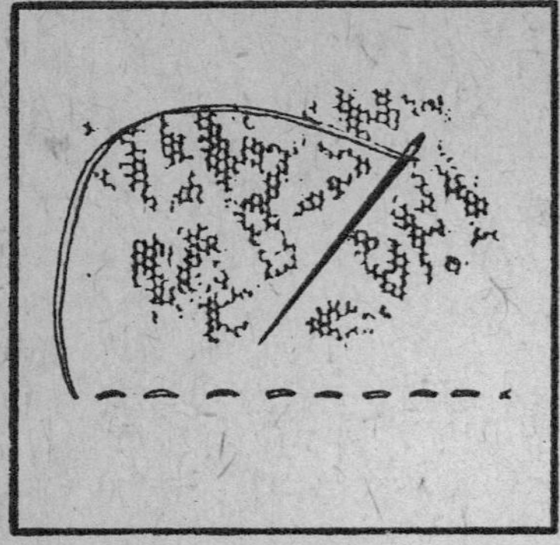

3 Continue the line of small running stitches to a point beyond the worn area on the left.

4 Turn the work round and run back again, keeping very close to the previous line of stitching. Do not pull the thread tight at the end of the row.

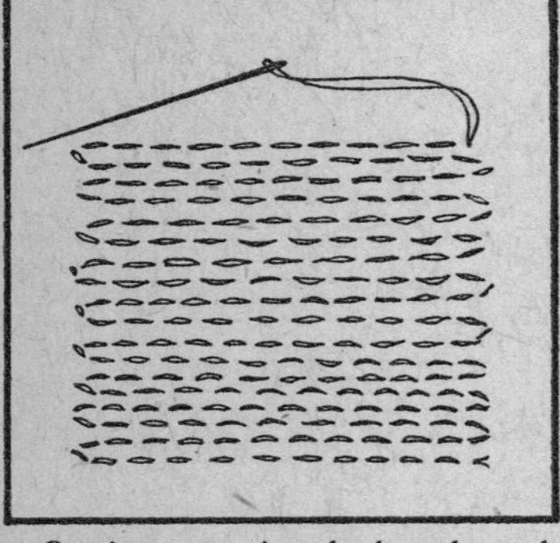

5 Continue running backwards and forwards across the worn area and finish when you reach firm fabric again.

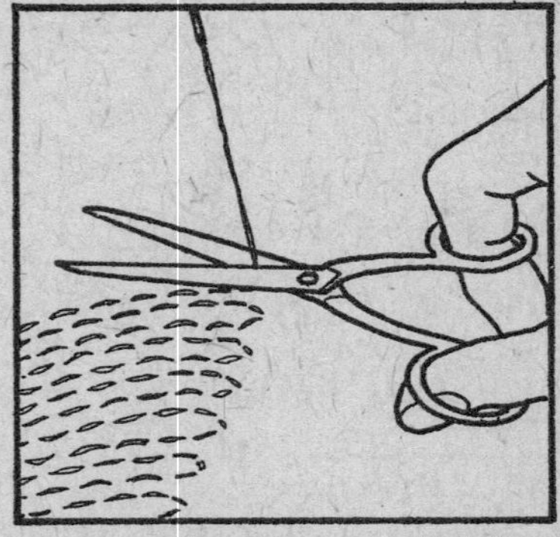

6 Do not make a heavy job of finishing off. Cut the threads close to the fabric.

tiny slits in sheets and pillowcases

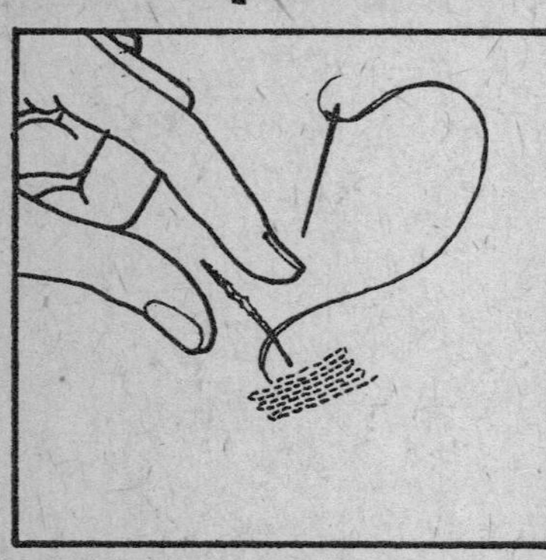

1 Hold the slit firmly together with your left hand and use the method described above, starting about ½ in. away from the slit.

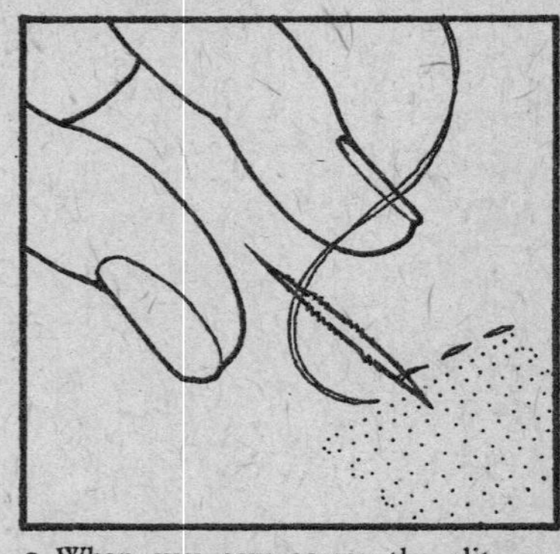

2 When you sew across the slit, go over one edge and under the other.

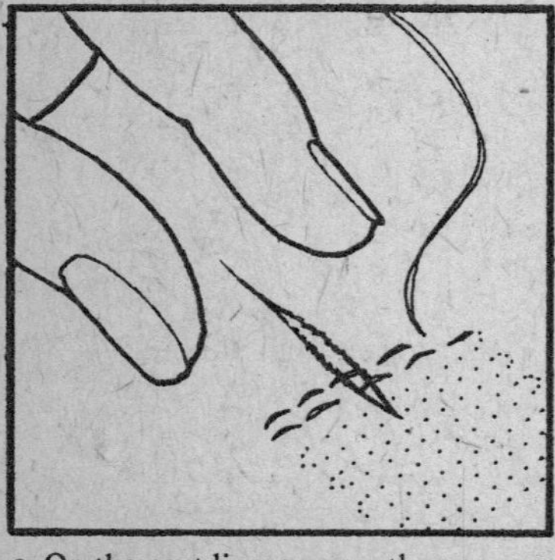

3 On the next line, go over the one you went under last time, and under the other.

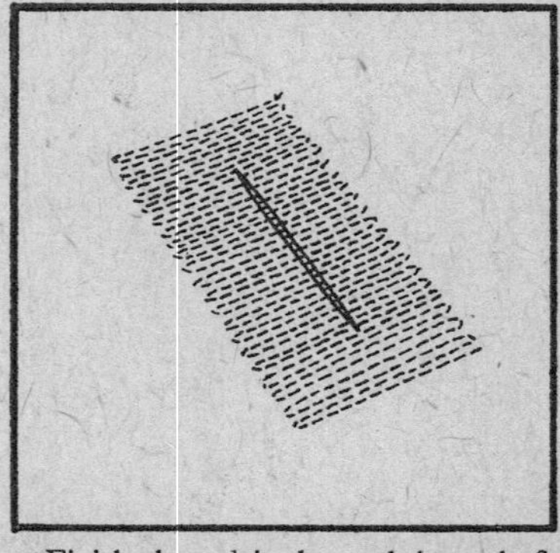

4 Finish about ½ in. beyond the end of the slit.

torn buttonhole – stitched

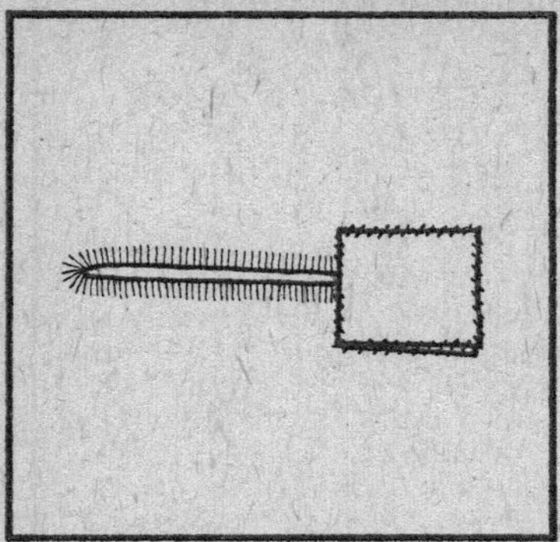

1 It's no use cobbling it together. Take a piece of tape about $1\frac{1}{2}$ in. long, fold it in half and sew it behind the torn end of the buttonhole.

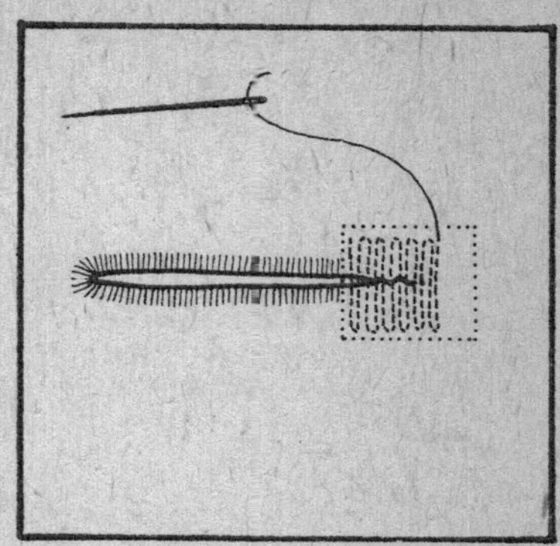

2 On the right side, stitch across the tear as on page 112, taking in the tape.

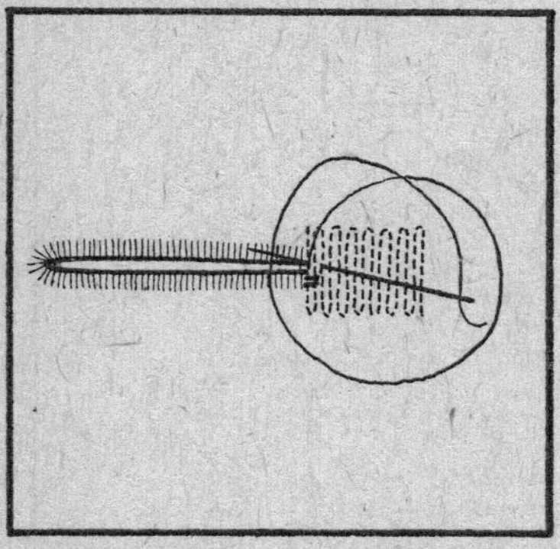

3 Buttonhole stitch the end of the buttonhole to the tape.

buttons tearing the fabric

1 Take a piece of wide tape or strong fabric, about $1\frac{1}{2}$ in. long, and fold it in half.

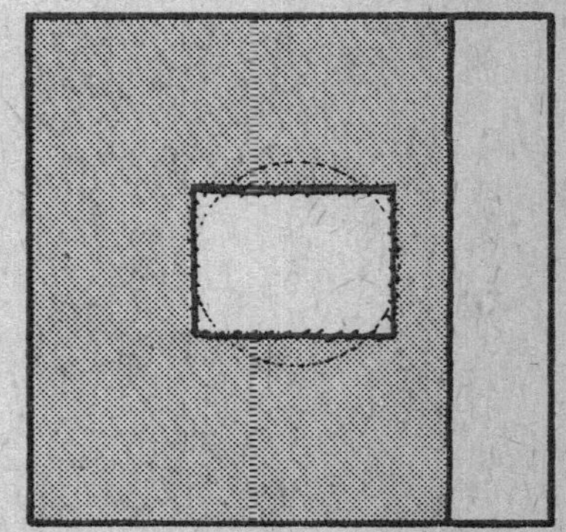

2 Hem it behind the button, on all four sides.

3 Stitch backwards and forwards across the tear as on page 112, taking in the backing.

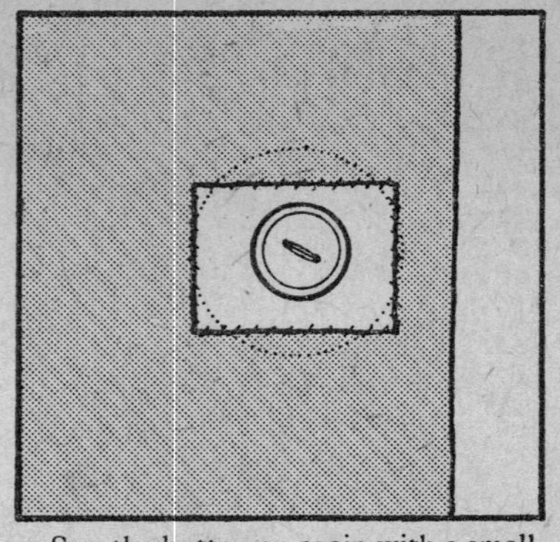

4 Sew the button on again with a small button behind it as on page 43.

seam coming unstitched

1 Don't try to sew it again on the outside.

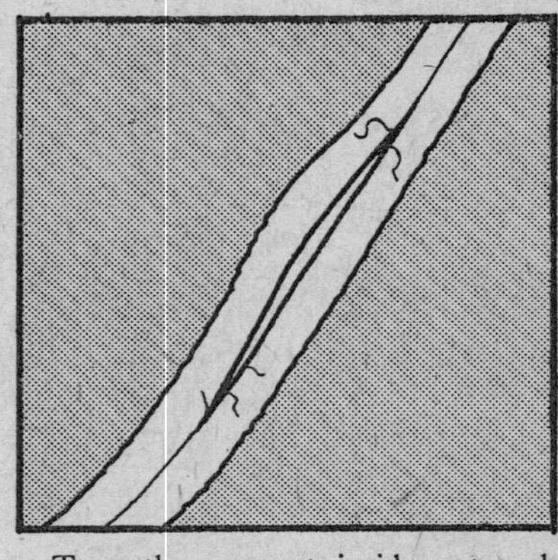

2 Turn the garment inside out and find the offending spot.

3 For neatness, pull any ends of thread to the inside.

4 Sew the unstitched seam again, beginning and ending about 1 in. either side of the open part.

invisible mending – slits and three-cornered tears

Until you can take the garment to a specialist this will do as a stop-gap, and may well do for ever.

1 Take a long human hair, red, blonde or brunette according to the colour of the fabric.

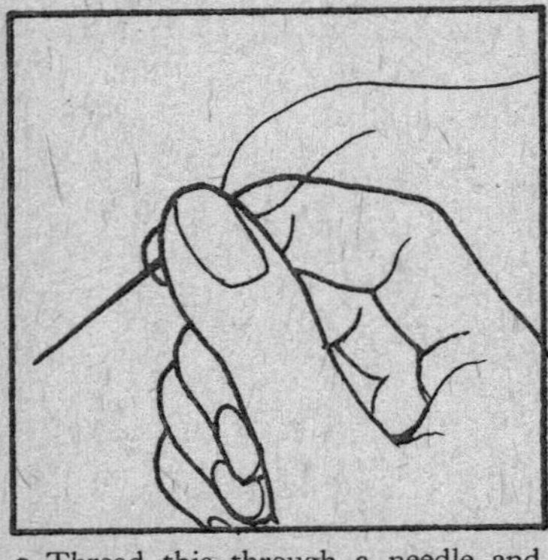

2 Thread this through a needle and hold it firmly by the eye, as hair is more slippery than thread.

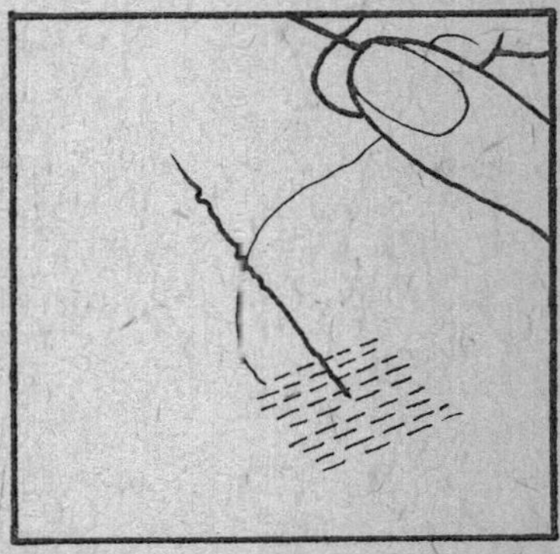

3 Weave backwards and forwards across the slit as on page 112. If the fabric is thick, weave *through* it rather than on top and underneath.

sheets – side to middle

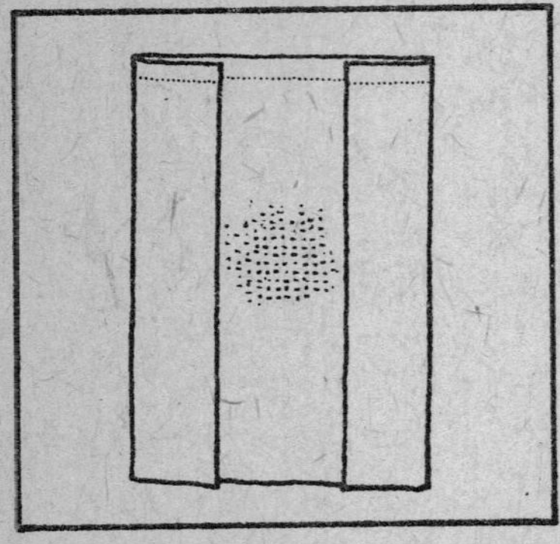

1 Lay the sheet out flat on the table, or on the floor. Fold over each side towards the middle, leaving only the worn part which you wish to cut away showing between them.

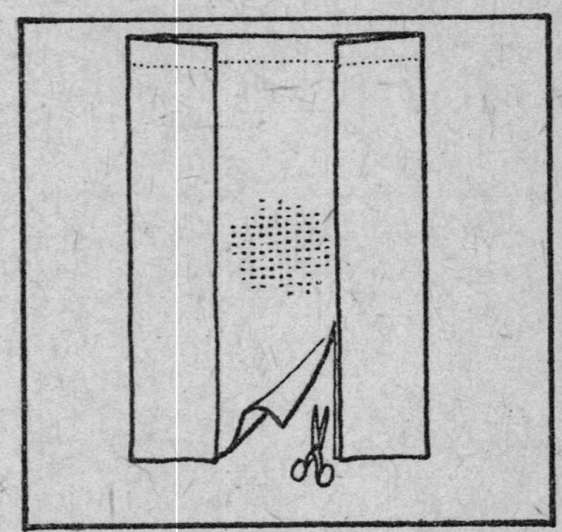

2 If you keep the folded-over pieces level with the top and bottom of the sheet, and cut against the folded-in edges down the length of the sheet, you will cut in a straight line.

3 As you are going to join the selvages together, you need only sew a plain seam as near as possible to the edge, to give the maximum width to the sheet which is left. Work on the wrong side.

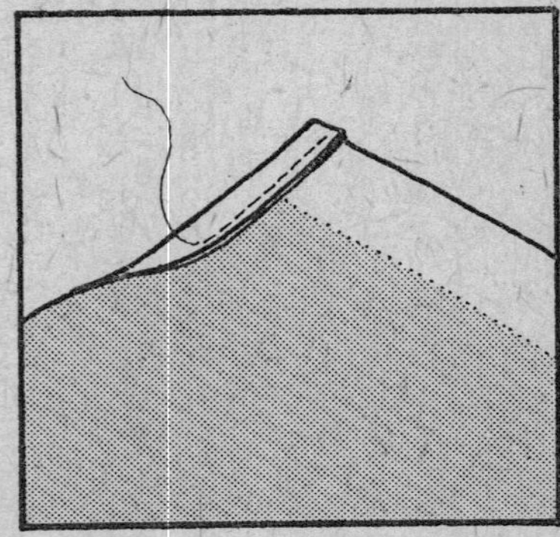

4 Fold over the side edges to a small hem, about ¼ in., on the wrong side, and sew down.

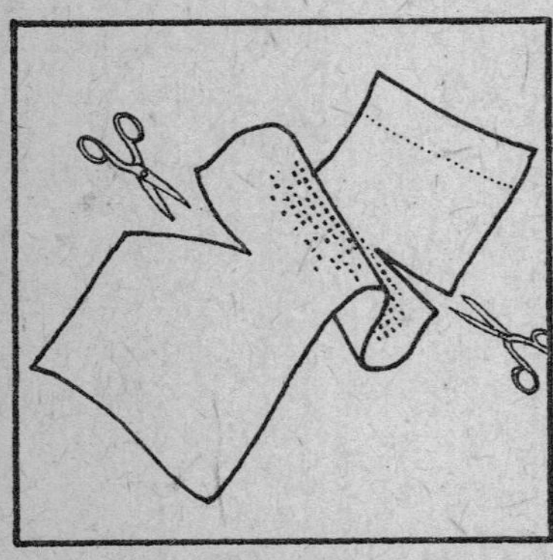

5 The sheet was very likely only worn in the middle, so, for future use, cut away the good pieces at either end of the worn part.

patching

1 Cut away, to a near square if possible, the worn part.

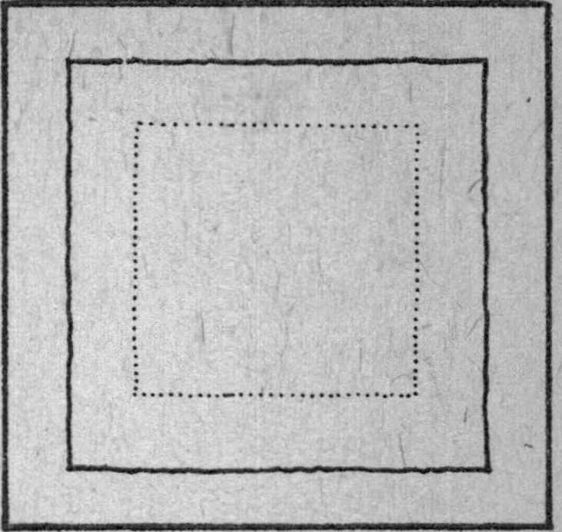

2 Take another piece of stout fabric and cut a square half as big again as the previous one.

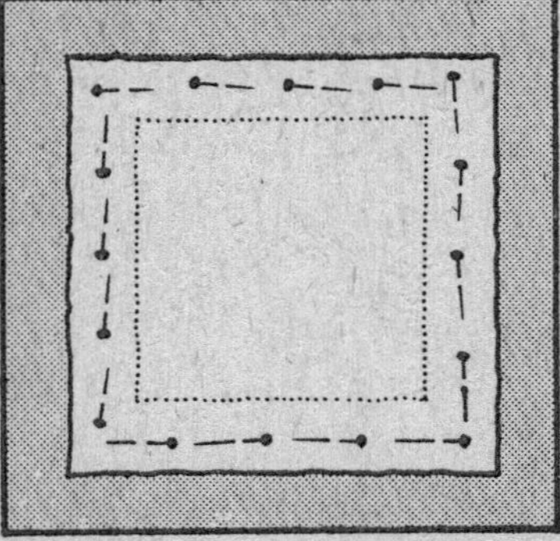

3 On the wrong side of the fabric, pin the square piece over the square hole.

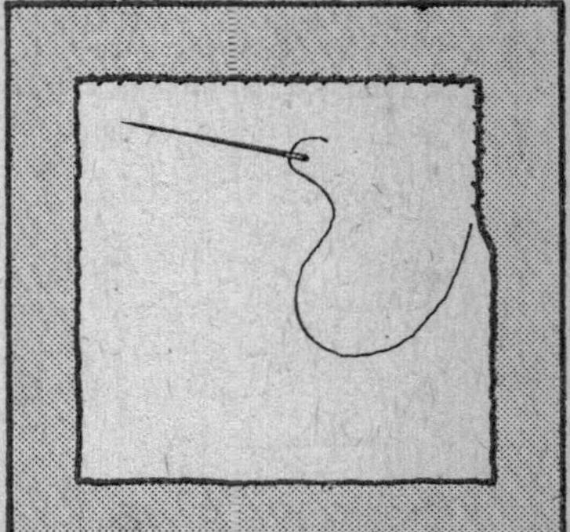

4 Turn this piece under at the edge and hem or machine sew all four sides very neatly to the main piece.

5 Turn the work back to the right side. Snip each corner about $\frac{1}{8}$ in. very carefully.

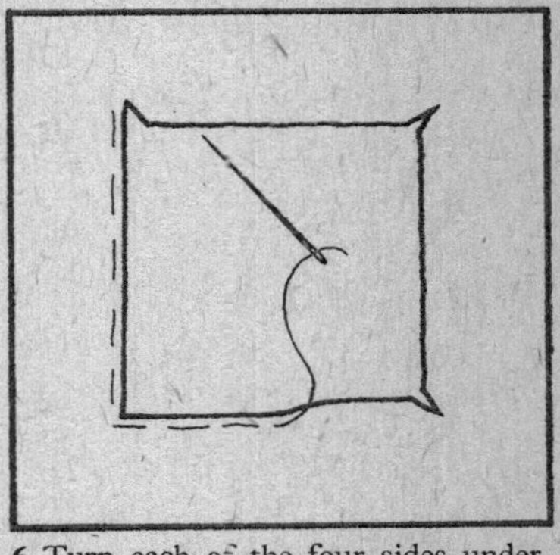

6 Turn each of the four sides under about $\frac{1}{8}$ in. and tack.

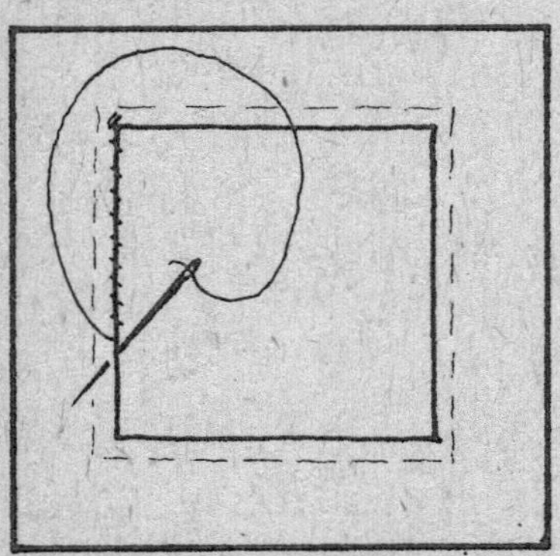

7 Hem neatly all round, putting a few extra stitches in each corner where you snipped the fabric.

three-cornered tear

Depending on where the tear is it can be dealt with in any of three ways.

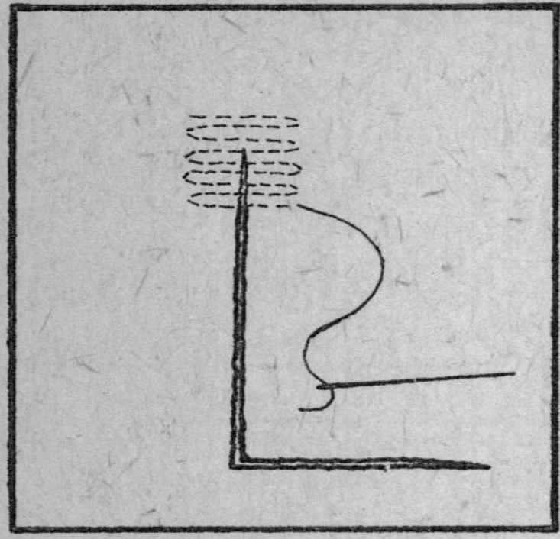

1 If there is no strain on the fabric sew backwards and forwards across the tear as on page 112.

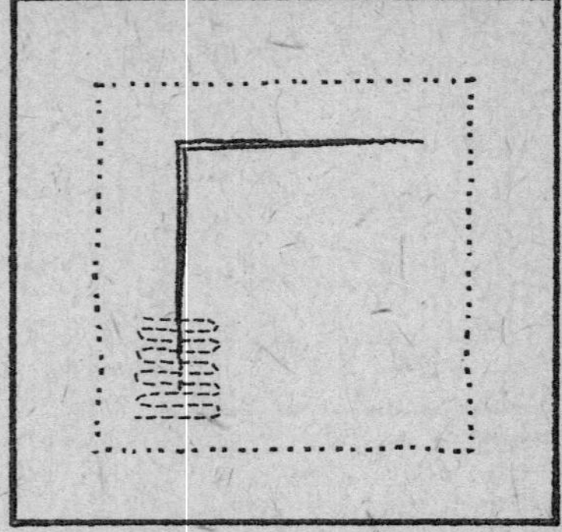

2 If it is at an elbow or knee, where it may incur further strain, place a piece of fabric behind the tear and sew as in 1, on the right side but taking in the backing as well.

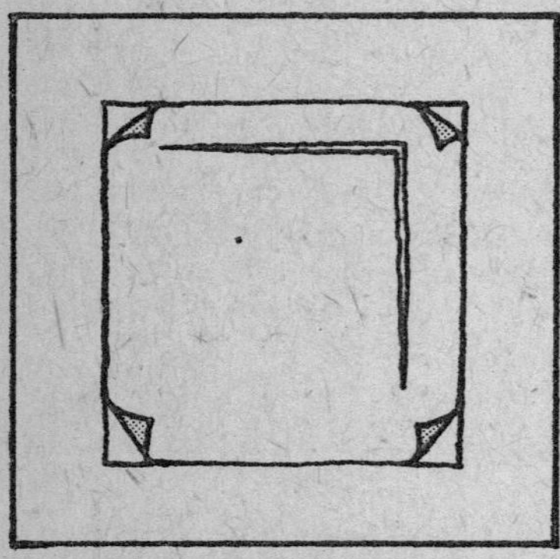

3 It could be more practical to cut out the torn area completely and put in a patch, as on page 117.

elasticated foundation garments

If you put your thumb through your foundation it doesn't have to be thrown away.

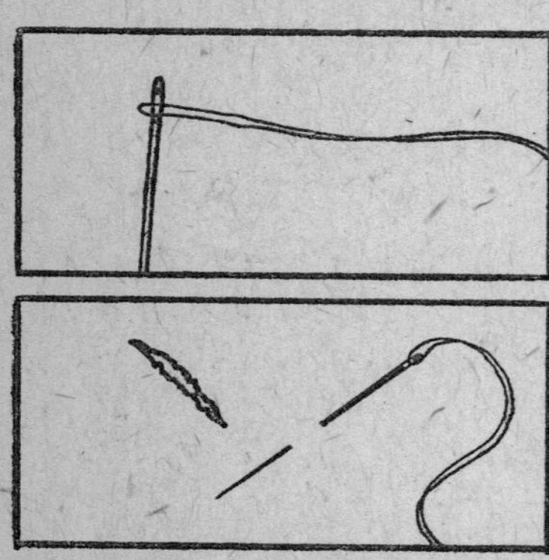

1 Use a strong double thread and prepare to deal with it as an ordinary slit as on page 112.

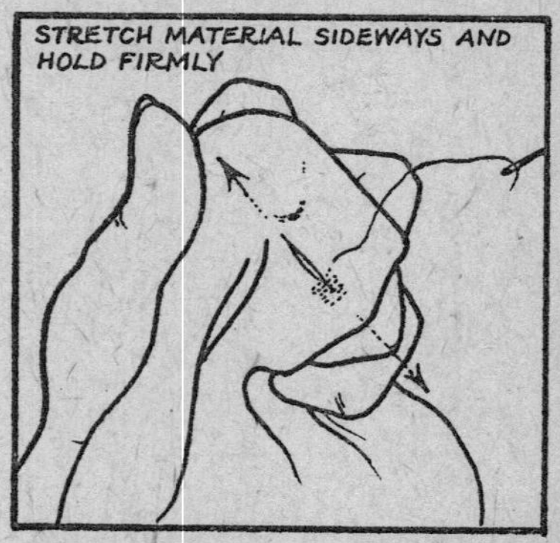

2 All the time you are sewing, keep the garment stretched to its maximum, otherwise it won't stretch when you put it on and your sewing will burst open.

re-lining a coat

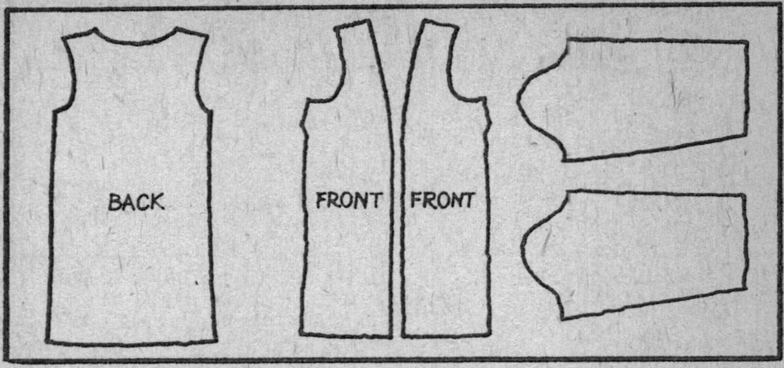

1 Very carefully take out the old lining and unpick every seam.

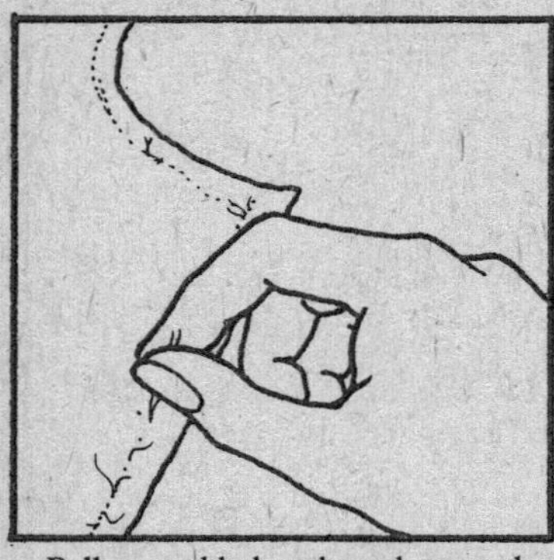

2 Pull out odd threads and press the pieces. They will be marked where the old seams and folds were.

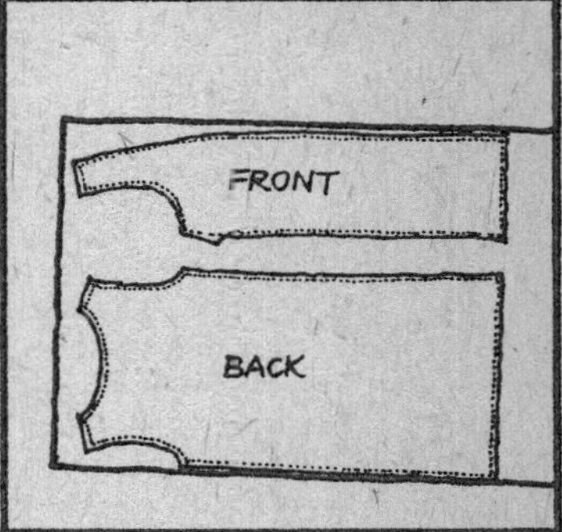

3 Use these pieces as patterns for cutting out a new lining, and cut exactly to size as the seam allowance is already there.

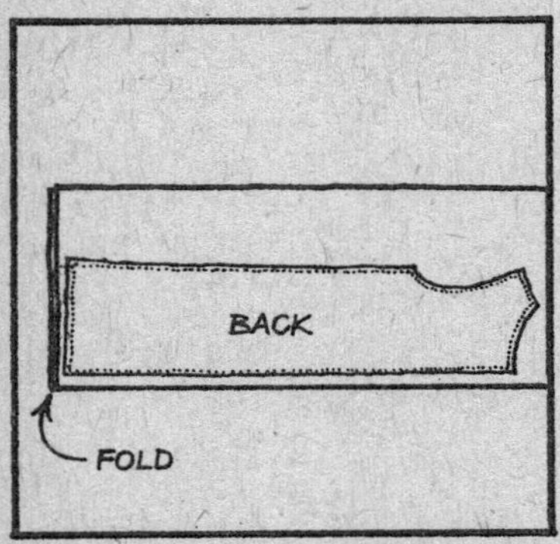

4 If the back consists of two pieces, use only one and cut on double fabric.

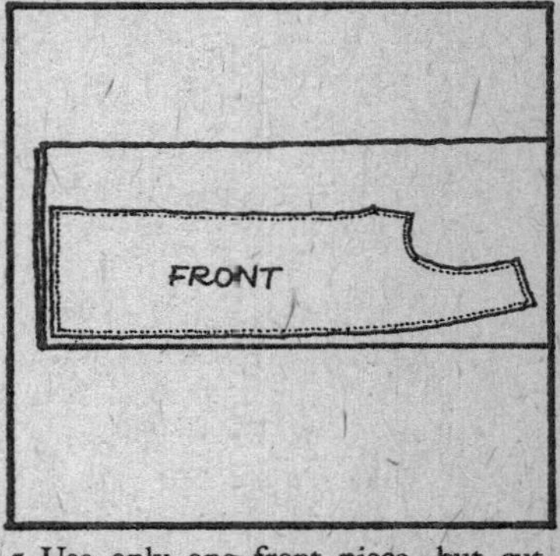

5 Use only one front piece, but cut on double fabric.

6 Use only one sleeve and cut on double fabric.

7 Sew any darts as outlined on the original.

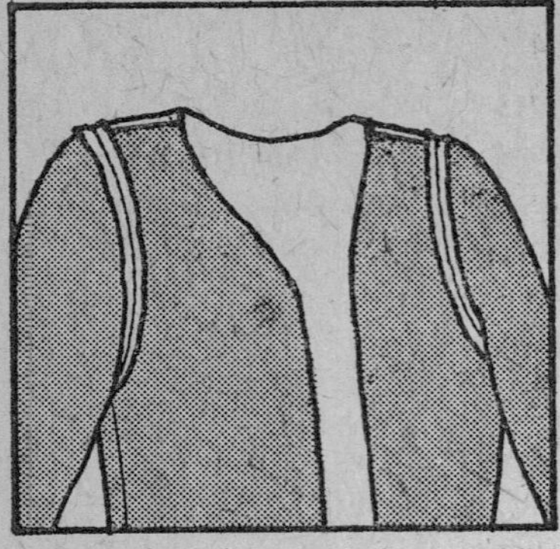

8 Sew the pieces together as the original.

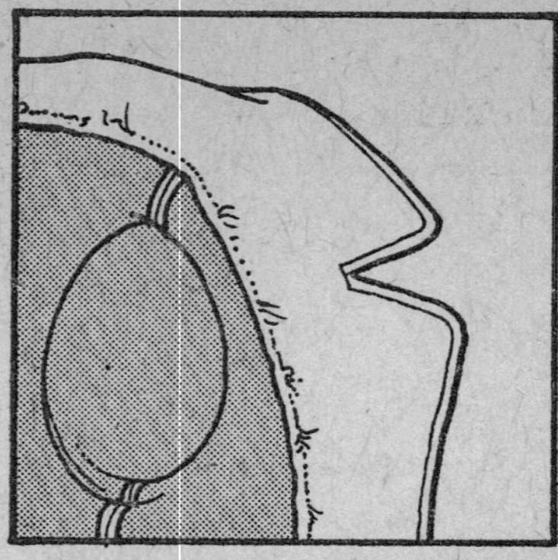

9 On the coat itself there will be a distinct line where the lining was originally sewn in. Pull out odd ends of thread.

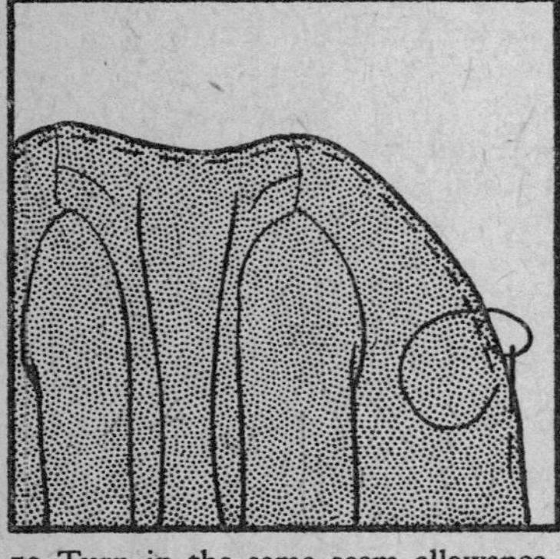

10 Turn in the same seam allowance as on the old lining, and tack.

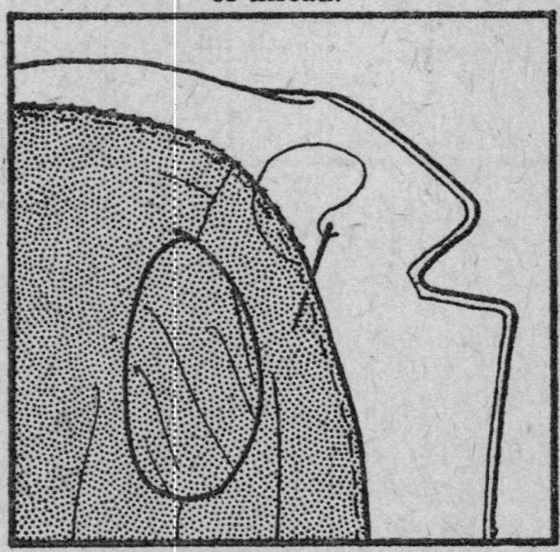

11 Sew in the new lining by hand, preferably with hem stitch, on the same sewing line as before.

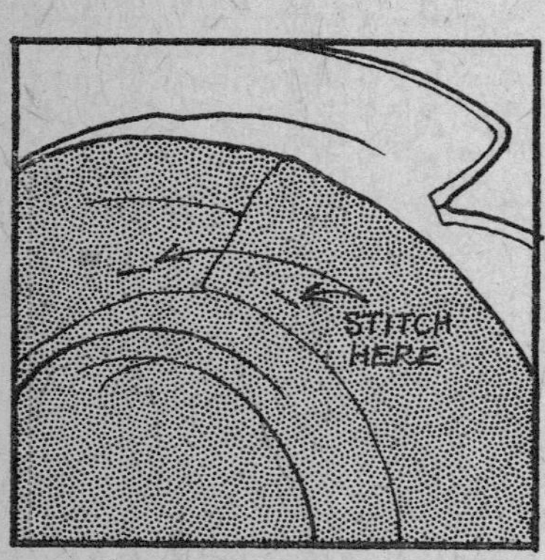

12 Anchor the lining at the shoulder by stitching to the padding.

frayed shirt collar

1 Unpick, stitch by stitch, the seams joining the collar to the shirt.

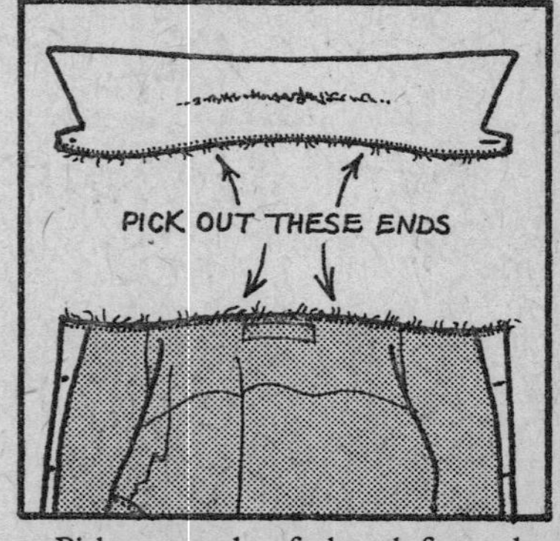

2 Pick out ends of thread from the collar and the shirt.

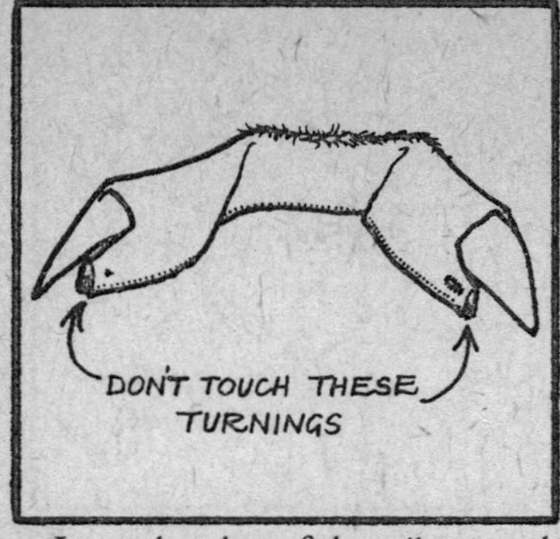

3 Leave the edges of the collar turned in as they were.

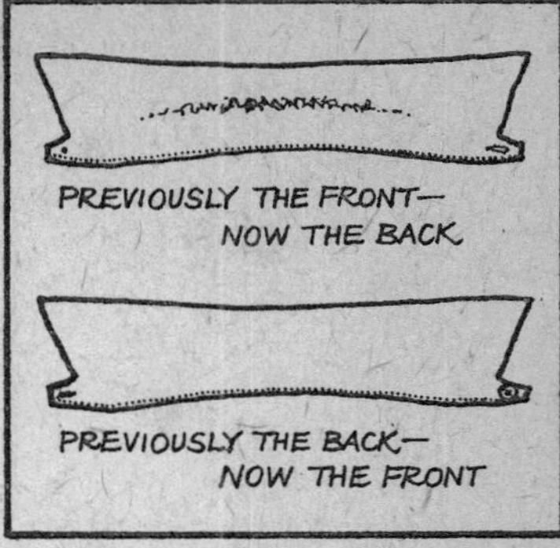

4 Turn the collar round so that the frayed side is at the back.

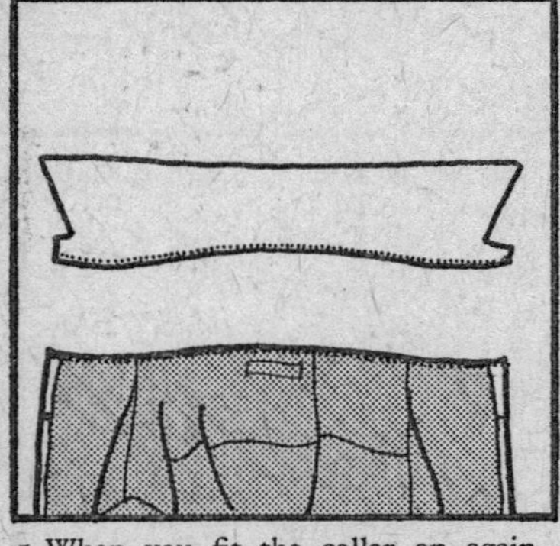

5 When you fit the collar on again, match up the old sewing lines which will look like rows of tiny holes.

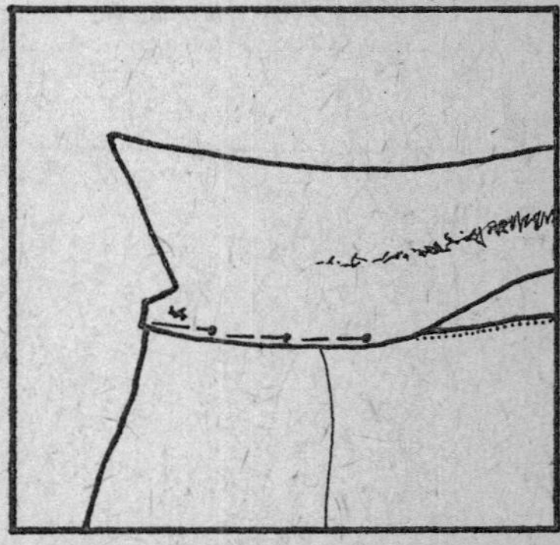

6 Pin the lower edge of what is now the back of the collar to the neck of the shirt on the outside of the shirt.

7 Sew down the back of the collar on the original sewing lines.

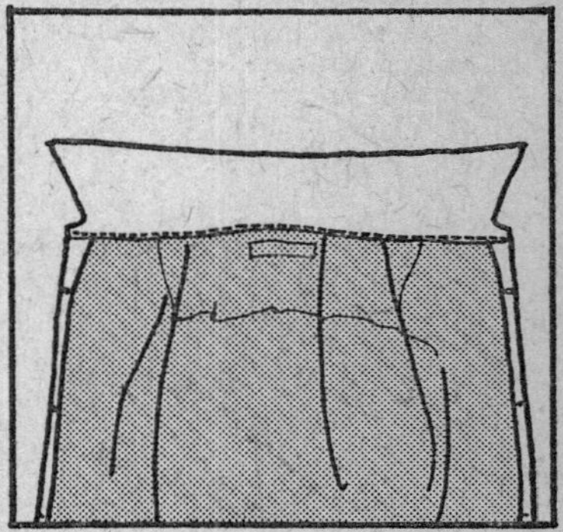

8 Place what is now the front of the collar in position and sew down on the original sewing line.

under-arm fraying

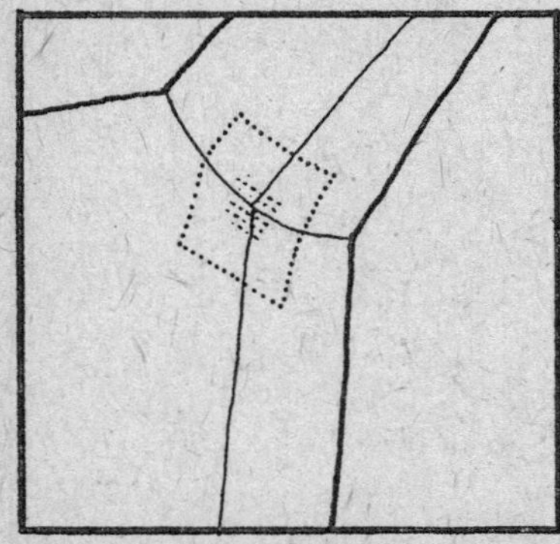

1 If it is in its early stages, place a piece of firm fabric behind the frayed part.

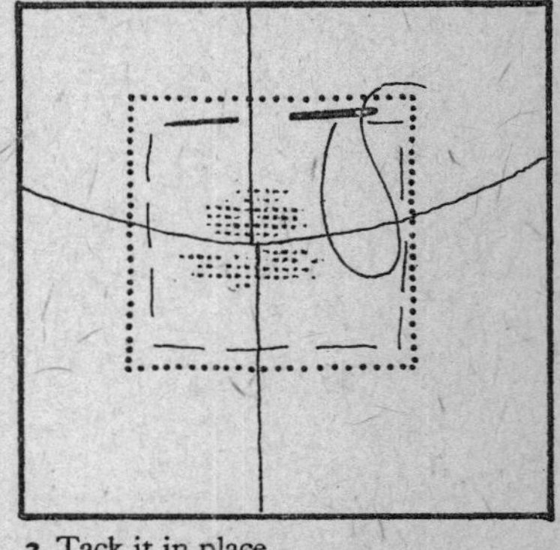

2 Tack it in place.

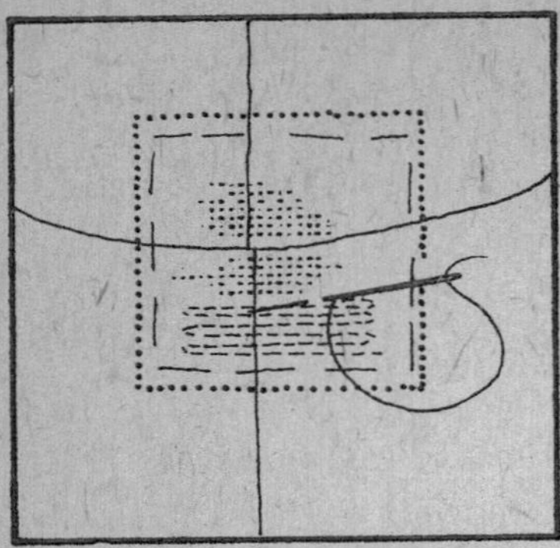

3 On the right side of the fabric, stitch backwards and forwards across the frayed part as on page 112, taking in the backing fabric as well, or

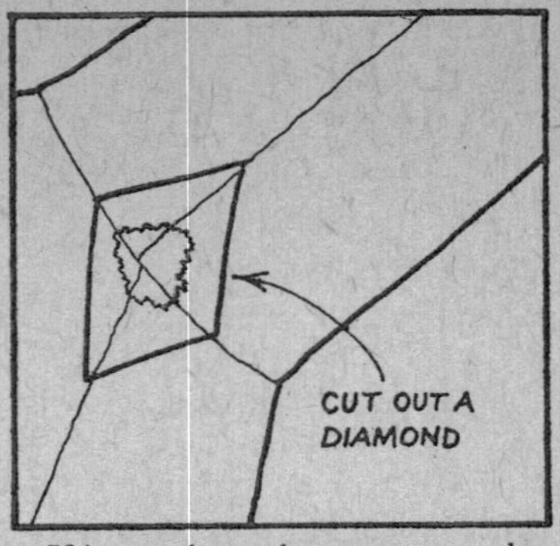

4 If in an advanced stage, cut out the worn part completely to form a diamond shape.

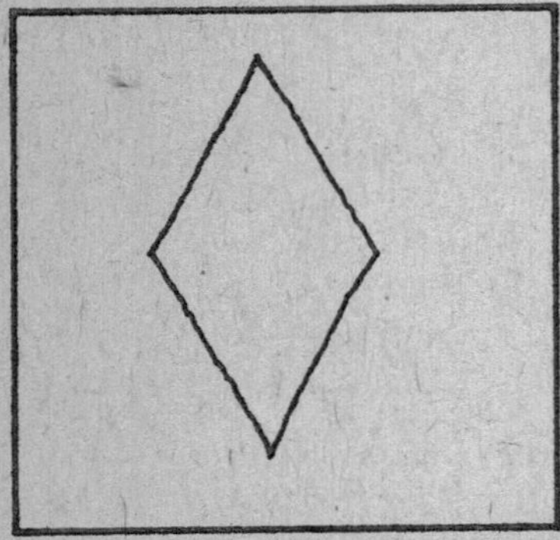

5 Cut from matching fabric a diamond ½ in. longer on each side than the diamond under the armhole.

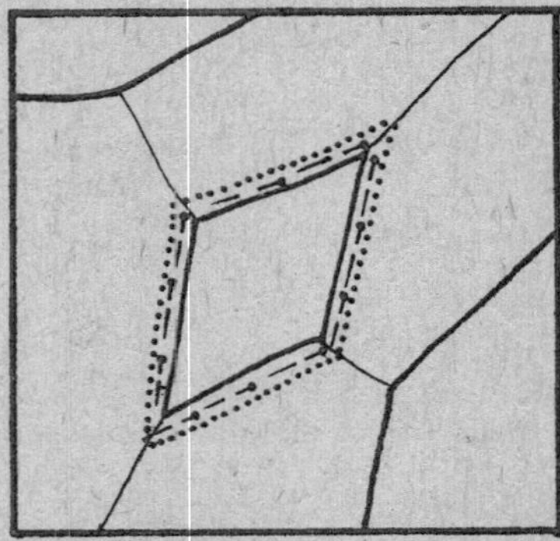

6 Pin the new diamond behind the cut out diamond so that its right side shows through to the right side of the garment.

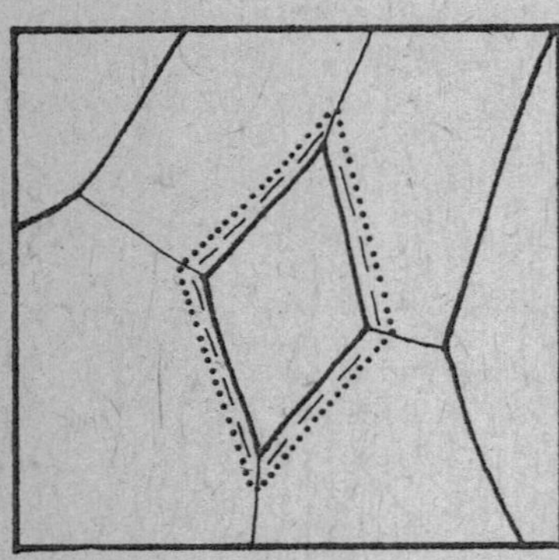

7 Tack this in place.

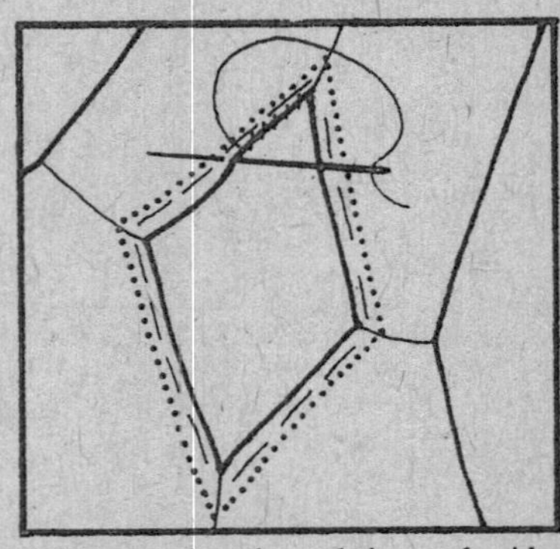

8 Turn under about ⅛ in. each side of the diamond you have cut out and hem them down to the garment.

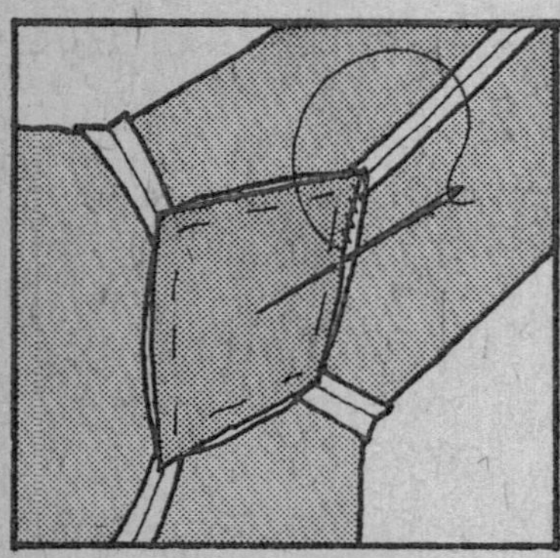

9 Turn to the wrong side, turn in the edges of the diamond piece and hem each side down neatly.

frayed trouser bottoms

WITHOUT TURN-UPS

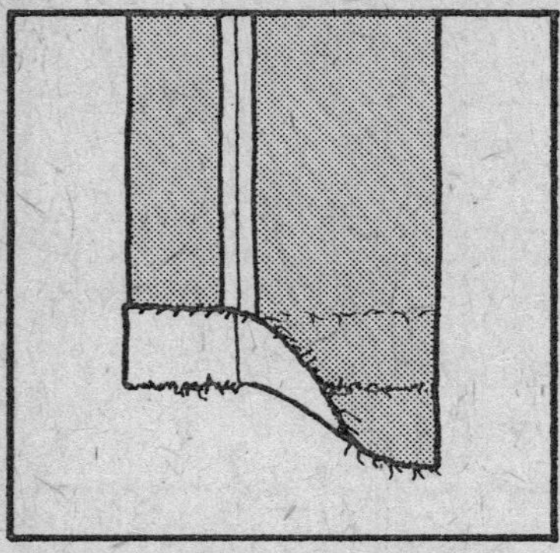

1 Unpick the original turning and press as in page 69-70.

2 Turn up the trouser bottom $\frac{1}{8}$ in. above the old frayed fold. Blind hem as on page 36 and press.

WITH TURN-UPS

This must be done without noticeably shortening the length of the leg and without the marks of old folds showing.

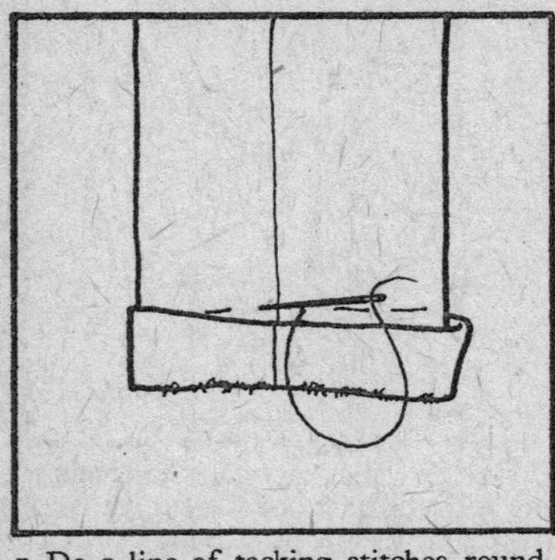

1 Do a line of tacking stitches round the leg at the point to which the turn-up reaches.

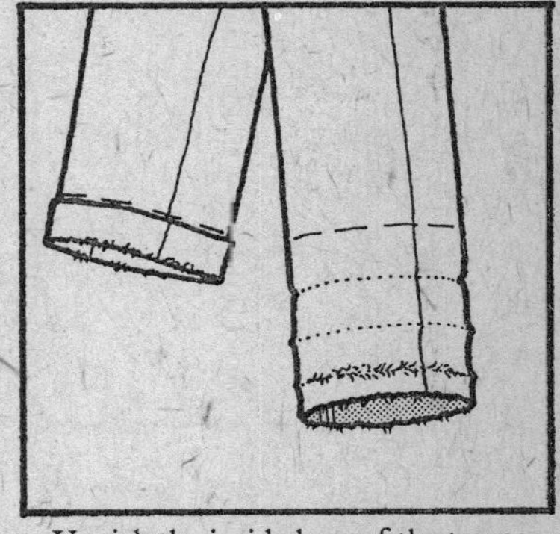

2 Unpick the inside hem of the trouser leg and unfold it. Brush out fluff and odd ends of thread. Do not press.

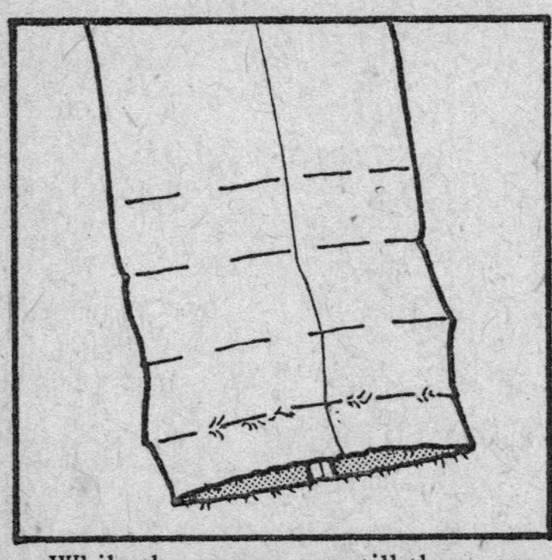

3 While the creases are still there, sew a line of tacking stitches along each one.

4 Press out the creases as on page 69-70.

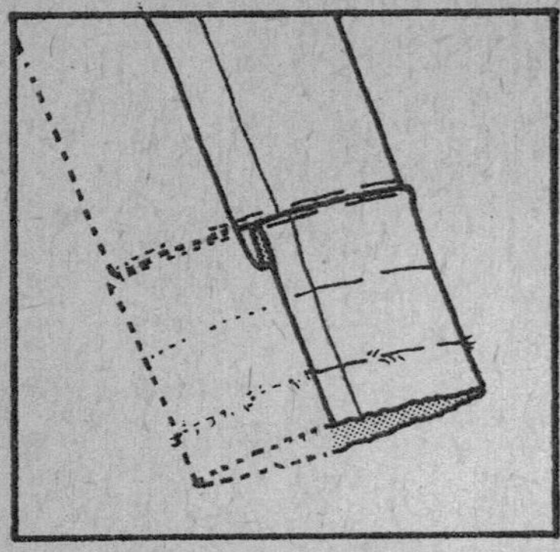

5 Working on the right side of the garment, take a tuck in the leg by bringing up the second line of tacking from the top to meet the top one. The top edge of this tuck will be the top of the new turn-up.

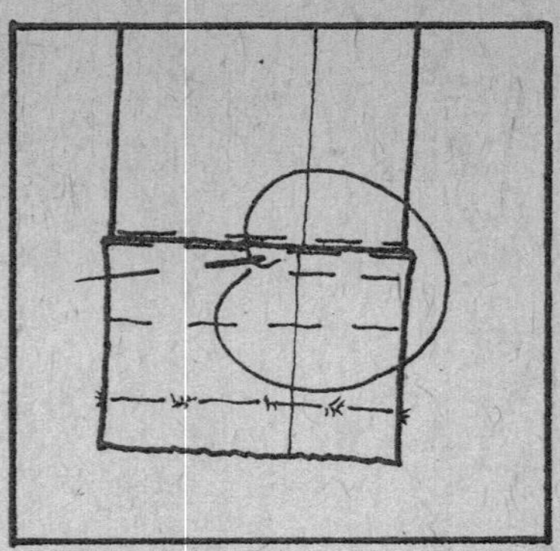

6 Tack this fold.

7 Turn back the leg and sew round the lower edge of the tuck you have just made with running stitches. Do not sew it to the outer fabric.

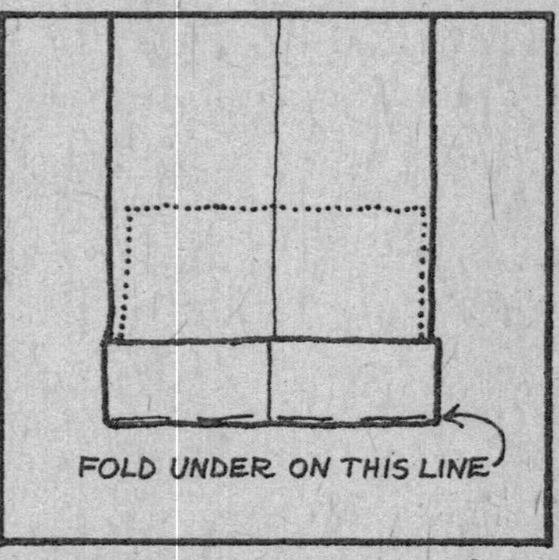

8 Working on the right side of the fabric fold in the bottom of the leg along the third line of tacking stitches, and tack along the fold.

9 Turn the leg inside out. Trim off the excess, turning along the bottom line of tacking.

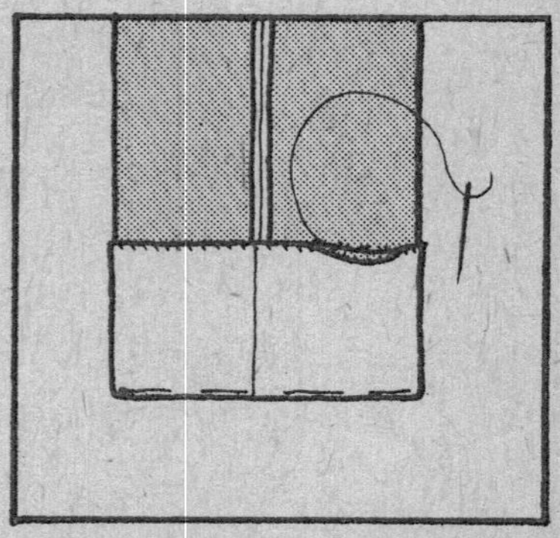

10 Oversew the cut edge and blind hem it to the outer fabric as page 36.

11 At the seams, just lightly catch the new turn-up to the trouser leg, but make sure that it doesn't show on the outside.

frayed shirt cuffs

This can only be done successfully with turn-back linked cuffs. Work one at a time, keeping the second one as a guide while you get the first one right.

1 Do not cut off the worn cuff, but unpick it, stitch by stitch.

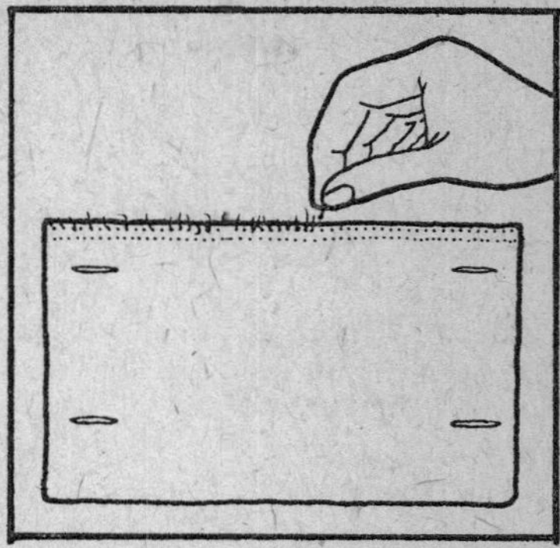

2 Pull out all loose ends of thread but do not press out the old sewing lines.

3 Turn the cuff round so that what was the outside is now inside and re-set the sleeve into it, matching the marks of the previous sewing lines. Tack in place.

4 Re-sew on the original sewing lines.

frayed jacket sleeves

WITHOUT BUTTONS

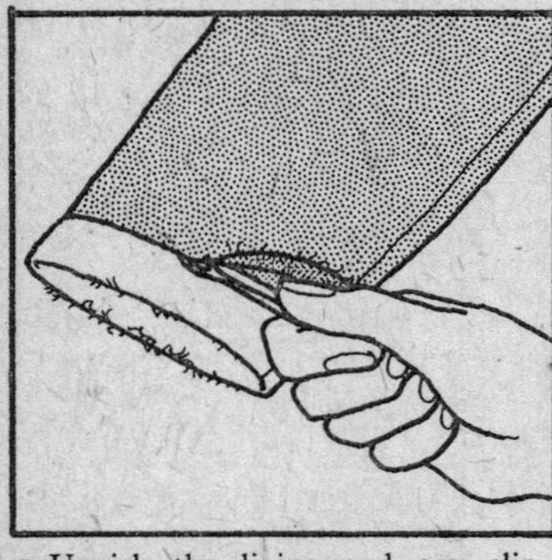

1 Unpick the lining and any slip-stitching. Press out old fold (see page 69-70).

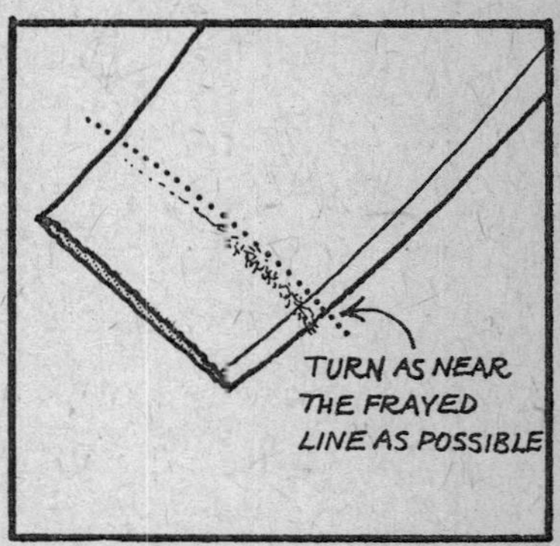

2 Turn up the sleeve not more than $\frac{1}{8}$ in. above the frayed line. Tack.

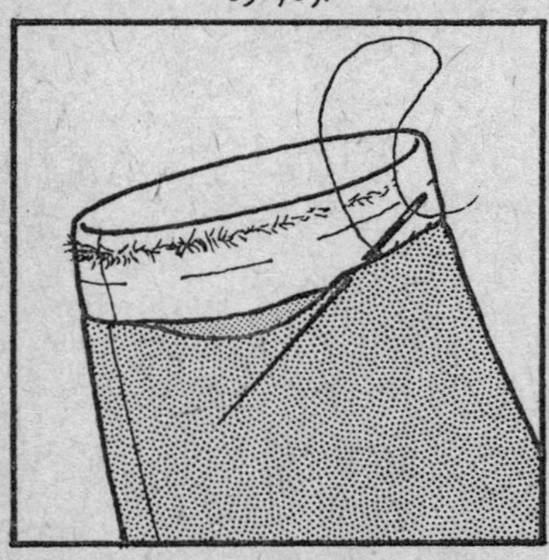

3 Blind hem and replace the lining as page 98.

WITH BUTTONS

Nowadays the buttons and buttonholes are sometimes only ornamental. With good suits you can actually unbutton the sleeve vent, but if the cuffs fray at the edges there isn't much a home sewer can do to make a neat job. However, there are many suits where the buttons on the sleeves are just a finishing touch – you can't unfasten them but you can at least do something about the frayed edges.

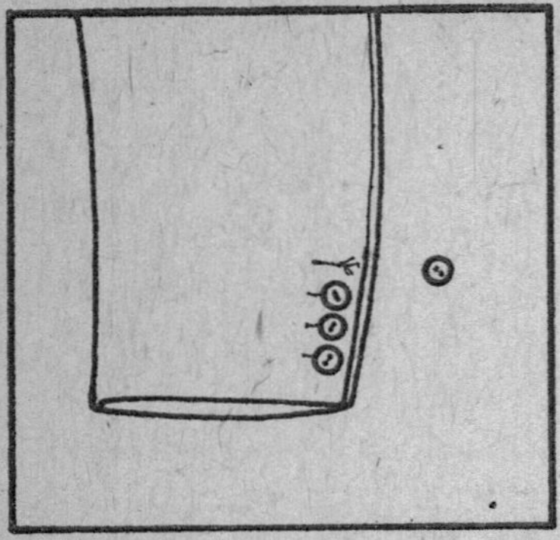

1 Remove the buttons.

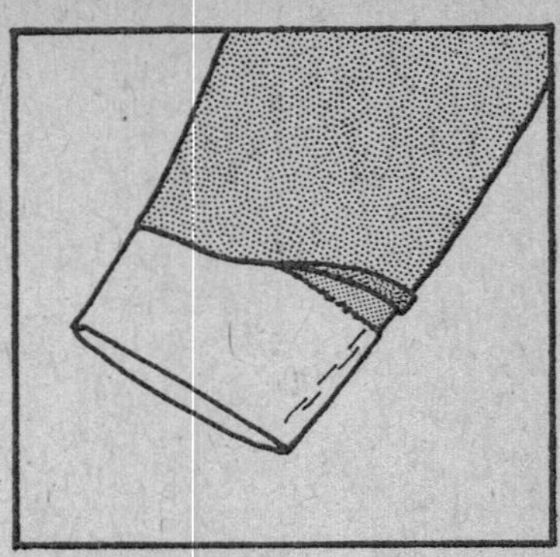

2 Unpick the lining.

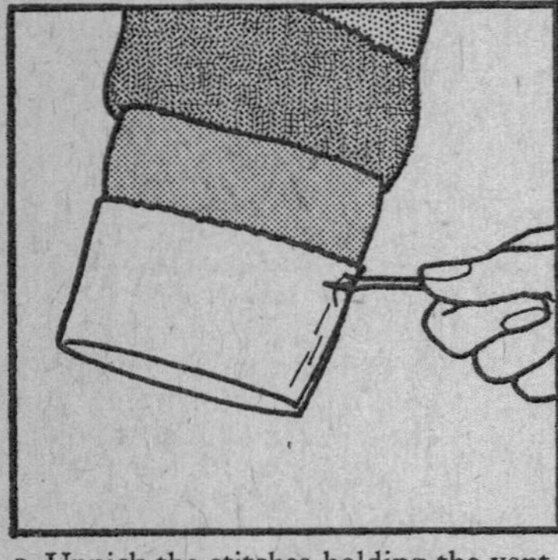

3 Unpick the stitches holding the vent together.

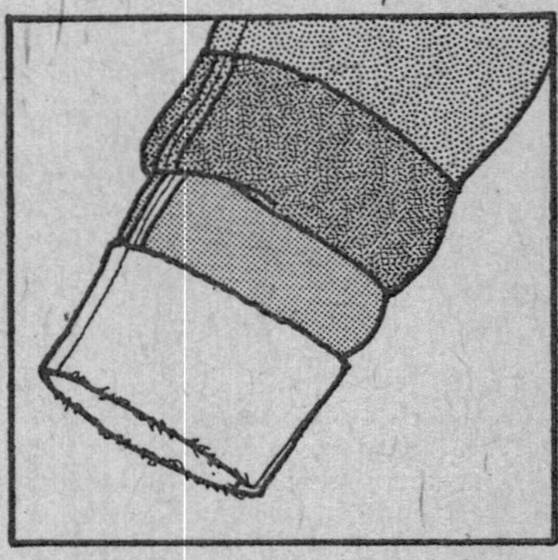

4 You will see that the buttonholes are sewn only on the outer sleeve – they do not take in the facing.

5 Unpick the fold-back inside the sleeve.

6 Unpick the facing either side of the vent.

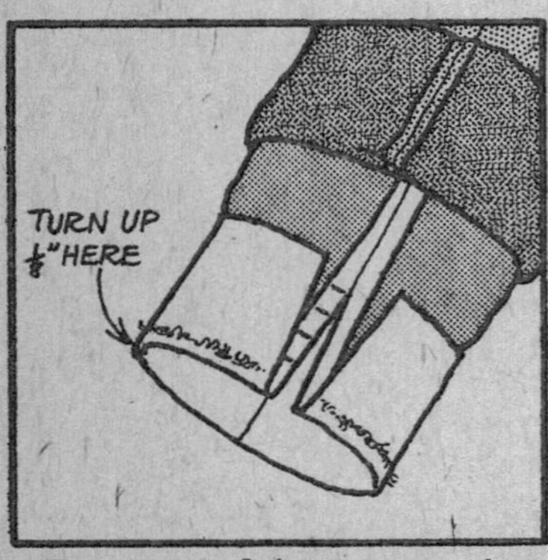

7 Turn up the facing not more than ⅛ in. or just enough to ensure that the frayed edge is out of sight.

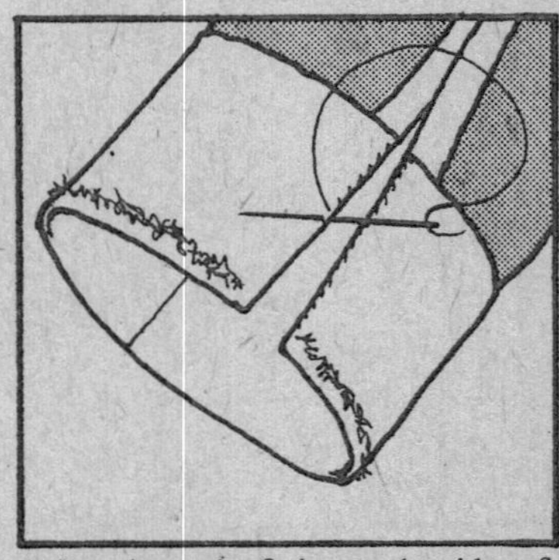

8 Sew down the facing at the sides of the vent.

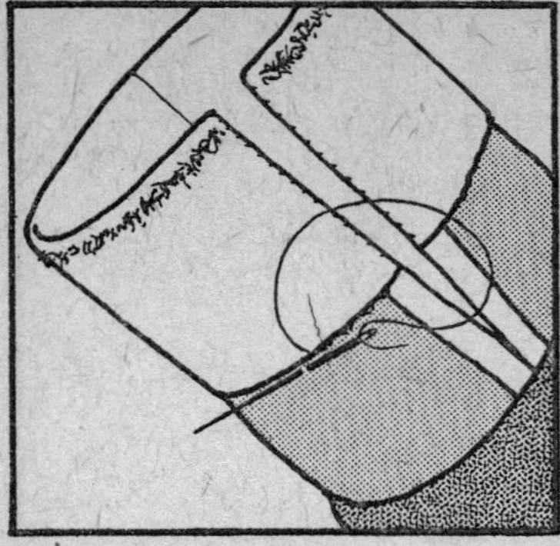

9 Slip stitch the fold-back very lightly to the outer sleeve.

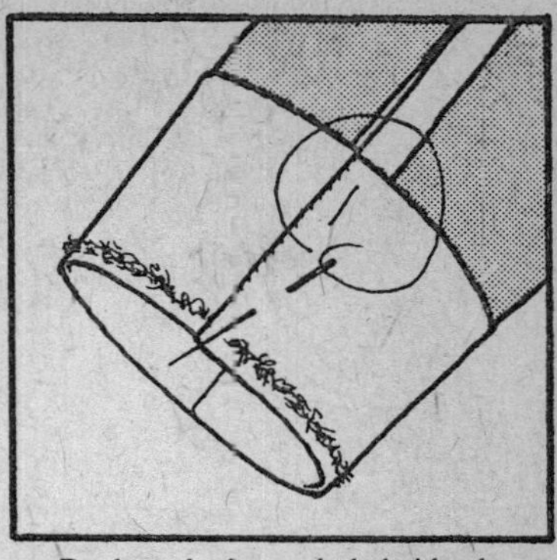

10 Replace the buttonholed side above the plain side and stitch in place without the stitches showing on the outside of the sleeve.

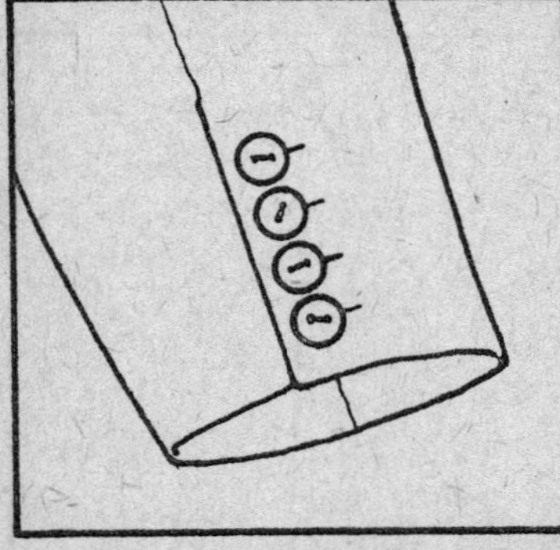

11 Turn to the outside of the sleeve and sew the buttons in place again above the buttonholes.

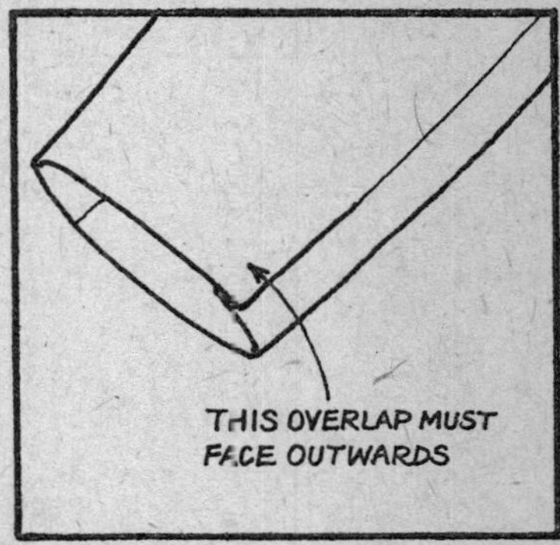

WITH A VENT AND NO BUTTONS

12 Work in exactly the same way as page 126, but ignore the reference to buttons. The buttonholed side referred to in 10 will be the upper side which overlaps the other.

top of pleat or vent frayed

Don't try stitching the seam together, it will only break out again, and you will have an even worse mess. The best method by far is to make a 'clock' at the top of the pleat or vent, worked over the frayed part. It must be worked on the right side of the garment.

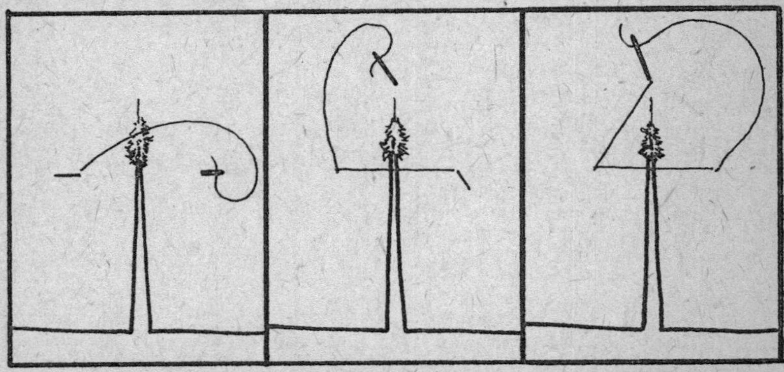

1 Using a contrasting thread, make three long stitches in the form of a triangle, as guide lines for your 'clock'. They can be pulled out afterwards.

2 The base of the triangle should come at least $\frac{1}{4}$ in. below the frayed part to be effective.

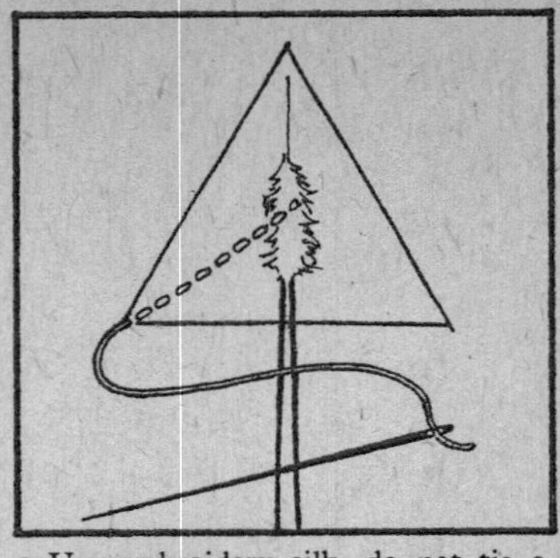

3 Use embroidery silk, do not tie a knot in the end, but start by sewing a few running stitches across the middle of the triangle, ending at the bottom left hand corner.

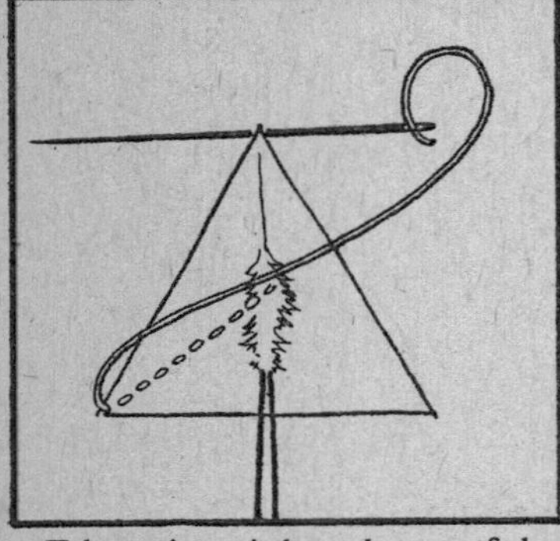

4 Take a tiny stitch at the top of the triangle. Pull the thread right through.

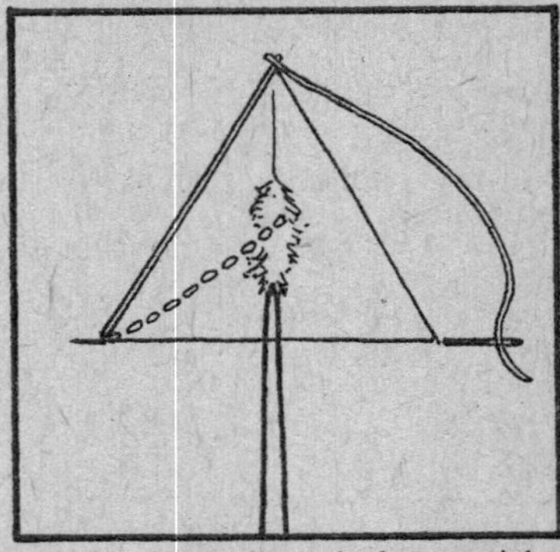

5 Insert the needle at the bottom right hand corner and bring it out alongside the point where you started the triangle.

6 Return to the top of the triangle and insert the needle outside the right-hand stitch, bringing it out again outside the left-hand stitch, in each case keeping the thread alongside the previous stitch.

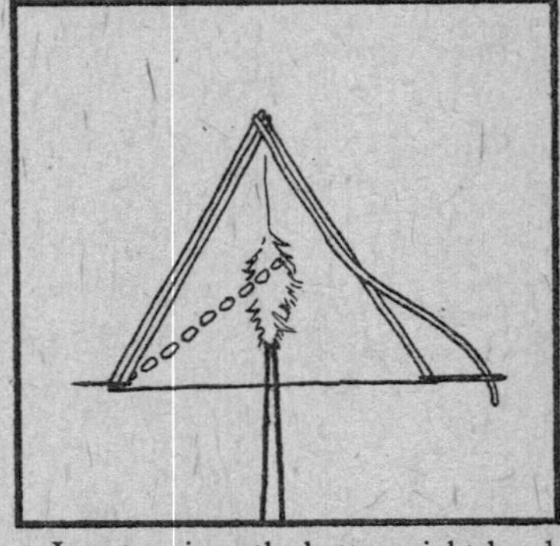

7 Insert again at the bottom right-hand corner, just inside the base of the previous stitch, bringing the needle out just inside the left-hand stitch.

8 Continue working in this way, gradually working towards the centre of the triangle, until you have covered it. Finish off at the back.

mending a zip

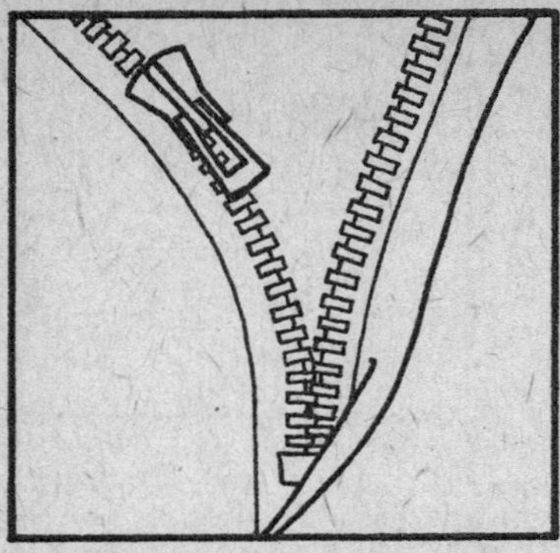

1 When a zip fastener breaks it is nearly always because one side has come out of the slider. You just can't get it back in again. But you can mend it, although the zip will be about 1 in. shorter than it was before.

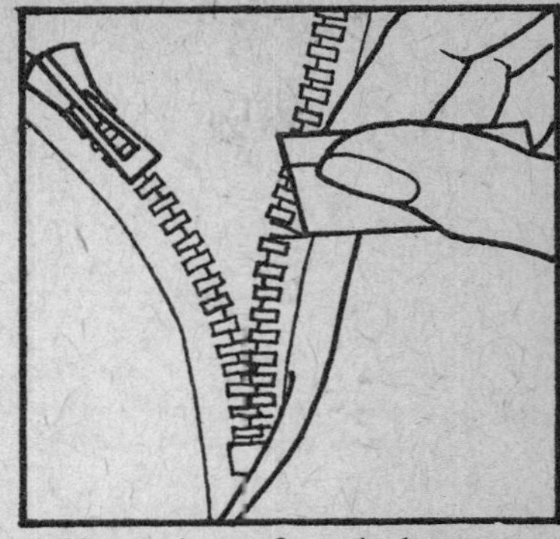

2 About 1 in. up from the bottom, on the side which has come out of the slider, slash through the webbing between two of the teeth with a sharp razor blade. (You must use a razor blade to get an absolutely clean cut).

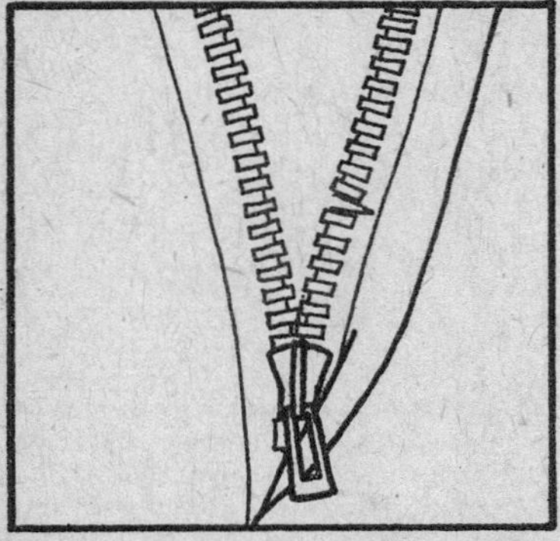

3 Bring the slider right down to the bottom.

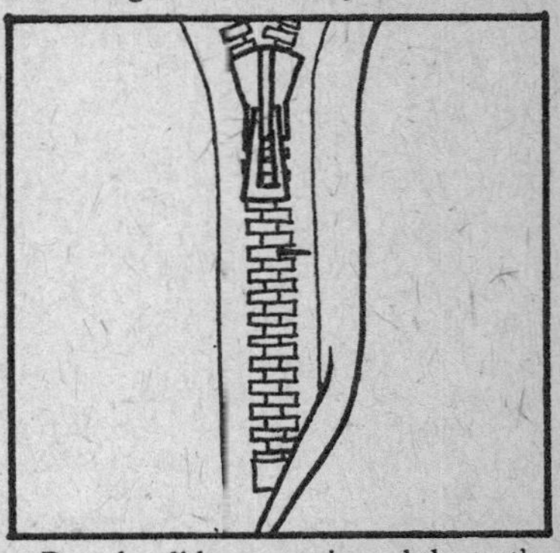

4 Run the slider up again and the teeth will start locking beyond the point where you cut the webbing.

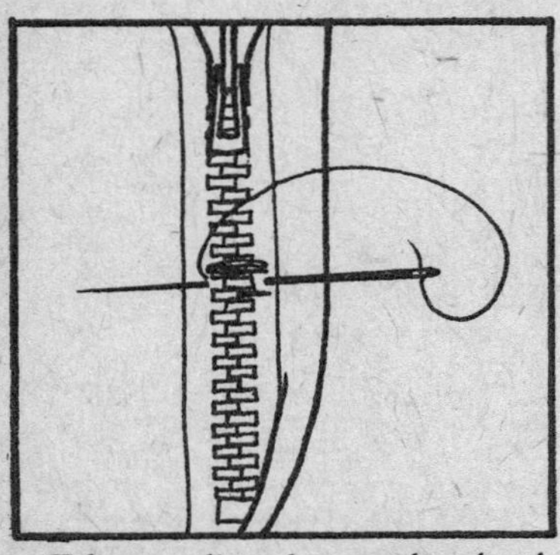

5 Take a needle and strong thread and sew, over and over again, across the zip just above where you cut it, to form a buffer beyond which the slider cannot go.

darning

For woollen garments use darning wool, and for thinner fabrics use double thread.

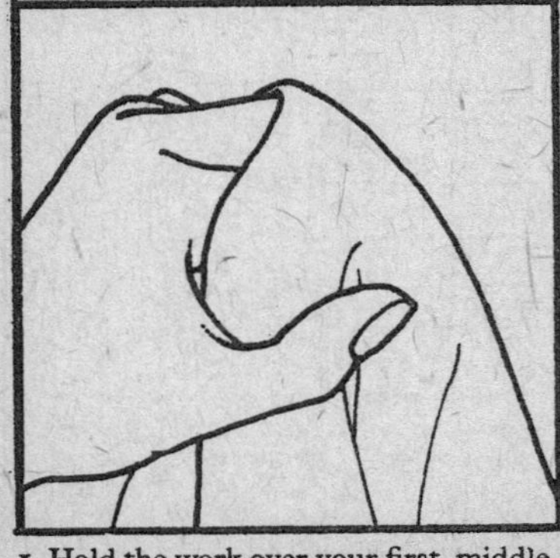

1 Hold the work over your first, middle and third fingers, gripped on one side by the thumb and on the other side by the little finger, or buy a 'mushroom'.

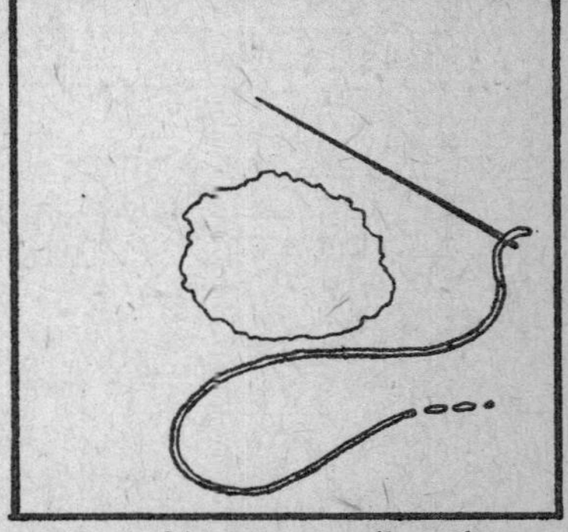

2 Take a fairly long needle and start just below the hole and to the right of it. Do not knot the thread, simply pull it until it is nearly out of sight.

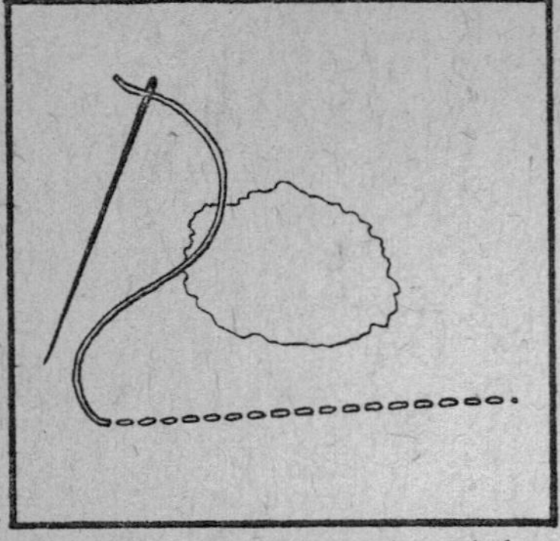

3 Do a line of small running stitches until you get to the other side of the hole.

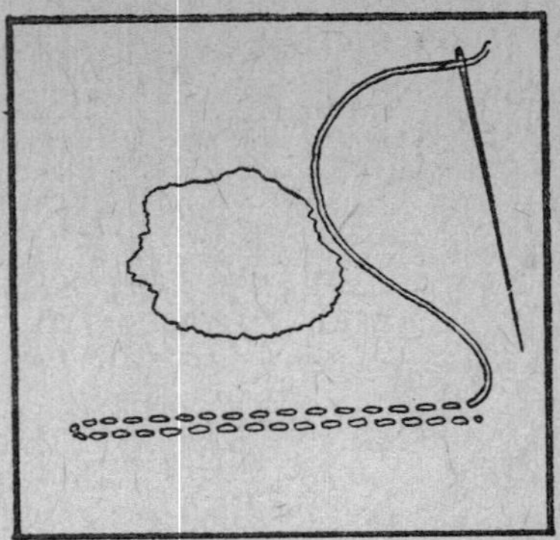

4 Turn the work round and go back again with another row of running stitches, this time a little nearer the hole.

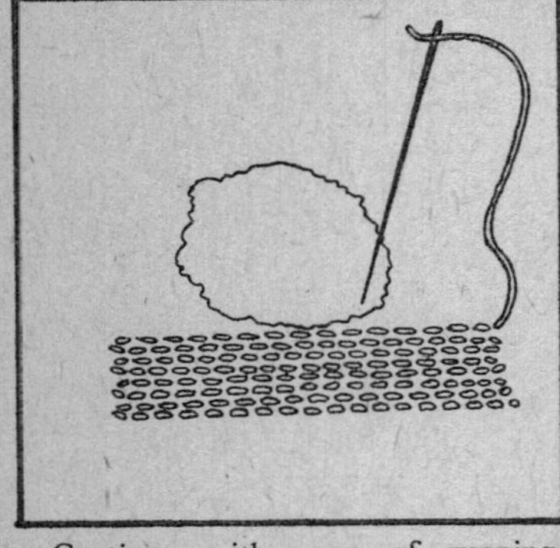

5 Continue with rows of running stitches until you reach the hole itself.

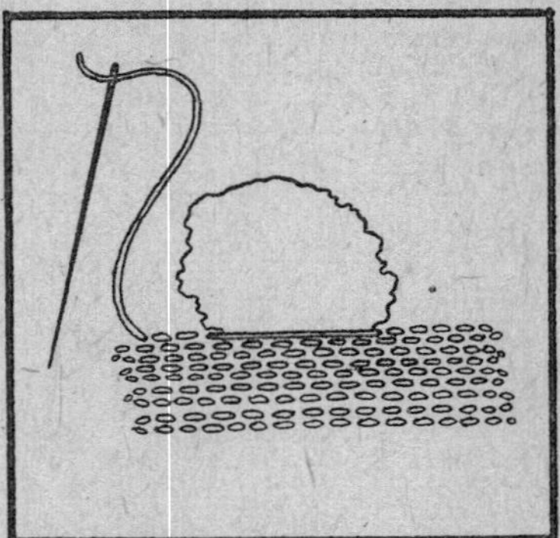

6 Now do running stitches as far as the hole, carry the thread across the hole and continue with running stitches the other side. Don't tug the thread.

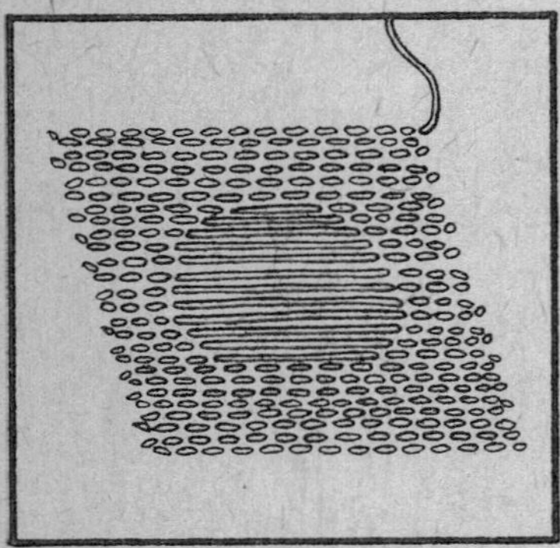

7 Continue in this way until you get beyond the hole, then do a few more rows of stitching for strengthening.

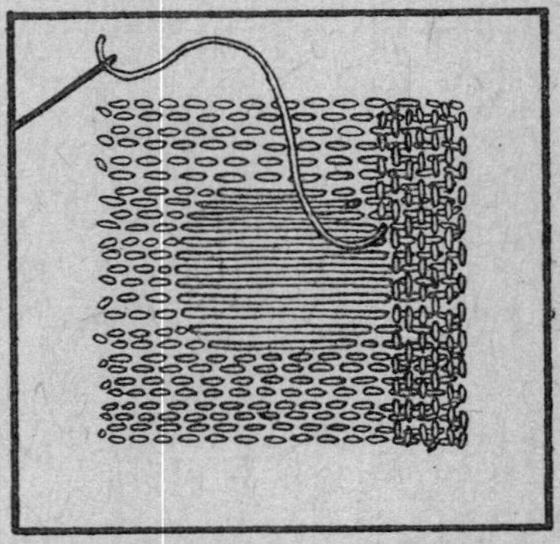

8 Turn the work round and work rows of running stitches across the previous ones until you reach the hole.

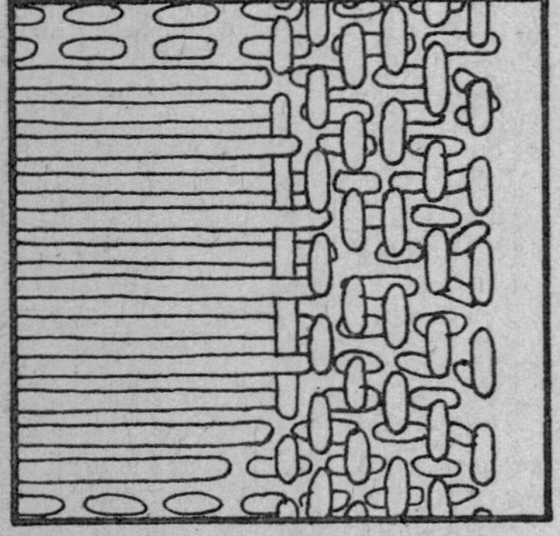

9 When you get to the rows of thread across the hole, put the needle under the first strand and over the next, under the next and over the next, until you reach the other side. Continue with a few more running stitches.

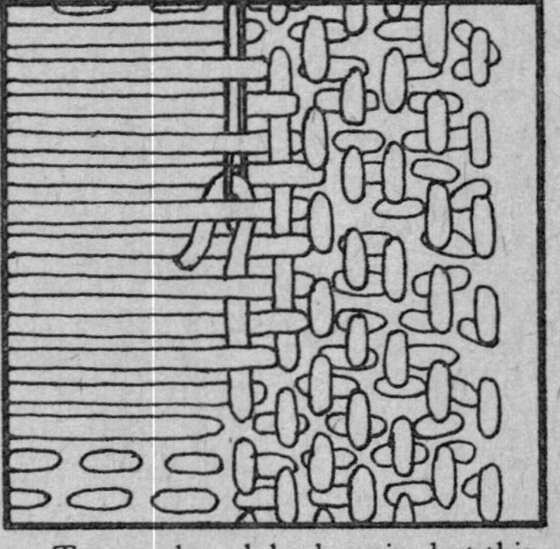

10 Turn and work back again, but this time put the needle under the thread you went over last time, and over the thread you went under. This is called weaving.

11 Weave your way across the hole and finish up with a few rows of running stitches.

trouser pocket replacement

Nowadays you can buy replacement pockets which only have to be ironed on, but if you have an economic turn of mind you can save even that small expense by making and sewing in a new one. Use an odd piece of cotton lining.

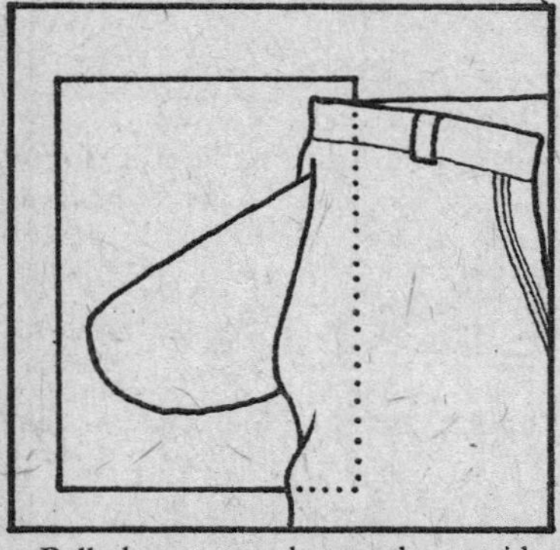

1 Pull the torn pocket to the outside and lay it flat on a piece of paper.

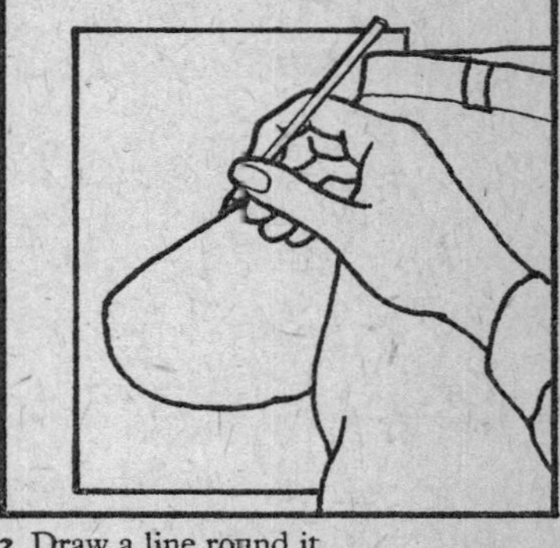

2 Draw a line round it.

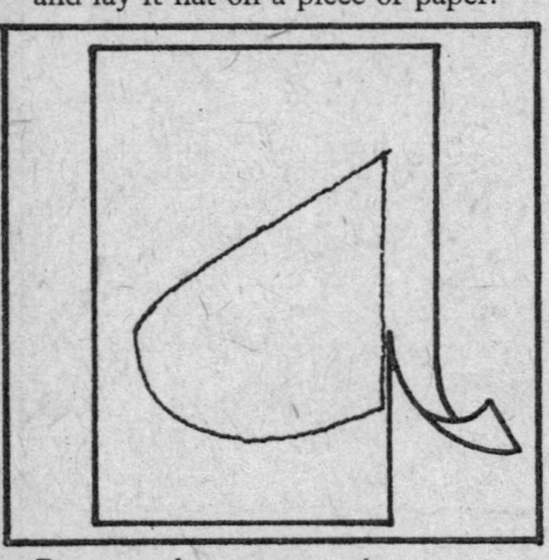

3 Remove the paper and cut out a pattern of the pocket.

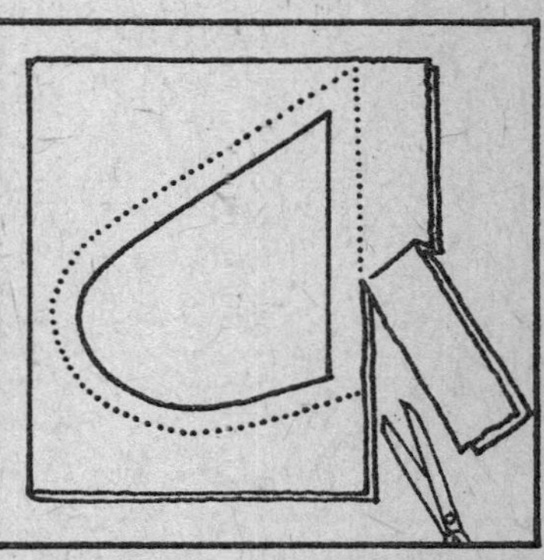

4 Fold the fabric in half, lay the pattern on it, and cut $\frac{1}{2}$ in. away from the pattern all the way round.

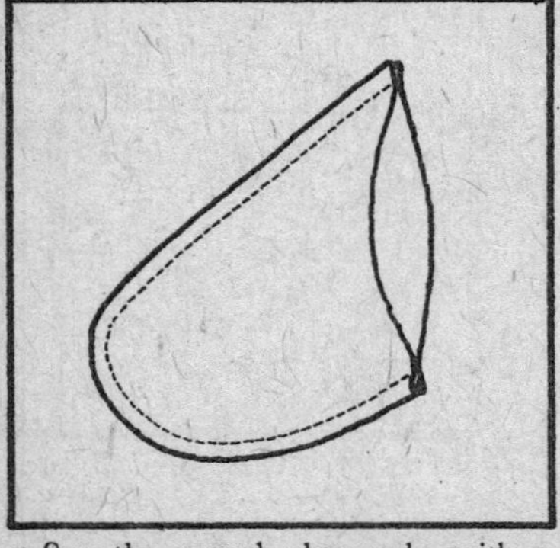

5 Sew the curved edges only, with a French seam, leaving the mouth of the pocket open.

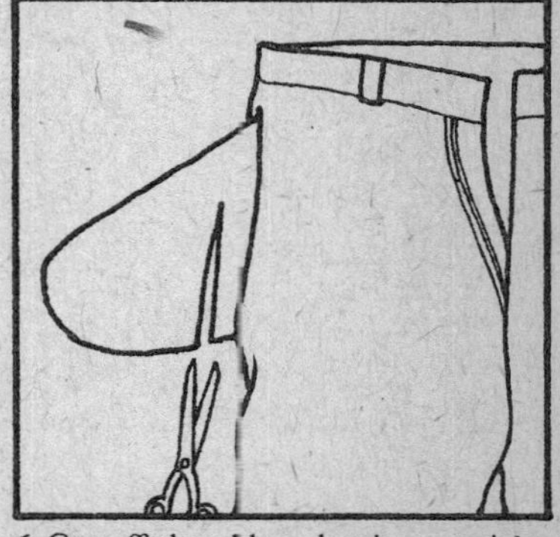

6 Cut off the old pocket in a straight line, $1\frac{1}{2}$ to 2 in. from the opening.

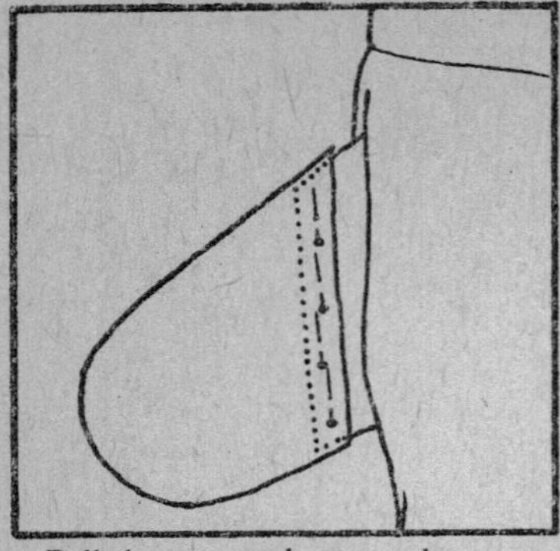

7 Pull the new pocket over the stump of the old one, overlapping about 1 in, and pin in place right side outwards.

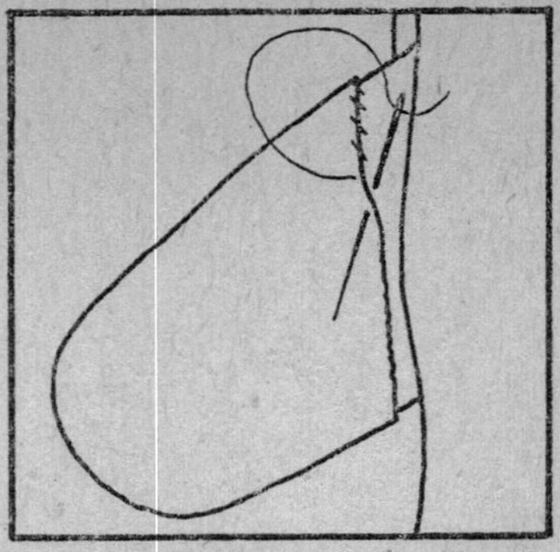

8 Turn under the raw edge and hem it down.

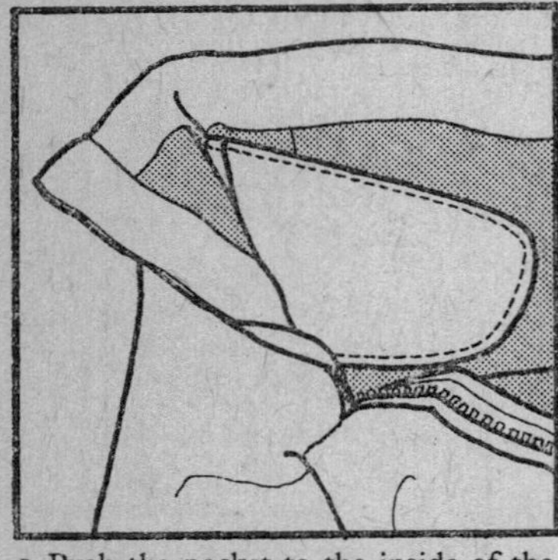

9 Push the pocket to the inside of the trousers.

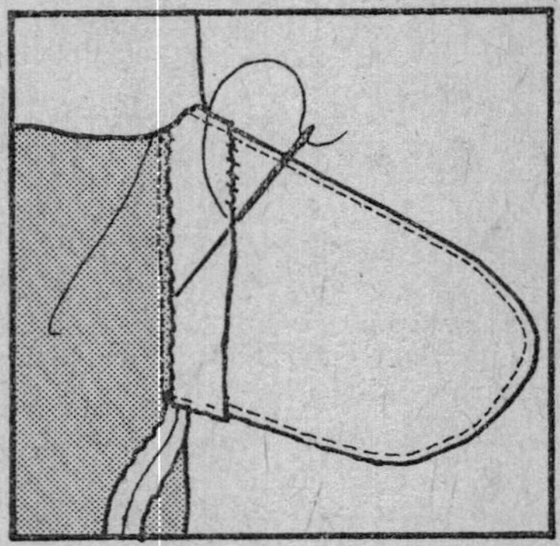

10 Working inside the trousers turn under the raw edge and hem it down.

three good ideas

an extra trouser seat

You give a pair of trousers a longer lease of life by inserting an extra seat on the inside. Use a strong, smooth fabric, not anything likely to cause chafing.

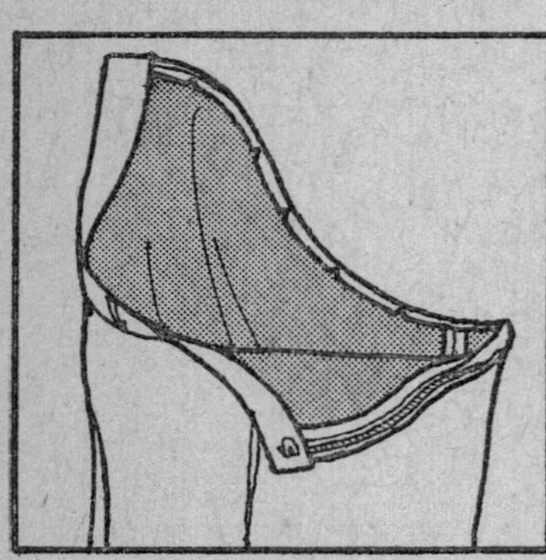

1 Fold the trousers in half down the centre back seam.

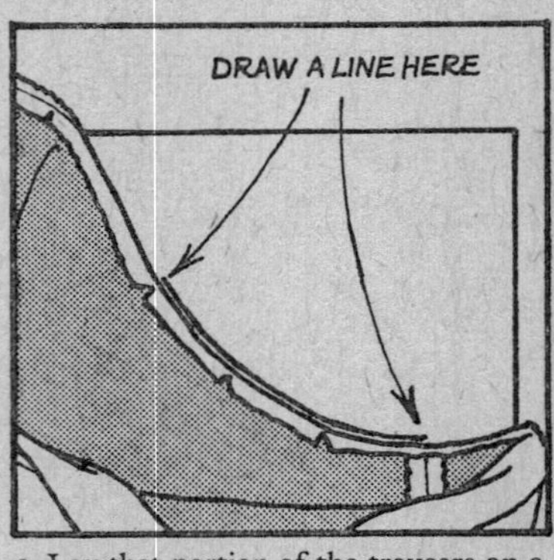

2 Lay that portion of the trousers on a piece of paper and draw a line round the curve from half way up the back to the centre seam.

3 Remove the paper and complete the pattern by drawing a half circle from one end of the line to the other.

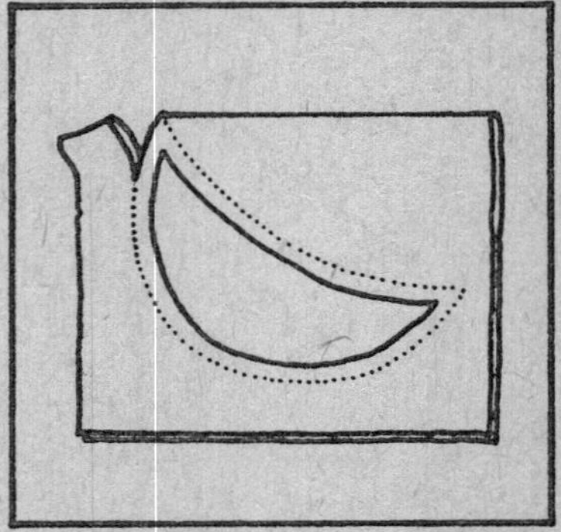

4 This is the pattern of the extra seat. Cut two pieces $\frac{1}{2}$ in. larger to allow for turnings.

5 Sew the centre seam, wrong sides outwards, with a single plain seam.

6 Snip the seam allowance, open out and press flat

7 Lay this piece, wrong side downwards, on the inside back of the trousers, with the two seams one on top of the other. Pin in place.

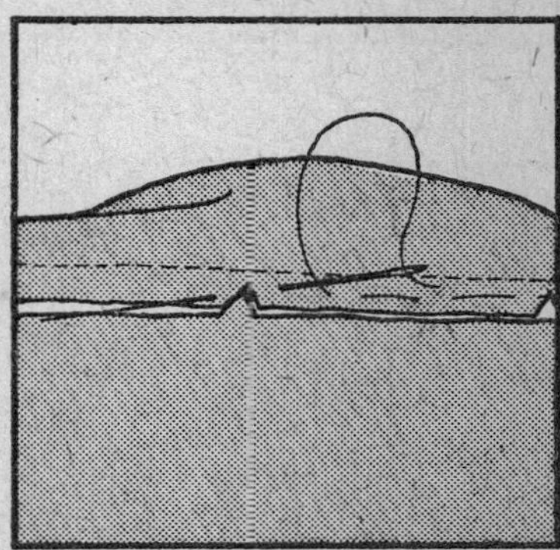

8 First fold back one side of the extra piece and tack the seam allowance of the new piece to the seam allowance in the trousers, then do the same on the other side.

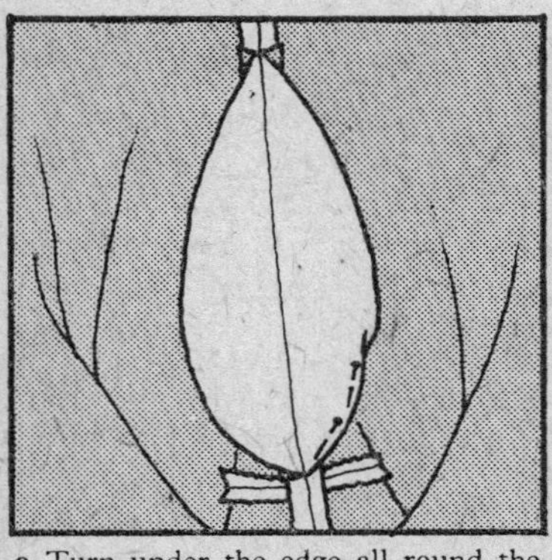

9 Turn under the edge all round the extra piece and pin it down.

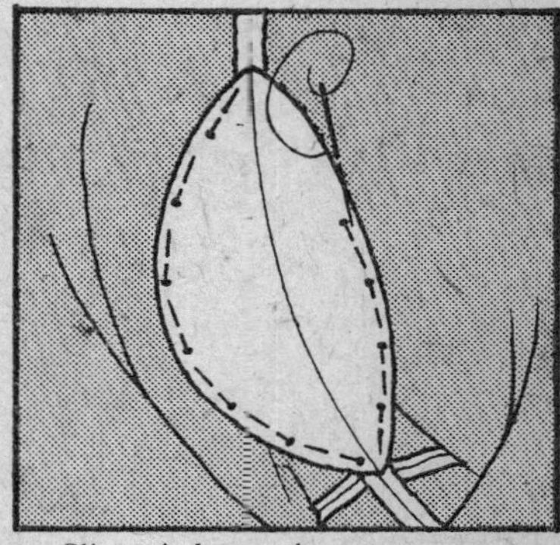

10 Slip stitch to the trousers, very lightly, all round.

lining a skirt

A skirt has twice the life with a lining. It keeps its shape better and, particularly jersey cloth, stands up to dry cleaning much better. If you buy one without a lining it will pay you to put one in. If you don't know how much lining to buy consult the shop assistant.

1 Fold the length of lining in half end to end.

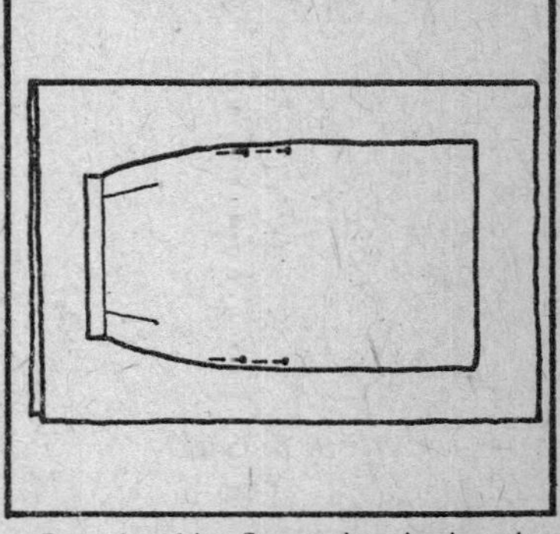

2 Lay the skirt flat on it, pinning the side seams at the widest part, flattened to their full width.

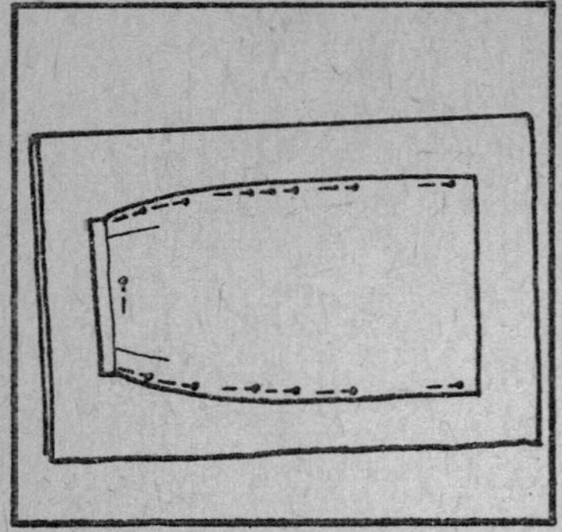

3 Flatten the side seams between the hip and the waist and pin them down to the lining. Pin the rest of the skirt here and there.

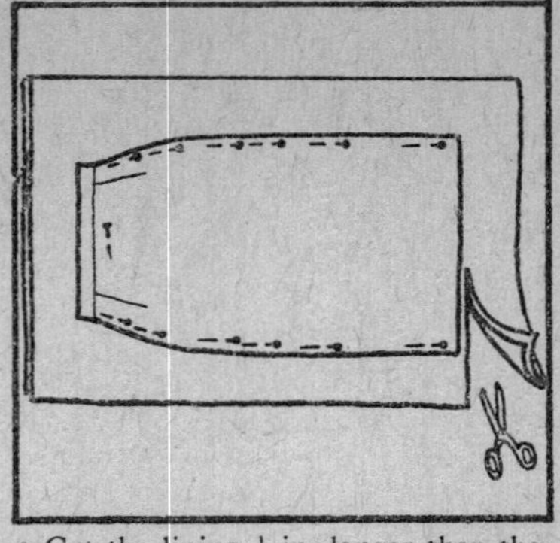

4 Cut the lining ½ in. longer than the skirt so that when it is turned up it will be a little shorter than the skirt.

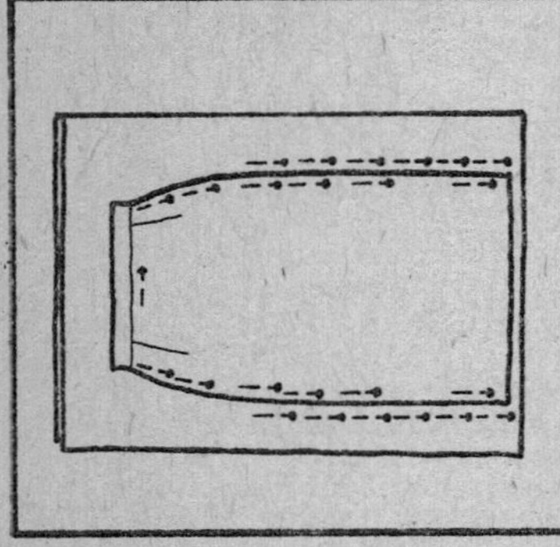

5 Make a line with pins ¾ in. away from the sides of the skirt until you get to the hips.

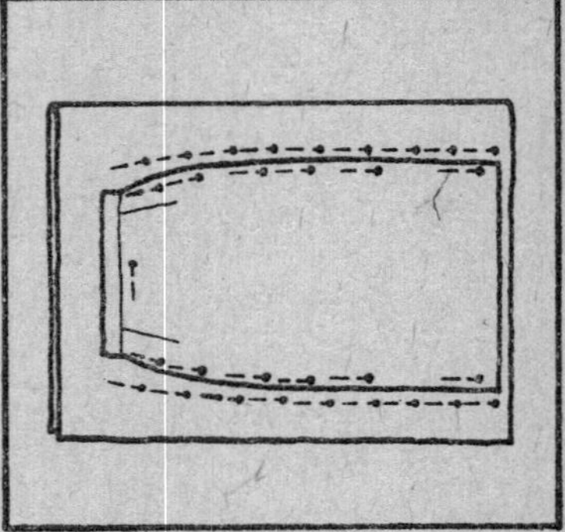

6 From the hips to the waist gently curve the sides inwards but finish about 1½ in. away from the sides of the skirt at the waist, because you must allow for putting in some darts.

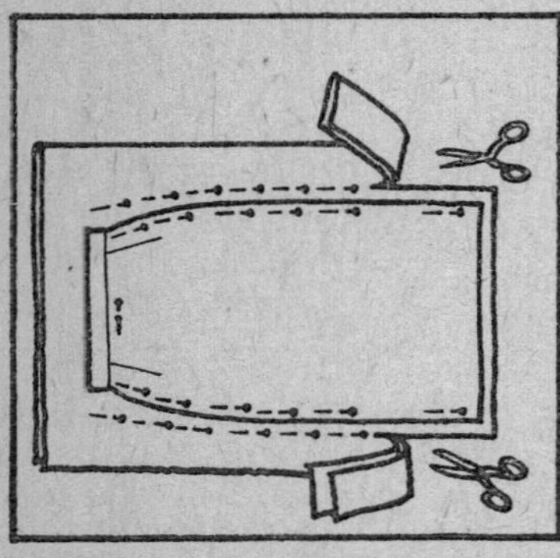

7 When you are satisfied your hip line is correct cut along the lines you have marked out with pins. Cut an extra ½ in. at the top for seam allowance.

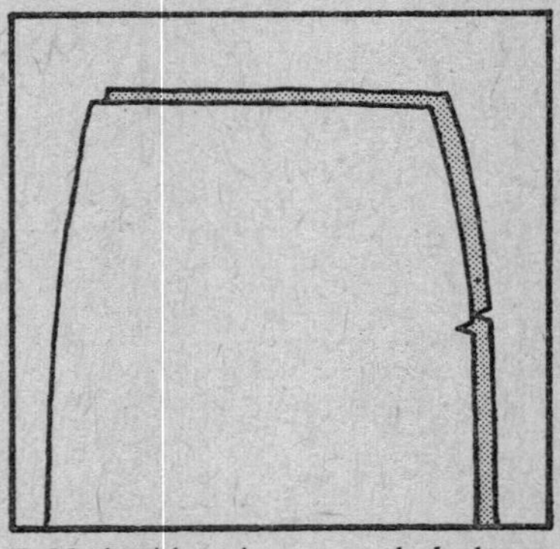

8 Mark with a pin or a notch the lower end of the side opening.

9 Sew together the left side seam as far as the placket mark, and the right side seam from top to bottom. Leave ½ in. seam allowance.

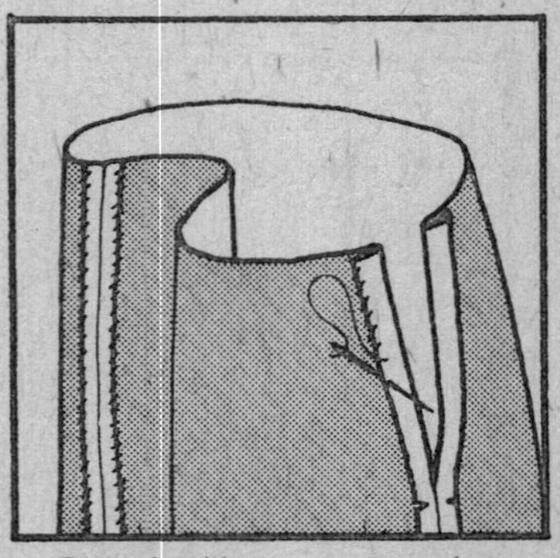

10 Press the side seams open and oversew the raw edges.

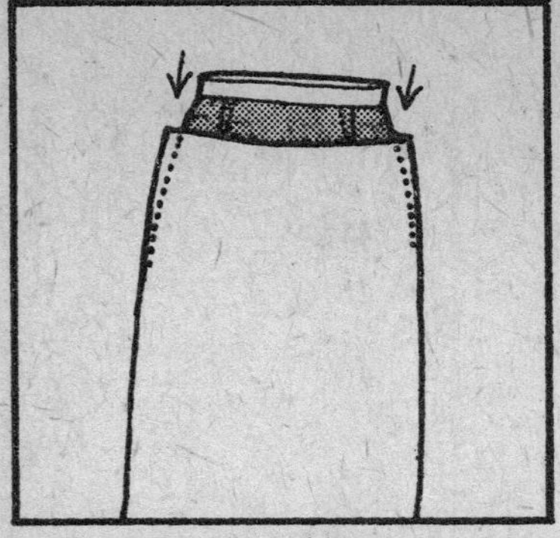

11 Turn the skirt inside out and, with the wrong side of the lining inwards, pull the lining over the skirt.

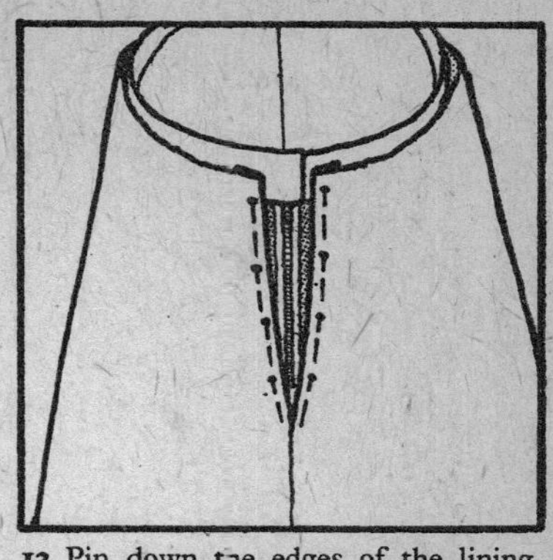

12 Pin down the edges of the lining placket either side of the zip fastener.

13 Pin the right-hand seam of the lining to the right-hand seam of the skirt.

14 The waist of the lining will be much larger than the waist of the skirt.

15 Make darts as on page 33 in the back and front of the lining in the same place as the darts on the skirt so that the lining is drawn in to fit the skirt waistband.

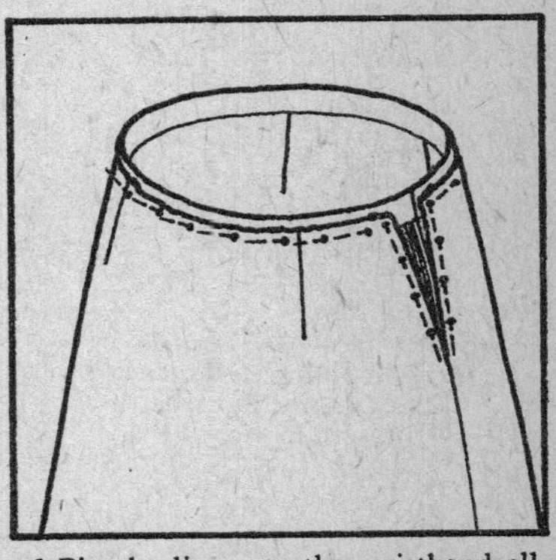

16 Pin the lining to the waistband all the way round. Remove the pins from the right side. Try on to make sure the lining is not dragging the skirt anywhere.

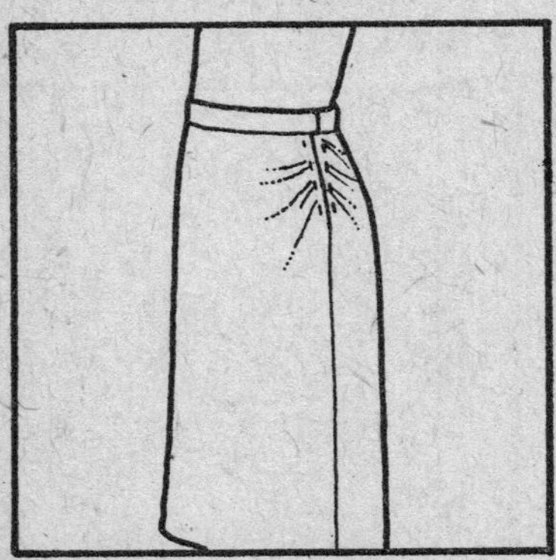

17 If there is any dragging it will probably be where you have pinned the lining to the placket, in which case remove the pins to release the dragging, and pin the lining again in the released position.

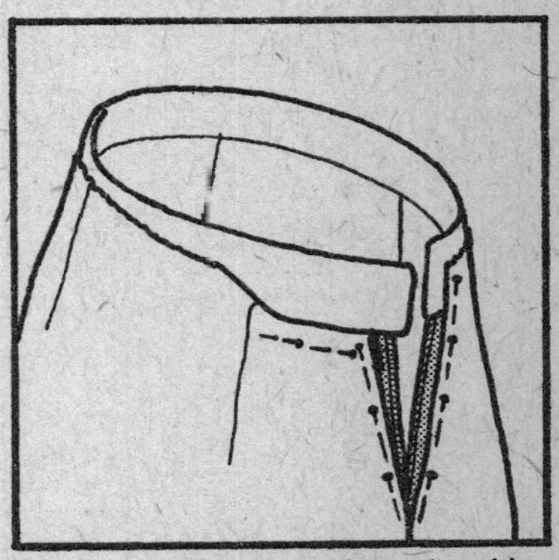

18 To sew the lining into the skirt turn in the top of the lining to meet the lower edge of the skirt waistband.

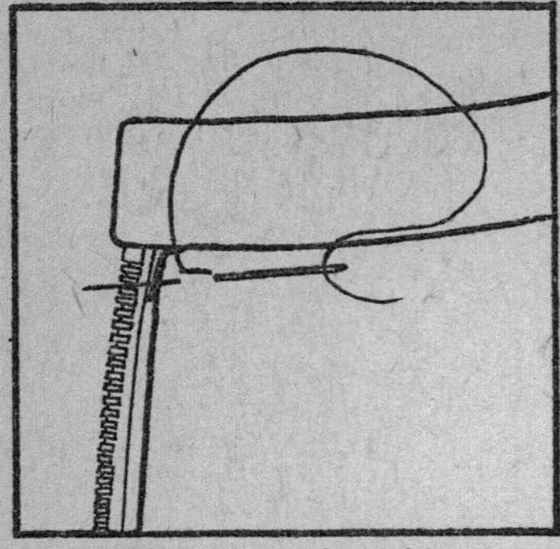

19 Sew the two together with a cross stitch. Starting at the left take two running stitches one on top of the other just below the top of the lining.

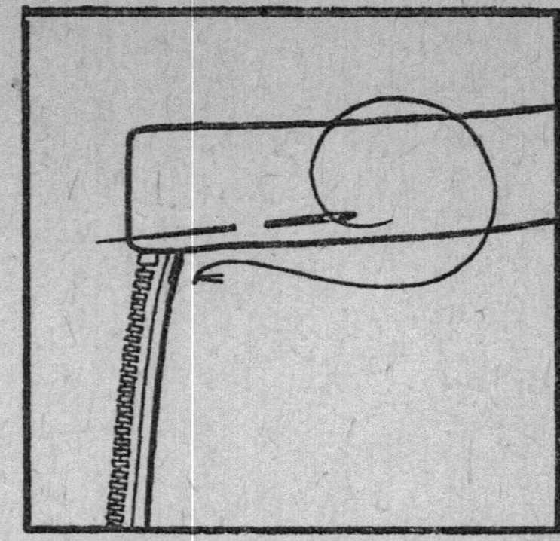

20 Now take a running stitch to the right of this, in the waistband.

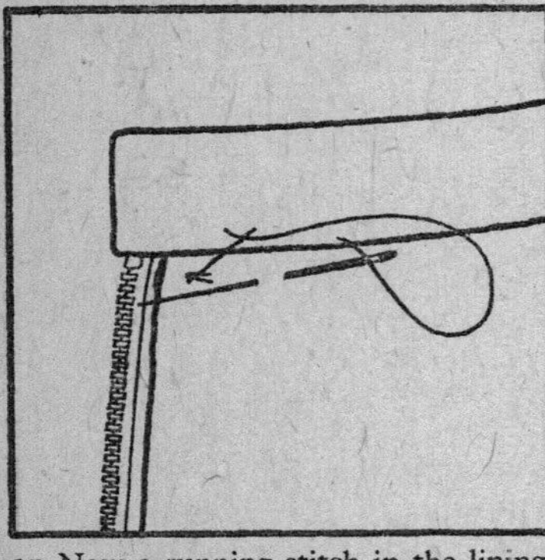

21 Now a running stitch in the lining a little to the right.

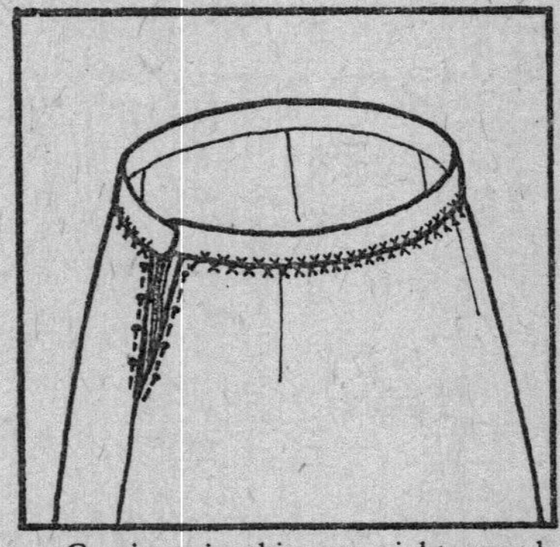

22 Continue in this way right round the waist.

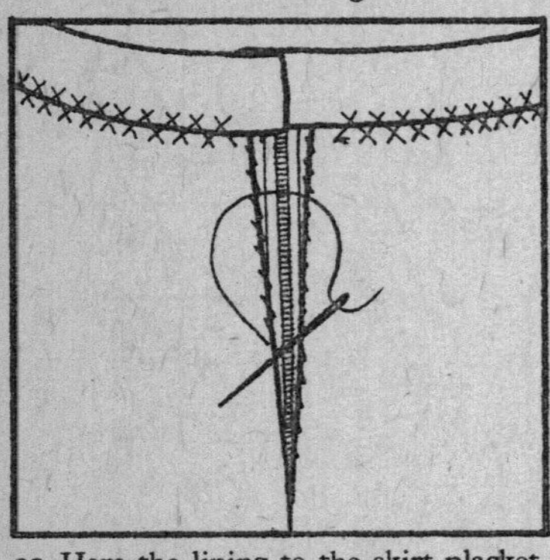

23 Hem the lining to the skirt placket either side of the zip.

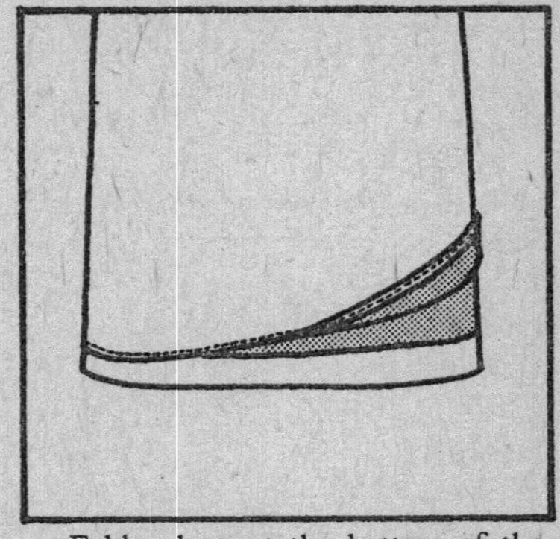

24 Fold a hem at the bottom of the lining so that it is about 1 in. shorter than the skirt, and machine it.

safety pocket

Beware of pickpockets! Men are particularly vulnerable, because everyone knows the whereabouts of the pockets in mens' suits. Ladies also would be well advised, particularly when travelling abroad, to carry their spare money where no one can easily find it. A handy place is inside the top *front* of your trousers, skirt or slacks. Use a lightweight fabric, preferably a cotton lining.

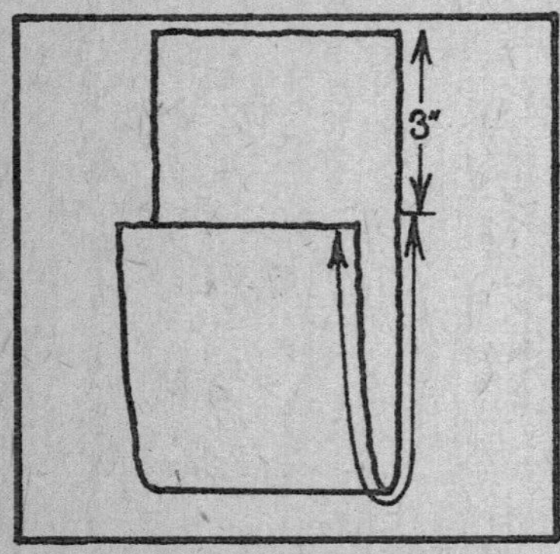

1 Make up your mind how big you want the pocket to be, and cut a strip $\frac{1}{2}$ in. wider than required, and 3 in. longer than twice the length required.

2 Turn a narrow hem on the wrong side at one end of the strip and either machine or hem it.

3 Turn the fabric over once on the wrong side at the other end, and only tack it.

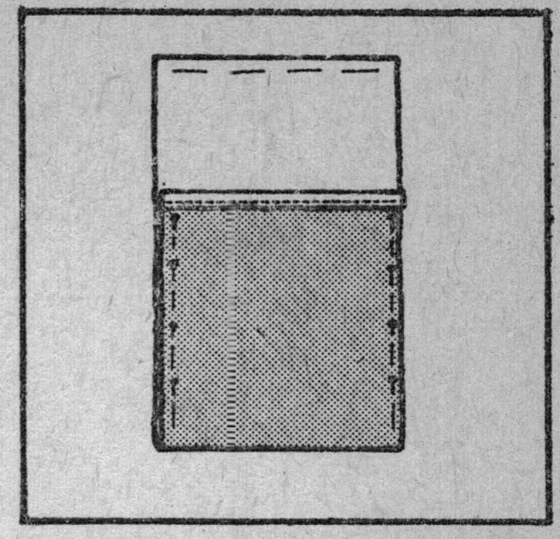

4 Working on the wrong side fold up the bottom edge to within 3 in. of the top, and pin.

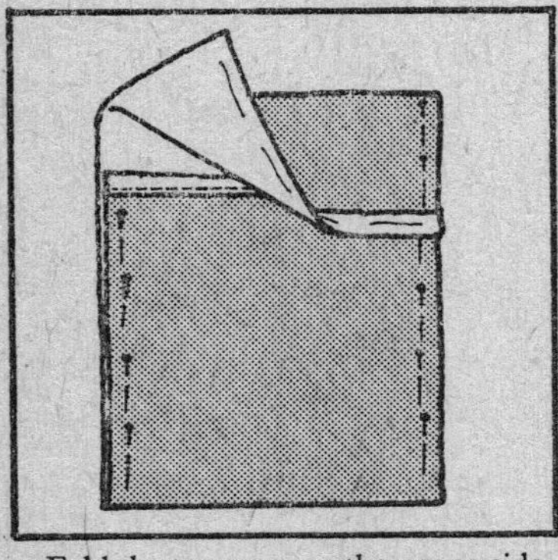

5 Fold the top over, on the wrong side, so that it overlaps the other edge by 1 in. and pin.

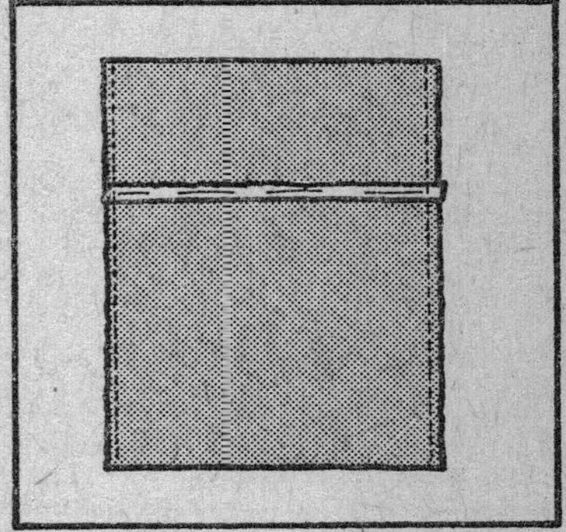

6 Sew down each side and fasten off securely as page 19-20.

7 Oversew the raw edges down either side.

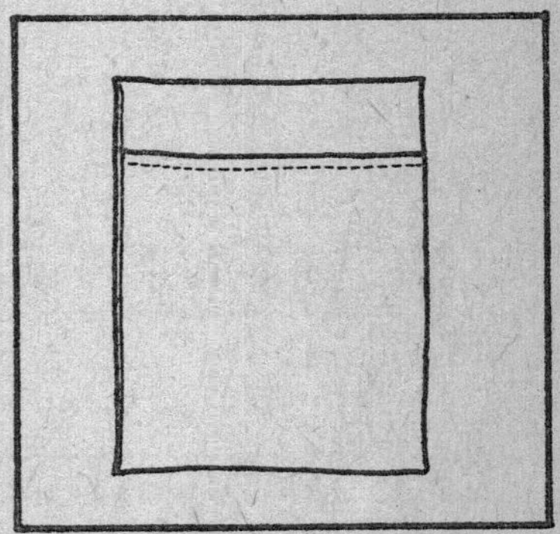

8 Turn the pocket inside out. Pick out the corners as page 186.

9 Inside the pocket, hem down the tacked fold to the back of the pocket.

10 To close the pocket sew press studs on the front edge and the back.

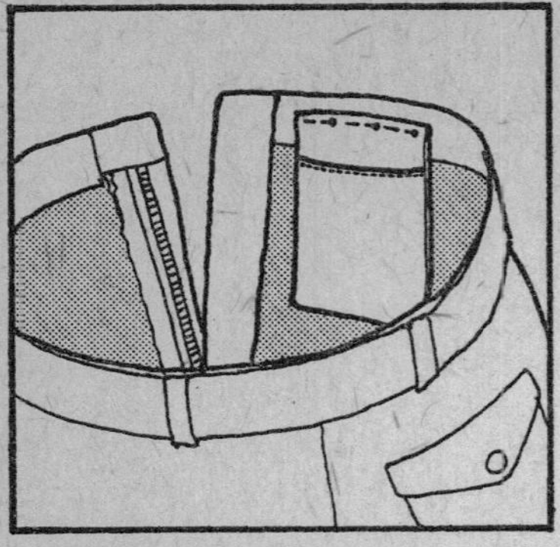

11 With the back of the pocket against the garment, pin the top edge to the inside waistband.

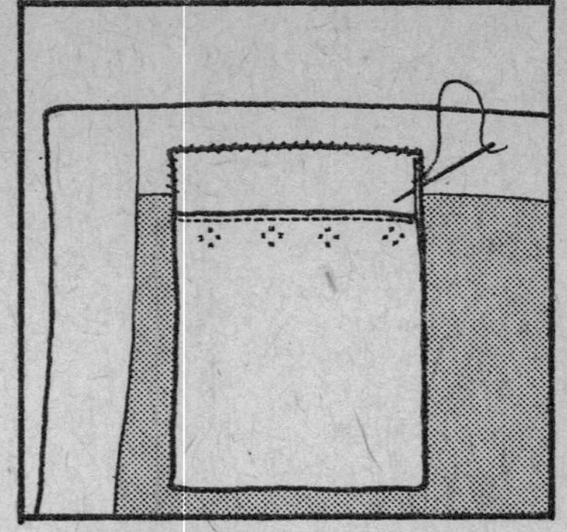

12 This must be attached firmly, but the stitches must not show on the outside. Hem to the upper surface of the waistband only, at the sides and along the top.

pattern jargon

Good patterns are in every way reliable, and contain a great deal of helpful information, but they do pre-suppose a certain amount of experience. This section explains and illustrates in greater detail some typical instructions from a good couture pattern.

When the pattern says 'match large O's,' or 'sew from ● to ●', you must do just this.

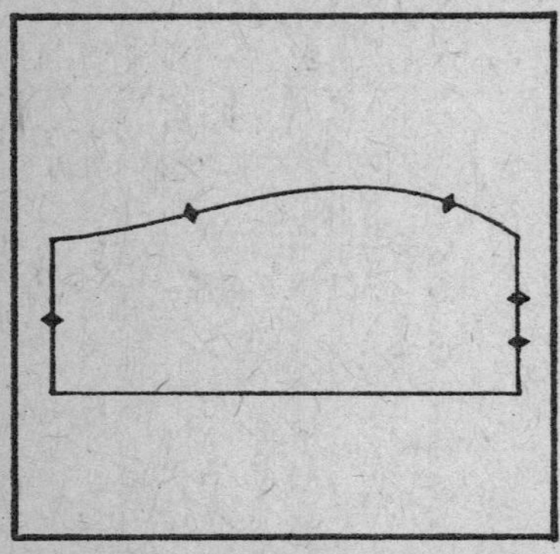

1 **Cutting line.** This is always clearly marked and is an unbroken line running right round the outer edge of the pattern piece, with notches here and there.

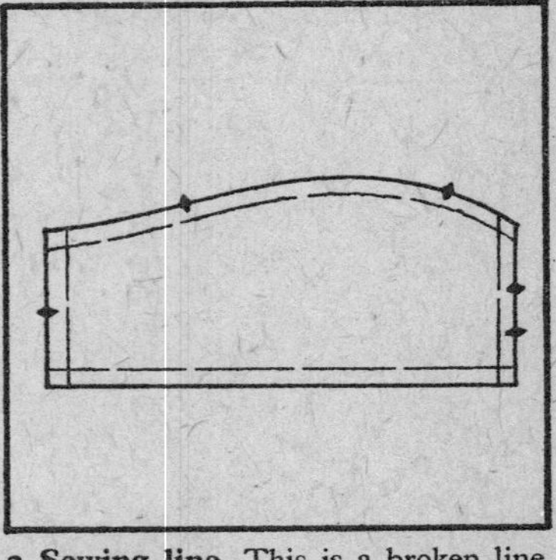

2 **Sewing line.** This is a broken line just over $\frac{1}{2}$ in. inside the cutting line.

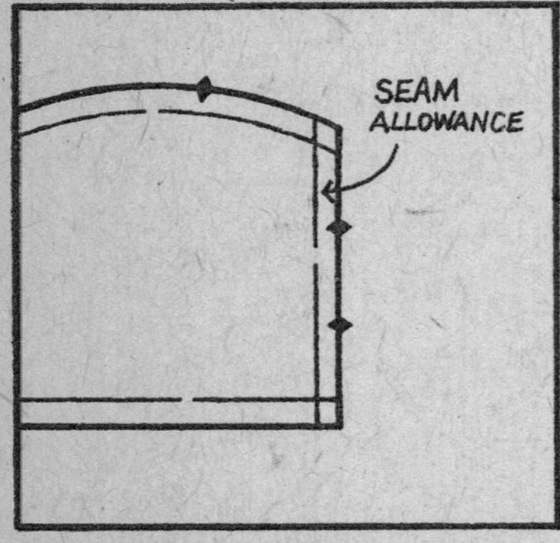

3 **Seam allowance.** This is the space between the cutting line and the sewing line.

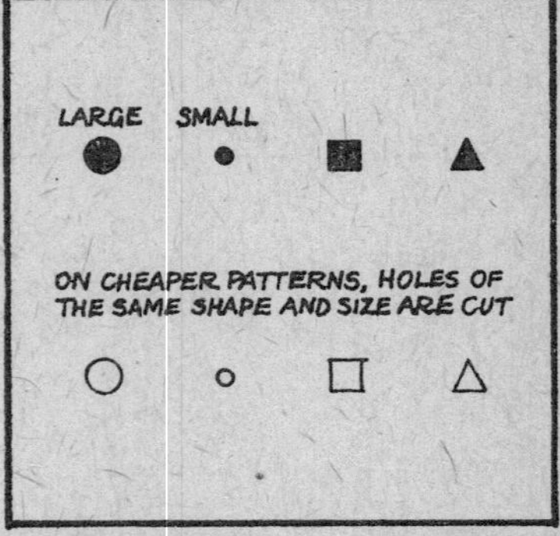

4 **Symbols.** Squares, holes and triangles all mean something, and are placed at points where one piece is required to match up with another, or where you stitch from one point to another. All symbols must be transferred to the fabric, see page 148-149.

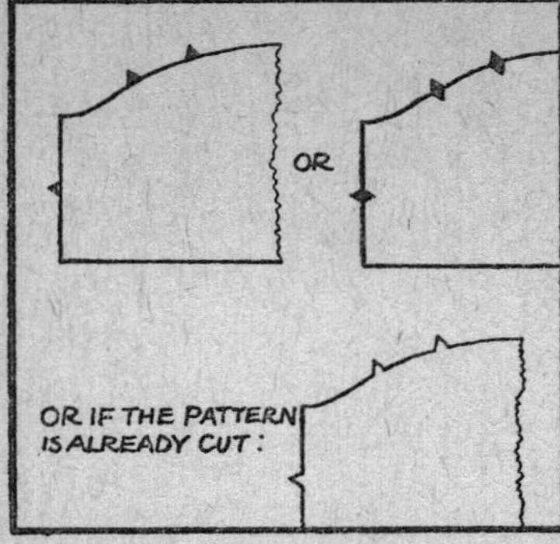

5 Notches. These also are important symbols and must be clearly marked on the fabric, see Cutting Out, page 144 to 149.

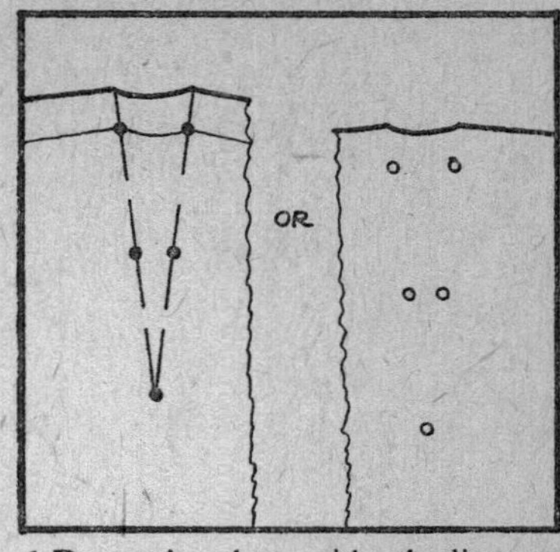

6 Darts. Are shown either by lines or just small o's or ●'s. To sew see page 33.

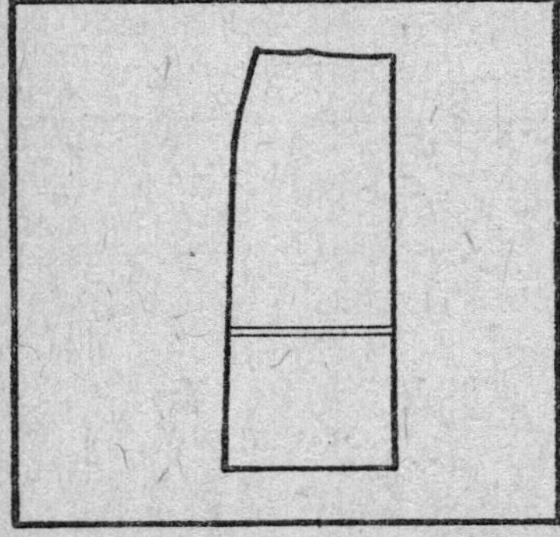

7 Adjustment line. This means that you can adjust the length at this point. It is quite normal for either the bodice, skirt or sleeve, even the trouser leg, of a pattern to need either shortening or lengthening. This has to be done in the proper place in order not to spoil the line, and the proper place is marked by a double line right across the piece.

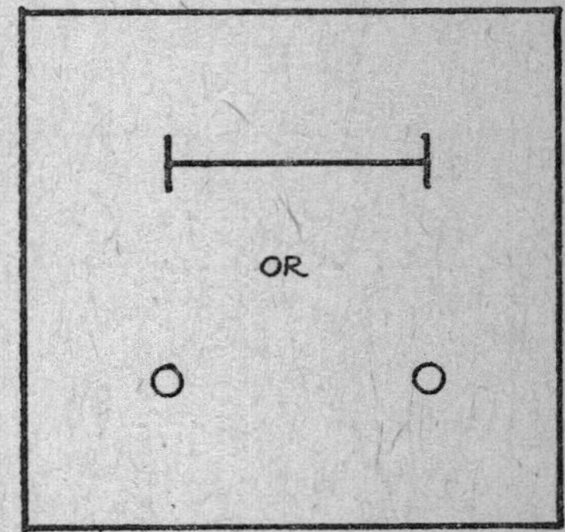

8 Buttonholes. The position of buttonholes is always marked, and it is advisable to follow the positioning on the pattern in order to maintain the style. However, if you adjust the length, you must also adjust the spacing of the buttonholes.

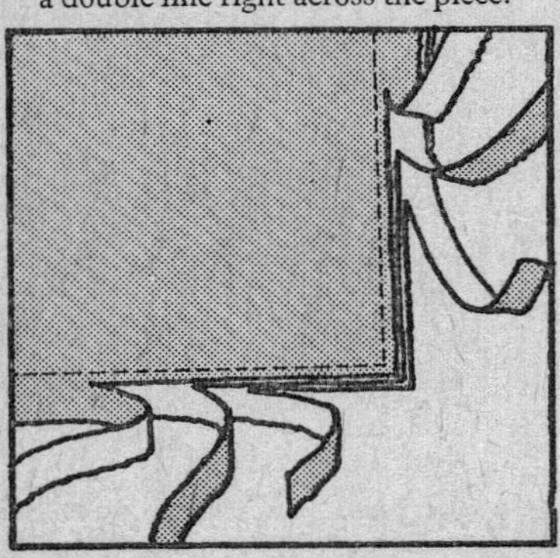

9 Trim. This means cut away unwanted seam allowances if they are likely to cause unsightly bulging, especially if you have more than two thicknesses of fabric. See page 154-156.

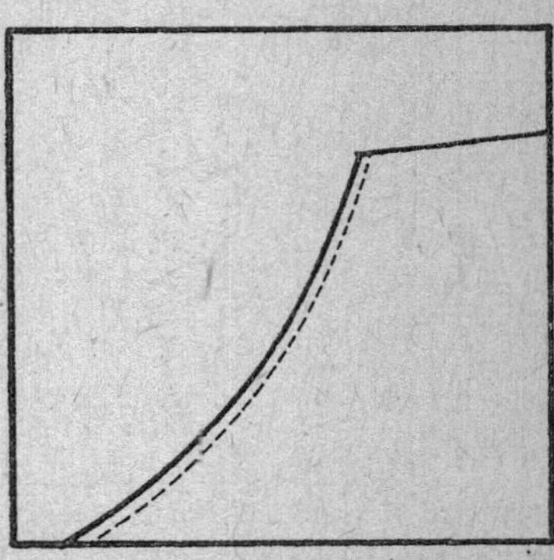

10 Stay stitch. This is a line of plain stitching just inside the outer edge of the fabric, usually done on curved edges to stop the fabric stretching as the garment is made up. It is important the tension of the sewing machine should not be too tight.

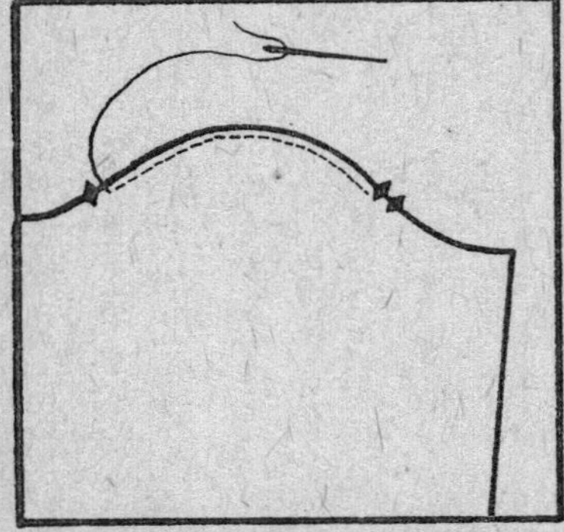

11 Ease stitch. Small running stitches done by hand which can be gathered slightly to fit into a given space. Generally done round the tops of sleeves when fitting them into armholes.

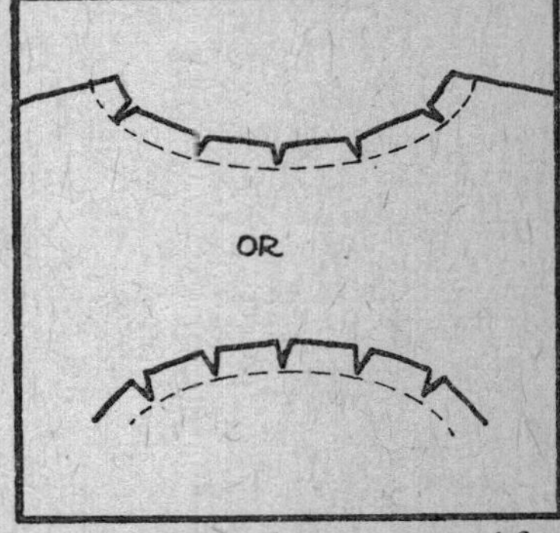

12 Clip and notch are terms used for cutting into the seam allowance to ease strain, see page 28-30.

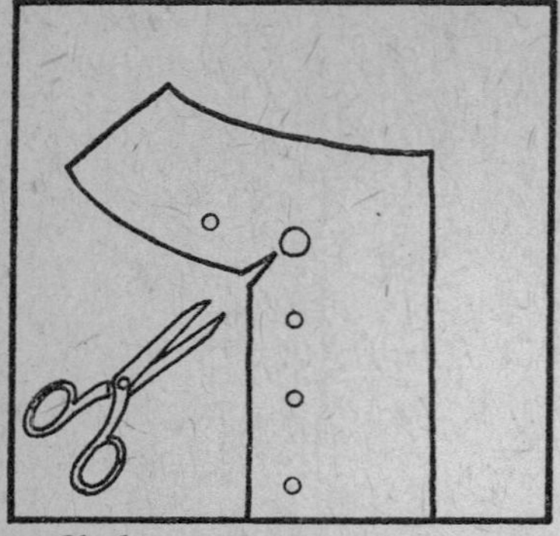

13 Slash means to cut the seam allowance with a straight cut from the outer edge to a given point, see page 30.

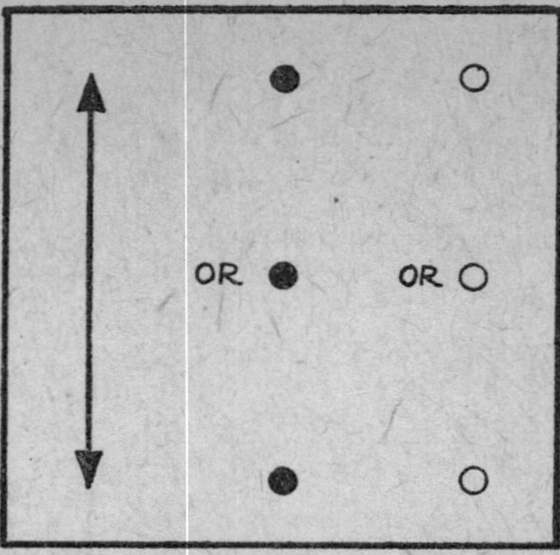

14 Grainline. This is shown by a straight line , or a line of well-spaced large O's or ●'s. If these markings are placed parallel to the selvage any design or marking on the fabric will be vertically straight in the made up garment.

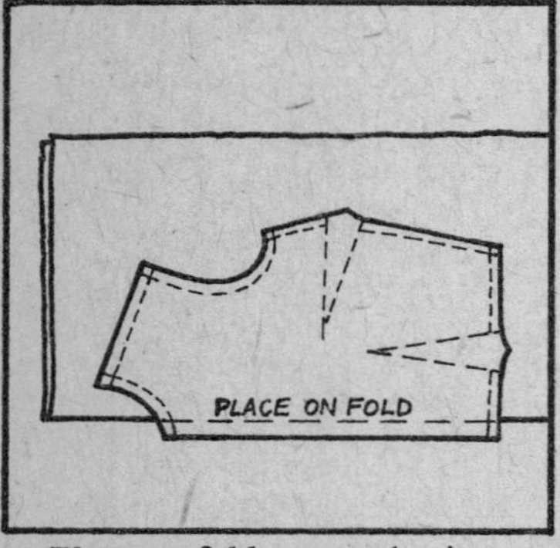

15 Place on fold means what it says. Lay the sewing line on the fold of the fabric, and do not cut it.

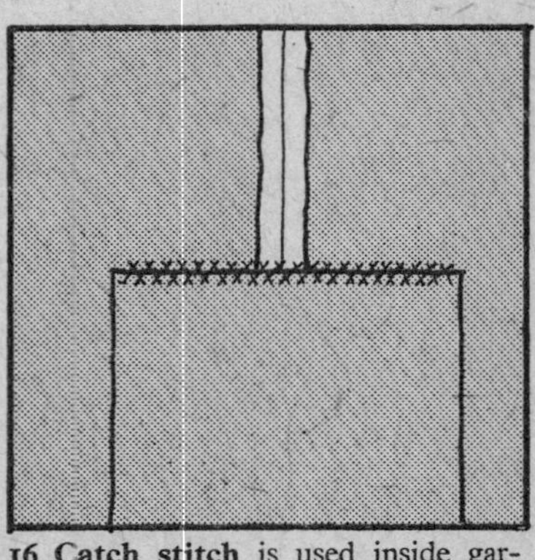

16 Catch stitch is used inside garments for holding facing, interfacing, pleats etc. in place, see page 17.

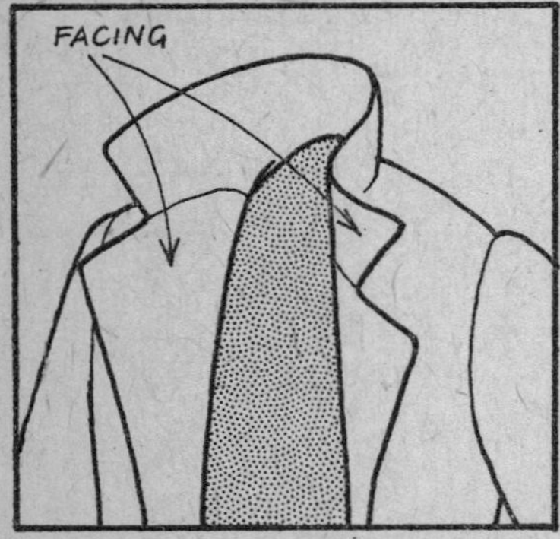

17 **Facing** is really a backing, but it gets its name from the fact that it often has to face outwards as part of the outer garment, like a coat revers.

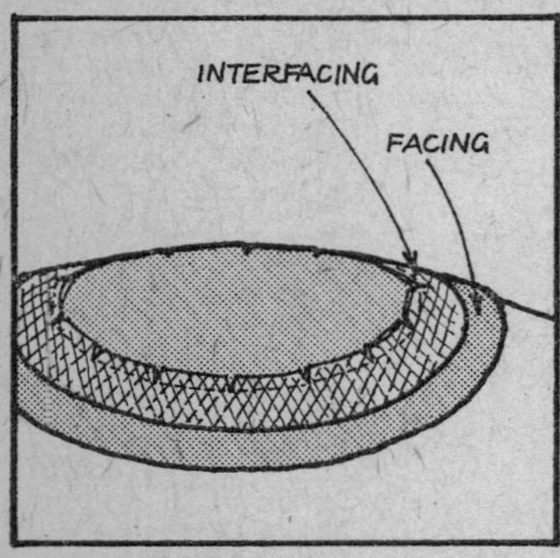

18 Interfacing is used to give a garment body. Most interfacing is slightly stiffened, like a well starched muslin, or for coats and mens' suits, stiffened linen, even hessian. Also nowadays, most commonly used for dresses, Vilene. Plays a great part in creating a professional look.

altering patterns

Alterations to patterns should be made on the adjustment lines (see 7 on page 139) and, unless you are very skilled, are best limited to shortening and lengthening. Therefore when buying a pattern it is wise to buy the correct *bust* size, because length can be adjusted, and the hips can be adjusted, but it can be tricky altering a bodice, although some simple instructions are given here.

shortening

1 Measure the pattern piece either against the person for whom the garment is being made, or against a garment which you know is a good fit, and decide exactly just how much too long it is.

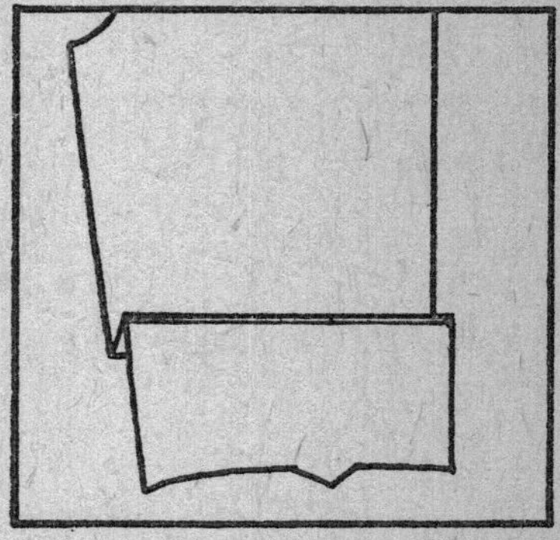

2 Take a tuck in the pattern along the adjustment line.

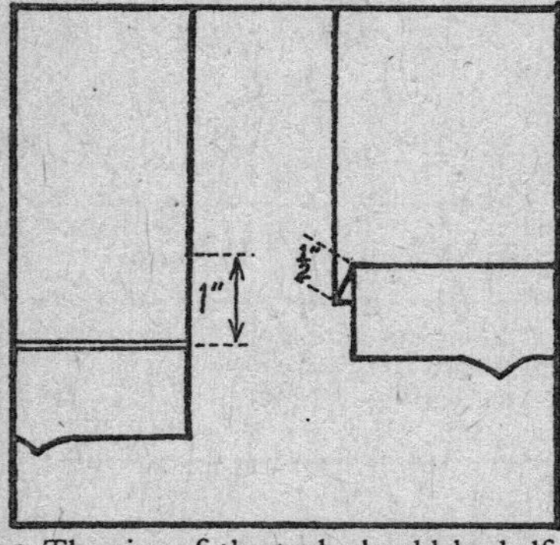

3 The size of the tuck should be half as much as the amount by which you are shortening, i.e., to shorten by 1 in. the tuck should be ½ in.

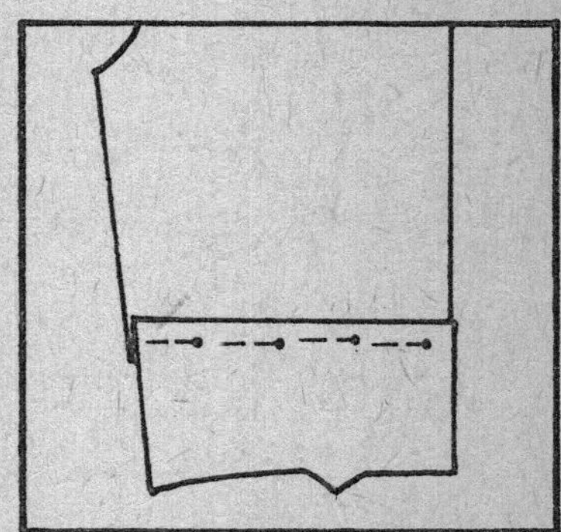

4 Pin in place

lengthening

1 After measuring as in 1 above, work out by how much the pattern is short. Cut the pattern along the adjustment line.

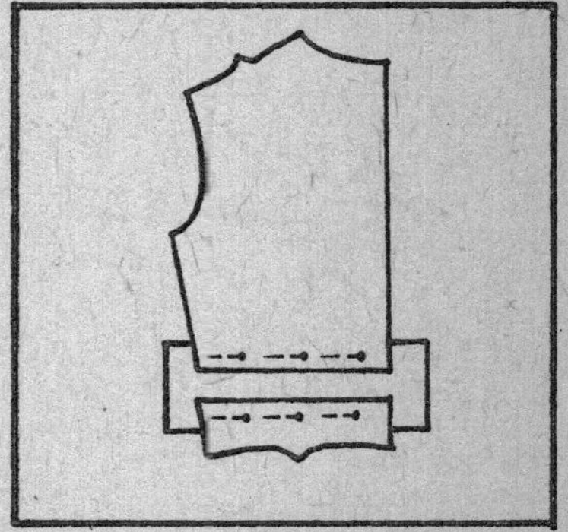

2 Lay a piece of paper underneath the two pattern pieces and pin them in position as far apart as you need them.

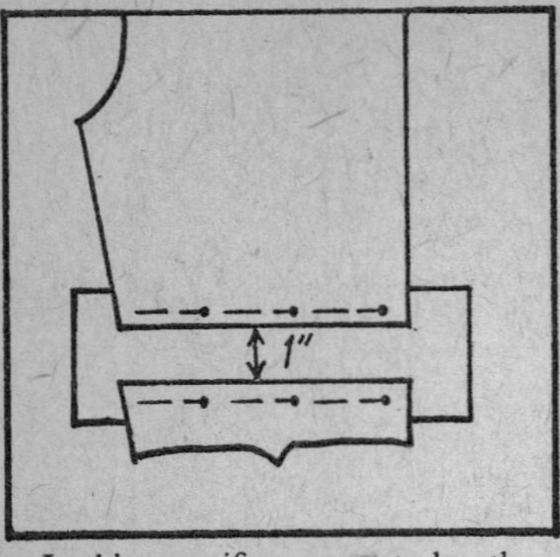

3 In this case, if you want to lengthen by 1 in. then you must pin the pieces 1 in. apart.

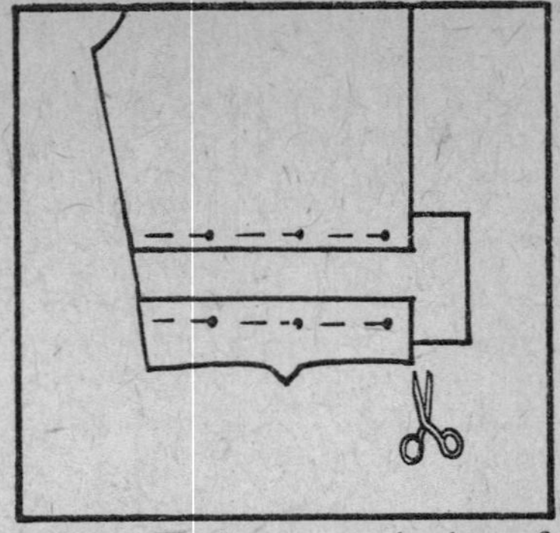

4 Cut away the unwanted edges of paper.

widening the hip but not the waist

You can make this adjustment by cutting wider than the pattern, but if you do, remember that the total amount by which you wish to extend will be divided by the number of cut edges.

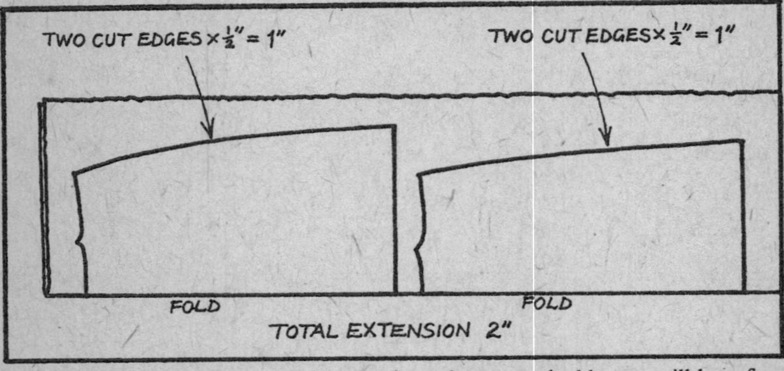

1 For instance, if you have two skirt panels, each one cut double, you will have four cut edges, so the total amount will be divided by four.
As an example, if you are extending the hip measurement by 2 in, you will only need to add ½ in. to each piece.

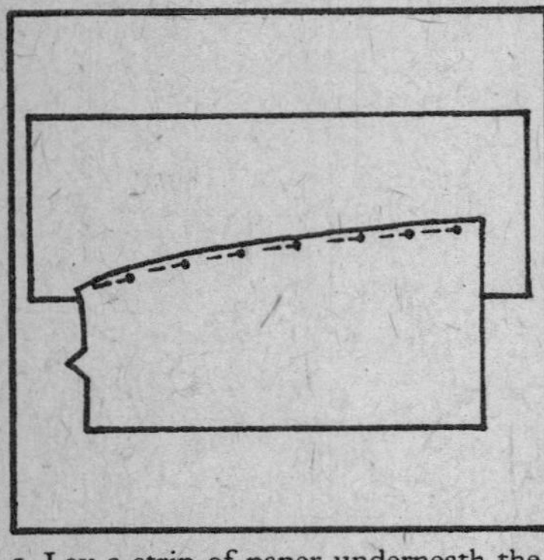

2 Lay a strip of paper underneath the side edge of the pattern, and pin the two together.

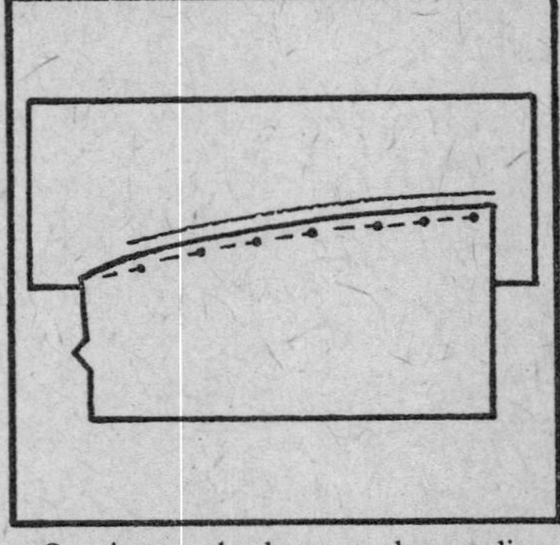

3 Starting at the bottom, draw a line the appropriate distance away from the cutting line up the side until you are round the hip bulge.

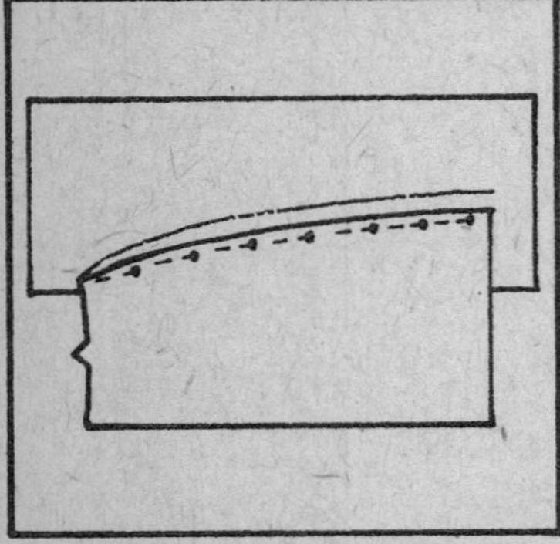

4 Once beyond the point where the extra width is no longer needed, taper the line towards the waist until it runs into the original cutting line.

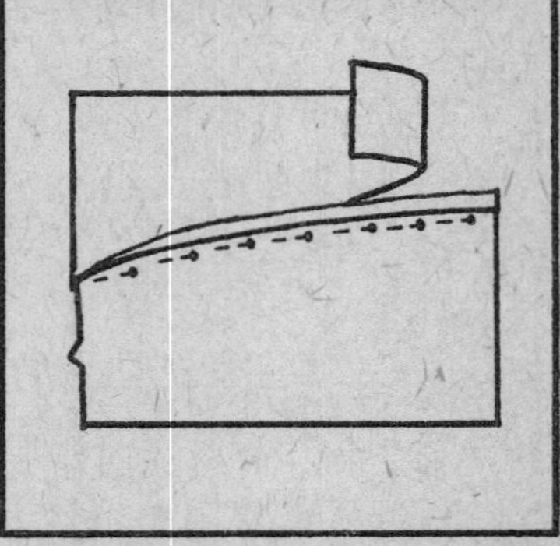

5 Cut away the waste paper each end, and cut out along new cutting line.

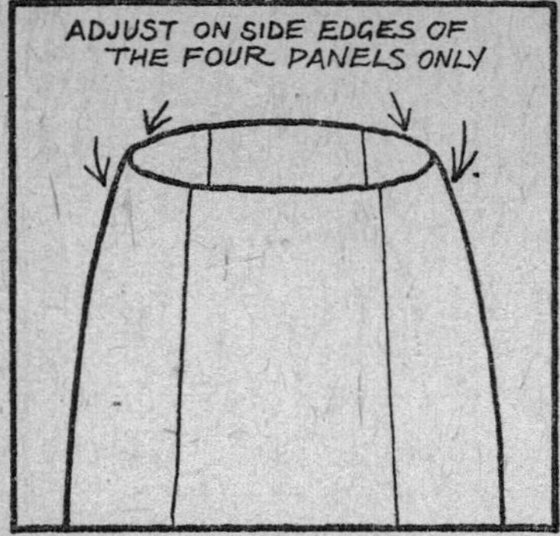

6 For a panelled skirt, use the above method, on the side panels, back and front. You will still have four cut edges.

For final fitting of the adjusted hip, see page 151.

widening the hip and waist

If you are making a dress, the bodice will have to be altered to match the skirt. There are two alternative methods. For the first, proceed as 1 to 3, page 142, then continue:

1 Instead of tapering towards the original cutting line, continue parallel with the cutting line until you reach the waist. Cut away waste as in 5.

Alternatively, for a skirt only you can allow extra on the straight edges. The same principle of dividing the total amount by the number of edges will apply. Do not alter the pattern but allow for cutting wider than the pattern when you lay it down on the fabric.

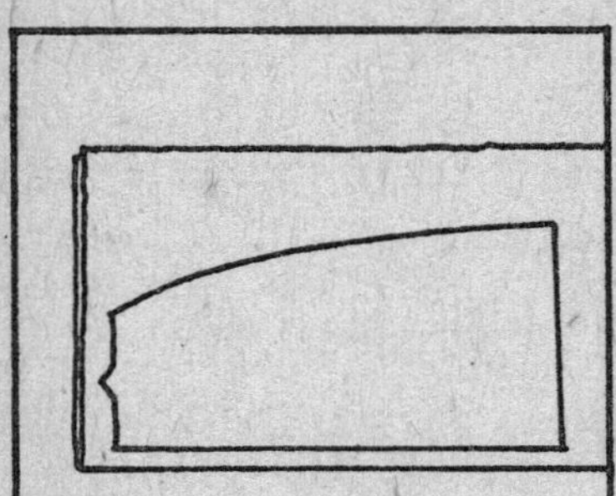

2 If you are placing one piece against the fold of the fabric, lay it with the *cutting* line an appropriate distance from the fold.

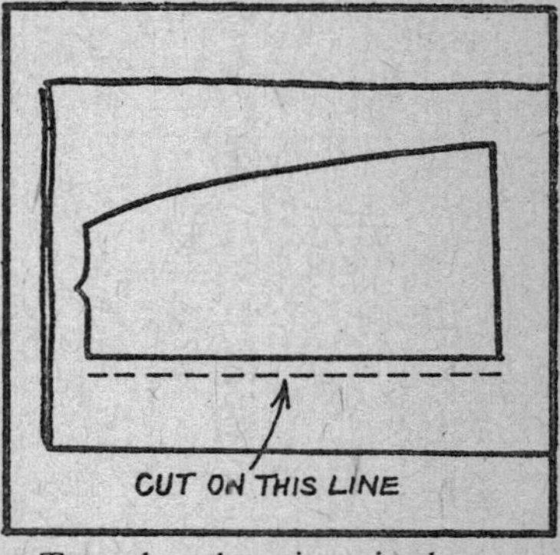

3 Treat the other pieces in the same way if they should lie against the fold, but if they do not, cut the straight edge an appropriate distance from the original cutting line.

If, by widening the skirt, the waist is too big, see page 84 to adjust the garment. If you now have to widen the bodice at the waist to match the skirt:

4 Pin paper behind your bodice pieces on the side edge, as you did with the skirt.

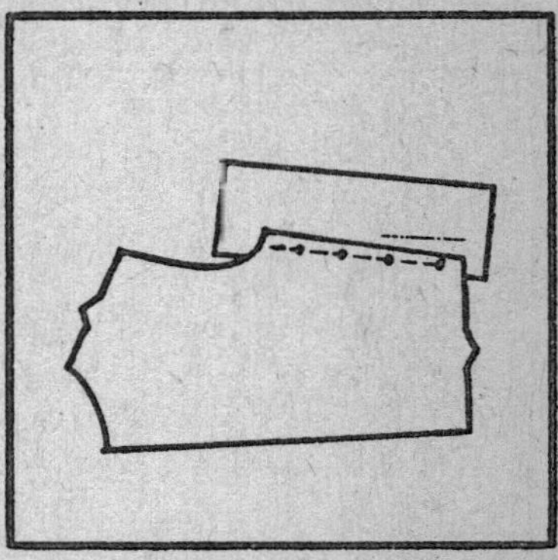

5 The same principle of dividing by four will apply, so starting at the waist, on the side edge, draw a line the same distance from the cutting line as you did for the skirt.

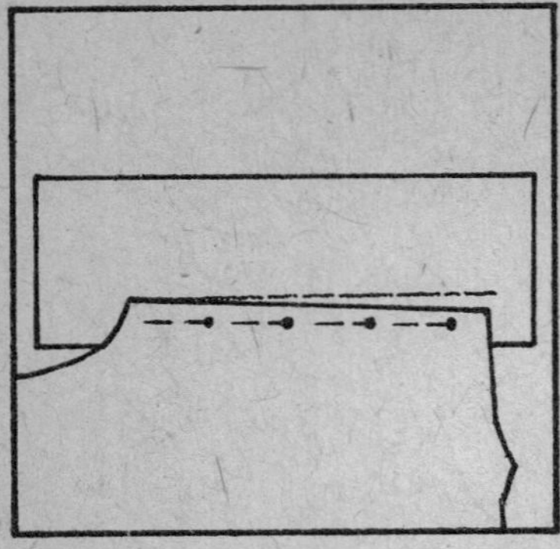

6 Keep this line straight so that it will taper into the original cutting line. Cut away the waste paper as on page 142.

taking in the hip and waist

Cut and make up the garment as it is, but leave the side seams open. Fit to the figure as on page 151.

lengthening and shortening sleeves

Don't take chances with sleeves. Adjust only on the lines indicated. Either take a tuck to shorten or let in a piece to lengthen, exactly as on page 141.

cutting out

All paper patterns give illustrated instructions on how to lay out the pattern pieces on varying widths of fabric. It is advisable to follow these instructions wherever possible. Even so, there are several pitfalls to watch out for, and mistakes made in cutting can be difficult to rectify.

First of all, establish which is the right and wrong side of the fabric (see page 25). If necessary, pin pieces of paper here and there on the right side so that odd pieces can be identified and properly used.

Get the cut edges of the fabric straight.

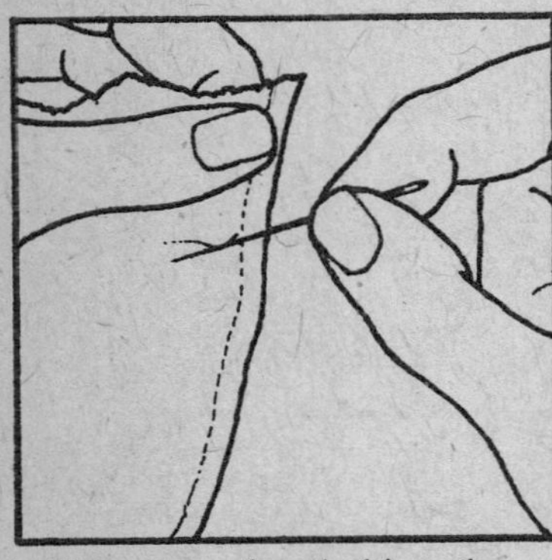

1 The most used method is to draw a thread just below the lowest point of the jagged edge. Lift a horizontal thread with a needle point just inside the selvage.

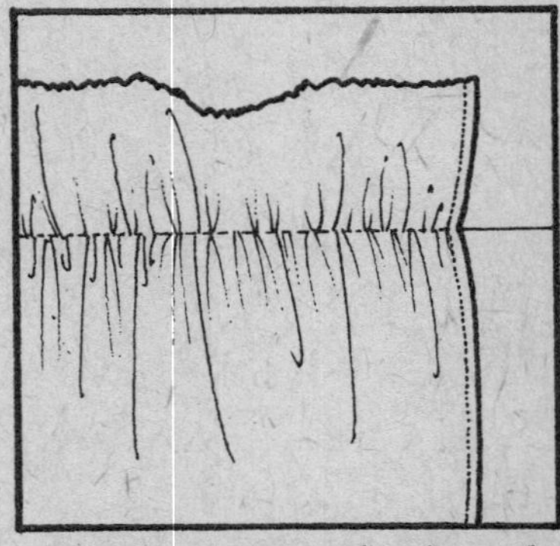

2 Pull this thread, easing it gently right across the piece.

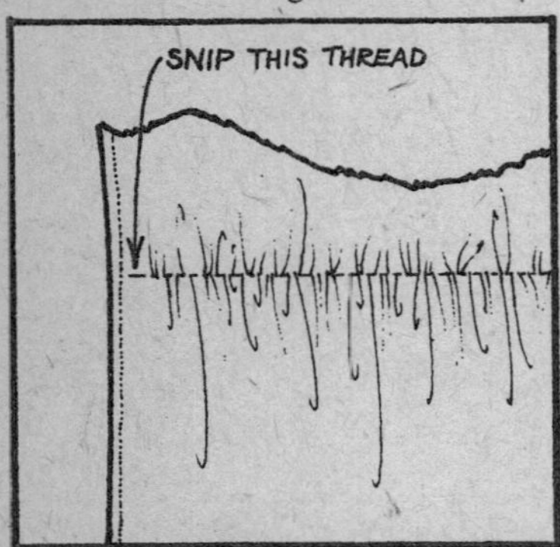

3 Find the same thread just inside the other selvage – it will be pulled very taut and easily seen – and snip it carefully.

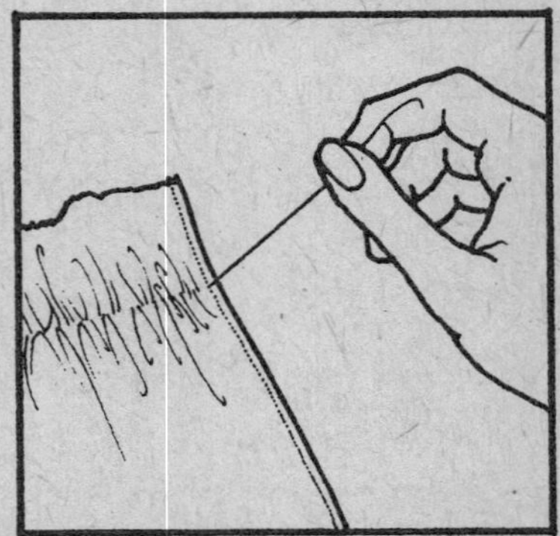

4 Pull the thread right out.

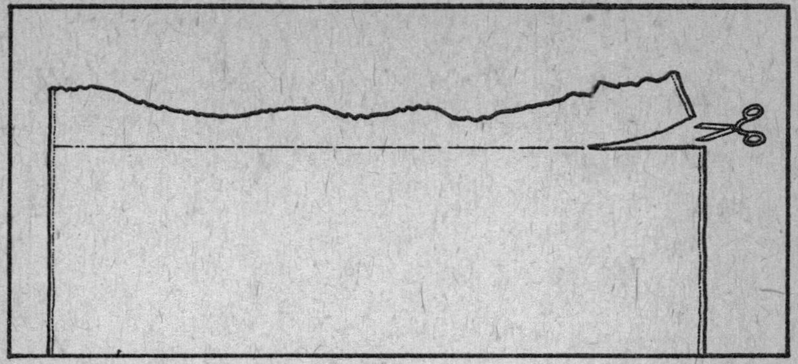

5 You will be left with a fine line right across the width of the fabric, which will be absolutely straight. Cut along here.

LACE AND FANCY FABRICS

6 Do not attempt the foregoing method with lace or any fabric with a fancy weave. First of all, fold the whole length of fabric in half, end to end.

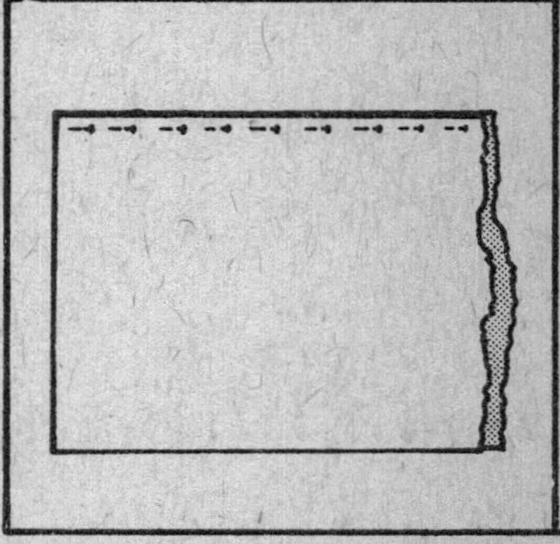

7 Pin the selvages together along one side.

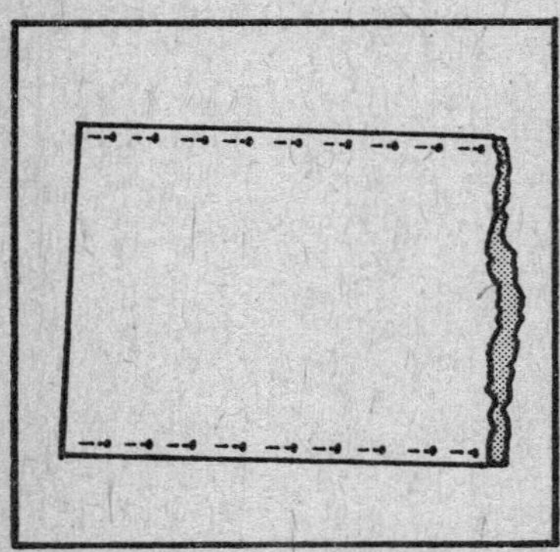

8 Smooth the fabric absolutely flat. The selvages along other side should now lay evenly one on top of the other. Pin them together.

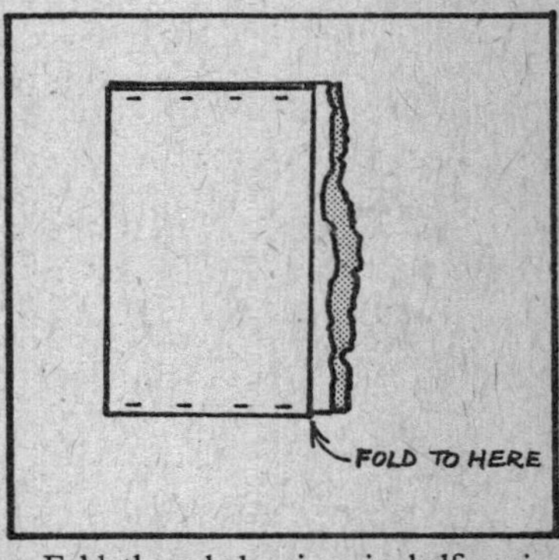

9 Fold the whole piece in half again with the first fold on a level with the lowest point of the uneven edge.

10 This should now show you a straight edge. Pin or mark with tailor's chalk all the way along, and then cut on that line.

SEAM ALLOWANCES

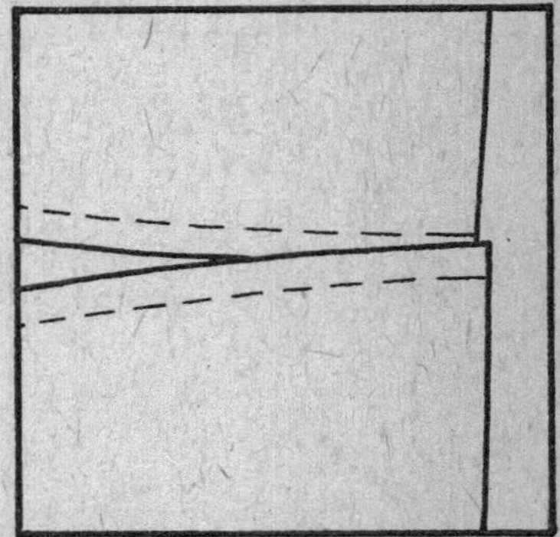

11 You can overlap these slightly if you are short of fabric.

VELVET AND FABRICS WITH A PILE

See page 26.

You can follow pattern instructions unless you are, for instance, cutting a child's dress out of an old evening dress, in which case, follow the basic rules given here.

ONE-WAY PATTERNED FABRICS

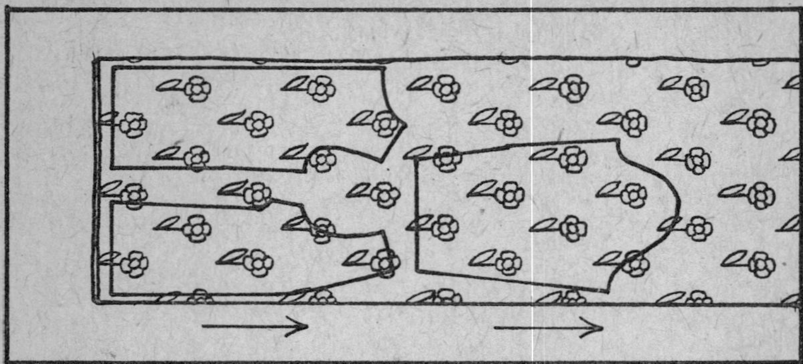

1 If the pattern is for this type of fabric the instructions will guide you so far as keeping the design facing in the right direction is concerned, but if you are working without such instructions remember to place all pattern pieces facing in the same direction. You must do your own matching up of patterned fabrics.

horizontal stripes

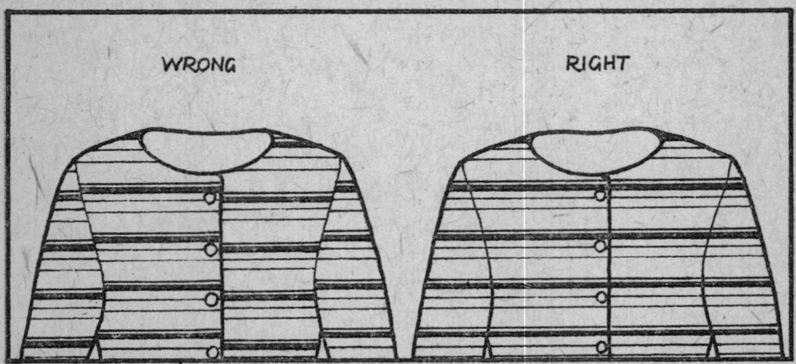

1 These must match at seams wherever possible, and across the front of an open bodice. This has to be taken care of at the cutting stage.

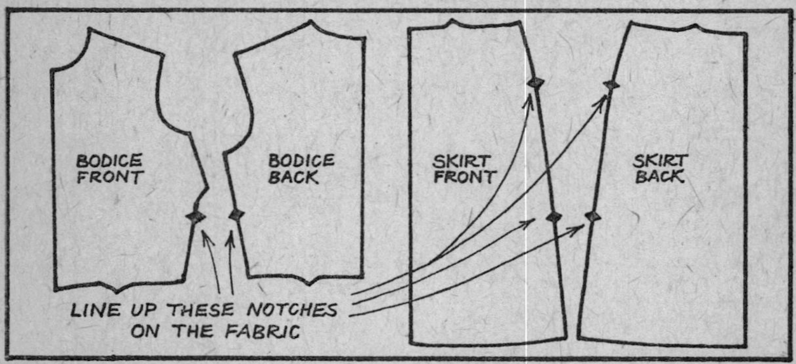

2 The notches on the outer edge of various pieces have to match up with each other, so use these notches as your guide. Examine the pattern pieces carefully and note the notches which will have to match up.

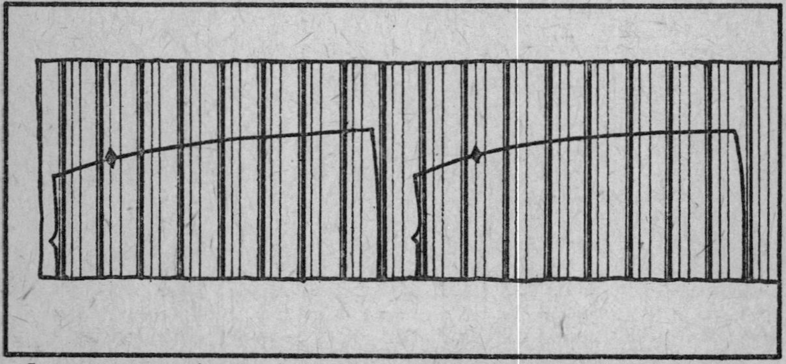

3 Lay your pattern pieces so that matching notches are placed on the same stripe.

4 At the waistline, remember it is the sewing line which counts, not the cutting line.

vertical stripes

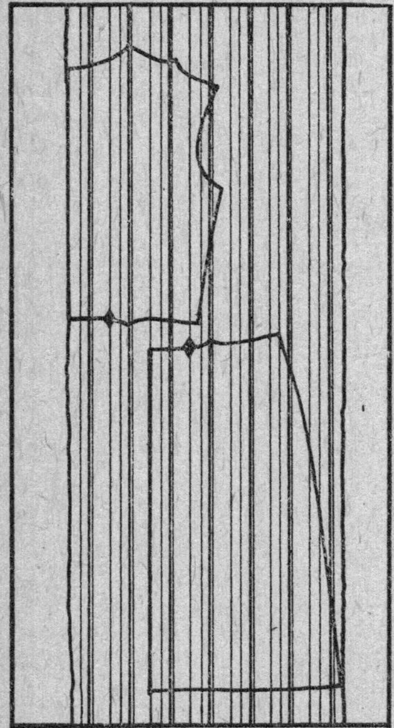

These also must match, but across the pattern instead of vertically. As most vertical stripes are made up into plain garments this will probably only apply at the waist.

checked fabrics

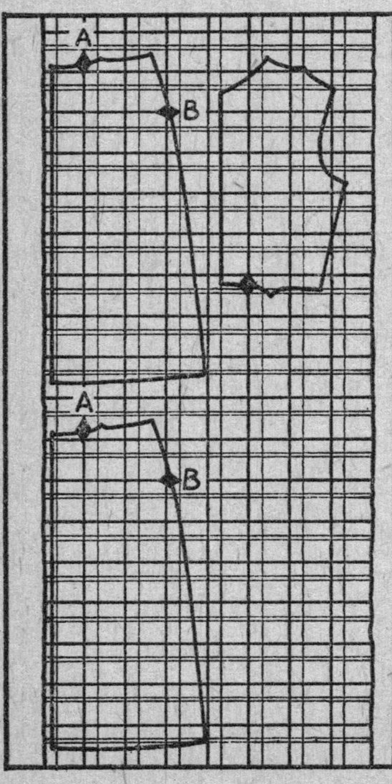

If there is a dominant stripe in the check, this must match vertically and horizontally. The same principles apply as for horizontal and vertical stripes, with care being taken at the waistline.

large floral and geometrical designs

Adopt the same principles as for stripes and checks, whichever is appropriate.

cutting identical pieces

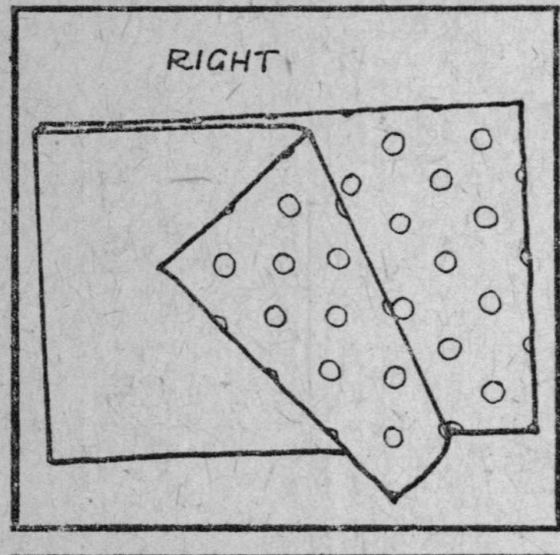

When two identical pieces are required, such as two sleeves or bodice pieces, and are cut together, the fabric is always placed 'face to face', that is, either the right sides facing inwards or the wrong sides facing inwards.

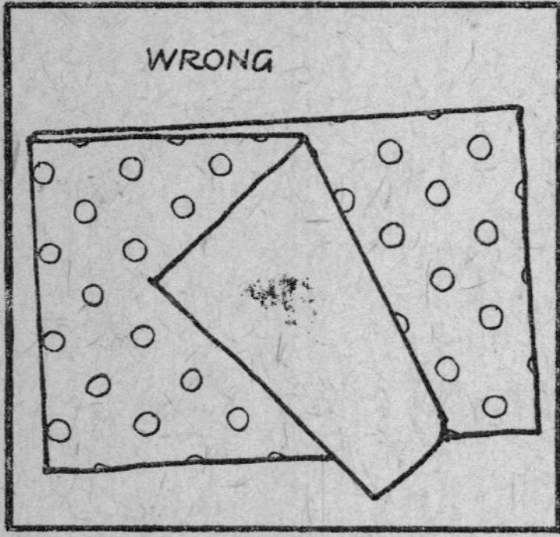

Identical pieces are never cut two at a time with both thicknesses of fabric facing the same way. If you make this mistake, this will be the result.

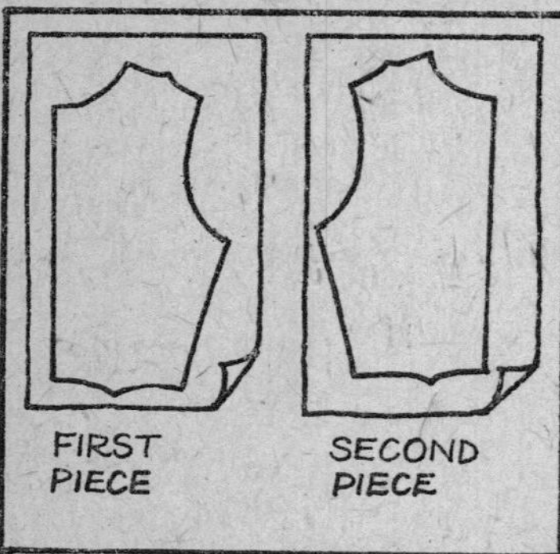

Alternatively, if you are making up from an old garment and have to cut two identical pieces entirely separately, cut with the right side of the fabric uppermost both times, but for the second piece turn the pattern over.

Where you have a paper pattern which has not been printed, use the smooth side and the rough side as identification.

marking pattern symbols on the fabric

By far the most simple method is to use tailor's tacks. Tailor's chalk is inclined to rub off, and the tracing wheel method requires carbon, but tailor's tacks only require tacking cotton, or any contrasting thread you have.

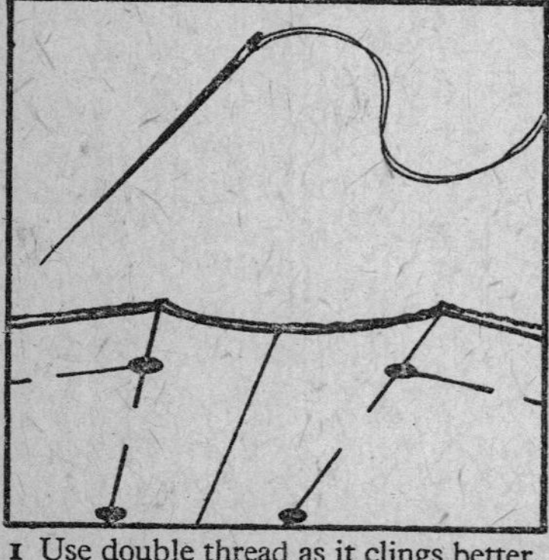

1 Use double thread as it clings better, and work with the paper pattern in place on the fabric.

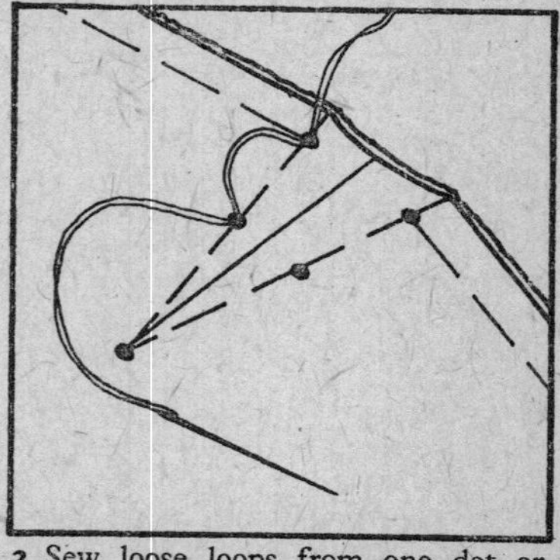

2 Sew loose loops from one dot or hole to another, making sure you go in and out of each dot or hole, and over the paper to the next one.

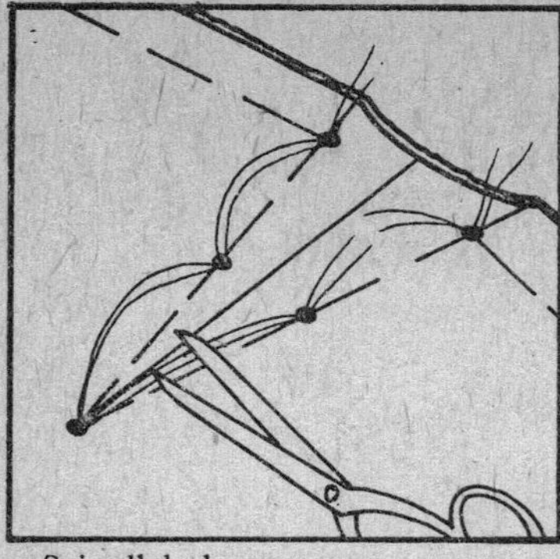
3 Snip all the loops.

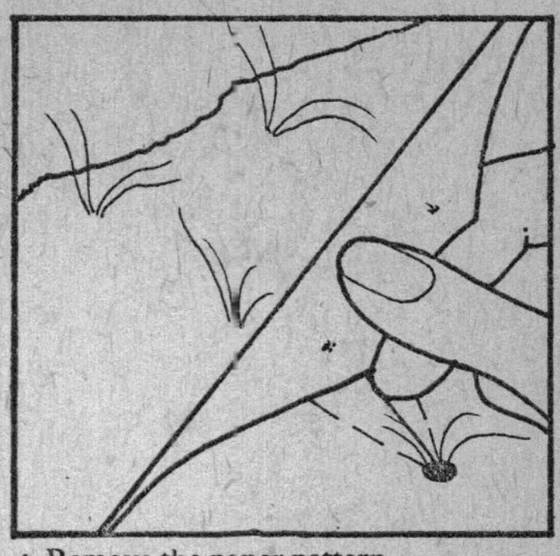
4 Remove the paper pattern.

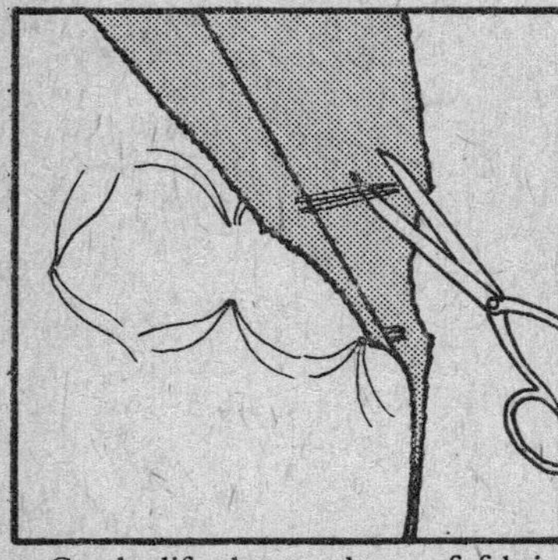
5 Gently lift the top layer of fabric and snip the threads between the two pieces.

notches round the edge

Cut round these as you go along.

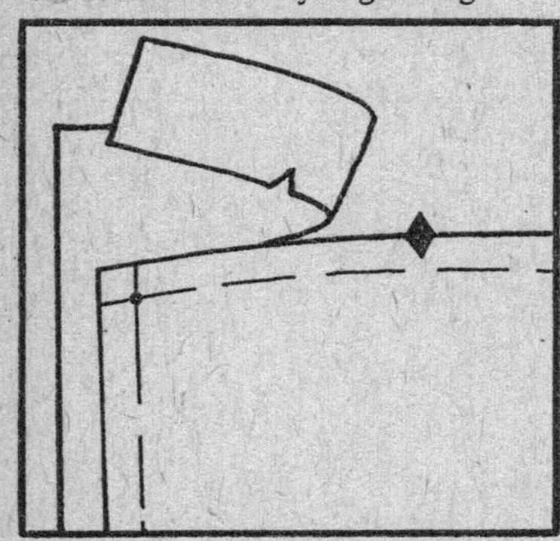

lining up the designs on the fabric

When you are folding patterned fabric in half preparatory to cutting out, remember that you will be cutting double, so get your stripes, checks or whatever, fair and square on top of each other. If necessary pin in place.

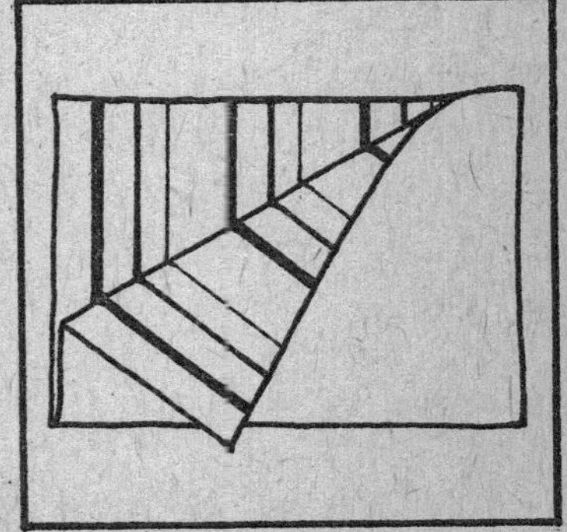

making a lined dress

All couture dresses are lined, so this is one of the ways in which a novice home dress-maker can produce an expensive looking garment for a modest outlay. All silks hang better if they are lined, so also do the rayons and tricels, but the quality lies in making the lining with the dress instead of putting it in afterwards. Do not line the sleeves, or the facings.

If the pattern does not give you the amount required for the lining consult the shop assistant who will be able to tell you how much you will need.

1 Cut out the dress and mark up all the notches and tailor's tacks before removing the pattern.

2 Lay out the pieces again on the lining and cut another dress, with the exception of facings and sleeves.

3 Mark up notches and tailor's tacks on the lining.

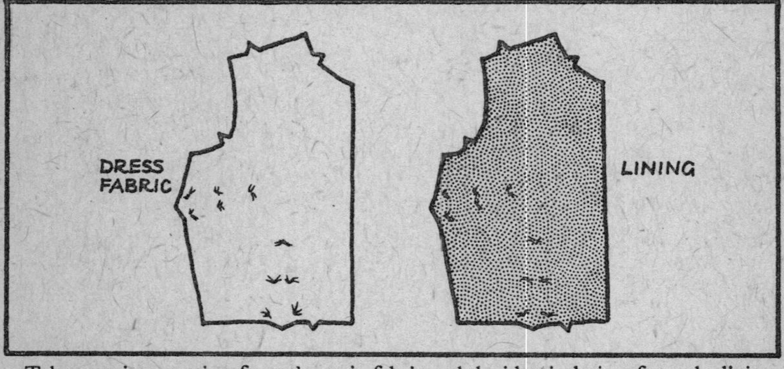

4 Take one piece at a time from the main fabric and the identical piece from the lining.

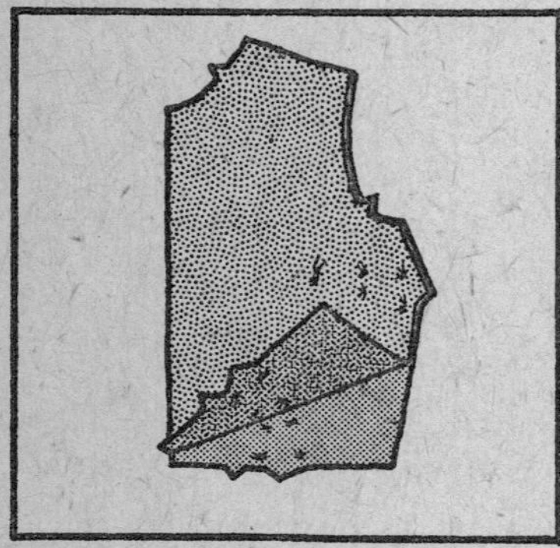

5 Lay the lining on the wrong side of the main fabric, matched notch for notch.

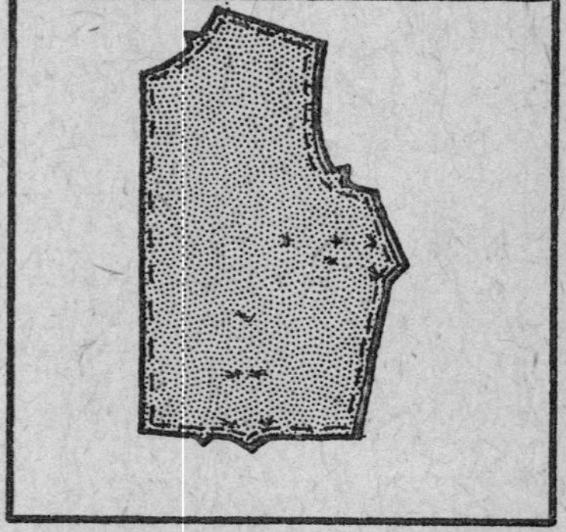

6 Tack the two pieces together all round the edge and work on them as one piece of fabric. These stitches can be removed afterwards.

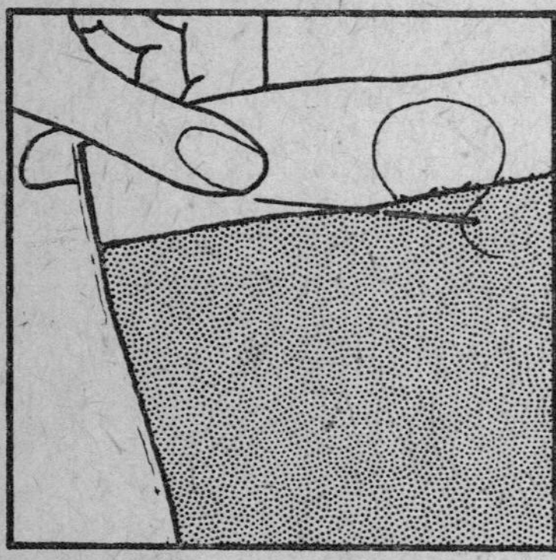

7 When slip-stitching facings and the hem, catch only a few threads from the lining. This will give a completely smooth surface on the outside.

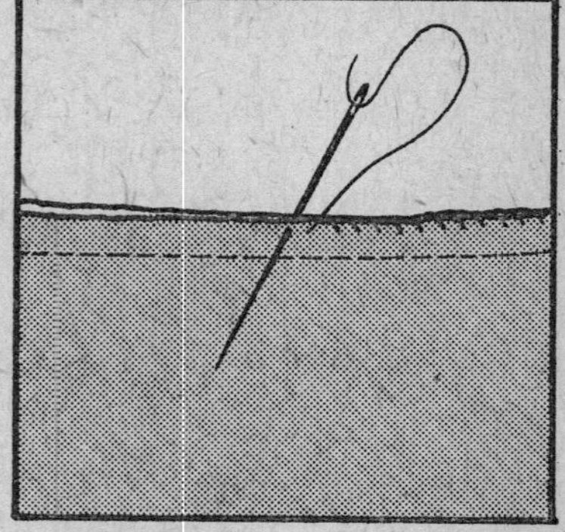

8 To finish off the raw edges neatly inside the dress, oversew the outer fabric and the lining together.

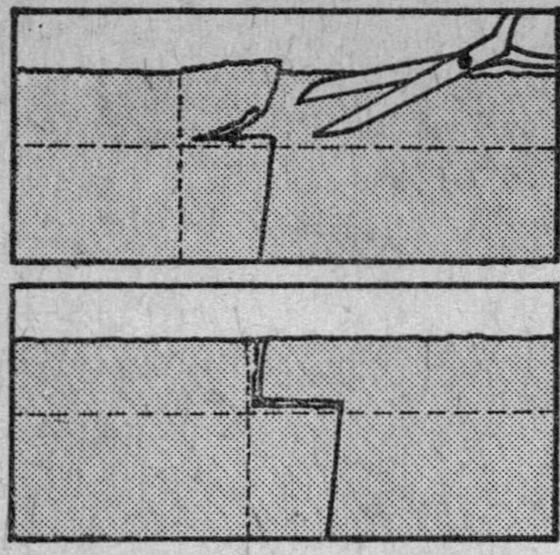

9 If you get too much thickness on folds, for instance, at the top of darts, cut away as on pages 154 and 156.

fitting a dress

This section assumes you are inexperienced and haven't got a dressmaker's dummy. Pattern instructions tell you to sew side seams as you go along, that is, you make up the bodice as a whole, and the skirt as a whole, having fitted them both perfectly, and then sew the two together.

This is fine if you are sure of yourself, but if you would prefer to fit the dress as a whole, and some professional dressmakers work this way, sew your shoulder seams, and sew the waist seams front and back, then hang the garment over your shoulders inside out. Get someone to help you.

1 Pin the back opening together if there is one, being careful to take in no more fabric than will be taken in when the zip is inserted.

2 Pin the side seams of the bodice from the armhole to the waist making sure the garment fits easily across the bust and at the waist.

3 Pin the skirt either side in the same way, following the natural hip line. This is particularly important where you have adjusted the hip and/or waist on the pattern.

Perform some contortions in it, swing your arms about, sit down, walk about in it, even try knees full bend, and when you are absolutely satisfied that the dress fits perfectly tack the side seams and sew them. The same principle applies when you are making alterations. Put on the dress, inside out, and get someone to fit it to your shape wherever you have unpicked and wish to re-sew.

the sleeves

Sleeves themselves are very seldom wrong, and if the bust fits and you matched the notches as instructed when fitting them in, they should not need any adjustment. Any other adjustments found to be necessary can be dealt with as in Alterations.

making underwear and nightwear

This section does not tell you how to make garments – the pattern instructions will do that – but there are several simple rules to follow to give you better results.

Some people still like to make their own lingerie. Cotton nightdresses are a rarity and expensive to buy, but very necessary in really hot weather, or in hospital.

There is one important thing to remember when making lingerie: don't ever leave raw edges anywhere. With the constant washing these garments have to bear, the insides of the seams would be a mass of shreds in no time. Oversewing them is not the answer. You must hide all raw edges completely.

Use a french seam (page 21-22) on fine fabrics, and a run and fell seam (see page 21) on tougher garments like pyjamas.

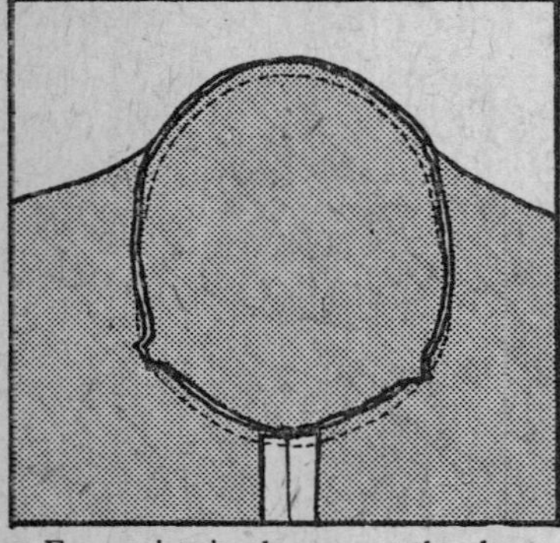

1 For sewing in sleeves, set the sleeve and sew once in the ordinary way.

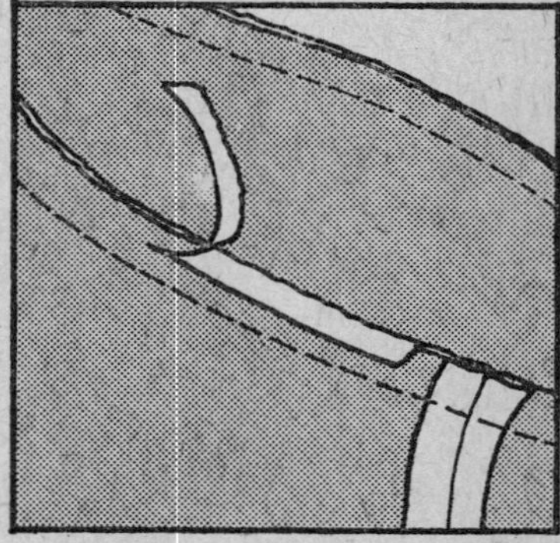

2 Trim off half the seam allowance of the bodice section only.

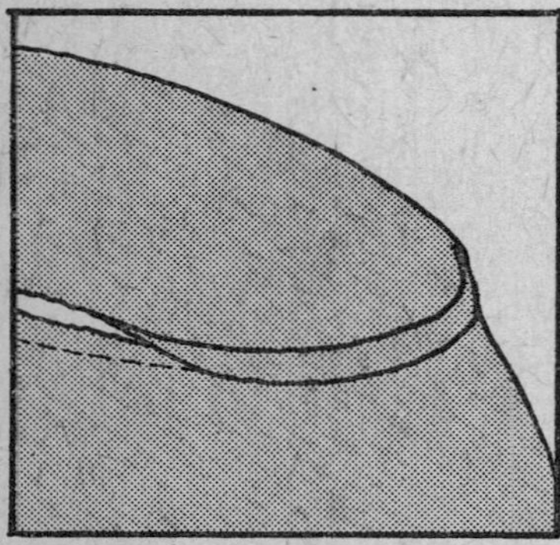

3 Fold the seam allowance of the sleeve over the cut-away seam allowance of the bodice.

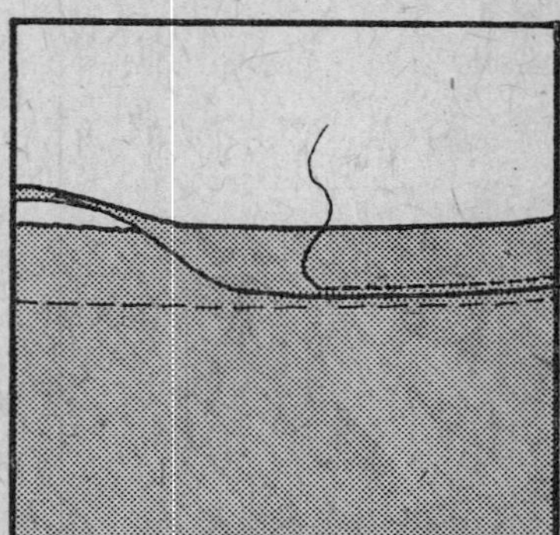

4 Turn under a small hem and sew it down.

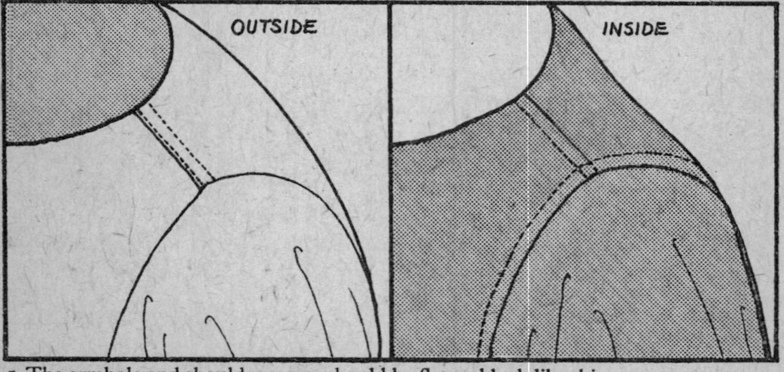

5 The armhole and shoulder seams should be flat and look like this.

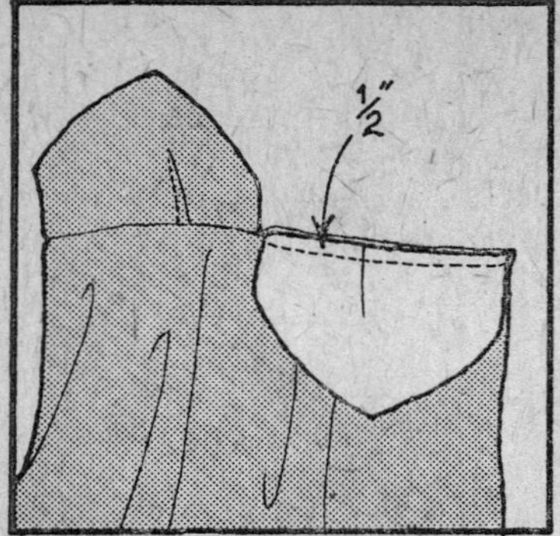

6 When sewing a french seam on fine fabrics, make this as small as possible. In the first instance, leave a ½ in. seam allowance if the pattern says so.

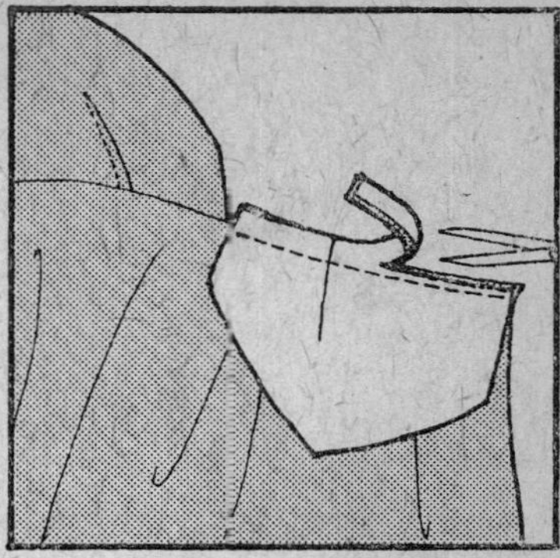

7 You must leave ½ in. seam allowance if that's what the pattern says, otherwise the garment will be too big, but trim it off to about ⅛ in. before you turn inside out to sew the second seam.

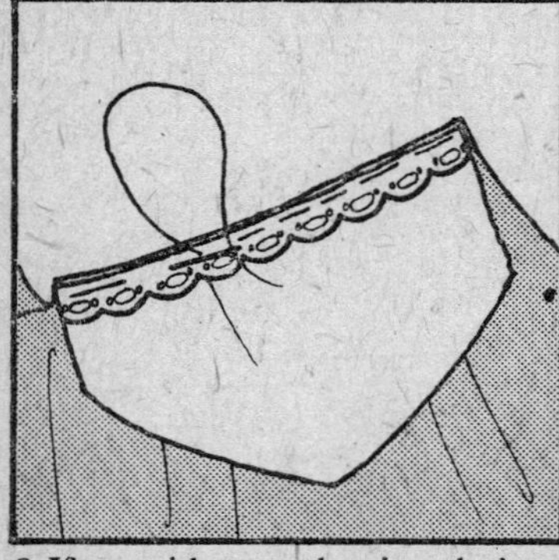

8 If you wish to sew lace into the bust seams instead of applying it afterwards, do this after you have trimmed off the seam allowance by tacking the lace to the small seam allowance.

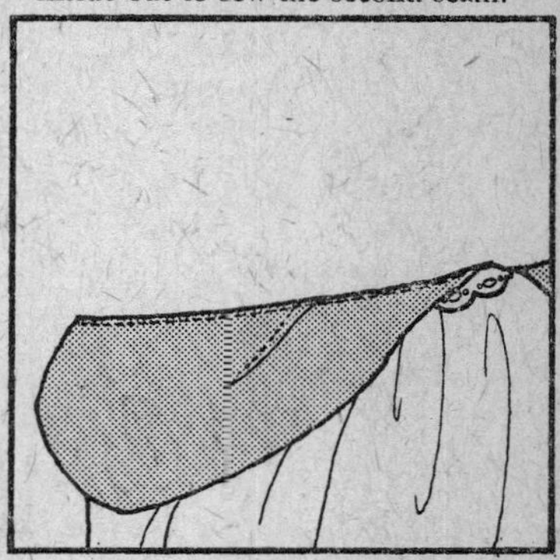

9 Turn the work inside out and sew the second seam. The lace will lie in place on the right side.

10 Press the french seams downwards on the wrong side so that the lace will face upwards on the right side.

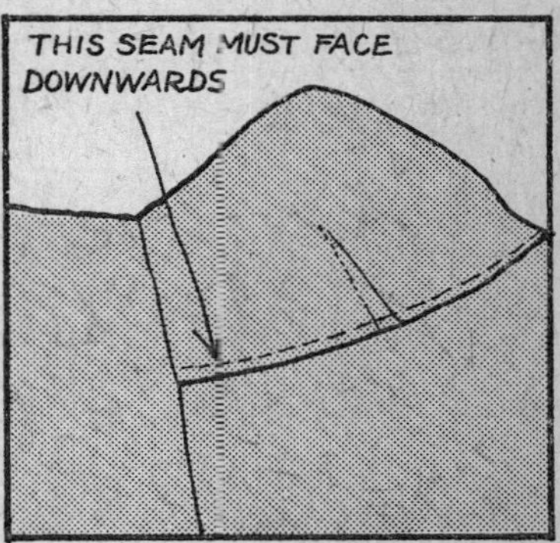

11 Sew the side seams with the bust seam in a downwards position to hold the lace in place.

finishing touches

PRESSING AS YOU GO
The most important finishing touch starts very nearly at the beginning. With dress-making, each stage in the putting together of a garment must be pressed as it is sewn. It doesn't mean you have to run to the ironing board at the end of every seam, but it does mean that you must press while you can still lay the garment flat on the ironing board.
For instance, press all the darts at the shoulder before you sew the shoulder seam, and press the shoulder seam open before you put in the sleeve.
This process gives a much more tailored look than you would get if you left it all until the garment is finished.

COTTON, RAYON AND SILK
Iron direct on to the wrong side of the fabric, with a cool iron.

MAN-MADE FIBRES
These are tougher than they look, particularly Crimplene. Even Tricel can be obstinate. To get really crisp, firm seams press over a damp cloth.

WOOLLEN FABRICS
Always press over a damp cloth, on the wrong side, with a cool iron.

finishing off raw edges

It is essential in dressmaking to tidy up all raw edges so that there is no likelihood of the garment fraying on the inside. Most couture gowns are hand finished, and even cheap ready-mades are machine sewn. There are five different methods.

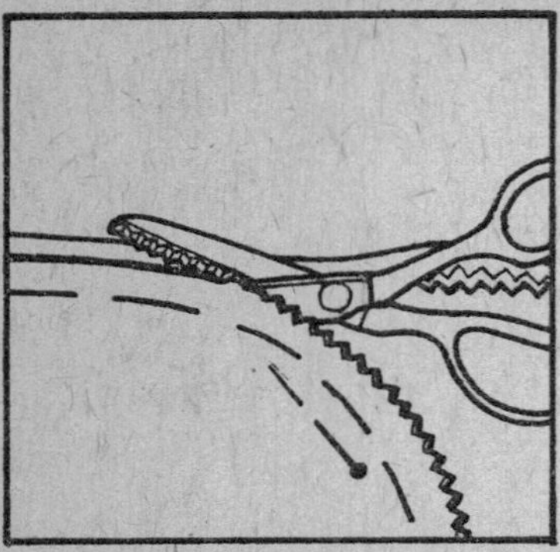

1 You can cut out the garment with pinking shears instead of ordinary scissors.

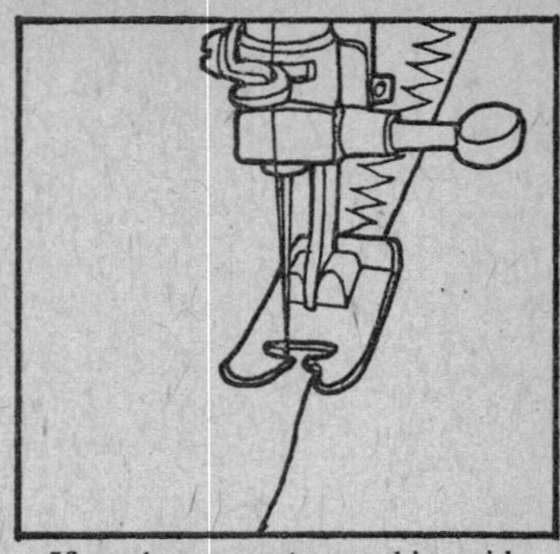

2 If you have a sewing machine with a zig-zag fitting, sew all the way round the raw edges with this before you start putting the garment together.

3 Plain machine stitch close to the edge, round every piece. Make sure the tension is fairly loose so that there is no chance of puckering.

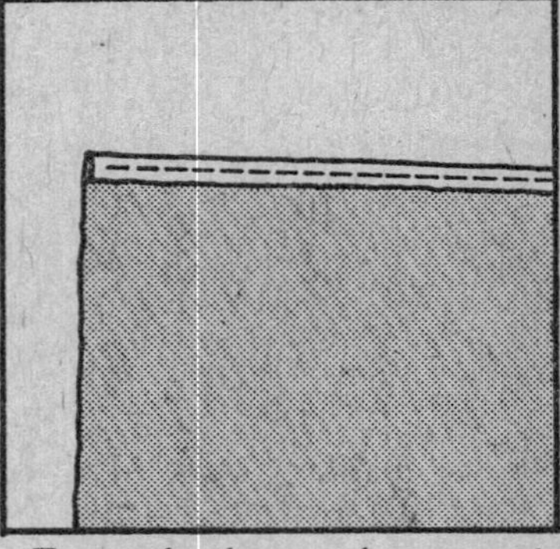

4 Turn under the raw edge once and machine along the fold. Again, make sure there is no puckering. This is not recommended for thick fabrics.

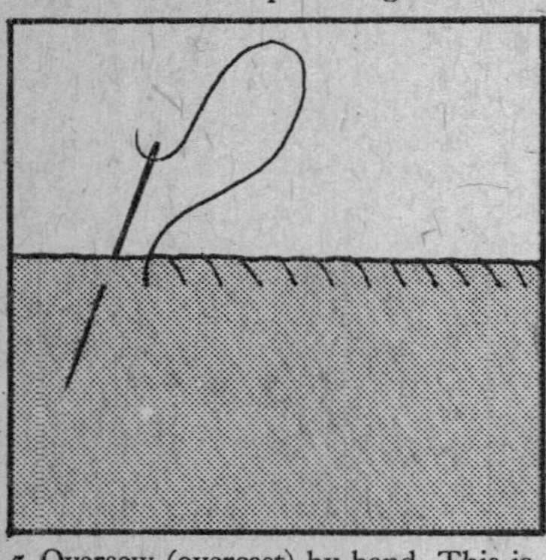

5 Oversew (overcast) by hand. This is the classiest method. Equally suitable on any thickness of fabric.

preventing lumps

A lot of good sewing is ruined by what are obviously lumps, which no amount of pressing will remove. In fact, the pressing often shows them up more. Far worse than the resulting home-made appearance of the garment is the discomfort of the wearer, who can feel a nasty knob of fabric digging in somewhere. The disappointment, and the knowledge that the much admired dress is not what it seems, is worst of all.

This can be avoided by careful trimming away as you go along. First of all, here is how they happen.

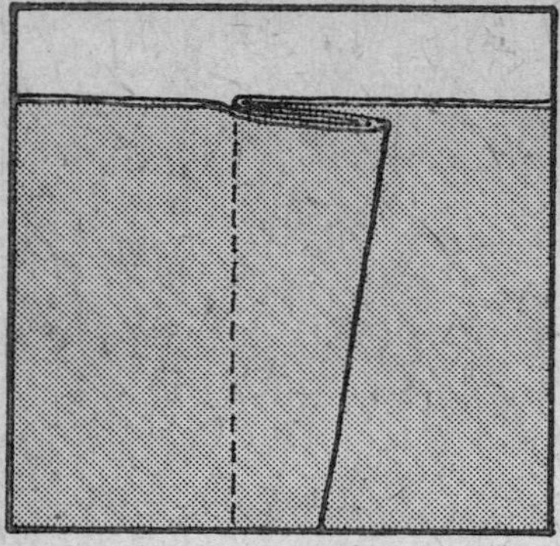

1 Take, for example, a jersey dress made with a lining. After you have made the darts and pressed them to one side, you will have six thicknesses of fabric.

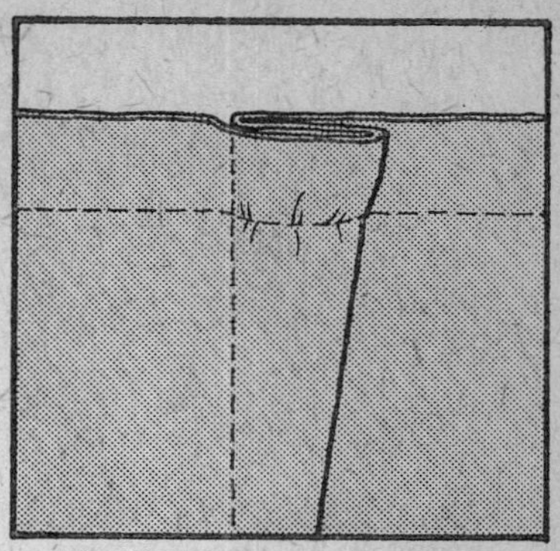

2 When you have sewn a seam across this you will have a thick wadge in the seam allowance, and this will happen all over the garment wherever you have darts.

There are two ways of dealing with this.

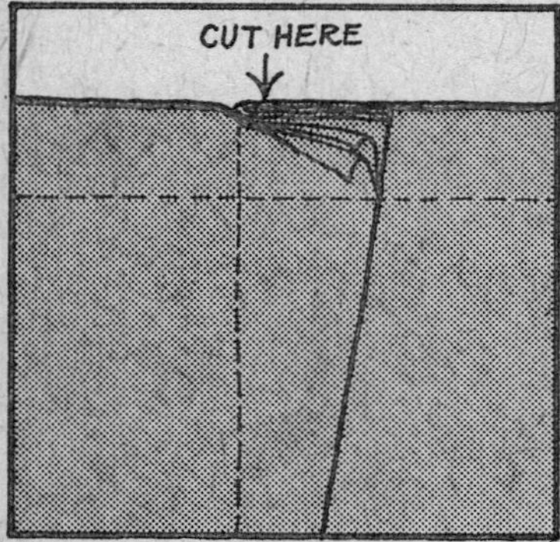

3 Cut out the upper two layers of the dart from the seam allowance, one at a time, and the lower layer a little way away from the upper layer.

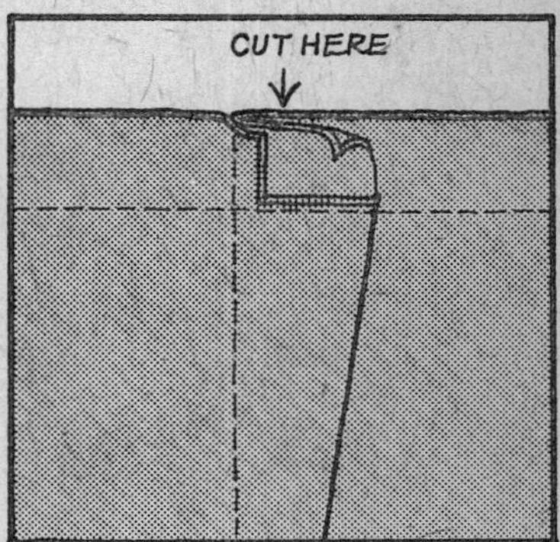

4 If there is still too much bulk, cut out the second layer of the dart top, but cut a little way away from the previous cut. This will avoid creating a ridge.

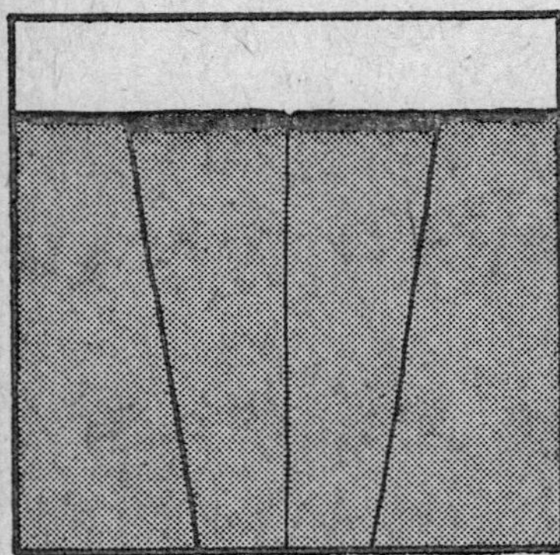

5 When you know you have thick fabrics, don't press the dart to one side. Instead, cut it down the middle and open it out, which will give you only four thicknesses.

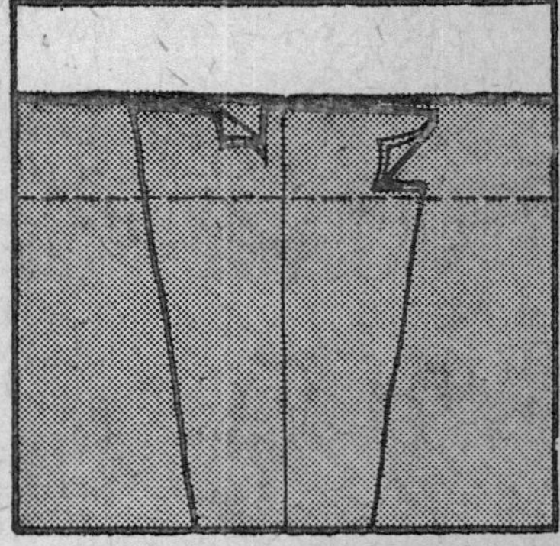

6 After you have sewn the seam across, you can then cut out the top of the dart before you open out the seam for pressing, as in 3. On fabrics such as jersey, which carry a shiny mark if pressed over a bulge, these operations must be done before pressing open the seams.

This same principle applies wherever you have several thicknesses as a result of folding. Coat facings create this problem at the hem.

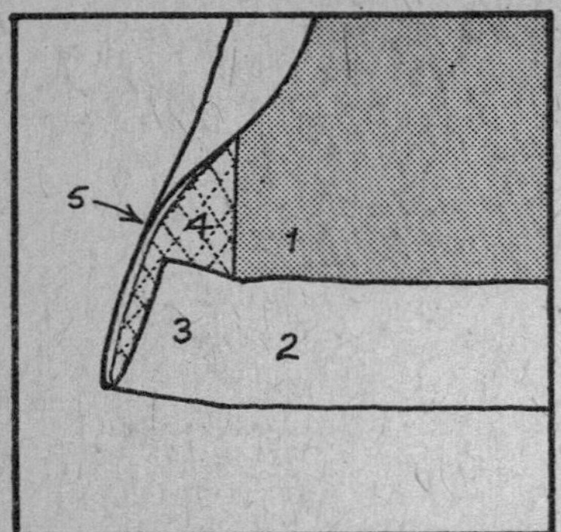

7 When you have turned up the hem and folded back the facing you will have at least four thicknesses of fabric, possibly plus interfacing as well.

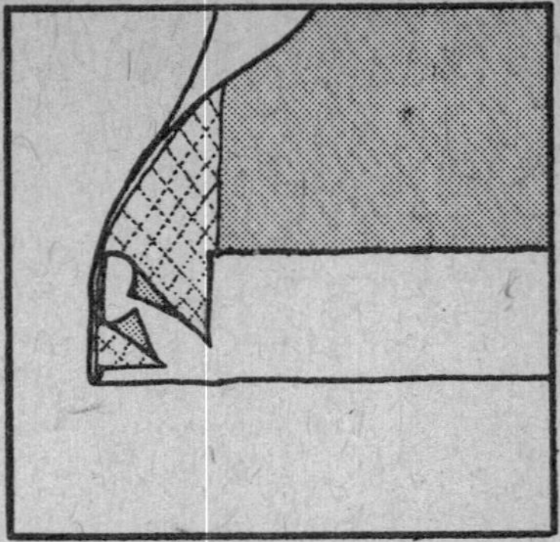

8 Cut away the inside fold of the hem of the facing so that it will fold round the cut edge of the hem. Leave just enough at the bottom to turn in neatly.

Provided the seams are sound, and you don't cut near enough to break the stitching, you can cut away seam allowances wherever you think the overall appearance would be improved, but you must cut in layers, and the thicker the bulge the more important this is.

mitred corners

There are several methods of doing this. Some are very complicated and some just don't work at all. This method is simple and it works.
For curtains where the two hems are not the same width.

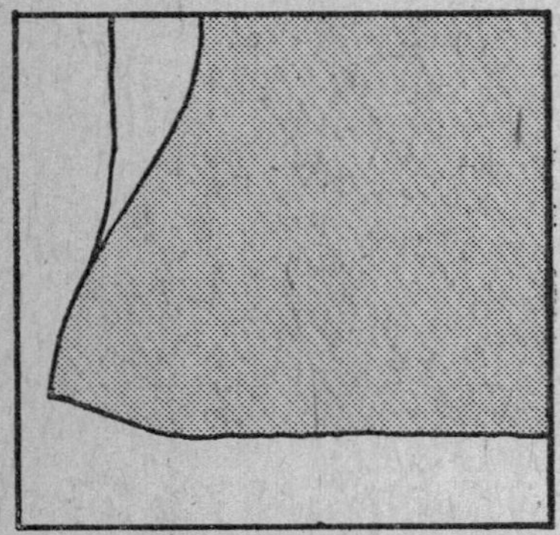

1 Leave the side hem of the curtain unstitched for about 10 in. until you are ready to hem the bottom.

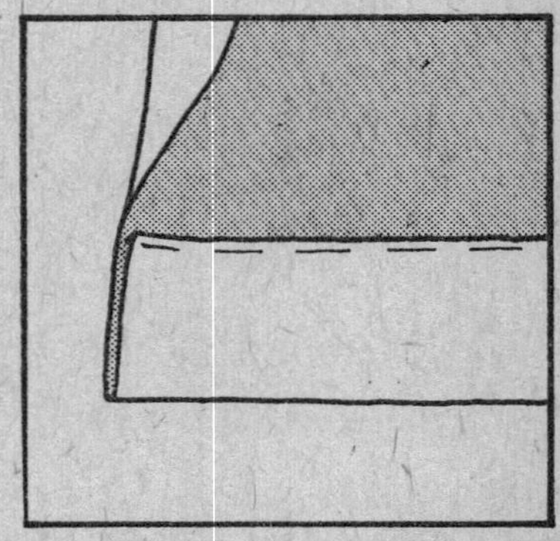

2 Turn up the bottom hem on the wrong side by the required amount, having already oversewn or turned it under. Tack.

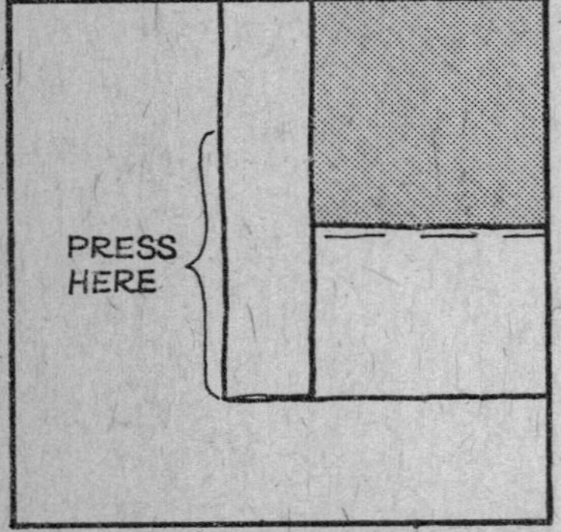

3 Fold over the side hem, and press the fold.

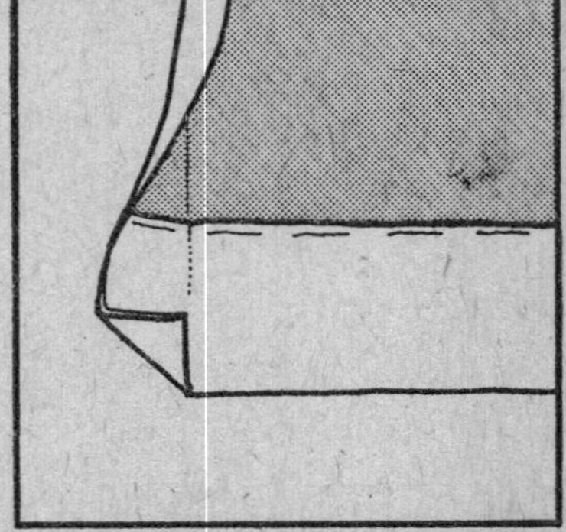

4 Fold under the bottom edge of the side fold so that it lies along the downward fold.

5 Press the diagonal fold.

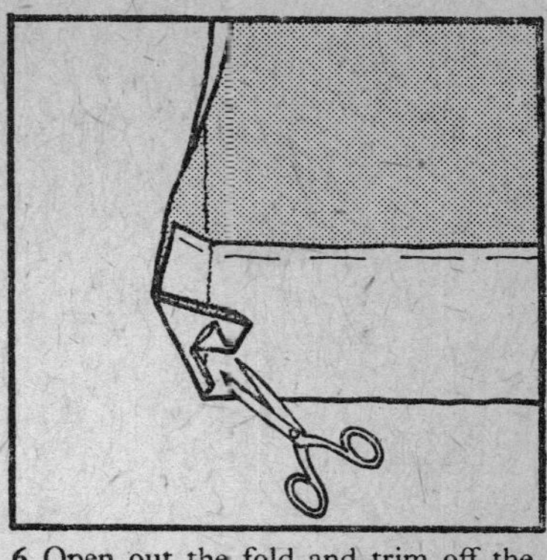

6 Open out the fold and trim off the triangular piece formed by the fold to within ¼ in. of the fold.

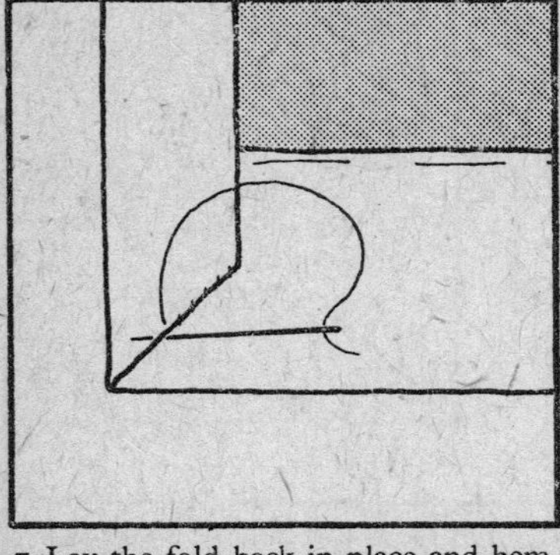

7 Lay the fold back in place and hem the diagonal fold down very lightly to the bottom hem, taking care not to penetrate more than the surface of the hem.

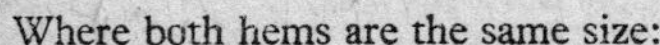

Where both hems are the same size:

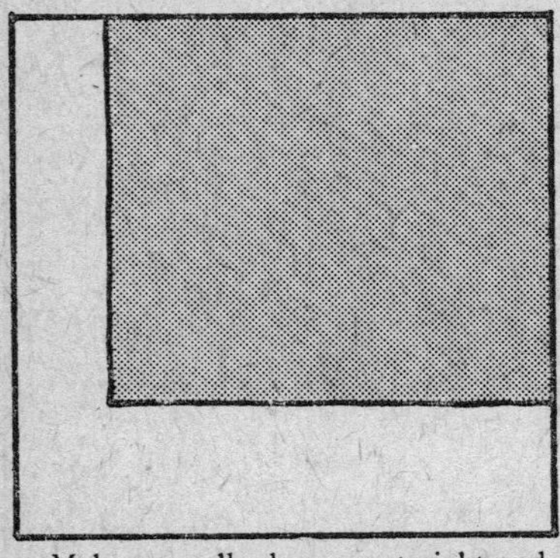

1 Make sure all edges are straight and that you already have good right-angled corners.

2 Fold both hems so that they are exactly the same width, and press the corner very firmly.

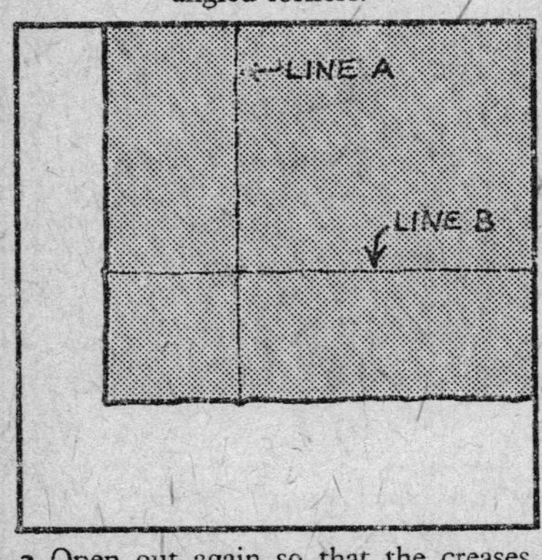

3 Open out again so that the creases show clearly.

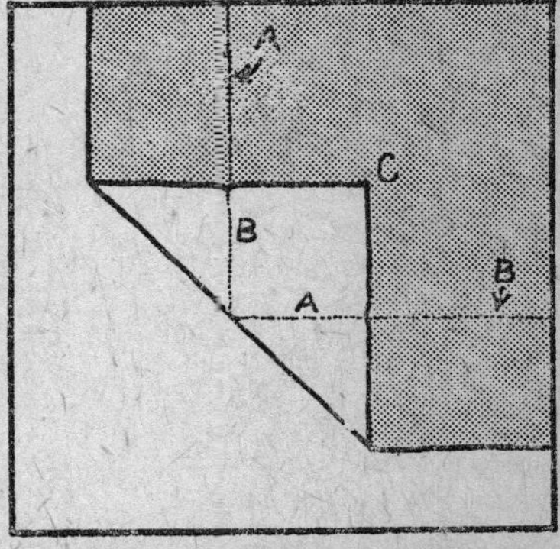

4 Take the point C and fold it forwards until the crease A lies along crease B, and crease B lies along crease A. Press.

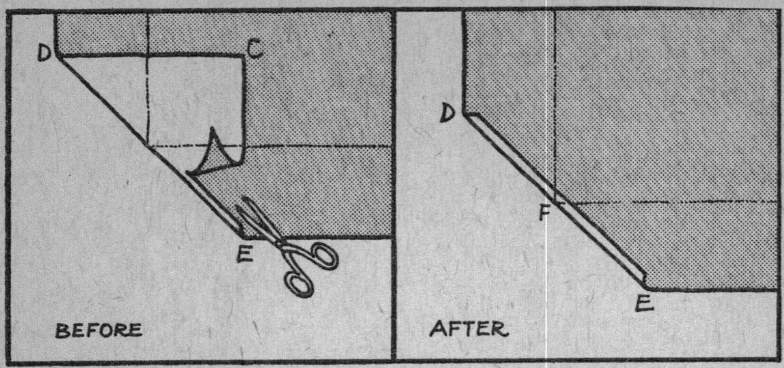

5 Trim away the triangle to within ¼ in. of the fold to avoid an ugly thickness of fabric at the corner.

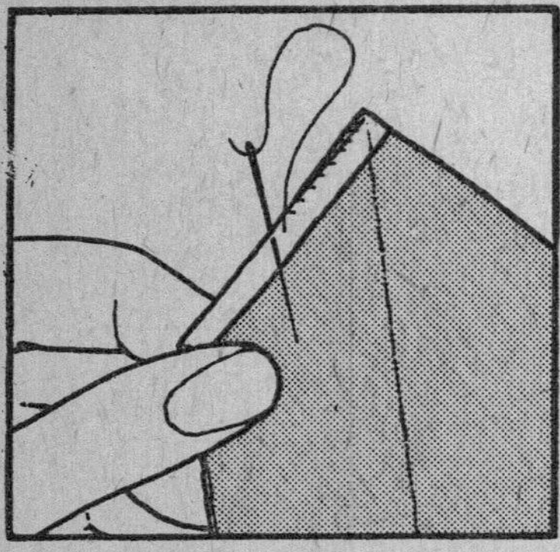

6 Fold the corner backwards at point F so that points D and E meet. Oversew the two edges together very lightly along the edge.

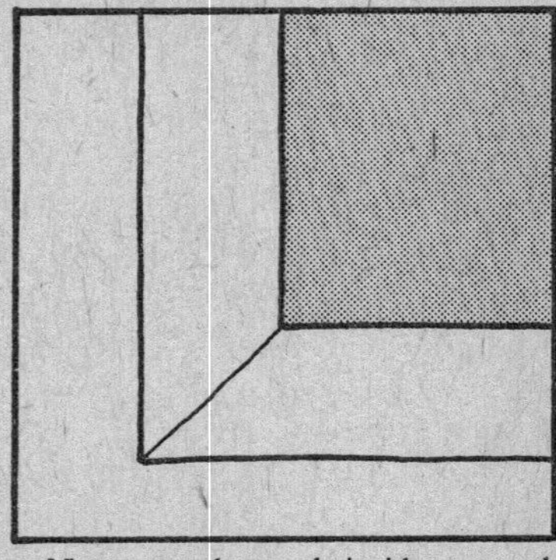

7 Now turn the work inside out and you will have a perfectly mitred corner.

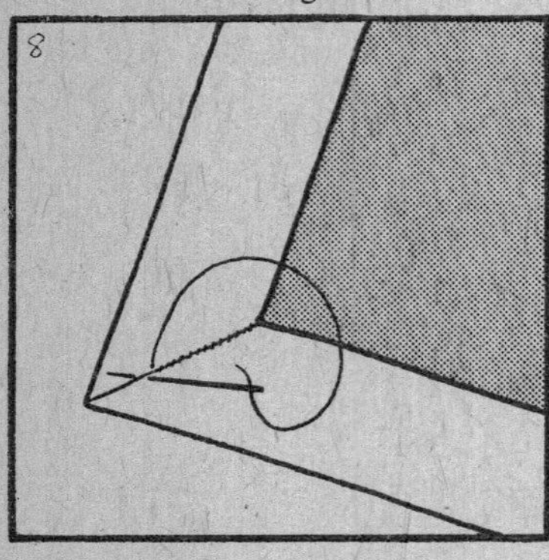

8 If you are nervous of turning the corner inside out work as above as far as 5. Fold over the hems on the wrong side of the work and stitch the diagonal folds together very lightly making sure no stitching shows on the outside.

belt slots and thread loops

Don't do these until you know how wide your belt is going to be.

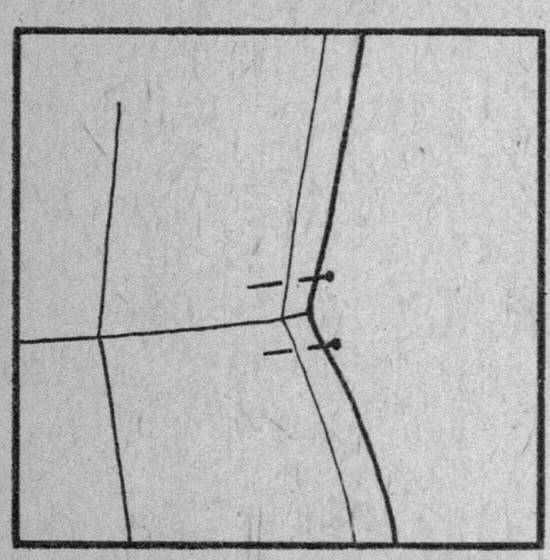

1 Allow for half the width of the belt above the waistline and half below. Mark with pins.

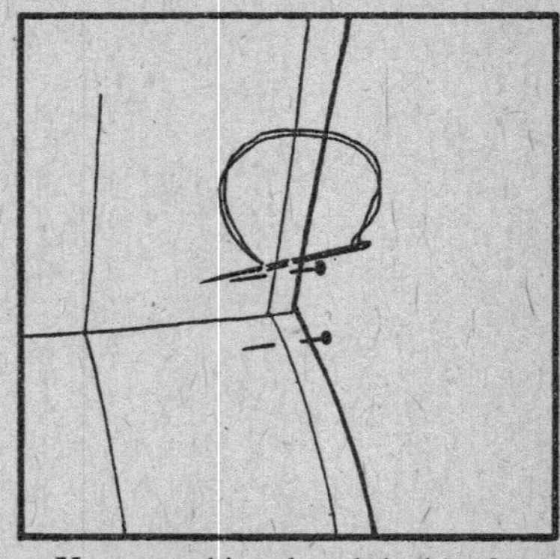

2 Use a matching thread double. Start at the upper pin by making a few stitches close together. If you tie a knot in the thread pull it through from the inside to hide the knot.

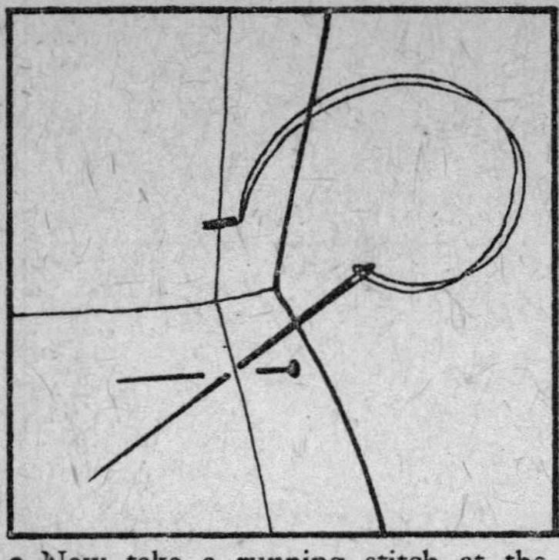

3 Now take a running stitch at the lower pin.

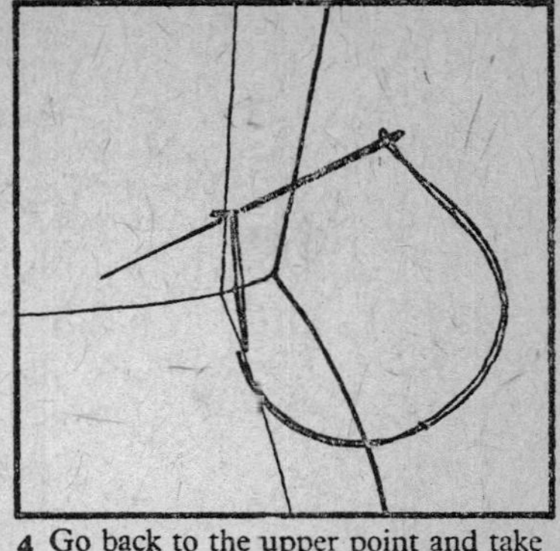

4 Go back to the upper point and take a running stitch.

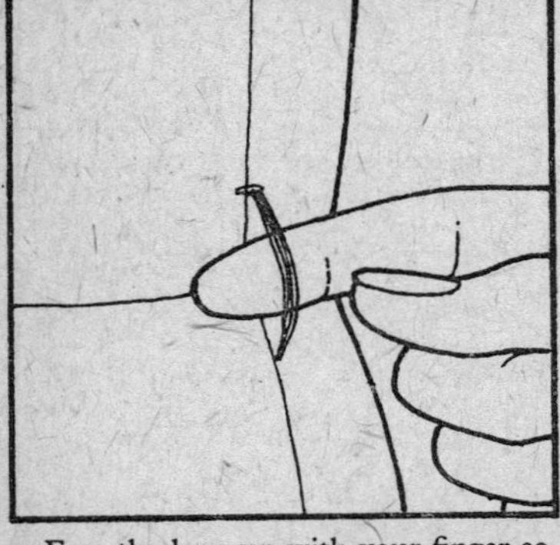

5 Ease the loop up with your finger so that it is not too tight. Make six loops all together.

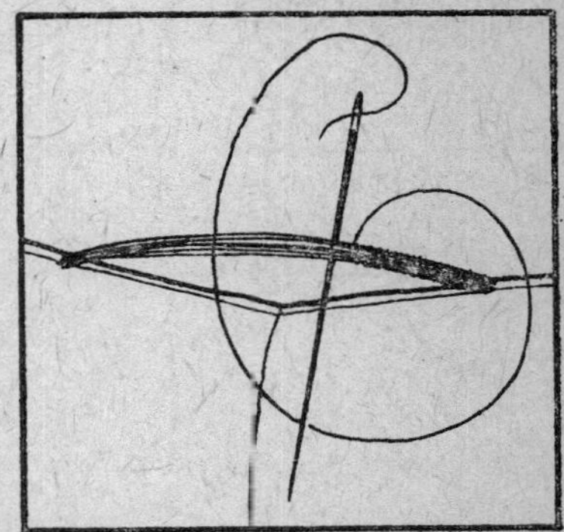

6 Work buttonhole stitches over the loops of thread all the way along. Make sure you have enough thread to do the job without a break, and keep the stitches pressed close together.

eyelet holes

1 There is no need to cut an eyelet hole. Jab the fabric with a knitting needle.

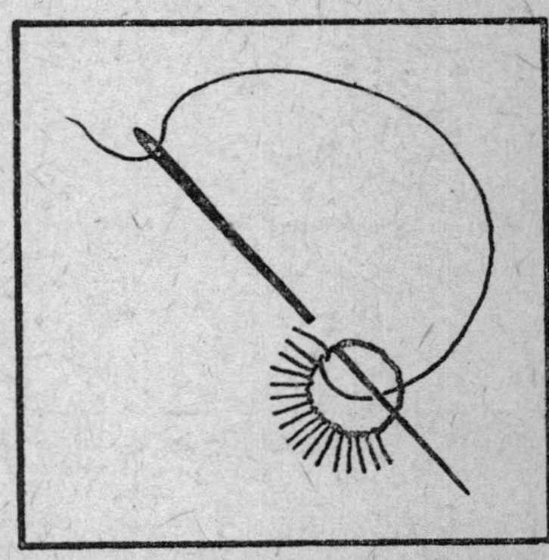

2 If you want perfection, buttonhole stitch around the hole as for stitched buttonholes, page 19. As you stitch you will make the hole a little bigger, which is why you don't need a big one to start with, or

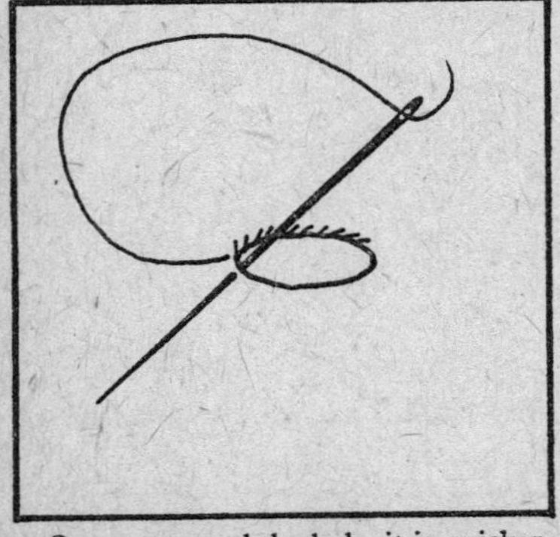

3 Oversew round the hole, it is quicker and expands the hole just the same.

saddle stitching

This does not form part of sewing the garment together, but is decorative and is done after the garment is made up. It is generally done round revers, pocket tops and alongside seams, and in a contrasting thick thread.

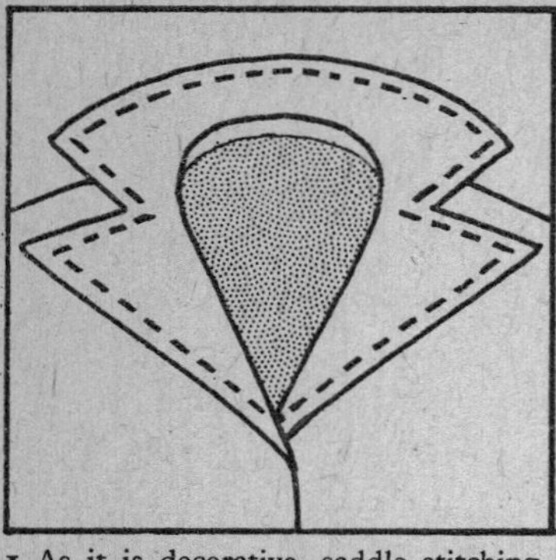

1 As it is decorative, saddle stitching must be even. It is ordinary running stitch, larger than usual and spread out.

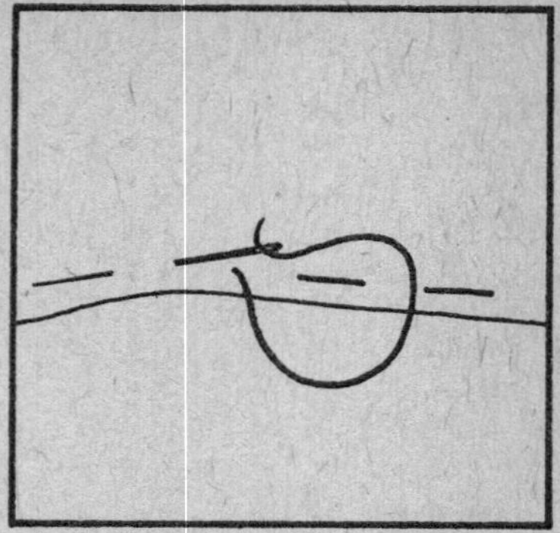

2 The space between the stitches must be the same size as the stitches themselves.

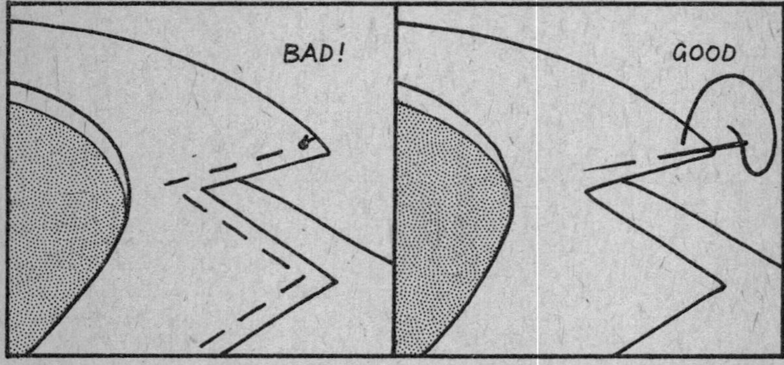

3 You must not have a knot in the end of the thread showing on the outside, or even a few starter stitches. Bring the thread through from the inside to start.

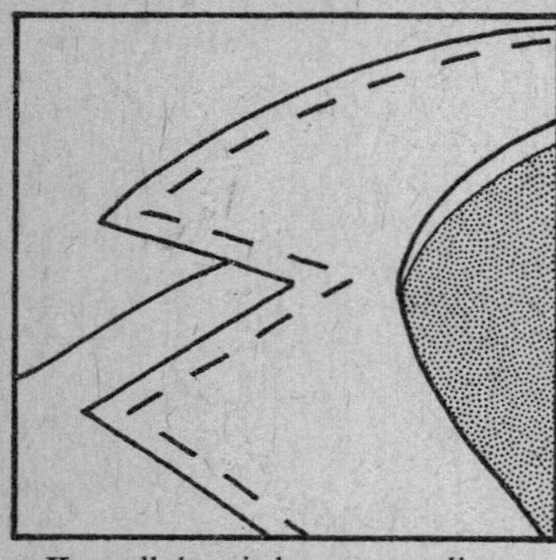

4 Keep all the stitches an even distance from the edge.

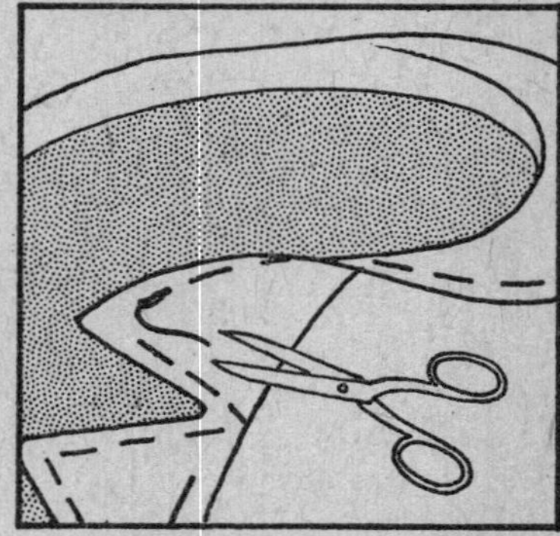

5 Always fasten off on an underneath surface.

picking out/hand picking

This is the term used for the tiny stitches all round the edge of the revers and collar, and down the front edges of a good tailored jacket. It is worked on the same principle as back stitch but with a space between the stitches.

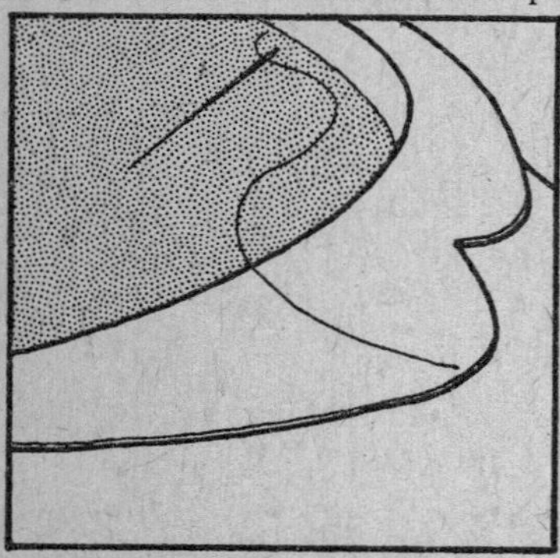

1 Bring the thread through from the back to the right side of the garment.

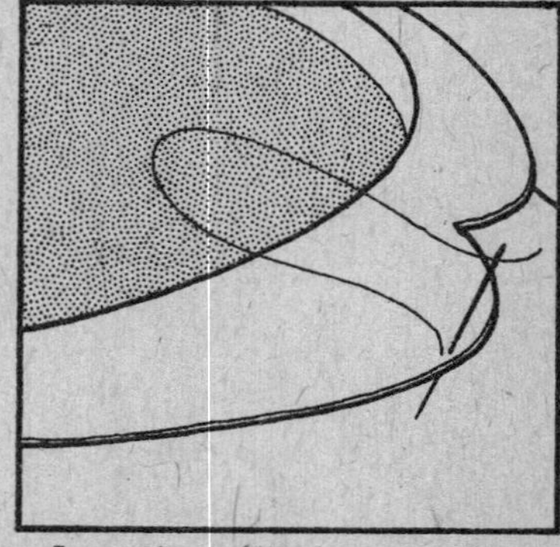

2 Insert the needle about two threads to the right of where the sewing thread emerges.

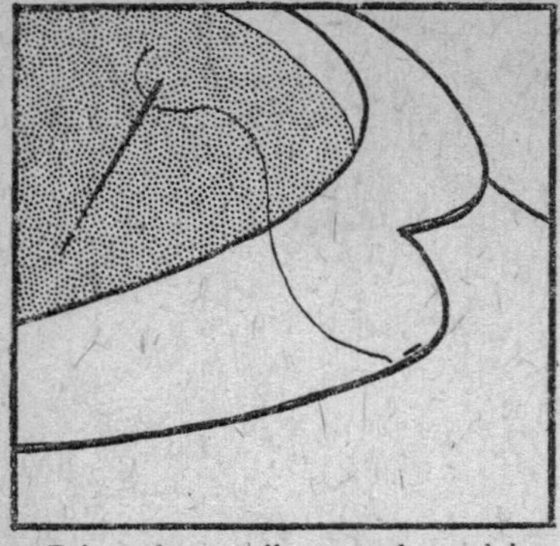

3 Bring the needle out about ¼ in. farther along.

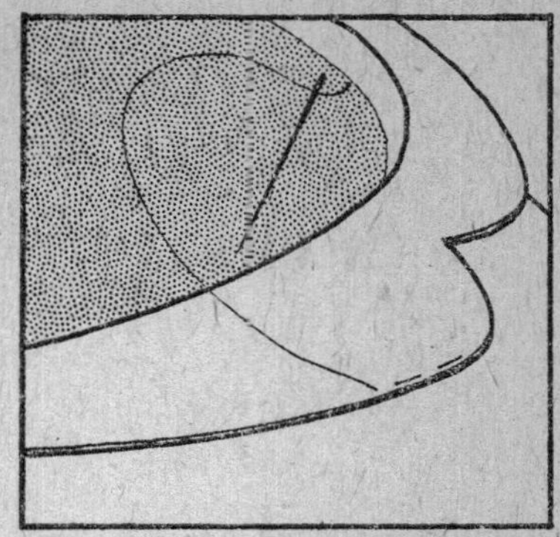

4 Insert the needle again two threads to the right of where the sewing thread emerges and bring it out ¼ in. farther on.

5 Each time go fairly deeply through all the thicknesses of fabric.

shell edging

This is a pretty edging for baby's and children's clothes.

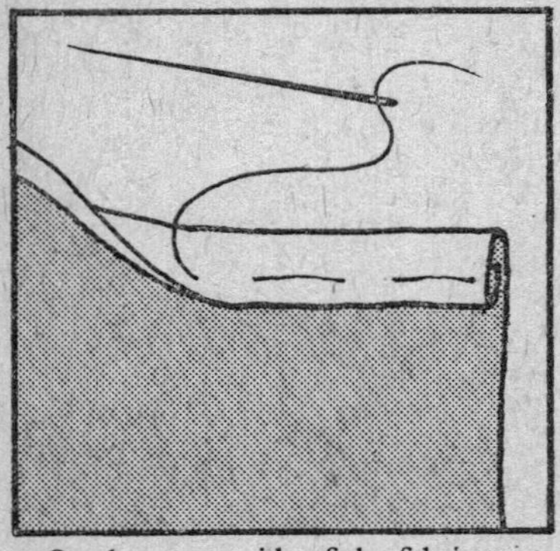

1 On the wrong side of the fabric turn a small hem not more than ¼ in. wide, and tack it down.

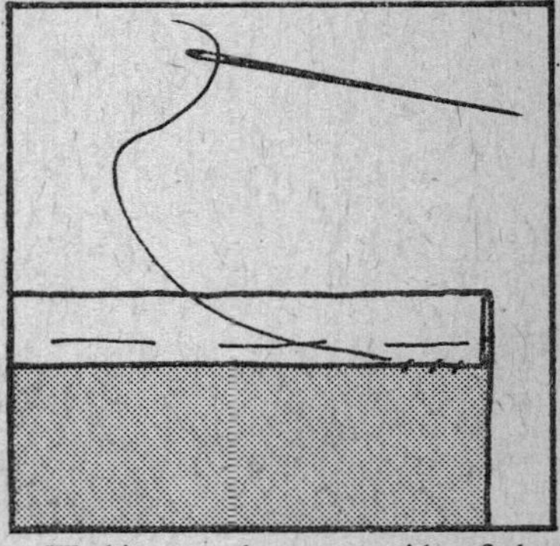

2 Working on the wrong side of the fabric, starting at the right, do three hem stitches.

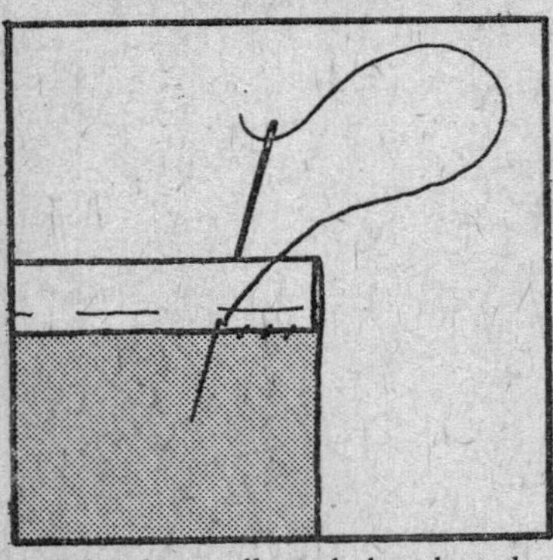

3 Take the needle and thread to the back of the work and insert the needle from the back to the front, bringing it out at the point where the thread previously came through.

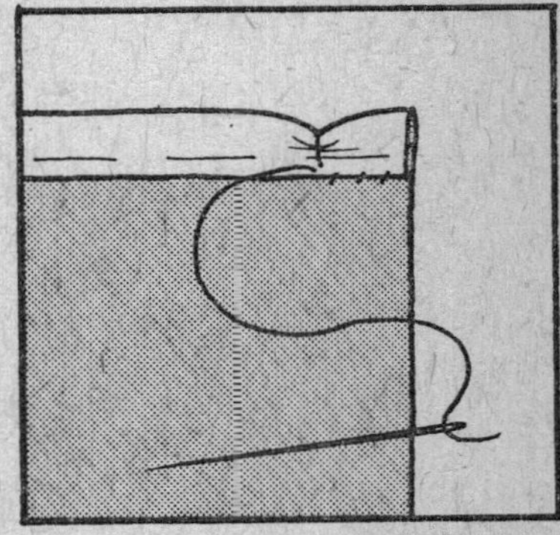

4 Bring the needle and thread right through, and pull the thread tight.

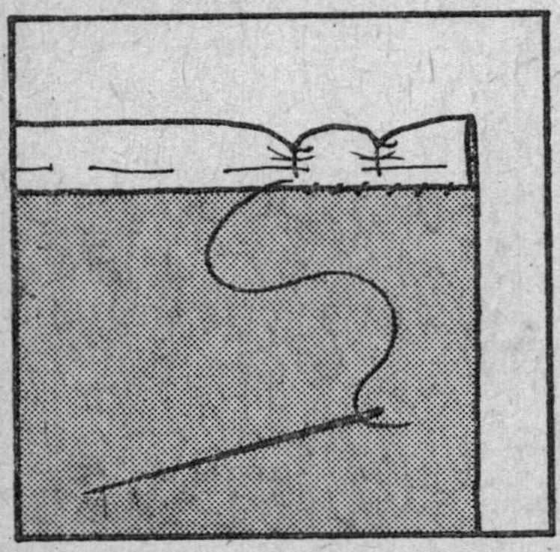

5 Do three more hem stitches then make a stitch over the hem as before.

6 Continue with three hem stitches and one tight stitch over the fold. Hem very lightly, and remove the tacking stitches when the shell edging is complete.

rolled edges

This is a delicate edging for delicate fabrics, and has to be done by hand. It is sewn as it is rolled and there is no preparatory pinning or tacking. Work from right to left, on the wrong side.

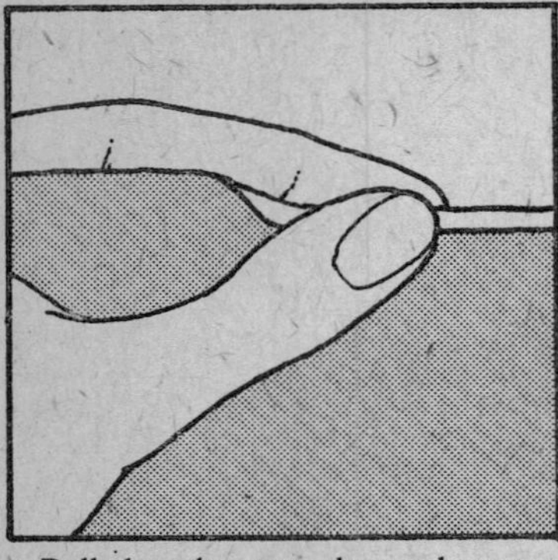

1 Roll the edge towards you between your finger and thumb.

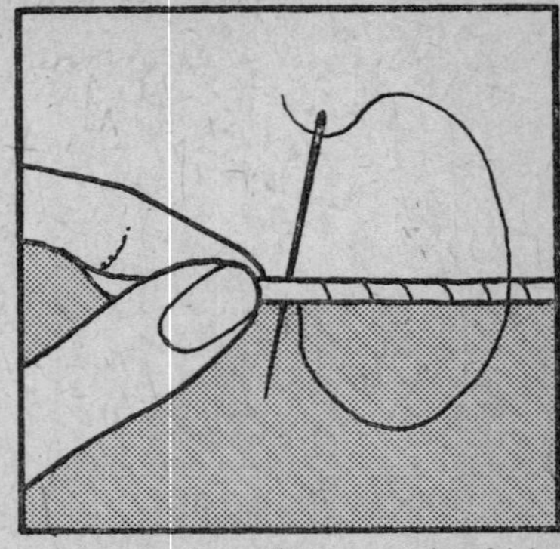

2 Oversew the rolled edge with fairly generously spaced stitches.

shoulder strap loops

It's true you can buy these now, but it does save money to make your own.

1 Before sewing in the loops try on the dress and see exactly where your shoulder straps come in relation to the dress. It is no use putting them too far on one side – they must be in the right place.

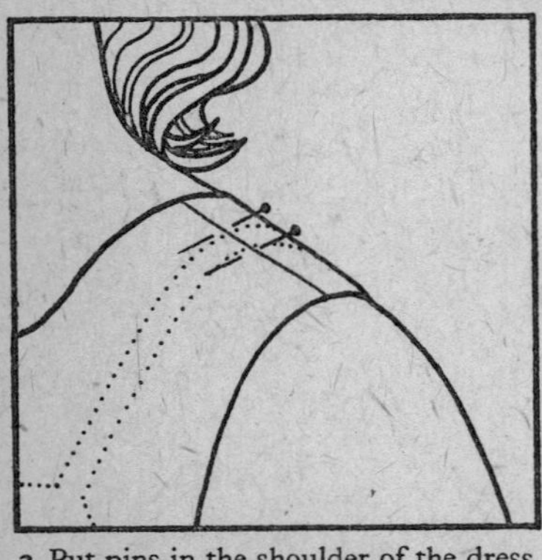

2 Put pins in the shoulder of the dress either side of where your shoulder straps lie.

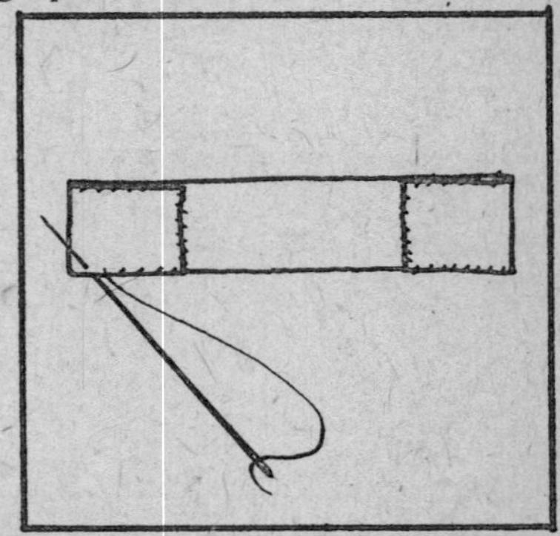

3 Take $1\frac{1}{2}$ in. of narrow tape or ribbon for each loop. Turn under each end $\frac{1}{4}$ in. and sew down.

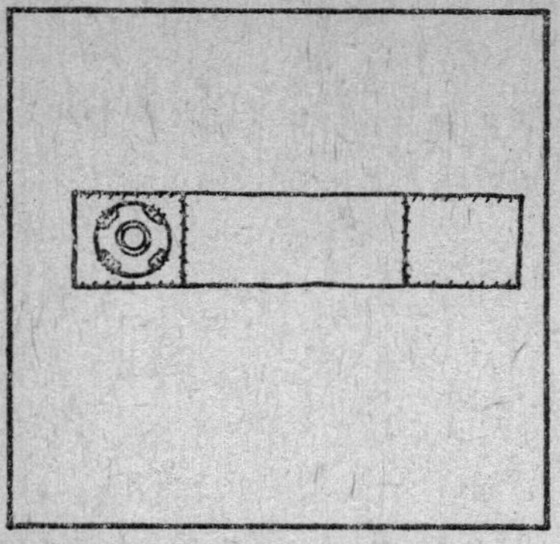

4 On the wrong side of one end sew one half of a small press stud.

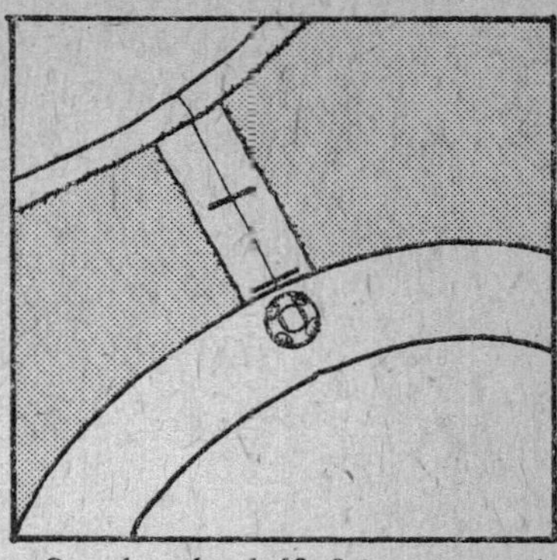

5 Sew the other half of the press stud to the seam allowance of the shoulder or the facing, just outside the marker pin nearest to the neckline. Remove the pins.

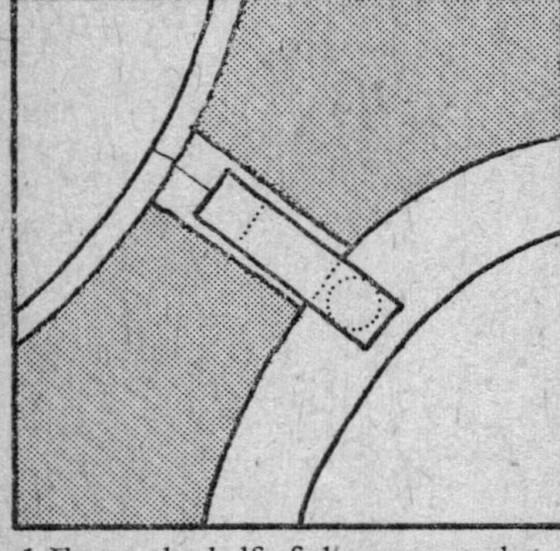

6 Fasten the half of the press stud on the loop to the half on the dress and lay the loop straight along the shoulder seam.

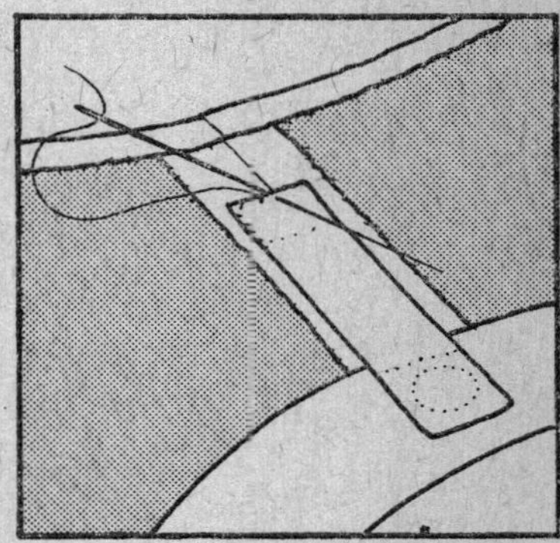

7 Sew the other end of the loop down to the seam allowance, keeping it flat and not dragging.

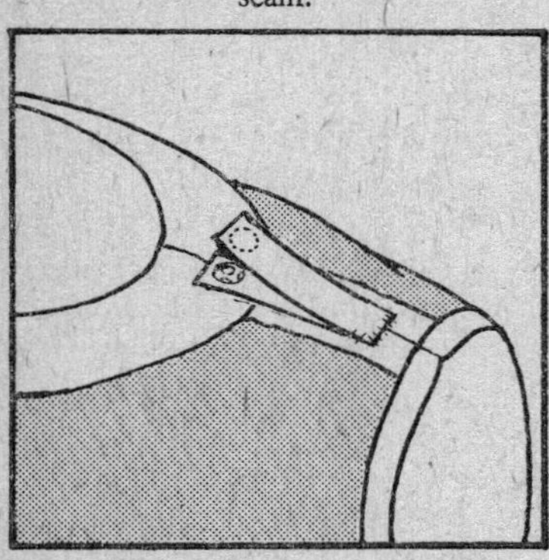

8 If you are using the bought variety, work as 1 and 2 above, and sew in place, with the press stud nearest to the neck.

loop for hanging coats

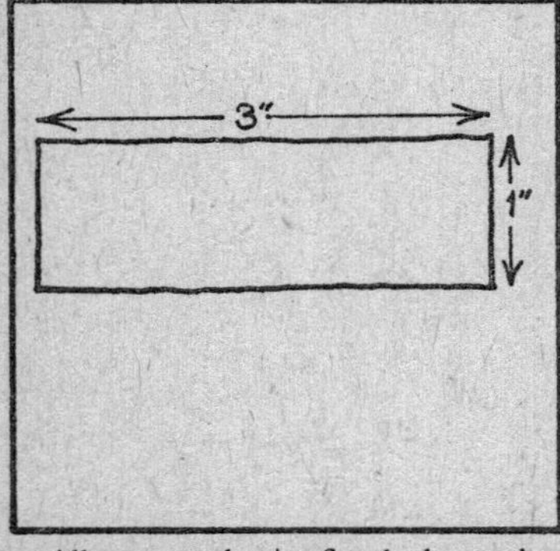

1 Allow a good 2 in. for the loop, plus ½ in. each end for turnings. Cut a piece of fabric 3 in. long by 1 in. wide.

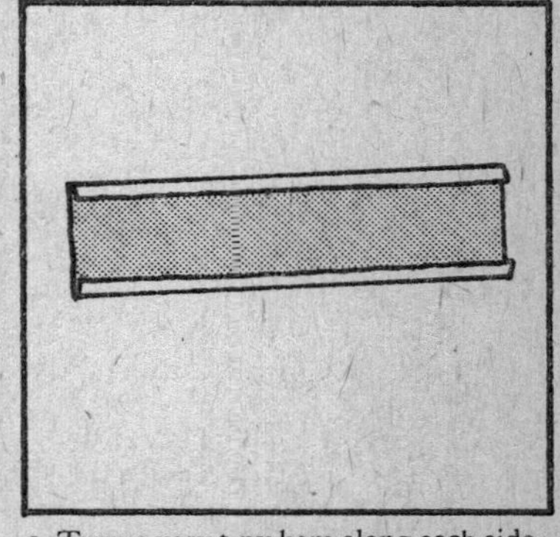

2 Turn a very tiny hem along each side. Press.

3 Fold each of the long edges in to the middle and press. The strip will then be slightly less than ½ in. wide.

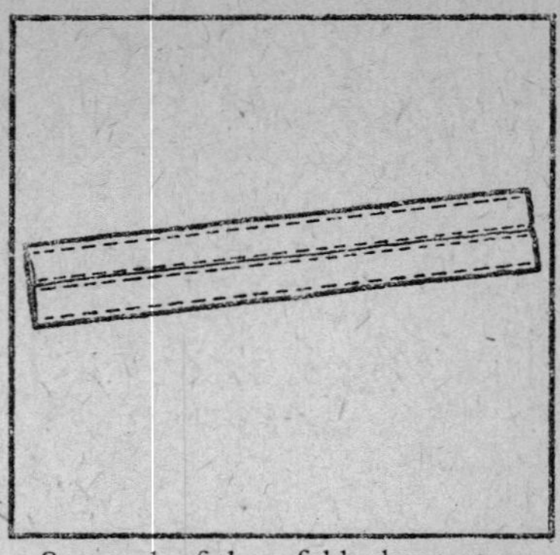

4 Sew each of these folds down separately. Sew each side of the strip.

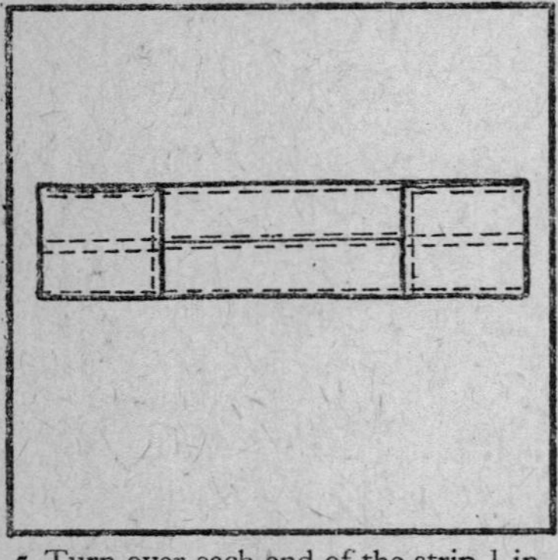

5 Turn over each end of the strip ½ in. and sew down.

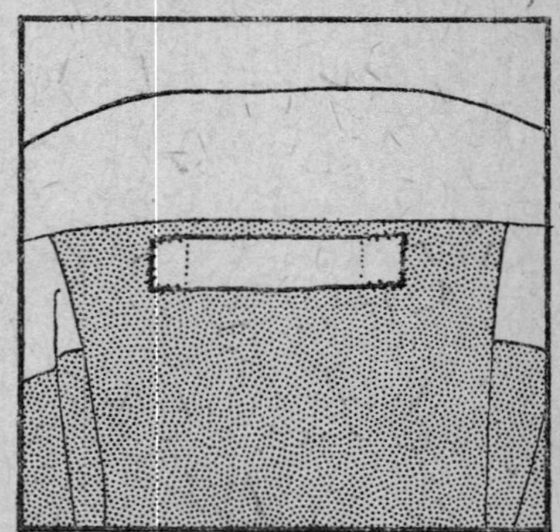

6 With the folded ends underneath, sew each end of the loop to the inside back of the coat at the centre neck edge of the back lining.

loops for hanging anything

You won't want these to be too bulky, so take a 3 in. strip of fabric, ¾ in. wide, and turn each side in to the middle as 2 page 163, but without the first small turning.

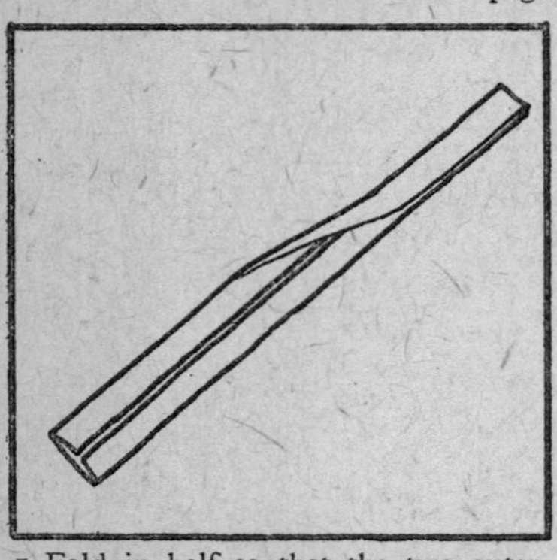

1 Fold in half so that the two outer edges meet.

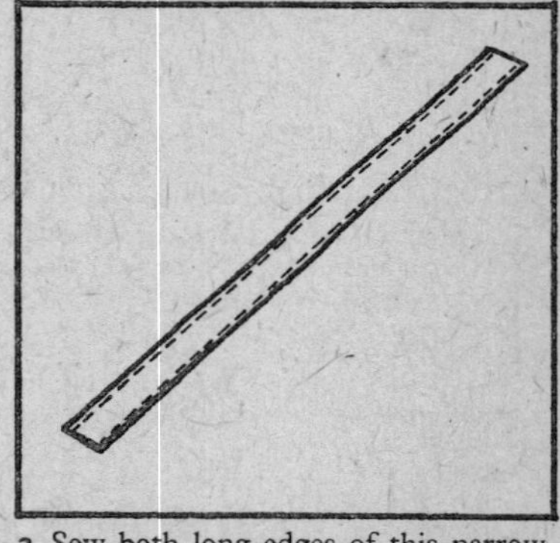

2 Sew both long edges of this narrow strip.

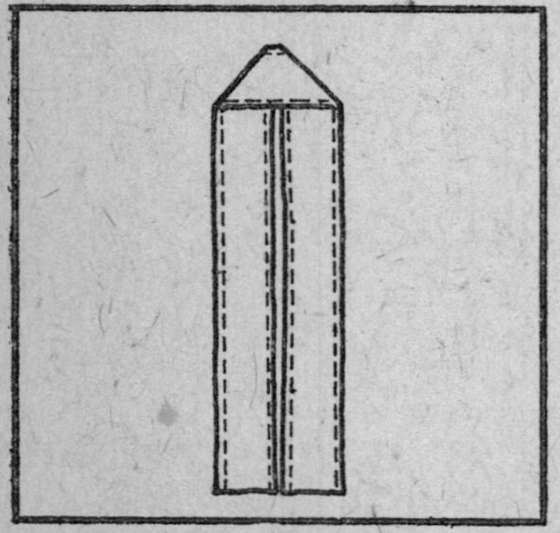

3 Bend the strip in the middle so that the two ends lie side by side.

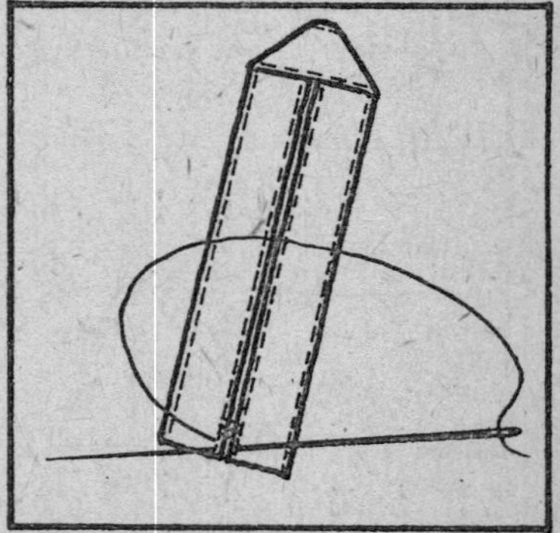

4 Do a few oversew stitches at the foot of the loop to hold the two edges in place.

5 Turn back the bottom of both ends of the loop and hem the turnings down neatly.

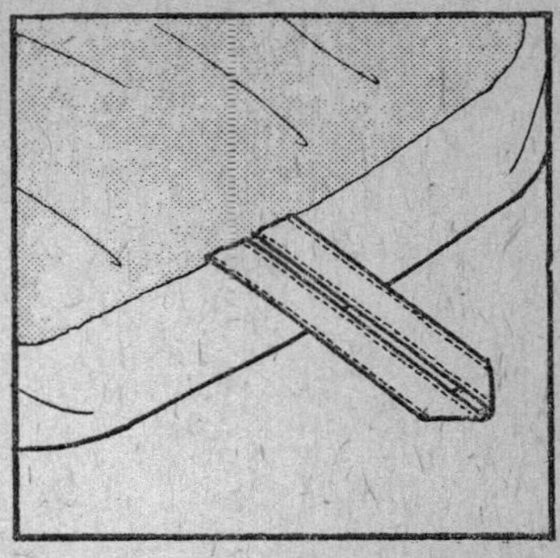

6 When you attach the loop, place it with the bottom folds inwards so that they are not seen.

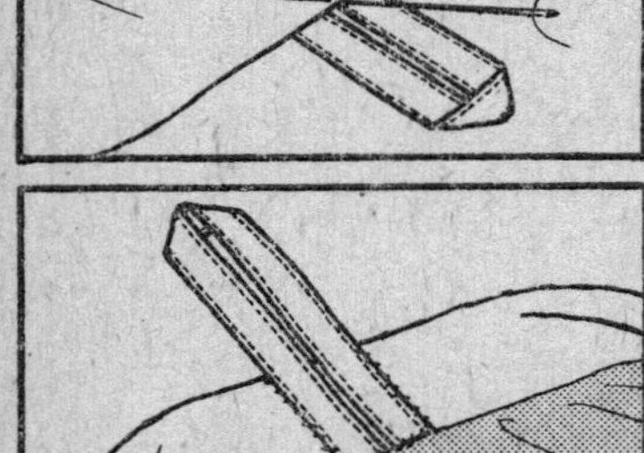

7 Hem the top edge of the main fabric to the loops on the outside first, then turn to the inside and hem all the way round.

turning narrow strips inside out

There are two ways of doing this.

METHOD ONE

Cut your strip to the required length and width, and fold in half on the wrong side.

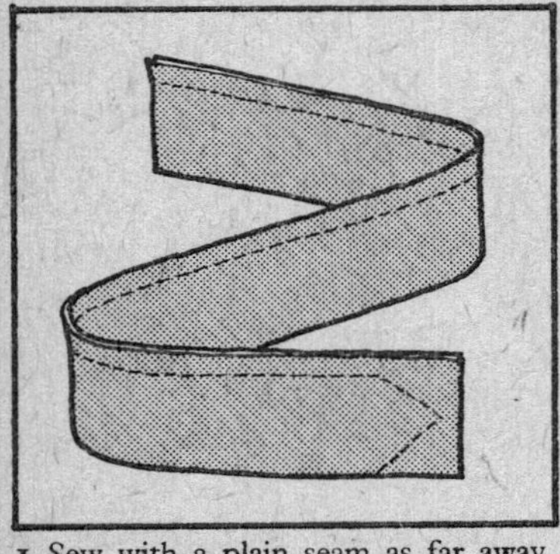

1 Sew with a plain seam as far away from the fold as you require your band to be, pointing it, if required, at one end.

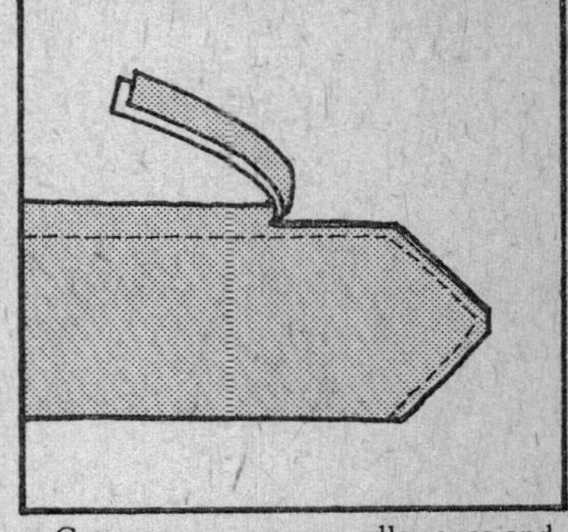

2 Cut away excess seam allowance and snip off as much of the point as you dare.

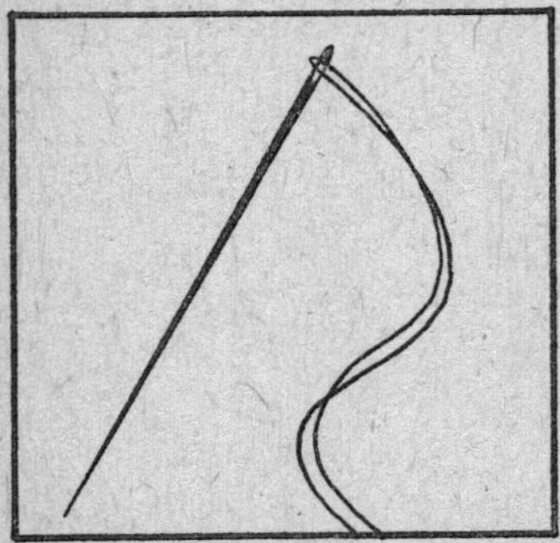

3 Take a length of strong thread which, when double, will be longer than the band you are making, and thread this through the stoutest darning needle you have.

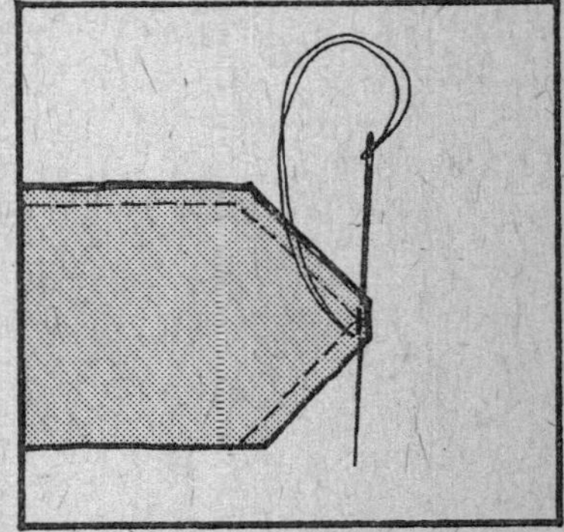

4 Anchor this thread to the point of the band by sewing a few stitches in the seam allowance.

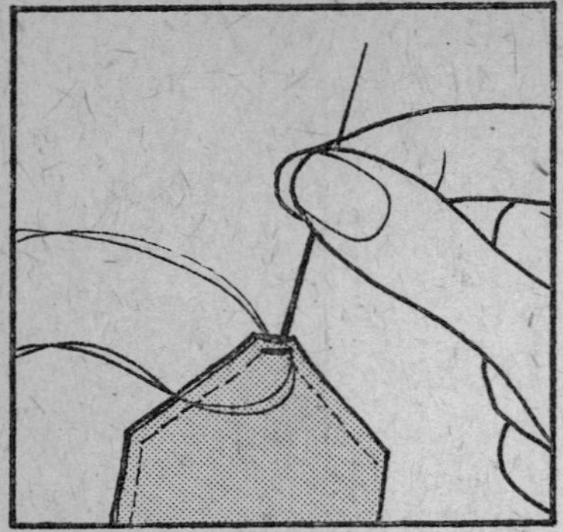

5 Push the needle, blunt end first, through the point of the band so that it goes out of sight between the two thicknesses.

6 Work the needle along the inside of the band until it comes out at the open end.

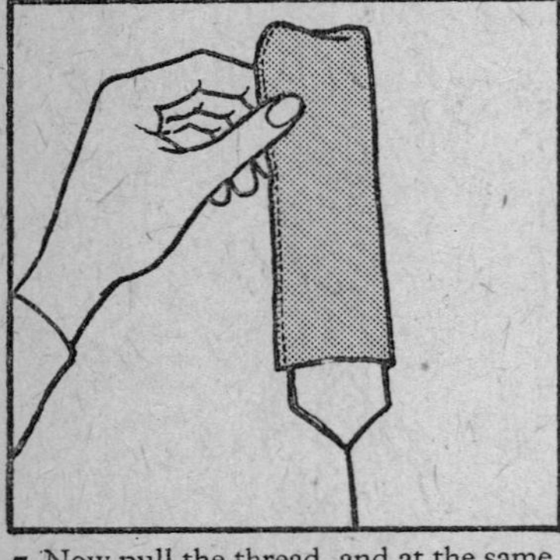

7 Now pull the thread, and at the same time work the band back in the opposite direction at the pointed end.

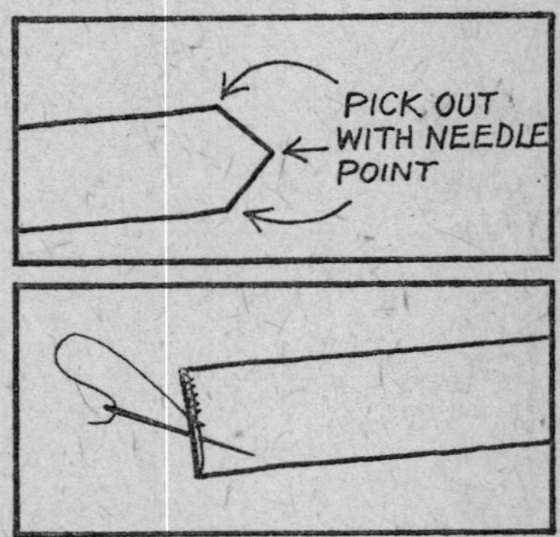

8 Eventually your band will be inside out. Snip the thread and leave it inside. Pick out the point, turn in the straight end and oversew it, or

METHOD TWO

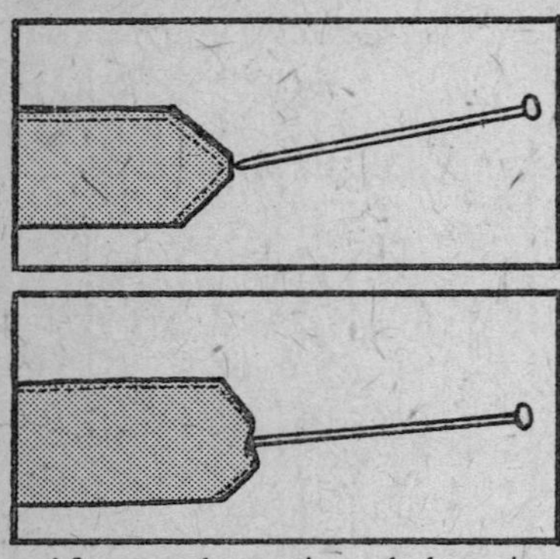

9 After you have trimmed the point and the seam allowance, dig the point of a knitting needle into the pointed end of the band and push the outside fabric to the inside.

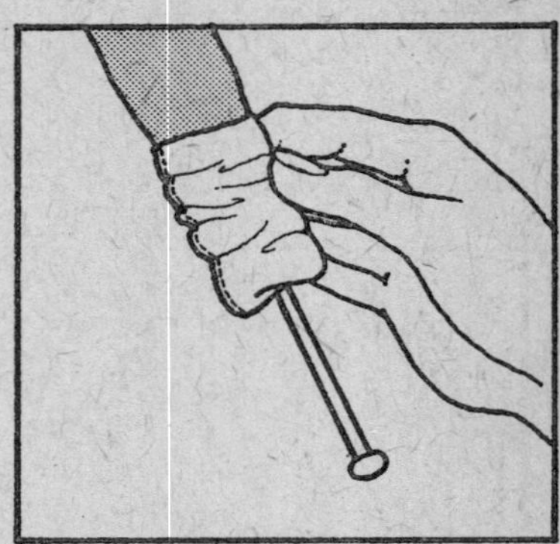

10 At the same time keep working the fabric down the knitting needle until the whole strip is inside out.

narrow strips for elastic to be threaded through

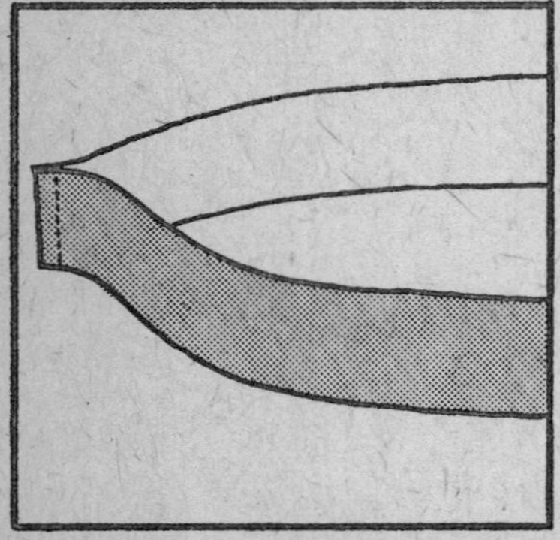

1 First cut your strip of fabric and join the ends together.

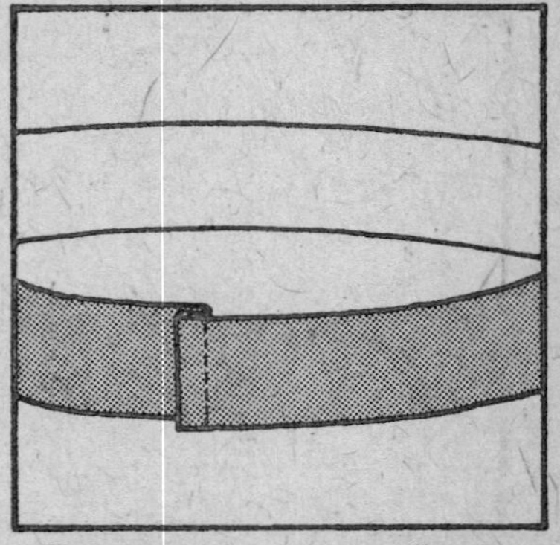

2 Do not open out the seam allowance, but fold both pieces in the same direction.

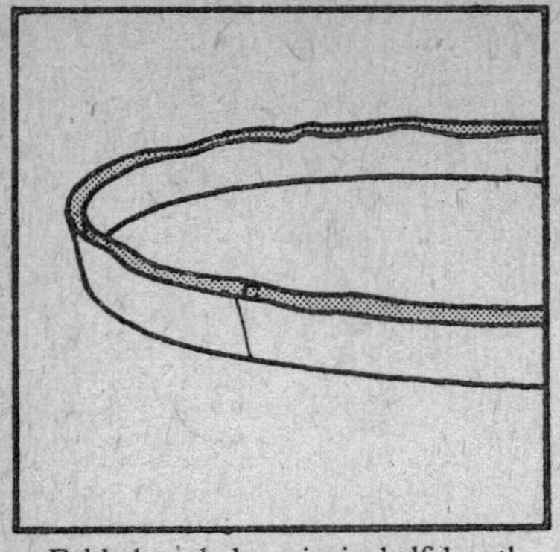
3 Fold the whole strip in half lengthways with the right side outside.

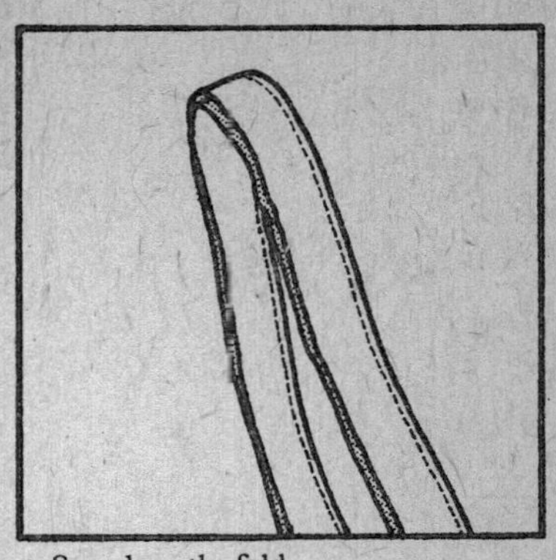
4 Sew along the fold.

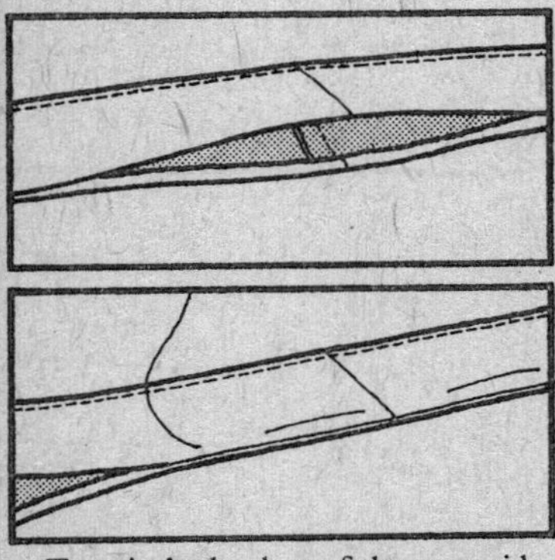
5 Turn in both edges of the open side so that they meet to form an even edge. Tack.

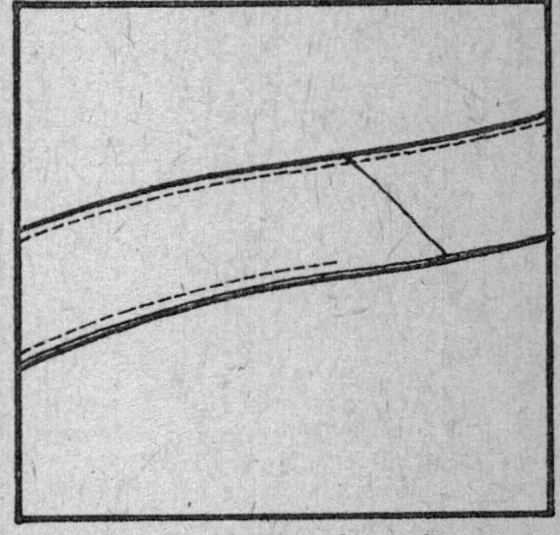
6 Sew this side together, the same distance from the edge as you did on the folded side, commencing just to one side of the join.

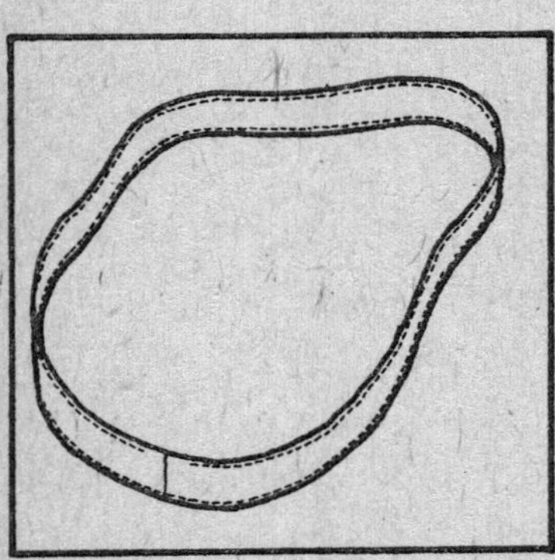
7 Sew right the way round and stop just before you get to the join.

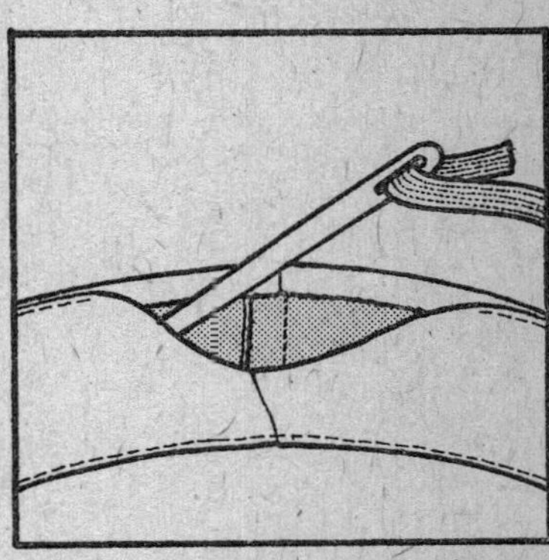
8 Insert the elastic through this gap, working it through in the same direction as you folded the seam allowance of the join. In this way you won't have difficulty getting the bodkin past the seam.

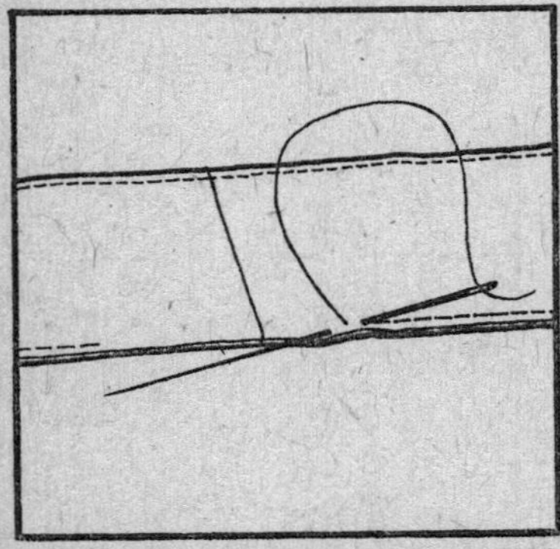
9 When you have joined both ends of the elastic, sew down the gap with back stitches.

sewing on tapes, ties and shoulder straps

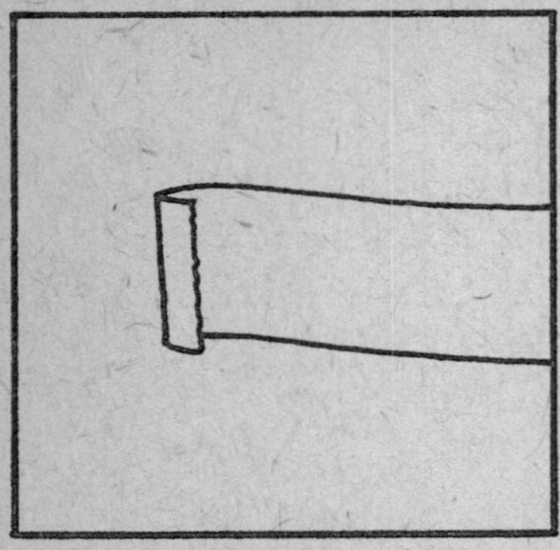

1 Turn under the end you wish to sew.

2 Place the end of the tape, with the fold inwards, on the wrong side of the garment so that the folded edge of the tape is level with the lower edge of the hem.

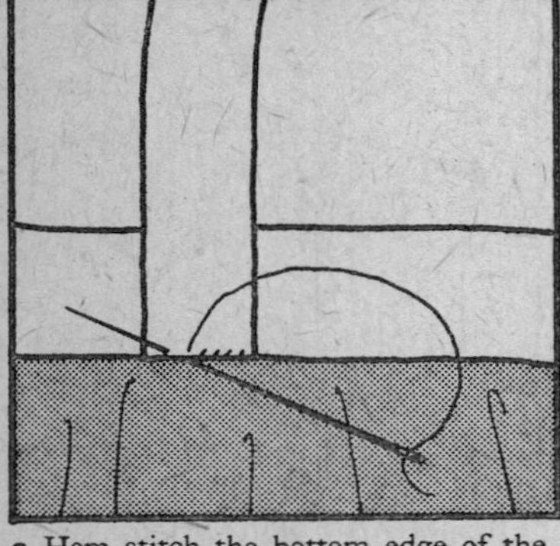

3 Hem stitch the bottom edge of the tape to the bottom edge of the hem.

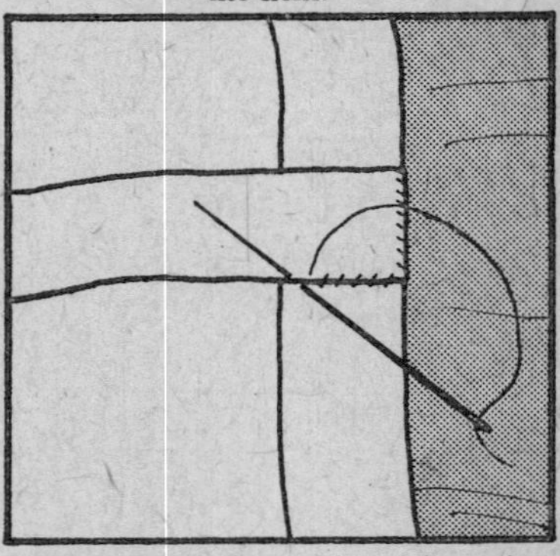

4 Turn the work round and hem the side of the tape to the garment.

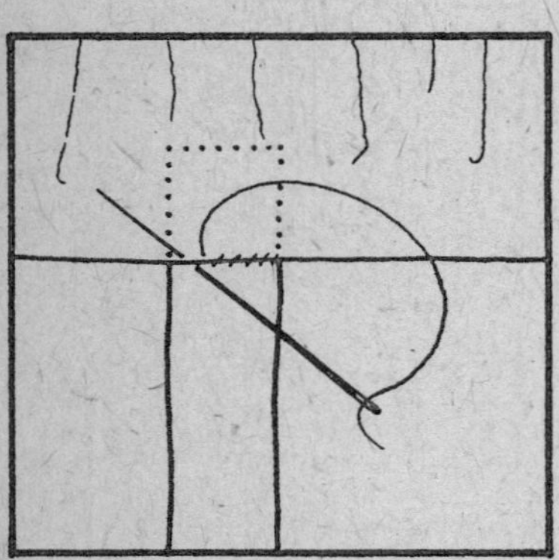

5 Now turn to the right side of the garment and hem the edge of the garment to the tape.

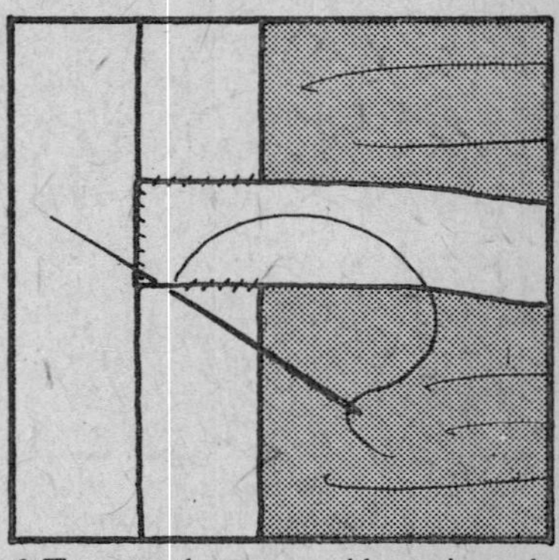

6 Turn to the wrong side again and hem down the last edge of the tape.

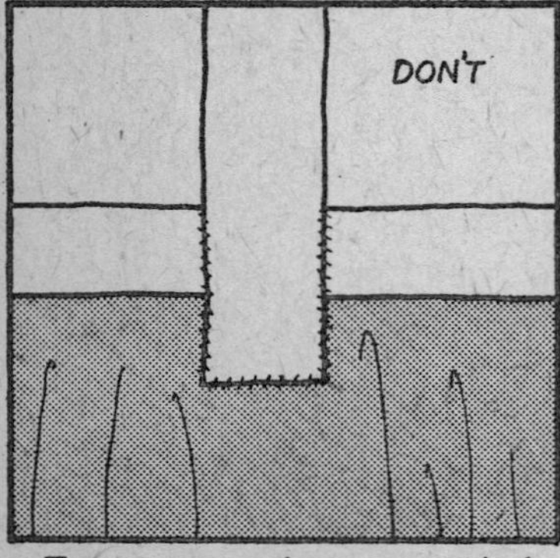

7 Try not to sew the tape to a single thickness of thin fabric because it will tear it.

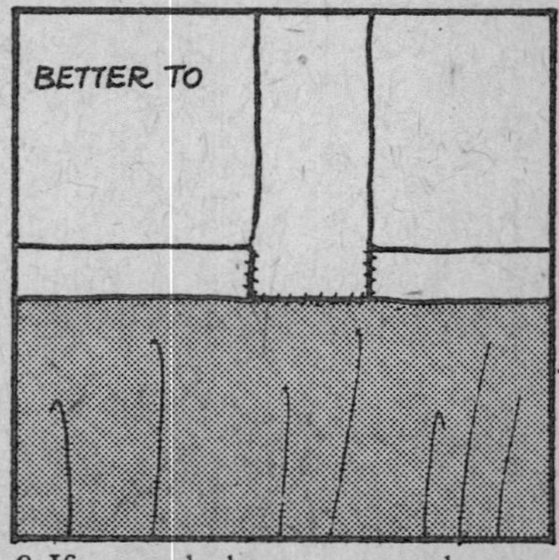

8 If you only have a narrow hem to which to sew the tape, sew it very firmly on a narrow hem.

If you are making a slip you can sew in the shoulder straps with the hem:

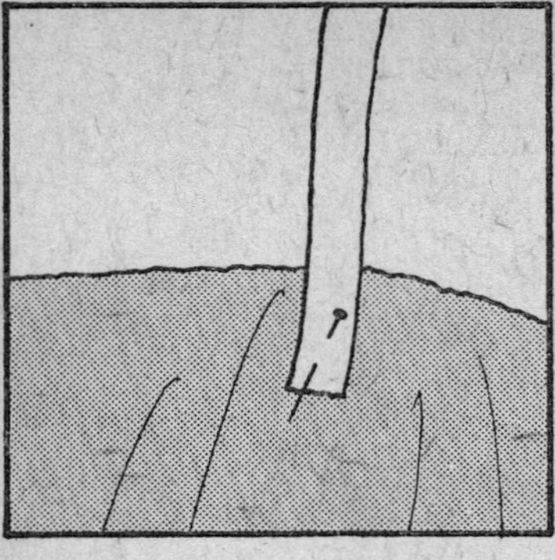

9 Pin the shoulder straps in place, on the wrong side of the garment, each end overlapping the raw edge by at least ½ in.

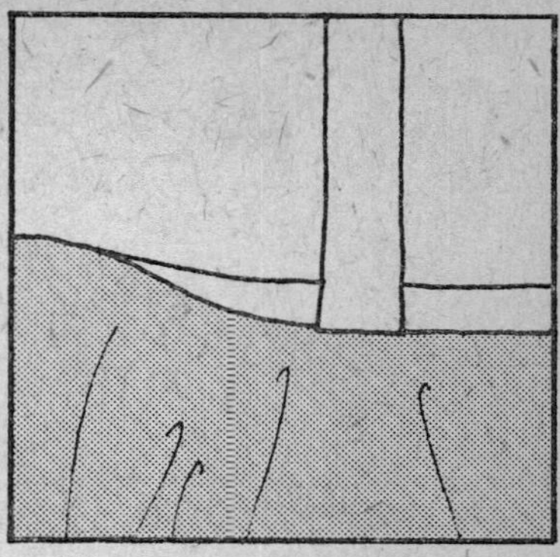

10 When you turn the hem, turn the shoulder straps with it as part of the fabric.

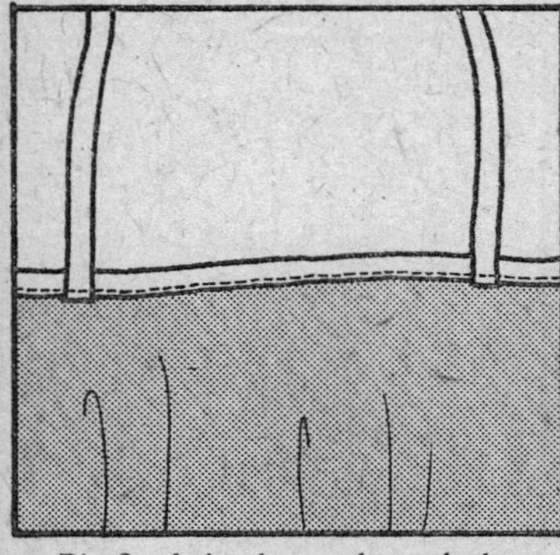

11 Pin firmly in place and sew the hem.

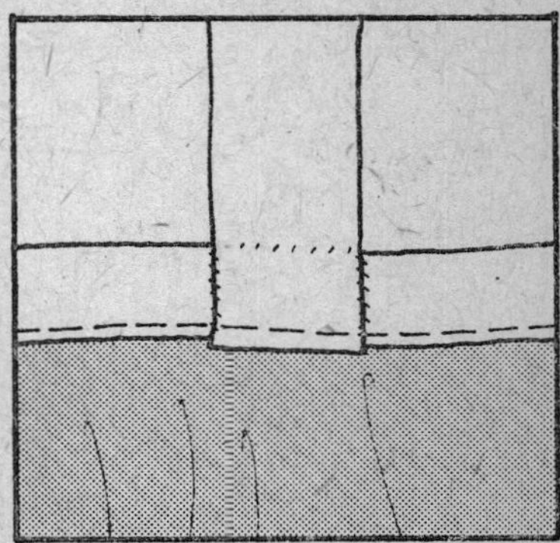

12 Finally add a few hem stitches to the other three sides to hold the strap firmly in place.

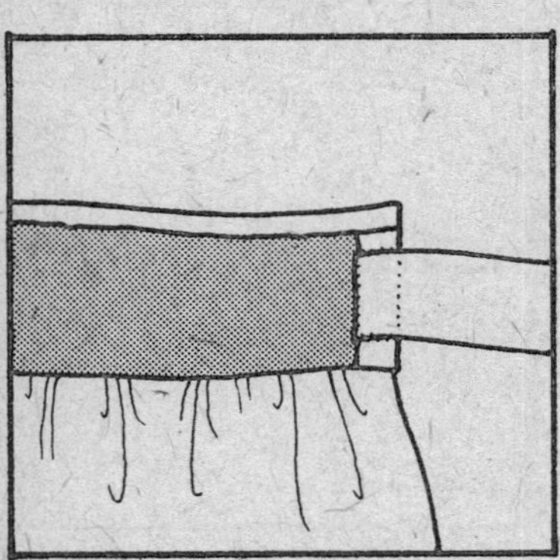

13 For aprons, the same principles apply if you are attaching to a single thickness of fabric.

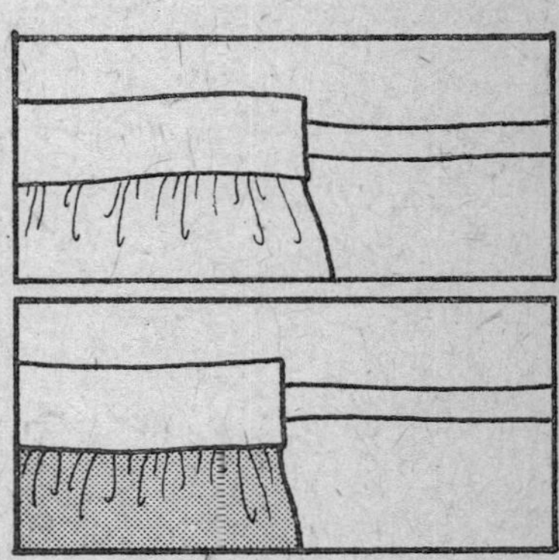

14 If you are using facing, try to sew the tape in as you make the garment.

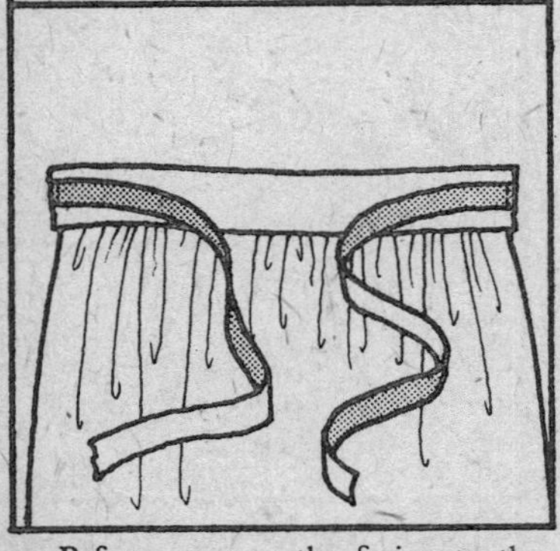

15 Before you sew the facing to the garment, tack the end of the tie to the side edge of the garment, right sides together.

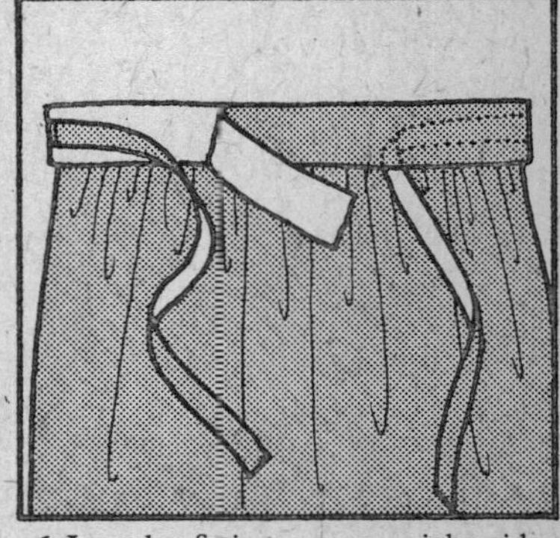

16 Lay the facing on top, right side downwards.

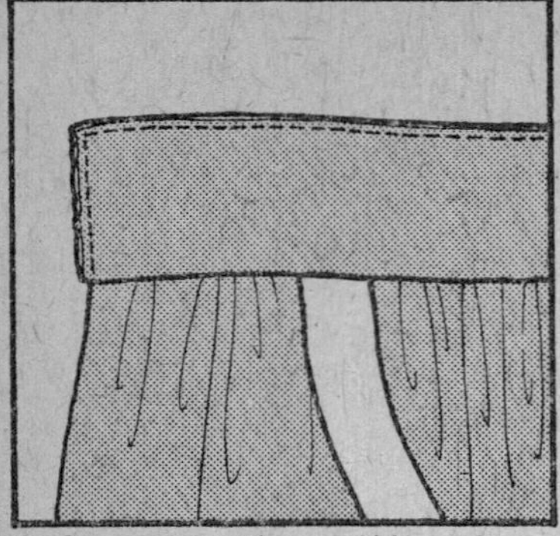

17 Sew together the two sides and top.

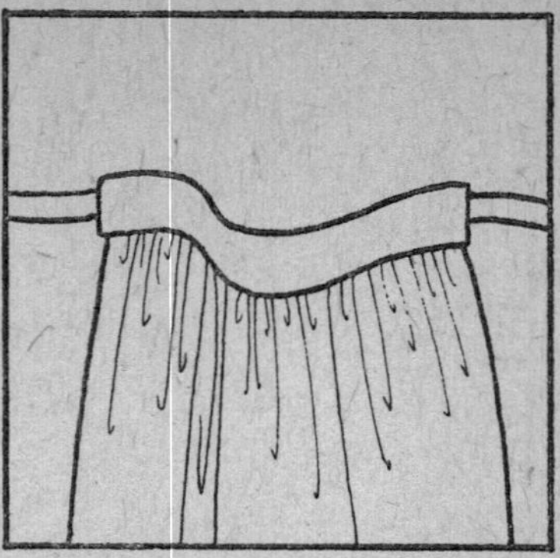

18 Turn inside out and ties will be in place.

sewing knitted pieces together

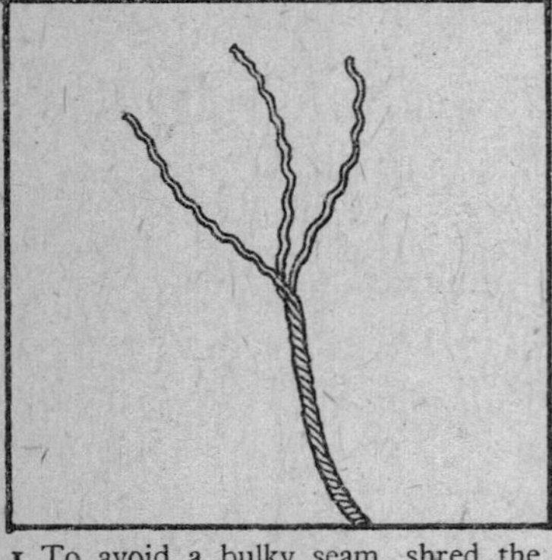

1 To avoid a bulky seam, shred the length of wool you propose to use for sewing. According to its strength, use only one ply or two ply.

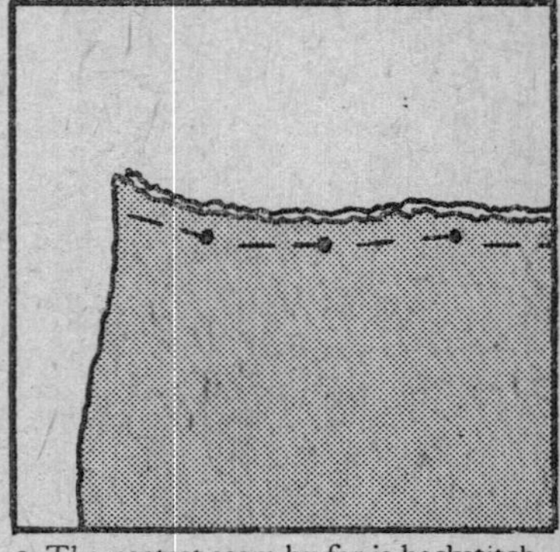

2 The neatest seam by far is backstitch. Place the two pieces together, wrong sides outwards, and pin in place.

3 Don't stretch anywhere unless the pattern says so, and backstitch just inside the edges of the knitting.

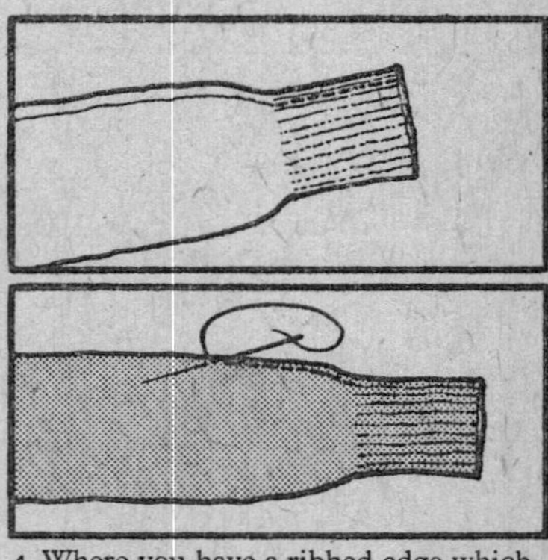

4 Where you have a ribbed edge which will be turned back when the garment is worn, like a cuff, sew the ribbed edges together on the outside, then turn the work inside out and continue the seam on the wrong side.

5 Never sew buttons or press studs on to knitting without a backing. Use a length of tape, about ½ in. wide.

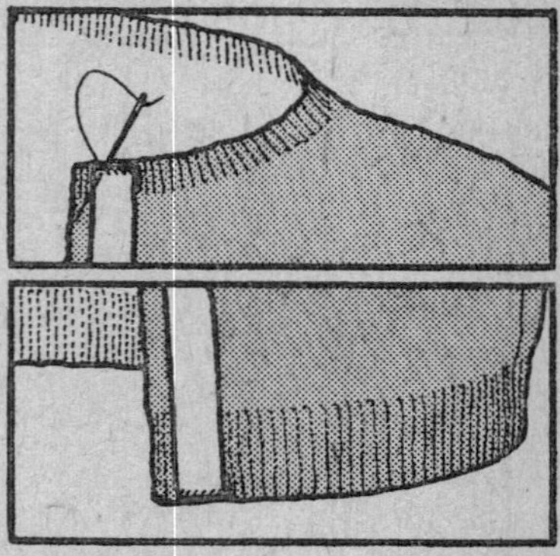

6 Place the tape behind the area where the buttons will be sewn and turn under each end. Sew this with matching cotton to the neck and bottom edges of the garment, making sure it doesn't drag.

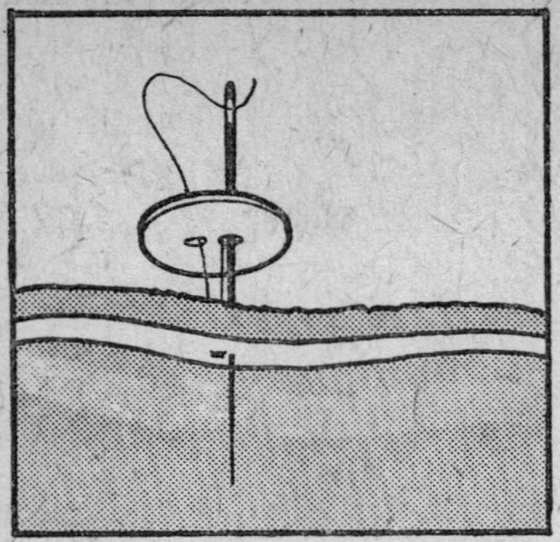

7 When you sew on the buttons or studs sew right through the knitting to take in the backing tape as well.

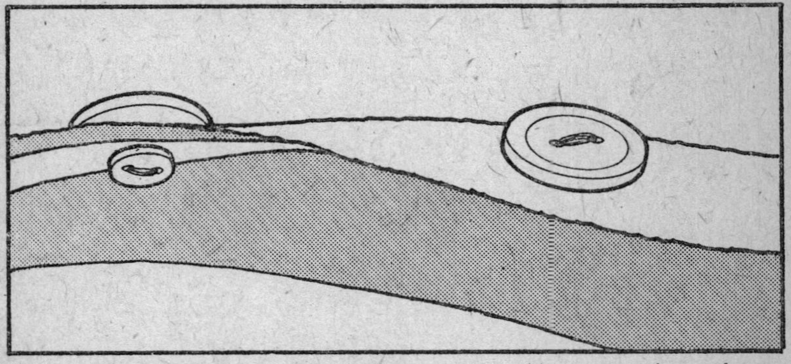

8 If you have knitted a heavy garment, like a coat, it would pay to use the two-button method as on page 43.

working with fur

1 Never cut fur with scissors.

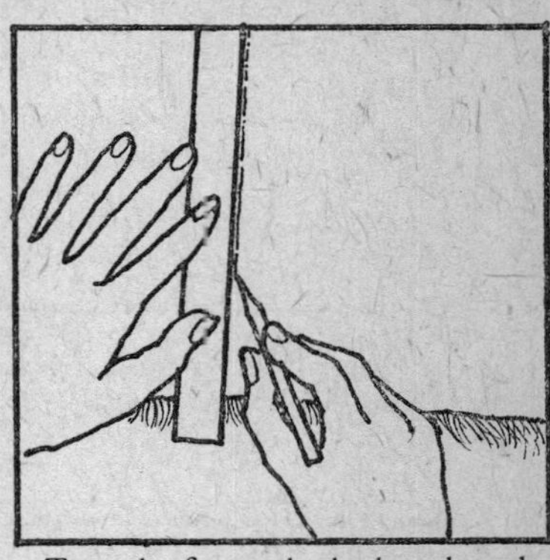

2 Turn the fur to the back and mark on the skin where you wish to cut.

3 With a razor blade cut the skin only, along the mark.

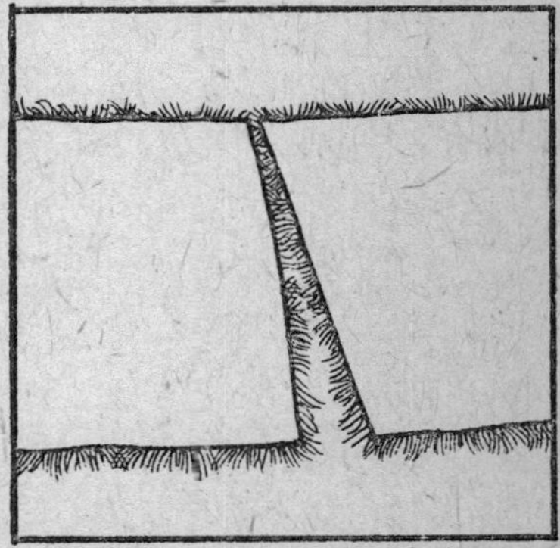

4 When you have completed the cut, gently pull the two pieces apart.

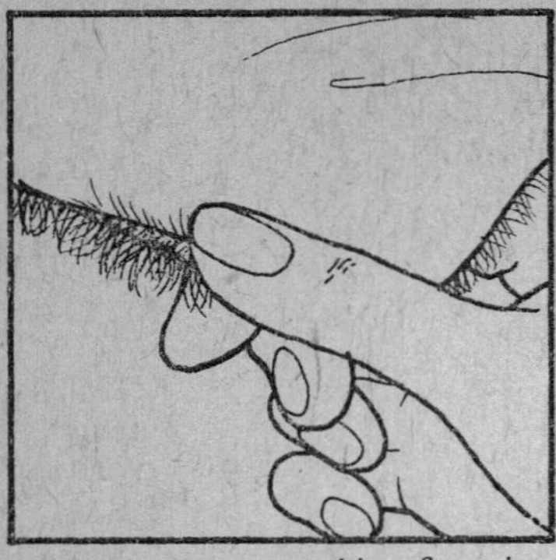

5 When you are attaching fur trimmings, turn the edge of the skin under by the smallest amount you can get away with.

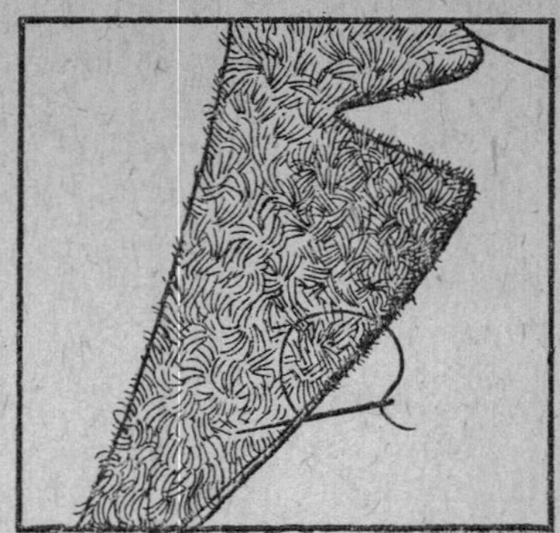

6 Hem the edge to the main fabric.

curtains

Curtains can make or mar a room so give a lot of thought to just what sort you want before you buy or make anything. You can have them from ceiling to floor, or from the top of the window frame to the sill, or from the top of the frame to just below the sill, or from the top of the frame to the floor.

The first step is to measure the area you actually need to cover, then add the required number of inches per curtain for turnings.

If you are not certain how much to buy take your measurements along to the shop and let the assistant advise you.

There are no golden rules about the length of curtains, but there are one or two points of commonsense you should consider.

1 If you have a wide window sill the curtain would look better resting on it rather than bulging over it.

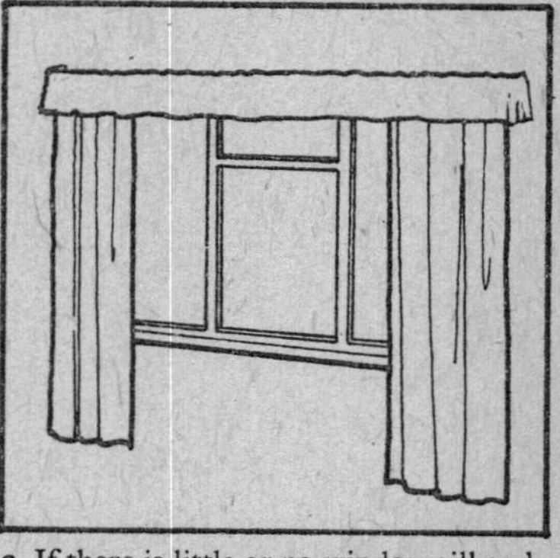

2 If there is little or no window sill and the curtain rail juts out so that the curtain hangs flat, it could look more elegant for the curtains to hang below the sill.

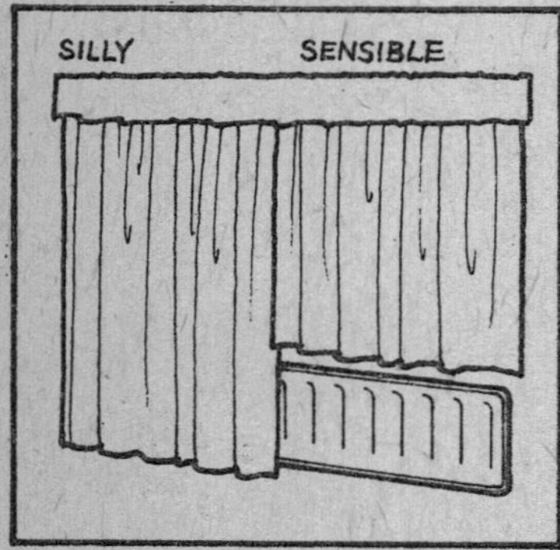

3 If you have a radiator under the window it would be more sensible to keep the curtains above it, otherwise heat would be lost when the curtains are drawn.

4 If you have a picture window you may not want the curtains to cover any part of it during the daytime so you must allow for the curtains to hang outside the frame instead of in front of it, and measure accordingly.

5 If you live in a cottage-type property, or a flat with a door and window on the same wall, it may look better to curtain the whole wall.

how much width to allow

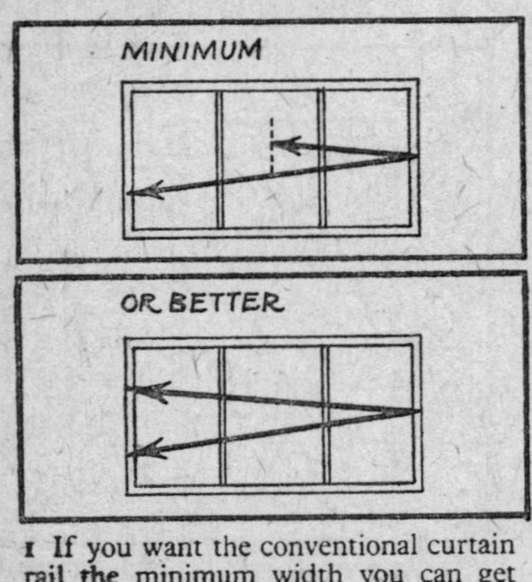

1 If you want the conventional curtain rail the minimum width you can get away with is the width of the curtain rail and half as much again. If you can afford it, have twice the width to give you really full curtains.

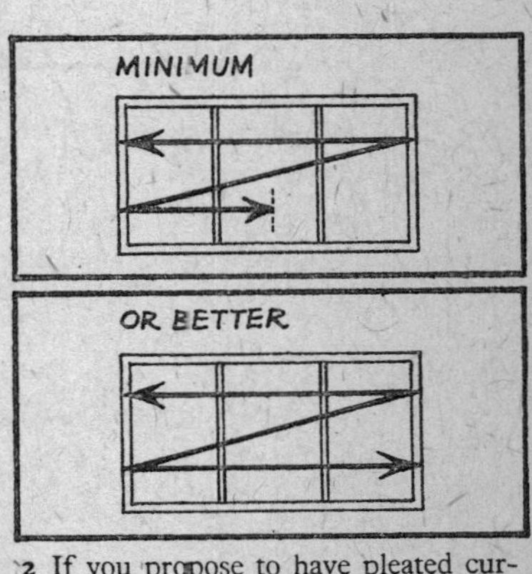

2 If you propose to have pleated curtains you must allow $2\frac{1}{2}$ to 3 times the width of the area to be curtained. To avoid wastage or disappointment take the advice of the shop assistant or the fitting manufacturers, who supply detailed leaflets.

how much length to allow

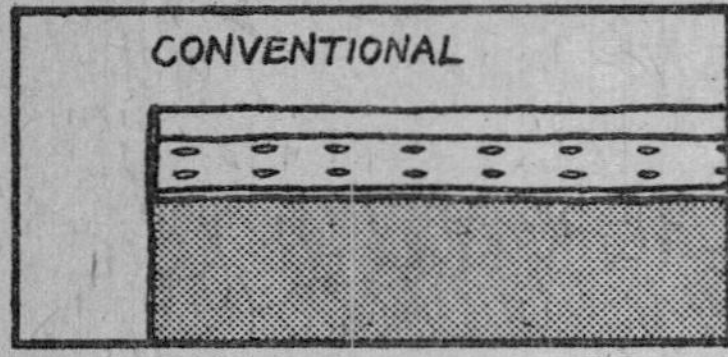

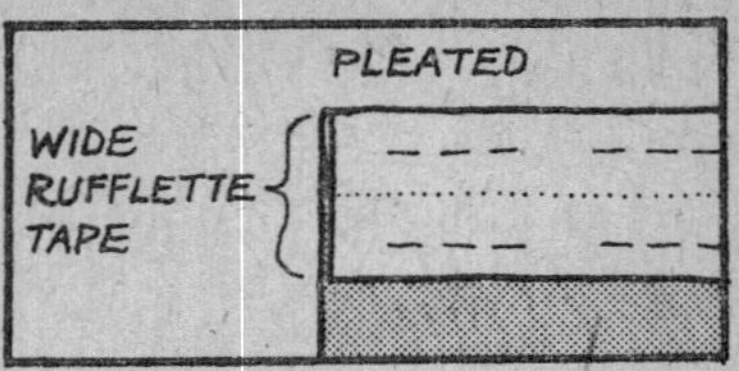

3 When making allowance for turnings at the top and bottom, you will need only a small turning at the top for both conventional fittings and for pleated curtains.

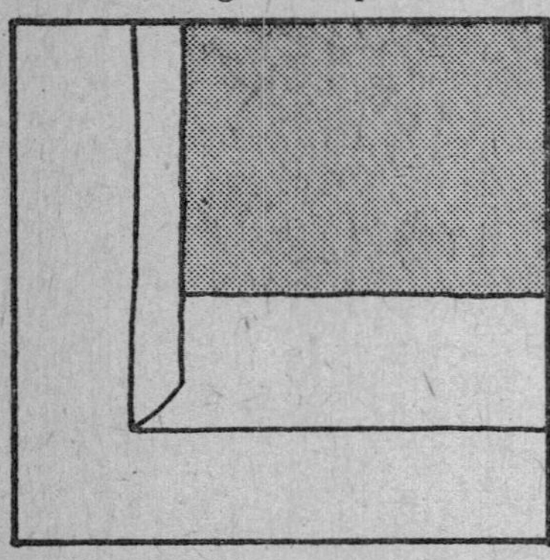

4 Take a good hem at the bottom to give weight to the curtain, and a look of luxury. Allow at least 4 in.

joining the lengths

Most curtaining is 48 in. wide, and some is 60 in. You can use as many widths as you like in one curtain, even half a width, to get the required fullness. If the fabric is patterned you must match the pattern so that the joins don't show. Work on a large table top or the floor.

1 Cut the first length.

2 Lay the length of fabric beside this piece and move it up and down until the patterns match. You will incur some wastage here.

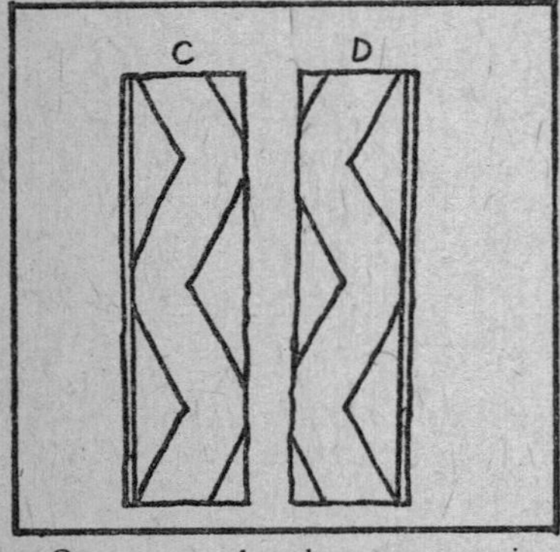

3 Cut as many lengths as you require for one curtain. If you require a half-width, line up the pattern and cut the length as before, then cut that piece in half lengthways.

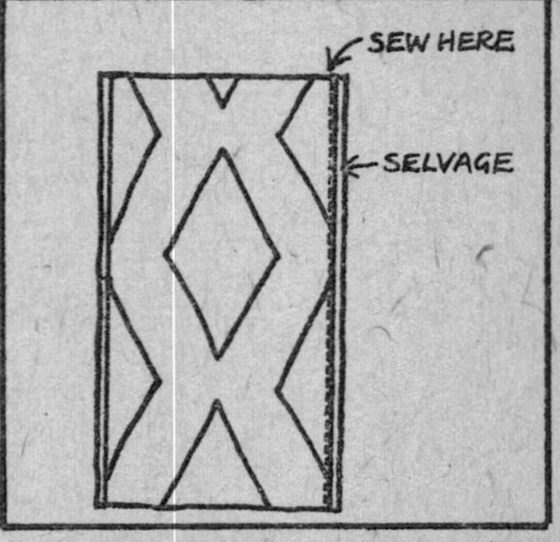

4 When you join the lengths, sew just clear of the selvage. This is particularly important on patterned fabrics because you will not want to encroach on the pattern, so keep as near the selvage as you can.

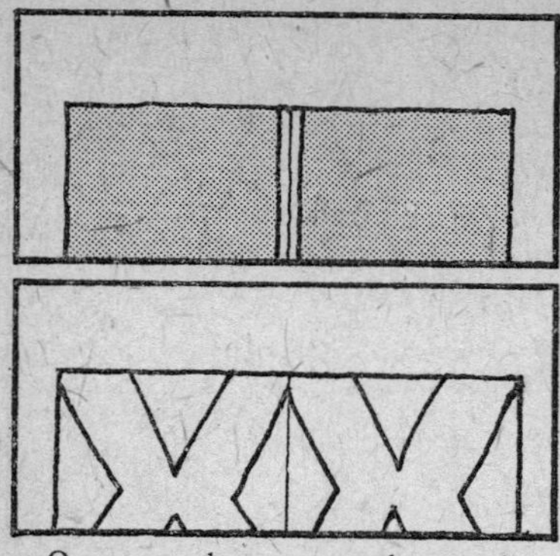

5 Open out the seams and press flat.

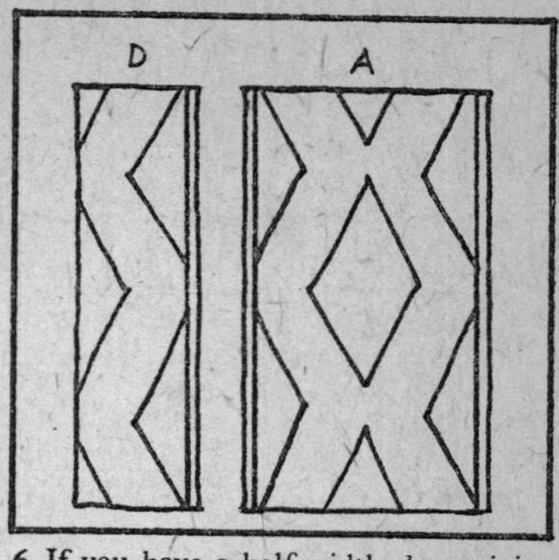

6 If you have a half width *do not* join the cut edge because you have no selvage. If you turn in the cut edge you will spoil the pattern. Join the right hand selvage edge to the left hand edge of the first piece you cut.

7 Make this the left hand curtain so that the cut edge will be at the far side.

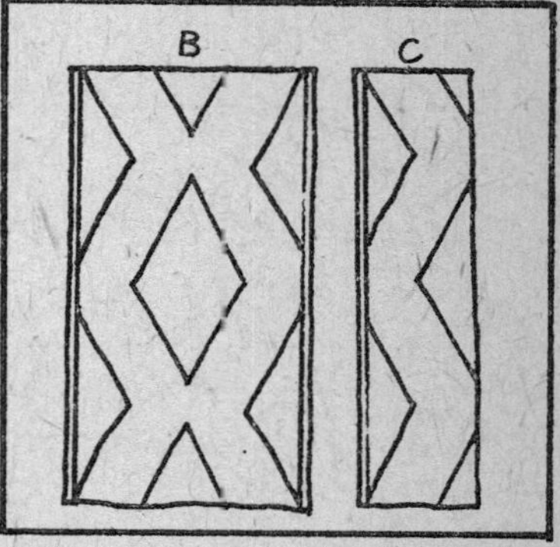

8 Utilise the other half width for the far side of the right hand curtain by joining its left hand selvage to the right hand selvage of the previous piece.

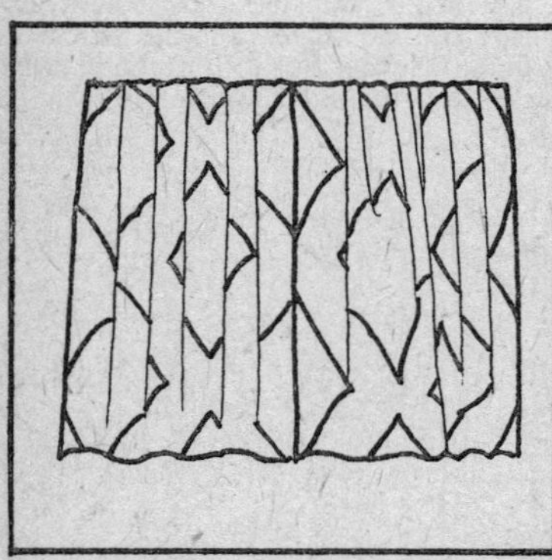

9 When the curtains are drawn they will look as if they are one continuous piece of fabric.

lining

It is advisable to line all curtains for several reasons, (a) they hang better, (b) the sun will bleach the lining instead of the more expensive curtaining, (c) the added substance will give them a richer and more professional look.

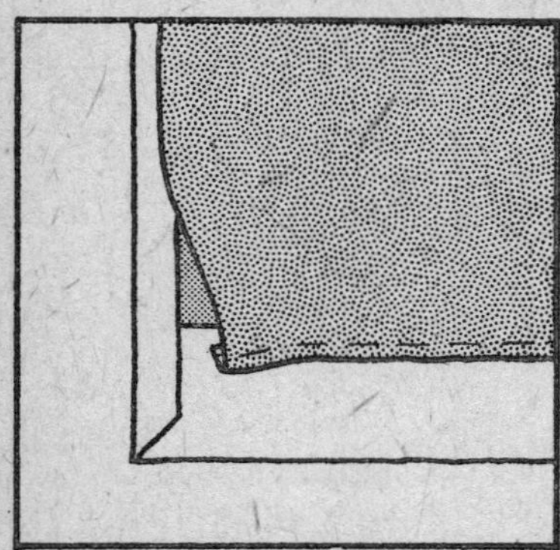

1 You can either have the lining hanging loose at the bottom with a narrow hem, or

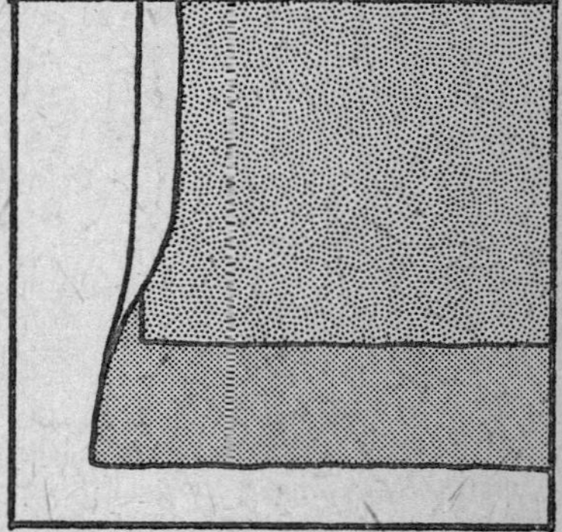

2 You can bring it to the point at which you turn up the hem of the curtain.

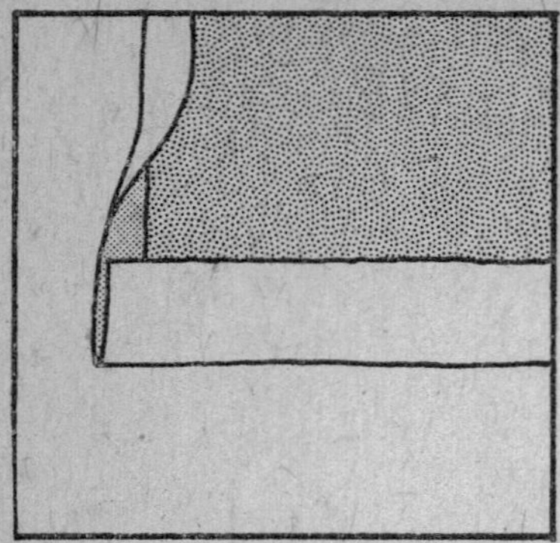

3 Fold the curtain over the lining. Do not fold up the lining.

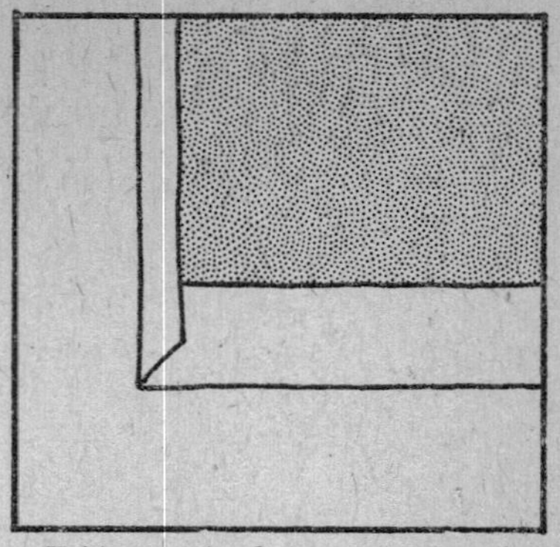

4 Fold over the facing and mitre the corner as on page 156-158.

5 The lining may not be the same width as the curtaining so join as many lengths as you need, plus part of a length to make the same width as the curtain.

making up

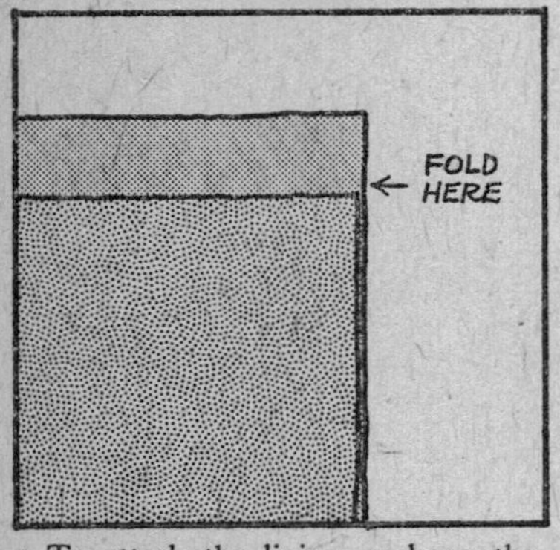

1 To attach the lining work on the wrong side of the fabric. Start with the top of the lining at the point where you will fold over the curtain for the top hem.

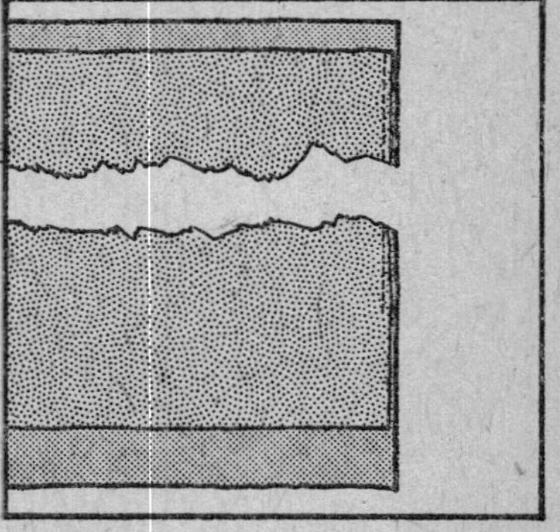

2 Sew the two pieces together, just clear of the selvage, from the top of the lining to about 10 in. from the bottom. Sew both sides in this way.

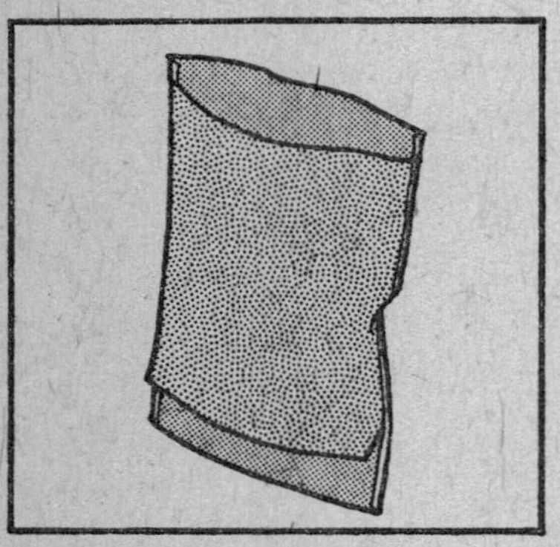

3 Turn the whole thing inside out.

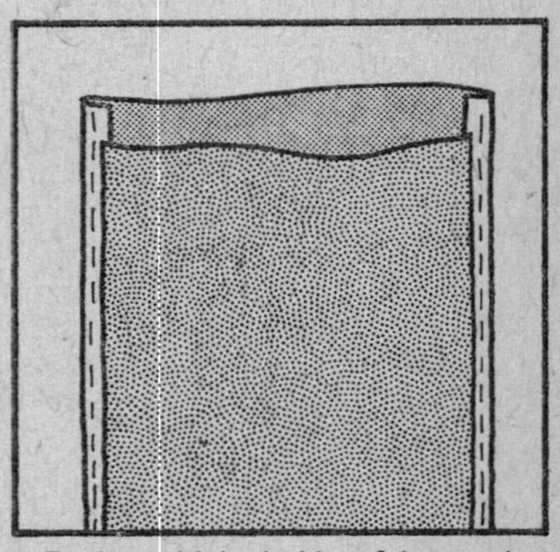

4 Dealing with both sides of the curtain in the same way, fold over the side of the curtain 1 in., and pin or tack it in place.

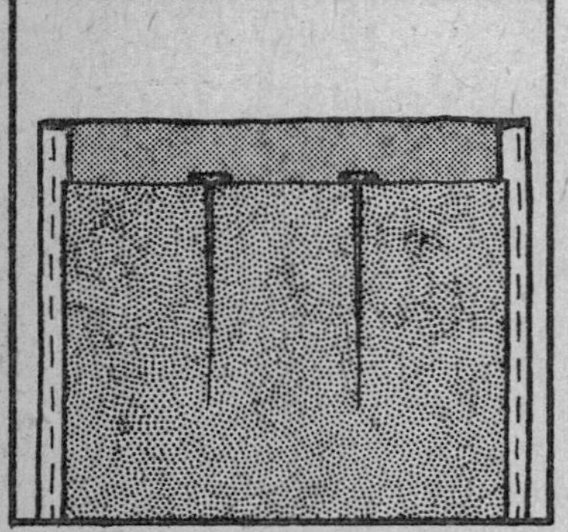

5 You will now have more width in the lining than the curtain so take one or two inverted pleats in the top of the lining until it lies flat against the curtain.

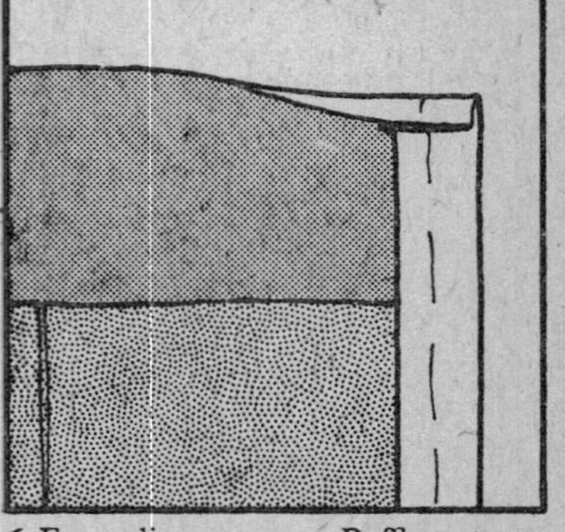

6 For ordinary narrow Rufflette tape, turn, towards the wrong side, a $\frac{1}{4}$ in. single hem at the top of the curtain.

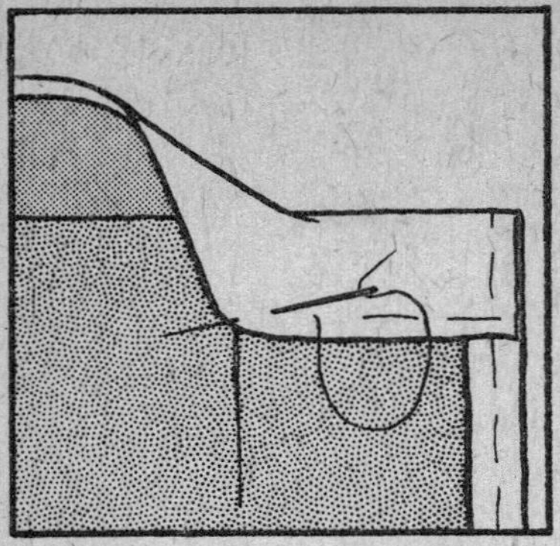

7 Turn the top over again along the top of the lining. Tack in place.

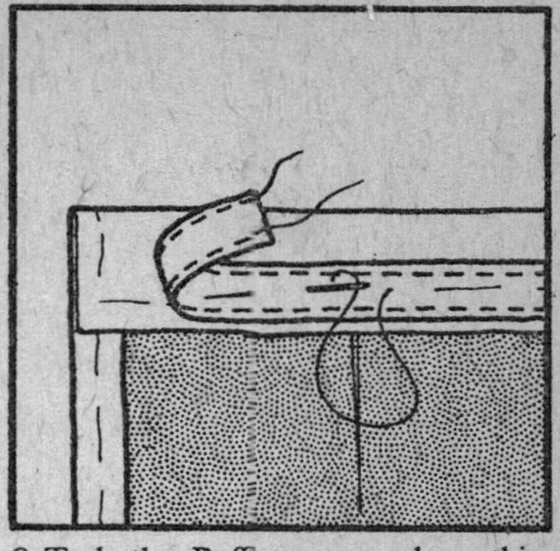

8 Tack the Rufflette tape along this hem, with the lower edge just above the lower edge of the hem.

9 Sew down the Rufflette tape and the hem at one and the same time by machining along both edges of the Rufflette tape.

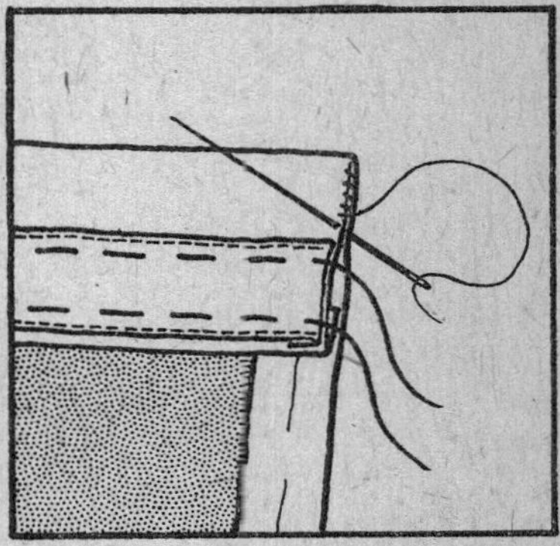

10 Tuck in the ends of the Rufflette tape and hem the folds together by hand leaving the two ends of cord free.

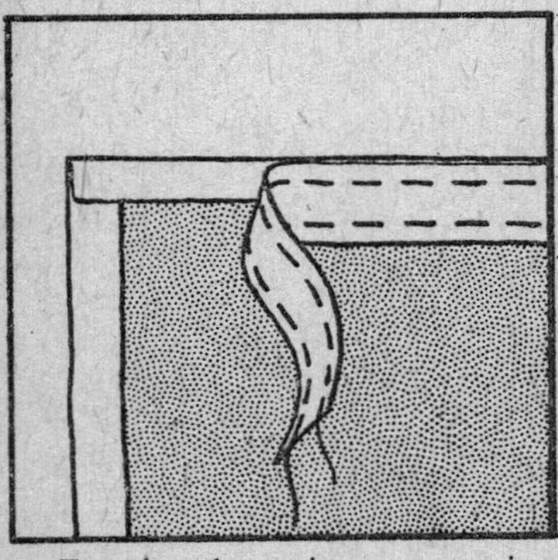

11 For pleated curtains turn a 1 in. single hem over the top of the lining, and attach appropriate Rufflette tape, upper edge to top of curtain.

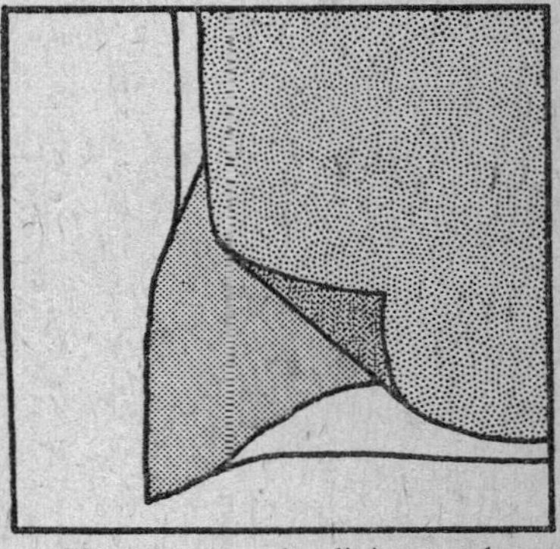

12 If you want the lining to hang separately turn up the bottom of the curtain, on the wrong side, at the required length.

13 Turn in the edge and slip stitch it to the main fabric

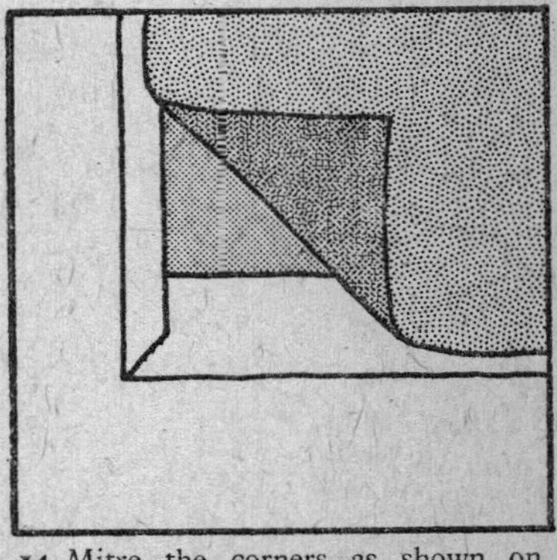

14 Mitre the corners as shown on page 156 -158.

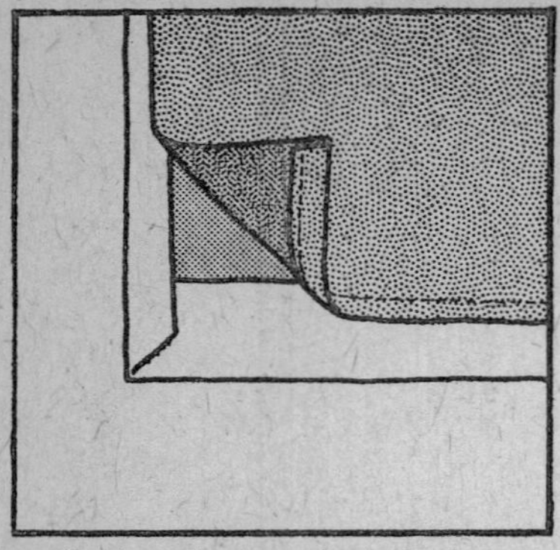

15 Fold a 1 in. hem along the bottom of the lining, turned towards the back of the lining. Sew.

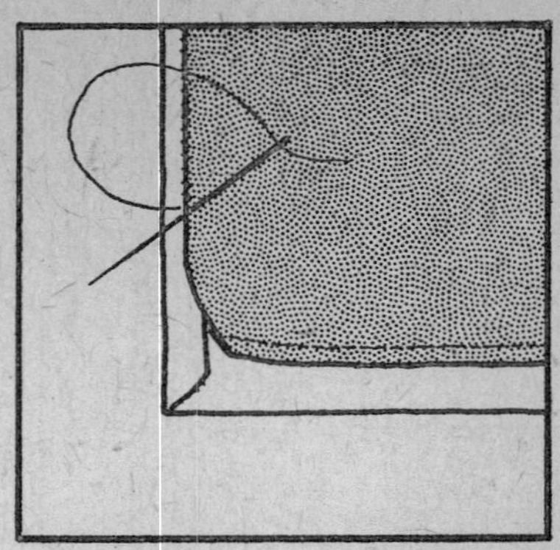

16 Finish off the side seams by hemming the curtain to the lining, to within 2 in. of the bottom of the lining.

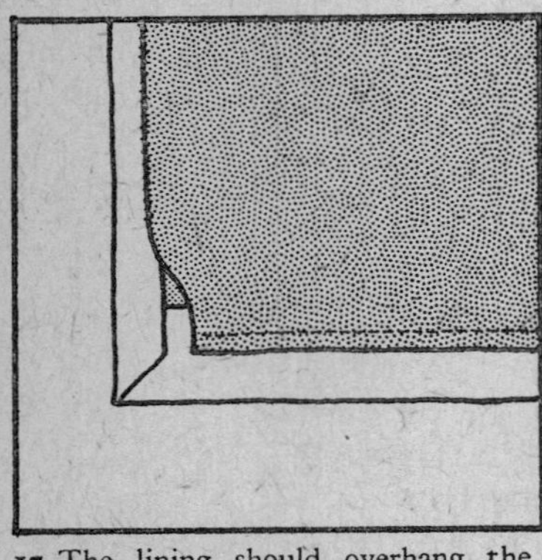

17 The lining should overhang the slip-stitched hem by about 1 in., or

It you wish to sew the lining inside the hem of the curtain, work as far as 10, then proceed as follows:

18 Lay the curtain flat on a table top or the floor.

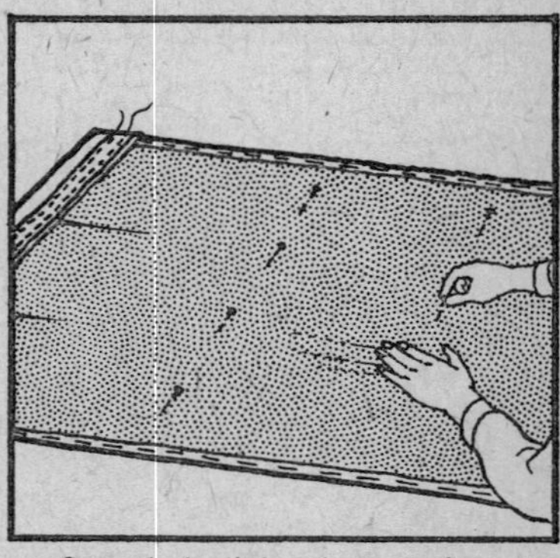

19 Smooth the lining downwards starting at the top and pinning it in stages. It must not drag when the curtain is hanging.

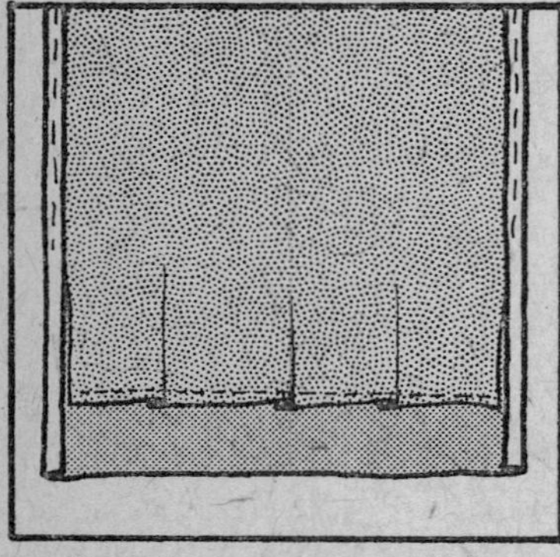

20 Tack the bottom of the lining in place, taking two or three small tucks to absorb the fullness.

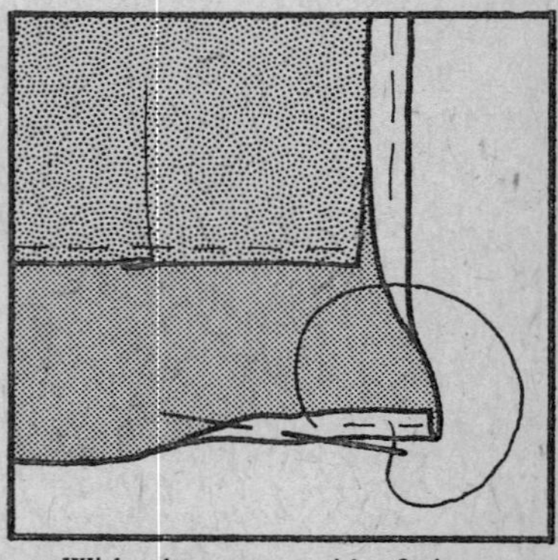

21 With the wrong side facing you turn up the bottom of the curtain ½ in. Tack.

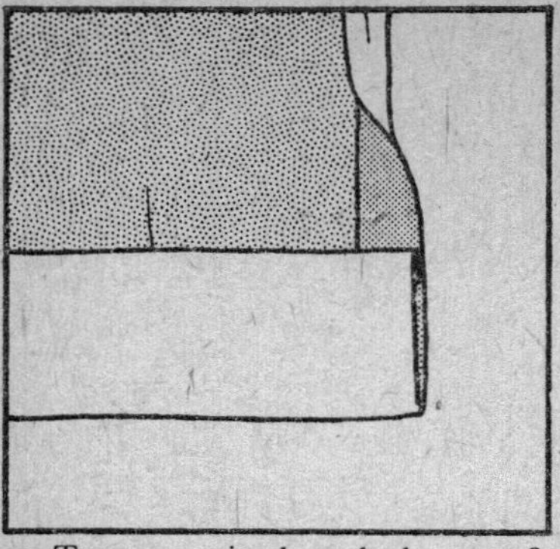

22 Turn up again along the bottom of the lining, bringing the hem up over the lining.

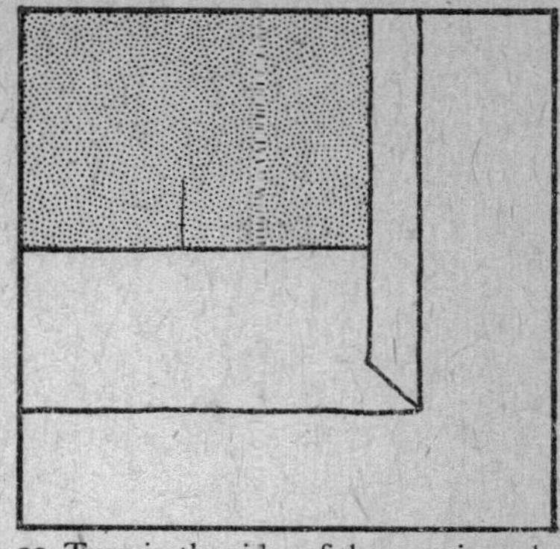

23 Turn in the sides of the curtain and mitre the corners as on page 156-158.

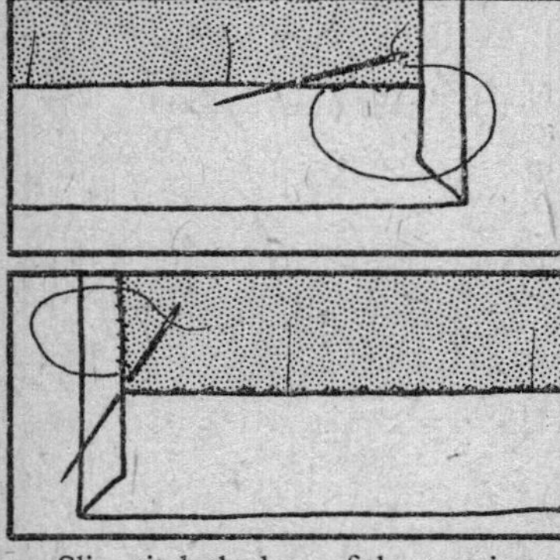

24 Slip stitch the hem of the curtain to the lining and hem down the sides.

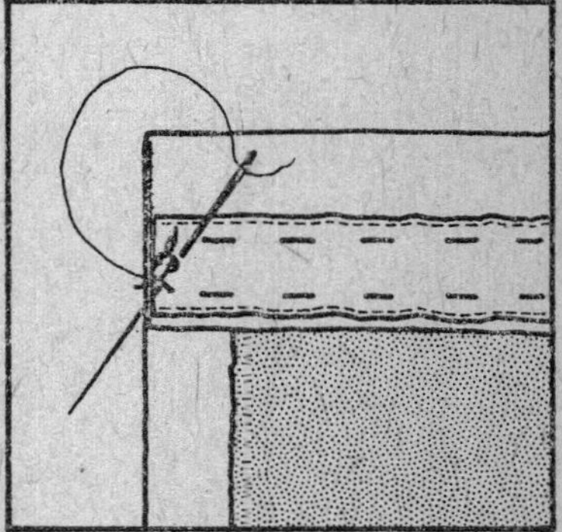

25 Before you pull the threads in the Rufflette tape to gather the curtain, tie together the two ends of thread at the centre edge, and sew down firmly, otherwise you will pull the threads right out.

firming the edges

The sides of curtains hang better with a little stiffening inside. This can be done by inserting a strip of stiffened muslin or Vilene all the way down the edges of the curtain.

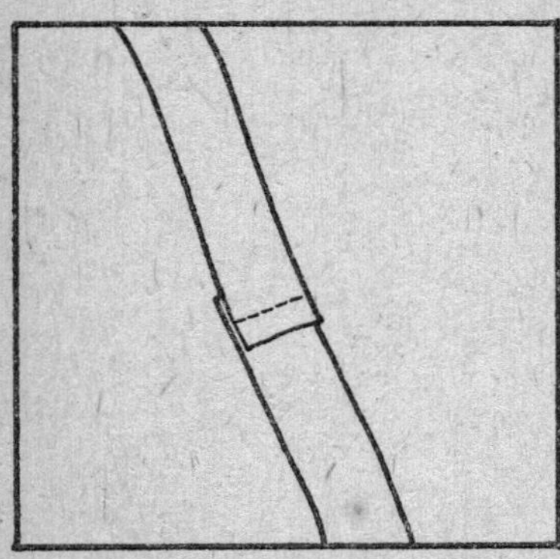

1 Cut 1 in. wide strips of stiffening. Join them by overlapping and stitching with one plain seam.

2 Before you attach the lining, tack a strip of stiffening against the outside edge of the curtain, on the wrong side, from the point where the top fold will come to the point where the bottom fold will be made.

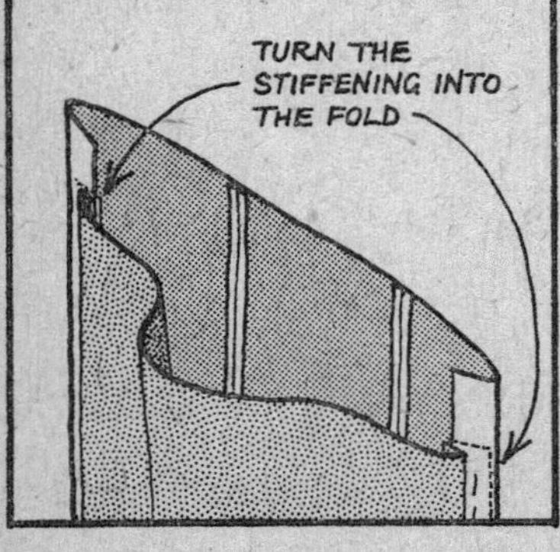

3 Attach the lining as on page 175, 176. When you turn the curtain inside out as on page 176, turn the stiffening outwards into the fold. When you fold the sides in 1 in. as step 4 in the making up section, you will be folding the curtain round the stiffening. Complete the curtain as on page 176-179.

net curtains–ready made

Fashions have changed considerably and very few net curtains are completely home-made nowadays. It is easier to buy the ready-made curtains which are sold by the yard 'sideways'.

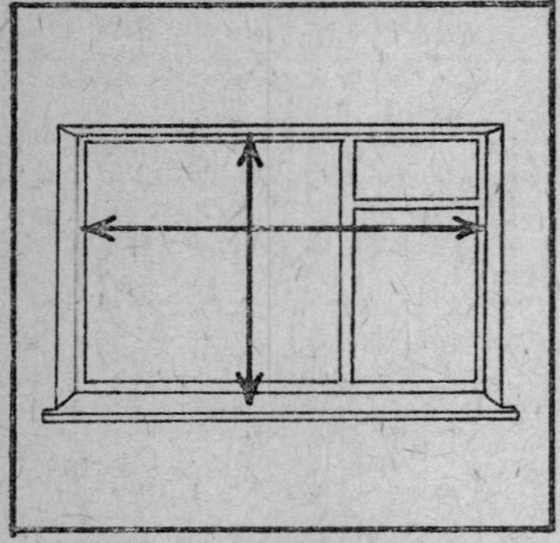

1 Net curtains should be hung close to the window and need only cover the glazed area. Allow for them to just touch the sill.

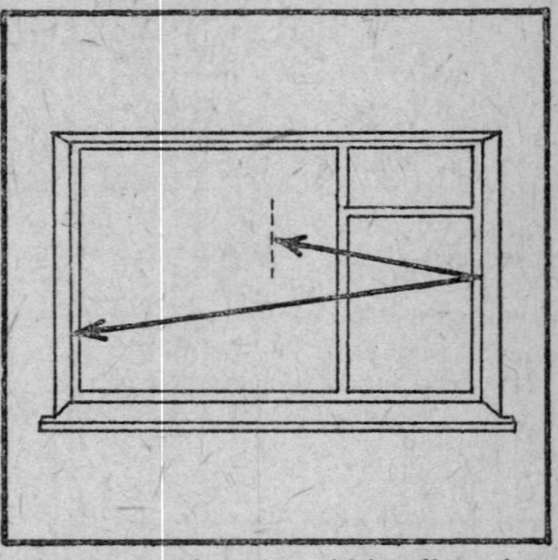

2 When gauging the width, allow the width of the window plus half as much again, as the minimum to give you any fullness. The yardage you buy will therefore be whatever the window measures from side to side, plus half as much again.

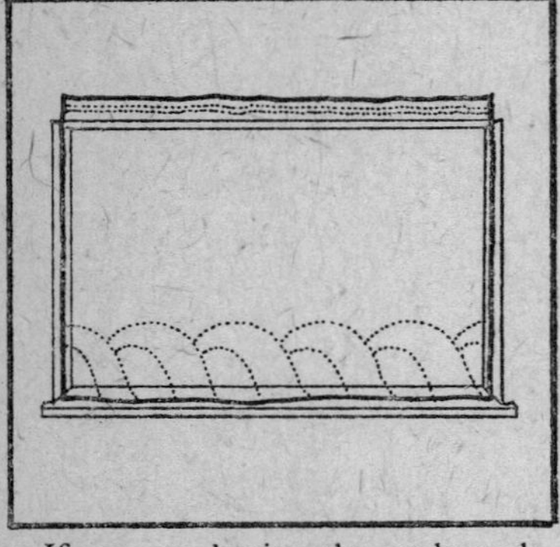

3 If you are buying the ready-made 'sideways' nets you will be looking for one which is the same depth as your window. If you are unable to obtain the exact depth, buy one about 3 in. deeper.

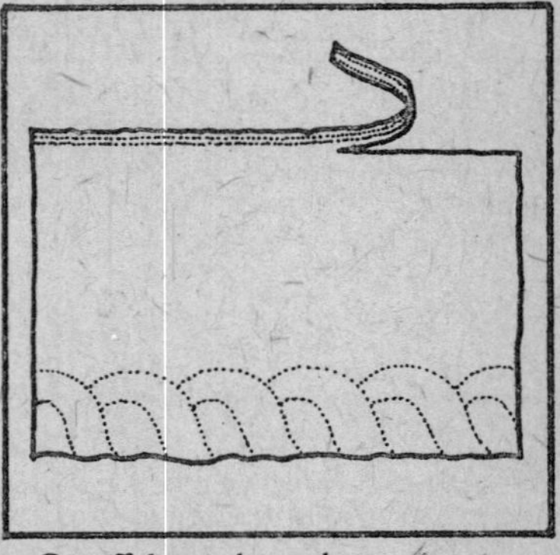

4 Cut off the ready-made top. Turn a new hem at the top of the curtain to give you the correct depth for your window as shown in 8, 9, 10 and 11 page 181, 182.

5 Turn under and sew, on the wrong side, a very small hem down each side of the curtain.

net curtains–hand made

Measure the window as in 1 and 2 above. Joins in net curtains do not look very nice so it is better to use one width of net per panel of the window. Allow 2 in. for the top hem and not less than 4 in. at the bottom.

1 If you have any difficulty in straightening the cut edge of the net, open out a double sheet of newspaper and lay it flat on the table. (Newspapers are machine cut and you would be very unlucky to get one which is not symetrical).

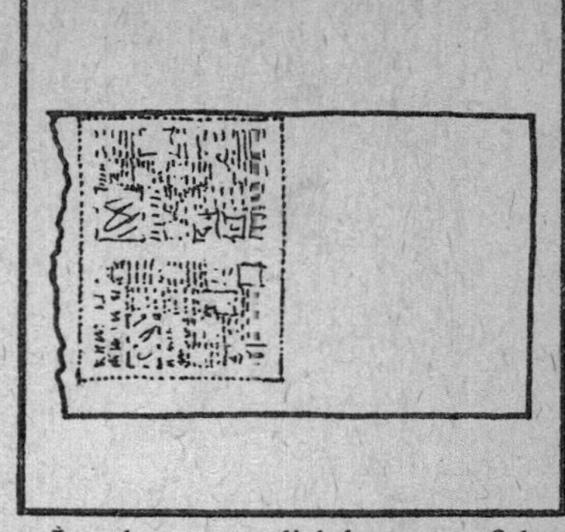

2 Lay the net very lightly on top of the newspaper with the top edge of the net just above the top edge of the paper. Do not press the net on the paper otherwise you may blacken it with the ink.

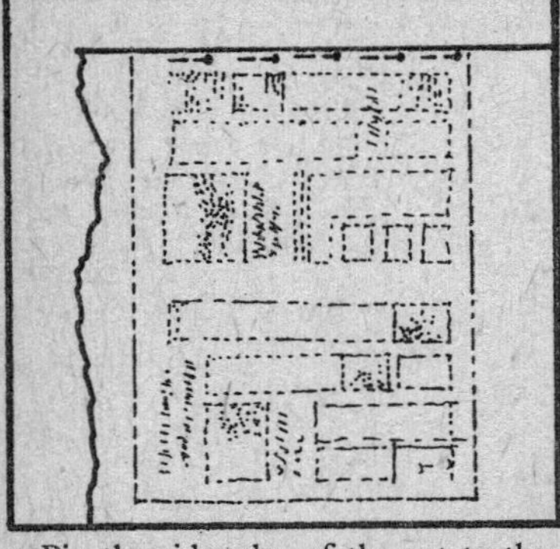

3 Pin the side edge of the net to the edge of the paper.

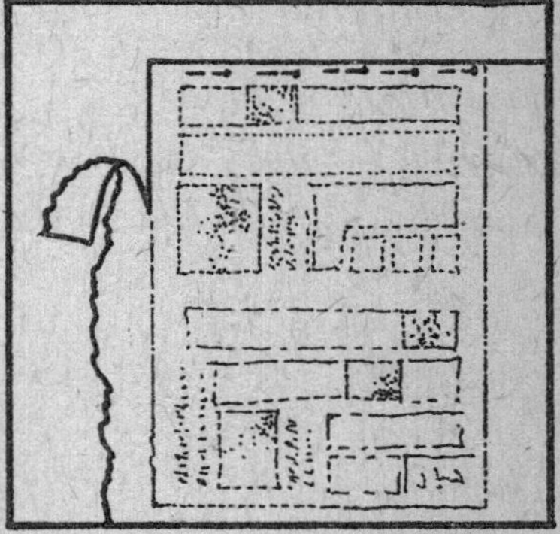

4 Lightly smooth the net across and cut it along the edge of the paper. When you get to the end of the paper it will not be difficult to keep straight for the rest of the width.

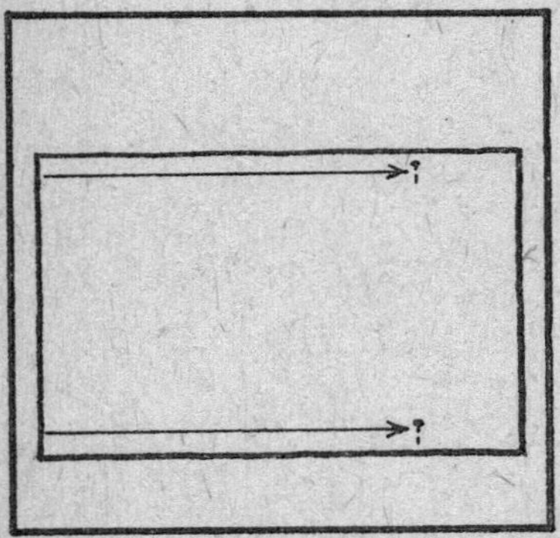

5 When you cut from then onwards, measure your length on both edges and mark the point with a pin on either side of the width.

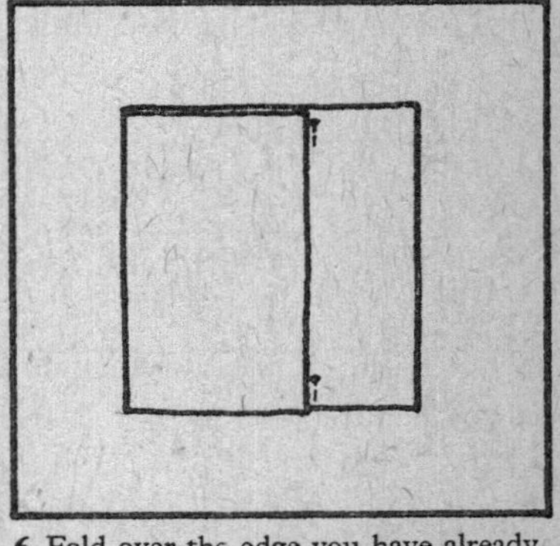

6 Fold over the edge you have already cut and bring it down to the point you have marked with pins.

7 Put a few pins in the folded edges, which must meet exactly, and cut across using the previous cut edge as a guide. Continue in this way until you have cut as many lengths as you need.

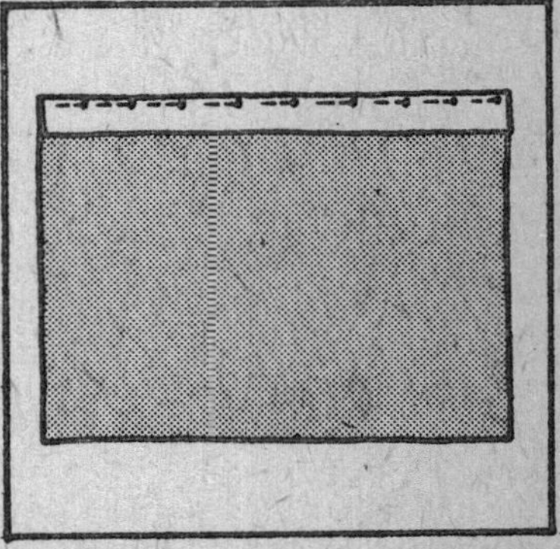

8 To make up, start at the top by turning down the edge 2 in. on the wrong side, and pin it along the fold.

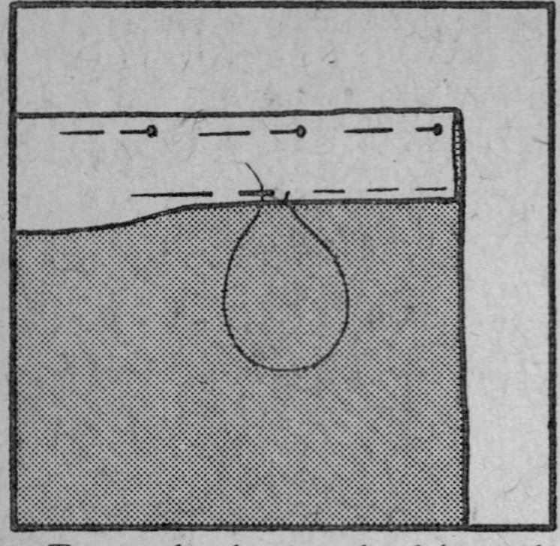

9 Turn under the raw edge ½ in., and tack.

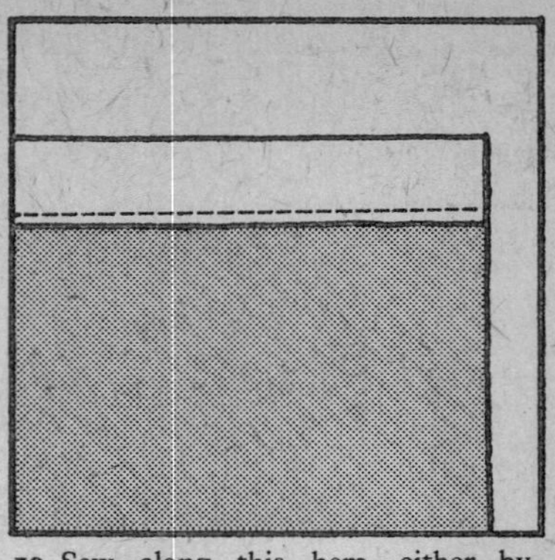

10 Sew along this hem, either by machine or b, hand in running stitch.

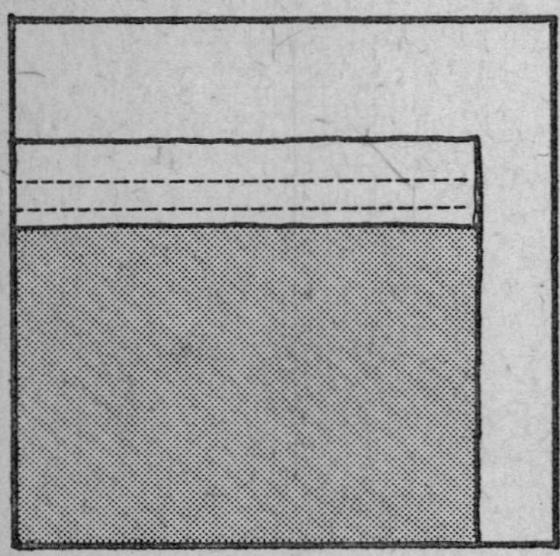

11 Sew another seam ½ in. above it.

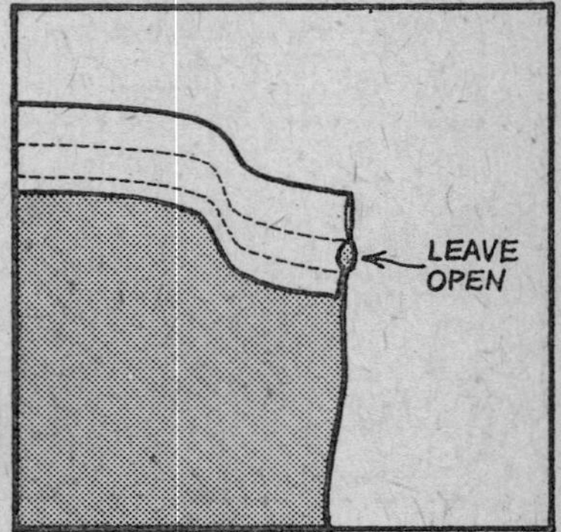

12 You will thread the wire between these two seams.

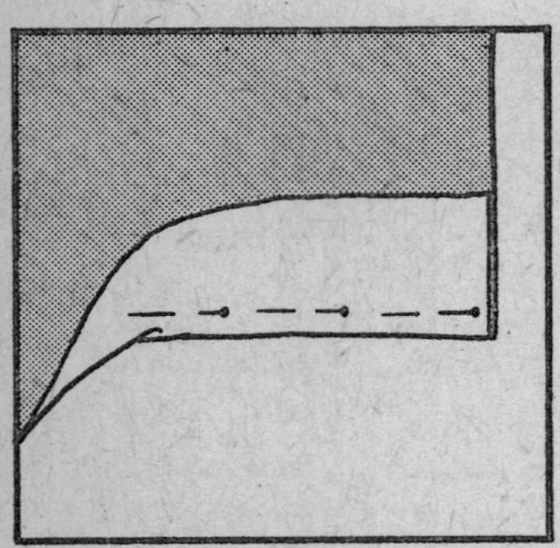

13 Turn up the bottom hem, on the wrong side, and pin along the fold.

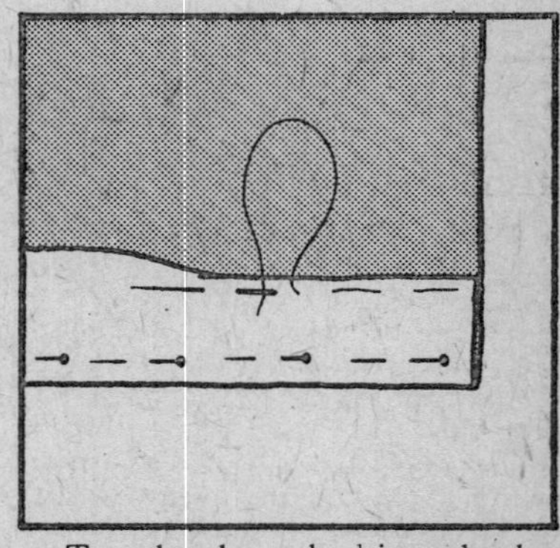

14 Turn the edge under ½ in. and tack.

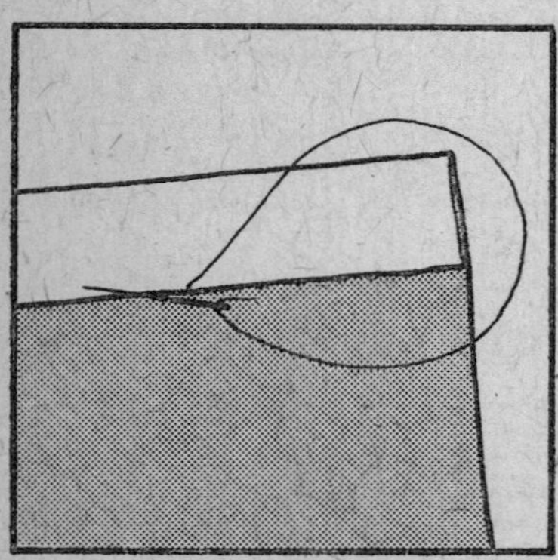

15 Slip stitch the hem. (You can machine it, but it looks rather ugly)

pelmets

You don't need fancy or expensive fittings to make your own pelmets.

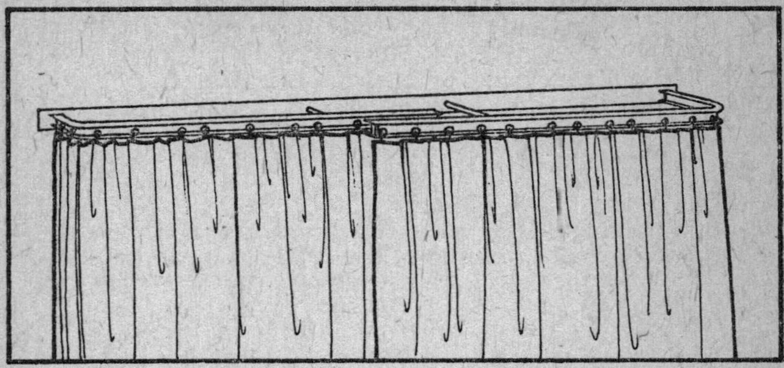

1 You need the old-fashioned type of curtain rail with bent ends, which stands out from the wall.

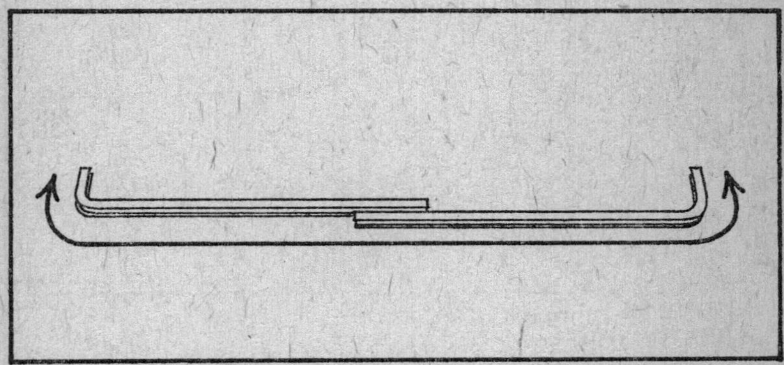

2 Measure the length of this rail from wall to wall, ignoring the overlap in the middle.

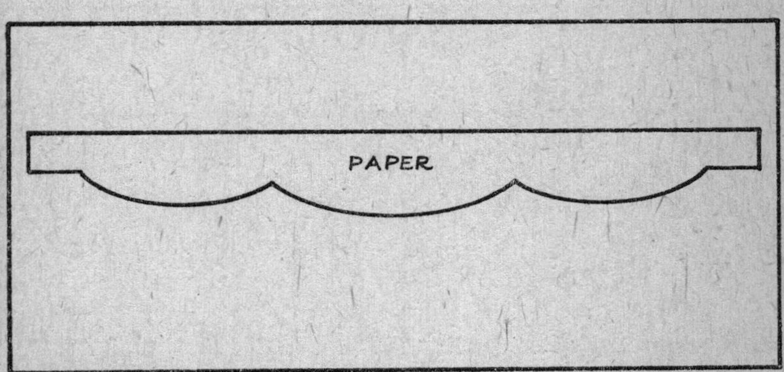

3 If you want a fancy shaped pelmet, cut out the pattern in brown paper first.

4 Try to make the pelmet without a join, but if you can't, better to have two joins, one at each end, both equi-distant from the corner. If you can't manage two, then go for the centre. But don't have one on its own anywhere else.

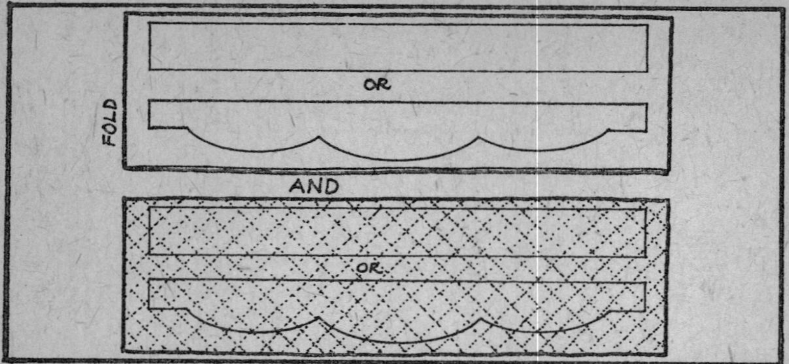

5 Cut two thicknesses of the main fabric, allowing ½ in. seam allowance all round, using whatever depth you wish, and one thickness of stiffening the same size.

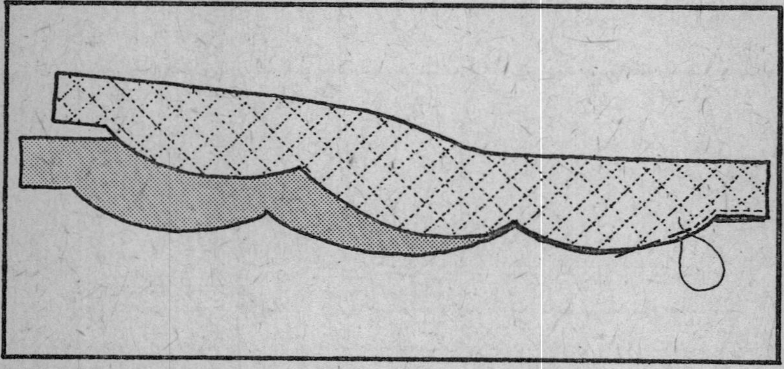

6 Tack the stiffening to the wrong side of one of the pelmet pieces.

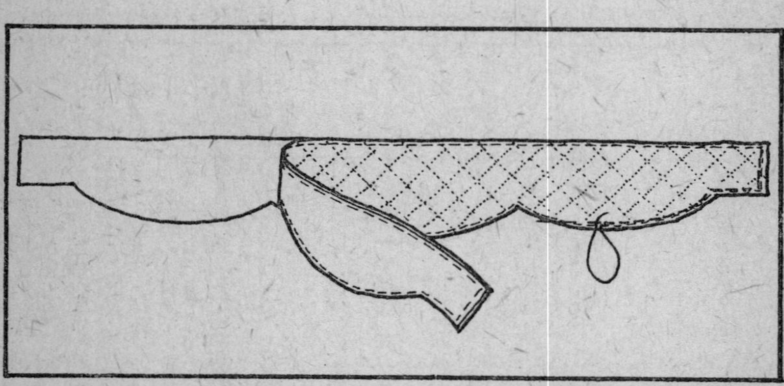

7 Place the two pelmet pieces together, wrong sides outside, and tack in place at ends and bottom edge.

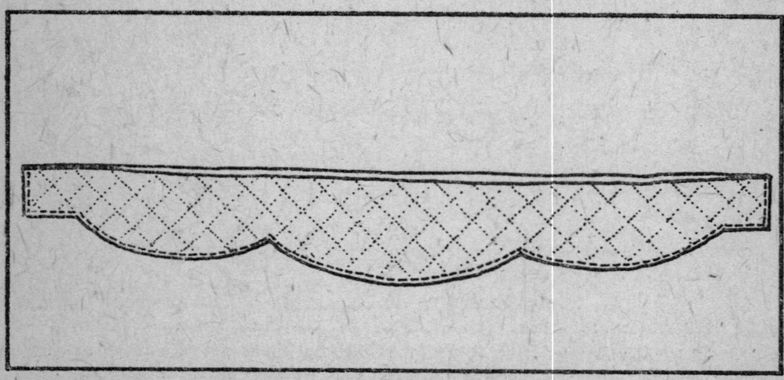

8 Sew the ends and the bottom edge. Leave the upper edge open.

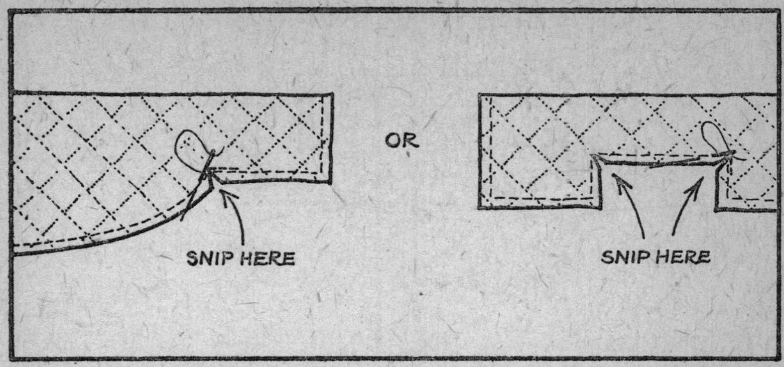

9 If you have a shaped edge at the bottom with scallops or angles, snip the seam allowance between the scallops, or into corners, and work a few little running stitches in those corners as reinforcement.

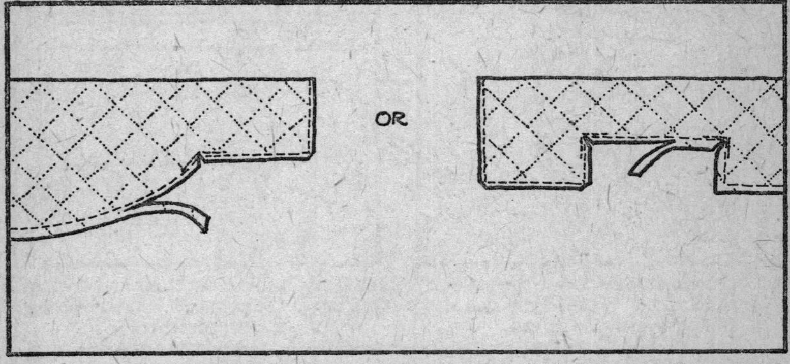

10 You are going to turn the work inside out, so trim back the seam allowance by about half, and slice off all the corners.

11 Turn the work inside out.

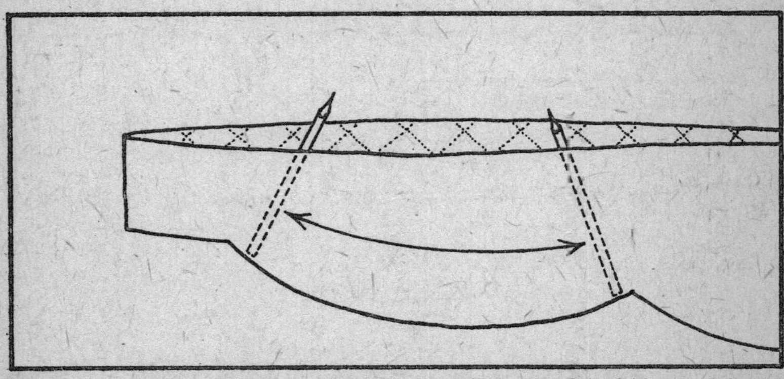

12 Run the unsharpened end of a pencil all round the inside of the fold to push it out. particularly the curves if there are any

13 Dig out corners carefully with the point of a needle, if the shape demands it.

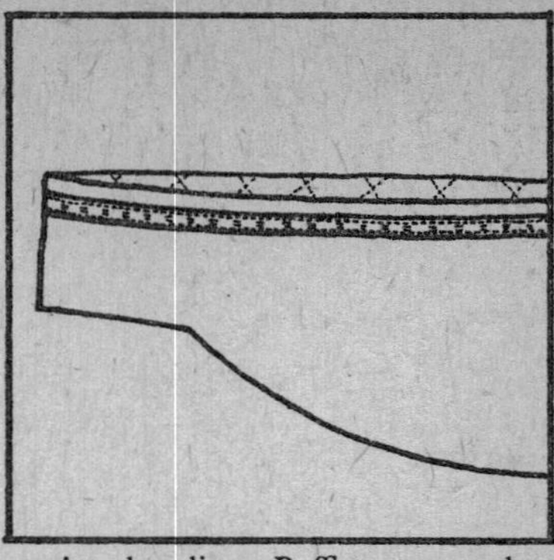

14 Attach ordinary Rufflette tape to the back of the pelmet, with the top edge $\frac{3}{4}$ in. down from the edge of the pelmet.

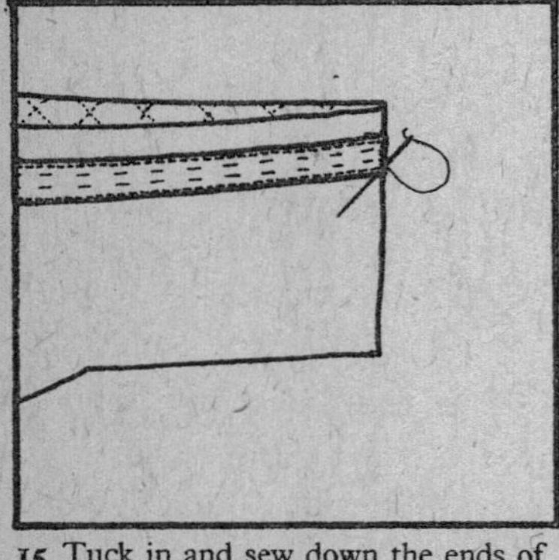

15 Tuck in and sew down the ends of the Rufflette tape because you will not need to pull the threads.

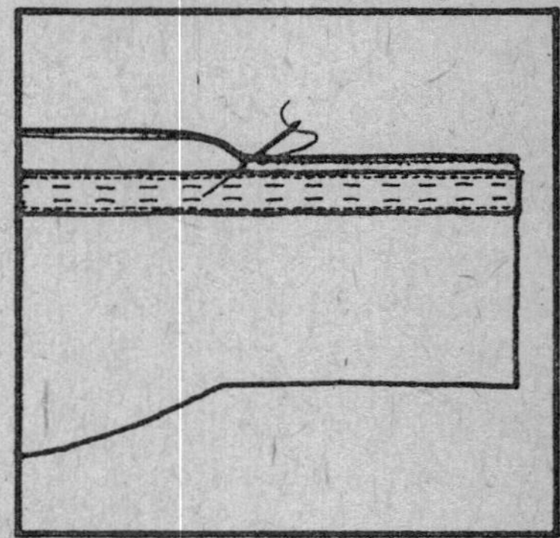

16 Turn in both the front and back of the top of the pelmet $\frac{1}{2}$ in. and oversew them together.

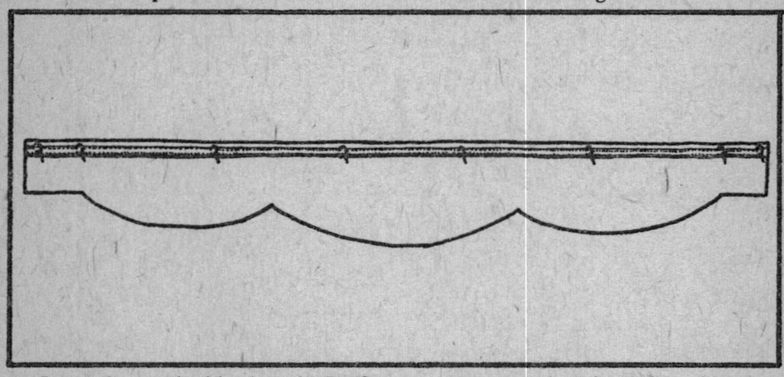

17 Insert the standard hook in the Rufflette tape, one at each end, one at each corner, and two or three more either side of the break in the centre of the frame.

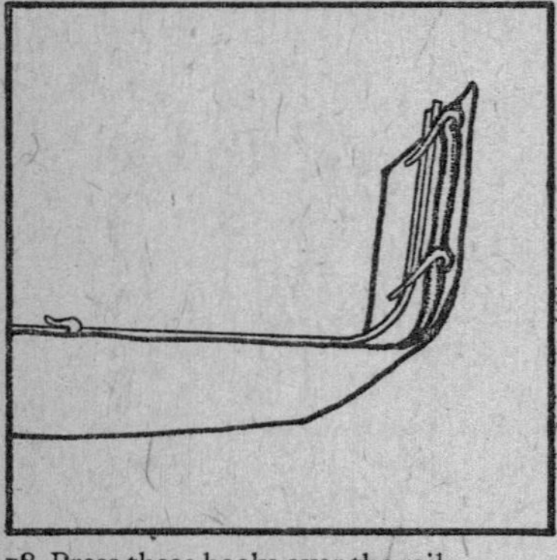

18 Press these hooks over the rail.

family measurements

Name:

Date:

Bust or chest:

Waist:

Hips:

Back bodice, armhole to armhole:

Bodice, shoulder to waist:

Skirt, waist to fashion length:
waist to ankle length:

Trousers, outside leg:
inside leg:

Sleeve length, armhole seam round elbow to wrist:
underarm to wrist:

Neck, for shirts:

Name:

Date:

Bust or chest:

Waist:

Hips:

Back bodice, armhole to armhole:

Bodice, shoulder to waist:

Skirt, waist to fashion length:
waist to ankle length:

Trousers, outside leg:
inside leg:

Sleeve length, armhole seam round elbow to wrist:
underarm to wrist:

Neck, for shirts:

Name:

Date:

Bust or chest:

Waist:

Hips:

Back bodice, armhole to armhole:

Bodice, shoulder to waist:

Skirt, waist to fashion length:
waist to ankle length:

Trousers, outside leg:
inside leg:

Sleeve length, armhole seam round elbow to wrist:
underarm to wrist:

Neck, for shirts:

Name:

Date:

Bust or chest:

Waist:

Hips:

Back bodice, armhole to armhole:

Bodice, shoulder to waist:

Skirt, waist to fashion length:
waist to ankle length:

Trousers, outside leg:
inside leg:

Sleeve length, armhole seam round elbow to wrist:
underarm to wrist:

Neck, for shirts:

Name:

Date:

Bust or chest:

Waist:

Hips:

Back bodice, armhole to armhole:

Bodice, shoulder to waist:

Skirt, waist to fashion length:
waist to ankle length:

Trousers, outside leg:
inside leg:

Sleeve length, armhole seam round elbow to wrist:
underarm to wrist:

Neck, for shirts:

Name:

Date:

Bust or chest:

Waist:

Hips:

Back bodice, armhole to armhole:

Bodice, shoulder to waist:

Skirt, waist to fashion length:
waist to ankle length:

Trousers, outside leg:
inside leg:

Sleeve length, armhole seam round elbow to wrist:
underarm to wrist:

Neck, for shirts:

Name:

Date:

Bust or chest:

Waist:

Hips:

Back bodice, armhole to armhole:

Bodice, shoulder to waist:

Skirt, waist to fashion length:
waist to ankle length:

Trousers, outside leg:
inside leg:

Sleeve length, armhole seam round elbow to wrist:
underarm to wrist:

Neck, for shirts:

Name:

Date:

Bust or chest:

Waist:

Hips:

Back bodice, armhole to armhole:

Bodice, shoulder to waist:

Skirt, waist to fashion length:
waist to ankle length:

Trousers, outside leg:
inside leg:

Sleeve length, armhole seam round elbow to wrist:
underarm to wrist:

Neck, for shirts:

Name:

Date:

Bust or chest:

Waist:

Hips:

Back bodice, armhole to armhole:

Bodice, shoulder to waist:

Skirt, waist to fashion length:
waist to ankle length:

Trousers, outside leg:
inside leg:

Sleeve length, armhole seam round elbow to wrist:
underarm to wrist:

Neck, for shirts:

Name:

Date:

Bust or chest:

Waist:

Hips:

Back bodice, armhole to armhole:

Bodice, shoulder to waist:

Skirt, waist to fashion length:
waist to ankle length:

Trousers, outside leg:
inside leg:

Sleeve length, armhole seam round elbow to wrist:
underarm to wrist:

Neck, for shirts:

Name:

Date:

Bust or chest:

Waist:

Hips:

Back bodice, armhole to armhole:

Bodice, shoulder to waist:

Skirt, waist to fashion length:
waist to ankle length:

Trousers, outside leg:
inside leg:

Sleeve length, armhole seam round elbow to wrist:
underarm to wrist:

Neck, for shirts:

Name:

Date:

Bust or chest:

Waist:

Hips:

Back bodice, armhole to armhole:

Bodice, shoulder to waist:

Skirt, waist to fashion length:
waist to ankle length:

Trousers, outside leg:
inside leg:

Sleeve length, armhole seam round elbow to wrist:
underarm to wrist:

Neck, for shirts: